Linux Kernel Networking

Implementation and Theory

Rami Rosen

Apress®

Linux Kernel Networking: Implementation and Theory

ISBN-13 (pbk): 978-1-4302-6196-4

ISBN-13 (electronic): 978-1-4302-6197-1

President and Publisher: Paul Manning
Lead Editor: Michelle Lowman
Technical Reviewer: Brendan Horan
Editorial Board: Steve Anglin, Ewan Buckingham, Gary Cornell, Louise Corrigan, James DeWolf,
    Jonathan Gennick, Jonathan Hassell, Robert Hutchinson, Michelle Lowman, James Markham,
    Matthew Moodie, Jeff Olson, Jeffrey Pepper, Douglas Pundick, Ben Renow-Clarke, Dominic Shakeshaft,
    Gwenan Spearing, Matt Wade, Steve Weiss, Tom Welsh
Coordinating Editor: Kevin Shea
Copy Editor: Corbin Collins
Compositor: SPi Global
Indexer: SPi Global
Artist: SPi Global
Cover Designer: Anna Ishchenko

Distributed to the book trade worldwide by Springer Science+Business Media New York, 233 Spring Street, 6th Floor, New York, NY 10013. Phone 1-800-SPRINGER, fax (201) 348-4505, e-mail orders-ny@springer-sbm.com, or visit www.springeronline.com.

For information on translations, please e-mail rights@apress.com, or visit www.apress.com.

Apress and friends of ED books may be purchased in bulk for academic, corporate, or promotional use. eBook versions and licenses are also available for most titles. For more information, reference our Special Bulk Sales–eBook Licensing web page at www.apress.com/bulk-sales.

Any source code or other supplementary materials referenced by the author in this text is available to readers at www.apress.com. For detailed information about how to locate your book's source code, go to www.apress.com/source-code.

To Dr. Joseph Shapira, Qualcomm Israel Founder and Ex-President, coauthor of "CDMA Radio with Repeaters"(Springer, 2007).

To Dr Ruth Shapira.

Iris & Dr. Shye Shapira, made of the stuff dreams are made of.

—Rami Rosen

Contents at a Glance

Contents

About the Author

Rami Rosen is a software engineer, a computer science graduate of the Technion, Israel High Institute of Technology. In the last 17 years he has been a software developer for three innovative startups and a semiconductor company. Rami lives in Israel and he has participated in highly advanced Linux kernel projects, in particular those related to networking. He has published several articles and given lectures about Linux kernel networking and virtualization.

About the Technical Reviewer

Brendan Horan is a hardware fanatic, with a full high rack of all types of machine architectures in his home. He has more than ten years of experience working with large UNIX systems and tuning the underlying hardware for optimal performance and stability. Brendan's love for all forms of hardware has helped him throughout his IT career, from fixing laptops to tuning servers and their hardware in order to suit the needs of high-availability designs and ultra low-latency applications. Brendan takes pride in the open source movement and is happy to say that every computer in his house is powered by open source technology. He resides in Hong Kong with his wife, Vikki, who continues daily to teach him more Cantonese.

Acknowledgments

Thanks to my editors for giving me the honor of writing this book; to Michelle Lowman, the lead editor, for believing in this book while it was still just an idea; to Kevin Shea, the coordinating editor, who guided and supported me from the initial stages until the book was fully realized; to Brendan Horan, the technical reviewer, for his helpful comments that helped me to improve the book by a lot; to Troy Mott, the development editor, for his many suggestions and for his hard work; to Corbin Collins and Roger LeBlanc, the copy editors, for shaping up the text; and to Kumar Dhaneesh from the production team.

I would like to thank the Linux kernel networking maintainer, David Miller, for the great work he has done over all these years and all the developers who continue to participate and contribute to the networking subsystem. I would like also to say thanks to the Linux kernel networking community and all its members who helped me by reviewing my text: Julian Anastasov, Timo Teras, Steffen Klassert, Gerrit Renker, Javier Cardona, Gao feng, Vlad Yasevich, Cong Wang, Florian Westphal, Reuben Hawkins, Pekka Savola, Andreas Steffen, Daniel Borkmann, Joachim Nilsson, David Hauweele, Maxime Ripard, Alexandre Belloni, Benjamin Zores, and too many others to mention. Thanks to Donald Wood and Eliezer Tamir from Intel for their help with the "Busy Polling Sockets" section, and to Samuel Ortiz from Intel for his advice in preparing the NFC section. Thanks for Dotan Barak, an InfiniBand expert, for contributing Chapter 13, "InfiniBand."

Rami Rosen

Preface

This book takes you on a guided, in-depth tour of the current Linux kernel networking implementation and the theory behind it. For almost a decade, no new book about Linux networking has been written. A decade of dynamic and fast-paced Linux kernel development is quite a long time. There are important kernel networking subsystems that are not described in any other book; for example, IPv6, IPsec, Wireless (IEEE 802.11), IEEE 802.15.4, NFC, InfiniBand, and more. There is also very little information on the Web about the implementation details of these subsystems. For all these reasons, I have written this book.

About ten years ago I made my first steps in kernel programming. I was a developer in a startup taking part in a VoIP project for a Linux-based set-top box (STB). There were crashes in the USB stack with some USB cameras, and we had to delve into the code to try to find a solution, because the vendors of that STB did not want to spend time to solve the problem. In fact, it was not that they did not want to, they simply did not know how to. In these days, there was almost no documentation about the USB stack. The *Linux Device Drivers* book from O'Reilly in those days was only in its second edition (the USB chapter was added only in the third edition). Success in that project was crucial for us as a startup. I had learned much about kernel programming in the process of solving the USB crash. Later on we had a project where a NAT traversal solution was needed. The userspace solution was so heavy that the device quickly crashed. When I suggested a kernel solution, my managers were very skeptical, but they did let me try. The kernel solution proved to be very stable and took much less CPU than the userspace solution. Since then I have taken part in many kernel networking projects. This book is a result of my many years of development and research.

Who This Book Is For

This book is intended for computer professionals, including developers, software architects, designers, project managers, and CTOs, who are working on networking-related projects. These projects can be in a wide range of professional areas, such as communication, data centers, embedded devices, virtualization, security, and more. In addition, students and academy researchers and theorists who deal with networking projects or networking research or operating systems research will find a lot of help in this book.

How This Book Is Structured

In Chapter 1 you will find a general overview of the Linux kernel and the Linux network stack. Other topics in this chapter include the implementation of the network device, the socket buffer, and the Rx and Tx paths. Chapter 1 concludes with a section about the Linux Kernel Networking Development Model.

In chapter 2 you will learn about netlink sockets, which provide a mechanism for bidirectional communication between userspace and the kernel, and which are used by the networking subsystem as well as by other subsystems. You will also find a section in this chapter about generic netlink sockets, which can be perceived as advanced netlink sockets, and which you will encounter in Chapter 12 and while browsing the kernel networking source code.

In Chapter 3 you will learn about the ICMP protocol, which helps to keep the system behaving correctly by sending error and control messages about the network layer (L3). You will learn about the implementation of the ICMP protocol both in IPv4 and in IPv6.

Chapter 4 delves into the IPv4 protocol—the Internet and modern life cannot be described without it. You will learn about the structure of IPv4 header, about the Rx and Tx path, about IP options, about fragmentation and defragmentation and why they are needed, and about forwarding packets, which is one of the important tasks of IPv4.

Chapters 5 and 6 are devoted to the IPv4 Routing Subsystem. In chapter 5 you will learn how a lookup in the routing subsystem is performed, how the routing tables are organized, which optimizations are used in the IPv4 routing subsystem and about the removal of the IPv4 routing cache. Chapter 6 discusses advanced routing topics such as Multicast Routing, Policy Routing, and Multipath Routing.

Chapter 7 endeavors to explain the neighbouring subsystem. You will learn about the ARP protocol, which is used in IPv4, and about the the NDISC protocol used in IPv6, and about some of the differences between the two protocols. You will also learn about the Duplicate Address Detection (DAD) mechanism in IPv6.

Chapter 8 discusses the IPv6 protocol, which seems to be the inevitable solution to the shortage of IPv4 addresses. This chapter describes the implementation of IPv6 and discusses topics such as IPv6 addresses, the IPv6 header and extension headers, autoconfiguration in IPv6, Rx path, and forwarding. It also describes the MLD protocol.

Chapter 9 deals with the netfilter subsystem. You will learn about netfilter hooks and how they are registered, about Connection Tracking, about IP tables and Network Address Translation (NAT), and about callback used by Connection Tracking and NAT.

Chapter 10 deals with IPsec, one of the most complex networking subsystems. Topics like the IKE protocol (which is implemented in userspace) and cryptography aspects of IPsec are discussed briefly (full treatment is beyond the scope of the book). You will learn about the XFRM framework, which is the basis of the Linux IPsec subsystem, and about its two most important structures: XFRM policy and XFRM state. The ESP protocol is briefly described, as well as the IPsec Rx path and Tx path in transport mode. The chapter concludes with a section about XFRM lookup and a short section about NAT traversal.

Chapter 11 describes four Layer 4 protocols, starting with the most commonly used protocols, UDP and TCP, and concluding with two newer protocols, SCTP and DCCP.

Chapter 12 deals with wireless in Linux (IEEE 802.11). You will learn about the mac80211 subsystem and its implementation, about various wireless network topologies, about power save mode, and about IEEE 802.11n and packet aggregation. There is also a section devoted to Wireless Mesh networks in this chapter.

Chapter 13 delves into the InfiniBand subsystem, a technology enjoying a rising popularity in datacenters. You will learn about the RDMA stack organization, about addressing in InfiniBand, about the organization of InfiniBand packets, and about the RDMA API.

Chapter 14 concludes the book with a discussion of advanced topics such as Linux namespaces and network namespaces in particular, Busy Poll Sockets, the Bluetooth subsystem, the IEEE 802.15.4 subsystem, the Near Field Communication (NFC) subsystem, the PCI subsystem, and more.

Appendices A, "Linux API," and C, "Glossary ," provide complete reference information for many topics dicussed in the book. Appendix B, "Network Administration," provides information about various tools which you will need while working with Linux kernel networking.

Conventions

Throughout the book, I've kept a consistent style. All code snippets, whether inside text paragraphs or on lines of their own, along with library paths, shell commands, URLs, and other code-related elements, are set in monospaced font, like this. New terms are set off in *italics*, and other emphasis may be given in **bold**.

CHAPTER 1

■ ■ ■

Introduction

This book deals with the implementation of the Linux Kernel Networking stack and the theory behind it. You will find in the following pages an in-depth and detailed analysis of the networking subsystem and its architecture. I will not burden you with topics not directly related to networking, which you may encounter while reading kernel networking code (for example, locking and synchronization, SMP, atomic operations, and so on). There are plenty of resources about such topics. On the other hand, there are very few up-to-date resources that focus on kernel networking proper. By this I mean primarily describing the traversal of the packet in the Linux Kernel Networking stack and its interaction with various networking layers and subsystems—and how various networking protocols are implemented.

This book is also not a cumbersome, line-by-line code walkthrough. I focus on the essence of the implementation of each network layer and the theory guidelines and principles that led to this implementation. The Linux operating system has proved itself in recent years as a successful, reliable, stable, and popular operating system. And it seems that its popularity is growing steadily, in a wide variety of flavors, from mainframes, data centers, core routers, and web servers to embedded devices like wireless routers, set-top boxes, medical instruments, navigation equipment (like GPS devices), and consumer electronics devices. Many semiconductor vendors use Linux as the basis for their Board Support Packages (BSPs). The Linux operating system, which started as a project of a Finnish student named Linus Torvalds back in 1991, based on the UNIX operating system, proved to be a serious and reliable operating system and a rival for veteran proprietary operating systems.

Linux began as an Intel x86-based operating system but has been ported to a very wide range of processors, including ARM, PowerPC, MIPS, SPARC, and more. The Android operating system, based upon the Linux kernel, is common today in tablets and smartphones, and seems likely to gain popularity in the future in smart TVs. Apart from Android, Google has also contributed some kernel networking features that were merged into the mainline kernel.

Linux is an open source project, and as such it has an advantage over other proprietary operating systems: its source code is freely available under the General Public License (GPL). Other open source operating systems, like the different types of BSD, have much less popularity. I should also mention in this context the OpenSolaris project, based on the Common Development and Distribution License (CDDL). This project, started by Sun Microsystems, has not achieved the popularity that Linux has. Among the large community of active Linux developers, some contribute code on behalf of the companies they work for, and some contribute code voluntarily. All of the kernel development process is accessible via the kernel mailing lists. There is one central mailing list, the Linux Kernel Mailing List (LKML), and many subsystems have their own mailing lists. Contributing code is done via sending patches to the appropriate kernel mailing lists and to the maintainers, and these patches are discussed over the mailing lists.

The Linux Kernel Networking stack is a very important subsystem of the Linux kernel. It is quite difficult to find a Linux-based system, whether it is a desktop, a server, a mobile device or any other embedded device, that does not use any kind of networking. Even in the rare case when a machine doesn't have any hardware network devices, you will still be using networking (maybe unconsciously) when you use X-Windows, as X-Windows itself is based upon client-server networking. A wide range of projects are related to the Linux Networking stack, from core routers to small embedded devices. Some of these projects deal with adding vendor-specific features. For example, some hardware vendors implement Generic Segmentation Offload (GSO) in some network devices. GSO is a networking feature of the kernel network stack that divides a large packet into smaller ones in the Tx path. Many hardware vendors implement checksumming in hardware in their network devices. *Checksum* is a mechanism to verify that a packet was not

1

damaged on transit by calculating some hash from the packet and attaching it to the packet. Many projects provide some security enhancements for Linux. Sometimes these enhancements require some changes in the networking subsystem, as you will see, for example, in Chapter 3, when discussing the Openwall GNU/*/Linux project. In the embedded device arena there are, for example, many wireless routers that are Linux based; one example is the WRT54GL Linksys router, which runs Linux. There is also an open source, Linux-based operating system that can run on this device (and on some other devices), named OpenWrt, with a large and active community of developers (see https://openwrt.org/). Learning about how the various protocols are implemented by the Linux Kernel Networking stack and becoming familiar with the main data structures and the main paths of a packet in it are essential to understanding it better.

The Linux Network Stack

There are seven logical networking layers according to the Open Systems Interconnection (OSI) model. The lowest layer is the physical layer, which is the hardware, and the highest layer is the application layer, where userspace software processes are running. Let's describe these seven layers:

1. *The physical layer:* Handles electrical signals and the low level details.

2. *The data link layer:* Handles data transfer between endpoints. The most common data link layer is Ethernet. The Linux Ethernet network device drivers reside in this layer.

3. *The network layer:* Handles packet forwarding and host addressing. In this book I discuss the most common network layers of the Linux Kernel Networking subsystem: IPv4 or IPv6. There are other, less common network layers which Linux implements, like DECnet, but they are not discussed.

4. *The protocol layer/transport layer:* Handles data sending between nodes. The TCP and UDP protocols are the best-known protocols.

5. *The session layer:* Handles sessions between endpoints.

6. *The presentation layer:* Handles delivery and formatting.

7. *The application layer:* Provides network services to end-user applications.

Figure 1-1 shows the seven layers according to the OSI model.

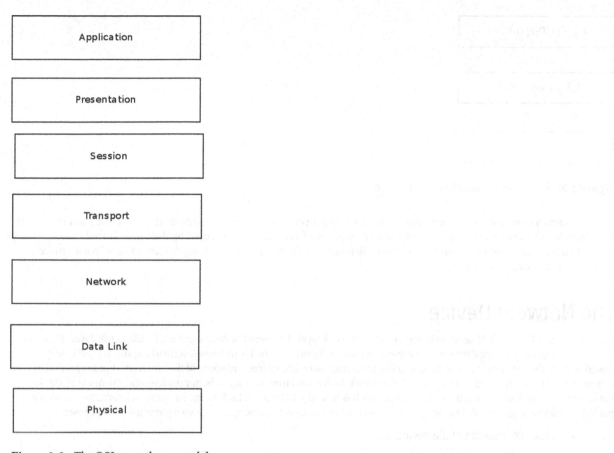

Figure 1-1. *The OSI seven-layer model*

Figure 1-2 shows the three layers that the Linux Kernel Networking stack handles. The L2, L3, and L4 layers in this figure correspond to the data link layer, the network layer, and the transport layer in the seven-layer model, respectively. The essence of the Linux kernel stack is passing incoming packets from L2 (the network device drivers) to L3 (the network layer, usually IPv4 or IPv6) and then to L4 (the transport layer, where you have, for example, TCP or UDP listening sockets) if they are for local delivery, or back to L2 for transmission when the packets should be forwarded. Outgoing packets that were locally generated are passed from L4 to L3 and then to L2 for actual transmission by the network device driver. Along this way there are many stages, and many things can happen. For example:

- The packet can be changed due to protocol rules (for example, due to an IPsec rule or to a NAT rule).

- The packet can be discarded.

- The packet can cause an error message to be sent.

- The packet can be fragmented.

- The packet can be defragmented.

- A checksum should be calculated for the packet.

```
┌─────────────────────────────────┐
│                                 │
│        L4 (TCP/UDP,...)          │
│                                 │
└─────────────────────────────────┘

┌─────────────────────────────────┐
│                                 │
│        L3 (IPv4, IPv6)           │
│                                 │
└─────────────────────────────────┘

┌─────────────────────────────────┐
│                                 │
│              L2                  │
│                                 │
└─────────────────────────────────┘
```

Figure 1-2. *The Linux Kernel Networking layers*

The kernel does not handle any layer above L4; those layers (the session, presentation, and application layers) are handled solely by userspace applications. The physical layer (L1) is also not handled by the Linux kernel.

If you feel overwhelmed, don't worry. You will learn a lot more about everything described here in a lot more depth in the following chapters.

The Network Device

The lower layer, Layer 2 (L2), as seen in Figure 1-2, is the link layer. The network device drivers reside in this layer. This book is not about network device driver development, because it focuses on the Linux kernel networking stack. I will briefly describe here the net_device structure, which represents a network device, and some of the concepts that are related to it. You should have a basic familiarity with the network device structure in order to better understand the network stack. Parameters of the device—like the size of MTU, which is typically 1,500 bytes for Ethernet devices—determine whether a packet should be fragmented. The net_device is a very large structure, consisting of device parameters like these:

- The IRQ number of the device.

- The MTU of the device.

- The MAC address of the device.

- The name of the device (like eth0 or eth1).

- The flags of the device (for example, whether it is up or down).

- A list of multicast addresses associated with the device.

- The promiscuity counter (discussed later in this section).

- The features that the device supports (like GSO or GRO offloading).

- An object of network device callbacks (net_device_ops object), which consists of function pointers, such as for opening and stopping a device, starting to transmit, changing the MTU of the network device, and more.

- An object of ethtool callbacks, which supports getting information about the device by running the command-line ethtool utility.

- The number of Tx and Rx queues, when the device supports multiqueues.

- The timestamp of the last transmit of a packet on this device.

- The timestamp of the last reception of a packet on this device.

The following is the definition of some of the members of the net_device structure to give you a first impression:

```
struct net_device {
    unsigned int            irq;            /* device IRQ number    */
    . . .
    const struct net_device_ops *netdev_ops;
    . . .
    unsigned int            mtu;
    . . .
    unsigned int            promiscuity;
    . . .
    unsigned char           *dev_addr;
    . . .
};
(include/linux/netdevice.h)
```

Appendix A of the book includes a very detailed description of the net_device structure and most of its members. In that appendix you can see the irq, mtu, and other members mentioned earlier in this chapter.

When the promiscuity counter is larger than 0, the network stack does not discard packets that are not destined to the local host. This is used, for example, by packet analyzers ("sniffers") like tcpdump and wireshark, which open raw sockets in userspace and want to receive also this type of traffic. It is a counter and not a Boolean in order to enable opening several sniffers concurrently: opening each such sniffer increments the counter by 1. When a sniffer is closed, the promiscuity counter is decremented by 1; and if it reaches 0, there are no more sniffers running, and the device exits the promiscuous mode.

When browsing kernel networking core source code, in various places you will probably encounter the term NAPI (New API), which is a feature that most network device drivers implement nowadays. You should know what it is and why network device drivers use it.

New API (NAPI) in Network Devices

The old network device drivers worked in interrupt-driven mode, which means that for every received packet, there was an interrupt. This proved to be inefficient in terms of performance under high load traffic. A new software technique was developed, called New API (NAPI), which is now supported on almost all Linux network device drivers. NAPI was first introduced in the 2.5/2.6 kernel and was backported to the 2.4.20 kernel. With NAPI, under high load, the network device driver works in polling mode and not in interrupt-driven mode. This means that each received packet does not trigger an interrupt. Instead the packets are buffered in the driver, and the kernel polls the driver from time to time to fetch the packets. Using NAPI improves performance under high load. For sockets applications that need the lowest possible latency and are willing to pay a cost of higher CPU utilization, Linux has added a capability for Busy Polling on Sockets from kernel 3.11 and later. This technology is discussed in Chapter 14, in the "Busy Poll Sockets" section.

With your new knowledge about network devices under your belt, it is time to learn about the traversal of a packet inside the Linux Kernel Networking stack.

Receiving and Transmitting Packets

The main tasks of the network device driver are these:

- To receive packets destined to the local host and to pass them to the network layer (L3), and from there to the transport layer (L4)

- To transmit outgoing packets generated on the local host and sent outside, or to forward packets that were received on the local host

For each packet, incoming or outgoing, a lookup in the routing subsystem is performed. The decision about whether a packet should be forwarded and on which interface it should be sent is done based on the result of the lookup in the routing subsystem, which I describe in depth in Chapters 5 and 6. The lookup in the routing subsystem is not the only factor that determines the traversal of a packet in the network stack. For example, there are five points in the network stack where callbacks of the netfilter subsystem (often referred to as netfilter hooks) can be registered. The first netfilter hook point of a received packet is NF_INET_PRE_ROUTING, before a routing lookup was performed. When a packet is handled by such a callback, which is invoked by a macro named NF_HOOK(), it will continue its traversal in the networking stack according to the result of this callback (also called verdict). For example, if the verdict is NF_DROP, the packet will be discarded, and if the verdict is NF_ACCEPT, the packet will continue its traversal as usual. Netfilter hooks callbacks are registered by the nf_register_hook() method or by the nf_register_hooks() method, and you will encounter these invocations, for example, in various netfilter kernel modules. The kernel netfilter subsystem is the infrastructure for the well-known iptables userspace package. Chapter 9 describes the netfilter subsystem and the netfilter hooks, along with the connection tracking layer of netfilter.

Besides the netfilter hooks, the packet traversal can be influenced by the IPsec subsystem—for example, when it matches a configured IPsec policy. IPsec provides a network layer security solution, and it uses the ESP and the AH protocols. IPsec is mandatory according to IPv6 specification and optional in IPv4, though most operating systems, including Linux, implemented IPsec also in IPv4. IPsec has two modes of operation: transport mode and tunnel mode. It is used as a basis for many virtual private network (VPN) solutions, though there are also non-IPsec VPN solutions. You learn about the IPsec subsystem and about IPsec policies in Chapter 10, which also discusses the problems that occur when working with IPsec through a NAT, and the IPsec NAT traversal solution.

Still other factors can influence the traversal of the packet—for example, the value of the ttl field in the IPv4 header of a packet being forwarded. This ttl is decremented by 1 in each forwarding device. When it reaches 0, the packet is discarded, and an ICMPv4 message of "Time Exceeded" with "TTL Count Exceeded" code is sent back. This is done to avoid an endless journey of a forwarded packet because of some error. Moreover, each time a packet is forwarded successfully and the ttl is decremented by 1, the checksum of the IPv4 header should be recalculated, as its value depends on the IPv4 header, and the ttl is one of the IPv4 header members. Chapter 4, which deals with the IPv4 subsystem, talks more about this. In IPv6 there is something similar, but the hop counter in the IPv6 header is named hop_limit and not ttl. You will learn about this in Chapter 8, which deals with the IPv6 subsystem. You will also learn about ICMP in IPv4 and in IPv6 in Chapter 3, which deals with ICMP.

A large part of the book discusses the traversal of a packet in the networking stack, whether it is in the receive path (Rx path, also known as *ingress* traffic) or the transmit path (Tx path, also known as *egress* traffic). This traversal is complex and has many variations: large packets could be fragmented before they are sent; on the other hand, fragmented packets should be assembled (discussed in Chapter 4). Packets of different types are handled differently. For example, multicast packets are packets that can be processed by a group of hosts (as opposed to unicast packets, which are destined to a specified host). Multicast can be used, for example, in applications of streaming media in order to consume less network resources. Handling IPv4 multicast traffic is discussed in Chapter 4. You will also learn how a host joins and leaves a multicast group; in IPv4, the Internet Group Management Protocol (IGMP) protocol handles multicast membership. Yet there are cases when the host is configured as a multicast router, and multicast traffic should be forwarded and not delivered to the local host. These cases are more complex as they should be handled in conjunction with a userspace multicast routing daemon, like the pimd daemon or the mrouted daemon. These cases, which are called multicast routing, are discussed in Chapter 6.

To better understand the packet traversal, you must learn about how a packet is represented in the Linux kernel. The sk_buff structure represents an incoming or outgoing packet, including its headers (include/linux/skbuff.h). I refer to an sk_buff object as SKB in many places along this book, as this is the common way to denote sk_buff objects (SKB stands for *socket buffer*). The socket buffer (sk_buff) structure is a large structure—I will only discuss a few members of this structure in this chapter.

The Socket Buffer

The sk_buff structure is described in depth in Appendix A. I recommend referring to this appendix when you need to know more about one of the SKB members or how to use the SKB API. Note that when working with SKBs, you must adhere to the SKB API. Thus, for example, when you want to advance the skb->data pointer, you do not do it directly, but with the skb_pull_inline() method or the skb_pull() method (you will see an example of this later in this section). And if you want to fetch the L4 header (transport header) from an SKB, you do it by calling the skb_transport_header() method. Likewise if you want to fetch the L3 header (network header), you do it by calling the skb_network_header() method, and if you want to fetch the L2 header (MAC header), you do it by calling the skb_mac_header() method. These three methods get an SKB as a single parameter.

Here is the (partial) definition of the sk_buff structure:

```
struct sk_buff {
    . . .
    struct sock          *sk;
    struct net_device    *dev;
    . . .
    __u8                 pkt_type:3,
    . . .
    __be16               protocol;
    . . .
    sk_buff_data_t       tail;
    sk_buff_data_t       end;
    unsigned char        *head,
                         *data;

    sk_buff_data_t       transport_header;
    sk_buff_data_t       network_header;
    sk_buff_data_t       mac_header;
    . . .
};
(include/linux/skbuff.h)
```

When a packet is received on the wire, an SKB is allocated by the network device driver, typically by calling the netdev_alloc_skb() method (or the dev_alloc_skb() method, which is a legacy method that calls the netdev_alloc_skb() method with the first parameter as NULL). There are cases along the packet traversal where a packet can be discarded, and this is done by calling kfree_skb() or dev_kfree_skb(), both of which get as a single parameter a pointer to an SKB. Some members of the SKB are determined in the link layer (L2). For example, the pkt_type is determined by the eth_type_trans() method, according to the destination Ethernet address. If this address is a multicast address, the pkt_type will be set to PACKET_MULTICAST; if this address is a broadcast address, the pkt_type will be set to PACKET_BROADCAST; and if this address is the address of the local host, the pkt_type will be set to PACKET_HOST. Most Ethernet network drivers call the eth_type_trans() method in their Rx path. The eth_type_trans() method also sets the protocol field of the SKB according to the ethertype of the Ethernet header. The eth_type_trans() method also advances the data pointer of the SKB by 14 (ETH_HLEN), which is the size of an Ethernet header, by calling the skb_pull_inline() method. The reason for this is that the skb->data should point to the header of the layer in which it currently resides. When the packet was in L2, in the network device driver Rx path, skb->data pointed to the L2 (Ethernet) header; now that the packet is going to be moved to Layer 3, immediately after the call to the eth_type_trans() method, skb->data should point to the network (L3) header, which starts immediately after the Ethernet header (see Figure 1-3).

Ethernet header 14 bytes	IPv4 header 20 bytes - 60 bytes	UDP header 8 bytes	Payload

Figure 1-3. *An IPv4 packet*

The SKB includes the packet headers (L2, L3, and L4 headers) and the packet payload. In the packet traversal in the network stack, a header can be added or removed. For example, for an IPv4 packet generated locally by a socket and transmitted outside, the network layer (IPv4) adds an IPv4 header to the SKB. The IPv4 header size is 20 bytes as a minimum. When adding IP options, the IPv4 header size can be up to 60 bytes. IP options are described in Chapter 4, which discusses the IPv4 protocol implementation. Figure 1-3 shows an example of an IPv4 packet with L2, L3, and L4 headers. The example in Figure 1-3 is a UDPv4 packet. First is the Ethernet header (L2) of 14 bytes. Then there's the IPv4 header (L3) of a minimal size of 20 bytes up to 60 bytes, and after that is the UDPv4 header (L4), of 8 bytes. Then comes the payload of the packet.

Each SKB has a dev member, which is an instance of the net_device structure. For incoming packets, it is the incoming network device, and for outgoing packets it is the outgoing network device. The network device attached to the SKB is sometimes needed to fetch information which might influence the traversal of the SKB in the Linux Kernel Networking stack. For example, the MTU of the network device may require fragmentation, as mentioned earlier. Each transmitted SKB has a sock object associated to it (sk). If the packet is a forwarded packet, then sk is NULL, because it was not generated on the local host.

Each received packet should be handled by a matching network layer protocol handler. For example, an IPv4 packet should be handled by the ip_rcv() method, and an IPv6 packet should be handled by the ipv6_rcv() method. You will learn about the registration of the IPv4 protocol handler with the dev_add_pack() method in Chapter 4, and about the registration of the IPv6 protocol handler also with the dev_add_pack() method in Chapter 8. Moreover, I will follow the traversal of incoming and outgoing packets both in IPv4 and in IPv6. For example, in the ip_rcv() method, mostly sanity checks are performed, and if everything is fine the packet proceeds to an NF_INET_PRE_ROUTING hook callback, if such a callback is registered, and the next step, if it was not discarded by such a hook, is the ip_rcv_finish() method, where a lookup in the routing subsystem is performed. A lookup in the routing subsystem builds a destination cache entry (dst_entry object). You will learn about the dst_entry and about the input and output callback methods associated with it in Chapters 5 and 6, which describe the IPv4 routing subsystem.

In IPv4 there is a problem of limited address space, as an IPv4 address is only 32 bit. Organizations use NAT (discussed in Chapter 9) to provide local addresses to their hosts, but the IPv4 address space still diminishes over the years. One of the main reasons for developing the IPv6 protocol was that its address space is huge compared to the IPv4 address space, because the IPv6 address length is 128 bit. But the IPv6 protocol is not only about a larger address space. The IPv6 protocol includes many changes and additions as a result of the experience gained over the years with the IPv4 protocol. For example, the IPv6 header has a fixed length of 40 bytes as opposed to the IPv4 header, which is variable in length (from a minimum of 20 bytes to 60 bytes) due to IP options, which can expand it. Processing IP options in IPv4 is complex and quite heavy in terms of performance. On the other hand, in IPv6 you cannot expand the IPv6 header at all (it is fixed in length, as mentioned). Instead there is a mechanism of extension headers which is much more efficient than the IP options in IPv4 in terms of performance. Another notable change is with the ICMP protocol; in IPv4 it was used only for error reporting and for informative messages. In IPv6, the ICMP protocol is used for many other purposes: for Neighbour Discovery (ND), for Multicast Listener Discovery (MLD), and more. Chapter 3 is dedicated to ICMP (both in IPv4 and IPv6). The IPv6 Neighbour Discovery protocol is described in Chapter 7, and the MLD protocol is discussed in Chapter 8, which deals with the IPv6 subsystem.

As mentioned earlier, received packets are passed by the network device driver to the network layer, which is IPv4 or IPv6. If the packets are for local delivery, they will be delivered to the transport layer (L4) for handling by listening sockets. The most common transport protocols are UDP and TCP, discussed in Chapter 11, which discusses Layer 4, the transport layer. This chapter also covers two newer transport protocols, the Stream Control Transmission Protocol (SCTP) and the Datagram Congestion Control Protocol (DCCP). Both SCTP and DCCP adopted some TCP features and some UDP features, as you will find out. The SCTP protocol is known to be used in conjunction with the Long Term Evolution (LTE) protocol; the DCCP has not been tested so far in larger-scale Internet setups.

Packets generated by the local host are created by Layer 4 sockets—for example, by TCP sockets or by UDP sockets. They are created by a userspace application with the Sockets API. There are two main types of sockets: **datagram** sockets and **stream** sockets. These two types of sockets and the POSIX-based socket API are also discussed in Chapter 11, where you will also learn about the kernel implementation of sockets (`struct socket`, which provides an interface to userspace, and `struct sock`, which provides an interface to Layer 3). The packets generated locally are passed to the network layer, L3 (described in Chapter 4, in the section "Sending IPv4 Packets") and then are passed to the network device driver (L2) for transmission. There are cases when fragmentation takes place in Layer 3, the network layer, and this is also discussed in chapter 4.

Every Layer 2 network interface has an L2 address that identifies it. In the case of Ethernet, this is a 48-bit address, the MAC address which is assigned for each Ethernet network interface, provided by the manufacturer, and said to be unique (though you should consider that the MAC address for most network interfaces can be changed by userspace commands like `ifconfig` or `ip`). Each Ethernet packet starts with an Ethernet header, which is 14 bytes long. It consists of the Ethernet type (2 bytes), the source MAC address (6 bytes), and the destination MAC address (6 bytes). The Ethernet type value is 0x0800, for example, for IPv4, or 0x86DD for IPv6. For each outgoing packet, an Ethernet header should be built. When a userspace socket sends a packet, it specifies its destination address (it can be an IPv4 or an IPv6 address). This is not enough to build the packet, as the destination MAC address should be known. Finding the MAC address of a host based on its IP address is the task of the neighbouring subsystem, discussed in Chapter 7. Neighbor Discovery is handled by the ARP protocol in IPv4 and by the NDISC protocol in IPv6. These protocols are different: the ARP protocol relies on sending broadcast requests, whereas the NDISC protocol relies on sending ICMPv6 requests, which are in fact multicast packets. Both the ARP protocol and the NDSIC protocol are also discussed in Chapter 7.

The network stack should communicate with the userspace for tasks such as adding or deleting routes, configuring neighboring tables, setting IPsec policies and states, and more. The communication between userspace and the kernel is done with netlink sockets, described in Chapter 2. The `iproute2` userspace package, based on netlink sockets, is also discussed in Chapter 2, as well as the generic netlink sockets and their advantages.

The wireless subsystem is discussed in Chapter 12. This subsystem is maintained separately, as mentioned earlier; it has a `git` tree of its own and a mailing list of its own. There are some unique features in the wireless stack that do not exist in the ordinary network stack, such as power save mode (which is when a station or an access point enters a sleep state). The Linux wireless subsystem also supports special topologies, like Mesh network, ad-hoc network, and more. These topologies sometimes require using special features. For example, Mesh networking uses a routing protocol called Hybrid Wireless Mesh Protocol (HWMP), discussed in Chapter 12. This protocol works in Layer 2 and deals with MAC addresses, as opposed to the IPV4 routing protocol. Chapter 12 also discusses the mac80211 framework, which is used by wireless device drivers. Another very interesting feature of the wireless subsystem is the block acknowledgment mechanism in IEEE 802.11n, also discussed in Chapter 12.

In recent years InfiniBand technology has gained in popularity with enterprise datacenters. InfiniBand is based on a technology called Remote Direct Memory Access (RDMA). The RDMA API was introduced to the Linux kernel in version 2.6.11. In Chapter 13 you will find a good explanation about the Linux Infiniband implementation, the RDMA API, and its fundamental data structures.

Virtualization solutions are also becoming popular, especially due to projects like Xen or KVM. Also hardware improvements, like VT-x for Intel processors or AMD-V for AMD processors, have made virtualization more efficient. There is another form of virtualization, which may be less known but has its own advantages. This virtualization is based on a different approach: process virtualization. It is implemented in Linux by namespaces. There is currently support for six namespaces in Linux, and there could be more in the future. The namespaces feature is already used by projects like Linux Containers (http://lxc.sourceforge.net/) and Checkpoint/Restore In Userspace (CRIU). In order to support namespaces, two system calls were added to the kernel: `unshare()` and `setns()`; and six new flags were added to the CLONE_* flags, one for each type of namespace. I discuss namespaces and network namespaces in particular in Chapter 14. Chapter 14 also deals with the Bluetooth subsystem and gives a brief overview about the PCI subsystem, because many network device drivers are PCI devices. I do not delve into the PCI subsystem internals, because that is out of the scope of this book. Another interesting subsystem discussed in Chapter 14 is the IEEE 8012.15.4, which is for low-power and low-cost devices. These devices are sometimes mentioned in conjunction with the *Internet of Things* (IoT) concept, which involves connecting IP-enabled embedded devices to IP networks. It turns out that using IPv6 for these devices might be a good idea. This solution is termed IPv6 over Low Power Wireless Personal Area Networks (6LoWPAN). It has its own challenges, such as expanding the IPv6 Neighbour Discovery protocol to be suitable for such devices, which occasionally enter sleep mode (as opposed to ordinary IPv6 networks). These changes to the IPv6 Neighbour Discovery protocol have not been implemented yet, but it is interesting to consider the theory behind these changes. Apart from this, in Chapter 14 there are sections about other advanced topics like NFC, cgroups, Android, and more.

To better understand the Linux Kernel Network stack or participate in its development, you must be familiar with how its development is handled.

The Linux Kernel Networking Development Model

The kernel networking subsystem is very complex, and its development is quite dynamic. Like any Linux kernel subsystem, the development is done by git patches that are sent over a mailing list (sometimes over more than one mailing list) and that are eventually accepted or rejected by the maintainer of that subsystem. Learning about the Kernel Networking Development Model is important for many reasons. To better understand the code, to debug and solve problems in Linux Kernel Networking-based projects, to implement performance improvements and optimizations patches, or to implement new features, in many cases you need to learn many things such as the following:

- How to apply a patch

- How to read and interpret a patch

- How to find which patches could cause a given problem

- How to revert a patch

- How to find which patches are relevant to some feature

- How to adjust a project to an older kernel version (backporting)

- How to adjust a project to a newer kernel version (upgrading)

- How to clone a git tree

- How to rebase a git tree

- How to find out in which kernel version a specified git patch was applied

There are cases when you need to work with new features that were just added, and for this you need to know how to work with the latest, bleeding-edge tree. And there are cases when you encounter some bug or you want to add some new feature to the network stack, and you need to prepare a patch and submit it. The Linux Kernel Networking subsystem, like the other parts of the kernel, is managed by git, a source code management (SCM) system, developed by Linus Torvalds. If you intend to send patches for the mainline kernel, or if your project is managed by git, you must learn to use the git tool.

Sometimes you may even need to install a git server for development of local projects. Even if you are not intending to send any patches, you can use the git tool to retrieve a lot of information about the code and about the history of the development of the code. There are many available resources on the web about git; I recommend the free online book *Pro Git*, by Scott Chacon, available at http://git-scm.com/book. If you intend to submit your patches to the mainline, you must adhere to some strict rules for writing, checking, and submitting patches so that your patch will be applied. Your patch should conform to the kernel coding style and should be tested. You also need to be patient, as sometimes even a trivial patch can be applied only after several days. I recommend learning to configure a host for using the git send-email command to submit patches (though submitting patches can be done with other mail clients, even with the popular Gmail webmail client). There are plenty of guides on the web about how to use git to prepare and send kernel patches. I also recommend reading Documentation/SubmittingPatches and Documentation/CodingStyle in the kernel tree before submitting your first patch.

And I recommended using the following PERL scripts:

- `scripts/checkpatch.pl` to check the correctness of a patch

- `scripts/get_maintainer.pl` to find out to which maintainers a patch should be sent

One of the most important resources of information is the Kernel Networking Development mailing list, netdev: `netdev@vger.kernel.org`, archived at `www.spinics.net/lists/netdev`. This is a high volume list. Most of the posts are patches and Request for Comments (RFCs) for new code, along with comments and discussions about patches. This mailing list handles the Linux Kernel Networking stack and network device drivers, except for cases when dealing with a subsystem that has a specific mailing list and a specific `git` repository (such as the wireless subsystem, discussed in Chapter 12). Development of the `iproute2` and the `ethtool` userspace packages is also handled in the `netdev` mailing list. It should be mentioned here that not every networking subsystem has a mailing list of its own; for example, the IPsec subsystem (discussed in Chapter 10), does not have a mailing list, nor does the IEEE 802.15.4 subsystem (Chapter 14). Some networking subsystems have their own specific `git` tree, maintainer, and mailing list, such as the wireless mailing list and the Bluetooth mailing list. From time to time the maintainers of these subsystems send a pull request for their `git` trees over the `netdev` mailing list. Another source of information is `Documentation/networking` in the kernel tree. It has a lot of information in many files about various networking topics, but keep in mind that the file that you find there is not always up to date.

The Linux Kernel Networking subsystem is maintained in two `git` repositories. Patches and RFCs are sent to the `netdev` mailing list for both repositories. Here are the two `git` trees:

- *net:* `http://git.kernel.org/?p=linux/kernel/git/davem/net.git`: for fixes to existing code already in the mainline tree

- *net-next:* `http://git.kernel.org/?p=linux/kernel/git/davem/net-next.git`: new code for the future kernel release

From time to time the maintainer of the networking subsystem, David Miller, sends pull requests for mainline for these `git` trees to Linus over the LKML. You should be aware that there are periods of time, during merge with mainline, when the net-next `git` tree is closed, and no patches should be sent. An announcement about when this period starts and another one when it ends is sent over the `netdev` mailing list.

■ **Note**   This book is based on kernel 3.9. All the code snippets are from this version, unless explicitly specified otherwise. The kernel tree is available from `www.kernel.org` as a `tar` file. Alternatively, you can download a kernel `git` tree with `git clone` (for example, using the URLs of the `git net` tree or the `git net-next` tree, which were mentioned earlier, or other `git` kernel repositories). There are plenty of guides on the Internet covering how to configure, build, and boot a Linux kernel. You can also browse various kernel versions online at `http://lxr.free-electrons.com/`. This website lets you follow where each method and each variable is referenced; moreover, you can navigate easily with a click of a mouse to previous versions of the Linux kernel. In case you are working with your own version of a Linux kernel tree, where some changes were made locally, you can locally install and configure a Linux Cross-Referencer server (LXR) on a local Linux machine. See `http://lxr.sourceforge.net/en/index.shtml`.

Summary

This chapter is a short introduction to the Linux Kernel Networking subsystem. I described the benefits of using Linux, a popular open source project, and the Kernel Networking Development Model. I also described the network device structure (net_device) and the socket buffer structure (sk_buff), which are the two most fundamental structures of the networking subsystem. You should refer to Appendix A for a detailed description of almost all the members of these structures and their uses. This chapter covered other important topics related to the traversal of a packet in the kernel networking stack, such as the lookup in the routing subsystem, fragmentation and defragmentation, protocol handler registration, and more. Some of these protocols are discussed in later chapters, including IPv4, IPv6, ICMP4 and ICMP6, ARP, and Neighbour Discovery. Several important subsystems, including the wireless subsystem, the Bluetooth subsystem, and the IEEE 812.5.4 subsystem, are also covered in later chapters. Chapter 2 starts the journey in the kernel network stack with netlink sockets, which provide a way for bidirectional communication between the userspace and the kernel, and which are talked about in several other chapters.

CHAPTER 2

■ ■ ■

Netlink Sockets

Chapter 1 discusses the roles of the Linux kernel networking subsystem and the three layers in which it operates. The netlink socket interface appeared first in the 2.2 Linux kernel as AF_NETLINK socket. It was created as a more flexible alternative to the awkward IOCTL communication method between userspace processes and the kernel. The IOCTL handlers cannot send asynchronous messages to userspace from the kernel, whereas netlink sockets can. In order to use IOCTL, there is another level of complexity: you need to define IOCTL numbers. The operation model of netlink is quite simple: you open and register a netlink socket in userspace using the socket API, and this netlink socket handles bidirectional communication with a kernel netlink socket, usually sending messages to configure various system settings and getting responses back from the kernel.

This chapter describes the netlink protocol implementation and API and discusses its advantages and drawbacks. I also talk about the new generic netlink protocol, discuss its implementation and its advantages, and give some illustrative examples using the libnl library. I conclude with a discussion of the socket monitoring interface.

The Netlink Family

The netlink protocol is a socket-based Inter Process Communication (IPC) mechanism, based on RFC 3549, "Linux Netlink as an IP Services Protocol." It provides a bidirectional communication channel between userspace and the kernel or among some parts of the kernel itself. Netlink is an extension of the standard socket implementation. The netlink protocol implementation resides mostly under net/netlink, where you will find the following four files:

- af_netlink.c
- af_netlink.h
- genetlink.c
- diag.c

Apart from them, there are a few header files. In fact, the af_netlink module is the most commonly used; it provides the netlink kernel socket API, whereas the genetlink module provides a new generic netlink API with which it should be easier to create netlink messages. The diag monitoring interface module (diag.c) provides an API to dump and to get information about the netlink sockets. I discuss the diag module later in this chapter in the section "Socket monitoring interface."

I should mention here that theoretically netlink sockets can be used to communicate between two userspace processes, or more (including sending multicast messages), though this is usually not used, and was not the original goal of netlink sockets. The UNIX domain sockets provide an API for IPC, and they are widely used for communication between two userspace processes.

Netlink has some advantages over other ways of communication between userspace and the kernel. For example, there is no need for polling when working with netlink sockets. A userspace application opens a socket and then calls recvmsg(), and enters a blocking state if no messages are sent from the kernel; see, for example, the rtnl_listen() method of the iproute2 package (lib/libnetlink.c). Another advantage is that the kernel can be the initiator of sending asynchronous messages to userspace, without any need for the userspace to trigger any action (for example, by calling some IOCTL or by writing to some sysfs entry). Yet another advantage is that netlink sockets support multicast transmission.

You create netlink sockets from userspace with the socket() system call. The netlink sockets can be SOCK_RAW sockets or SOCK_DGRAM sockets.

Netlink sockets can be created in the kernel or in userspace; kernel netlink sockets are created by the netlink_kernel_create() method; and userspace netlink sockets are created by the socket() system call. Creating a netlink socket from userspace or from the kernel creates a netlink_sock object. When the socket is created from userspace, it is handled by the netlink_create() method. When the socket is created in the kernel, it is handled by __netlink_kernel_create(); this method sets the NETLINK_KERNEL_SOCKET flag. Eventually both methods call __netlink_create() to allocate a socket in the common way (by calling the sk_alloc() method) and initialize it. Figure 2-1 shows how a netlink socket is created in the kernel and in userspace.

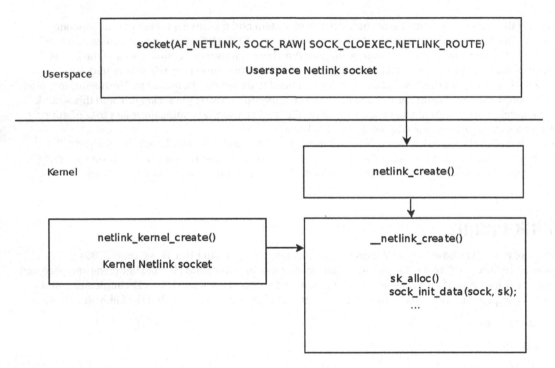

Figure 2-1. *Creating a netlink socket in the kernel and in userspace*

You can create a netlink socket from userspace in a very similar way to ordinary BSD-style sockets, like this, for example: socket(AF_NETLINK, SOCK_RAW, NETLINK_ROUTE). Then you should create a sockaddr_nl object (instance of the netlink socket address structure), initialize it, and use the standard BSD sockets API (such as bind(), sendmsg(), recvmsg(), and so on). The sockaddr_nl structure represents a netlink socket address in userspace or in the kernel.

Netlink socket libraries provide a convenient API to netlink sockets. I discuss them in the next section.

Netlink Sockets Libraries

I recommend you use the libnl API to develop userspace applications, which send or receive data by netlink sockets. The libnl package is a collection of libraries providing APIs to the netlink protocol-based Linux kernel interfaces. The iproute2 package uses the libnl library, as mentioned. Besides the core library (libnl), it includes support for the generic netlink family (libnl-genl), routing family (libnl-route), and netfilter family (libnl-nf). The package was developed mostly by Thomas Graf (www.infradead.org/~tgr/libnl/). I should mention here also that there is a library called libmnl, which is a minimalistic userspace library oriented to netlink developers. The libmnl library was mostly written by Pablo Neira Ayuso, with contributions from Jozsef Kadlecsik and Jan Engelhardt. (http://netfilter.org/projects/libmnl/).

The sockaddr_nl Structure

Let's take a look at the sockaddr_nl structure, which represents a netlink socket address:

```
struct sockaddr_nl {
    __kernel_sa_family_t    nl_family;      /* AF_NETLINK            */
    unsigned short          nl_pad;         /* zero                  */
    __u32                   nl_pid;         /* port ID               */
    __u32                   nl_groups;      /* multicast groups mask */
};
```

(include/uapi/linux/netlink.h)

- nl_family: Should always be AF_NETLINK.

- nl_pad: Should always be 0.

- nl_pid: The unicast address of a netlink socket. For kernel netlink sockets, it should be 0. Userspace applications sometimes set the nl_pid to be their process id (pid). In a userspace application, when you set nl_pid explicitly to 0, or don't set it at all, and afterwards call bind(), the kernel method netlink_autobind() assigns a value to nl_pid. It tries to assign the process id of the current thread. If you're creating two sockets in userspace, then you are responsible that their nl_pids are unique in case you don't call bind. Netlink sockets are not used only for networking; other subsystems, such as SELinux, audit, uevent, and others, use netlink sockets. The rtnelink sockets are netlink sockets specifically used for networking; they are used for routing messages, neighbouring messages, link messages, and more networking subsystem messages.

- nl_groups: The multicast group (or multicast group mask).

The next section discusses the iproute2 and the older net-tools packages. The iproute2 package is based upon netlink sockets, and you'll see an example of using netlink sockets in iproute2 in the section "Adding and deleting a routing entry in a routing table", later in this chapter. I mention the net-tools package, which is older and might be deprecated in the future, to emphasize that as an alternative to iproute2, it has less power and less abilities.

Userspace Packages for Controlling TCP/IP Networking

There are two userspace packages for controlling TCP/IP networking and handling network devices: net-tools and iproute2. The iproute2 package includes commands like the following:

- ip: For management of network tables and network interfaces

- tc: For traffic control management

- ss: For dumping socket statistics

- lnstat: For dumping linux network statistics

- bridge: For management of bridge addresses and devices

The iproute2 package is based mostly on sending requests to the kernel from userspace and getting replies back over netlink sockets. There are a few exceptions where IOCTLs are used in iproute2. For example, the ip tuntap command uses IOCTLs to add/remove a TUN/TAP device. If you look at the TUN/TAP software driver code, you'll find that it defines some IOCTL handlers, but it does not use the rtnetlink sockets. The net-tools package is based on IOCTLs and includes known commands like these:

- ifconifg

- arp

- route

- netstat

- hostname

- rarp

Some of the advanced functionalities of the iproute2 package are not available in the net-tools package.

The next section discusses kernel netlink sockets—the core engine of handling communication between userspace and the kernel by exchanging netlink messages of different types. Learning about kernel netlink sockets is essential for understanding the interface that the netlink layer provides to userspace.

Kernel Netlink Sockets

You create several netlink sockets in the kernel networking stack. Each kernel socket handles messages of different types: so for example, the netlink socket, which should handle NETLINK_ROUTE messages, is created in rtnetlink_net_init():

```
static int __net_init rtnetlink_net_init(struct net *net) {
    ...
    struct netlink_kernel_cfg cfg = {
        .groups     = RTNLGRP_MAX,
        .input      = rtnetlink_rcv,
        .cb_mutex   = &rtnl_mutex,
        .flags      = NL_CFG_F_NONROOT_RECV,
    };

    sk = netlink_kernel_create(net, NETLINK_ROUTE, &cfg);
    ...
}
```

Note that the rtnetlink socket is aware of network namespaces; the network namespace object (struct net) contains a member named rtnl (rtnetlink socket). In the rtnetlink_net_init() method, after the rtnetlink socket was created by calling netlink_kernel_create(), it is assigned to the rtnl pointer of the corresponding network namespace object.

Let's look in netlink_kernel_create() prototype:

```
struct sock *netlink_kernel_create(struct net *net, int unit, struct netlink_kernel_cfg *cfg)
```

- The first parameter (net) is the network namespace.

- The second parameter is the netlink protocol (for example, NETLINK_ROUTE for rtnetlink messages, or NETLINK_XFRM for IPsec or NETLINK_AUDIT for the audit subsystem). There are over 20 netlink protocols, but their number is limited by 32 (MAX_LINKS). This is one of the reasons for creating the generic netlink protocol, as you'll see later in this chapter. The full list of netlink protocols is in include/uapi/linux/netlink.h.

- The third parameter is a reference to netlink_kernel_cfg, which consists of optional parameters for the netlink socket creation:

```
struct netlink_kernel_cfg {
    unsigned int    groups;
    unsigned int    flags;
    void            (*input)(struct sk_buff *skb);
    struct mutex    *cb_mutex;
    void            (*bind)(int group);
};
(include/uapi/linux/netlink.h)
```

The groups member is for specifying a multicast group (or a mask of multicast groups). It's possible to join a multicast group by setting nl_groups of the sockaddr_nl object (you can also do this with the nl_join_groups() method of libnl). However, in this way you are limited to joining only 32 groups. Since kernel version 2.6.14, you can use the NETLINK_ADD_MEMBERSHIP/ NETLINK_DROP_MEMBERSHIP socket option to join/leave a multicast group, respectively. Using the socket option enables you to join a much higher number of groups. The nl_socket_add_memberships()/nl_socket_drop_membership() methods of libnl use this socket option.

The flags member can be NL_CFG_F_NONROOT_RECV or NL_CFG_F_NONROOT_SEND.

When CFG_F_NONROOT_RECV is set, a non-superuser can bind to a multicast group; in netlink_bind() there is the following code:

```
static int netlink_bind(struct socket *sock, struct sockaddr *addr,
                        int addr_len)
{
  ...
  if (nladdr->nl_groups) {
        if (!netlink_capable(sock, NL_CFG_F_NONROOT_RECV))
                    return -EPERM;
  }
```

For a non-superuser, if the NL_CFG_F_NONROOT_RECV is not set, then when binding to a multicast group the netlink_capable() method will return 0, and you get –EPRM error.

When the NL_CFG_F_NONROOT_SEND flag is set, a non-superuser is allowed to send multicasts.

The input member is for a callback; when the input member in netlink_kernel_cfg is NULL, the kernel socket won't be able to receive data from userspace (sending data from the kernel to userspace is possible, though). For the rtnetlink kernel socket, the rtnetlink_rcv() method was declared to be the input callback; as a result, data sent from userspace over the rtnelink socket will be handled by the rtnetlink_rcv() callback.

For uevent kernel events, you need only to send data from the kernel to userspace; so, in lib/kobject_uevent.c, you have an example of a netlink socket where the input callback is undefined:

```
static int uevent_net_init(struct net *net)
{
    struct uevent_sock *ue_sk;
    struct netlink_kernel_cfg cfg = {
        .groups    = 1,
        .flags     = NL_CFG_F_NONROOT_RECV,
    };

    ...
    ue_sk->sk = netlink_kernel_create(net, NETLINK_KOBJECT_UEVENT, &cfg);
    ...
}
```
(lib/kobject_uevent.c)

The mutex (cb_mutex) in the netlink_kernel_cfg object is optional; when not defining a mutex, you use the default one, cb_def_mutex (an instance of a mutex structure; see net/netlink/af_netlink.c). In fact, most netlink kernel sockets are created without defining a mutex in the netlink_kernel_cfg object. For example, the uevent kernel netlink socket (NETLINK_KOBJECT_UEVENT), mentioned earlier. Also, the audit kernel netlink socket (NETLINK_AUDIT) and other netlink sockets don't define a mutex. The rtnetlink socket is an exception—it uses the rtnl_mutex. Also the generic netlink socket, discussed in the next section, defines a mutex of its own: genl_mutex.

The netlink_kernel_create() method makes an entry in a table named nl_table by calling the netlink_insert() method. Access to the nl_table is protected by a read write lock named nl_table_lock; lookup in this table is done by the netlink_lookup() method, specifying the protocol and the port id. Registration of a callback for a specified message type is done by rtnl_register(); there are several places in the networking kernel code where you register such callbacks. For example, in rtnetlink_init() you register callbacks for some messages, like RTM_NEWLINK (creating a new link), RTM_DELLINK (deleting a link), RTM_GETROUTE (dumping the route table), and more. In net/core/neighbour.c, you register callbacks for RTM_NEWNEIGH messages (creating a new neighbour), RTM_DELNEIGH (deleting a neighbour), RTM_GETNEIGHTBL message (dumping the neighbour table), and more. I discuss these actions in depth in Chapters 5 and 7. You also register callbacks to other types of messages in the FIB code (ip_fib_init()), in the multicast code (ip_mr_init()), in the IPv6 code, and in other places.

The first step you should take to work with a netlink kernel socket is to register it. Let's take a look at the rtnl_register() method prototype:

```
extern void rtnl_register(int protocol, int msgtype,
                    rtnl_doit_func,
                    rtnl_dumpit_func,
                    rtnl_calcit_func);
```

The first parameter is the protocol family (when you don't aim at a specific protocol, it is PF_UNSPEC); you'll find a list of all the protocol families in include/linux/socket.h.

The second parameter is the netlink message type, like RTM_NEWLINK or RTM_NEWNEIGH. These are private netlink message types which the rtnelink protocol added. The full list of message types is in include/uapi/linux/rtnetlink.h.

The last three parameters are callbacks: doit, dumpit, and calcit. The callbacks are the actions you want to perform for handling the message, and you usually specify only one callback.

The doit callback is for actions like addition/deletion/modification; the dumpit callback is for retrieving information, and the calcit callback is for calculation of buffer size. The rtnetlink module has a table named rtnl_msg_handlers. This table is indexed by protocol number. Each entry in the table is a table in itself, indexed by message type. Each element in the table is an instance of rtnl_link, which is a structure that consists of pointers for these three callbacks. When registering a callback with rtnl_register(), you add the specified callback to this table.

Registering a callback is done like this, for example: rtnl_register(PF_UNSPEC, RTM_NEWLINK, rtnl_newlink, NULL, NULL) in net/core/rtnetlink.c. This adds rtnl_newlink as the doit callback for RTM_NEWLINK messages in the corresponding rtnl_msg_handlers entry.

Sending of rtnelink messages is done with rtmsg_ifinfo(). For example, in dev_open() you create a new link, so you call: rtmsg_ifinfo(RTM_NEWLINK, dev, IFF_UP|IFF_RUNNING); in the rtmsg_ifinfo() method, first the nlmsg_new() method is called to allocate an sk_buff with the proper size. Then two objects are created: the netlink message header (nlmsghdr) and an ifinfomsg object, which is located immediately after the netlink message header. These two objects are initialized by the rtnl_fill_ifinfo() method. Then rtnl_notify() is called to send the packet; sending the packet is actually done by the generic netlink method, nlmsg_notify() (in net/netlink/af_netlink.c). Figure 2-2 shows the stages of sending rtnelink messages with the rtmsg_ifinfo() method.

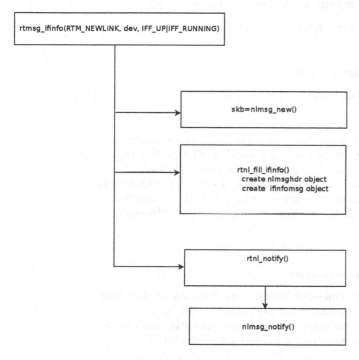

Figure 2-2. *Sending of rtnelink messages with the* rtmsg_ifinfo() *method*

The next section is about netlink messages, which are exchanged between userspace and the kernel. A netlink message always starts with a netlink message header, so your first step in learning about netlink messages will be to study the netlink message header format.

The Netlink Message Header

A netlink message should obey a certain format, specified in RFC 3549, "Linux Netlink as an IP Services Protocol", section 2.2, "Message Format." A netlink message starts with a fixed size netlink header, and after it there is a payload. This section describes the Linux implementation of the netlink message header.

The netlink message header is defined by struct nlmsghdr in include/uapi/linux/netlink.h:

```
struct nlmsghdr
{
    __u32 nlmsg_len;
    __u16 nlmsg_type;
```

```
    __u16 nlmsg_flags;
    __u32 nlmsg_seq;
    __u32 nlmsg_pid;
};
(include/uapi/linux/netlink.h)
```

Every netlink packet starts with a netlink message header, which is represented by struct nlmsghdr. The length of nlmsghdr is 16 bytes. It contains five fields:

- nlmsg_len is the length of the message including the header.

- nlmsg_type is the message type; there are four basic netlink message header types:

    - NLMSG_NOOP: No operation, message must be discarded.

    - NLMSG_ERROR: Error occurred.

    - NLMSG_DONE: A multipart message is terminated.

    - NLMSG_OVERRUN: Overrun notification: error, data was lost.

        (include/uapi/linux/netlink.h)

        However, families can add netlink message header types of their own. For example, the rtnetlink protocol family adds message header types such as RTM_NEWLINK, RTM_DELLINK, RTM_NEWROUTE, and a lot more (see include/uapi/linux/rtnetlink.h). For a full list of the netlink message header types that were added by the rtnelink family with detailed explanation on each, see: man 7 rtnetlink. Note that message type values smaller than NLMSG_MIN_TYPE (0x10) are reserved for control messages and may not be used.

- nlmsg_flags field can be as follows:

    - NLM_F_REQUEST: When it's a request message.

    - NLM_F_MULTI: When it's a multipart message. Multipart messages are used for table dumps. Usually the size of messages is limited to a page (PAGE_SIZE). So large messages are divided into smaller ones, and each of them (except the last one) has the NLM_F_MULTI flag set. The last message has the NLMSG_DONE flag set.

    - NLM_F_ACK: When you want the receiver of the message to reply with ACK. Netlink ACK messages are sent by the netlink_ack() method (net/netlink/af_netlink.c).

    - NLM_F_DUMP: Retrieve information about a table/entry.

    - NLM_F_ROOT: Specify the tree root.

    - NLM_F_MATCH: Return all matching entries.

    - NLM_F_ATOMIC: This flag is deprecated.

        The following flags are modifiers for creation of an entry:

    - NLM_F_REPLACE: Override existing entry.

    - NLM_F_EXCL: Do not touch entry, if it exists.

    - NLM_F_CREATE: Create entry, if it does not exist.

- NLM_F_APPEND: Add entry to end of list.

- NLM_F_ECHO: Echo this request.

    I've shown the most commonly used flags. For a full list, see
    include/uapi/linux/netlink.h.

- nlmsg_seq is the sequence number (for message sequences). Unlike some Layer 4 transport protocols, there is no strict enforcement of the sequence number.

- nlmsg_pid is the sending port id. When a message is sent from the kernel, the nlmsg_pid is 0. When a message is sent from userspace, the nlmsg_pid can be set to be the process id of that userspace application which sent the message.

    Figure 2-3 shows the netlink message header.

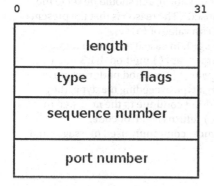

Figure 2-3. *nlmsg header*

After the header comes the payload. The payload of netlink messages is composed of a set of attributes which are represented in Type-Length-Value (TLV) format. With TLV, the type and length are fixed in size (typically 1–4 bytes), and the value field is of variable size. The TLV representation is used also in other places in the networking code—for example, in IPv6 (see RFC 2460). TLV provides flexibility which makes future extensions easier to implement. Attributes can be nested, which enables complex tree structures of attributes.

Each netlink attribute header is defined by struct nlattr:

```
struct nlattr {
    __u16    nla_len;
    __u16    nla_type;
};
(include/uapi/linux/netlink.h)
```

- nla_len: The size of the attribute in bytes.

- nla_type: The attribute type. The value of nla_type can be, for example, NLA_U32 (for a 32-bit unsigned integer), NLA_STRING for a variable length string, NLA_NESTED for a nested attribute, NLA_UNSPEC for arbitrary type and length, and more. You can find the list of available types in include/net/netlink.h.

Every netlink attribute must be aligned by a 4-byte boundary (NLA_ALIGNTO).

Each family can define an attribute validation policy, which represents the expectations regarding the received attributes. This validation policy is represented by the nla_policy object. In fact, the nla_policy struct has exactly the same content as struct nlattr:

```
struct nla_policy {
    u16    type;
    u16    len;
};
(include/uapi/linux/netlink.h)
```

The attribute validation policy is an array of nla_policy objects; this array is indexed by the attribute number. For each attribute (except the fixed-length attributes), if the value of len in the nla_policy object is 0, no validation should be performed. If the attribute is one of the string types (such as NLA_STRING), len should be the maximum length of the string, without the terminating NULL byte. If the attribute type is NLA_UNSPEC or unknown, len should be set to the exact length of the attribute's payload. If the attribute type is NLA_FLAG, len is unused. (The reason is that the presence of the attribute itself implies a value of true, and the absence of the attribute implies a value of false).

Receiving a generic netlink message in the kernel is handled by genl_rcv_msg(). In case it is a dump request (when the NLM_F_DUMP flag is set), you dump the table by calling the netlink_dump_start() method. If it's not a dump request, you parse the payload by the nlmsg_parse() method. The nlmsg_parse() method performs attribute validation by calling validate_nla() (lib/nlattr.c). If there are attributes with a type exceeding maxtype, they will be silently ignored for backwards compatibility. In case validation fails, you don't continue to the next step in genl_rcv_msg() (which is running the doit() callback), and the genl_rcv_msg() returns an error code.

The next section describes the NETLINK_ROUTE messages, which are the most commonly used messages in the networking subsystem.

NETLINK_ROUTE Messages

The rtnetlink (NETLINK_ROUTE) messages are not limited to the networking routing subsystem: there are neighbouring subsystem messages as well, interface setup messages, firewalling message, netlink queuing messages, policy routing messages, and many other types of rtnetlink messages, as you'll see in later chapters.

The NETLINK_ROUTE messages can be divided into families:

- LINK (network interfaces)

- ADDR (network addresses)

- ROUTE (routing messages)

- NEIGH (neighbouring subsystem messages)

- RULE (policy routing rules)

- QDISC (queueing discipline)

- TCLASS (traffic classes)

- ACTION (packet action API, see net/sched/act_api.c)

- NEIGHTBL (neighbouring table)

- ADDRLABEL (address labeling)

Each of these families has three types of messages: for creation, deletion, and retrieving information. So, for routing messages, you have the RTM_NEWROUTE message type for creating a route, the RTM_DELROUTE message type for deleting a route, and the RTM_GETROUTE message type for retrieving a route. With LINK messages there is, apart from the three methods for creation, deletion and information retrieval, an additional message for modifying a link: RTM_SETLINK.

There are cases in which an error occurs, and you send an error message as a reply. The netlink error message is represented by the nlmsgerr struct:

```
struct nlmsgerr {
    int         error;
    struct nlmsghdr msg;
};
(include/uapi/linux/netlink.h)
```

In fact, as you can see in Figure 2-4, the netlink error message is built from a netlink message header and an error code. When the error code is not 0, the netlink message header of the original request which caused the error is appended after the error code field.

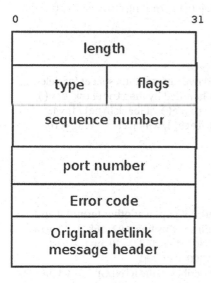

Figure 2-4. *Netlink error message*

If you send a message that was constructed erroneously (for example, the nlmsg_type is not valid) then a netlink error message is sent back, and the error code is set according to the error that occurred. For example, when the nlmsg_type is not valid (a negative value, or a value higher than the maximum value permitted) the error code is set to –EOPNOTSUPP. See the rtnetlink_rcv_msg() method in net/core/rtnetlink.c. In error messages, the sequence number is set to be the sequence number of the request that caused the error.

The sender can request to get an ACK for a netlink message. This is done by setting the netlink message header type (nlmsg_type) to be NLM_F_ACK. When the kernel sends an ACK, it uses an error message (the netlink message header type of this message is set to be NLMSG_ERROR) with an error code of 0. In this case, the original netlink header of the request is not appended to the error message. For implementation details, see the netlink_ack() method implementation in net/netlink/af_netlink.c.

After learning about NETLINK_ROUTE messages, you're ready to look at an example of adding and deleting a routing entry in a routing table using NETLINK_ROUTE messages.

Adding and Deleting a Routing Entry in a Routing Table

Behind the scenes, let's see what happens in the kernel in the context of netlink protocol when adding and deleting a routing entry. You can add a routing entry to the routing table by running, for example, the following:

```
ip route add 192.168.2.11 via 192.168.2.20
```

This command sends a netlink message from userspace (RTM_NEWROUTE) over an rtnetlink socket for adding a routing entry. The message is received by the rtnetlink kernel socket and handled by the `rtnetlink_rcv()` method. Eventually, adding the routing entry is done by invoking `inet_rtm_newroute()` in `net/ipv4/fib_frontend.c`. Subsequently, insertion into the Forwarding Information Base (FIB), which is the routing database, is accomplished with the `fib_table_insert()` method; however, inserting into the routing table is not the only task of `fib_table_insert()`. You should notify all listeners who performed registration for RTM_NEWROUTE messages. How? When inserting a new routing entry, you call the `rtmsg_fib()` method with RTM_NEWROUTE. The `rtmsg_fib()` method builds a netlink message and sends it by calling `rtnl_notify()` to notify all listeners who are registered to the RTNLGRP_IPV4_ROUTE group. These RTNLGRP_IPV4_ROUTE listeners can be registered in the kernel as well as in userspace (as is done in iproute2, or in some userspace routing daemons, like xorp). You'll see shortly how userspace daemons of iproute2 can subscribe to various rtnelink multicast groups.

When deleting a routing entry, something quite similar happens. You can delete the routing entry earlier by running the following:

```
ip route del 192.168.2.11
```

That command sends a netlink message from userspace (RTM_DELROUTE) over an rtnetlink socket for deleting a routing entry. The message is again received by the rtnetlink kernel socket and handled by the `rtnetlink_rcv()` callback. Eventually, deleting the routing entry is done by invoking `inet_rtm_delroute()` callback in `net/ipv4/fib_frontend.c`. Subsequently, deletion from the FIB is done with `fib_table_delete()`, which calls `rtmsg_fib()`, this time with the RTM_DELROUTE message.

You can monitor networking events with iproute2 ip command like this:

```
ip monitor route
```

For example, if you open one terminal and run `ip monitor route` there, and then open another terminal and run `ip route add 192.168.1.10 via 192.168.2.200`, on the first terminal you'll see this line: `192.168.1.10 via 192.168.2.200 dev em1`. And when you run, on the second terminal, `ip route del 192.168.1.10`, on the first terminal the following text will appear: `Deleted 192.168.1.10 via 192.168.2.200 dev em1`.

Running `ip monitor route` runs a daemon that opens a netlink socket and subscribes to the RTNLGRP_IPV4_ROUTE multicast group. Now, adding/deleting a route, as done in this example, will result in this: the message that was sent with `rtnl_notify()` will be received by the daemon and displayed on the terminal.

You can subscribe to other multicast groups in this way. For example, to subscribe to the RTNLGRP_LINK multicast group, run `ip monitor link`. This daemon receives netlink messages from the kernel—when adding/deleting a link, for example. So if you open one terminal and run `ip monitor link`, and then open another terminal and add a VLAN interface by `vconfig add eth1 200,` on the first terminal you'll see lines like this:

```
4: eth1.200@eth1: <BROADCAST,MULTICAST> mtu 1500 qdisc noop state DOWN
    link/ether 00:e0:4c:53:44:58 brd ff:ff:ff:ff:ff:ff
```

And if you will add a bridge on the second terminal by brctl addbr mybr, on the first terminal you'll see lines like this:

```
5: mybr: <BROADCAST,MULTICAST> mtu 1500 qdisc noop state DOWN
    link/ether a2:7c:be:62:b5:b6 brd ff:ff:ff:ff:ff:ff
```

You've seen what a netlink message is and how it is created and handled. You've seen how netlink sockets are handled. Next you'll learn why the generic netlink family (introduced in kernel 2.6.15) was created, and you'll learn about its Linux implementation.

Generic Netlink Protocol

One of the drawbacks of the netlink protocol is that the number of protocol families is limited to 32 (MAX_LINKS). This is one of the main reasons that the generic netlink family was created—to provide support for adding a higher number of families. It acts as a netlink multiplexer and works with a single netlink family (NETLINK_GENERIC). The generic netlink protocol is based on the netlink protocol and uses its API.

To add a netlink protocol family, you should add a protocol family definition in include/linux/netlink.h. But with generic netlink protocol, there is no need for that. The generic netlink protocol is also intended to be used in other subsystems besides networking, because it provides a general purpose communication channel. For example, it's used also by the acpi subsystem (see the definition of acpi_event_genl_family in drivers/acpi/event.c), by the task stats code (see kernel/taskstats.c), by the thermal events code, and more.

The generic netlink kernel socket is created by the netlink_kernel_create() method like this:

```
static int __net_init genl_pernet_init(struct net *net) {
    ..
        struct netlink_kernel_cfg cfg = {
                .input       = genl_rcv,
                .cb_mutex    = &genl_mutex,
                .flags       = NL_CFG_F_NONROOT_RECV,
        };
        net->genl_sock = netlink_kernel_create(net, NETLINK_GENERIC, &cfg);
    ...
}
(net/netlink/genetlink.c)
```

Note that, like the netlink sockets described earlier, the generic netlink socket is also aware of network namespaces; the network namespace object (struct net) contains a member named genl_sock (a generic netlink socket). As you can see, the network namespace genl_sock pointer is assigned in the genl_pernet_init() method.

The genl_rcv() method is defined to be the input callback of the genl_sock object, which was created earlier by the genl_pernet_init() method. As a result, data sent from userspace over generic netlink sockets is handled in the kernel by the genl_rcv() callback.

You can create a generic netlink userspace socket with the socket() system call, though it is better to use the libnl-genl API (discussed later in this section).

Immediately after creating the generic netlink kernel socket, register the controller family (genl_ctrl):

```
static struct genl_family genl_ctrl = {
        .id = GENL_ID_CTRL,
        .name = "nlctrl",
```

```
        .version = 0x2,
        .maxattr = CTRL_ATTR_MAX,
        .netnsok = true,
};

static int __net_init genl_pernet_init(struct net *net) {
...
err = genl_register_family_with_ops(&genl_ctrl, &genl_ctrl_ops, 1)
...
```

The genl_ctrl has a fixed id of 0x10 (GENL_ID_CTRL); it is in fact the only instance of genl_family that's initialized with a fixed id; all other instances are initialized with GENL_ID_GENERATE as an id, which subsequently is replaced by a dynamically assigned value.

There is support for registering multicast groups in generic netlink sockets by defining a genl_multicast_group object and calling genl_register_mc_group(); for example, in the Near Field Communication (NFC) subsystem, you have the following:

```
static struct genl_multicast_group nfc_genl_event_mcgrp = {
        .name = NFC_GENL_MCAST_EVENT_NAME,
 };

int __init nfc_genl_init(void)
{
...
 rc = genl_register_mc_group(&nfc_genl_family, &nfc_genl_event_mcgrp);
...
}
(net/nfc/netlink.c)
```

The name of a multicast group should be unique, because it is the primary key for lookups.

In the multicast group, the id is also generated dynamically when registering a multicast group by calling the find_first_zero_bit() method in genl_register_mc_group(). There is only one multicast group, the notify_grp, that has a fixed id, GENL_ID_CTRL.

To work with generic netlink sockets in the kernel, you should do the following:

- Create a genl_family object and register it by calling genl_register_family().

- Create a genl_ops object and register it by calling genl_register_ops().

Alternatively, you can call genl_register_family_with_ops() and pass to it a genl_family object, an array of genl_ops, and its size. This method will first call genl_register_family() and then, if successful, will call genl_register_ops() for each genl_ops element of the specified array of genl_ops.

The genl_register_family() and genl_register_ops() as well as the genl_family and genl_ops are defined in include/net/genetlink.h.

The wireless subsystem uses generic netlink sockets:

```
int nl80211_init(void)
{
    int err;
```

```
    err = genl_register_family_with_ops(&nl80211_fam,
        nl80211_ops, ARRAY_SIZE(nl80211_ops));
...
}
(net/wireless/nl80211.c)
```

The generic netlink protocol is used by some userspace packages, such as the hostapd package and the iw package. The hostapd package (http://hostap.epitest.fi) provides a userspace daemon for wireless access point and authentication servers. The iw package is for manipulating wireless devices and their configuration (see http://wireless.kernel.org/en/users/Documentation/iw).

The iw package is based on nl80211 and the libnl library. Chapter 12 discusses nl80211 in more detail. The old userspace wireless package is called wireless-tools and is based on sending IOCTLs.

Here are the genl_family and genl_ops definitions in nl80211:

```
static struct genl_family nl80211_fam = {
    .id         = GENL_ID_GENERATE, /* don't bother with a hardcoded ID */
    .name       = "nl80211",     /* have users key off the name instead */
    .hdrsize    = 0,         /* no private header */
    .version    = 1,         /* no particular meaning now */
    .maxattr    = NL80211_ATTR_MAX,
    .netnsok    = true,
    .pre_doit   = nl80211_pre_doit,
    .post_doit  = nl80211_post_doit,
};
```

- name: Must be a unique name.

- id: id is GENL_ID_GENERATE in this case, which is in fact 0. GENL_ID_GENERATE tells the generic netlink controller to assign the channel a unique channel number when you register the family with genl_register_family(). The genl_register_family() assigns an id in the range 16 (GENL_MIN_ID, which is 0x10) to 1023 (GENL_MAX_ID).

- hdrsize: Size of a private header.

- maxattr: NL80211_ATTR_MAX, which is the maximum number of attributes supported.

    The nl80211_policy validation policy array has NL80211_ATTR_MAX elements (each attribute has an entry in the array):

- netnsok: true, which means the family can handle network namespaces.

- pre_doit: A hook that's called before the doit() callback.

- post_doit: A hook that can, for example, undo locking or any required private tasks after the doit() callback.

    You can add a command or several commands with the genl_ops structure. Let's take a look at the definition of genl_ops struct and then at its usage in nl80211:

```
struct genl_ops {
    u8                      cmd;
    u8                      internal_flags;
    unsigned int            flags;
    const struct nla_policy *policy;
    int                     (*doit)(struct sk_buff *skb,
```

```
                                              struct genl_info *info);
        int                   (*dumpit)(struct sk_buff *skb,
                                              struct netlink_callback *cb);
        int                   (*done)(struct netlink_callback *cb);
        struct list_head       ops_list;
};
```

- cmd: Command identifier (the genl_ops struct defines a single command and its doit/dumpit handlers).

- internal_flags: Private flags which are defined and used by the family. For example, in nl80211, there are many operations that define internal flags (such as NL80211_FLAG_ NEED_NETDEV_UP, NL80211_FLAG_NEED_RTNL, and more). The nl80211 pre_doit() and post_doit() callbacks perform actions according to these flags. See net/wireless/nl80211.

- flags: Operation flags. Values can be the following:

  - GENL_ADMIN_PERM: When this flag is set, it means that the operation requires the CAP_NET_ADMIN privilege; see the genl_rcv_msg() method in net/netlink/genetlink.c.

  - GENL_CMD_CAP_DO: This flag is set if the genl_ops struct implements the doit() callback.

  - GENL_CMD_CAP_DUMP: This flag is set if the genl_ops struct implements the dumpit() callback.

  - GENL_CMD_CAP_HASPOL: This flag is set if the genl_ops struct defines attribute validation policy (nla_policy array).

- policy : Attribute validation policy is discussed later in this section when describing the payload.

- doit: Standard command callback.

- dumpit: Callback for dumping.

- done: Completion callback for dumps.

- ops_list: Operations list.

```
static struct genl_ops nl80211_ops[] = {
    {

    ...
      {
        .cmd = NL80211_CMD_GET_SCAN,
        .policy = nl80211_policy,
        .dumpit = nl80211_dump_scan,
      },
    ...
    }
```

Note that either a doit or a dumpit callback must be specified for every element of genl_ops (nl80211_ops in this case) or the function will fail with -EINVAL.

This entry in genl_ops adds the nl80211_dump_scan() callback as a handler of the NL80211_CMD_GET_SCAN command. The nl80211_policy is an array of nla_policy objects and defines the expected datatype of the attributes and their length.

When running a scan command from userspace, for example by iw dev wlan0 scan, you send from userspace a generic netlink message whose command is NL80211_CMD_GET_SCAN over a generic netlink socket. Messages are sent by the nl_send_auto_complete() method or by nl_send_auto() in the newer libnl versions. nl_send_auto() fills the missing bits and pieces in the netlink message header. If you don't require any of the automatic message completion functionality, you can use nl_send() directly.

The message is handled by the nl80211_dump_scan() method, which is the dumpit callback for this command (net/wireless/nl80211.c). There are more than 50 entries in the nl80211_ops object for handling commands, including NL80211_CMD_GET_INTERFACE, NL80211_CMD_SET_INTERFACE, NL80211_CMD_START_AP, and so on.

To send commands to the kernel, a userspace application should know the family id. The family name is known in the userspace, but the family id is unknown in the userspace because it's determined only in runtime in the kernel. To get the family id, the userspace application should send a generic netlink CTRL_CMD_GETFAMILY request to the kernel. This request is handled by the ctrl_getfamily() method. It returns the family id as well as other information, such as the operations the family supports. Then the userspace can send commands to the kernel specifying the family id that it got in the reply. I discuss this more in the next section.

Creating and Sending Generic Netlink Messages

A generic netlink message starts with a netlink header, followed by the generic netlink message header, and then there is an optional user specific header. Only after all that do you find the optional payload, as you can see in Figure 2-5.

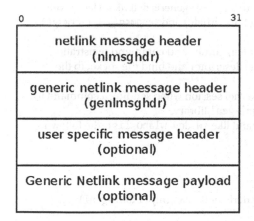

0   31

| netlink message header (nlmsghdr) |
| generic netlink message header (genlmsghdr) |
| user specific message header (optional) |
| Generic Netlink message payload (optional) |

Figure 2-5. *Generic netlink message.*

This is the generic netlink message header:

```
struct genlmsghdr {
    __u8    cmd;
    __u8    version;
    __u16   reserved;
};
(include/uapi/linux/genetlink.h)
```

- cmd is a generic netlink message type; each generic family that you register adds its own commands. For example, for the nl80211_fam family mentioned above, the commands it adds (like NL80211_CMD_GET_INTERFACE) are represented by the nl80211_commands enum. There are more than 60 commands (see include/linux/nl80211.h).

- version can be used for versioning support. With nl80211 it is 1, with no particular meaning. The version member allows changing the format of a message without breaking backward compatibility.

- reserved is for future use.

Allocating a buffer for a generic netlink message is done by the following method:

```
sk_buff *genlmsg_new(size_t payload, gfp_t flags)
```

This is in fact a wrapper around nlmsg_new().

After allocating a buffer with genlmsg_new(), the genlmsg_put() is called to create the generic netlink header, which is an instance of genlmsghdr. You send a unicast generic netlink message with genlmsg_unicast(), which is in fact a wrapper around nlmsg_unicast(). You can send a multicast generic netlink message in two ways:

- genlmsg_multicast(): This method sends the message to the default network namespace, net_init.

- genlmsg_multicast_allns(): This method sends the message to all network namespaces.

(All prototypes of the methods mentioned in this section are in include/net/genetlink.h.)

You can create a generic netlink socket from userspace like this: socket(AF_NETLINK, SOCK_RAW, NETLINK_GENERIC); this call is handled in the kernel by the netlink_create() method, like an ordinary, non-generic netlink socket, as you saw in the previous section. You can use the socket API to perform further calls like bind() and sendmsg() or recvmsg(); however, using the libnl library instead is recommended.

libnl-genl provides generic netlink API, for management of controller, family, and command registration. With libnl-genl, you can call genl_connect() to create a local socket file descriptor and bind the socket to the NETLINK_GENERIC netlink protocol.

Let's take a brief look at what happens in a short typical userspace-kernel session when sending a command to the kernel via generic netlink sockets using the libnl library and the libnl-genl library.

The iw package uses the libnl-genl library. When you run a command like iw dev wlan0 list, the following sequence occurs (omitting unimportant details):

```
state->nl_sock = nl_socket_alloc()
```

Allocate a socket (note the use here of libnl core API and not the generic netlink family (libnl-genl) yet.

```
genl_connect(state->nl_sock)
```

Call socket() with NETLINK_GENERIC and call bind() on this socket; the genl_connect() is a method of the libnl-genl library.

```
genl_ctrl_resolve(state->nl_sock, "nl80211");
```

This method resolves the generic netlink family name ("nl80211") to the corresponding numeric family identifier. The userspace application must send its subsequent messages to the kernel, specifying this id.

The genl_ctrl_resolve() method calls genl_ctrl_probe_by_name(), which in fact sends a generic netlink message to the kernel with the CTRL_CMD_GETFAMILY command.

In the kernel, the generic netlink controller ("nlctrl") handles the CTRL_CMD_GETFAMILY command by the ctrl_getfamily() method and returns the family id to userspace. This id was generated when the socket was created.

■ **Note** You can get various parameters (such as generated id, header size, max attributes, and more) of all the registered generic netlink families with the userspace tool genl (of iproute2) by running genl ctrl list.

You're now ready to learn about the socket monitoring interface, which lets you get information about sockets. The socket monitoring interface is used in userspace tools like ss, which displays socket information and statistics for various socket types, and in other projects, as you'll see in the next section.

Socket Monitoring Interface

The sock_diag netlink sockets provide a netlink-based subsystem that can be used to get information about sockets. This feature was added to the kernel to support checkpoint/restore functionality for Linux in userspace (CRIU). To support this functionality, additional data about sockets was needed. For example, /procfs doesn't say which are the peers of a UNIX domain socket (AF_UNIX), and this info is needed for checkpoint/restore support. This additional data is not exported via /proc, and to make changes to procfs entries isn't always desirable because it might break userspace applications. The sock_diag netlink sockets give an API which enables access to this additional data. This API is used in the CRIU project as well as in the ss util. Without the sock_diag, after *checkpointing* a process (saving the state of a process to the filesystem), you can't reconstruct its UNIX domain sockets because you don't know who the peers are.

To support the monitoring interface used by the ss tool, a netlink-based kernel socket is created (NETLINK_SOCK_DIAG). The ss tool, which is part of the iproute2 package, enables you to get socket statistics in a similar way to netstat. It can display more TCP and state information than other tools.

You create a netlink kernel socket for sock_diag like this:

```
static int __net_init diag_net_init(struct net *net)
{
    struct netlink_kernel_cfg cfg = {
        .input    = sock_diag_rcv,
    };

    net->diag_nlsk = netlink_kernel_create(net, NETLINK_SOCK_DIAG, &cfg);
    return net->diag_nlsk == NULL ? -ENOMEM : 0;
}
(net/core/sock_diag.c)
```

The sock_diag module has a table of sock_diag_handler objects named sock_diag_handlers. This table is indexed by the protocol number (for the list of protocol numbers, see include/linux/socket.h).

The sock_diag_handler struct is very simple:

```
struct sock_diag_handler {
__u8 family;
int (*dump)(struct sk_buff *skb, struct nlmsghdr *nlh);
};
(net/core/sock_diag.c)
```

Each protocol that wants to add a socket monitoring interface entry to this table first defines a handler and then calls sock_diag_register(), specifying its handler. For example, for UNIX sockets, there is the following in net/unix/diag.c:

The first step is definition of the handler:

```
static const struct sock_diag_handler unix_diag_handler = {
    .family = AF_UNIX,
    .dump = unix_diag_handler_dump,
};
```

The second step is registration of the handler:

```
static int __init unix_diag_init(void)
{
    return sock_diag_register(&unix_diag_handler);
}
```

Now, with ss -x or ss --unix, you can dump the statistics that are gathered by the UNIX diag module. In quite a similar way, there are diag modules for other protocols, such as UDP (net/ipv4/udp_diag.c), TCP (net/ipv4/tcp_diag.c), DCCP (/net/dccp/diag.c), and AF_PACKET (net/packet/diag.c).

There's also a diag module for the netlink sockets themselves. The /proc/net/netlink entry provides information about the netlink socket (netlink_sock object) like the portid, groups, the inode number of the socket, and more. If you want the details, dumping /proc/net/netlink is handled by netlink_seq_show() in net/netlink/af_netlink.c. There are some netlink_sock fields which /proc/net/netlink doesn't provide—for example, dst_group or dst_portid or groups above 32. For this reason, the netlink socket monitoring interface was added (net/netlink/diag.c). You should be able to use the ss tool of iproute2 to read netlink sockets information. The netlink diag code can be built also as a kernel module.

Summary

This chapter covered netlink sockets, which provide a mechanism for bidirectional communication between the userspace and the kernel and are widely used by the networking subsystem. You've seen some examples of netlink sockets usage. I also discussed netlink messages, how they're created and handled. Another important subject the chapter dealt with is the generic netlink sockets, including their advantages and their usage. The next chapter covers the ICMP protocol, including its usage and its implementation in IPv4 and IPv6.

Quick Reference

I conclude this chapter with a short list of important methods of the netlink and generic netlink subsystems. Some of them were mentioned in this chapter:

int netlink_rcv_skb(struct sk_buff *skb, int (*cb)(struct sk_buff *, struct nlmsghdr *))

This method handles receiving netlink messages. It's called from the input callback of netlink families (for example, in the rtnetlink_rcv() method for the rtnetlink family, or in the sock_diag_rcv() method for the sock_diag family. The method performs sanity checks, like making sure that the length of the netlink message header does not exceed the permitted max length (NLMSG_HDRLEN). It also avoids invoking the specified callback in case that the message is a control message. In case the ACK flag (NLM_F_ACK) is set, it sends an error message by invoking the netlink_ack() method.

struct sk_buff *netlink_alloc_skb(struct sock *ssk, unsigned int size, u32 dst_portid, gfp_t gfp_mask)

This method allocates an SKB with the specified size and gfp_mask; the other parameters (ssk, dst_portid) are used when working with memory mapped netlink IO (NETLINK_MMAP). This feature is not discussed in this chapter, and is located here: net/netlink/af_netlink.c.

struct netlink_sock *nlk_sk(struct sock *sk)

This method returns the netlink_sock object, which has an sk as a member, and is located here: net/netlink/af_netlink.h.

struct sock *netlink_kernel_create(struct net *net, int unit, struct netlink_kernel_cfg *cfg)

This method creates a kernel netlink socket.

struct nlmsghdr *nlmsg_hdr(const struct sk_buff *skb)

This method returns the netlink message header pointed to by skb->data.

struct nlmsghdr *__nlmsg_put(struct sk_buff *skb, u32 portid, u32 seq, int type, int len, int flags)

This method builds a netlink message header according to the specified parameters, and puts it in the skb, and is located here: include/linux/netlink.h.

struct sk_buff *nlmsg_new(size_t payload, gfp_t flags)

This method allocates a new netlink message with the specified message payload by calling alloc_skb(). If the specified payload is 0, alloc_skb() is called with NLMSG_HDRLEN (after alignment with the NLMSG_ALIGN macro).

int nlmsg_msg_size(int payload)

This method returns the length of a netlink message (message header length and payload), not including padding.

void rtnl_register(int protocol, int msgtype, rtnl_doit_func doit, rtnl_dumpit_func dumpit, rtnl_calcit_func calcit)

This method registers the specified rtnetlink message type with the three specified callbacks.

static int rtnetlink_rcv_msg(struct sk_buff *skb, struct nlmsghdr *nlh)

This method processes an rtnetlink message.

static int rtnl_fill_ifinfo(struct sk_buff *skb, struct net_device *dev, int type, u32 pid, u32 seq, u32 change, unsigned int flags, u32 ext_filter_mask)

This method creates two objects: a netlink message header (nlmsghdr) and an ifinfomsg object, located immediately after the netlink message header.

void rtnl_notify(struct sk_buff *skb, struct net *net, u32 pid, u32 group, struct nlmsghdr *nlh, gfp_t flags)

This method sends an rtnetlink message.

int genl_register_mc_group(struct genl_family *family, struct genl_multicast_group *grp)

This method registers the specified multicast group, notifies the userspace, and returns 0 on success or a negative error code. The specified multicast group must have a name. The multicast group id is generated dynamically in this method by the find_first_zero_bit() method for all multicast groups, except for notify_grp, which has a fixed id of 0x10 (GENL_ID_CTRL).

void genl_unregister_mc_group(struct genl_family *family, struct genl_multicast_group *grp)

This method unregisters the specified multicast group and notifies the userspace about it. All current listeners on the group are removed. It's not necessary to unregister all multicast groups before unregistering the family—unregistering the family causes all assigned multicast groups to be unregistered automatically.

int genl_register_ops(struct genl_family *family, struct genl_ops *ops)

This method registers the specified operations and assigns them to the specified family. Either a doit() or a dumpit() callback must be specified or the operation will fail with -EINVAL. Only one operation structure per command identifier may be registered. It returns 0 on success or a negative error code.

int genl_unregister_ops(struct genl_family *family, struct genl_ops *ops)

This method unregisters the specified operations and unassigns them from the specified family. The operation blocks until the current message processing has finished and doesn't start again until the unregister process has finished. It's not necessary to unregister all operations before unregistering the family—unregistering the family causes all assigned operations to be unregistered automatically. It returns 0 on success or a negative error code.

int genl_register_family(struct genl_family *family)

This method registers the specified family after validating it first. Only one family may be registered with the same family name or identifier. The family id may equal GENL_ID_GENERATE, causing a unique id to be automatically generated and assigned.

int genl_register_family_with_ops(struct genl_family *family, struct genl_ops *ops, size_t n_ops)

This method registers the specified family and operations. Only one family may be registered with the same family name or identifier. The family id may equal GENL_ID_GENERATE, causing a unique id to be automatically generated and assigned. Either a `doit` or a `dumpit` callback must be specified for every registered operation or the function will fail. Only one operation structure per command identifier may be registered. This is equivalent to calling `genl_register_family()` followed by `genl_register_ops()` for every operation entry in the table, taking care to unregister the family on the error path. The method returns 0 on success or a negative error code.

int genl_unregister_family(struct genl_family *family)

This method unregisters the specified family and returns 0 on success or a negative error code.

void *genlmsg_put(struct sk_buff *skb, u32 portid, u32 seq, struct genl_family *family, int flags, u8 cmd)

This method adds a generic netlink header to a netlink message.

int genl_register_family(struct genl_family *family) int genl_unregister_family(struct genl_family *family)

This method registers/unregisters a generic netlink family.

int genl_register_ops(struct genl_family *family, struct genl_ops *ops) int genl_unregister_ops(struct genl_family *family, struct genl_ops *ops)

This method registers/unregisters generic netlink operations.

void genl_lock(void)
void genl_unlock(void)

This method locks/unlocks the generic netlink mutex (`genl_mutex`). Used for example in `net/l2tp/l2tp_netlink.c`.

CHAPTER 3

■ ■ ■

Internet Control Message Protocol (ICMP)

Chapter 2 discusses the netlink sockets implementation and how netlink sockets are used as a communication channel between the kernel and userspace. This chapter deals with the ICMP protocol, which is a Layer 4 protocol. Userspace applications can use the ICMP protocol (to send and receive ICMP packets) by using the sockets API (the best-known example is probably the ping utility). This chapter discusses how these ICMP packets are handled in the kernel and gives some examples.

The ICMP protocol is used primarily as a mandatory mechanism for sending error and control messages about the network layer (L3). The protocol enables getting feedback about problems in the communication environment by sending ICMP messages. These messages provide error handling and diagnostics. The ICMP protocol is relatively simple but is very important for assuring correct system behavior. The basic definition of ICMPv4 is in RFC 792, "Internet Control Message Protocol." This RFC defines the goals of the ICMPv4 protocol and the format of various ICMPv4 messages. I also mention in this chapter RFC 1122 ("Requirements for Internet Hosts—Communication Layers") which defines some requirements about several ICMP messages; RFC 4443, which defines the ICMPv6 protocol; and RFC 1812, which defines requirements for routers. I also describe which types of ICMPv4 and ICMPv6 messages exist, how they are sent, and how they are processed. I cover ICMP sockets, including why they were added and how they are used. Keep in mind that the ICMP protocol is also used for various security attacks; for example, the Smurf Attack is a denial-of-service attack in which large numbers of ICMP packets with the intended victim's spoofed source IP are sent as broadcasts to a computer network using an IP broadcast address.

ICMPv4

ICMPv4 messages can be classified into two categories: error messages and information messages (they are termed "query messages" in RFC 1812). The ICMPv4 protocol is used in diagnostic tools like ping and traceroute. The famous ping utility is in fact a userspace application (from the iputils package) which opens a raw socket and sends an ICMP_ECHO message and should get back an ICMP_REPLY message as a response. Traceroute is a utility to find the path between a host and a given destination IP address. The traceroute utility is based on setting varying values to the Time To Live (TTL), which is a field in the IP header representing the hop count. The traceroute utility takes advantage of the fact that a forwarding machine will send back an ICMP_TIME_EXCEED message when the TTL of the packet reaches 0. The traceroute utility starts by sending messages with a TTL of 1, and with each received ICMP_DEST_UNREACH with code ICMP_TIME_EXCEED as a reply, it increases the TTL by 1 and sends again to the same destination. It uses the returned ICMP "Time Exceeded" messages to build a list of the routers that the packets traverse, until the destination is reached and returns an ICMP "Echo Reply" message. Traceroute uses the UDP protocol by default. The ICMPv4 module is net/ipv4/icmp.c. Note that ICMPv4 cannot be built as a kernel module.

ICMPv4 Initialization

ICMPv4 initialization is done in the inet_init() method, which is invoked in boot phase. The inet_init() method invokes the icmp_init() method, which in turn calls the icmp_sk_init() method to create a kernel ICMP socket for sending ICMP messages and to initialize some ICMP procfs variables to their default values. (You will encounter some of these procfs variables later in this chapter.)

Registration of the ICMPv4 protocol, like registration of other IPv4 protocols, is done in inet_init():

```
static const struct net_protocol icmp_protocol = {
    .handler        =  icmp_rcv,
    .err_handler    =  icmp_err,
    .no_policy      =  1,
    .netns_ok       =  1,
};
```

(net/ipv4/af_inet.c)

- icmp_rcv: The handler callback. This means that for incoming packets whose protocol field in the IP header equals IPPROTO_ICMP (0x1), icmp_rcv() will be invoked.

- no_policy: This flag is set to 1, which implies that there is no need to perform IPsec policy checks; for example, the xfrm4_policy_check() method is not called in ip_local_deliver_finish() because the no_policy flag is set.

- netns_ok: This flag is set to 1, which indicates that the protocol is aware of network namespaces. Network namespaces are described in Appendix A, in the net_device section. The inet_add_protocol() method will fail for protocols whose netns_ok field is 0 with an error of -EINVAL.

```
static int __init inet_init(void) {
. . .
    if (inet_add_protocol(&icmp_protocol, IPPROTO_ICMP) < 0)
        pr_crit("%s: Cannot add ICMP protocol\n", __func__);
. . .

int __net_init icmp_sk_init(struct net *net)
{
    . . .
    for_each_possible_cpu(i) {
        struct sock *sk;

        err = inet_ctl_sock_create(&sk, PF_INET,
                    SOCK_RAW, IPPROTO_ICMP, net);
        if (err < 0)
            goto fail;

            net->ipv4.icmp_sk[i] = sk;
            . . .
            sock_set_flag(sk, SOCK_USE_WRITE_QUEUE);
        inet_sk(sk)->pmtudisc = IP_PMTUDISC_DONT;
    }
    . . .

}
```

In the `icmp_sk_init()` method, a raw ICMPv4 socket is created for each CPU and is kept in an array. The current sk can be accessed with the `icmp_sk(struct net *net)` method. These sockets are used in the `icmp_push_reply()` method. The ICMPv4 procfs entries are initialized in the `icmp_sk_init()` method; I mention them in this chapter and summarize them in the "Quick Reference" section at the end of this chapter. Every ICMP packet starts with an ICMPv4 header. Before discussing how ICMPv4 messages are received and transmitted, the following section describes the ICMPv4 header, so that you better understand how ICMPv4 messages are built.

ICMPv4 Header

The ICMPv4 header consists of type (8 bits), code (8 bits), and checksum (16 bits), and a 32 bits variable part member (its content varies based on the ICMPv4 type and code), as you can see in Figure 3-1. After the ICMPv4 header comes the payload, which should include the IPv4 header of the originating packet and a part of its payload. According to RFC 1812, it should contain as much of the original datagram as possible without the length of the ICMPv4 datagram exceeding 576 bytes. This size is in accordance to RFC 791, which specifies that "All hosts must be prepared to accept datagrams of up to 576 octets."

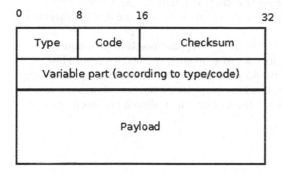

Figure 3-1. *The ICMPv4 header*

The ICMPv4 header is represented by `struct icmphdr`:

```
struct icmphdr {
    __u8        type;
    __u8        code;
    __sum16     checksum;
  union {
    struct {
        __be16      id;
        __be16      sequence;
    } echo;
    __be32      gateway;
    struct {
        __be16      __unused;
        __be16      mtu;
    } frag;
  } un;
};
```

(include/uapi/linux/icmp.h)

You'll find the current complete list of assigned ICMPv4 message type numbers and codes at www.iana.org/assignments/icmp-parameters/icmp-parameters.xml.

The ICMPv4 module defines an array of icmp_control objects, named icmp_pointers, which is indexed by ICMPv4 message type. Let's take a look at the icmp_control structure definition and at the icmp_pointers array:

```
struct icmp_control {
    void (*handler)(struct sk_buff *skb);
    short error;        /* This ICMP is classed as an error message */
};
```

```
static const struct icmp_control icmp_pointers[NR_ICMP_TYPES+1];
```

NR_ICMP_TYPES is the highest ICMPv4 type, which is 18.

(include/uapi/linux/icmp.h)

The error field of the icmp_control objects of this array is 1 only for error message types, like the "Destination Unreachable" message (ICMP_DEST_UNREACH), and it is 0 (implicitly) for information messages, like echo (ICMP_ECHO). Some handlers are assigned to more than one type. Next I discuss handlers and the ICMPv4 message types they manage.

ping_rcv() handles receiving a ping reply (ICMP_ECHOREPLY). The ping_rcv() method is implemented in the ICMP sockets code, net/ipv4/ping.c. In kernels prior to 3.0, in order to send ping, you had to create a raw socket in userspace. When receiving a reply to a ping (ICMP_ECHOREPLY message), the raw socket that sent the ping processed it. In order to understand how this is implemented, let's take a look in ip_local_deliver_finish(), which is the method which handles incoming IPv4 packets and passes them to the sockets which should process them:

```
static int ip_local_deliver_finish(struct sk_buff *skb)
{
    . . .
        int protocol = ip_hdr(skb)->protocol;
        const struct net_protocol *ipprot;
        int raw;

    resubmit:
        raw = raw_local_deliver(skb, protocol);
        ipprot = rcu_dereference(inet_protos[protocol]);
            if (ipprot != NULL) {
                    int ret;
                    . . .
                    ret = ipprot->handler(skb);
                    . . .
```

(net/ipv4/ip_input.c)

When the ip_local_deliver_finish() method receives an ICMP_ECHOREPLY packet, it first tries to deliver it to a listening raw socket, which will process it. Because a raw socket that was opened in userspace handles the ICMP_ECHOREPLY message, there is no need to do anything further with it. So when the ip_local_deliver_finish() method receives ICMP_ECHOREPLY, the raw_local_deliver() method is invoked first to process it by a raw socket, and afterwards the ipprot->handler(skb) is invoked (this is the icmp_rcv() callback in the case of ICMPv4 packet). And because the packet was already processed by a raw socket, there is nothing more to do with it. So the packet is discarded silently by calling the icmp_discard() method, which is the handler for ICMP_ECHOREPLY messages.

When the ICMP sockets ("ping sockets") were integrated into the Linux kernel in kernel 3.0, this was changed. Ping sockets are discussed in the "ICMP Sockets ("Ping Sockets")" section later in this chapter. In this context I should note that with ICMP sockets, the sender of ping can be also *not a raw socket*. For example, you can create a socket like this: socket (PF_INET, SOCK_DGRAM, PROT_ICMP) and use it to send ping packets. This socket is not a raw socket. As a result, the echo reply is not delivered to any raw socket, since there is no corresponding raw socket which listens. To avoid this problem, the ICMPv4 module handles receiving ICMP_ECHOREPLY messages with the ping_rcv() callback. The ping module is located in the IPv4 layer (net/ipv4/ping.c). Nevertheless, most of the code in net/ipv4/ping.c is a dual-stack code (intended for both IPv4 and IPv6). As a result, the ping_rcv() method also handles ICMPV6_ECHO_REPLY messages for IPv6 (see icmpv6_rcv() in net/ipv6/icmp.c). I talk more about ICMP sockets later in this chapter.

icmp_discard() is an empty handler used for nonexistent message types (message types whose numbers are without corresponding declarations in the header file) and for some messages that do not need any handling, for example ICMP_TIMESTAMPREPLY. The ICMP_TIMESTAMP and the ICMP_TIMESTAMPREPLY messages are used for time synchronization; the sender sends the originate timestamp in an ICMP_TIMESTAMP request; the receiver sends ICMP_TIMESTAMPREPLY with three timestamps: the originating timestamp which was sent by the sender of the timestamp request, as well as a receive timestamp and a transmit timestamp. There are more commonly used protocols for time synchronization than ICMPv4 timestamp messages, like the Network Time Protocol (NTP). I should also mention the Address Mask request (ICMP_ADDRESS), which is normally sent by a host to a router in order to obtain an appropriate subnet mask. Recipients should reply to this message with an address mask reply message. The ICMP_ADDRESS and the ICMP_ADDRESSREPLY messages, which were handled in the past by the icmp_address() method and by the icmp_address_reply() method, are now handled also by icmp_discard(). The reason is that there are other ways to get the subnet masks, such as with DHCP.

icmp_unreach() handles ICMP_DEST_UNREACH, ICMP_TIME_EXCEED, ICMP_PARAMETERPROB, and ICMP_QUENCH message types.

An ICMP_DEST_UNREACH message can be sent under various conditions. Some of these conditions are described in the "Sending ICMPv4 Messages: Destination Unreachable" section in this chapter.

An ICMP_TIME_EXCEEDED message is sent in two cases:

In ip_forward(), each packet decrements its TTL. According to RFC 1700, the recommended TTL for the IPv4 protocol is 64. If the TTL reaches 0, this is indication that the packet should be dropped because probably there was some loop. So, if the TTL reaches 0 in ip_forward(), the icmp_send() method is invoked:

```
icmp_send(skb, ICMP_TIME_EXCEEDED, ICMP_EXC_TTL, 0);
```

(net/ipv4/ip_forward.c)

In such a case, an ICMP_TIME_EXCEEDED message with code ICMP_EXC_TTL is sent, the SKB is freed, the InHdrErrors SNMP counter (IPSTATS_MIB_INHDRERRORS) is incremented, and the method returns NET_RX_DROP.

In ip_expire(), the following occurs when a timeout of a fragment exists:

```
icmp_send(head, ICMP_TIME_EXCEEDED, ICMP_EXC_FRAGTIME, 0);
```

(net/ipv4/ip_fragment.c)

An ICMP_PARAMETERPROB message is sent when parsing the options of an IPv4 header fails, in the ip_options_compile() method or in the ip_options_rcv_srr() method (net/ipv4/ip_options.c). The options are an optional, variable length field (up to 40 bytes) of the IPv4 header. IP options are discussed in Chapter 4.

An ICMP_QUENCH message type is in fact deprecated. According to RFC 1812, section 4.3.3.3 (Source Quench): "A router SHOULD NOT originate ICMP Source Quench messages", and also, "A router MAY ignore any ICMP Source Quench messages it receives." The ICMP_QUENCH message was intended to reduce congestion, but it turned out that this is an ineffective solution.

icmp_redirect() handles ICMP_REDIRECT messages; according to RFC 1122, section 3.2.2.2, hosts should not send an ICMP redirect message; redirects are to be sent only by gateways. icmp_redirect() handles ICMP_REDIRECT messages. In the past, icmp_redirect() called ip_rt_redirect(), but an ip_rt_redirect()

invocation is not needed anymore as the protocol handlers now all properly propagate the redirect back into the routing code. In fact, in kernel 3.6, the ip_rt_redirect() method was removed. So the icmp_redirect() method first performs sanity checks and then calls icmp_socket_deliver(), which delivers the packet to the raw sockets and invokes the protocol error handler (in case it exists). Chapter 6 discusses ICMP_REDIRECT messages in more depth.

icmp_echo() handles echo ("ping") requests (ICMP_ECHO) by sending echo replies (ICMP_ECHOREPLY) with icmp_reply(). If case net->ipv4.sysctl_icmp_echo_ignore_all is set, a reply will not be sent. For configuring ICMPv4 procfs entries, see the "Quick Reference" section at the end of this chapter, and also Documentation/networking/ip-sysctl.txt.

icmp_timestamp() handles ICMP Timestamp requests (ICMP_TIMESTAMP) by sending ICMP_TIMESTAMPREPLY with icmp_reply().

Before discussing sending ICMP messages by the icmp_reply() method and by the icmp_send() method, I should describe the icmp_bxm ("ICMP build xmit message") structure, which is used in both methods:

```
struct icmp_bxm {
    struct sk_buff *skb;
    int offset;
    int data_len;

    struct {
        struct icmphdr icmph;
        __be32          times[3];
    } data;
    int head_len;
    struct ip_options_data replyopts;
};
```

- skb: For the icmp_reply() method, this skb is the request packet; the icmp_param object (instance of icmp_bxm) is built from it (in the icmp_echo() method and in the icmp_timestamp() method). For the icmp_send() method, this skb is the one that triggered sending an ICMPv4 message due to some conditions; you will see several examples of such messages in this section.

- offset: Difference (offset) between skb_network_header(skb) and skb->data.

- data_len: ICMPv4 packet payload size.

- icmph: The ICMP v4 header.

- times[3]: Array of three timestamps, filled in icmp_timestamp().

- head_len: Size of the ICMPv4 header (in case of icmp_timestamp(), there are additional 12 bytes for the timestamps).

- replyopts: An ip_options data object. IP options are optional fields after the IP header, up to 40 bytes. They enable advanced features like strict routing/loose routing, record routing, time stamping, and more. They are initialized with the ip_options_echo() method. Chapter 4 discusses IP options.

Receiving ICMPv4 Messages

The ip_local_deliver_finish() method handles packets for the local machine. When getting an ICMP packet, the method delivers the packet to the raw sockets that had performed registration of ICMPv4 protocol. In the icmp_rcv() method, first the InMsgs SNMP counter (ICMP_MIB_INMSGS) is incremented. Subsequently, the checksum correctness is verified. If the checksum is not correct, two SNMP counters are incremented, InCsumErrors and InErrors (ICMP_MIB_CSUMERRORS and ICMP_MIB_INERRORS, respectively), the SKB is freed, and the method returns 0. The icmp_rcv() method does not return an error in this case. In fact, the icmp_rcv() method always returns 0; the reason for returning 0 in case of checksum error is that no special thing should be done when receiving an erroneous ICMP message except to discard it; when a protocol handler returns a negative error, another attempt to process the packet is performed, and it is not needed in this case. For more details, refer to the implementation of the ip_local_deliver_finish() method. Then the ICMP header is examined in order to find its type; the corresponding procfs message type counter is incremented (each ICMP message type has a procfs counter), and a sanity check is performed to verify that it is not higher than the highest permitted value (NR_ICMP_TYPES). According to section 3.2.2 of RFC 1122, if an ICMP message of unknown type is received, it must be silently discarded. So if the message type is out of range, the InErrors SNMP counter (ICMP_MIB_INERRORS) is incremented, and the SKB is freed.

In case the packet is a broadcast or a multicast, and it is an ICMP_ECHO message or an ICMP_TIMESTAMP message, there is a check whether broadcast/multicast echo requests are permitted by reading the variable net->ipv4.sysctl_icmp_echo_ignore_broadcasts. This variable can be configured via procfs by writing to /proc/sys/net/ipv4/icmp_echo_ignore_broadcasts, and by default its value is 1. If this variable is set, the packet is dropped silently. This is done according to section 3.2.2.6 of RFC 1122: "An ICMP Echo Request destined to an IP broadcast or IP multicast address MAY be silently discarded." And according to section 3.2.2.8 of this RFC, "An ICMP Timestamp Request message to an IP broadcast or IP multicast address MAY be silently discarded." Then a check is performed to detect whether the type is allowed for broadcast/multicast (ICMP_ECHO, ICMP_TIMESTAMP, ICMP_ADDRESS, and ICMP_ADDRESSREPLY). If it is not one of these message types, the packet is dropped and 0 is returned. Then according to its type, the corresponding entry in the icmp_pointers array is fetched and the appropriate handler is called. Let's take a look in the ICMP_ECHO entry in the icmp_control dispatch table:

```
static const struct icmp_control icmp_pointers[NR_ICMP_TYPES + 1] = {
...
  [ICMP_ECHO] = {
        .handler = icmp_echo,
    },
...
}
```

So when receiving a ping (the type of the message is "Echo Request," ICMP_ECHO), it is handled by the icmp_echo() method. The icmp_echo() method changes the type in the ICMP header to be ICMP_ECHOREPLY and sends a reply by calling the icmp_reply() method. Apart from ping, the only other ICMP message which requires a response is the timestamp message (ICMP_TIMESTAMP); it is handled by the icmp_timestamp() method, which, much like in the ICMP_ECHO case, changes the type to ICMP_TIMESTAMPREPLY and sends a reply by calling the icmp_reply() method. Sending is done by ip_append_data() and by ip_push_pending_frames(). Receiving a ping reply (ICMP_ECHOREPLY) is handled by the ping_rcv() method.

You can disable replying to pings with the following:

```
echo 1 >  /proc/sys/net/ipv4/icmp_echo_ignore_all
```

There are some callbacks that handle more than one ICMP type. The icmp_discard() callback, for example, handles ICMPv4 packets whose type is not handled by the Linux ICMPv4 implementation, and messages like ICMP_TIMESTAMPREPLY, ICMP_INFO_REQUEST , ICMP_ADDRESSREPLY, and more.

Sending ICMPv4 Messages: "Destination Unreachable"

There are two methods for sending an ICMPv4 message: the first is the icmp_reply() method, which is sent as a response for two types of ICMP requests, ICMP_ECHO and ICMP_TIMESTAMP. The second one is the icmp_send() method, where the local machine initiates sending an ICMPv4 message under certain conditions (described in this section). Both these methods eventually invoke icmp_push_reply() for actually sending the packet. The icmp_reply() method is called as a response to an ICMP_ECHO message from the icmp_echo() method, and as a response to an ICMP_TIMESTAMP message from the icmp_timestamp() method. The icmp_send() method is invoked from many places in the IPv4 network stack—for example, from netfilter, from the forwarding code (ip_forward.c), from tunnels like ipip and ip_gre, and more.

This section looks into some of the cases when a "Destination Unreachable" message is sent (the type is ICMP_DEST_UNREACH).

Code 2: ICMP_PROT_UNREACH (Protocol Unreachable)

When the protocol of the IP header (which is an 8-bit field) is a nonexistent protocol, an ICMP_DEST_UNREACH/ICMP_PROT_UNREACH is sent back to the sender because there is no protocol handler for such a protocol (the protocol handler array is indexed by the protocol number, so for nonexistent protocols there will be no handler). By *nonexistent* protocol I mean either that because of some error indeed the protocol number of the IPv4 header does not appear in the protocol number list (which you can find in include/uapi/linux/in.h, for IPv4), or that the kernel was built without support for that protocol, and, as a result, this protocol is not registered and there is no entry for it in the protocol handlers array. Because such a packet can't be handled, an ICMPv4 message of "Destination Unreachable" should be replied back to the sender; the ICMP_PROT_UNREACH code in the ICMPv4 reply signifies the cause of the error, "protocol is unreachable." See the following:

```
static int ip_local_deliver_finish(struct sk_buff *skb)
  {
    ...
    int protocol = ip_hdr(skb)->protocol;
    const struct net_protocol *ipprot;
    int raw;

resubmit:
    raw = raw_local_deliver(skb, protocol);

    ipprot = rcu_dereference(inet_protos[protocol]);
    if (ipprot != NULL) {
      ...
    } else {
    if (!raw) {
    if (xfrm4_policy_check(NULL, XFRM_POLICY_IN, skb)) {
          IP_INC_STATS_BH(net, IPSTATS_MIB_INUNKNOWNPROTOS);
          icmp_send(skb, ICMP_DEST_UNREACH,ICMP_PROT_UNREACH, 0);
          }
      ...
  }
```

(net/ipv4/ip_input.c)

In this example, a lookup in the inet_protos array by protocol is performed; and because no entry was found, this means that the protocol is not registered in the kernel.

Code 3: ICMP_PORT_UNREACH ("Port Unreachable")

When receiving UDPv4 packets, a matching UDP socket is searched for. If no matching socket is found, the checksum correctness is verified. If it is wrong, the packet is dropped silently. If it is correct, the statistics are updated and a "Destination Unreachable"/"Port Unreachable" ICMP message is sent back:

```
int __udp4_lib_rcv(struct sk_buff *skb, struct udp_table *udptable, int proto)
{
        struct sock *sk;
        ...
        sk = __udp4_lib_lookup_skb(skb, uh->source, uh->dest, udptable)
        ...
        if (sk != NULL) {
        ...
        }

        /* No socket. Drop packet silently, if checksum is wrong */
    if (udp_lib_checksum_complete(skb))
        goto csum_error;

        UDP_INC_STATS_BH(net, UDP_MIB_NOPORTS, proto == IPPROTO_UDPLITE);
        icmp_send(skb, ICMP_DEST_UNREACH, ICMP_PORT_UNREACH, 0);
        ...
        }
...

}
```

(net/ipv4/udp.c)

A lookup is being performed by the __udp4_lib_lookup_skb() method, and if there is no socket, the statistics are updated and an ICMP_DEST_UNREACH message with ICMP_PORT_UNREACH code is sent back.

Code 4: ICMP_FRAG_NEEDED

When forwarding a packet with a length larger than the MTU of the outgoing link, if the don't fragment (DF) bit in the IPv4 header (IP_DF) is set, the packet is discarded and an ICMP_DEST_UNREACH message with ICMP_FRAG_NEEDED code is sent back to the sender:

```
int ip_forward(struct sk_buff *skb)
{
        ...
        struct rtable *rt;      /* Route we use */
        ...
        if (unlikely(skb->len > dst_mtu(&rt->dst) && !skb_is_gso(skb) &&
                    (ip_hdr(skb)->frag_off & htons(IP_DF))) && !skb->local_df) {
            IP_INC_STATS(dev_net(rt->dst.dev), IPSTATS_MIB_FRAGFAILS);
```

```
            icmp_send(skb, ICMP_DEST_UNREACH, ICMP_FRAG_NEEDED,
                    htonl(dst_mtu(&rt->dst)));
            goto drop;
    }
    ...
}
```

(net/ipv4/ip_forward.c)

Code 5: ICMP_SR_FAILED

When forwarding a packet with the strict routing option and gatewaying set, a "Destination Unreachable" message with ICMP_SR_FAILED code is sent back, and the packet is dropped:

```
int ip_forward(struct sk_buff *skb)
{
        struct ip_options *opt  = &(IPCB(skb)->opt);
        ...
        if (opt->is_strictroute && rt->rt_uses_gateway)
                goto sr_failed;
        ...
sr_failed:
        icmp_send(skb, ICMP_DEST_UNREACH, ICMP_SR_FAILED, 0);
        goto drop;
}
```

(net/ipv4/ip_forward.c)

For a full list of all IPv4 "Destination Unreachable" codes, see Table 3-1 in the "Quick Reference" section at the end of this chapter. Note that a user can configure some rules with the iptables REJECT target and the --reject-with qualifier, which can send "Destination Unreachable" messages according to the selection; more in the "Quick Reference" section at the end of this chapter.

Both the icmp_reply() and the icmp_send() methods support rate limiting; they call icmpv4_xrlim_allow(), and if the rate limiting check allows sending the packet (the icmpv4_xrlim_allow() returns true), they send the packet. It should be mentioned here that rate limiting is not performed automatically on all types of traffic. Here are the conditions under which rate limiting check will not be performed:

- The message type is unknown.

- The packet is of PMTU discovery.

- The device is a loopback device.

- The ICMP type is not enabled in the rate mask.

If all these conditions are not matched, rate limiting is performed by calling the inet_peer_xrlim_allow() method. You'll find more info about rate mask in the "Quick Reference" section at the end of this chapter.

Let's look inside the icmp_send() method. First, this is its prototype:

```
void icmp_send(struct sk_buff *skb_in, int type, int code, __be32 info)
```

skb_in is the SKB which caused the invocation of the icmp_send() method, type and code are the ICMPv4 message type and code, respectively. The last parameter, info, is used in the following cases:

- For the ICMP_PARAMETERPROB message type it is the offset in the IPv4 header where the parsing problem occurred.

- For the ICMP_DEST_UNREACH message type with ICMP_FRAG_NEEDED code, it is the MTU.

- For the ICMP_REDIRECT message type with ICMP_REDIR_HOST code, it is the IP address of the destination address in the IPv4 header of the provoking SKB.

When further looking into the icmp_send() method, first there are some sanity checks. Then multicast/broadcast packets are rejected. A check of whether the packet is a fragment is performed by inspecting the frag_off field of the IPv4 header. If the packet is fragmented, an ICMPv4 message is sent, but only for the first fragment. According to section 4.3.2.7 of RFC 1812, an ICMP error message must not be sent as the result of receiving an ICMP error message. So first a check is performed to find out whether the ICMPv4 message to be sent is an error message, and if it is so, another check is performed to find out whether the provoking SKB contained an error ICMPv4 message, and if so, then the method returns without sending the ICMPv4 message. Also if the type is an unknown ICMPv4 type (higher than NR_ICMP_TYPES), the method returns without sending the ICMPv4 message, though this isn't specified explicitly by the RFC. Then the source address is determined according to the value of net->ipv4.sysctl_icmp_errors_use_inbound_ifaddr value (more details in the "Quick Reference" section at the end of this chapter). Then the ip_options_echo() method is invoked to copy the IP options of the IPv4 header of the invoking SKB. An icmp_bxm object (icmp_param) is being allocated and initialized, and a lookup in the routing subsystem is performed with the icmp_route_lookup() method. Then the icmp_push_reply() method is invoked.

Let's take a look at the icmp_push_reply() method, which actually sends the packet. The icmp_push_reply() first finds the socket on which the packet should be sent by calling:

```
sk = icmp_sk(dev_net((*rt)->dst.dev));
```

The dev_net() method returns the network namespace of the outgoing network device. (The dev_net() method and network namespaces are discussed in chapter 14 and in Appendix A.) Then, the icmp_sk() method fetches the socket (because in SMP there is a socket per CPU). Then the ip_append_data() method is called to move the packet to the IP layer. If the ip_append_data() method fails, the statistics are updated by incrementing the ICMP_MIB_OUTERRORS counter and the ip_flush_pending_frames() method is called to free the SKB. I discuss the ip_append_data() method and the ip_flush_pending_frames() method in Chapter 4.

Now that you know all about ICMPv4, it's time to move on to ICMPv6.

ICMPv6

ICMPv6 has many similarities to ICMPv4 when it comes to reporting errors in the network layer (L3). There are additional tasks for ICMPv6 which are not performed in ICMPv4. This section discusses the ICMPv6 protocol, its new features (which are not implemented in ICMPv4), and the features which are similar. ICMPv6 is defined in RFC 4443. If you delve into ICMPv6 code you will probably encounter, sooner or later, comments that mention RFC 1885. In fact, RFC 1885, "Internet Control Message Protocol (ICMPv6) for the Internet Protocol Version 6 (IPv6)," is the base ICMPv6 RFC. It was obsoleted by RFC 2463, which was in turn obsoleted by RFC 4443. The ICMPv6 implementation is based upon IPv4, but it is more complicated; the changes and additions that were added are discussed in this section.

The ICMPv6 protocol has a next header value of 58, according to RFC 4443, section 1 (Chapter 8 discusses IPv6 next headers). ICMPv6 is an integral part of IPv6 and must be fully implemented by every IPv6 node. Apart from error handling and diagnostics, ICMPv6 is used for the Neighbour Discovery (ND) protocol in IPv6, which replaces and enhances functions of ARP in IPv4, and for the Multicast Listener Discovery (MLD) protocol, which is the counterpart of the IGMP protocol in IPv4, shown in Figure 3-2.

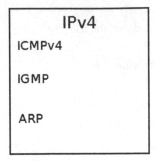 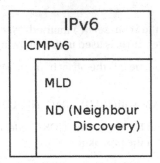

Figure 3-2. *ICMP in IPv4 and IPv6. The counterpart of the IGMP protocol in IPv6 is the MLD protocol, and the counterpart of the ARP protocol in IPv6 is the ND protocol*

This section covers the ICMPv6 implementation. As you will see, it has many things in common with the ICMPv4 implementation in the way messages are handled and sent. There are even cases when the same methods are called in ICMPv4 and in ICMPv6 (for example, `ping_rcv()` and `inet_peer_xrlim_allow()`). There are some differences, and some topics are unique to ICMPv6. The `ping6` and `traceroute6` utilities are based on ICMPv6 and are the counterparts of `ping` and `traceroute` utilities of IPv4 (mentioned in the ICMPv4 section in the beginning of this chapter). ICMPv6 is implemented in `net/ipv6/icmp.c` and in `net/ipv6/ip6_icmp.c`. As with ICMPv4, ICMPv6 cannot be built as a kernel module.

ICMPv6 Initialization

ICMPv6 initialization is done by the `icmpv6_init()` method and by the `icmpv6_sk_init()` method. Registration of the ICMPv6 protocol is done by `icmpv6_init()` (`net/ipv6/icmp.c`):

```
static const struct inet6_protocol icmpv6_protocol = {
        .handler        =       icmpv6_rcv,
        .err_handler    =       icmpv6_err,
        .flags          =       INET6_PROTO_NOPOLICY|INET6_PROTO_FINAL,
};
```

The `handler` callback is `icmpv6_rcv()`; this means that for incoming packets whose protocol field equals IPPROTO_ICMPV6 (58), `icmpv6_rcv()` will be invoked.

When the INET6_PROTO_NOPOLICY flag is set, this implies that IPsec policy checks should not be performed; for example, the `xfrm_policy_check()` method is not called in `ip6_input_finish()` because the INET6_PROTO_NOPOLICY flag is set:

```
int __init icmpv6_init(void)
{
        int err;
        ...
        if (inet6_add_protocol(&icmpv6_protocol, IPPROTO_ICMPV6) < 0)
                goto fail;
        return 0;
}
```

```
static int __net_init icmpv6_sk_init(struct net *net)
{
    struct sock *sk;
    ...
    for_each_possible_cpu(i) {
        err = inet_ctl_sock_create(&sk, PF_INET6,
                        SOCK_RAW, IPPROTO_ICMPV6, net);
        ...
        net->ipv6.icmp_sk[i] = sk;
        ...

}
```

As in ICMPv4, a raw ICMPv6 socket is created for each CPU and is kept in an array. The current sk can be accessed by the icmpv6_sk() method.

ICMPv6 Header

The ICMPv6 header consists of type (8 bits), code (8 bits), and checksum (16 bits), as you can see in Figure 3-3.

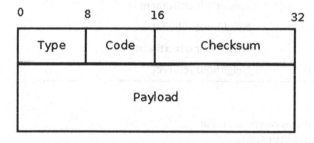

Figure 3-3. *ICMPv6 header*

The ICMPv6 header is represented by struct icmp6hdr:

```
struct icmp6hdr {
    __u8        icmp6_type;
    __u8        icmp6_code;
    __sum16     icmp6_cksum;
    ...
}
```

There is not enough room to show all the fields of struct icmp6hdr because it is too large (it is defined in include/uapi/linux/icmpv6.h). When the high-order bit of the type field is 0 (values in the range from 0 to 127), it indicates an error message; when the high-order bit is 1 (values in the range from 128 to 255), it indicates an information message. Table 3-1 shows the ICMPv6 message types by their number and kernel symbol.

Table 3-1. ICMPv6 Messages

Type	Kernel symbol	Error/Info	Description
1	ICMPV6_DEST_UNREACH	Error	Destination Unreachable
2	ICMPV6_PKT_TOOBIG	Error	Packet too big
3	ICMPV6_TIME_EXCEED	Error	Time Exceeded
4	ICMPV6_PARAMPROB	Error	Parameter problem
128	ICMPV6_ECHO_REQUEST	Info	Echo Request
129	ICMPV6_ECHO_REPLY	Info	Echo Reply
130	ICMPV6_MGM_QUERY	Info	Multicast group membership management query
131	ICMPV6_MGM_REPORT	Info	Multicast group membership management report
132	ICMPV6_MGM_REDUCTION	Info	Multicast group membership management reduction
133	NDISC_ROUTER_SOLICITATION	Info	Router solicitation
134	NDISC_ROUTER_ADVERTISEMENT	Info	Router advertisement
135	NDISC_NEIGHBOUR_SOLICITATION	Info	Neighbour solicitation
136	NDISC_NEIGHBOUR_ADVERTISEMENT	Info	Neighbour advertisement
137	NDISC_REDIRECT	Info	Neighbour redirect

The current complete list of assigned ICMPv6 types and codes can be found at www.iana.org/assignments/icmpv6-parameters/icmpv6-parameters.xml.

ICMPv6 performs some tasks that are not performed by ICMPv4. For example, Neighbour Discovery is done by ICMPv6, whereas in IPv4 it is done by the ARP/RARP protocols. Multicast group memberships are handled by ICMPv6 in conjunction with the MLD (Multicast Listener Discovery) protocol, whereas in IPv4 this is performed by IGMP (Internet Group Management Protocol). Some ICMPv6 messages are similar in meaning to ICMPv4 messages; for example, ICMPv6 has these messages: "Destination Unreachable," (ICMPV6_DEST_UNREACH), "Time Exceeded" (ICMPV6_TIME_EXCEED), "Parameter Problem" (ICMPV6_PARAMPROB), "Echo Request" (ICMPV6_ECHO_REQUEST), and more. On the other hand, some ICMPv6 messages are unique to IPv6, such as the NDISC_NEIGHBOUR_SOLICITATION message.

Receiving ICMPv6 Messages

When getting an ICMPv6 packet, it is delivered to the icmpv6_rcv() method, which gets only an SKB as a parameter. Figure 3-4 shows the Rx path of a received ICMPv6 message.

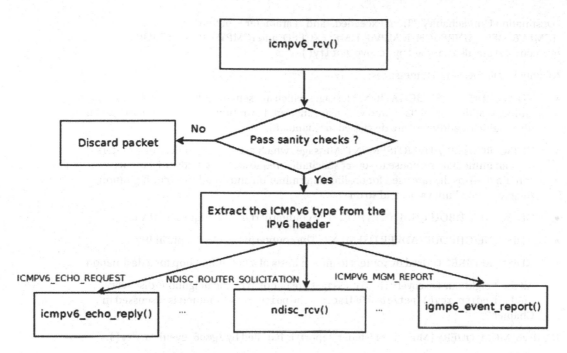

Figure 3-4. *Receive path of ICMPv6 message*

In the icmpv6_rcv() method, after some sanity checks, the InMsgs SNMP counter (ICMP6_MIB_INMSGS) is incremented. Subsequently, the checksum correctness is verified. If the checksum is not correct, the InErrors SNMP counter (ICMP6_MIB_INERRORS) is incremented, and the SKB is freed. The icmpv6_rcv() method does not return an error in this case (in fact it always returns 0, much like its IPv4 counterpart, icmp_rcv()).Then the ICMPv6 header is read in order to find its type; the corresponding procfs message type counter is incremented by the ICMP6MSGIN_INC_STATS_BH macro (each ICMPv6 message type has a procfs counter). For example, when receiving ICMPv6 ECHO requests ("pings"), the /proc/net/snmp6/Icmp6InEchos counter is incremented, and when receiving ICMPv6 Neighbour Solicitation requests, the /proc/net/snmp6/Icmp6InNeighborSolicits counter is incremented.

In ICMPv6, there is no dispatch table like the icmp_pointers table in ICMPv4. The handlers are invoked according to the ICMPv6 message type, in a long switch(type) command:

- "Echo Request" (ICMPV6_ECHO_REQUEST) is handled by the icmpv6_echo_reply() method.

- "Echo Reply" (ICMPV6_ECHO_REPLY) is handled by the ping_rcv() method. The ping_rcv() method is in the IPv4 ping module (net/ipv4/ping.c); this method is a dual-stack method (it handles both IPv4 and IPv6—discussed in the beginning of this chapter).

- Packet too big (ICMPV6_PKT_TOOBIG).

  - First a check is done to verify that the data block area (pointed to by skb->data) contains a block of data whose size is at least as big as an ICMP header. This is done by the pskb_may_pull() method. If this condition is not met, the packet is dropped.

  - Then the icmpv6_notify() method is invoked. This method eventually calls the raw6_icmp_error() method so that the registered raw sockets will handle the ICMP messages.

- "Destination Unreachable," "Time Exceeded," and "Parameter Problem" (ICMPV6_DEST_UNREACH, ICMPV6_TIME_EXCEED, and ICMPV6_PARAMPROB respectively) are also handled by `icmpv6_notify()`.

- Neighbour Discovery (ND) messages:

  - NDISC_ROUTER_SOLICITATION: Messages which are sent usually to the `all-routers` multicast address of FF02::2, and which are answered by router advertisements. (Special IPv6 multicast addresses are discussed in Chapter 8).

  - NDISC_ROUTER_ADVERTISEMENT: Messages which are sent periodically by routers or as an immediate response to router solicitation requests. Router advertisements contain prefixes that are used for on-link determination and/or address configuration, a suggested hop limit value, and so on.

  - NDISC_NEIGHBOUR_SOLICITATION: The counterpart of ARP request in IPv4.

  - NDISC_NEIGHBOUR_ADVERTISEMENT: The counterpart of ARP reply in IPv4.

  - NDISC_REDIRECT: Used by routers to inform hosts of a better first hop for a destination.

  - All the Neighbour Discovery (ND) messages are handled by the neighbour discovery method, `ndisc_rcv()` (`net/ipv6/ndisc.c`). The `ndisc_rcv()` method is discussed in Chapter 7.

- ICMPV6_MGM_QUERY (Multicast Listener Report) is handled by `igmp6_event_query()`.

- ICMPV6_MGM_REPORT (Multicast Listener Report) is handled by `igmp6_event_report()`. Note: Both ICMPV6_MGM_QUERY and ICMPV6_MGM_REPORT are discussed in more detail in Chapter 8.

- Messages of unknown type, and the following messages, are all handled by the `icmpv6_notify()` method:

  - ICMPV6_MGM_REDUCTION: When a host leaves a multicast group, it sends an MLDv2 ICMPV6_MGM_REDUCTION message; see the `igmp6_leave_group()` method in `net/ipv6/mcast.c`.

  - ICMPV6_MLD2_REPORT: MLDv2 Multicast Listener Report packet; usually sent with destination address of the all MLDv2-capable routers Multicast Group Address (FF02::16).

  - ICMPV6_NI_QUERY- ICMP: Node Information Query.

  - ICMPV6_NI_REPLY: ICMP Node Information Response.

  - ICMPV6_DHAAD_REQUEST: ICMP Home Agent Address Discovery Request Message; see section 6.5, RFC 6275, "Mobility Support in IPv6."

  - ICMPV6_DHAAD_REPLY: ICMP Home Agent Address Discovery Reply Message; See section 6.6, RFC 6275.

  - ICMPV6_MOBILE_PREFIX_SOL: ICMP Mobile Prefix Solicitation Message Format; see section 6.7, RFC 6275.

  - ICMPV6_MOBILE_PREFIX_ADV: ICMP Mobile Prefix Advertisement Message Format; see section 6.8, RFC 6275.

Notice that the switch(type) command ends like this:

```
default:
    LIMIT_NETDEBUG(KERN_DEBUG "icmpv6: msg of unknown type\n");

    /* informational */
    if (type & ICMPV6_INFOMSG_MASK)
        break;

    /*
     * error of unknown type.
     * must pass to upper level
     */

    icmpv6_notify(skb, type, hdr->icmp6_code, hdr->icmp6_mtu);
}
```

Informational messages fulfill the condition (type & ICMPV6_INFOMSG_MASK), so they are discarded, whereas the other messages which do not fulfill this condition (and therefore should be error messages) are passed to the upper layer. This is done in accordance with section 2.4 ("Message Processing Rules") of RFC 4443.

Sending ICMPv6 Messages

The main method for sending ICMPv6 messages is the icmpv6_send() method. The method is called when the local machine initiates sending an ICMPv6 message under conditions described in this section. There is also the icmpv6_echo_reply() method, which is called only as a response to an ICMPV6_ECHO_REQUEST ("ping") message. The icmp6_send() method is invoked from many places in the IPv6 network stack. This section looks at several examples.

Example: Sending "Hop Limit Time Exceeded" ICMPv6 Messages

When forwarding a packet, every machine decrements the Hop Limit Counter by 1. The Hop Limit Counter is a member of the IPv6 header—it is the IPv6 counterpart to Time To Live in IPv4. When the value of the Hop Limit Counter header reaches 0, an ICMPV6_TIME_EXCEED message is sent with ICMPV6_EXC_HOPLIMIT code by calling the icmpv6_send() method, then the statistics are updated and the packet is dropped:

```
int ip6_forward(struct sk_buff *skb)
{
    ...
    if (hdr->hop_limit <= 1) {
            /* Force OUTPUT device used as source address */
            skb->dev = dst->dev;
            icmpv6_send(skb, ICMPV6_TIME_EXCEED, ICMPV6_EXC_HOPLIMIT, 0);
            IP6_INC_STATS_BH(net,
                            ip6_dst_idev(dst), IPSTATS_MIB_INHDRERRORS);

            kfree_skb(skb);
            return -ETIMEDOUT;
    }
    ...
}
```

(net/ipv6/ip6_output.c)

Example: Sending "Fragment Reassembly Time Exceeded" ICMPv6 Messages

When a timeout of a fragment occurs, an ICMPV6_TIME_EXCEED message with ICMPV6_EXC_FRAGTIME code is sent back, by calling the icmpv6_send() method:

```
void ip6_expire_frag_queue(struct net *net, struct frag_queue *fq,
                           struct inet_frags *frags)
{
       ...
       icmpv6_send(fq->q.fragments, ICMPV6_TIME_EXCEED, ICMPV6_EXC_FRAGTIME, 0);
       ...
}
```

(net/ipv6/reassembly.c)

Example: Sending "Destination Unreachable"/"Port Unreachable" ICMPv6 Messages

When receiving UDPv6 packets, a matching UDPv6 socket is searched for. If no matching socket is found, the checksum correctness is verified. If it is wrong, the packet is dropped silently. If it is correct, the statistics (UDP_MIB_NOPORTS MIB counter, which is exported to procfs by /proc/net/snmp6/Udp6NoPorts) is updated and a "Destination Unreachable"/"Port Unreachable" ICMPv6 message is sent back with icmpv6_send():

```
int __udp6_lib_rcv(struct sk_buff *skb, struct udp_table *udptable, int proto)
{
       ...
       sk = __udp6_lib_lookup_skb(skb, uh->source, uh->dest, udptable);
       if (sk != NULL) {
       ...
       }
       ...
       if (udp_lib_checksum_complete(skb))
               goto discard;

       UDP6_INC_STATS_BH(net, UDP_MIB_NOPORTS, proto == IPPROTO_UDPLITE);
       icmpv6_send(skb, ICMPV6_DEST_UNREACH, ICMPV6_PORT_UNREACH, 0);
       ...

}
```

This case is very similar to the UDPv4 example given earlier in this chapter.

Example: Sending "Fragmentation Needed" ICMPv6 Messages

When forwarding a packet, if its size is larger than the MTU of the outgoing link, and the local_df bit in the SKB is not set, the packet is discarded and an ICMPV6_PKT_TOOBIG message is sent back to the sender. The information in this message is used as part of the Path MTU (PMTU) discovery process.

Note that as opposed to the parallel case in IPv4, where an ICMP_DEST_UNREACH message with ICMP_FRAG_NEEDED code is sent, in this case an ICMPV6_PKT_TOOBIG message is sent back, and not a "Destination Unreachable" (ICMPV6_DEST_UNREACH) message. The ICMPV6_PKT_TOOBIG message has a message type number of its own in ICMPv6:

```
int ip6_forward(struct sk_buff *skb)
{
...
        if ((!skb->local_df && skb->len > mtu && !skb_is_gso(skb)) ||
            (IP6CB(skb)->frag_max_size && IP6CB(skb)->frag_max_size > mtu)) {
                /* Again, force OUTPUT device used as source address */
                skb->dev = dst->dev;
                icmpv6_send(skb, ICMPV6_PKT_TOOBIG, 0, mtu);
                IP6_INC_STATS_BH(net,
                                 ip6_dst_idev(dst), IPSTATS_MIB_INTOOBIGERRORS);
                IP6_INC_STATS_BH(net,
                                 ip6_dst_idev(dst), IPSTATS_MIB_FRAGFAILS);
                kfree_skb(skb);
                return -EMSGSIZE;
        }
...
}
```

(net/ipv6/ip6_output.c)

Example: Sending "Parameter Problem" ICMPv6 Messages

When encountering a problem in parsing extension headers, an ICMPV6_PARAMPROB message with ICMPV6_UNK_OPTION code is sent back:

```
static bool ip6_tlvopt_unknown(struct sk_buff *skb, int optoff) {
        switch ((skb_network_header(skb)[optoff] & 0xC0) >> 6) {
        ...
        case 2: /* send ICMP PARM PROB regardless and drop packet */
                icmpv6_param_prob(skb, ICMPV6_UNK_OPTION, optoff);
                return false;
        }
```

(net/ipv6/exthdrs.c)

The icmpv6_send() method supports rate limiting by calling icmpv6_xrlim_allow(). I should mention here that, as in ICMPv4, rate limiting is not performed automatically in ICMPv6 on all types of traffic. Here are the conditions under which rate limiting check will not be performed:

- Informational messages
- PMTU discovery
- Loopback device

If all these conditions are not matched, rate limiting is performed by calling the inet_peer_xrlim_allow() method, which is shared between ICMPv4 and ICMPv6. Note that unlike IPv4, you can't set a rate mask in IPv6. It is not forbidden by the ICMPv6 spec, RFC 4443, but it was never implemented.

Let's look inside the `icmp6_send()` method. First, this is its prototype:

```
static void icmp6_send(struct sk_buff *skb, u8 type, u8 code, __u32 info)
```

The parameters are similar to those of the `icmp_send()` method of IPv4, so I won't repeat the explanation here. When further looking into the `icmp6_send()` code, you find some sanity checks. Checking whether the provoking message is an ICMPv6 error message is done by calling the `is_ineligible()` method; if it is, the `icmp6_send()` method terminates. The length of the message should not exceed 1280, which is IPv6 minimum MTU (IPV6_MIN_MTU, defined in `include/linux/ipv6.h`). This is done in accordance with RFC 4443, section 2.4 (c), which says that every ICMPv6 error message must include as much of the IPv6 offending (invoking) packet (the packet that caused the error) as possible without making the error message packet exceed the minimum IPv6 MTU. Then the message is passed to the IPv6 layer, by the `ip6_append_data()` method and by the `icmpv6_push_pending_frame()` method, to free the SKB.

Now I'll turn to the `icmpv6_echo_reply()` method; as a reminder, this method is called as a response to an ICMPV6_ECHO message. The `icmpv6_echo_reply()` method gets only one parameter, the SKB. It builds an `icmpv6_msg` object and sets its type to ICMPV6_ECHO_REPLY. Then it passes the message to the IPv6 layer, by the `ip6_append_data()` method and by the `icmpv6_push_pending_frame()` method. If the `ip6_append_data()` method fails, an SNMP counter (ICMP6_MIB_OUTERRORS) is incremented, and `ip6_flush_pending_frames()` is invoked to free the SKB.

Chapters 7 and 8 also discuss ICMPv6. The next section introduces ICMP sockets and the purpose they serve.

ICMP Sockets ("Ping sockets")

A new type of sockets (IPPROTO_ICMP) was added by a patch from the Openwall GNU/*/Linux distribution (Owl), which provides security enhancements over other distributions. The ICMP sockets enable a `setuid-less` "ping." For Openwall GNU/*/Linux, it was the last step on the road to a `setuid-less` distribution. With this patch, a new ICMPv4 ping socket (which is not a raw socket) is created with:

```
socket(PF_INET, SOCK_DGRAM, IPPROTO_ICMP);
```

instead of with:

```
socket(PF_INET, SOCK_RAW, IPPROTO_ICMP);
```

There is also support for IPPROTO_ICMPV6 sockets, which was added later, in `net/ipv6/icmp.c`. A new ICMPv6 ping socket is created with:

```
socket(PF_INET6, SOCK_DGRAM, IPPROTO_ICMPV6);
```

instead of with:

```
socket(PF_INET6, SOCK_RAW, IPPROTO_ICMP6);
```

Similar functionality (non-privileged ICMP) is implemented in Mac OS X; see: `www.manpagez.com/man/4/icmp/`.

Most of the code for ICMP sockets is in `net/ipv4/ping.c`; in fact, large parts of the code in `net/ipv4/ping.c` are dual-stack (IPv4 and IPv6). In `net/ipv6/ping.c` there are only few IPv6-specific bits. Using ICMP sockets is disabled by default. You can enable ICMP sockets by setting the following procfs entry: `/proc/sys/net/ipv4/ping_group_range`. It is "1 0" by default, meaning that nobody (not even root) may create ping sockets. So, if you want to allow a user with uid and gid of 1000 to use the ICMP socket, you should run this from the command line (with root privileges): `echo 1000 1000 > /proc/sys/net/ipv4/ping_group_range`, and then you can ping from this user account using ICMP sockets. If you want to set privileges for a user in the system, you should run from the command line echo 0 2147483647 > /proc/sys/net/ipv4/ping_group_range. (2147483647 is the value of GID_T_MAX; see include/net/ping.h.) There are no separate security settings for IPv4 and IPv6; everything is controlled by /proc/sys/net/ipv4/ping_group_range. The ICMP sockets support only ICMP_ECHO for IPv4 or ICMPV6_ECHO_REQUEST for IPv6, and the code of the ICMP message must be 0 in both cases.

The ping_supported() helper method checks whether the parameters for building the ICMP message (both for IPv4 and IPv6) are valid. It is invoked from ping_sendmsg():

```
static inline int ping_supported(int family, int type, int code)
{
    return (family == AF_INET && type == ICMP_ECHO && code == 0) ||
           (family == AF_INET6 && type == ICMPV6_ECHO_REQUEST && code == 0);
}
```

(net/ipv4/ping.c)

ICMP sockets export the following entries to procfs: /proc/net/icmp for IPv4 and /proc/net/icmp6 for IPv6.

For more info about ICMP sockets see http://openwall.info/wiki/people/segoon/ping and http://lwn.net/Articles/420799/.

Summary

This chapter covered the implementation of ICMPv4 and ICMPv6. You learned about the ICMP header format of both protocols and about receiving and sending messages with both protocols. The new features of ICMPv6, which you will encounter in upcoming chapters, were also discussed. The Neighbouring Discovery protocol, which uses ICMPv6 messages, is discussed in Chapter 7, and the MLD protocol, which also uses ICMPv6 messages, is covered in Chapter 8. The next chapter, Chapter 4, talks about the implementation of the IPv4 network layer.

In the "Quick Reference" section that follows, I cover the top methods related to the topics discussed in this chapter, ordered by their context. Then two tables mentioned in the chapter, some important relevant procfs entries and a short section about ICMP messages usage in iptables reject rules are all covered.

Quick Reference

I conclude this chapter with a short list of important methods of ICMPv4 and ICMPv6, 6 tables, a section about procfs entries, and a short section about using a reject target in iptables and ip6tables to create ICMP "Destination Unreachable" messages.

Methods

The following methods were covered in this chapter.

int icmp_rcv(struct sk_buff *skb);

This method is the main handler for processing incoming ICMPv4 packets.

extern void icmp_send(struct sk_buff *skb_in, int type, int code, __be32 info);

This method sends an ICMPv4 message. The parameters are the provoking SKB, ICMPv4 message type, ICMPv4 message code, and info (which is dependent on type).

struct icmp6hdr *icmp6_hdr(const struct sk_buff *skb);

This method returns the ICMPv6 header, which the specified skb contains.

void icmpv6_send(struct sk_buff *skb, u8 type, u8 code, __u32 info);

This method sends an ICMPv6 message. The parameters are the provoking SKB, ICMPv6 message type, ICMPv6 message code, and info (which is dependent on type).

void icmpv6_param_prob(struct sk_buff *skb, u8 code, int pos);

This method is a convenient version of the icmp6_send() method, which all it does is call icmp6_send() with ICMPV6_PARAMPROB as a type, and with the other specified parameters, skb, code and pos, and frees the SKB afterwards.

Tables

The following tables were covered in this chapter.

Table 3-2. *ICMPv4 "Destination Unreachable" (ICMP_DEST_UNREACH) Codes*

Code	Kernel Symbol	Description
0	ICMP_NET_UNREACH	Network Unreachable
1	ICMP_HOST_UNREACH	Host Unreachable
2	ICMP_PROT_UNREACH	Protocol Unreachable
3	ICMP_PORT_UNREACH	Port Unreachable
4	ICMP_FRAG_NEEDED	Fragmentation Needed, but the DF flag is set.
5	ICMP_SR_FAILED	Source route failed
6	ICMP_NET_UNKNOWN	Destination network unknown
7	ICMP_HOST_UNKNOWN	Destination host unknown
8	ICMP_HOST_ISOLATED	Source host isolated
9	ICMP_NET_ANO	The destination network is administratively prohibited.
10	ICMP_HOST_ANO	The destination host is administratively prohibited.
11	ICMP_NET_UNR_TOS	The network is unreachable for Type Of Service.
12	ICMP_HOST_UNR_TOS	The host is unreachable for Type Of Service.
13	ICMP_PKT_FILTERED	Packet filtered
14	ICMP_PREC_VIOLATION	Precedence violation
15	ICMP_PREC_CUTOFF	Precedence cut off
16	NR_ICMP_UNREACH	Number of unreachable codes

Table 3-3. *ICMPv4 Redirect (ICMP_REDIRECT) Codes*

Code	Kernel Symbol	Description
0	ICMP_REDIR_NET	Redirect Net
1	ICMP_REDIR_HOST	Redirect Host
2	ICMP_REDIR_NETTOS	Redirect Net for TOS
3	ICMP_REDIR_HOSTTOS	Redirect Host for TOS

Table 3-4. *ICMPv4 Time Exceeded (ICMP_TIME_EXCEEDED) Codes*

Code	Kernel Symbol	Description
0	ICMP_EXC_TTL	TTL count exceeded
1	ICMP_EXC_FRAGTIME	Fragment Reassembly time exceeded

Table 3-5. *ICMPv6 "Destination Unreachable" (ICMPV6_DEST_UNREACH) Codes*

Code	Kernel Symbol	Description
0	ICMPV6_NOROUTE	No route to destination
1	ICMPV6_ADM_PROHIBITED	Communication with destination administratively prohibited
2	ICMPV6_NOT_NEIGHBOUR	Beyond scope of source address
3	ICMPV6_ADDR_UNREACH	Address Unreachable
4	ICMPV6_PORT_UNREACH	Port Unreachable

Note that ICMPV6_PKT_TOOBIG, which is the counterpart of IPv4 ICMP_DEST_UNREACH /ICMP_FRAG_NEEDED, is not a code of ICMPV6_DEST_UNREACH, but an ICMPv6 type in itself.

Table 3-6. *ICMPv6 Time Exceeded (ICMPV6_TIME_EXCEED) Codes*

Code	Kernel Symbol	Description
0	ICMPV6_EXC_HOPLIMIT	Hop limit exceeded in transit
1	ICMPV6_EXC_FRAGTIME	Fragment reassembly time exceeded

Table 3-7. *ICMPv6 Parameter Problem (ICMPV6_PARAMPROB) Codes*

Code	Kernel Symbol	Description
0	ICMPV6_HDR_FIELD	Erroneous header field encountered
1	ICMPV6_UNK_NEXTHDR	Unknown Next Header type encountered
2	ICMPV6_UNK_OPTION	Unknown IPv6 option encountered

procfs entries

The kernel provides a way of configuring various settings for various subsystems from the userspace by way of writing values to entries under /proc. These entries are referred to as procfs entries. All of the ICMPv4 procfs entries are represented by variables in the netns_ipv4 structure (include/net/netns/ipv4.h), which is an object in the network namespace (struct net). Network namespaces and their implementation are discussed in Chapter 14. The following are the names of the sysctl variables that correspond to the ICMPv4 netns_ipv4 elements, explanations about their usage, and the default values to which they are initialized, specifying also in which method the initialization takes place.

sysctl_icmp_echo_ignore_all

When icmp_echo_ignore_all is set, echo requests (ICMP_ECHO) will not be replied.
    procfs entry: /proc/sys/net/ipv4/icmp_echo_ignore_all
    Initialized to 0 in icmp_sk_init()

sysctl_icmp_echo_ignore_broadcasts

When receiving a broadcast or a multicast echo (ICMP_ECHO) message or a timestamp (ICMP_TIMESTAMP) message, you check whether broadcast/multicast requests are permitted by reading sysctl_icmp_echo_ignore_broadcasts. If this variable is set, you drop the packet and return 0.
    procfs entry: /proc/sys/net/ipv4/icmp_echo_ignore_broadcasts
    Initialized to 1 in icmp_sk_init()

sysctl_icmp_ignore_bogus_error_responses

Some routers violate RFC1122 by sending bogus responses to broadcast frames. In the icmp_unreach() method, you check this flag. If this flag is set to TRUE, the kernel will not log these warnings ("<IPv4Addr>sent an invalid ICMP type...").
    procfs entry: /proc/sys/net/ipv4/icmp_ignore_bogus_error_responses
    Initialized to 1 in icmp_sk_init()

sysctl_icmp_ratelimit

Limit the maximal rates for sending ICMP packets whose type matches the icmp ratemask (icmp_ratemask, see later in this section) to specific targets.
    A value of 0 means disable any limiting; otherwise it is the minimal space between responses in milliseconds.
    procfs entry: /proc/sys/net/ipv4/icmp_ratelimit
    Initialized to 1 * HZ in icmp_sk_init()

sysctl_icmp_ratemask

Mask made of ICMP types for which rates are being limited. Each bit is an ICMPv4 type.
    procfs entry: /proc/sys/net/ipv4/icmp_ratemask
    Initialized to 0x1818 in icmp_sk_init()

sysctl_icmp_errors_use_inbound_ifaddr

The value of this variable is checked in icmp_send(). When it's not set, the ICMP error messages are sent with the primary address of the interface on which the packet will be sent. When it is set, the ICMP message will be sent with the primary address of the interface that received the packet that caused the icmp error.
    procfs entry: /proc/sys/net/ipv4/icmp_errors_use_inbound_ifaddr
    Initialized to 0 in icmp_sk_init()

■ **Note**   See also more about the ICMP `sysctl` variables, their types and their default values in

`Documentation/networking/ip-sysctl.txt`.

Creating "Destination Unreachable" Messages with iptables

The `iptables` userspace tool enables us to set rules which dictate what the kernel should do with traffic according to filters set by these rules. Handling `iptables` rules is done in the netfilter subsystem, and is discussed in Chapter 9. One of the `iptables` rules is the reject rule, which discards packets without further processing them. When setting an `iptables  reject` target, the user can set a rule to send a "Destination Unreachable" ICMPv4 messages with various codes using the `-j REJECT` and `--reject-with` qualifiers. For example, the following `iptables` rule will discard any packet from any source with sending back an ICMP message of "ICMP Host Prohibited":

`iptables -A INPUT -j REJECT --reject-with icmp-host-prohibited`

These are the possible values to the `--reject-with` qualifier for setting an ICMPV4 message which will be sent in reply to the sending host:

```
icmp-net-unreachable   - ICMP_NET_UNREACH
icmp-host-unreachable  - ICMP_HOST_UNREACH
icmp-port-unreachable  - ICMP_PORT_UNREACH
icmp-proto-unreachable - ICMP_PROT_UNREACH
icmp-net-prohibited    - ICMP_NET_ANO
icmp-host-prohibited   - ICMP_HOST_ANO
icmp-admin-prohibited  - ICMP_PKT_FILTERED
```

You can also use `--reject-with  tcp-reset` which will send a TCP RST packet in reply to the sending host.

`(net/ipv4/netfilter/ipt_REJECT.c)`

With `ip6tables` in IPv6, there is also a REJECT target. For example:

`ip6tables -A INPUT -s 2001::/64 -p ICMPv6  -j REJECT --reject-with icmp6-adm-prohibited`

These are the possible values to the `--reject-with` qualifier for setting an ICMPv6 message which will be sent in reply to the sending host:

```
no-route, icmp6-no-route                  - ICMPV6_NOROUTE.
adm-prohibited, icmp6-adm-prohibited      - ICMPV6_ADM_PROHIBITED.
port-unreach, icmp6-port-unreachable      - ICMPV6_NOT_NEIGHBOUR.
addr-unreach, icmp6-addr-unreachable      - ICMPV6_ADDR_UNREACH.
```

`(net/ipv6/netfilter/ip6t_REJECT.c)`

CHAPTER 4

■ ■ ■

IPv4

Chapter 3 deals with the implementation of the ICMP protocol in IPv4 and in IPv6. This chapter, which deals with the IPv4 protocol, shows how ICMP messages are used for reporting Internet protocol errors under certain circumstances. The IPv4 protocol (Internet Protocol version 4) is one of the core protocols of today's standards-based Internet and routes most of the traffic on the Internet. The base definition is in RFC 791, "Internet Protocol," from 1981. The IPv4 protocol provides an end-to-end connectivity between any two hosts. Another important function of the IP layer is forwarding packets (also called routing) and managing tables that store routing information. Chapters 5 and 6 discuss IPv4 routing. This chapter describes the IPv4 Linux implementation: receiving and sending IPv4 packets, including multicast packets, IPv4 forwarding, and handling IPv4 options. There are cases when the packet to be sent is bigger than the MTU of the outgoing interface; in such cases the packet should be fragmented into smaller fragments. When fragmented packets are received, they should be assembled into one big packet, which should be identical to the packet that was sent before it was fragmented. These are also important tasks of the IPv4 protocol discussed in this chapter.

Every IPv4 packet starts with an IP header, which is at least 20 bytes long. If IP options are used, the IPv4 header can be up to 60 bytes. After the IP header, there is the transport header (TCP header or UDP header, for example), and after it is the payload data. To understand the IPv4 protocol, you must first learn how the IPv4 header is built. In Figure 4-1 you can see the IPv4 header, which consists of two parts: the first part of 20 bytes (until the beginning of the options field in the IPv4 header) is the basic IPv4 header, and after it there is the IP options part, which can be from 0 to 40 bytes in length.

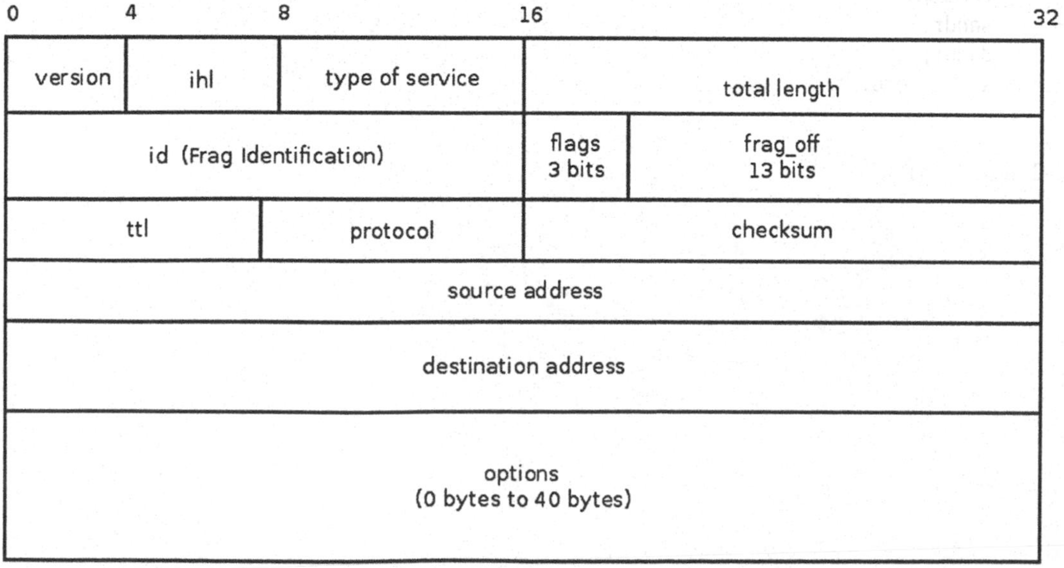

Figure 4-1. *IPv4 header*

IPv4 Header

The IPv4 header consists of information that defines how a packet should be handled by the kernel network stack: the protocol being used, the source and destination address, the checksum, the identification (id) of the packet that is needed for fragmentation, the ttl that helps avoiding packets being forwarded endlessly because of some error, and more. This information is stored in 13 members of the IPv4 header (the 14th member, IP Options, which is an extension to the IPv4 header, is optional). The various members of the IPv4 and the various IP options are described next. The IPv4 header is represented by the iphdr structure. Its members, which appear in Figure 4-1, are described in the next section. The IP options and their use are described in the "IP Options" section later in this chapter.

Figure 4-1 shows the IPv4 header. All members always exist—except for the last one, the IP options, which is optional. The content of the IPv4 members determines how it will be handled in the IPv4 network stack: the packet is discarded when there is some problem (for example, if the version, which is the first member, is not 4, or if the checksum is incorrect). Each IPv4 packet starts with IPv4 header, and after it there is the payload:

```
struct iphdr {
#if defined(__LITTLE_ENDIAN_BITFIELD)
    __u8    ihl:4,
            version:4;
#elif defined (__BIG_ENDIAN_BITFIELD)
    __u8    version:4,
            ihl:4;
#else
#error    "Please fix <asm/byteorder.h>"
#endif
    __u8        tos;
    __be16      tot_len;
    __be16      id;
    __be16      frag_off;
    __u8        ttl;
    __u8        protocol;
    __sum16     check;
    __be32      saddr;
    __be32      daddr;
    /*The options start here. */
};
```

(include/uapi/linux/ip.h)

The following is a description of the IPv4 header members:

- ihl: This stands for Internet Header Length. The length of the IPv4 header, measured in multiples of 4 bytes. The length of the IPv4 header is not fixed, as opposed to the header of IPv6, where the length is fixed (40 bytes). The reason is that the IPv4 header can include optional, varying length options. The minimum size of the IPv4 header is 20 bytes, when there are no options, and the maximum size is 60 bytes. The corresponding ihl values are 5 for minimum IPv4 header size, and 15 for the maximum size. The IPv4 header must be aligned to a 4-byte boundary.

- version: Should be 4.

- tos: The tos field of the IPv4 header was originally intended for Quality of Service (QoS) services; tos stands for Type of Service. Over the years this field took on a different meaning, as follows: RFC 2474 defines the Differentiated Services Field (DS Field) in the IPv4 and IPv6 headers, which is bits 0–5 of the tos. It is also named Differentiated Services Code Point (DSCP). RFC 3168 from 2001 defines the Explicit Congestion Notification (ECN) of the IP header; it is bits 6 and 7 of the tos field.

- tot_len: The total length, including the header, measured in bytes. Because tot_len is a 16-bit field, it can be up to 64KB. According to RFC 791, the minimum size is 576 bytes.

- id: Identification of the IPv4 header. The id field is important for fragmentation: when fragmenting an SKB, the id value of all the fragments of that SKB should be the same. Reassembling fragmented packets is done according to the id of the fragments.

- frag_off: The fragment offset, a 16-bit field. The lower 13 bits are the offset of the fragment. In the first fragment, the offset is 0. The offset is measured in units of 8 bytes. The higher 3 bits are the flags:

  - 001 is MF (More Fragments). It is set for all fragments, except the last one.

  - 010 is DF (Don't Fragment).

  - 100 is CE (Congestion).

  See the IP_MF, IP_DF, and IP_CE flags declaration in include/net/ip.h.

- ttl: Time To Live: this is a hop counter. Each forwarding node decreases the ttl by 1. When it reaches 0, the packet is discarded, and a time exceeded ICMPv4 message is sent back; this avoids packets from being forwarded endlessly, for this reason or another.

- protocol: The L4 protocol of the packet—for example, IPPROTO_TCP for TCP traffic or IPPROTO_UDP for UDP traffic (for a list of all available protocols see include/linux/in.h).

- check: The checksum (16-bit field). The checksum is calculated only over the IPv4 header bytes.

- saddr: Source IPv4 address, 32 bits.

- daddr: Destination IPv4 address, 32 bits.

In this section you have learned about the various IPv4 header members and their purposes. The initialization of the IPv4 protocol, which sets the callback to be invoked when receiving an IPv4 header, is discussed in the next section.

IPv4 Initialization

IPv4 packets are packets with Ethernet type 0x0800 (Ethernet type is stored in the first two bytes of the 14-byte Ethernet header). Each protocol should define a protocol handler, and each protocol should be initialized so that the network stack can handle packets that belong to this protocol. So that you understand what causes received IPv4 packets to be handled by IPv4 methods, this section describes the registration of the IPv4 protocol handler :

```
static struct packet      _type ip_packet_type __read_mostly = {
    .type = cpu_to_be16(ETH_P_IP),
    .func = ip_rcv,
};

static int __init inet_init(void)
{
  ...
  dev_add_pack(&ip_packet_type);
  ...
}
```

(net/ipv4/af_inet.c)

The dev_add_pack() method adds the ip_rcv() method as a protocol handler for IPv4 packets. These are packets with Ethernet type 0x0800 (ETH_P_IP, defined in include/uapi/linux/if_ether.h). The inet_init() method performs various IPv4 initializations and is called during the boot phase.

The main functionality of the IPv4 protocol is divided into the Rx (receive) path and the Tx (transmit) path. Now that you learned about the registration of the IPv4 protocol handler, you know which protocol handler manages IPv4 packets (the ip_rcv callback) and how this protocol handler is registered. You are ready now to start to learn about the IPv4 Rx path and how received IPv4 packets are handled. The Tx path is described in a later section, "Sending IPv4 Packets."

Receiving IPv4 Packets

The main IPv4 receive method is the ip_rcv() method, which is the handler for all IPv4 packets (including multicasts and broadcasts). In fact, this method consists mostly of sanity checks. The real work is done in the ip_rcv_finish() method it invokes. Between the ip_rcv() method and the ip_rcv_finish() method is the NF_INET_PRE_ROUTING netfilter hook, invoked by calling the NF_HOOK macro (see code snippet later in this section). In this chapter, you will encounter many invocations of the NF_HOOK macros—these are the netfilter hooks. The netfilter subsystem allows you to register callbacks in five points along the journey of a packet in the network stack. These points will be mentioned by their names shortly. The reason for adding the netfilter hooks is to enable loading the netfilter kernel modules at runtime. The NF_HOOK macro invokes the callbacks of a specified point, if such callbacks were registered. You might also encounter the NF_HOOK macro called NF_HOOK_COND, which is a variation of the NF_HOOK macro. In some places in the network stack, the NF_HOOK_COND macro includes a Boolean parameter (the last parameter), which must be true for the hook to be executed (Chapter 9 discusses netfilter hooks). Note that the netfilter hooks can discard the packet and in such a case it will not continue on its ordinary path. Figure 4-2 shows the receiving path (Rx) of a packet received by the network driver. This packet can either be delivered to the local machine or be forwarded to another host. It is the lookup in the routing table that determines which of these two options will take place.

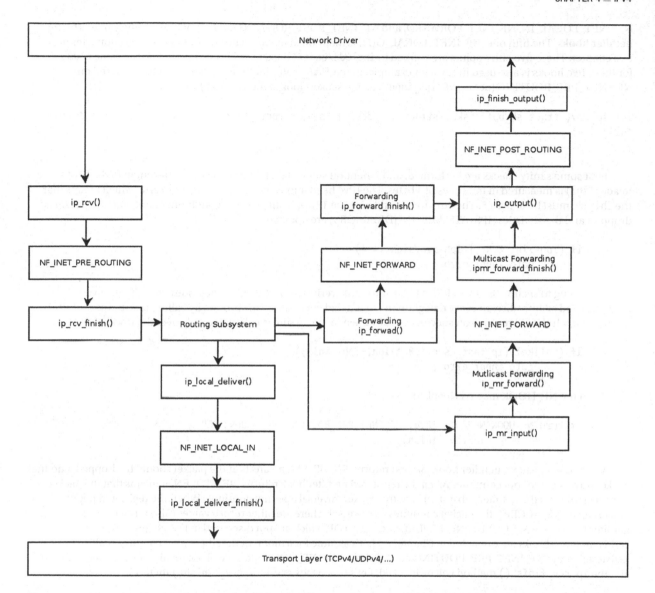

Figure 4-2. *Receiving IPv4 packets. For simplicity, the diagram does not include the fragmentation/defragmentation/ options/IPsec methods*

Figure 4-2 shows the paths for a received IPv4 packet. The packet is received by the IPv4 protocol handler, the ip_rcv() method (see the upper left side of the figure). First of all, a lookup in the routing subsystem should be performed, immediately after calling the ip_rcv_finish() method. The result of the routing lookup determines whether the packet is for local delivery to the local host or is to be forwarded (routing lookup is explained in Chapter 5). If the packet is destined for the local host, it will first reach the ip_local_deliver() method, and subsequently it will reach the ip_local_deliver_finish() method. When the packet is to be forwarded, it will be handled by the ip_forward() method. Some netfilter hooks appear in the figure, like NF_INET_PRE_ROUTING and NF_INET_LOCAL_IN. Note that multicast traffic is handled by the ip_mr_input() method, discussed in the "Receiving IPv4 Multicast Packets" section later in this chapter. The NF_INET_PRE_ROUTING,

NF_INET_LOCAL_IN, NF_INET_FORWARD, and NF_INET_POST_ROUTING are four of the five entry points of the netfilter hooks. The fifth one, NF_INET_LOCAL_OUT, is mentioned in the "Sending IPv4 packets" section later in this chapter. These five entry points are defined in include/uapi/linux/netfilter.h. Note that the same enum for these five hooks is also used in IPv6; for example, in the ipv6_rcv() method, a hook is being registered on NF_INET_PRE_ROUTING (net/ipv6/ip6_input.c). Let's take a look at the ip_rcv() method:

```
int ip_rcv(struct sk_buff *skb, struct net_device *dev, struct packet_type *pt, struct net_device *orig_dev)
{
```

First some sanity checks are performed, and I mention some of them in this section. The length of the IPv4 header (ihl) is measured in multiples of 4 bytes. The IPv4 header must be at least 20 bytes in size, which means that the ihl size must be at least 5. The version should be 4 (for IPv4). If one of these conditions is not met, the packet is dropped and the statistics (IPSTATS_MIB_INHDRERRORS) are updated.

```
if (iph->ihl < 5 || iph->version != 4)
        goto inhdr_error;
```

According to section 3.2.1.2 of RFC 1122, a host must verify the IPv4 header checksum on every received datagram and silently discard every datagram that has a bad checksum. This is done by calling the ip_fast_csum() method, which should return 0 on success. The IPv4 header checksum is calculated only over the IPv4 header bytes:

```
if (unlikely(ip_fast_csum((u8 *)iph, iph->ihl)))
        goto inhdr_error;
```

Then the NF_HOOK macro is invoked:

```
return NF_HOOK(NFPROTO_IPV4, NF_INET_PRE_ROUTING, skb, dev, NULL,
                ip_rcv_finish);
```

When the registered netfilter hook method returns NF_DROP, it means that the packet should be dropped, and the packet traversal does not continue. When the registered netfilter hook returns NF_STOLEN, it means that the packet was taken over by the netfilter subsystem, and the packet traversal does not continue. When the registered netfilter hook returns NF_ACCEPT, the packet continues its traversal. There are other return values (also termed *verdicts*) from netfilter hooks, like NF_QUEUE, NF_REPEAT, and NF_STOP, which are not discussed in this chapter. (As mentioned earlier, netfilter hooks are discussed in Chapter 9.) Let's assume for a moment that there are no netfilter callbacks registered in the NF_INET_PRE_ROUTING entry point, so the NF_HOOK macro will not invoke any netfilter callbacks and the ip_rcv_finish() method will be invoked. Let's take a look at the ip_rcv_finish() method:

```
static int ip_rcv_finish(struct sk_buff *skb)
{
        const struct iphdr *iph = ip_hdr(skb);
        struct rtable *rt;
```

The skb_dst() method checks whether there is a dst object attached to the SKB; dst is an instance of dst_entry (include/net/dst.h) and represents the result of a lookup in the routing subsystem. The lookup is done according to the routing tables and the packet headers. The lookup in the routing subsystem also sets the input and /or the output callbacks of the dst. For example, if the packet is to be forwarded, the lookup in the routing subsystem will set the input callback to be ip_forward(). When the packet is destined to the local machine, the lookup in the routing subsystem will set the input callback to be ip_local_deliver(). For a multicast packet it can be ip_mr_input() under some conditions (I discuss multicast packets in the next section). The contents of the dst object determine how the packet will proceed in its journey; for example, when forwarding a packet, the decision about which input callback should be called when invoking dst_input(), or on which interface it should be transmitted, is taken according to the dst.(I discuss the routing subsystem in depth in the next chapter).

If there is no dst attached to the SKB, a lookup in the routing subsystem is performed by the ip_route_input_noref() method. If the lookup fails, the packet is dropped. Note that handling multicast packets is different than handling unicast packets (discussed in the section "Receiving IPv4 Multicast Packets" later in this chapter).

```
...
if (!skb_dst(skb)) {
```

Perform a lookup in the routing subsystem:

```
        int err = ip_route_input_noref(skb, iph->daddr, iph->saddr,
                                       iph->tos, skb->dev);
        if (unlikely(err)) {
            if (err == -EXDEV)
                NET_INC_STATS_BH(dev_net(skb->dev),
                                 LINUX_MIB_IPRPFILTER);
            goto drop;
        }
}
```

■ **Note** The -EXDEV ("Crossdevice link") error is returned by the __fib_validate_source() method under certain circumstances when the Reverse Path Filter (RPF) is set. The RPF can be set via an entry in the procfs. In such cases the packet is dropped, the statistics (LINUX_MIB_IPRPFILTER) are updated, and the method returns NET_RX_DROP. Note that you can display the LINUX_MIB_IPRPFILTER counter by looking in the IPReversePathFilter column in the output of cat /proc/net/netstat.

Now a check is performed to see whether the IPv4 header includes options. Because the length of the IPv4 header (ihl) is measured in multiples of 4 bytes, if it is greater than 5 this means that it includes options, so the ip_rcv_options() method should be invoked to handle these options. Handling IP options is discussed in depth in the "IP Options" section later in this chapter. Note that the ip_rcv_options() method can fail, as you will shortly see. If it is a multicast entry or a broadcast entry, the IPSTATS_MIB_INMCAST statistics or the IPSTATS_MIB_INBCAST statistics is updated, respectively. Then the dst_input() method is invoked. This method in turn simply invokes the input callback method by calling skb_dst(skb)->input(skb):

```
if (iph->ihl > 5 && ip_rcv_options(skb))
        goto drop;

rt = skb_rtable(skb);
if (rt->rt_type == RTN_MULTICAST) {
    IP_UPD_PO_STATS_BH(dev_net(rt->dst.dev), IPSTATS_MIB_INMCAST,
            skb->len);
} else if (rt->rt_type == RTN_BROADCAST)
    IP_UPD_PO_STATS_BH(dev_net(rt->dst.dev), IPSTATS_MIB_INBCAST,
            skb->len);

return dst_input(skb);
```

In this section you learned about the various stages in the reception of IPv4 packets: the sanity checks performed, the lookup in the routing subsystem, the ip_rcv_finish() method which performs the actual work. You also learned about which method is called when the packet should be forwarded and which method is called when the packet is for local delivery. IPv4 multicasting is a special case. Handling the reception of IPv4 multicast packets is discussed in the next section.

Receiving IPv4 Multicast Packets

The ip_rcv() method is also a handler for multicast packets. As mentioned earlier, after some sanity checks, it invokes the ip_rcv_finish() method, which performs a lookup in the routing subsystem by calling ip_route_input_noref(). In the ip_route_input_noref() method, first a check is performed to see whether the local machine belongs to a multicast group of the destination multicast address, by calling the ip_check_mc_rcu() method. If it is so, or if the local machine is a multicast router (CONFIG_IP_MROUTE is set), the ip_route_input_mc() method is invoked; let's take a look at the code:

```
int ip_route_input_noref(struct sk_buff *skb, __be32 daddr, __be32 saddr,
                         u8 tos, struct net_device *dev)
{
        int res;
        rcu_read_lock();
        . . .
        if (ipv4_is_multicast(daddr)) {
                struct in_device *in_dev = __in_dev_get_rcu(dev);
                if (in_dev) {
                        int our = ip_check_mc_rcu(in_dev, daddr, saddr,
                                                  ip_hdr(skb)->protocol);
                        if (our
#ifdef CONFIG_IP_MROUTE
                                ||
                            (!ipv4_is_local_multicast(daddr) &&
                             IN_DEV_MFORWARD(in_dev))
#endif
                            ) {
                                int res = ip_route_input_mc(skb, daddr, saddr,
                                                            tos, dev, our);
                                rcu_read_unlock();
                                return res;
                        }
                }
        . . .
        }
        . . .
```

Let's further look into the ip_route_input_mc() method. If the local machine belongs to a multicast group of the destination multicast address (the value of the variable our is 1), then the input callback of dst is set to be ip_local_deliver. If the local host is a multicast router and IN_DEV_MFORWARD(in_dev) is set, then the input callback of dst is set to be ip_mr_input. The ip_rcv_finish() method, which calls dst_input(skb), invokes thus either the ip_local_deliver() method or the ip_mr_input() method, according to the input callback of dst. The IN_DEV_MFORWARD macro checks the procfs multicast forwarding entry. Note that the procfs multicast forwarding entry, /proc/sys/net/ipv4/conf/all/mc_forwarding , is a read-only entry (as opposed to the IPv4 unicast procfs forwarding entry), so you cannot set it simply by running from the command line: echo 1 > /proc/sys/net/ipv4/conf/all/mc_forwarding. Starting the pimd daemon, for example, sets it to 1, and stopping the daemon sets it to 0. pimd is a lightweight standalone PIM-SM v2 multicast routing daemon. If you are interested in learning about multicast routing daemon implementation, you might want to look into the pimd source code in https://github.com/troglobit/pimd/:

```
static int ip_route_input_mc(struct sk_buff *skb, __be32 daddr, __be32 saddr,
                            u8 tos, struct net_device *dev, int our)
{
        struct rtable *rth;
        struct in_device *in_dev = __in_dev_get_rcu(dev);

        . . .

        if (our) {
                rth->dst.input= ip_local_deliver;
                rth->rt_flags |= RTCF_LOCAL;
        }
#ifdef CONFIG_IP_MROUTE
        if (!ipv4_is_local_multicast(daddr) && IN_DEV_MFORWARD(in_dev))
                rth->dst.input = ip_mr_input;
#endif
        . . .
```

The multicast layer holds a data structure called the Multicast Forwarding Cache (MFC). I don't discuss the details of the MFC or of the ip_mr_input() method here (I discuss them in Chapter 6). What is important in this context is that if a valid entry is found in the MFC, the ip_mr_forward() method is called. The ip_mr_forward() method performs some checks and eventually calls the ipmr_queue_xmit() method. In the ipmr_queue_xmit() method, the ttl is decreased, and the checksum is updated by calling the ip_decrease_ttl() method (the same is done in the ip_forward() method, as you will see later in this chapter). Then the ipmr_forward_finish() method is invoked by calling the NF_INET_FORWARD NF_HOOK macro (let's assume that there are no registered IPv4 netfilter hooks on NF_INET_FORWARD):

```
static void ipmr_queue_xmit(struct net *net, struct mr_table *mrt,
                            struct sk_buff *skb, struct mfc_cache *c, int vifi)
{
        . . .

        ip_decrease_ttl(ip_hdr(skb));
        ...
        NF_HOOK(NFPROTO_IPV4, NF_INET_FORWARD, skb, skb->dev, dev,
                        ipmr_forward_finish);
        return;

}
```

The `ipmr_forward_finish()` method is very short and is shown here in its entirety. All it does is update the statistics, call the `ip_forward_options()` method if there are options in the IPv4 header (IP options are described in the next section), and call the `dst_output()` method:

```
static inline int ipmr_forward_finish(struct sk_buff *skb)
{
        struct ip_options *opt = &(IPCB(skb)->opt);

        IP_INC_STATS_BH(dev_net(skb_dst(skb)->dev), IPSTATS_MIB_OUTFORWDATAGRAMS);
        IP_ADD_STATS_BH(dev_net(skb_dst(skb)->dev), IPSTATS_MIB_OUTOCTETS, skb->len);

        if (unlikely(opt->optlen))
                ip_forward_options(skb);

        return dst_output(skb);
}
```

This section discussed how receiving IPv4 multicast packets is handled. The `pimd` was mentioned as an example of a multicast routing daemon, which interacts with the kernel in multicast packet forwarding. The next section describes the various IP options, which enable using special features of the network stack, such as tracking the route of a packet, tracking timestamps of packets, specifying network nodes which a packet should traverse. I also discuss how these IP options are handled in the network stack.

IP Options

The IP options field of the IPv4 header is optional and is not often used for security reasons and because of processing overhead. Which options might be helpful? Suppose, for example, that your packets are being dropped by a certain firewall. You may be able to specify a different route with the Strict or Loose Source Routing options. Or if you want to find out the packets' path to some destination addresses, you can use the Record Route option.

The IPv4 header may contain zero, one, or more options. The IPv4 header size is 20 bytes when there are no options. The length of the IP options field can be 40 bytes at most. The reason the IPv4 maximum length is 60 bytes is because the IPv4 header length is a 4-bit field, which expresses the length in multiples of 4 bytes. Hence the maximum value of the field is 15, which gives an IPv4 maximum header length of 60 bytes. When using more than one option, options are simply concatenated one after the other. The IPv4 header must be aligned to a 4-byte boundary, so sometimes padding is needed. The following RFCs discuss IP options: 781 (Timestamp Option), 791, 1063, 1108, 1393 (Traceroute Using an IP Option), and 2113 (IP Router Alert Option). There are two forms of IP options:

- *Single byte option (option type)*: The "End of Option List" and "No Operation" are the only single byte options.

- *Multibyte option*: When using a multibyte option after the option type byte there are the following three fields:

  - *Length (1 byte)*: Length of the option in bytes.

  - *Pointer (1 byte)*: Offset from option start.

  - *Option data*: This is a space where intermediate hosts can store data, for example, timestamps or IP addresses.

In Figure 4-3 the Option type is shown.

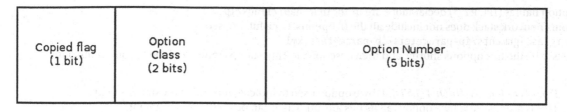

Copied flag (1 bit)	Option Class (2 bits)	Option Number (5 bits)

Figure 4-3. *Option type*

When set, copied flag means that the option should be copied in all fragments. When it is not set, the option should be copied only in the first fragment. The IPOPT_COPIED macro checks whether the copied flag of a specified IP option is set. It is used in the ip_options_fragment() method for detecting options which may not be copied and for inserting IPOPT_NOOP instead. The ip_options_fragment() method is discussed later in this section.

The option class can be one of the following 4 values:

- 00: control class (IPOPT_CONTROL)

- 01: reserved1 (IPOPT_RESERVED1)

- 10: debugging and measurement (IPOPT_MEASUREMENT)

- 11: reserved2 (IPOPT_RESERVED2)

In the Linux network stack, only the IPOPT_TIMESTAMP option belongs to the debugging and measurement class. All the other options are control classes.

The Option Number specifies an option by a unique number; possible values are 0–31, but not all are used by the Linux kernel.

Table 4-1 shows all options according to their Linux symbol, option number, option class, and copied flag.

Table 4-1. *Options Table*

Linux Symbol	Option Number	Class	Copied Flag	Description
IPOPT_END	0	0	0	End of Option List
IPOPT_NOOP	1	0	0	No Operation
IPOPT_SEC	2	0	1	Security
IPOPT_LSRR	3	0	1	Loose Source Record Route
IPOPT_TIMESTAMP	4	2	0	Timestamp
IPOPT_CIPSO	6	0	1	Commercial Internet Protocol Security Option
IPOPT_RR	7	0	0	Record Route
IPOPT_SID	8	0	1	Stream ID
IPOPT_SSRR	9	0	1	Strict Source Record Route
IPOPT_RA	20	0	1	Router Alert

The option names (IPOPT_*) declarations are in `include/uapi/linux/ip.h`.

The Linux network stack does not include all the IP options. For a full list, see `www.iana.org/assignments/ip-parameters/ip-parameters.xml`.

I will describe the five options shortly, and then describe the Timestamp Option and the Record Route option in depth:

- *End of Option List (IPOPT_END)*: 1-byte option used to indicate the end of the options field. This is a single zero byte option (all its bits are '0'). There can be no IP options after it.

- *No Operation (IPOPT_NOOP)*: 1-byte option is used for internal padding, which is used for alignment.

- *Security (IPOPT_SEC)*: This option provides a way for hosts to send security, handling restrictions, and TCC (closed user group) parameters. See RFC 791 and RFC 1108. Initially intended to be used by military applications.

- *Loose Source Record Route (IPOPT_LSRR)*: This option specifies a list of routers that the packet should traverse. Between each two adjacent nodes in the list there can be intermediate routers which do not appear in the list, but the order should be kept.

- *Commercial Internet Protocol Security Option (IPOPT_CIPSO)*: CIPSO is an IETF draft that has been adopted by several vendors. It deals with a network labeling standard. CIPSO labeling of a socket means adding the CIPSO IP options to all packets leaving the system through that socket. This option is validated upon reception of the packet. For more info about the CIPSO option, see `Documentation/netlabel/draft-ietf-cipso-ipsecurity-01.txt` and `Documentation/netlabel/cipso_ipv4.txt`.

Timestamp Option

Timestamp (IPOPT_TIMESTAMP): The Timestamp option is specified in RFC 781, "A Specification of the Internet Protocol (IP) Timestamp Option." This option stores timestamps of hosts along the packet route. The stored timestamp is a 32-bit timestamp in milliseconds since midnight UTC of the current day. In addition, it can also store the addresses of all hosts in the packet route or timestamps of only selected hosts along the route. The maximum Timestamp option length is 40. The Timestamp option is not copied for fragments; it is carried only in the first fragment. The Timestamp option begins with three bytes of option type, length, and pointer (offset). The higher 4 bits of the fourth byte are the overflow counter, which is incremented in each hop where there is no available space to store the required data. When the overflow counter exceeds 15, an ICMP message of Parameter Problem is sent back. The lower 4 bits is the flag. The value of the flag can be one of the following:

- *0*: Timestamp only (IPOPT_TS_TSONLY)

- *1*: Timestamps and addresses (IPOPT_TS_TSANDADDR)

- *3*: Timestamps of specified hops only (IPOPT_TS_PRESPEC)

■ **Note**   You can use the command-line `ping` utility with the Timestamp option and with the three subtypes mentioned earlier:

```
ping -T tsonly     (IPOPT_TS_TSONLY)

ping -T tsandaddr  (IPOPT_TS_TSANDADDR)

ping -T tsprespec  (IPOPT_TS_PRESPEC)
```

Figure 4-4 shows the Timestamp option with timestamp only (the IPOPT_TS_TSONLY flag is set). Each router on the path adds its IPv4 address. When there is no more space, the overflow counter is incremented.

Option Type (1 byte)	Option Length (1 byte)	Pointer Offset from Option Start (1 byte)	Overflow Counter 4 bits	Flag 0 4 bits
First node TIMESTAMP 4 bytes				
Second node TIMESTAMP 4 bytes				

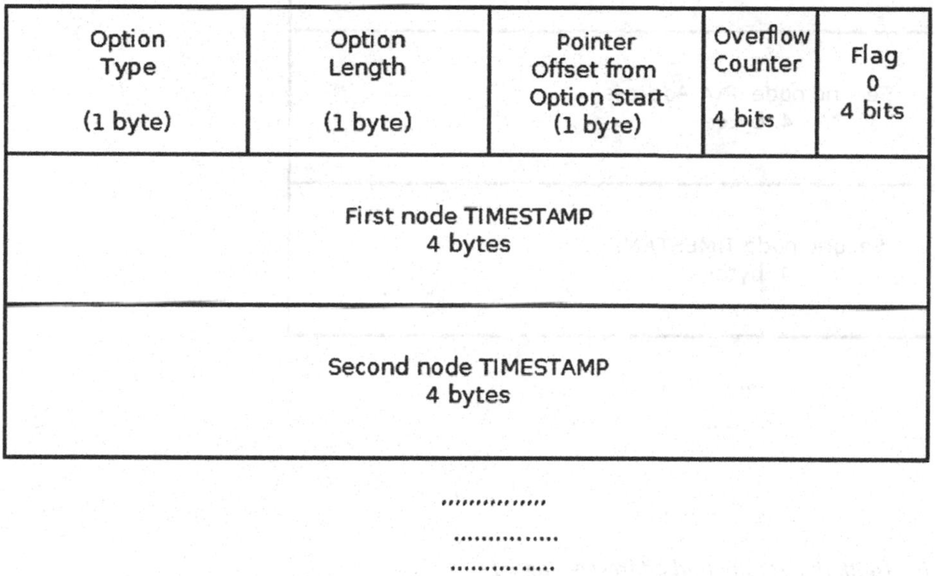

Figure 4-4. *Timestamp option (with timestamp only, flag = 0)*

Figure 4-5 shows the Timestamp option with timestamps and addresses (the IPOPT_TS_TSANDADDR flag is set). Each router on the path adds its IPv4 address and its timestamp. Again, when there is no more space, the overflow counter is incremented.

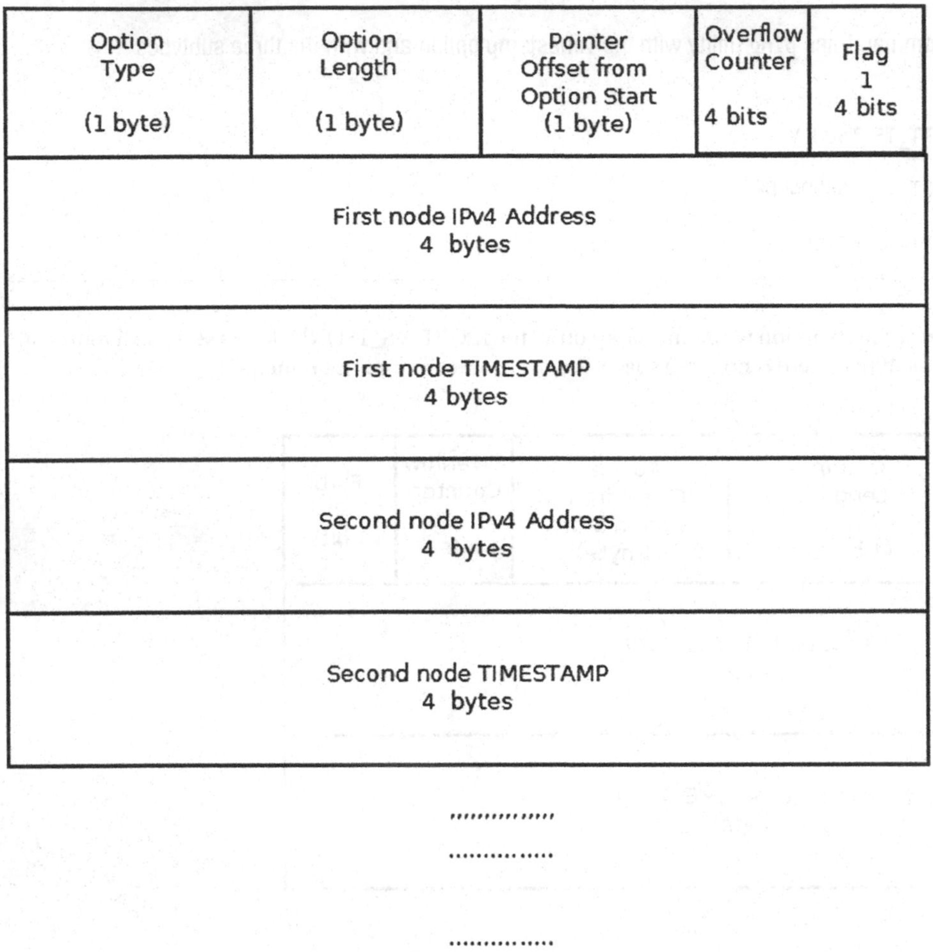

Option Type (1 byte)	Option Length (1 byte)	Pointer Offset from Option Start (1 byte)	Overflow Counter 4 bits	Flag 1 4 bits
First node IPv4 Address 4 bytes				
First node TIMESTAMP 4 bytes				
Second node IPv4 Address 4 bytes				
Second node TIMESTAMP 4 bytes				

,,,,,,,,,,,,,,,,,

....

....

Figure 4-5. *Timestamp option (with timestamps and addresses, flag = 1)*

Figure 4-6 shows the Timestamp option with timestamps (the IPOPT_TS_PRESPEC flag is set). Each router on the path adds its timestamp only if it is in the pre-specified list. Again, when there is no more space, the overflow counter is incremented.

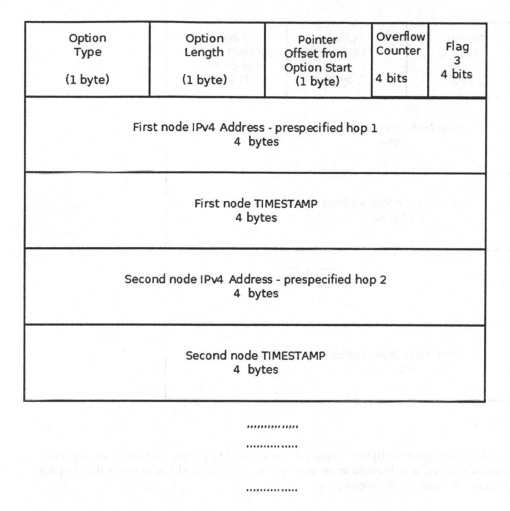

Option Type (1 byte)	Option Length (1 byte)	Pointer Offset from Option Start (1 byte)	Overflow Counter 4 bits	Flag 3 4 bits
First node IPv4 Address - prespecified hop 1 4 bytes				
First node TIMESTAMP 4 bytes				
Second node IPv4 Address - prespecified hop 2 4 bytes				
Second node TIMESTAMP 4 bytes				

Figure 4-6. *Timestamp option (with timestamps of specified hops only, flag = 3)*

Record Route Option

Record Route (IPOPT_RR): The route of a packet is recorded. Each router on the way adds its address (see Figure 4-7). The length is set by the sending device. The command-line utility ping -R uses the Record Route IP Option. Note that the IPv4 header is only large enough for nine such routes (or even less, if more options are used). When the header is full and there is no room to insert an additional address, the datagram is forwarded without inserting the address to the IP options. See section 3.1, RFC 791.

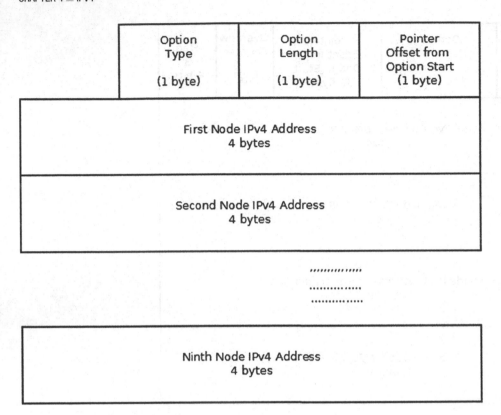

Figure 4-7. *Record Route option*

Though ping -R uses the Record Route IP Option, in many cases, if you will try it, you will not get the expected result of all the network nodes along the way, because for security reasons many network nodes ignore this IP option. The manpage of ping mentions this explicitly. From man ping:

. . .
-R
Includes the RECORD_ROUTE option in the ECHO_REQUEST packet and displays the route buffer on returned packets.
. . .
Many hosts ignore or discard this option.
. . .

- *Stream ID (IPOPT_SID)*: This option provides a way for the 16-bit SATNET stream identifier to be carried through networks that do not support the stream concept.

- *Strict Source Record Route (IPOPT_SSRR)*: This option specifies a list of routers that the packet should traverse. The order should be kept, and no changes in traversal are permitted. Many routers block the Loose Source Record Route (LSRR) and Strict Source Record Route (SSRR) options because of security reasons.

- *Router Alert (IPOPT_RA)*: The IP Router Alert option can be used to notify transit routers to more closely examine the contents of an IP packet. This is useful, for example, for new protocols but requires relatively complex processing in routers along the path. Specified in RFC 2113, "IP Router Alert Option."

IP options are represented in Linux by the `ip_options` structure:

```
struct ip_options {
        __be32          faddr;
        __be32          nexthop;
        unsigned char   optlen;
        unsigned char   srr;
        unsigned char   rr;
        unsigned char   ts;
        unsigned char   is_strictroute:1,
        srr_is_hit:1,
        is_changed:1,
        rr_needaddr:1,
        ts_needtime:1,
        ts_needaddr:1;
        unsigned char   router_alert;
        unsigned char   cipso;
        unsigned char   __pad2;
        unsigned char   __data[0];
};
```

(include/net/inet_sock.h)

Here are short descriptions of the members of the IP options structure:

- faddr: Saved first hop address. Set in `ip_options_compile()` when handling loose and strict routing, when the method was not invoked from the Rx path (SKB is NULL).

- nexthop: Saved nexthop address in LSRR and SSRR.

- optlen: The option length, in bytes. Cannot exceed 40 bytes.

- is_strictroute: A flag specifing usage of strict source route. The flag is set in the `ip_options_compile()` method when parsing strict route option type (IPOPT_SSRR); note that it is not set for loose route (IPOPT_LSRR).

- srr_is_hit: A flag specifing that the packet destination addr was the local host The srr_is_hit flag is set in `ip_options_rcv_srr()`.

- is_changed: IP checksum is not valid anymore (the flag is set when one of the IP options is changed).

- rr_needaddr: Need to record IPv4 address of the outgoing device. The flag is set for the Record Route option (IPOPT_RR).

- ts_needtime: Need to record timestamp. The flag is set for these flags of the Timestamp IP Option: IPOPT_TS_TSONLY, IPOPT_TS_TSANDADDR and IPOPT_TS_PRESPEC (see a detailed explanation about the difference between these flags later in this section).

- ts_needaddr: Need to record IPv4 address of the outgoing device. This flag is set only when the IPOPT_TS_TSANDADDR flag is set, and it indicates that the IPv4 address of each node along the route of the packet should be added.

- router_alert: Set in the `ip_options_compile()` method when parsing a router alert option (IPOPT_RR).

- __data[0]: A buffer to store options that are received from userspace by `setsockopt()`.

See `ip_options_get_from_user()` and `ip_options_get_finish()` (net/ipv4/ip_options.c).

Let's take a look at the ip_rcv_options() method:

```
static inline bool ip_rcv_options(struct sk_buff *skb)
{
        struct ip_options *opt;
        const struct iphdr *iph;
        struct net_device *dev = skb->dev;
    . . .
```

Fetch the IPv4 header from the SKB:

```
        iph = ip_hdr(skb);
```

Fetch the ip_options object from the inet_skb_parm object which is associated to the SKB:

```
        opt = &(IPCB(skb)->opt);
```

Calculate the expected options length:

```
        opt->optlen = iph->ihl*4 - sizeof(struct iphdr);
```

Call the ip_options_compile() method to build an ip_options object out of the SKB:

```
        if (ip_options_compile(dev_net(dev), opt, skb)) {
                IP_INC_STATS_BH(dev_net(dev), IPSTATS_MIB_INHDRERRORS);
                goto drop;
        }
```

When the ip_options_compile() method is called in the Rx path (from the ip_rcv_options() method), it parses the IPv4 header of the specified SKB and builds an ip_options object out of it, according to the IPv4 header content, after verifying the validity of the options. The ip_options_compile() method can also be invoked from the ip_options_get_finish() method when getting options from userspace via the setsockopt() system call with IPPROTO_IP and IP_OPTIONS. In this case, data is copied from userspace into opt->data, and the third parameter for ip_options_compile(), the SKB, is NULL; the ip_options_compile() method builds the ip_options object in such a case from opt->__data. If some error is found while parsing the options, and it is in the Rx path (the ip_options_compile() method was invoked from ip_rcv_options()), a "Parameter Problem" ICMPv4 message (ICMP_PARAMETERPROB) is sent back. An error with the code –EINVAL is returned in case of error, regardless of how the method was invoked. Naturally, it is more convenient to work with the ip_options object than with the raw IPv4 header, because access to the IP options fields is much simpler this way. In the Rx path, the ip_options object that the ip_options_compile() method builds is stored in the control buffer (cb) of the SKB; this is done by setting the opt object to &(IPCB(skb)->opt). The IPCB(skb) macro is defined like this:

```
#define IPCB(skb) ((struct inet_skb_parm*)((skb)->cb))
```

And the inet_skb_parm structure (which includes an ip_options object) is defined like this:

```
struct inet_skb_parm {
        struct ip_options       opt;            /* Compiled IP options          */
        unsigned char           flags;
        u16                     frag_max_size;
};
```

(include/net/ip.h)

So &(IPCB(skb)->opt points to the ip_options object inside the inet_skb_parm object. I will not delve into all the small, tedious technical details of parsing the IPv4 header in the ip_options_compile() method in this book, because there is an abundance of such details and they are self-explanatory. I will discuss briefly how the ip_options_compile() parses some single byte options, like IPOPT_END and IPOPT_NOOP, and some more complex options like IPOPT_RR and IPOPT_TIMESTAMP in the Rx path and show some examples of which checks are done in this method and how it is implemented in the following code snippet:

```
int ip_options_compile(struct net *net, struct ip_options *opt, struct sk_buff *skb)
{

        ...
        unsigned char *pp_ptr = NULL;
        struct rtable *rt = NULL;
        unsigned char *optptr;
        unsigned char *iph;
        int optlen, l;
```

For starting the parsing process, the optptr pointer should point to the start of the IP options object and iterate over all the options in a loop. For the Rx path (when the ip_options_compile() method is invoked from the ip_rcv_options() method), the SKB that was received in the ip_rcv() method is passed as a parameter to ip_options_compile() and, needless to say, cannot be NULL. In such a case, the IP options start immediately after the initial fixed size (20 bytes) of the IPv4 header. When the ip_options_compile() was invoked from ip_options_get_finish(), the optptr pointer was set to opt->__data, because the ip_options_get_from_user() method copied the options that were sent from userspace into opt->__data. To be accurate, I should mention that if alignment is needed, the ip_options_get_finish() method also writes into opt->__data (it writes IPOPT_END in the proper place).

```
        if (skb != NULL) {
            rt = skb_rtable(skb);
            optptr = (unsigned char *)&(ip_hdr(skb)[1]);
        } else
            optptr = opt->__data;
```

In this case, iph = ip_hdr(skb) cannot be used instead, because the case when SKB is NULL should be considered. The following assignment is correct also for the non-Rx path:

```
        iph = optptr - sizeof(struct iphdr);
```

The variable l is initialized to be the options length (it can be 40 bytes at most). It is decremented by the length of the current option in each iteration of the following for loop:

```
        for (l = opt->optlen; l > 0; ) {
            switch (*optptr) {
```

If an IPOPT_END option is encountered, it indicates that this is the end of the options list—there must be no other option after it. In such a case you write IPOPT_END for each byte which is different than IPOPT_END until the end of the options list. The is_changed Boolean flag should also be set, because it indicates that the IPv4 header was changed (and as a result, recalculation of checksum is pending—there is no justification for calculating the checksum right now or inside the for loop, because there might be other changes in the IPv4 header during the loop):

```
        case IPOPT_END:
            for (optptr++, l--; l>0; optptr++, l--) {
                if (*optptr != IPOPT_END) {
                    *optptr = IPOPT_END;
                    opt->is_changed = 1;
                }
            }
    goto eol;
```

If an option type of No Operation (IPOPT_NOOP), which is a single byte option, is encountered, simply decrement l by 1, increment optptr by 1, and move forward to the next option type:

```
        case IPOPT_NOOP:
            l--;
            optptr++;
            continue;
    }
```

Optlen is set to be the length of the option that is read (as optptr[1] holds the option length):

```
        optlen = optptr[1];
```

The No Operation (IPOPT_NOOP) option and the End of Option List (IPOPT_END) option are the only single byte options. All other options are multibyte options and must have at least two bytes (option type and option length). Now a check is made that there are at least two option bytes and the option list length was not exceeded. If there was some error, the pp_ptr pointer is set to point to the source of the problem and exit the loop. If it is in the Rx path, an ICMPv4 message of "Parameter Problem" is sent back, passing as a parameter the offset where the problem occurred, so that the other side can analyze the problem:

```
        if (optlen<2 || optlen>l) {
            pp_ptr = optptr;
            goto error;
        }
        switch (*optptr) {
            case IPOPT_SSRR:
            case IPOPT_LSRR:
            ...
            case IPOPT_RR:
```

The option length of the Record Route option must be at least 3 bytes: option type, option length, and pointer (offset):

```
            if (optlen < 3) {
                pp_ptr = optptr + 1;
                goto error;
            }
```

The option pointer offset of the Record Route option must be at least 4 bytes, since the space reserved for the address list must start after the three initial bytes (option type, option length, and pointer):

```
if (optptr[2] < 4) {
        pp_ptr = optptr + 2;
        goto error;
}
if (optptr[2] <= optlen) {
```

If the offset (optptr[2]) plus the three initial bytes exceeds the option length, there is an error:

```
if (optptr[2]+3 > optlen) {
    pp_ptr = optptr + 2;
    goto error;
}
if (rt) {
    spec_dst_fill(&spec_dst, skb);
```

Copy the IPv4 address to the Record Route buffer:

```
memcpy(&optptr[optptr[2]-1], &spec_dst, 4);
```

Set the is_changed Boolean flag, which indicates that the IPv4 header was changed (recalculation of checksum is pending):

```
    opt->is_changed = 1;
}
```

Increment the pointer (offset) by 4 for the next address in the Record Route buffer (each IPv4 address is 4 bytes):

```
optptr[2] += 4;
```

Set the rr_needaddr flag (this flag is checked in the ip_forward_options() method):

```
    opt->rr_needaddr = 1;
}
opt->rr = optptr - iph;
break;

    case IPOPT_TIMESTAMP:
        ...
```

The option length for Timestamp option must be at least 4 bytes: option type, option length, pointer (offset), and the fourth byte is divided into two fields: the higher 4 bits are the overflow counter, which is incremented in each hop where there is no available space to store the required data, and the lower 4 bits are the flag: timestamp only, timestamp and address, and timestamp by a specified hop:

```
if (optlen < 4) {
        pp_ptr = optptr + 1;
        goto error;
}
```

optptr[2] is the pointer (offset). Because, as stated earlier, each Timestamp option starts with 4 bytes, it implies that the pointer (offset) must be at least 5:

```
                    if (optptr[2] < 5) {
                            pp_ptr = optptr + 2;
                            goto error;
                    }
                    if (optptr[2] <= optlen) {
                            unsigned char *timeptr = NULL;
                            if (optptr[2]+3 > optptr[1]) {
                                    pp_ptr = optptr + 2;
                                    goto error;
                            }
```

In the switch command, the value of optptr[3]&0xF is checked. It is the flag (4 lower bits of the fourth byte) of the Timestamp option:

```
                switch (optptr[3]&0xF) {
                    case IPOPT_TS_TSONLY:
                        if (skb)
                                timeptr = &optptr[optptr[2]-1];
                        opt->ts_needtime = 1;
```

For the Timestamp option with timestamps only flag (IPOPT_TS_TSONLY), 4 bytes are needed; so the pointer (offset) is incremented by 4:

```
                        optptr[2] += 4;
                        break;

                    case IPOPT_TS_TSANDADDR:
                        if (optptr[2]+7 > optptr[1]) {
                                pp_ptr = optptr + 2;
                                goto error;
                        }
                        if (rt)  {
                                spec_dst_fill(&spec_dst, skb);
                                memcpy(&optptr[optptr[2]-1],
                                        &spec_dst, 4);
                                timeptr = &optptr[optptr[2]+3];
                        }
                        opt->ts_needaddr = 1;
                        opt->ts_needtime = 1;
```

For the Timestamp option with timestamps and addresses flag (IPOPT_TS_TSANDADDR), 8 bytes are needed; so the pointer (offset) is incremented by 8:

```
                        optptr[2] += 8;
                        break;

                    case IPOPT_TS_PRESPEC:
                        if (optptr[2]+7 > optptr[1]) {
```

```
                        pp_ptr = optptr + 2;
                        goto error;
                }
                {
                __be32 addr;
                memcpy(&addr, &optptr[optptr[2]-1], 4);
                    if (inet_addr_type(net,addr) == RTN_UNICAST)
                        break;
                if (skb)
                        timeptr = &optptr[optptr[2]+3];
                }
                opt->ts_needtime = 1;
```

For the Timestamp option with timestamps and pre-specified hops flag (IPOPT_TS_PRESPEC), 8 bytes are needed, so the pointer (offset) is incremented by 8:

```
                        optptr[2] += 8;
                        break;
                default:
                    ...
        }
    ...
```

After the ip_options_compile() method has built the ip_options object, strict routing is handled. First, a check is performed to see whether the device supports source routing. This means that the /proc/sys/net/ipv4/conf/all/accept_source_route is set, and the /proc/sys/net/ipv4/conf/<deviceName>/accept_source_route is set. If these conditions are not met, the packet is dropped:

```
    . . .
    if (unlikely(opt->srr)) {
        struct in_device *in_dev = __in_dev_get_rcu(dev);

        if (in_dev) {
                if (!IN_DEV_SOURCE_ROUTE(in_dev)) {
                . . .
                        goto drop;
                }
        }

        if (ip_options_rcv_srr(skb))
                goto drop;
    }
```

Let's take a look at the ip_options_rcv_srr() method (again, I will focus on the important points, not little details). The list of source route addresses is iterated over. During the parsing process some sanity checks are made in the loop to see if there are errors. When the first nonlocal address is encountered, the loop is exited, and the following actions take place:

- Set the srr_is_hit flag of the IP option object (opt->srr_is_hit = 1).

- Set opt->nexthop to be the nexthop address that was found.

- Set the opt->is_changed flag to 1.

The packet should be forwarded. When the method ip_forward_finish() is reached, the ip_forward_options() method is called. In this method, if the srr_is_hit flag of the IP option object is set, the daddr of the ipv4 header is changed to be opt->nexthop, the offset is incremented by 4 (to point to the next address in the source route addresses list), and—because the IPv4 header was changed—the checksum is recalculated by calling the ip_send_check() method.

IP Options and Fragmentation

When describing the option type in the beginning of this section, I mentioned a copied flag in the option type byte which indicates whether or not to copy the option when forwarding a fragmented packet. Handling IP options in fragmentation is done by the ip_options_fragment() method, which is invoked from the method which prepares fragments, ip_fragment(). It is called only for the first fragment. Let's take a look at the ip_options_fragment() method, which is very simple:

```
void ip_options_fragment(struct sk_buff *skb)
{
        unsigned char *optptr = skb_network_header(skb) + sizeof(struct iphdr);
        struct ip_options *opt = &(IPCB(skb)->opt);
        int  l = opt->optlen;
        int  optlen;
```

The while loop simply iterates over the options, reading each option type. optptr is a pointer to the option list (which starts at the end of the 20 first bytes of the IPv4 header). l is the size of the option list, which is being decremented by 1 in each loop iteration:

```
        while (l > 0) {
                switch (*optptr) {
```

When the option type is IPOPT_END, which terminates the option string, it means that reading the options is finished:

```
                case IPOPT_END:
                        return;

                case IPOPT_NOOP:
```

When the option type is IPOPT_NOOP, used for padding between options, the optptr pointer is incremented by 1, l is decremented, and the next option is processed:

```
                        l--;
                        optptr++;
                        continue;
                }
```

Perform a sanity check on the option length:

```
                       optlen = optptr[1];
                       if (optlen<2 || optlen>l)
                          return;
```

Check whether the option should be copied; if not, simply put one or several IPOPT_NOOP options instead of it with the memset() function. The number of IPOPT_NOOP bytes that memset() writes is the size of the option that was read, namely optlen:

```
                       if (!IPOPT_COPIED(*optptr))
                              memset(optptr, IPOPT_NOOP, optlen);
```

Now go to the next option:

```
                       l -= optlen;
                       optptr += optlen;            }
```

IPOPT_TIMESTAMP and IPOPT_RR are options for which the copied flag is 0 (see Table 4-1). They are replaced by IPOPT_NOOP in the loop you saw earlier, and their relevant fields in the IP option object are reset to 0:

```
                 opt->ts = 0;
                 opt->rr = 0;
                 opt->rr_needaddr = 0;
                 opt->ts_needaddr = 0;
                 opt->ts_needtime = 0;
}
```

(net/ipv4/ip_options.c)

In this section you have learned how the ip_rcv_options() handles the reception of packets with IP options and how IP options are parsed by the ip_options_compile() method. Fragmentation in IP options was also discussed. The next section covers the process of building IPv4 options, which involves setting the IP options of an IPv4 header based on a specified ip_options object.

Building IP Options

The ip_options_build() method can be thought of as the reverse of the ip_options_compile() method you saw earlier in this chapter. It takes an ip_options object as an argument and writes its content to the IPv4 header. Let's take a look at it:

```
void ip_options_build(struct sk_buff *skb, struct ip_options *opt,
                      __be32 daddr, struct rtable *rt, int is_frag)
{
        unsigned char *iph = skb_network_header(skb);

        memcpy(&(IPCB(skb)->opt), opt, sizeof(struct ip_options));
        memcpy(iph+sizeof(struct iphdr), opt->__data, opt->optlen);
        opt = &(IPCB(skb)->opt);
```

```
        if (opt->srr)
                memcpy(iph+opt->srr+iph[opt->srr+1]-4, &daddr, 4);

        if (!is_frag) {
                if (opt->rr_needaddr)
                        ip_rt_get_source(iph+opt->rr+iph[opt->rr+2]-5, skb, rt);
                if (opt->ts_needaddr)
                        ip_rt_get_source(iph+opt->ts+iph[opt->ts+2]-9, skb, rt);
                if (opt->ts_needtime) {
                        struct timespec tv;
                        __be32 midtime;
                        getnstimeofday(&tv);
                        midtime = htonl((tv.tv_sec % 86400) *
                                        MSEC_PER_SEC + tv.tv_nsec / NSEC_PER_MSEC);
                        memcpy(iph+opt->ts+iph[opt->ts+2]-5, &midtime, 4);
                }
                return;
        }
        if (opt->rr) {
                memset(iph+opt->rr, IPOPT_NOP, iph[opt->rr+1]);
                opt->rr = 0;
                opt->rr_needaddr = 0;
        }
        if (opt->ts) {
                memset(iph+opt->ts, IPOPT_NOP, iph[opt->ts+1]);
                opt->ts = 0;
                opt->ts_needaddr = opt->ts_needtime = 0;
        }
}
```

The ip_forward_options() method handles forwarding fragmented packets (net/ipv4/ip_options.c). In this method the Record Route and Strict Record route options are handled, and the ip_send_check() method is invoked to calculate the checksum for packets whose IPv4 header was changed (the opt->is_changed flag is set) and to reset the opt->is_changed flag to 0. The IPv4 Tx path—namely, how packets are sent—is discussed in the next section.

My discussion on the Rx path is finished. The next section talks about the Tx path—what happens when IPv4 packets are sent.

Sending IPv4 Packets

The IPv4 layer provides the means for the layer above it, the transport layer (L4), to send packets by passing these packets to the link layer (L2). I discuss how that is implemented in this section, and you'll see some differences between handling transmission of TCPv4 packets in IPv4 and handling transmission of UDPv4 packets in IPv4. There are two main methods for sending IPv4 packets from Layer 4, the transport layer: The first one is the ip_queue_xmit() method, used by the transport protocols that handle fragmentation by themselves, like TCPv4. The ip_queue_xmit() method is not the only transmission method used by TCPv4, which uses also the ip_build_and_send_pkt() method, for example, to send SYN ACK messages (see the `tcp_v4_send_synack()` method implementation in `net/ipv4/tcp_ipv4.c`). The second method is the `ip_append_data()` method, used by the transport protocols that do not handle fragmentation, like the UDPv4 protocol or the ICMPv4 protocol. The `ip_append_data()` method does not send any packet—it only prepares the packet. The `ip_push_pending_frames()` method is for actually sending the packet, and it is used by ICMPv4 or raw sockets, for example. Calling `ip_push_pending_frames()` actually starts the transmission process by calling the `ip_send_skb()` method, which eventually calls the `ip_local_out()` method. The `ip_push_pending_frames()` method was used for carrying out the transmission in UDPv4 prior to kernel 2.6.39; with the new `ip_finish_skb` API in 2.6.39, the `ip_send_skb()` method is used instead. Both methods are implemented in `net/ipv4/ip_output.c`.

There are cases where the `dst_output()` method is called directly, without using the `ip_queue_xmit()` method or the `ip_append_data()` method; for example, when sending with a raw socket which uses IP_HDRINCL socket option, there is no need to prepare an IPv4 header. Userspace applications that build an IPv4 by their own use the IPv4 IP_HDRINCL socket option. For example, the well-known `ping` of `iputils` and `nping` of `nmap` both enable the user to set the `ttl` of the IPv4 header like this:

```
ping -ttl ipDestAddress
```

   or:

```
nping -ttl ipDestAddress
```

Sending packets by raw sockets whose IP_HDRINCL socket option is set is done like this:

```
static int raw_send_hdrinc(struct sock *sk, struct flowi4 *fl4,
              void *from, size_t length,
              struct rtable **rtp,
              unsigned int flags)
{
      ...
      err = NF_HOOK(NFPROTO_IPV4, NF_INET_LOCAL_OUT, skb, NULL,
          rt->dst.dev, dst_output);
      ...
}
```

Figure 4-8 shows the paths for sending IPv4 packets from the transport layer.

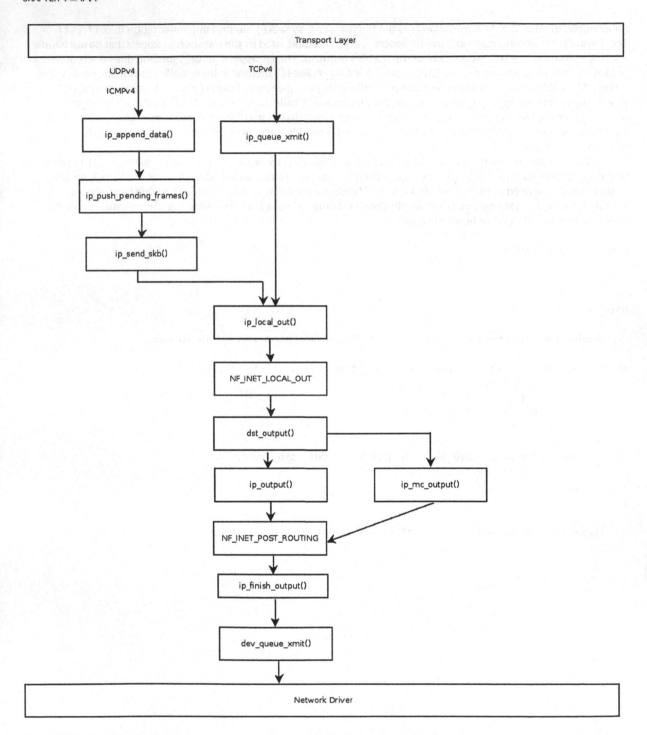

Figure 4-8. *Sending IPv4 packets*

In figure 4-8 you can see the different paths for transmitted packets that come from the transport layer (L4); these packets are handled by the ip_queue_xmit() method or by the ip_append_data() method.

Let's start with the ip_queue_xmit() method, which is the simpler method of the two:

```
int ip_queue_xmit(struct sk_buff *skb, struct flowi *fl)
. . .
/* Make sure we can route this packet. */
rt = (struct rtable *)__sk_dst_check(sk, 0);
```

The rtable object is the result of a lookup in the routing subsystem. First I discuss the case where the rtable instance is NULL and you need to perform a lookup in the routing subsystem. If the strict routing option flag is set, the destination address is set to be the first address of the IP options:

```
if (rt == NULL) {
    __be32 daddr;

    /* Use correct destination address if we have options. */
    daddr = inet->inet_daddr;
    if (inet_opt && inet_opt->opt.srr)
        daddr = inet_opt->opt.faddr;
```

Now a lookup in the routing subsystem is performed with the ip_route_output_ports() method: if the lookup fails, the packet is dropped, and an error of –EHOSTUNREACH is returned:

```
    /* If this fails, retransmit mechanism of transport layer will
     * keep trying until route appears or the connection times
     * itself out.
     */
    rt = ip_route_output_ports(sock_net(sk), fl4, sk,
                    daddr, inet->inet_saddr,
                    inet->inet_dport,
                    inet->inet_sport,
                    sk->sk_protocol,
                    RT_CONN_FLAGS(sk),
                    sk->sk_bound_dev_if);
    if (IS_ERR(rt))
        goto no_route;
    sk_setup_caps(sk, &rt->dst);
}
skb_dst_set_noref(skb, &rt->dst);
. . .
```

If the lookup succeeds, but both the is_strictroute flag in the options and the rt_uses_gateway flag in the routing entry are set, the packet is dropped, and an error of –EHOSTUNREACH is returned:

```
if (inet_opt && inet_opt->opt.is_strictroute && rt->rt_uses_gateway)
    goto no_route;
```

Now the IPv4 header is being built. You should remember that the packet arrived from Layer 4, where skb->data pointed to the transport header. The skb->data pointer is moved back by the skb_push() method; the offset needed to move it back is the size of the IPv4 header plus the size of the IP options list (optlen), if IP options are used:

```
/* OK, we know where to send it, allocate and build IP header. */
skb_push(skb, sizeof(struct iphdr) + (inet_opt ? inet_opt->opt.optlen : 0));
```

Set the L3 header (skb->network_header) to point to skb->data:

```
skb_reset_network_header(skb);
iph = ip_hdr(skb);
*((__be16 *)iph) = htons((4 << 12) | (5 << 8) | (inet->tos & 0xff));
if (ip_dont_fragment(sk, &rt->dst) && !skb->local_df)
    iph->frag_off = htons(IP_DF);
else
    iph->frag_off = 0;
iph->ttl      = ip_select_ttl(inet, &rt->dst);
iph->protocol = sk->sk_protocol;
ip_copy_addrs(iph, fl4);
```

The options length (optlen) is divided by 4, and the result is added to the IPv4 header length (iph->ihl) because the IPv4 header is measured in multiples of 4 bytes. Then the ip_options_build() method is invoked to build the options in the IPv4 header based on the content of the specified IP options. The last parameter of the ip_options_build() method, is_frag, specifies that there are no fragments. The ip_options_build() method was discussed in the "IP Option" section earlier in this chapter.

```
        if (inet_opt && inet_opt->opt.optlen) {
        iph->ihl += inet_opt->opt.optlen >> 2;
        ip_options_build(skb, &inet_opt->opt, inet->inet_daddr, rt, 0);
        }
```

Set the id in the IPv4 header:

```
        ip_select_ident_more(iph, &rt->dst, sk,
                (skb_shinfo(skb)->gso_segs ?: 1) - 1);

        skb->priority = sk->sk_priority;
        skb->mark = sk->sk_mark;
```

Send the packet:

```
        res = ip_local_out(skb);
```

Before discussing the ip_append_data() method, I want to mention a callback which is a parameter to the ip_append_data() method: the getfrag() callback. The getfrag() method is a callback to copy the actual data from userspace into the SKB. In UDPv4, the getfrag() callback is set to be the generic method, ip_generic_getfrag(). In ICMPv4, the getfrag() callback is set to be a protocol-specific method, icmp_glue_bits(). Another issue I should mention here is the UDPv4 corking feature. The UDP_CORK socket option was added in kernel 2.5.44; when this option is enabled, all data output on this socket is accumulated into a single datagram that is transmitted when the option is disabled. You can enable and disable this socket option with the setsockopt() system call; see man 7 udp. In kernel 2.6.39, a lockless transmit fast path was added to the UDPv4 implementation. With this addition, when the corking feature is not used, the socket lock is not used. So when the UDP_CORK socket option is set (with the setsockopt() system call), or the MSG_MORE flag is set, the ip_append_data() method is invoked. And when the UDP_CORK socket option is not set, another path in the udp_sendmsg() method is used, which does not hold the socket lock and is faster as a result, and the ip_make_skb() method is invoked. Calling the ip_make_skb() method is similar to the ip_append_data() and the ip_push_pending_frames() methods rolled into one, except that it does not send the SKB produced. Sending the SKB is carried out by the ip_send_skb() method.

Let's take a look now at the ip_append_data() method:

```
int ip_append_data(struct sock *sk, struct flowi4 *fl4,
                   int getfrag(void *from, char *to, int offset, int len,
                               int odd, struct sk_buff *skb),
                   void *from, int length, int transhdrlen,
                   struct ipcm_cookie *ipc, struct rtable **rtp,
                   unsigned int flags)
{
        struct inet_sock *inet = inet_sk(sk);
        int err;
```

If the MSG_PROBE flag us used, it means that the caller is interested only in some information (usually MTU, for PMTU discovery), so there is no need to actually send the packet, and the method returns 0:

```
        if (flags&MSG_PROBE)
                return 0;
```

The value of transhdrlen is used to indicate whether it is a first fragment or not. The ip_setup_cork() method creates a cork IP options object if it does not exist and copies the IP options of the specified ipc (ipcm_cookie object) to the cork IP options:

```
        if (skb_queue_empty(&sk->sk_write_queue)) {
                err = ip_setup_cork(sk, &inet->cork.base, ipc, rtp);
                if (err)
                        return err;
        } else {
                transhdrlen = 0;
        }
```

The real work is done by the __ip_append_data() method; this is a long and a complex method, and I can't delve into all its details. I will mention that there are two different ways to handle fragments in this method, according to whether the network device supports Scatter/Gather (NETIF_F_SG) or not. When the NETIF_F_SG flag is set, skb_shinfo(skb)->frags is used, whereas when the NETIF_F_SG flag is not set, skb_shinfo(skb)->frag_list is used. There is also a different memory allocation when the MSG_MORE flag is set. The MSG_MORE flag indicates that soon another packet will be sent. Since Linux 2.6, this flag is also supported for UDP sockets.

```
        return __ip_append_data(sk, fl4, &sk->sk_write_queue, &inet->cork.base,
                                sk_page_frag(sk), getfrag,
                                from, length, transhdrlen, flags);
}
```

In this section you have learned about the Tx path—how sending IPv4 packets is implemented. When the packet length is higher than the network device MTU, the packet can't be sent as is. The next section covers fragmentation in the Tx path and how it is handled.

Fragmentation

The network interface has a limit on the size of a packet. Usually in 10/100/1000 Mb/s Ethernet networks, it is 1500 bytes, though there are network interfaces that allow using an MTU of up to 9K (called *jumbo frames*). When sending a packet that is larger than the MTU of the outgoing network card, it should be broken into smaller pieces. This is done within the ip_fragment() method (net/ipv4/ip_output.c). Received fragmented packets should be reassembled into one packet. This is done by the ip_defrag() method, (net/ipv4/ip_fragment.c), discussed in the next section, "Defragmentation."

Let's take a look first at the ip_fragment() method. Here's its prototype:

```
int ip_fragment(struct sk_buff *skb, int (*output)(struct sk_buff *))
```

The output callback is the method of transmission to be used. When the ip_fragment() method is invoked from ip_finish_output(), the output callback is the ip_finish_output2() method. There are two paths in the ip_fragment() method: the fast path and the slow path. The fast path is for packets where the frag_list of the SKB is not NULL, and the slow path is for packets that do not meet this condition.

First a check is performed to see whether fragmentation is permitted, and if not, a "Destination Unreachable" ICMPv4 message with code of fragmentation needed is sent back to the sender, the statistics (IPSTATS_MIB_FRAGFAILS) are updated, the packet is dropped, and an error code of –EMSGSIZE is returned:

```
int ip_fragment(struct sk_buff *skb, int (*output)(struct sk_buff *))
    {
    unsigned int mtu, hlen, left, len, ll_rs;
    . . .
    struct rtable *rt = skb_rtable(skb);
    int err = 0;

    dev = rt->dst.dev;

    . . .

    iph = ip_hdr(skb);

    if (unlikely((((iph->frag_off & htons(IP_DF)) && !skb->local_df) ||
        (IPCB(skb)->frag_max_size &&
          IPCB(skb)->frag_max_size > dst_mtu(&rt->dst)))) {
    IP_INC_STATS(dev_net(dev), IPSTATS_MIB_FRAGFAILS);
    icmp_send(skb, ICMP_DEST_UNREACH, ICMP_FRAG_NEEDED,
            htonl(ip_skb_dst_mtu(skb)));
    kfree_skb(skb);
    return -EMSGSIZE;
}
. . .
. . .
```

The next section discusses the fast path in fragmentation and its implementation.

Fast Path

Now let's look into the fast path. First a check is performed to see whether the packet should be handled in the fast path by calling the skb_has_frag_list() method, which simply checks that skb_shinfo(skb)->frag_list is not NULL; if it is NULL, some sanity checks are made, and if something is not valid, the fallback to the slow path mechanism is activated (simply by calling goto slow_path). Then an IPv4 header is built for the first fragment. The frag_off of this IPv4 header is set to be htons(IP_MF), which indicates more fragments ahead. The frag_off field of the IPv4 header is a 16-bit field; the lower 13 bits are the fragment offset, and the higher 3 bits are the flags. For the first fragment, the offset should be 0, and the flag should be IP_MF (More Fragments). For all other fragments except the last one, the IP_MF flag should be set, and the lower 13 bits should be the fragment offset (measured in units of 8 bytes). For the last fragment, the IP_MF flag should not be set, but the lower 13 bits will still hold the fragment offset.

Here's how to set hlen to the IPv4 header size in bytes:

```
hlen = iph->ihl * 4;
. . .
if (skb_has_frag_list(skb)) {
    struct sk_buff *frag, *frag2;
    int first_len = skb_pagelen(skb);
    . . .
    err   = 0;
    offset = 0;
    frag = skb_shinfo(skb)->frag_list;
```

set skb_shinfo(skb)->frag_list to NULL by skb_frag_list_init(skb):

```
skb_frag_list_init(skb);
skb->data_len = first_len - skb_headlen(skb);
skb->len = first_len;
iph->tot_len = htons(first_len);
```

Set the IP_MF (More Fragments) flag for the first fragment:

```
iph->frag_off = htons(IP_MF);
```

Because the value of some IPv4 header fields were changed, the checksum needs to be recalculated:

```
ip_send_check(iph);
```

Now take a look at the loop that traverses frag_list and builds fragments:

```
for (;;) {
    /* Prepare header of the next frame,
     * before previous one went down. */
    if (frag) {
        frag->ip_summed = CHECKSUM_NONE;
        skb_reset_transport_header(frag);
```

The ip_fragment() was invoked from the transport layer (L4), so skb->data points to the transport header. The skb->data pointer should be moved back by hlen bytes so that it will point to the IPv4 header (hlen is the size of the IPv4 header in bytes):

```
        __skb_push(frag, hlen);
```

95

Set the L3 header (skb->network_header) to point to skb->data:

```
skb_reset_network_header(frag);
```

Copy the IPv4 header which was created into the L3 network header; in the first iteration of this for loop, it is the header which was created outside the loop for the first fragment:

```
memcpy(skb_network_header(frag), iph, hlen);
```

Now the IPv4 header and its tot_len of the next frag are initialized:

```
iph = ip_hdr(frag);
iph->tot_len = htons(frag->len);
```

Copy various SKB fields (like pkt_type, priority, protocol) from SKB into frag:

```
ip_copy_metadata(frag, skb);
```

Only for the first fragment (where the offset is 0) should the ip_options_fragment() method be called:

```
if (offset == 0)
    ip_options_fragment(frag);
offset += skb->len - hlen;
```

The frag_off field of the IPv4 header is measured in multiples of 8 bytes, so divide the offset by 8:

```
iph->frag_off = htons(offset>>3);
```

Each fragment, except the last one, should have the IP_MF flag set:

```
if (frag->next != NULL)
    iph->frag_off |= htons(IP_MF);
```

The value of some IPv4 header fields were changed, so the checksum should be recalculated:

```
/* Ready, complete checksum */
ip_send_check(iph);
}
```

Now send the fragment with the output callback. If sending it succeeded, increment IPSTATS_MIB_FRAGCREATES. If there was an error, exit the loop:

```
err = output(skb);

if (!err)
    IP_INC_STATS(dev_net(dev), IPSTATS_MIB_FRAGCREATES);
if (err || !frag)
    break;
```

Fetch the next SKB:

```
skb = frag;
frag = skb->next;
skb->next = NULL;
```

The following closing bracket is the end of the for loop:

```
}
```

The for loop is terminated, and the return value of the last call to output(skb) should be checked. If it is successful, the statistics (IPSTATS_MIB_FRAGOKS) are updated, and the method returns 0:

```
if (err == 0) {
    IP_INC_STATS(dev_net(dev), IPSTATS_MIB_FRAGOKS);
    return 0;
}
```

If the last call to output(skb) failed in one of the loop iterations, including the last one, the SKBs are freed, the statistics (IPSTATS_MIB_FRAGFAILS) are updated, and the error code (err) is returned:

```
while (frag) {
    skb = frag->next;
    kfree_skb(frag);
    frag = skb;
}
IP_INC_STATS(dev_net(dev), IPSTATS_MIB_FRAGFAILS);
return err;
```

You should now have a good understanding of the fast path in fragmentation and how it is implemented.

Slow Path

Let's now take a look at how to implement the slow path in fragmentation:

```
    . . .

    iph = ip_hdr(skb);

    left = skb->len - hlen;          /* Space per frame */
    . . .

    while (left > 0) {
            len = left;
            /* IF: it doesn't fit, use 'mtu' - the data space left */
            if (len > mtu)
                    len = mtu;
```

Each fragment (except the last one) should be aligned on a 8-byte boundary:

```
if (len < left) {
        len &= ~7;
}
```

Allocate an SKB:

```
if ((skb2 = alloc_skb(len+hlen+ll_rs, GFP_ATOMIC)) == NULL) {
        NETDEBUG(KERN_INFO "IP: frag: no memory for new fragment!\n");
        err = -ENOMEM;
        goto fail;
}

/*
 *        Set up data on packet
 */
```

Copy various SKB fields (like pkt_type, priority, protocol) from skb into skb2:

```
ip_copy_metadata(skb2, skb);
skb_reserve(skb2, ll_rs);
skb_put(skb2, len + hlen);
skb_reset_network_header(skb2);
skb2->transport_header = skb2->network_header + hlen;

/*
 *        Charge the memory for the fragment to any owner
 *        it might possess
 */

if (skb->sk)
        skb_set_owner_w(skb2, skb->sk);

/*
 *        Copy the packet header into the new buffer.
 */

skb_copy_from_linear_data(skb, skb_network_header(skb2), hlen);

/*
 *        Copy a block of the IP datagram.
 */
if (skb_copy_bits(skb, ptr, skb_transport_header(skb2), len))
        BUG();
left -= len;

/*
 *        Fill in the new header fields.
 */
iph = ip_hdr(skb2);
```

frag_off is measured in multiples of 8 bytes, so divide the offset by 8:

```
iph->frag_off = htons((offset >> 3));
. . .
```

Handle options only once for the first fragment:

```
if (offset == 0)
        ip_options_fragment(skb);
```

The MF flag (More Fragments) should be set on any fragment but the last:

```
if (left > 0 || not_last_frag)
        iph->frag_off |= htons(IP_MF);
ptr += len;
offset += len;

/*
 *      Put this fragment into the sending queue.
 */
iph->tot_len = htons(len + hlen);
```

Because the value of some IPv4 header fields were changed, the checksum should be recalculated:

```
ip_send_check(iph);
```

Now send the fragment with the output callback. If sending it succeeded, increment IPSTATS_MIB_FRAGCREATES. If there was an error, then free the packet, update the statistics (IPSTATS_MIB_FRAGFAILS), and return the error code:

```
err = output(skb2);
if (err)
        goto fail;

IP_INC_STATS(dev_net(dev), IPSTATS_MIB_FRAGCREATES);
}
```

Now the while (left > 0) loop has terminated, and the consume_skb() method is invoked to free the SKB, the statistics (IPSTATS_MIB_FRAGOKS) are updated, and the value of err is returned:

```
consume_skb(skb);
IP_INC_STATS(dev_net(dev), IPSTATS_MIB_FRAGOKS);
return err;
```

This section dealt with the implementation of slow path in fragmentation, and this ends the discussion of fragmentation in the Tx path. Remember that received fragmented packets, which are received on a host, should be reconstructed again so that applications can handle the original packet. The next section discusses defragmentation—the opposite of fragmentation.

Defragmentation

Defragmentation is the process of reassembling all the fragments of a packet, which all have the same id in the IPv4 header, into one buffer. The main method that handles defragmentation in the Rx path is ip_defrag() (net/ipv4/ip_fragment.c), which is called from ip_local_deliver(). There are other places where defragmentation might be needed, such as in firewalls, where the content of the packet should be known in order to be able to inspect it. In the ip_local_deliver() method, the ip_is_fragment() method is invoked to check whether the packet is fragmented; if it is, the ip_defrag() method is invoked. The ip_defrag() method has two arguments: the first is the SKB and the second is a 32-bit field which indicates the point where the method was invoked. Its value can be the following:

- IP_DEFRAG_LOCAL_DELIVER when it was called from ip_local_deliver().

- IP_DEFRAG_CALL_RA_CHAIN when it was called from ip_call_ra_chain().

- IP_DEFRAG_VS_IN or IP_DEFRAG_VS_FWD or IP_DEFRAG_VS_OUT when it was called from IPVS.

For a full list of possible values for the second argument of ip_defrag(), look in the ip_defrag_users enum definition in include/net/ip.h.

Let's look at the ip_defrag() invocation in ip_local_deliver():

```
int ip_local_deliver(struct sk_buff *skb)
{
    /*
     *    Reassemble IP fragments.
     */

    if (ip_is_fragment(ip_hdr(skb))) {
        if (ip_defrag(skb, IP_DEFRAG_LOCAL_DELIVER))
            return 0;
    }

    return NF_HOOK(NFPROTO_IPV4, NF_INET_LOCAL_IN, skb, skb->dev, NULL,
            ip_local_deliver_finish);
}
```

(net/ipv4/ip_input.c)

The ip_is_fragment() is a simple helper method that takes as a sole argument the IPv4 header and returns true when it is a fragment, like this:

```
static inline bool ip_is_fragment(const struct iphdr *iph)
{
        return (iph->frag_off & htons(IP_MF | IP_OFFSET)) != 0;
}
```

(include/net/ip.h)

The ip_is_fragment() method returns true in either of two cases (or both):

- The IP_MF flag is set.

- The fragment offset is not 0.

Thus it will return true on all fragments:

- On the first fragment, where frag_off is 0 but the IP_MF flag is set.

- On the last fragment, where frag_off is not 0 but the IP_MF flag is not set.

- On all other fragments, where frag_off is not 0 and the IP_MF flag is set.

The implementation of defragmentation is based on a hash table of ipq objects. The hash function (ipqhashfn) has four arguments: fragment id, source address, destination address, and protocol:

```
struct ipq {
        struct inet_frag_queue q;

        u32                 user;
        __be32              saddr;
        __be32              daddr;
        __be16              id;
        u8                  protocol;
        u8                  ecn; /* RFC3168 support */
        int                 iif;
        unsigned int        rid;
        struct inet_peer    *peer;
};
```

Note that the logic of IPv4 defragmentation is shared with its IPv6 counterpart. So, for example, the inet_frag_queue structure and methods like the inet_frag_find() method and the inet_frag_evictor() method are not specific to IPv4; they are also used in IPv6 (see net/ipv6/reassembly.c and net/ipv6/nf_conntrack_reasm.c).

The ip_defrag() method is quite short. First it makes sure there is enough memory by calling the ip_evictor() method. Then it tries to find an ipq for the SKB by calling the ip_find() method; if it does not find one, it creates an ipq object. The ipq object that the ip_find() method returns is assigned to a variable named qp (a pointer to an ipq object). Then it calls the ip_frag_queue() method to add the fragment to a linked list of fragments (qp->q.fragments). The addition to the list is done according to the fragment offset, because the list is sorted by the fragment offset. After all fragments of an SKB were added, the ip_frag_queue() method calls the ip_frag_reasm() method to build a new packet from all its fragments. The ip_frag_reasm() method also stops the timer (of ip_expire()) by calling the ipq_kill() method. If there was some error, and the size of the new packet exceeds the highest permitted size (which is 65535), the ip_frag_reasm() method updates the statistics (IPSTATS_MIB_REASMFAILS) and returns -E2BIG. If the call to skb_clone() method in ip_frag_reasm() fails, it returns –ENOMEM. The IPSTATS_MIB_REASMFAILS statistics is updated in this case as well. Constructing a packet from all its fragments should be done in a specified time interval. If it's not completed within that interval, the ip_expire() method will send an ICMPv4 message of "Time Exceeded" with "Fragment Reassembly Time Exceeded" code. The defragmentation time interval can be set by the following procfs entry: /proc/sys/net/ipv4/ipfrag_time. It is 30 seconds by default.

Let's take a look at the ip_defrag() method:

```
int ip_defrag(struct sk_buff *skb, u32 user)
{
        struct ipq *qp;
        struct net *net;

        net = skb->dev ? dev_net(skb->dev) : dev_net(skb_dst(skb)->dev);
        IP_INC_STATS_BH(net, IPSTATS_MIB_REASMREQDS);

        /* Start by cleaning up the memory. */
        ip_evictor(net);
```

```
            /* Lookup (or create) queue header */
            if ((qp = ip_find(net, ip_hdr(skb), user)) != NULL) {
                    int ret;

                    spin_lock(&qp->q.lock);
                    ret = ip_frag_queue(qp, skb);
                    spin_unlock(&qp->q.lock);
                    ipq_put(qp);
                    return ret;
            }

            IP_INC_STATS_BH(net, IPSTATS_MIB_REASMFAILS);
            kfree_skb(skb);
            return -ENOMEM;
    }
```

Before looking at the ip_frag_queue() method, consider the following macro, which simply returns the ipfrag_skb_cb object which is associated with the specified SKB:

```
#define FRAG_CB(skb)     ((struct ipfrag_skb_cb *)((skb)->cb))
```

Now let's look at the ip_frag_queue() method. I will not describe all the details because the method is very complicated and takes into account problems that might arise from overlapping (overlapping fragments may occur due to retransmissions). In the following snippet, qp->q.len is set to be the total length of the packet, including all its fragments; when the IP_MF flag is not set, this means that this is the last fragment:

```
static int ip_frag_queue(struct ipq *qp, struct sk_buff *skb)
{
        struct sk_buff *prev, *next;
        . . .
        /* Determine the position of this fragment. */
        end = offset + skb->len - ihl;
        err = -EINVAL;

        /* Is this the final fragment? */
        if ((flags & IP_MF) == 0) {
                /* If we already have some bits beyond end
                 * or have different end, the segment is corrupted.
                 */
                if (end < qp->q.len ||
                    ((qp->q.last_in & INET_FRAG_LAST_IN) && end != qp->q.len))
                        goto err;
                qp->q.last_in |= INET_FRAG_LAST_IN;
                qp->q.len = end;
        } else {
            . . .
        }
```

Now the location for adding the fragment is found by looking for the first place which is after the fragment offset (the linked list of fragments is ordered by offset):

```
. . .
prev = NULL;
for (next = qp->q.fragments; next != NULL; next = next->next) {
        if (FRAG_CB(next)->offset >= offset)
                break;  /* bingo! */
        prev = next;
}
```

Now, prev points to where to add the new fragment if it is not NULL. Skipping handling overlapping and some other checks, let's continue to the insertion of the fragment into the list:

```
FRAG_CB(skb)->offset = offset;
/* Insert this fragment in the chain of fragments. */
skb->next = next;
if (!next)
    qp->q.fragments_tail = skb;
if (prev)
    prev->next = skb;
else
    qp->q.fragments = skb;
. . .
qp->q.meat += skb->len;
```

Note that the qp->q.meat is incremented by skb->len for each fragment. As mentioned earlier, qp->q.len is the total length of all fragments, and when it is equal to qp->q.meat, it means that all fragments were added and should be reassembled into one packet with the ip_frag_reasm() method.

Now you can see how and where reassembly takes place: (reassembly is done by calling the ip_frag_reasm() method):

```
if (qp->q.last_in == (INET_FRAG_FIRST_IN | INET_FRAG_LAST_IN) &&
    qp->q.meat == qp->q.len) {
    unsigned long orefdst = skb->_skb_refdst;

    skb->_skb_refdst = OUL;
    err = ip_frag_reasm(qp, prev, dev);
    skb->_skb_refdst = orefdst;
    return err;
}
```

Let's take a look at the ip_frag_reasm() method:

```
static int ip_frag_reasm(struct ipq *qp, struct sk_buff *prev,
                         struct net_device *dev)
{
    struct net *net = container_of(qp->q.net, struct net, ipv4.frags);
    struct iphdr *iph;
    struct sk_buff *fp, *head = qp->q.fragments;
    int len;
    ...
```

```
/* Allocate a new buffer for the datagram. */
ihlen = ip_hdrlen(head);
len = ihlen + qp->q.len;

err = -E2BIG;
if (len > 65535)
        goto out_oversize;
...
skb_push(head, head->data - skb_network_header(head));
```

Forwarding

The main handler for forwarding a packet is the ip_forward() method:

```
int ip_forward(struct sk_buff *skb)
{
    struct iphdr        *iph;      /* Our header */
    struct rtable       *rt;       /* Route we use */
    struct ip_options   *opt     = &(IPCB(skb)->opt);
```

I should describe why Large Receive Offload (LRO) packets are dropped in forwarding. LRO is a performance-optimization technique that merges packets together, creating one large SKB, before they are passed to higher network layers. This reduces CPU overhead and thus improves the performance. Forwarding a large SKB, which was built by LRO, is not acceptable because it will be larger than the outgoing MTU. Therefore, when LRO is enabled the SKB is freed and the method returns NET_RX_DROP. Generic Receive Offload (GRO) design included forwarding ability, but LRO did not:

```
if (skb_warn_if_lro(skb))
    goto drop;
```

If the router_alert option is set, the ip_call_ra_chain() method should be invoked to handle the packet. When calling setsockopt() with IP_ROUTER_ALERT on a raw socket, the socket is added to a global list named ip_ra_chain (see include/net/ip.h). The ip_call_ra_chain() method delivers the packet to all raw sockets. You might wonder why is the packet delivered to all raw sockets and not to a single raw socket? In raw sockets there are no ports on which the sockets listen, as opposed to TCP or UDP.

If the pkt_type—which was determined by the eth_type_trans() method, which should be called from the network driver, and which is discussed in Appendix A—is not PACKET_HOST, the packet is discarded:

```
if (IPCB(skb)->opt.router_alert && ip_call_ra_chain(skb))
    return NET_RX_SUCCESS;

if (skb->pkt_type != PACKET_HOST)
    goto drop;
```

The ttl (Time To Live) field of the IPv4 header is a counter which is decreased by 1 in each forwarding device. If the ttl reaches 0, that is an indication that the packet should be dropped and that a corresponding time exceeded ICMPv4 message with "TTL Count Exceeded" code should be sent:

```
if (ip_hdr(skb)->ttl <= 1)
    goto too_many_hops; . . .
        . . .
```

```
too_many_hops:
    /* Tell the sender its packet died... */
    IP_INC_STATS_BH(dev_net(skb_dst(skb)->dev), IPSTATS_MIB_INHDRERRORS);
    icmp_send(skb, ICMP_TIME_EXCEEDED, ICMP_EXC_TTL, O);
    . . .
```

Now a check is performed if both the strict route flag (is_strictroute) is set and the rt_uses_gateway flag is set; in such a case, strict routing cannot be applied, and a "Destination Unreachable" ICMPv4 message with "Strict Routing Failed" code is sent back:

```
    rt = skb_rtable(skb);

    if (opt->is_strictroute && rt->rt_uses_gateway)
        goto sr_failed;
    . . .
sr_failed:
    icmp_send(skb, ICMP_DEST_UNREACH, ICMP_SR_FAILED, O);
    goto drop;
    . . .
```

Now a check is performed to see whether the length of the packet is larger than the outgoing device MTU. If it is, that means the packet is not permitted to be sent as it is. Another check is performed to see whether the DF (Don't Fragment) field in the IPv4 header is set and whether the local_df flag in the SKB is not set. If these conditions are met, it means that when the packet reaches the ip_output() method, it will not be fragmented with the ip_fragment() method. This means the packet cannot be sent as is, and it also cannot be fragmented; so a destination unreachable ICMPv4 message with "Fragmentation Needed" code is sent back, the packet is dropped, and the statistics (IPSTATS_MIB_FRAGFAILS) are updated:

```
    if (unlikely(skb->len > dst_mtu(&rt->dst) &&
        !skb_is_gso(skb) && (ip_hdr(skb)->frag_off & htons(IP_DF)))
            && !skb->local_df) {
    IP_INC_STATS(dev_net(rt->dst.dev), IPSTATS_MIB_FRAGFAILS);
    icmp_send(skb, ICMP_DEST_UNREACH, ICMP_FRAG_NEEDED,
            htonl(dst_mtu(&rt->dst)));
    goto drop;    }
```

Because the ttl and checksum of the IPv4 header are going to be changed, a copy of the SKB should be kept:

```
    /* We are about to mangle packet. Copy it! */
    if (skb_cow(skb, LL_RESERVED_SPACE(rt->dst.dev)+rt->dst.header_len))
            goto drop;
    iph = ip_hdr(skb);
```

As mentioned earlier, each node that forwards the packet should decrease the ttl. As a result of the ttl change, the checksum is also updated accordingly in the ip_decrease_ttl() method:

```
    /* Decrease ttl after skb cow done */
    ip_decrease_ttl(iph);
```

Now a redirect ICMPv4 message is sent back. If the RTCF_DOREDIRECT flag of the routing entry is set then a "Redirect To Host" code is used for this message (I discuss ICMPv4 redirect messages in Chapter 5).

```
/*
 *      We now generate an ICMP HOST REDIRECT giving the route
 *      we calculated.
 */
if (rt->rt_flags&RTCF_DOREDIRECT && !opt->srr && !skb_sec_path(skb))
        ip_rt_send_redirect(skb);
```

The skb->priority in the Tx path is set to be the socket priority (sk->sk_priority)—see, for example, the ip_queue_xmit() method. The socket priority, in turn, can be set by calling the setsockopt() system call with SOL_SOCKET and SO_PRIORITY. However, when forwarding the packet, there is no socket attached to the SKB. So, in the ip_forward() method, the skb->priority is set according to a special table called ip_tos2prio. This table has 16 entries (see include/net/route.h).

```
skb->priority = rt_tos2priority(iph->tos);
```

Now, assuming that there are no netfilter NF_INET_FORWARD hooks, the ip_forward_finish() method is invoked:

```
return NF_HOOK(NFPROTO_IPV4, NF_INET_FORWARD, skb, skb->dev,
                  rt->dst.dev, ip_forward_finish);
```

In ip_forward_finish(), the statistics are updated, and we check that the IPv4 packet includes IP options. If it does, the ip_forward_options() method is invoked to handle the options. If it does not have options, the dst_output() method is called. The only thing this method does is invoke skb_dst(skb)->output(skb):

```
static int ip_forward_finish(struct sk_buff *skb)
    {
    struct ip_options *opt  = &(IPCB(skb)->opt);

    IP_INC_STATS_BH(dev_net(skb_dst(skb)->dev), IPSTATS_MIB_OUTFORWDATAGRAMS);

    IP_ADD_STATS_BH(dev_net(skb_dst(skb)->dev), IPSTATS_MIB_OUTOCTETS, skb->len);


    if (unlikely(opt->optlen))
            ip_forward_options(skb);

    return dst_output(skb);
    }
```

In this section you learned about the methods for forwarding packets (ip_forward() and ip_forward_finish()), about cases when a packet is discarded in forwarding, about cases when an ICMP redirect is sent, and more.

Summary

This chapter dealt with the IPv4 protocol—how an IPv4 packet is built, the IPv4 header structure and IP options, and how they are handled. You learned how the IPv4 protocol handler is registered. You also learned about the Rx path (how the reception of IPv4 packets is handled) and about the Tx path in IPv4 (how the transmission of IPv4 packets is handled). There are cases when packets are larger than the network interface MTU, and as a result they can't be sent without being fragmented on the sender side and later defragmented on the receiver side. You learned about the implementation of fragmentation in IPv4 (including how the slow path and the fast path are implemented and when they are used) and the implementation of defragmentation in IPv4. The chapter also covered IPv4 forwarding— sending an incoming packet on a different network interface without passing it to the upper layer. And you saw some examples of when a packet is discarded in the forwarding process and when an ICMP redirect is sent. The next chapter discusses the IPv4 routing subsystem. The "Quick Reference" section that follows covers the top methods that are related to the topics discussed in this chapter, ordered by their context.

Quick Reference

I conclude this chapter with a short list of important methods and macros of the IPv4 subsystem that were mentioned in this chapter.

Methods

The following is a short list of important methods of the IPv4 layer, which were mentioned in this chapter.

int ip_queue_xmit(struct sk_buff *skb, struct flowi *fl);

This method moves packets from L4 (the transport layer) to L3 (the network layer), invoked for example from TCPv4.

int ip_append_data(struct sock *sk, struct flowi4 *fl4, int getfrag(void *from, char *to, int offset, int len, int odd, struct sk_buff *skb), void *from, int length, int transhdrlen, struct ipcm_cookie *ipc, struct rtable **rtp, unsigned int flags);

This method moves packets from L4 (the transport layer) to L3 (the network layer); invoked for example from UDPv4 when working with corked UDP sockets and from ICMPv4.

struct sk_buff *ip_make_skb(struct sock *sk, struct flowi4 *fl4, int getfrag(void *from, char *to, int offset, int len, int odd, struct sk_buff *skb), void *from, int length, int transhdrlen, struct ipcm_cookie *ipc, struct rtable **rtp, unsigned int flags);

This method was added in kernel 2.6.39 for enabling lockless transmit fast path to the UDPv4 implementation; called when not using the UDP_CORK socket option.

int ip_generic_getfrag(void *from, char *to, int offset, int len, int odd, struct sk_buff *skb);

This method is a generic method for copying data from userspace into the specified skb.

static int icmp_glue_bits(void *from, char *to, int offset, int len, int odd, struct sk_buff *skb);

This method is the ICMPv4 getfrag callback. The ICMPv4 module calls the ip_append_data() method with icmp_glue_bits() as the getfrag callback.

int ip_options_compile(struct net *net,struct ip_options *opt, struct sk_buff *skb);

This method builds an ip_options object by parsing IP options.

void ip_options_fragment(struct sk_buff *skb);

This method fills the options whose copied flag is not set with NOOPs and resets the corresponding fields of these IP options. Invoked only for the first fragment.

void ip_options_build(struct sk_buff *skb, struct ip_options *opt, __be32 daddr, struct rtable *rt, int is_frag);

This method takes the specified ip_options object and writes its content to the IPv4 header. The last parameter, is_frag, is in practice 0 in all invocations of the ip_options_build() method.

void ip_forward_options(struct sk_buff *skb);

This method handles IP options forwarding.

int ip_rcv(struct sk_buff *skb, struct net_device *dev, struct packet_type *pt, struct net_device *orig_dev);

This method is the main Rx handler for IPv4 packets.

ip_rcv_options(struct sk_buff *skb);

This method is the main method for handling receiving a packet with options.

int ip_options_rcv_srr(struct sk_buff *skb);

This method handles receiving a packet with strict route option.

int ip_forward(struct sk_buff *skb);

This method is the main handler for forwarding IPv4 packets.

static void ipmr_queue_xmit(struct net *net, struct mr_table *mrt, struct sk_buff *skb, struct mfc_cache *c, int vifi);

This method is the multicast transmission method.

static int raw_send_hdrinc(struct sock *sk, struct flowi4 *fl4, void *from, size_t length, struct rtable **rtp, unsigned int flags);

This method is used by raw sockets for transmission when the IPHDRINC socket option is set. It calls the dst_output() method directly.

int ip_fragment(struct sk_buff *skb, int (*output)(struct sk_buff *));

This method is the main fragmentation method.

int ip_defrag(struct sk_buff *skb, u32 user);

This method is the main defragmentation method. It processes an incoming IP fragment. The second parameter, user, indicates where this method was invoked from. For a full list of possible values for the second parameter, look in the ip_defrag_users enum definition in include/net/ip.h.

bool skb_has_frag_list(const struct sk_buff *skb);

This method returns true if skb_shinfo(skb)->frag_list is not NULL. The method skb_has_frag_list() was named skb_has_frags() in the past, and was renamed skb_has_frag_list() in kernel 2.6.37. (The reason was that the name was confusing.) SKBs can be fragmented in two ways: via a page array (called skb_shinfo(skb)->frags[]) and via a list of SKBs (called skb_shinfo(skb)->frag_list). Because skb_has_frags() tests the latter, its name is confusing because it sounds more like it's testing the former.

int ip_local_deliver(struct sk_buff *skb);

This method handles delivering packets to Layer 4.

int ip_options_get_from_user(struct net *net, struct ip_options_rcu **optp, unsigned char __user *data, int optlen);

This method handles setting options from userspace by the setsockopt() system call with IP_OPTIONS.

bool ip_is_fragment(const struct iphdr *iph);

This method returns true if the packet is a fragment.

int ip_decrease_ttl(struct iphdr *iph);

This method decrements the `ttl` of the specified IPv4 header by 1 and, because one of the IPv4 header fields had changed (`ttl`), recalculates the IPv4 header checksum.

int ip_build_and_send_pkt(struct sk_buff *skb, struct sock *sk, __be32 saddr, __be32 daddr, struct ip_options_rcu *opt);

This method is used by TCPv4 to send SYN ACK. See the `tcp_v4_send_synack()` method in `net/ipv4/tcp_ipv4.c`.

int ip_mr_input(struct sk_buff *skb);

This method handles incoming multicast packets.

int ip_mr_forward(struct net *net, struct mr_table *mrt, struct sk_buff *skb, struct mfc_cache *cache, int local);

This method forwards multicast packets.

bool ip_call_ra_chain(struct sk_buff *skb);

This method handles the Router Alert IP option.

Macros

This section mentions some macros from this chapter that deal with mechanisms encountered in the IPv4 stack, such as fragmentation, netfilter hooks, and IP options.

IPCB(skb)

This macro returns the `inet_skb_parm` object which `skb->cb` points to. It is used to access the `ip_options` object stored in the `inet_skb_parm` object (`include/net/ip.h`).

FRAG_CB(skb)

This macro returns the `ipfrag_skb_cb` object which `skb->cb` points to (`net/ipv4/ip_fragment.c`).

int NF_HOOK(uint8_t pf, unsigned int hook, struct sk_buff *skb, struct net_device *in, struct net_device *out, int (*okfn)(struct sk_buff *))

This macro is the netfilter hook; the first parameter, `pf`, is the protocol family; for IPv4 it is NFPROTO_IPV4, and for IPv6 it is NFPROTO_IPV6. The second parameter is one of the five netfilter hook points in the network stack; these five points are defined in `include/uapi/linux/netfilter.h` and can be used both by IPv4 and IPv6. The `okfn` callback is to be called if there is no hook registered or if the registered netfilter hook does not discard or reject the packet.

int NF_HOOK_COND(uint8_t pf, unsigned int hook, struct sk_buff *skb, struct net_device *in, struct net_device *out, int (*okfn)(struct sk_buff *), bool cond)

This macro is same as the NF_HOOK() macro, but with an additional Boolean parameter, cond, which must be true so that the netfilter hook will be called.

IPOPT_COPIED()

This macro returns the copied flag of the option type.

CHAPTER 5

■ ■ ■

The IPv4 Routing Subsystem

Chapter 4 discussed the IPv4 subsystem. In this chapter and the next I discuss one of the most important Linux subsystems, the routing subsystem, and its implementation in Linux. The Linux routing subsystem is used in a wide range of routers—from home and small office routers, to enterprise routers (which connect organizations or ISPs) and core high speed routers on the Internet backbone. It is impossible to imagine the modern world without these devices. The discussion in these two chapters is limited to the IPv4 routing subsystem, which is very similar to the IPv6 implementation. This chapter is mainly an introduction and presents the main data structures that are used by the IPv4 routing subsystem, like the routing tables, the Forwarding Information Base (FIB) info and the FIB alias, the FIB TRIE and more. (TRIE is not an acronym, by the way, but it is derived from the word *retrieval*). The TRIE is a data structure, a special tree that replaced the FIB hash table. You will learn how a lookup in the routing subsystem is performed, how and when ICMP Redirect messages are generated, and about the removal of the routing cache code. Note that the discussion and the code examples in this chapter relate to kernel 3.9, except for two sections where a different kernel version is explicitly mentioned.

Forwarding and the FIB

One of the important goals of the Linux Networking stack is to forward traffic. This is relevant especially when discussing core routers, which operate in the Internet backbone. The Linux IP stack layer, responsible for forwarding packets and maintaining the forwarding database, is called the routing subsystem. For small networks, management of the FIB can be done by a system administrator, because most of the network topology is static. When discussing core routers, the situation is a bit different, as the topology is dynamic and there is a vast amount of ever-changing information. In this case, management of the FIB is done usually by userspace routing daemons, sometimes in conjunction with special hardware enhancements. These userspace daemons usually maintain routing tables of their own, which sometimes interact with the kernel routing tables.

Let's start with the basics: what is routing? Take a look at a very simple forwarding example: you have two Ethernet Local Area Networks, LAN1 and LAN2. On LAN1 you have a subnet of 192.168.1.0/24, and on LAN2 you have a subnet of 192.168.2.0/24. There is a machine between these two LANs, which will be called a "forwarding router." There are two Ethernet network interface cards (NICs) in the forwarding router. The network interface connected to LAN1 is eth0 and has an IP address of 192.168.1.200, and the network interface connected to LAN2 is eth1 and has an IP address of 192.168.2.200, as you can see in Figure 5-1. For the sake of simplicity, let's assume that no firewall daemon runs on the forwarding router. You start sending traffic from LAN1, which is destined to LAN2. The process of forwarding incoming packets, which are sent from LAN1 and which are destined to LAN2 (or vice versa), according to data structures that are called routing tables, is called *routing*. I discuss this process and the routing table data structures in this chapter and in the next as well.

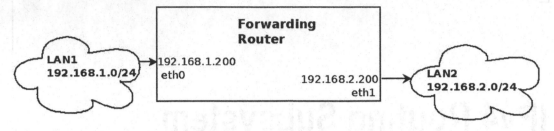

Figure 5-1. *Forwarding packets between two LANs*

In Figure 5-1, packets that arrive on eth0 from LAN1, which are destined to LAN2, are forwarded via eth1 as the outgoing device. In this process, the incoming packets move from Layer 2 (the link layer) in the kernel networking stack, to Layer 3, the network layer, in the forwarding router machine. As opposed to the case where the traffic is destined to the forwarding router machine ("Traffic to me"), however, there is no need to move the packets to Layer 4 (the transport layer) because this traffic in not intended to be handled by any Layer 4 transport socket. This traffic should be forwarded. Moving to Layer 4 has a performance cost, which is better to avoid whenever possible. This traffic is handled in Layer 3, and, according to the routing tables configured on the forwarding router machine, packets are forwarded on eth1 as the outgoing interface (or rejected).

Figure 5-2 shows the three network layers handled by the kernel that were mentioned earlier.

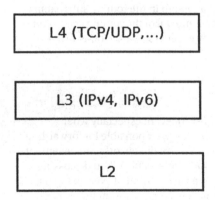

Figure 5-2. *The three layers that are handled by the networking kernel stack*

Two additional terms that I should mention here, which are commonly used in routing, are *default gateway* and *default route*. When you are defining a default gateway entry in a routing table, every packet that is not handled by the other routing entries (if there are such entries) must be forwarded to it, regardless of the destination address in the IP header of this packet. The default route is designated as 0.0.0.0/0 in Classless Inter-Domain Routing (CIDR) notation. As a simple example, you can add a machine with an IPv4 address of 192.168.2.1 as a default gateway as follows:

```
ip route add default via 192.168.2.1
```

Or, when using the route command, like this:

```
route add default gateway 192.168.2.1
```

In this section you learned what forwarding is and saw a simple example illustrating how packets are forwarded between two LANs. You also learned what a default gateway is and what a default route is, and how to add them. Now that you know the basic terminology and what forwarding is, let's move on and see how a lookup in the routing subsystem is performed.

Performing a Lookup in the Routing Subsystem

A lookup in the routing subsystem is done for each packet, both in the Rx path and in the Tx path. In kernels prior to 3.6, each lookup, both in the Rx path and in the Tx path, consisted of two phases: a lookup in the routing cache and, in case of a cache miss, a lookup in the routing tables (I discuss the routing cache at the end of this chapter, in the "IPv4 Routing Cache" section). A lookup is done by the fib_lookup() method. When the fib_lookup() method finds a proper entry in the routing subsystem, it builds a fib_result object, which consists of various routing parameters, and it returns 0. I discuss the fib_result object in this section and in other sections of this chapter. Here is the fib_lookup() prototype:

```
int fib_lookup(struct net *net, const struct flowi4 *flp, struct fib_result *res)
```

The flowi4 object consists of fields that are important to the IPv4 routing lookup process, including the destination address, source address, Type of Service (TOS), and more. In fact the flowi4 object defines the key to the lookup in the routing tables and should be initialized prior to performing a lookup with the fib_lookup() method. For IPv6 there is a parallel object named flowi6; both are defined in include/net/flow.h. The fib_result object is built in the IPv4 lookup process. The fib_lookup() method first searches the local FIB table. If the lookup fails, it performs a lookup in the main FIB table (I describe these two tables in the next section, "FIB tables"). After a lookup is successfully done, either in the Rx path or the Tx path, a dst object is built (an instance of the dst_entry structure, the destination cache, defined in include/net/dst.h). The dst object is embedded in a structure called rtable, as you will soon see. The rtable object, in fact, represents a routing entry which can be associated with an SKB. The most important members of the dst_entry object are two callbacks named input and output. In the routing lookup process, these callbacks are assigned to be the proper handlers according to the routing lookup result. These two callbacks get only an SKB as a parameter:

```
struct dst_entry {
    ...
    int   (*input)(struct sk_buff *);
    int   (*output)(struct sk_buff *);
    ...
}
```

The following is the rtable structure; as you can see, the dst object is the first object in this structure:

```
struct rtable {
    struct dst_entry   dst;

    int                rt_genid;
    unsigned int       rt_flags;
    __u16              rt_type;
    __u8               rt_is_input;
    __u8               rt_uses_gateway;

    int                rt_iif;

    /* Info on neighbour */
    __be32             rt_gateway;
```

```
    /* Miscellaneous cached information */
    u32            rt_pmtu;

    struct list_head  rt_uncached;
};
```

(include/net/route.h)

The following is a description of the members of the rtable structure:

- rt_flags: The rtable object flags; some of the important flags are mentioned here:

    - RTCF_BROADCAST: When set, the destination address is a broadcast address. This flag is set in the __mkroute_output() method and in the ip_route_input_slow() method.

    - RTCF_MULTICAST: When set, the destination address is a multicast address. This flag is set in the ip_route_input_mc() method and in the __mkroute_output() method.

    - RTCF_DOREDIRECT: When set, an ICMPv4 Redirect message should be sent as a response for an incoming packet. Several conditions should be fulfilled for this flag to be set, including that the input device and the output device are the same and the corresponding procfs send_redirects entry is set. There are more conditions, as you will see later in this chapter. This flag is set in the __mkroute_input() method.

    - RTCF_LOCAL: When set, the destination address is local. This flag is set in the following methods: ip_route_input_slow(), __mkroute_output(), ip_route_input_mc() and __ip_route_output_key(). Some of the RTCF_XXX flags can be set simultaneously. For example, RTCF_LOCAL can be set when RTCF_BROADCAST or RTCF_MULTICAST are set. For the complete list of RTCF_XXX flags, look in include/uapi/linux/in_route.h. Note that some of them are unused.

- rt_is_input: A flag that is set to 1 when this is an input route.

- rt_uses_gateway: Gets a value according to the following:

    - When the nexthop is a gateway, rt_uses_gateway is 1.

    - When the nexthop is a direct route, rt_uses_gateway is 0.

- rt_iif: The ifindex of the incoming interface. (Note that the rt_oif member was removed from the rtable structure in kernel 3.6; it was set to the oif of the specified flow key, but was used in fact only in one method).

- rt_pmtu: The Path MTU (the smallest MTU along the route).

    Note that in kernel 3.6, the fib_compute_spec_dst() method was added, which gets an SKB as a parameter. This method made the rt_spec_dst member of the rtable structure unneeded, and rt_spec_dst was removed from the rtable structure as a result. The fib_compute_spec_dst() method is needed in special cases, such as in the icmp_reply() method, when replying to the sender using its source address as a destination for the reply.

For incoming unicast packets destined to the local host, the input callback of the dst object is set to ip_local_deliver(), and for incoming unicast packets that should be forwarded, this input callback is set to ip_forward(). For a packet generated on the local machine and sent away, the output callback is set to be ip_output(). For a multicast packet, the input callback can be set to ip_mr_input() (under some conditions which are not detailed in this chapter). There are cases when the input callback is set to be ip_error(), as you will see later in the PROHIBIT rule example in this chapter. Let's take a look in the fib_result object:

```
struct fib_result {
        unsigned char    prefixlen;
        unsigned char    nh_sel;
        unsigned char    type;
        unsigned char    scope;
        u32              tclassid;
        struct fib_info  *fi;
        struct fib_table *table;
        struct list_head *fa_head;
};
```

(include/net/ip_fib.h)

- prefixlen: The prefix length, which represents the netmask. Its values are in the range 0 to 32. It is 0 when using the default route. When adding, for example, a routing entry by ip route add 192.168.2.0/24 dev eth0, the prefixlen is 24, according to the netmask which was specified when adding the entry. The prefixlen is set in the check_leaf() method (net/ipv4/fib_trie.c).

- nh_sel: The nexthop number. When working with one nexthop only, it is 0. When working with Multipath Routing, there can be more than one nexthop. The nexthop objects are stored in an array in the routing entry (inside the fib_info object), as discussed in the next section.

- type: The type of the fib_result object is the most important field because it determines in fact how to handle the packet: whether to forward it to a different machine, deliver it locally, discard it silently, discard it with replying with an ICMPv4 message, and so on. The type of the fib_result object is determined according to the packet content (most notably the destination address) and according to routing rules set by the administrator, routing daemons, or a Redirect message. You will see how the type of the fib_result object is determined in the lookup process later in this chapter and in the next. The two most common types of the fib_result objects are the RTN_UNICAST type, which is set when the packet is for forwarding via a gateway or a direct route, and the RTN_LOCAL type, which is set when the packet is for the local host. Other types you will encounter in this book are the RTN_BROADCAST type, for packets that should be accepted locally as broadcasts, the RTN_MULTICAST type, for multicast routes, the RTN_UNREACHABLE type, for packets which trigger sending back an ICMPv4 "Destination Unreachable" message, and more. There are 12 route types in all. For a complete list of all available route types, see include/uapi/linux/rtnetlink.h.

- fi: A pointer to a fib_info object, which represents a routing entry. The fib_info object holds a reference to the nexthop (fib_nh). I discuss the FIB info structure in the section "FIB Info" later in this chapter.

- table: A pointer to the FIB table on which the lookup is done. It is set in the check_leaf() method (net/ipv4/fib_trie.c).

- fa_head: A pointer to a fib_alias list (a list of fib_alias objects associated with this route); optimization of routing entries is done when using fib_alias objects, which avoids creating a separate fib_info object for each routing entry, regardless of the fact that there are other fib_info objects which are very similar. All FIB aliases are sorted by fa_tos descending and fib_priority (metric) ascending. Aliases whose fa_tos is 0 are the last and can match any TOS. I discuss the fib_alias structure in the section "FIB Alias" later in this chapter.

In this section you learned how a lookup in the routing subsystem is performed. You also found out about important data structures that relate to the routing lookup process, like fib_result and rtable. The next section discusses how the FIB tables are organized.

FIB Tables

The main data structure of the routing subsystem is the routing table, which is represented by the fib_table structure. A routing table can be described, in a somewhat simplified way, as a table of entries where each entry determines which nexthop should be chosen for traffic destined to a subnet (or to a specific IPv4 destination address). This entry has other parameters, of course, discussed later in this chapter. Each routing entry contains a fib_info object (include/net/ip_fib.h), which stores the most important routing entry parameters (but not all, as you will see later in this chapter). The fib_info object is created by the fib_create_info() method (net/ipv4/fib_semantics.c) and is stored in a hash table named fib_info_hash. When the route uses prefsrc, the fib_info object is added also to a hash table named fib_info_laddrhash.

There is a global counter of fib_info objects named fib_info_cnt which is incremented when creating a fib_info object, by the fib_create_info() method, and decremented when freeing a fib_info object, by the free_fib_info() method. The hash table is dynamically resized when it grows over some threshold. A lookup in the fib_info_hash hash table is done by the fib_find_info() method (it returns NULL when not finding an entry). Serializing access to the fib_info members is done by a spinlock named fib_info_lock. Here's the fib_table structure:

```
struct fib_table {
        struct hlist_node       tb_hlist;
        u32                     tb_id;
        int                     tb_default;
        int                     tb_num_default;
        unsigned long           tb_data[0];
};
```

(include/net/ip_fib.h)

- tb_id: The table identifier. For the main table, tb_id is 254 (RT_TABLE_MAIN), and for the local table, tb_id is 255 (RT_TABLE_LOCAL). I talk about the main table and the local table soon—for now, just note that when working without Policy Routing, only these two FIB tables, the main table and the local table, are created in boot.

- tb_num_default: The number of the default routes in the table. The fib_trie_table() method, which creates a table, initializes tb_num_default to 0. Adding a default route increments tb_num_default by 1, by the fib_table_insert() method. Deleting a default route decrements tb_num_default by 1, by the fib_table_delete() method.

- tb_data[0] : A placeholder for a routing entry (trie) object.

This section covered how a FIB table is implemented. Next you will learn about the FIB info, which represents a single routing entry.

FIB Info

A routing entry is represented by a fib_info structure. It consists of important routing entry parameters, such as the outgoing network device (fib_dev), the priority (fib_priority), the routing protocol identifier of this route (fib_protocol), and more. Let's take a look at the fib_info structure:

```
struct fib_info {
    struct hlist_node    fib_hash;
    struct hlist_node    fib_lhash;
    struct net           *fib_net;
    int                  fib_treeref;
    atomic_t             fib_clntref;
    unsigned int         fib_flags;
    unsigned char        fib_dead;
    unsigned char        fib_protocol;
    unsigned char        fib_scope;
    unsigned char        fib_type;
    __be32               fib_prefsrc;
    u32                  fib_priority;
    u32                  *fib_metrics;
#define fib_mtu fib_metrics[RTAX_MTU-1]
#define fib_window fib_metrics[RTAX_WINDOW-1]
#define fib_rtt fib_metrics[RTAX_RTT-1]
#define fib_advmss fib_metrics[RTAX_ADVMSS-1]
    int                  fib_nhs;
#ifdef CONFIG_IP_ROUTE_MULTIPATH
    int                  fib_power;
#endif
    struct rcu_head      rcu;
    struct fib_nh        fib_nh[0];
#define fib_dev          fib_nh[0].nh_dev
};
```

(include/net/ip_fib.h)

- fib_net: The network namespace the fib_info object belongs to.

- fib_treeref: A reference counter that represents the number of fib_alias objects which hold a reference to this fib_info object. This reference counter is incremented in the fib_create_info() method and decremented in the fib_release_info() method. Both methods are in net/ipv4/fib_semantics.c.

- fib_clntref: A reference counter that is incremented by the fib_create_info() method (net/ipv4/fib_semantics.c) and decremented by the fib_info_put() method (include/net/ip_fib.h). If, after decrementing it by 1 in the fib_info_put() method, it reaches zero, than the associated fib_info object is freed by the free_fib_info() method.

- fib_dead: A flag that indicates whether it is permitted to free the fib_info object with the free_fib_info() method; fib_dead must be set to 1 before calling the free_fib_info() method. If the fib_dead flag is not set (its value is 0), then it is considered alive, and trying to free it with the free_fib_info() method will fail.

- `fib_protocol`: The routing protocol identifier of this route. When adding a routing rule from userspace without specifying the routing protocol ID, the `fib_protocol` is assigned to be RTPROT_BOOT. The administrator may add a route with the "proto static" modifier, which indicates that the route was added by an administrator; this can be done, for example, like this: `ip route add proto static 192.168.5.3 via 192.168.2.1`. The `fib_protocol` can be assigned one of these flags:

  - RTPROT_UNSPEC: An error value.

  - RTPROT_REDIRECT: When set, the routing entry was created as a result of receiving an ICMP Redirect message. The RTPROT_REDIRECT protocol identifier is used only in IPv6.

  - RTPROT_KERNEL: When set, the routing entry was created by the kernel (for example, when creating the local IPv4 routing table, explained shortly).

  - RTPROT_BOOT: When set, the admin added a route without specifying the "proto static" modifier.

  - RTPROT_STATIC: Route installed by system administrator.

  - RTPROT_RA: Don't misread this— this protocol identifier is not for Router Alert; it is for RDISC/ND Router Advertisements, and it is used in the kernel by the IPv6 subsystem only; see: `net/ipv6/route.c`. I discuss it in Chapter 8.

  The routing entry could also be added by userspace routing daemons, like ZEBRA, XORP, MROUTED, and more. Then it will be assigned the corresponding value from a list of protocol identifiers (see the RTPROT_XXX definitions in `include/uapi/linux/rtnetlink.h`). For example, for the XORP daemon it will be RTPROT_XORP. Note that these flags (like RTPROT_KERNEL or RTPROT_STATIC) are also used by IPv6, for the parallel field (the `rt6i_protocol` field in the `rt6_info` structure; the `rt6_info` object is the IPv6 parallel to the `rtable` object).

- `fib_scope`: The scope of the destination address. In short, scopes are assigned to addresses and routes. Scope indicates the distance of the host from other nodes. The `ip address show` command shows the scopes of all configured IP addresses on a host. The `ip route show` command displays the scopes of all the route entries of the main table. A scope can be one of these:

  - host (RT_SCOPE_HOST): The node cannot communicate with the other network nodes. The loopback address has scope host.

  - global (RT_SCOPE_UNIVERSE): The address can be used anywhere. This is the most common case.

  - link (RT_SCOPE_LINK): This address can be accessed only from directly attached hosts.

  - site (RT_SCOPE_SITE): This is used in IPv6 only (I discuss it in Chapter 8).

  - nowhere (RT_SCOPE_NOWHERE): Destination doesn't exist.

  When a route is added by an administrator without specifying a scope, the `fib_scope` field is assigned a value according to these rules:

  - global scope (RT_SCOPE_UNIVERSE): For all gatewayed unicast routes.

  - scope link (RT_SCOPE_LINK): For direct unicast and broadcast routes.

  - scope host (RT_SCOPE_HOST): For local routes.

- `fib_type`: The type of the route. The `fib_type` field was added to the `fib_info` structure as a key to make sure there is differentiation among `fib_info` objects by their type. The `fib_type` field was added to the `fib_info` struct in kernel 3.7. Originally this type was stored only in the `fa_type` field of the FIB alias object (`fib_alias`). You can add a rule to block traffic according to a specified category, for example, by: `ip route add prohibit 192.168.1.17 from 192.168.2.103`.

  - The `fib_type` of the generated `fib_info` object is RTN_PROHIBIT.

  - Sending traffic from 192.168.2.103 to 192.168.1.17 results in an ICMPv4 message of "Packet Filtered" (ICMP_PKT_FILTERED).

- `fib_prefsrc`: There are cases when you want to provide a specific source address to the lookup key. This is done by setting `fib_prefsrc`.

- `fib_priority`: The priority of the route, by default, is 0, which is the highest priority. The higher the value of the priority, the lower the priority is. For example, a priority of 3 is lower than a priority of 0, which is the highest priority. You can configure it, for example, with the `ip` command, in one of the following ways:

  - `ip route add 192.168.1.10 via 192.168.2.1 metric 5`

  - `ip route add 192.168.1.10 via 192.168.2.1 priority 5`

  - `ip route add 192.168.1.10 via 192.168.2.1 preference 5`

  Each of these three commands sets the `fib_priority` to 5; there is no difference at all between them. Moreover, the `metric` parameter of the `ip route` command is not related in any way to the `fib_metrics` field of the `fib_info` structure.

- `fib_mtu`, `fib_window`, `fib_rtt`, and `fib_advmss` simply give more convenient names to commonly used elements of the `fib_metrics` array.

  `fib_metrics` is an array of 15 (RTAX_MAX) elements consisting of various metrics. It is initialized to be `dst_default_metrics` in `net/core/dst.c`. Many metrics are related to the TCP protocol, such as the Initial Congestion Window (`initcwnd`) metric. Table 5-1, at the end of the chapter shows all the available metrics and displays whether each is a TCP-related metric or not.

  From userspace, the TCPv4 `initcwnd` metric can be set thus, for example:

  `ip route add 192.168.1.0/24 initcwnd 35`

  There are metrics which are not TCP specific—for example, the `mtu` metric, which can be set from userspace like this:

  `ip route add 192.168.1.0/24 mtu 800`

  or like this:

  `ip route add 192.168.1.0/24 mtu lock 800`

The difference between the two commands is that when specifying the modifier lock, no path MTU discovery will be tried. When not specifying the modifier lock, the MTU may be updated by the kernel due to Path MTU discovery. For more about how this is implemented, see the __ip_rt_update_pmtu() method, in net/ipv4/route.c:

```
static void __ip_rt_update_pmtu(struct rtable *rt, struct flowi4 *fl4, u32 mtu)
{
```

Avoiding Path MTU update when specifying the mtu lock modifier is achieved by calling the dst_metric_locked() method:

```
. . .
if (dst_metric_locked(dst, RTAX_MTU))
        return;
. . .
}
```

- fib_nhs: The number of nexthops. When Multipath Routing (CONFIG_IP_ROUTE_MULTIPATH) is not set, it cannot be more than 1. The Multipath Routing feature sets multiple alternative paths for a route, possibly assigning different weights to these paths. This feature provides benefits such as fault tolerance, increased bandwidth, or improved security (I discuss it in Chapter 6).

- fib_dev: The network device that will transmit the packet to the nexthop.

- fib_nh[0]: The fib_nh[0] member represents the nexthop. When working with Multipath Routing, you can define more than one nexthop in a route, and in this case there is an array of nexthops. Defining two nexthop nodes can be done like this, for example: ip route add default scope global nexthop dev eth0 nexthop dev eth1.

As mentioned, when the fib_type is RTN_PROHIBIT, an ICMPv4 message of "Packet Filtered" (ICMP_PKT_FILTERED) is sent. How is it implemented? An array named fib_props consists of 12 (RTN_MAX) elements (defined in net/ipv4/fib_semantics.c). The index of this array is the route type. The available route types, such as RTN_PROHIBIT or RTN_UNICAST, can be found in include/uapi/linux/rtnetlink.h. Each element in the array is an instance of struct fib_prop; the fib_prop structure is a very simple structure:

```
struct fib_prop {
        int     error;
        u8      scope;
};
```

(net/ipv4/fib_lookup.h)

For every route type, the corresponding fib_prop object contains the error and the scope for that route. For example, for the RTN_UNICAST route type (gateway or direct route), which is a very common route, the error value is 0, which means that there is no error, and the scope is RT_SCOPE_UNIVERSE. For the RTN_PROHIBIT route type (a rule which a system administrator configures in order to block traffic), the error is –EACCES, and the scope is RT_SCOPE_UNIVERSE:

```
const struct fib_prop fib_props[RTN_MAX + 1] = {
. . .
        [RTN_PROHIBIT] = {
                .error  = -EACCES,
                .scope  = RT_SCOPE_UNIVERSE,
        },
. . .
```

Table 5-2 at the end of this chapter shows all available route types, their error codes, and their scopes.

When you configure a rule like the one mentioned earlier, by ip route add prohibit 192.168.1.17 from 192.168.2.103—and when a packet is sent from 192.168.2.103 to 192.168.1.17, what happens is the following: a lookup in the routing tables is performed in the Rx path. When a corresponding entry, which is in fact a leaf in the FIB TRIE, is found, the check_leaf() method is invoked. This method accesses the fib_props array with the route type of the packet as an index (fa->fa_type):

```
static int check_leaf(struct fib_table *tb, struct trie *t, struct leaf *l,
                      t_key key,  const struct flowi4 *flp,
                      struct fib_result *res, int fib_flags)
{
    . . .
    fib_alias_accessed(fa);
    err = fib_props[fa->fa_type].error;
    if (err) {
            . . .
            return err;
            }
    . . .
```

Eventually, the fib_lookup() method, which initiated the lookup in the IPv4 routing subsystem, returns an error of –EACCES (in our case). It propagates all the way back from check_leaf() via fib_table_lookup() and so on until it returns to the method which triggered this chain, namely the fib_lookup() method. When the fib_lookup() method returns an error in the Rx path, it is handled by the ip_error() method. According to the error, an action is taken. In the case of –EACCES, an ICMPv4 of destination unreachable with code of Packet Filtered (ICMP_PKT_FILTERED) is sent back, and the packet is dropped.

This section covered the FIB info, which represents a single routing entry. The next section discusses caching in the IPv4 routing subsystem (not to be confused with the IPv4 routing cache, which was removed from the network stack, and is discussed in the "IPv4 Routing Cache" section at the end of this chapter).

Caching

Caching the results of a routing lookup is an optimization technique that improves the performance of the routing subsystem. The results of a routing lookup are usually cached in the nexthop (fib_nh) object; when the packet is not a unicast packet or realms are used (the packet itag is not 0), the results are not cached in the nexthop. The reason is that if all types of packets are cached, then the same nexthop can be used by different kinds of routes—that should be avoided. There are some minor exceptions to this which I do not discuss in this chapter. Caching in the Rx and the Tx path are performed as follows:

- In the Rx path, caching the fib_result object in the nexthop (fib_nh) object is done by setting the nh_rth_input field of the nexthop (fib_nh) object.

- In the Tx path, caching the fib_result object in the nexthop (fib_nh) object is done by setting the nh_pcpu_rth_output field of the nexthop (fib_nh) object.

- Both nh_rth_input and nh_pcpu_rth_output are instances of the rtable structure.

- Caching the fib_result is done by the rt_cache_route() method both in the Rx and the Tx paths (net/ipv4/route.c).

- Caching of Path MTU and ICMPv4 redirects is done with FIB exceptions.

For performance, the nh_pcpu_rth_output is a per-CPU variable, meaning there is a copy for each CPU of the output dst entry. Caching is used almost always. The few exceptions are when an ICMPv4 Redirect message is sent, or itag (tclassid) is set, or there is not enough memory.

In this section you have learned how caching is done using the nexthop object. The next section discusses the fib_nh structure, which represents the nexthop, and the FIB nexthop exceptions.

Nexthop (fib_nh)

The fib_nh structure represents the nexthop. It consists of information such as the outgoing nexthop network device (nh_dev), outgoing nexthop interface index (nh_oif), the scope (nh_scope), and more. Let's take a look:

```
struct fib_nh {
    struct net_device       *nh_dev;
    struct hlist_node       nh_hash;
    struct fib_info         *nh_parent;
    unsigned int            nh_flags;
    unsigned char           nh_scope;
#ifdef CONFIG_IP_ROUTE_MULTIPATH
    int                     nh_weight;
    int                     nh_power;
#endif
#ifdef CONFIG_IP_ROUTE_CLASSID
    __u32                   nh_tclassid;
#endif
    int                     nh_oif;
    __be32                  nh_gw;
    __be32                  nh_saddr;
    int                     nh_saddr_genid;
    struct rtable __rcu * __percpu *nh_pcpu_rth_output;
    struct rtable __rcu     *nh_rth_input;
    struct fnhe_hash_bucket *nh_exceptions;
};
```

(include/net/ip_fib.h)

The nh_dev field represents the network device (net_device object) on which traffic to the nexthop will be transmitted. When a network device associated with one or more routes is disabled, a NETDEV_DOWN notification is sent. The FIB callback for handling this event is the fib_netdev_event() method; it is the callback of the fib_netdev_notifier notifier object, which is registered in the ip_fib_init() method by calling the register_netdevice_notifier() method (notification chains are discussed in Chapter 14). The fib_netdev_event() method calls the fib_disable_ip() method upon receiving a NETDEV_DOWN notification. In the fib_disable_ip() method, the following steps are performed:

- First, the fib_sync_down_dev() method is called (net/ipv4/fib_semantics.c). In the fib_sync_down_dev() method, the RTNH_F_DEAD flag of the nexthop flags (nh_flags) is set and the FIB info flags (fib_flags) is set.

- The routes are flushed by the fib_flush() method.

- The rt_cache_flush() method and the arp_ifdown() method are invoked. The arp_ifdown() method is not on any notifier chain.

FIB Nexthop Exceptions

FIB nexthop exceptions were added in kernel 3.6 to handle cases when a routing entry is changed not as a result of a userspace action, but as a result of an ICMPv4 Redirect message or as a result of Path MTU discovery. The hash key is the destination address. The FIB nexthop exceptions are based on a 2048 entry hash table; reclaiming (freeing hash entries) starts at a chain depth of 5. Each nexthop object (fib_nh) has a FIB nexthop exceptions hash table, nh_exceptions (an instance of the fnhe_hash_bucket structure). Let's take a look at the fib_nh_exception structure:

```
struct fib_nh_exception {
    struct fib_nh_exception __rcu    *fnhe_next;
    __be32                           fnhe_daddr;
    u32                              fnhe_pmtu;
    __be32                           fnhe_gw;
    unsigned long                    fnhe_expires;
    struct rtable __rcu              *fnhe_rth;
    unsigned long                    fnhe_stamp;
};
```

(include/net/ip_fib.h)

The fib_nh_exception objects are created by the update_or_create_fnhe() method (net/ipv4/route.c). Where are FIB nexthop exceptions generated? The first case is when receiving an ICMPv4 Redirect message ("Redirect to Host") in the __ip_do_redirect() method. The "Redirect to Host" message includes a new gateway. The fnhe_gw field of the fib_nh_exception is set to be the new gateway when creating the FIB nexthop exception object (in the update_or_create_fnhe() method):

```
static void __ip_do_redirect(struct rtable *rt, struct sk_buff *skb, struct flowi4 *fl4,
                 bool kill_route)
{
    ...
    __be32 new_gw = icmp_hdr(skb)->un.gateway;
    ...
    update_or_create_fnhe(nh, fl4->daddr, new_gw, 0, 0);
    ...
}
```

The second case of generating FIB nexthop exceptions is when the Path MTU has changed, in the __ip_rt_update_pmtu() method. In such a case, the fnhe_pmtu field of the fib_nh_exception object is set to be the new MTU when creating the FIB nexthop exception object (in the update_or_create_fnhe() method). PMTU value is expired if it was not updated in the last 10 minutes (ip_rt_mtu_expires). This period is checked on every dst_mtu() call via the ipv4_mtu() method, which is a dst->ops->mtu handler. The ip_rt_mtu_expires, which is by default 600 seconds, can be configured via the procfs entry /proc/sys/net/ipv4/route/mtu_expires:

```
static void __ip_rt_update_pmtu(struct rtable *rt, struct flowi4 *fl4, u32 mtu)
{
    . . .
    if (fib_lookup(dev_net(dst->dev), fl4, &res) == 0) {
        struct fib_nh *nh = &FIB_RES_NH(res);

        update_or_create_fnhe(nh, fl4->daddr, 0, mtu,
                    jiffies + ip_rt_mtu_expires);
    }
    . . .
}
```

■ **Note**   FIB nexthop exceptions are used in the Tx path. Starting with Linux 3.11, they are also used in the Rx path. As a result, instead of fnhe_rth, there are fnhe_rth_input and fnhe_rth_output.

Since kernel 2.4, Policy Routing is supported. With Policy Routing, the routing of a packet depends not only on the destination address, but on several other factors, such as the source address or the TOS. The system administrator can add up to 255 routing tables.

Policy Routing

When working without Policy Routing (CONFIG_IP_MULTIPLE_TABLES is not set), two routing tables are created: the local table and the main table. The main table id is 254 (RT_TABLE_MAIN), and the local table id is 255 (RT_TABLE_LOCAL). The local table contains routing entries of local addresses. These routing entries can be added to the local table only by the kernel. Adding routing entries to the main table (RT_TABLE_MAIN) is done by a system administrator (via ip route add, for example). These tables are created by the fib4_rules_init() method of net/ipv4/fib_frontend.c. These tables were called ip_fib_local_table and ip_fib_main_table in kernels prior to 2.6.25, but they were removed in favor of using unified access to the routing tables with the fib_get_table() method with appropriate argument. By *unified access*, I mean that access to the routing tables is done in the same way, with the fib_get_table() method, both when Policy Routing support is enabled and when it is disabled. The fib_get_table() method gets only two arguments: the network namespace and the table id. Note that there is a different method with the same name, fib4_rules_init(), for the Policy Routing case, in net/ipv4/fib_rules.c, which is invoked when working with Policy Routing support. When working with Policy Routing support (CONFIG_IP_MULTIPLE_TABLES is set), there are three initial tables (local, main, and default), and there can be up to 255 routing tables. I talk more about Policy Routing in Chapter 6. Access to the main routing table can be done as follows:

- By a system administrator command (using ip route or route):

    - Adding a route by ip route add is implemented by sending RTM_NEWROUTE message from userspace, which is handled by the inet_rtm_newroute() method. Note that a route is not necessarily always a rule that permits traffic. You can also add a route that blocks traffic, for example, by ip route add prohibit 192.168.1.17 from 192.168.2.103. As a result of applying this rule, all packets sent from 192.168.2.103 to 192.168.1.17 will be blocked.

    - Deleting a route by ip route del is implemented by sending RTM_DELROUTE message from userspace, which is handled by the inet_rtm_delroute() method.

    - Dumping a routing table by ip route show is implemented by sending RTM_GETROUTE message from userspace, which is handled by the inet_dump_fib() method.

    Note that ip route show displays the main table. For displaying the local table, you should run ip route show table local.

    - Adding a route by route add is implemented by sending SIOCADDRT IOCTL, which is handled by the ip_rt_ioctl() method (net/ipv4/fib_frontend.c).

    - Deleting a route by route del is implemented by sending SIOCDELRT IOCTL, which is handled by the ip_rt_ioctl() method (net/ipv4/fib_frontend.c).

- By userspace routing daemons which implement routing protocols like BGP (Border Gateway Protocol), EGP (Exterior Gateway Protocol), OSPF (Open Shortest Path First), or others. These routing daemons run on core routers, which operate in the Internet backbone, and can handle hundreds of thousands of routes.

I should mention here that routes that were changed as a result of an ICMPv4 REDIRECT message or as a result of Path MTU discovery are cached in the nexthop exception table, discussed shortly. The next section describes the FIB alias, which helps in routing optimizations.

FIB Alias (fib_alias)

There are cases when several routing entries to the same destination address or to the same subnet are created. These routing entries differ only in the value of their TOS. Instead of creating a fib_info for each such route, a fib_alias object is created. A fib_alias is smaller, which reduces memory consumption. Here is a simple example of creating 3 fib_alias objects:

```
ip route add 192.168.1.10 via 192.168.2.1 tos 0x2
ip route add 192.168.1.10 via 192.168.2.1 tos 0x4
ip route add 192.168.1.10 via 192.168.2.1 tos 0x6
```

Let's take a look at the fib_alias structure definition:

```
struct fib_alias {
        struct list_head        fa_list;
        struct fib_info         *fa_info;
        u8                      fa_tos;
        u8                      fa_type;
        u8                      fa_state;
        struct rcu_head         rcu;
};
```

(net/ipv4/fib_lookup.h)

Note that there was also a scope field in the fib_alias structure (fa_scope), but it was moved in kernel 2.6.39 to the fib_info structure.

The fib_alias object stores routes to the same subnet but with different parameters. You can have one fib_info object which will be shared by many fib_alias objects. The fa_info pointer in all these fib_alias objects, in this case, will point to the same shared fib_info object. In Figure 5-3, you can see one fib_info object which is shared by three fib_alias objects, each with a different fa_tos. Note that the reference counter value of the fib_info object is 3 (fib_treeref).

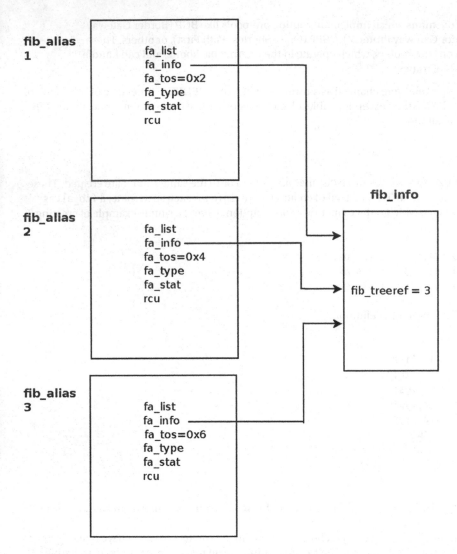

Figure 5-3. *A fib_info which is shared by three fib_alias objects. Each fib_alias object has a different fa_tos value*

Let's take a look at what happens when you try to add a key for which a fib_node was already added before (as in the earlier example with the three TOS values 0x2, 0x4, and 0x6); suppose you had created the first rule with TOS of 0x2, and now you create the second rule, with TOS of 0x4.

A fib_alias object is created by the fib_table_insert() method, which is the method that handles adding a routing entry:

```
int fib_table_insert(struct fib_table *tb, struct fib_config *cfg)
{
        struct trie *t = (struct trie *) tb->tb_data;
        struct fib_alias *fa, *new_fa;
        struct list_head *fa_head = NULL;
        struct fib_info *fi;
    . . .
```

First, a `fib_info` object is created. Note that in the `fib_create_info()` method, after allocating and creating a `fib_info` object, a lookup is performed to check whether a similar object already exists by calling the `fib_find_info()` method. If such an object exists, it will be freed, and the reference counter of the object that was found (`ofi` in the code snippet you will shortly see) will be incremented by 1:

```
fi = fib_create_info(cfg);
```

Let's take a look at the code snippet in the `fib_create_info()` method mentioned earlier; for creating the second TOS rule, the `fib_info` object of the first rule and the `fib_info` object of the second rule are identical. You should remember that the TOS field exists in the `fib_alias` object but not in the `fib_info` object:

```
struct fib_info *fib_create_info(struct fib_config *cfg)
{
    struct fib_info *fi = NULL;
    struct fib_info *ofi;
    . . .
    fi = kzalloc(sizeof(*fi)+nhs*sizeof(struct fib_nh), GFP_KERNEL);
    if (fi == NULL)
            goto failure;
    . . .
link_it:
        ofi = fib_find_info(fi);
```

If a similar object is found, free the `fib_info` object and increment the `fib_treeref` reference count:

```
    if (ofi) {
            fi->fib_dead = 1;
            free_fib_info(fi);
            ofi->fib_treeref++;
            return ofi;
    }
    . . .
}
```

Now a check is performed to find out whether there is an alias to the `fib_info` object; in this case, there will be no alias because the TOS of the second rule is different than the TOS of the first rule:

```
    l = fib_find_node(t, key);
    fa = NULL;

    if (l) {
            fa_head = get_fa_head(l, plen);
            fa = fib_find_alias(fa_head, tos, fi->fib_priority);
    }
if (fa && fa->fa_tos == tos &&
    fa->fa_info->fib_priority == fi->fib_priority) {
    . . .
    }
```

Now a `fib_alias` is created, and its `fa_info` pointer is assigned to point the `fib_info` of the first rule that was created:

```
new_fa = kmem_cache_alloc(fn_alias_kmem, GFP_KERNEL);
if (new_fa == NULL)
    goto out;

new_fa->fa_info = fi;
. . .
```

Now that I have covered the FIB Alias, you are ready to look at the ICMPv4 redirect message, which is sent when there is a suboptimal route.

ICMPv4 Redirect Message

There are cases when a routing entry is suboptimal. In such cases, an ICMPv4 redirect message is sent. The main criterion for a suboptimal entry is that the input device and the output device are the same. But there are more conditions that should be fulfilled so that an ICMPv4 redirect message is sent, as you will see in this section. There are four codes of ICMPv4 redirect message:

- ICMP_REDIR_NET: Redirect Net

- ICMP_REDIR_HOST: Redirect Host

- ICMP_REDIR_NETTOS: Redirect Net for TOS

- ICMP_REDIR_HOSTTOS: Redirect Host for TOS

Figure 5-4 shows a setup where there is a suboptimal route. There are three machines in this setup, all on the same subnet (192.168.2.0/24) and all connected via a gateway (192.168.2.1). The AMD server (192.168.2.200) added the Windows server (192.168.2.10) as a gateway for accessing 192.168.2.7 (the laptop) by `ip route add 192.168.2.7 via 192.168.2.10`. The AMD server sends traffic to the laptop, for example, by `ping 192.168.2.7`. Because the default gateway is `192.168.2.10`, the traffic is sent to `192.168.2.10`. The Windows server detects that this is a suboptimal route, because the AMD server could send directly to 192.168.2.7, and sends back to the AMD server an ICMPv4 redirect message with ICMP_REDIR_HOST code.

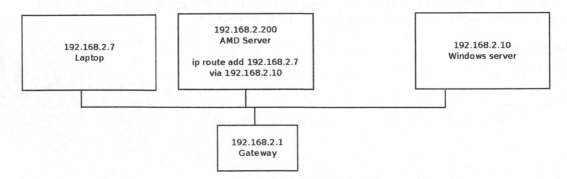

Figure 5-4. *Redirect to Host (ICMP_REDIR_HOST), a simple setup*

Now that you have a better understanding of redirects, let's look at how an ICMPv4 message is generated.

Generating an ICMPv4 Redirect Message

An ICMPv4 Redirect message is sent when there is some suboptimal route. The most notable condition for a suboptimal route is that the input device and the output device are the same, but there are some more conditions which should be met. Generating an ICMPv4 Redirect message is done in two phases:

- In the __mkroute_input() method: Here the RTCF_DOREDIRECT flag is set if needed.

- In the ip_forward() method: Here the ICMPv4 Redirect message is actually sent by calling the ip_rt_send_redirect() method.

```
static int __mkroute_input(struct sk_buff *skb,
                    const struct fib_result *res,
                    struct in_device *in_dev,
                    __be32 daddr, __be32 saddr, u32 tos)
{
    struct rtable *rth;
    int err;
    struct in_device *out_dev;
    unsigned int flags = 0;
    bool do_cache;
```

All of the following conditions should be sustained so that the RTCF_DOREDIRECT flag is set:

- The input device and the output device are the same.

- The procfs entry, /proc/sys/net/ipv4/conf/<deviceName>/send_redirects, is set.

- Either this outgoing device is a shared media or the source address (saddr) and the nexthop gateway address (nh_gw) are on the same subnet:

```
if (out_dev == in_dev && err && IN_DEV_TX_REDIRECTS(out_dev) &&
    (IN_DEV_SHARED_MEDIA(out_dev) ||
     inet_addr_onlink(out_dev, saddr, FIB_RES_GW(*res)))) {

    flags |= RTCF_DOREDIRECT;
    do_cache = false;
}
    . . .
```

Setting the rtable object flags is done by:

```
rth->rt_flags = flags;
. . .
```

```
}
```

Sending the ICMPv4 Redirect message is done in the second phase, by the ip_forward() method:

```
int ip_forward(struct sk_buff *skb)
{
    struct iphdr        *iph;    /* Our header */
    struct rtable       *rt;     /* Route we use */
    struct ip_options   *opt     = &(IPCB(skb)->opt);
```

Next a check is performed to see whether the RTCF_DOREDIRECT flag is set, whether an IP option of strict route does not exist (see chapter 4), and whether it is not an IPsec packet. (With IPsec tunnels, the input device of the tunneled packet can be the same as the decapsulated packet outgoing device; see http://lists.openwall.net/netdev/2007/08/24/29):

```
if (rt->rt_flags&RTCF_DOREDIRECT && !opt->srr && !skb_sec_path(skb))
    ip_rt_send_redirect(skb);
```

In the ip_rt_send_redirect() method, the ICMPv4 Redirect message is actually sent. The third parameter is the IP address of the advised new gateway, which will be 192.168.2.7 in this case (The address of the laptop):

```
void ip_rt_send_redirect(struct sk_buff *skb)
  {
      . . .
      icmp_send(skb, ICMP_REDIRECT, ICMP_REDIR_HOST,
            rt_nexthop(rt, ip_hdr(skb)->daddr))
      . . .
  }
```

(net/ipv4/route.c)

Receiving an ICMPv4 Redirect Message

For an ICMPv4 Redirect message to be processed, it should pass some sanity checks. Handling an ICMPv4 Redirect message is done by the __ip_do_redirect() method:

```
static void __ip_do_redirect(struct rtable *rt, struct sk_buff *skb, struct flowi4
    *fl4,bool kill_route)
{
    __be32 new_gw = icmp_hdr(skb)->un.gateway;
    __be32 old_gw = ip_hdr(skb)->saddr;
    struct net_device *dev = skb->dev;
    struct in_device *in_dev;
    struct fib_result res;
    struct neighbour *n;
    struct net *net;
      . . .
```

Various checks are performed, such as that the network device is set to accept redirects. The redirect is rejected if necessary:

```
if (rt->rt_gateway != old_gw)
    return;

in_dev = __in_dev_get_rcu(dev);
if (!in_dev)
    return;

net = dev_net(dev);
if (new_gw == old_gw || !IN_DEV_RX_REDIRECTS(in_dev) ||
    ipv4_is_multicast(new_gw) || ipv4_is_lbcast(new_gw) ||
```

```
        ipv4_is_zeronet(new_gw))
        goto reject_redirect;

if (!IN_DEV_SHARED_MEDIA(in_dev)) {
    if (!inet_addr_onlink(in_dev, new_gw, old_gw))
        goto reject_redirect;
    if (IN_DEV_SEC_REDIRECTS(in_dev) && ip_fib_check_default(new_gw, dev))
        goto reject_redirect;
} else {
    if (inet_addr_type(net, new_gw) != RTN_UNICAST)
        goto reject_redirect;
}
```

A lookup in the neighboring subsystem is performed; the key to the lookup is the address of the advised gateway, new_gw, which was extracted from the ICMPv4 message in the beginning of this method:

```
n = ipv4_neigh_lookup(&rt->dst, NULL, &new_gw);
if (n) {
    if (!(n->nud_state & NUD_VALID)) {
        neigh_event_send(n, NULL);
    } else {
        if (fib_lookup(net, fl4, &res) == 0) {
            struct fib_nh *nh = &FIB_RES_NH(res);
```

Create / update a FIB nexthop exception, specifying the IP address of an advised gateway (new_gw):

```
                update_or_create_fnhe(nh, fl4->daddr, new_gw,
                                0, 0);
            }
            if (kill_route)
                rt->dst.obsolete = DST_OBSOLETE_KILL;
            call_netevent_notifiers(NETEVENT_NEIGH_UPDATE, n);
        }
        neigh_release(n);
    }
    return;

reject_redirect:
    . . .
```

(net/ipv4/route.c)

Now that we've covered how a received ICMPv4 message is handled, we can next tackle the IPv4 routing cache and the reasons for its removal.

IPv4 Routing Cache

In kernels prior to 3.6, there was an IPv4 routing cache with a garbage collector. The IPv4 routing cache was removed in kernel 3.6 (around July 2012). The FIB TRIE / FIB hash was a choice in the kernel for years, but not as the default. Having the FIB TRIE made it possible to remove the IPv4 routing cache, as it had Denial of Service (DoS) issues. FIB TRIE (also known as LC-trie) is the longest matching prefix lookup algorithm that performs better than FIB hash for large routing tables. It consumes more memory and is more complex, but since it performs better, it made the removal of the routing cache feasible. The FIB TRIE code was in the kernel for a long time before it was merged, but it was not the default. The main reason for the removal of the IPv4 routing cache was that launching DoS attacks against it was easy because the IPv4 routing cache created a cache entry for each unique flow. Basically that meant that by sending packets to random destinations, you could generate an unlimited amount of routing cache entries.

Merging the FIB TRIE entailed the removal of the routing cache and of some of the cumbersome FIB hash tables and of the routing cache garbage collector methods. This chapter discusses the routing cache very briefly. Because the novice reader may wonder what it is needed for, note that in the Linux-based software industry, in commercial distributions like RedHat Enterprise, the kernels are fully maintained and fully supported for a very long period of time (RedHat, for example, gives support for its distributions for up to seven years). So it is very likely that some readers will be involved in projects based on kernels prior to 3.6, where you will find the routing cache and the FIB hash-based routing tables. Delving into the theory and implementation details of the FIB TRIE data structure is beyond the scope of this book. To learn more, I recommend the article "TRASH—A dynamic LC-trie and hash data structure" by Robert Olsson and Stefan Nilsson, www.nada.kth.se/~snilsson/publications/TRASH/trash.pdf.

Note that with the IPv4 routing cache implementation, there is a single cache, regardless of how many routing tables are used (there can be up to 255 routing tables when using Policy Routing). Note that there was also support for IPv4 Multipath Routing cache, but it was removed in kernel 2.6.23, in 2007. In fact, it never did work very well and never got out of the experimental state.

For kernels prior to the 3.6 kernel, where the FIB TRIE is not yet merged, the lookup in the IPv4 routing subsystem was different: access to routing tables was preceded by access to the routing cache, the tables were organized differently, and there was a routing cache garbage collector, which was both asynchronous (periodic timer) and synchronous (activated under specific conditions, for example when the number of the cache entries exceeded some threshold). The cache was basically a big hash with the IP flow source address, destination address, and TOS as a key, associated with all flow-specific information like neighbor entry, PMTU, redirect, TCPMSS info, and so on. The benefit here is that cached entries were fast to look up and contained all the information needed by higher layers.

■ **Note**　The following two sections ("Rx Path" and "Tx Path") refer to the 2.6.38 kernel.

Rx Path

In the Rx path, first the ip_route_input_common() method is invoked. This method performs a lookup in the IPv4 routing cache, which is much quicker than the lookup in the IPv4 routing tables. Lookup in these routing tables is based on the Longest Prefix Match (LPM) search algorithm. With the LPM search, the most specific table entry—the one with the highest subnet mask—is called the Longest Prefix Match. In case the lookup in the routing cache fails ("cache miss"), a lookup in the routing tables is being performed by calling the ip_route_input_slow() method. This method calls the fib_lookup() method to perform the actual lookup. Upon success, it calls the ip_mkroute_input() method which (among other actions) inserts the routing entry into the routing cache by calling the rt_intern_hash() method.

Tx Path

In the Tx path, first the ip_route_output_key() method is invoked. This method performs a lookup in the IPv4 routing cache. In case of a cache miss, it calls the ip_route_output_slow() method, which calls the fib_lookup() method to perform a lookup in the routing subsystem. Subsequently, upon success, it calls the ip_mkroute_output() method which (among other actions) inserts the routing entry into the routing cache by calling the rt_intern_hash() method.

Summary

This chapter covered various topics of the IPv4 routing subsystem. The routing subsystem is essential for handling both incoming and outgoing packets. You learned about various topics like forwarding, lookup in the routing subsystem, organization of the FIB tables, Policy Routing and the routing subsystem, and ICMPv4 Redirect message. You also learned about optimization which is gained with the FIB alias and the fact that the routing cache was removed, and why. The next chapter covers advanced topics of the IPv4 routing subsystem.

Quick Reference

I conclude this chapter with a short list of important methods, macros, and tables of the IPv4 routing subsystem, along with a short explanation about routing flags.

■ **Note** The IPv4 routing subsystem is implemented in these modules under net/ipv4: fib_frontend.c, fib_trie.c, fib_semantics.c, route.c.

The fib_rules.c module implements Policy Routing and is compiled only when CONFIG_IP_MULTIPLE_TABLES is set. Among the most important header files are fib_lookup.h, include/net/ip_fib.h, and include/net/route.h.

The destination cache (dst) implementation is in net/core/dst.c and in include/net/dst.h.

CONFIG_IP_ROUTE_MULTIPATH should be set for Multipath Routing Support.

Methods

This section lists the methods that were mentioned in this chapter.

int fib_table_insert(struct fib_table *tb, struct fib_config *cfg);

This method inserts an IPv4 routing entry to the specified FIB table (fib_table object), based on the specified fib_config object.

int fib_table_delete(struct fib_table *tb, struct fib_config *cfg);

This method deletes an IPv4 routing entry from the specified FIB table (fib_table object), based on the specified fib_config object.

struct fib_info *fib_create_info(struct fib_config *cfg);

This method creates a fib_info object derived from the specified fib_config object.

void free_fib_info(struct fib_info *fi);

This method frees a fib_info object in condition that it is not alive (the fib_dead flag is not 0) and decrements the global fib_info objects counter (fib_info_cnt).

void fib_alias_accessed(struct fib_alias *fa);

This method sets the fa_state flag of the specified fib_alias to be FA_S_ACCESSED. Note that the only fa_state flag is FA_S_ACCESSED.

void ip_rt_send_redirect(struct sk_buff *skb);

This method sends an ICMPV4 Redirect message, as a response to a suboptimal path.

void __ip_do_redirect(struct rtable *rt, struct sk_buff *skb, struct flowi4*fl4, bool kill_route);

This method handles receiving an ICMPv4 Redirect message.

void update_or_create_fnhe(struct fib_nh *nh, __be32 daddr, __be32 gw, u32 pmtu, unsigned long expires);

This method creates a FIB nexthop exception table (fib_nh_exception) in the specified nexthop object (fib_nh), if it does not already exist, and initializes it. It is invoked when there should be a route update due to ICMPv4 redirect or due to PMTU discovery.

u32 dst_metric(const struct dst_entry *dst, int metric);

This method returns a metric of the specified dst object.

struct fib_table *fib_trie_table(u32 id);

This method allocates and initializes a FIB TRIE table.

struct leaf *fib_find_node(struct trie *t, u32 key);

This method performs a TRIE lookup with the specified key. It returns a leaf object upon success, or NULL in case of failure.

Macros

This section is a list of macros of the IPv4 routing subsystem, some of which were mentioned in this chapter.

FIB_RES_GW()

This macro returns the nh_gw field (nexthop gateway address) associated with the specified fib_result object.

FIB_RES_DEV()

This macro returns the nh_dev field (Next hop net_device object) associated with the specified fib_result object.

FIB_RES_OIF()

This macro returns the nh_oif field (nexthop output interface index) associated with the specified fib_result object.

FIB_RES_NH()

This macro returns the nexthop (fib_nh object) of the fib_info of the specified fib_result object. When Multipath Routing is set, you can have multiple nexthops; the value of nh_sel field of the specified fib_result object is taken into account in this case, as an index to the array of the nexthops which is embedded in the fib_info object.

(include/net/ip_fib.h)

IN_DEV_FORWARD()

This macro checks whether the specified network device (in_device object) supports IPv4 forwarding.

IN_DEV_RX_REDIRECTS()

This macro checks whether the specified network device (in_device object) supports accepting ICMPv4 Redirects.

IN_DEV_TX_REDIRECTS()

This macro checks whether the specified network device (in_device object) supports sending ICMPv4 Redirects.

IS_LEAF()

This macro checks whether the specified tree node is a leaf.

IS_TNODE()

This macro checks whether the specified tree node is an internal node (trie node or tnode).

change_nexthops()

This macro iterates over the nexthops of the specified fib_info object (net/ipv4/fib_semantics.c).

Tables

There are 15 (RTAX_MAX) metrics for routes. Some of them are TCP related, and some are general. Table 5-1 shows which of these metrics are related to TCP.

Table 5-1. *Route Metrics*

Linux Symbol	TCP Metric (Y/N)
RTAX_UNSPEC	N
RTAX_LOCK	N
RTAX_MTU	N
RTAX_WINDOW	Y
RTAX_RTT	Y
RTAX_RTTVAR	Y
RTAX_SSTHRESH	Y
RTAX_CWND	Y
RTAX_ADVMSS	Y
RTAX_REORDERING	Y
RTAX_HOPLIMIT	N
RTAX_INITCWND	Y
RTAX_FEATURES	N
RTAX_RTO_MIN	Y
RTAX_INITRWND	Y

(include/uapi/linux/rtnetlink.h)

Table 5-2 shows the error value and the scope of all the route types.

Table 5-2. *Route Types*

Linux Symbol	Error	Scope
RTN_UNSPEC	0	RT_SCOPE_NOWHERE
RTN_UNICAST	0	RT_SCOPE_UNIVERSE
RTN_LOCAL	0	RT_SCOPE_HOST
RTN_BROADCAST	0	RT_SCOPE_LINK
RTN_ANYCAST	0	RT_SCOPE_LINK
RTN_MULTICAST	0	RT_SCOPE_UNIVERSE
RTN_BLACKHOLE	-EINVAL	RT_SCOPE_UNIVERSE
RTN_UNREACHABLE	-EHOSTUNREACH	RT_SCOPE_UNIVERSE
RTN_PROHIBIT	-EACCES	RT_SCOPE_UNIVERSE
RTN_THROW	-EAGAIN	RT_SCOPE_UNIVERSE
RTN_NAT	-EINVAL	RT_SCOPE_NOWHERE
RTN_XRESOLVE	-EINVAL	RT_SCOPE_NOWHERE

Route Flags

When running the route -n command, you get an output that shows the route flags. Here are the flag values and a short example of the output of route -n:

U (Route is up)

H (Target is a host)

G (Use gateway)

R (Reinstate route for dynamic routing)

D (Dynamically installed by daemon or redirect)

M (Modified from routing daemon or redirect)

A (Installed by addrconf)

! (Reject route)

Table 5-3 shows an example of the output of running route -n (the results are organized into a table form):

Table 5-3. *Kernel IP Routing Table*

Destination	Gateway	Genmask	Flags	Metric	Ref	Use	Iface
169.254.0.0	0.0.0.0	255.255.0.0	U	1002	0	0	eth0
192.168.3.0	192.168.2.1	255.255.255.0	UG	0	0	0	eth1

CHAPTER 6

■ ■ ■

Advanced Routing

Chapter 5 dealt with the IPv4 routing subsystem. This chapter continues with the routing subsystem and discusses advanced IPv4 routing topics such as Multicast Routing, Multipath Routing, Policy Routing, and more. This book deals with the Linux Kernel Networking implementation—it does not delve into the internals of userspace Multicast Routing daemons implementation, which are quite complex and beyond the scope of the book. I do, however, discuss to some extent the interaction between a userspace multicast routing daemon and the multicast layer in the kernel. I also briefly discuss the Internet Group Management Protocol (IGMP) protocol, which is the basis of multicast group membership management; adding and deleting multicast group members is done by the IGMP protocol. Some basic knowledge of IGMP is needed to understand the interaction between a multicast host and a multicast router.

Multipath Routing is the ability to add more than one nexthop to a route. Policy Routing enables configuring routing policies that are not based solely on the destination address. I start with describing Multicast Routing.

Multicast Routing

Chapter 4 briefly mentions Multicast Routing, in the "Receiving IPv4 Multicast Packets" section. I will now discuss it in more depth. Sending multicast traffic means sending the same packet to multiple recipients. This feature can be useful in streaming media, audio/video conferencing, and more. It has a clear advantage over unicast traffic in terms of saving network bandwidth. Multicast addresses are defined as Class D addresses. The Classless Inter-Domain Routing (CIDR) prefix of this group is 224.0.0.0/4. The range of IPv4 multicast addresses is from 224.0.0.0 to 239.255.255.255. Handling Multicast Routing must be done in conjunction with a userspace routing daemon which interacts with the kernel. According to the Linux implementation, Multicast Routing cannot be handled solely by the kernel code without this userspace Routing daemon, as opposed to Unicast Routing. There are various multicast daemons: for example: mrouted, which is based on an implementation of the Distance Vector Multicast Routing Protocol (DVMRP), or pimd, which is based on the Protocol-Independent Multicast protocol (PIM). The DVMRP protocol is defined in RFC 1075, and it was the first multicast routing protocol. It is based on the Routing Information Protocol (RIP) protocol.

The PIM protocol has two versions, and the kernel supports both of them (CONFIG_IP_PIMSM_V1 and CONFIG_IP_PIMSM_V2). PIM has four different modes: PIM-SM (PIM Sparse Mode), PIM-DM (PIM Dense Mode), PIM Source-Specific Multicast (PIM-SSM) and Bidirectional PIM. The protocol is called *protocol-independent* because it is not dependent on any particular routing protocol for topology discovery. This section discusses the interaction between the userspace daemon and the kernel multicast routing layer. Delving into the internals of the PIM protocol or the DVMRP protocol (or any other Multicast Routing protocol) is beyond the scope of this book. Normally, the Multicast Routing lookup is based on the source and destination addresses. There is a "Multicast Policy Routing" kernel feature, which is the parallel to the unicast policy routing kernel feature that was mentioned in Chapter 5 and which is also discussed in the course of this chapter. The multicast policy routing protocol is implemented using the Policy Routing API (for example, it calls the fib_rules_lookup() method to perform a lookup, creates a fib_rules_ops object, and registers it with the fib_rules_register() method, and so on). With Multicast Policy Routing, the routing can be based on additional criteria, like the ingress network interfaces. Moreover, you can work with more than one multicast routing table. In order to work with Multicast Policy Routing, IP_MROUTE_MULTIPLE_TABLES must be set.

Figure 6-1 shows a simple IPv4 Multicast Routing setup. The topology is very simple: the laptop, on the left, joins a multicast group (224.225.0.1) by sending an IGMP packet (IP_ADD_MEMBERSHIP). The IGMP protocol is discussed in the next section, "The IGMP Protocol." The AMD server, in the middle, is configured as a multicast router, and a userspace multicast routing daemon (like pimd or mrouted) runs on it. The Windows server, on the right, which has an IP address of 192.168.2.10, sends multicast traffic to 224.225.0.1; this traffic is forwarded to the laptop via the multicast router. Note that the Windows server itself did not join the 224.225.0.1 multicast group. Running ip route add 224.0.0.0/4 dev <networkDeviceName> tells the kernel to send all multicast traffic via the specified network device.

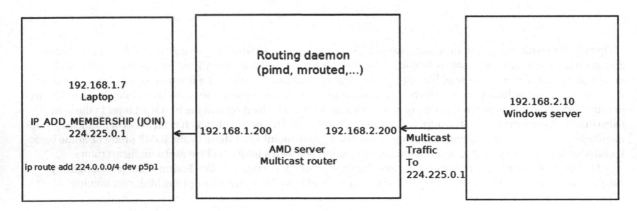

Figure 6-1. *Simple Multicast Routing setup*

The next section discusses the IGMP protocol, which is used for the management of multicast group membership.

The IGMP Protocol

The IGMP protocol is an integral part of IPv4 multicast. It must be implemented on each node that supports IPv4 multicast. In IPv6, multicast management is handled by the MLD (Multicast Listener Discovery) protocol, which uses ICMPv6 messages, discussed in Chapter 8. With the IGMP protocol, multicast group memberships are established and managed. There are three versions of IGMP:

1. *IGMPv1 (RFC 1112):* Has two types of messages—host membership report and host membership query. When a host wants to join a multicast group, it sends a membership report message. Multicast routers send membership queries to discover which host multicast groups have members on their attached local networks. Queries are addressed to the all-hosts group address (224.0.0.1, IGMP_ALL_HOSTS) and carry a TTL of 1 so that the membership query will not travel outside of the LAN.

2. *IGMPv2 (RFC 2236):* This is an extension of IGMPv1. The IGMPv2 protocol adds three new messages:

   a. Membership Query (0x11): There are two sub-types of Membership Query messages: General Query, used to learn which groups have members on an attached network, and Group-Specific Query, used to learn whether a particular group has any members on an attached network.

   b. Version 2 Membership Report (0x16).

   c. Leave Group (0x17).

■ **Note**   IGMPv2 also supports Version 1 Membership Report message, for backward compatibility with IGMPv1. See RFC 2236, section 2.1.

---

3. *IGMPv3 (RFC 3376, updated by RFC 4604):* This major revision of the protocol adds a feature called source filtering. This means that when a host joins a multicast group, it can specify a set of source addresses from which it will receive multicast traffic. The source filters can also exclude source addresses. To support the source filtering feature, the socket API was extended; see RFC 3678, "Socket Interface Extensions for Multicast Source Filters." I should also mention that the multicast router periodically (about every two minutes) sends a membership query to 224.0.0.1, the all-hosts multicast group address. A host that receives a membership query responds with a membership report. This is implemented in the kernel by the `igmp_rcv()` method: getting an IGMP_HOST_MEMBERSHIP_QUERY message is handled by the `igmp_heard_query()` method.

■ **Note**   The kernel implementation of IPv4 IGMP is in `net/core/igmp.c`, `include/linux/igmp.h` and `include/uapi/linux/igmp.h`.

The next section examines the fundamental data structure of IPv4 Multicast Routing, the multicast routing table, and its Linux implementation.

The Multicast Routing Table

The multicast routing table is represented by a structure named `mr_table`. Let's take a look at it:

```
struct mr_table {
    struct list_head        list;
#ifdef CONFIG_NET_NS
    struct net              *net;
#endif
    u32                     id;
    struct sock     __rcu   *mroute_sk;
    struct timer_list       ipmr_expire_timer;
    struct list_head        mfc_unres_queue;
```

```
    struct list_head    mfc_cache_array[MFC_LINES];
    struct vif_device   vif_table[MAXVIFS];
    . . .
};
```

(net/ipv4/ipmr.c)

The following is a description of some members of the mr_table structure:

- net: The network namespace associated with the multicast routing table; by default it is the initial network namespace, init_net. Network namespaces are discussed in Chapter 14.

- id: The multicast routing table id; it is RT_TABLE_DEFAULT (253) when working with a single table.

- mroute_sk: This pointer represents a reference to the userspace socket that the kernel keeps. The mroute_sk pointer is initialized by calling setsockopt() from the userspace with the MRT_INIT socket option and is nullified by calling setsockopt() with the MRT_DONE socket option. The interaction between the userspace and the kernel is based on calling the setsockopt() method, on sending IOCTLs from userspace, and on building IGMP packets and passing them to the Multicast Routing daemon by calling the sock_queue_rcv_skb() method from the kernel.

- ipmr_expire_timer: Timer of cleaning unresolved multicast routing entries. This timer is initialized when creating a multicast routing table, in the ipmr_new_table() method, and removed when removing a multicast routing table, by the ipmr_free_table() method.

- mfc_unres_queue: A queue of unresolved routing entries.

- mfc_cache_array: A cache of the routing entries, with 64 (MFC_LINES) entries, discussed shortly in the next section.

- vif_table[MAXVIFS]: An array of 32 (MAXVIFS) vif_device objects. Entries are added by the vif_add() method and deleted by the vif_delete() method. The vif_device structure represents a virtual multicast routing network interface; it can be based on a physical device or on an IPIP (IP over IP) tunnel. The vif_device structure is discussed later in "The Vif Device" section.

I have covered the multicast routing table and mentioned its important members, such as the Multicast Forwarding Cache (MFC) and the queue of unresolved routing entries. Next I will look at the MFC, which is embedded in the multicast routing table object and plays an important role in Multicast Routing.

The Multicast Forwarding Cache (MFC)

The most important data structure in the multicast routing table is the MFC, which is in fact an array of cache entries (mfc_cache objects). This array, named mfc_cache_array, is embedded in the multicast routing table (mr_table) object. It has 64 (MFC_LINES) elements. The index of this array is the hash value (the hash function takes two parameters—the multicast group address and the source IP address; see the description of the MFC_HASH macro in the "Quick Reference" section at the end of this chapter).

Usually there is only one multicast routing table, which is an instance of the mr_table structure, and a reference to it is kept in the IPv4 network namespace (net->ipv4.mrt). The table is created by the ipmr_rules_init() method, which also assigns net->ipv4.mrt to point to the multicast routing table that was created. When working with the multicast policy routing feature mentioned earlier, there can be multiple multicast policy routing tables. In both cases, you get the routing table using the same method, ipmr_fib_lookup(). The ipmr_fib_lookup() method gets three parameters as an input: the network namespace, the flow, and a pointer to the mr_table object which it should fill. Normally, it simply sets the specified mr_table pointer to be net->ipv4.mrt; when working with multiple tables (IP_MROUTE_MULTIPLE_TABLES is set), the implementation is more complex. Let's take a look at the mfc_cache structure:

```
struct mfc_cache {
    struct list_head list;
    __be32 mfc_mcastgrp;
    __be32 mfc_origin;
    vifi_t mfc_parent;
    int mfc_flags;
    union {
            struct {
                    unsigned long expires;
                    struct sk_buff_head unresolved; /* Unresolved buffers */
            } unres;
            struct {
                    unsigned long last_assert;
                    int minvif;
                    int maxvif;
                    unsigned long bytes;
                    unsigned long pkt;
                    unsigned long wrong_if;
                    unsigned char ttls[MAXVIFS];    /* TTL thresholds */
            } res;
    } mfc_un;
    struct rcu_head rcu;
};
```

(include/linux/mroute.h)

The following is a description of some members of the mfc_cache structure:

- mfc_mcastgrp: the address of the multicast group that the entry belongs to.

- mfc_origin: The source address of the route.

- mfc_parent: The source interface.

- mfc_flags: The flags of the entry. Can have one of these values:

    - MFC_STATIC: When the route was added statically and not by a multicast routing daemon.

    - MFC_NOTIFY: When the RTM_F_NOTIFY flag of the routing entry was set. See the rt_fill_info() method and the ipmr_get_route() method for more details.

- The mfc_un union consists of two elements:

    - unres: Unresolved cache entries.

    - res: Resolved cache entries.

The first time an SKB of a certain flow reaches the kernel, it is added to the queue of unresolved entries (mfc_un.unres.unresolved), where up to three SKBs can be saved. If there are three SKBs in the queue, the packet is not appended to the queue but is freed, and the ipmr_cache_unresolved() method returns -ENOBUFS ("No buffer space available"):

```
static int ipmr_cache_unresolved(struct mr_table *mrt, vifi_t vifi, struct sk_buff *skb)
{
        . . .
        if (c->mfc_un.unres.unresolved.qlen > 3) {
                kfree_skb(skb);
                err = -ENOBUFS;
        } else {
            . . .

}
```

(net/ipv4/ipmr.c)

This section described the MFC and its important members, including the queue of resolved entries and the queue of unresolved entries. The next section briefly describes what a multicast router is and how it is configured in Linux.

Multicast Router

In order to configure a machine as a multicast router, you should set the CONFIG_IP_MROUTE kernel configuration option. You should also run some routing daemon such as pimd or mrouted, as mentioned earlier. These routing daemons create a socket to communicate with the kernel. In pimd, for example, you create a raw IGMP socket by calling socket(AF_INET, SOCK_RAW, IPPROTO_IGMP). Calling setsockopt() on this socket triggers sending commands to the kernel, which are handled by the ip_mroute_setsockopt() method. When calling setsockopt() on this socket from the routing daemon with MRT_INIT, the kernel is set to keep a reference to the userspace socket in the mroute_sk field of the mr_table object that is used, and the mc_forwarding procfs entry (/proc/sys/net/ipv4/conf/all/mc_forwarding) is set by calling IPV4_DEVCONF_ALL(net, MC_FORWARDING)++. Note that the mc_forwarding procfs entry is a read-only entry and can't be set from userspace. You can't create another instance of a multicast routing daemon: when handling the MRT_INIT option, the ip_mroute_setsockopt() method checks whether the mroute_sk field of the mr_table object is initialized and returns -EADDRINUSE if so. Adding a network interface is done by calling setsockopt() on this socket with MRT_ADD_VIF, and deleting a network interface is done by calling setsockopt() on this socket with MRT_DEL_VIF. You can pass the parameters of the network interface to these setsockopt() calls by passing a vifctl object as the optval parameter of the setsockopt() system call. Let's take a look at the vifctl structure:

```
struct vifctl {
    vifi_t    vifc_vifi;                /* Index of VIF */
    unsigned char vifc_flags;          /* VIFF_ flags */
    unsigned char vifc_threshold;      /* ttl limit */
    unsigned int vifc_rate_limit;      /* Rate limiter values (NI) */
    union {
        struct in_addr vifc_lcl_addr;    /* Local interface address */
        int            vifc_lcl_ifindex; /* Local interface index   */
    };
    struct in_addr vifc_rmt_addr;    /* IPIP tunnel addr */
};
```

(include/uapi/linux/mroute.h)

The following is a description of some members of the vifctl structure:

- vifc_flags can be:

  - VIFF_TUNNEL: When you want to use an IPIP tunnel.

  - VIFF_REGISTER: When you want to register the interface.

  - VIFF_USE_IFINDEX: When you want to use the local interface index and not the local interface IP address; in such a case, you will set the vifc_lcl_ifindex to be the local interface index. The VIFF_USE_IFINDEX flag is available for 2.6.33 kernel and above.

- vifc_lcl_addr: The local interface IP address. (This is the default—no flag should be set for using it).

- vifc_lcl_ifindex: The local interface index. It should be set when the VIFF_USE_IFINDEX flag is set in vifc_flags.

- vifc_rmt_addr: The address of the remote node of a tunnel.

When the multicast routing daemon is closed, the setsockopt() method is called with an MRT_DONE option. This triggers calling the mrtsock_destruct() method to nullify the mroute_sk field of the mr_table object that is used and to perform various cleanups.

This section covered what a multicast router is and how it is configured in Linux. I also examined the vifctl structure. Next, I look at the Vif device, which represents a multicast network interface.

The Vif Device

Multicast Routing supports two modes: direct multicast and multicast encapsulated in a unicast packet over a tunnel. In both cases, the same object is used (an instance of the vif_device structure) to represent the network interface. When working over a tunnel, the VIFF_TUNNEL flag will be set. Adding and deleting a multicast interface is done by the vif_add() method and by the vif_delete() method, respectively. The vif_add() method also sets the device to support multicast by calling the dev_set_allmulti(dev, 1) method, which increments the allmulti counter of the specified network device (net_device object). The vif_delete() method calls dev_set_allmulti(dev, -1) to decrement the allmulti counter of the specified network device (net_device object). For more details about the dev_set_allmulti() method, see appendix A. Let's take a look at the vif_device structure; its members are quite self-explanatory:

```
struct vif_device {
        struct net_device    *dev;         /* Device we are using */
        unsigned long    bytes_in,bytes_out;
        unsigned long    pkt_in,pkt_out;    /* Statistics              */
        unsigned long    rate_limit;        /* Traffic shaping (NI)    */
        unsigned char    threshold;         /* TTL threshold           */
        unsigned short   flags;             /* Control flags           */
        __be32           local,remote;      /* Addresses(remote for tunnels)*/
        int              link;              /* Physical interface index */
};
```

(include/linux/mroute.h)

In order to receive multicast traffic, a host must join a multicast group. This is done by creating a socket in userspace and calling setsockopt() with IPPROTO_IP and with the IP_ADD_MEMBERSHIP socket option. The userspace application also creates an ip_mreq object where it initializes the request parameters, like the desired group multicast address and the source IP address of the host (see the netinet/in.h userspace header). The setsockopt() call is handled in the kernel by the ip_mc_join_group() method, in net/ipv4/igmp.c. Eventually, the multicast address is added by the `ip_mc_join_group()` method to a list of multicast addresses (`mc_list`), which is a member of the `in_device` object. A host can leave a multicast group by calling `setsockopt()` with IPPROTO_IP and with the IP_DROP_MEMBERSHIP socket option. This is handled in the kernel by the `ip_mc_leave_group()` method, in net/ipv4/igmp.c. A single socket can join up to 20 multicast groups (`sysctl_igmp_max_memberships`). Trying to join more than 20 multicast groups by the same socket will fail with the -ENOBUFS error ("No buffer space available.") See the `ip_mc_join_group()` method implementation in net/ipv4/igmp.c.

IPv4 Multicast Rx Path

Chapter 4's "Receiving IPv4 Multicast Packets" section briefly discusses how multicast packets are handled. I will now describe this in more depth. My discussion assumes that our machine is configured as a multicast router; this means, as was mentioned earlier, that CONFIG_IP_MROUTE is set and a routing daemon like pimd or mrouted runs on this host. Multicast packets are handled by the `ip_route_input_mc()` method, in which a routing table entry (an rtable object) is allocated and initialized, and in which the input callback of the dst object is set to be `ip_mr_input()`, in case CONFIG_IP_MROUTE is set. Let's take a look at the `ip_mr_input()` method:

```
int ip_mr_input(struct sk_buff *skb)
{
        struct mfc_cache *cache;
        struct net *net = dev_net(skb->dev);
```

First the `local` flag is set to `true` if the packet is intended for local delivery, as the `ip_mr_input()` method also handles local multicast packets.

```
int local = skb_rtable(skb)->rt_flags & RTCF_LOCAL;
struct mr_table *mrt;

/* Packet is looped back after forward, it should not be
* forwarded second time, but still can be delivered locally.
*/
if (IPCB(skb)->flags & IPSKB_FORWARDED)
        goto dont_forward;
```

Normally, when working with a single multicast routing table, the `ipmr_rt_fib_lookup()` method simply returns the `net->ipv4.mrt` object:

```
mrt = ipmr_rt_fib_lookup(net, skb);
if (IS_ERR(mrt)) {
        kfree_skb(skb);
        return PTR_ERR(mrt);
}
if (!local) {
```

IGMPv3 and some IGMPv2 implementations set the router alert option (IPOPT_RA) in the IPv4 header when sending JOIN or LEAVE packets. See the `igmpv3_newpack()` method in net/ipv4/igmp.c:

```
if (IPCB(skb)->opt.router_alert) {
```

The `ip_call_ra_chain()` method (net/ipv4/ip_input.c) calls the `raw_rcv()` method to pass the packet to the userspace raw socket, which listens. The `ip_ra_chain` object contains a reference to the multicast routing socket, which is passed as a parameter to the raw_rcv() method. For more details, look at the ip_call_ra_chain() method implementation, in net/ipv4/ip_input.c:

```
if (ip_call_ra_chain(skb))
        return 0;
```

There are implementations where the router alert option is not set, as explained in the following comment; these cases must be handled as well, by calling the raw_rcv() method directly:

```
} else if (ip_hdr(skb)->protocol == IPPROTO_IGMP) {
        /* IGMPv1 (and broken IGMPv2 implementations sort of
         * Cisco IOS <= 11.2(8)) do not put router alert
         * option to IGMP packets destined to routable
         * groups. It is very bad, because it means
         * that we can forward NO IGMP messages.
         */
        struct sock *mroute_sk;
```

The mrt->mroute_sk socket is a copy in the kernel of the socket that the multicast routing userspace application created:

```
mroute_sk = rcu_dereference(mrt->mroute_sk);
        if (mroute_sk) {
        nf_reset(skb);
        raw_rcv(mroute_sk, skb);
        return 0;
        }
    }
}
```

First a lookup in the multicast routing cache, mfc_cache_array, is performed by calling the ipmr_cache_find() method. The hash key is the destination multicast group address and the source IP address of the packet, taken from the IPv4 header:

```
cache = ipmr_cache_find(mrt, ip_hdr(skb)->saddr, ip_hdr(skb)->daddr);
if (cache == NULL) {
```

A lookup in the virtual devices array (vif_table) is performed to see whether there is a corresponding entry which matches the incoming network device (skb->dev):

```
int vif = ipmr_find_vif(mrt, skb->dev);
```

The ipmr_cache_find_any() method handles the advanced feature of multicast proxy support (which is not discussed in this book):

```
        if (vif >= 0)
                cache = ipmr_cache_find_any(mrt, ip_hdr(skb)->daddr,
                                            vif);
}
```

```
/*
 *       No usable cache entry
 */
if (cache == NULL) {
        int vif;
```

If the packet is destined to the local host, deliver it:

```
if (local) {
        struct sk_buff *skb2 = skb_clone(skb, GFP_ATOMIC);
        ip_local_deliver(skb);
        if (skb2 == NULL)
                return -ENOBUFS;
        skb = skb2;
}

read_lock(&mrt_lock);
vif = ipmr_find_vif(mrt, skb->dev);
if (vif >= 0) {
```

The ipmr_cache_unresolved() method creates a multicast routing entry (mfc_cache object) by calling the ipmr_cache_alloc_unres() method. This method creates a cache entry (mfc_cache object) and initializes its expiration time interval (by setting mfc_un.unres.expires). Let's take a look at this very short method, ipmr_cache_alloc_unres():

```
static struct mfc_cache *ipmr_cache_alloc_unres(void)
{
    struct mfc_cache *c = kmem_cache_zalloc(mrt_cachep, GFP_ATOMIC);

    if (c) {
        skb_queue_head_init(&c->mfc_un.unres.unresolved);
```

Setting the expiration time interval:

```
        c->mfc_un.unres.expires = jiffies + 10*HZ;
    }
    return c;
}
```

If the routing daemon does not resolve the routing entry within its expiration interval, the entry is removed from the queue of the unresolved entries. When creating a multicast routing table (by the ipmr_new_table() method), its timer (ipmr_expire_timer) is set. This timer invokes the ipmr_expire_process() method periodically. The ipmr_expire_process() method iterates over all the unresolved cache entries in the queue of unresolved entries (mfc_unres_queue of the mrtable object) and removes the expired unresolved cache entries.

After creating the unresolved cache entry, the ipmr_cache_unresolved() method adds it to the queue of unresolved entries (mfc_unres_queue of the multicast table, mrtable) and increments by 1 the unresolved queue length (cache_resolve_queue_len of the multicast table, mrtable). It also calls the ipmr_cache_report() method, which builds an IGMP message (IGMPMSG_NOCACHE) and delivers it to the userspace multicast routing daemon by calling eventually the sock_queue_rcv_skb() method.

I mentioned that the userspace routing daemon should resolve the routing within some time interval. I will not delve into how this is implemented in userspace. Note, however, that once the routing daemon decides it should resolve an unresolved entry, it builds the cache entry parameters (in an mfcctl object) and calls setsockopt() with the MRT_ADD_MFC socket option, then it passes the mfcctl object embedded in the optval parameter of the setsockopt() system call; this is handled in the kernel by the ipmr_mfc_add() method:

```
            int err2 = ipmr_cache_unresolved(mrt, vif, skb);
            read_unlock(&mrt_lock);

            return err2;
        }
    read_unlock(&mrt_lock);
    kfree_skb(skb);
    return -ENODEV;
}

read_lock(&mrt_lock);
```

If a cache entry was found in the MFC, call the ip_mr_forward() method to continue the packet traversal:

```
    ip_mr_forward(net, mrt, skb, cache, local);
    read_unlock(&mrt_lock);

    if (local)
            return ip_local_deliver(skb);

    return 0;

dont_forward:
    if (local)
            return ip_local_deliver(skb);
    kfree_skb(skb);
    return 0;
}
```

This section detailed the IPv4 Multicast Rx path and the interaction with the routing daemon in this path. The next section describes the multicast routing forwarding method, ip_mr_forward().

The ip_mr_forward() Method

Let's take a look at the ip_mr_forward() method:

```
static int ip_mr_forward(struct net *net, struct mr_table *mrt,
            struct sk_buff *skb, struct mfc_cache *cache,
            int local)
{
    int psend = -1;
    int vif, ct;
    int true_vifi = ipmr_find_vif(mrt, skb->dev);

    vif = cache->mfc_parent;
```

Here you can see update statistics of the resolved cache object (mfc_un.res):

```
cache->mfc_un.res.pkt++;
cache->mfc_un.res.bytes += skb->len;

if (cache->mfc_origin == htonl(INADDR_ANY) && true_vifi >= 0) {
    struct mfc_cache *cache_proxy;
```

The expression (*, G) means traffic from any source sending to the group G:

```
    /* For an (*,G) entry, we only check that the incomming
     * interface is part of the static tree.
     */
    cache_proxy = ipmr_cache_find_any_parent(mrt, vif);
    if (cache_proxy &&
        cache_proxy->mfc_un.res.ttls[true_vifi] < 255)
        goto forward;
}
/*
 * Wrong interface: drop packet and (maybe) send PIM assert.
 */
if (mrt->vif_table[vif].dev != skb->dev) {
    if (rt_is_output_route(skb_rtable(skb))) {
        /* It is our own packet, looped back.
         * Very complicated situation...
         *
         * The best workaround until routing daemons will be
         * fixed is not to redistribute packet, if it was
         * send through wrong interface. It means, that
         * multicast applications WILL NOT work for
         * (S,G), which have default multicast route pointing
         * to wrong oif. In any case, it is not a good
         * idea to use multicasting applications on router.
         */
        goto dont_forward;
    }

    cache->mfc_un.res.wrong_if++;

    if (true_vifi >= 0 && mrt->mroute_do_assert &&
        /* pimsm uses asserts, when switching from RPT to SPT,
         * so that we cannot check that packet arrived on an oif.
         * It is bad, but otherwise we would need to move pretty
         * large chunk of pimd to kernel. Ough... --ANK
         */
        (mrt->mroute_do_pim ||
        cache->mfc_un.res.ttls[true_vifi] < 255) &&
        time_after(jiffies,
                cache->mfc_un.res.last_assert + MFC_ASSERT_THRESH)) {
        cache->mfc_un.res.last_assert = jiffies;
```

Call the `ipmr_cache_report()` method to build an IGMP message (IGMPMSG_WRONGVIF) and to deliver it to the userspace multicast routing daemon by calling the `sock_queue_rcv_skb()` method:

```
        ipmr_cache_report(mrt, skb, true_vifi, IGMPMSG_WRONGVIF);
    }
    goto dont_forward;
}
```

The frame is now ready to be forwarded:

```
forward:
    mrt->vif_table[vif].pkt_in++;
    mrt->vif_table[vif].bytes_in += skb->len;

    /*
     *    Forward the frame
     */
    if (cache->mfc_origin == htonl(INADDR_ANY) &&
        cache->mfc_mcastgrp == htonl(INADDR_ANY)) {
        if (true_vifi >= 0 &&
            true_vifi != cache->mfc_parent &&
            ip_hdr(skb)->ttl >
                cache->mfc_un.res.ttls[cache->mfc_parent]) {
            /* It's an (*,*) entry and the packet is not coming from
             * the upstream; forward the packet to the upstream
             * only.
             */
            psend = cache->mfc_parent;
            goto last_forward;
        }
        goto dont_forward;
    }
    for (ct = cache->mfc_un.res.maxvif - 1;
         ct >= cache->mfc_un.res.minvif; ct--) {
        /* For (*,G) entry, don't forward to the incoming interface */
        if ((cache->mfc_origin != htonl(INADDR_ANY) ||
            ct != true_vifi) &&
            ip_hdr(skb)->ttl > cache->mfc_un.res.ttls[ct]) {
            if (psend != -1) {
                struct sk_buff *skb2 = skb_clone(skb, GFP_ATOMIC);
```

Call the `ipmr_queue_xmit()` method to continue with the packet forwarding:

```
                if (skb2)
                    ipmr_queue_xmit(net, mrt, skb2, cache,
                            psend);
            }
            psend = ct;
        }
    }
last_forward:
```

```
        if (psend != -1) {
            if (local) {
                struct sk_buff *skb2 = skb_clone(skb, GFP_ATOMIC);

                if (skb2)
                    ipmr_queue_xmit(net, mrt, skb2, cache, psend);
            } else {
                ipmr_queue_xmit(net, mrt, skb, cache, psend);
                return 0;
            }
        }
    }

dont_forward:
    if (!local)
        kfree_skb(skb);
    return 0;
}
```

Now that I have covered the multicast routing forwarding method, ip_mr_forward(), it is time to examine the ipmr_queue_xmit() method.

The ipmr_queue_xmit() Method

Let's take a look at the ipmr_queue_xmit() method:

```
static void ipmr_queue_xmit(struct net *net, struct mr_table *mrt,
                            struct sk_buff *skb, struct mfc_cache *c, int vifi)
{
        const struct iphdr *iph = ip_hdr(skb);
        struct vif_device *vif = &mrt->vif_table[vifi];
        struct net_device *dev;
        struct rtable *rt;
        struct flowi4 fl4;
```

The encap field is used when working with a tunnel:

```
        int encap = 0;

        if (vif->dev == NULL)
                goto out_free;

#ifdef CONFIG_IP_PIMSM
        if (vif->flags & VIFF_REGISTER) {
                vif->pkt_out++;
                vif->bytes_out += skb->len;
                vif->dev->stats.tx_bytes += skb->len;
                vif->dev->stats.tx_packets++;
                ipmr_cache_report(mrt, skb, vifi, IGMPMSG_WHOLEPKT);
                goto out_free;
        }
#endif
```

When working with a tunnel, a routing lookup is performed with the vif->remote and vif->local, which represent the destination and local addresses, respectively. These addresses are the end points of the tunnel. When working with a vif_device object which represents a physical device, a routing lookup is performed with the destination of the IPv4 header and 0 as a source address:

```
if (vif->flags & VIFF_TUNNEL) {
        rt = ip_route_output_ports(net, &fl4, NULL,
                                   vif->remote, vif->local,
                                   0, 0,
                                   IPPROTO_IPIP,
                                   RT_TOS(iph->tos), vif->link);
        if (IS_ERR(rt))
                goto out_free;
        encap = sizeof(struct iphdr);
} else {
        rt = ip_route_output_ports(net, &fl4, NULL, iph->daddr, 0,
                                   0, 0,
                                   IPPROTO_IPIP,
                                   RT_TOS(iph->tos), vif->link);
        if (IS_ERR(rt))
                goto out_free;
}

dev = rt->dst.dev;
```

Note that if the packet size is higher than the MTU, an ICMPv4 message is not sent (as is done in such a case under unicast forwarding); only the statistics are updated, and the packet is discarded:

```
if (skb->len+encap > dst_mtu(&rt->dst) && (ntohs(iph->frag_off) & IP_DF)) {
        /* Do not fragment multicasts. Alas, IPv4 does not
         * allow to send ICMP, so that packets will disappear
         * to blackhole.
         */

        IP_INC_STATS_BH(dev_net(dev), IPSTATS_MIB_FRAGFAILS);
        ip_rt_put(rt);
        goto out_free;
}

encap += LL_RESERVED_SPACE(dev) + rt->dst.header_len;

if (skb_cow(skb, encap)) {
        ip_rt_put(rt);
        goto out_free;
}

vif->pkt_out++;
vif->bytes_out += skb->len;

skb_dst_drop(skb);
skb_dst_set(skb, &rt->dst);
```

The TTL is decreased, and the IPv4 header checksum is recalculated (because the TTL is one of the IPv4 fields) when forwarding the packet; the same is done in the ip_forward() method for unicast packets:

```
ip_decrease_ttl(ip_hdr(skb));

/* FIXME: forward and output firewalls used to be called here.
 * What do we do with netfilter? -- RR
 */
if (vif->flags & VIFF_TUNNEL) {
        ip_encap(skb, vif->local, vif->remote);
        /* FIXME: extra output firewall step used to be here. --RR */
        vif->dev->stats.tx_packets++;
        vif->dev->stats.tx_bytes += skb->len;
}

IPCB(skb)->flags |= IPSKB_FORWARDED;

/*
 * RFC1584 teaches, that DVMRP/PIM router must deliver packets locally
 * not only before forwarding, but after forwarding on all output
 * interfaces. It is clear, if mrouter runs a multicasting
 * program, it should receive packets not depending to what interface
 * program is joined.
 * If we will not make it, the program will have to join on all
 * interfaces. On the other hand, multihoming host (or router, but
 * not mrouter) cannot join to more than one interface - it will
 * result in receiving multiple packets.
 */
```

Invoke the NF_INET_FORWARD hook:

```
        NF_HOOK(NFPROTO_IPV4, NF_INET_FORWARD, skb, skb->dev, dev,
                ipmr_forward_finish);
        return;

out_free:
        kfree_skb(skb);
}
```

The ipmr_forward_finish() Method

Let's take a look at the ipmr_forward_finish() method, which is a very short method—it is in fact identical to the ip_forward() method:

```
static inline int ipmr_forward_finish(struct sk_buff *skb)
{
        struct ip_options *opt = &(IPCB(skb)->opt);

        IP_INC_STATS_BH(dev_net(skb_dst(skb)->dev), IPSTATS_MIB_OUTFORWDATAGRAMS);
        IP_ADD_STATS_BH(dev_net(skb_dst(skb)->dev), IPSTATS_MIB_OUTOCTETS, skb->len);
```

Handle IPv4 options, if set (see Chapter 4):

```
    if (unlikely(opt->optlen))
            ip_forward_options(skb);

    return dst_output(skb);
}
```

Eventually, `dst_output()` sends the packet via the `ip_mc_output()` method, which calls the `ip_finish_output()` method (both methods are in `net/ipv4/route.c`).

Now that I have covered these multicast methods, let's get a better understanding of how the value of the TTL field is used in multicast traffic.

The TTL in Multicast Traffic

The TTL field of the IPv4 header has a double meaning when discussing multicast traffic. The first is the same as in unicast IPV4 traffic: the TTL represents a hop counter which is decreased by 1 on every device that is forwarding the packet. When it reaches 0, the packet is discarded. This is done to avoid endless travelling of packets due to some error. The second meaning of the TTL, which is unique to multicast traffic, is a threshold. The TTL values are divided into scopes. Routers have a TTL threshold assigned to each of their interfaces, and only packets with a TTL greater than the interface's threshold are forwarded. Here are the values of these thresholds:

- *0:* Restricted to the same host (cannot be sent out by any interface)

- *1:* Restricted to the same subnet (will not be forwarded by a router)

- *32:* Restricted to the same site

- *64:* Restricted to the same region

- *128:* Restricted to the same continent

- *255:* Unrestricted in scope (global)

See: "IP Multicast Extensions for 4.3BSD UNIX and related systems," by Steve Deering, available at www.kohala.com/start/mcast.api.txt.

■ **Note** IPv4 Multicast Routing is implemented in `net/ipv4/ipmr.c`, `include/linux/mroute.h`, and `include/uapi/linux/mroute.h`.

This completes my discussion of Multicast Routing. The chapter now moves on to Policy Routing, which enables you to configure routing policies that are not based solely on the destination address.

Policy Routing

With Policy Routing, a system administrator can define up to 255 routing tables. This section discusses IPv4 Policy Routing; IPv6 Policy Routing is discussed in Chapter 8. In this section, I use the terms *policy* or *rule* for entries that are created by Policy Routing, in order to avoid confusing the ordinary routing entries (discussed in Chapter 5) with policy rules.

Policy Routing Management

Policy Routing management is done with the `ip rule` command of the `iproute2` package (there is no parallel for Policy Routing management with the `route` command). Let's see how to add, delete, and dump all Policy Routing rules:

- You add a rule with the `ip rule add` command; for example: `ip rule add tos 0x04 table 252`. After this rule is inserted, every packet which has an IPv4 TOS field matching 0x04 will be handled according to the routing rules of table 252. You can add routing entries to this table by specifying the table number when adding a route; for example: `ip route add default via 192.168.2.10 table 252`. This command is handled in the kernel by the `fib_nl_newrule()` method, in `net/core/fib_rules.c`. The `tos` modifier in the `ip rule` command earlier is one of the available SELECTOR modifiers of the `ip rule` command; see `man 8 ip rule`, and also Table 6-1 in the "Quick Reference" section at the end of this chapter.

- You delete a rule with the `ip rule del` command; for example: `ip rule del tos 0x04 table 252`. This command is handled in the kernel by the `fib_nl_delrule()` method in `net/core/fib_rules.c`.

- You dump all the rules with the `ip rule list` command or the `ip rule show` command. Both these commands are handled in the kernel by the `fib_nl_dumprule()` method in `net/core/fib_rules.c`.

You now have a good idea about the basics of Policy Routing management, so let's examine the Linux implementation of Policy Routing.

Policy Routing Implementation

The core infrastructure of Policy Routing is the `fib_rules` module, `net/core/fib_rules.c`. It is used by three protocols of the kernel networking stack: IPv4 (including the multicast module, which has a multicast policy routing feature, as mentioned in the "Multicast Routing" section earlier in this chapter), IPv6, and DECnet. The IPv4 Policy Routing is implemented also in a file named `fib_rules.c`. Don't be confused by the identical name (`net/ipv4/fib_rules.c`). In IPv6, policy routing is implemented in `net/ipv6/fib6_rules.c`. The header file, `include/net/fib_rules.h`, contains the data structures and methods of the Policy Routing core. Here is the definition of the `fib4_rule` structure, which is the basis for IPv4 Policy Routing:

```
struct fib4_rule {
    struct fib_rule    common;
    u8              dst_len;
    u8              src_len;
    u8              tos;
    __be32             src;
    __be32             srcmask;
    __be32             dst;
    __be32             dstmask;
#ifdef CONFIG_IP_ROUTE_CLASSID
    u32                tclassid;
#endif
};
```

(net/ipv4/fib_rules.c)

Three policies are created by default at boot time, by calling the `fib_default_rules_init()` method: the local (RT_TABLE_LOCAL) table, the main (RT_TABLE_MAIN) table, and the default (RT_TABLE_DEFAULT) table. Lookup is done by the `fib_lookup()` method. Note that there are two different implementations of the `fib_lookup()` method in include/net/ip_fib.h. The first one, which is wrapped in the #ifndef CONFIG_IP_MULTIPLE_TABLES block, is for non-Policy Routing, and the second is for Policy Routing. When working with Policy Routing, the lookup is performed like this: if there were no changes to the initial policy routing rules (`net->ipv4.fib_has_custom_rules` is not set), that means the rule must be in one of the three initial routing tables. So, first a lookup is done in the local table, then in the main table, and then the default table. If there is no corresponding entry, a network unreachable (-ENETUNREACH) error is returned. If there was some change in the initial policy routing rules (`net->ipv4.fib_has_custom_rules` is set), the_fib_lookup() method is invoked, which is a heavier method, because it iterates over the list of rules and calls `fib_rule_match()` for each rule in order to decide whether it matches or not. See the implementation of the `fib_rules_lookup()` method in net/core/fib_rules.c. (The `fib_rules_lookup()` method is invoked from the `__fib_lookup()` method). I should mention here that the `net->ipv4.fib_has_custom_rules` variable is set to false in the initialization phase, by the `fib4_rules_init()` method, and to true in the `fib4_rule_configure()` method and the `fib4_rule_delete()` method. Note that CONFIG_IP_MULTIPLE_TABLES should be set for working with Policy Routing.

This concludes my Multicast Routing discussion. The next section talks about Multipath Routing, which is the ability to add more than one nexthop to a route.

Multipath Routing

Multipath Routing provides the ability to add more than one nexthop to a route. Defining two nexthop nodes can be done like this, for example: `ip route add default scope global nexthop dev eth0 nexthop dev eth1`. A system administrator can also assign weights for each nexthop—like this, for example: `ip route add 192.168.1.10 nexthop via 192.168.2.1 weight 3 nexthop via 192.168.2.10 weight 5`. The `fib_info` structure represents an IPv4 routing entry that can have more than one FIB nexthop. The `fib_nhs` member of the `fib_info` object represents the number of FIB nexthop objects; the `fib_info` object contains an array of FIB nexthop objects named `fib_nh`. So in this case, a single `fib_info` object is created, with an array of two FIB nexthop objects. The kernel keeps the weight of each next hop in the nh_weight field of the FIB nexthop object (`fib_nh`). If weight was not specified when adding a multipath route, it is set by default to 1, in the `fib_create_info()` method. The `fib_select_multipath()` method is called to determine the nexthop when working with Multipath Routing. This method is invoked from two places: from the `__ip_route_output_key()` method, in the Tx path, and from the `ip_mkroute_input()` method, in the Rx path. Note that when the output device is set in the flow, the `fib_select_multipath()` method is not invoked, because the output device is known:

```
struct rtable *__ip_route_output_key(struct net *net, struct flowi4 *fl4) {
. . .
#ifdef CONFIG_IP_ROUTE_MULTIPATH
    if (res.fi->fib_nhs > 1 && fl4->flowi4_oif == 0)
        fib_select_multipath(&res);
    else
#endif
. . .

}
```

In the Rx path there is no need for checking whether fl4->flowi4_oif is 0, because it is set to 0 in the beginning of this method. I won't delve into the details of the `fib_select_multipath()` method. I will only mention that there is an element of randomness in the method, using `jiffies`, for helping in creating a fair weighted route distribution, and that the weight of each next hop is taken in account. The FIB nexthop to use is assigned by setting the FIB nexthop selector (nh_sel) of the specified `fib_result` object. In contrast to Multicast Routing, which is handled by a dedicated module (`net/ipv4/ipmr.c`), the code of Multipath Routing appears scattered in the existing routing code, enclosed in `#ifdef CONFIG_IP_ROUTE_MULTIPATH` conditionals, and no separate module was added in the source code for supporting it. As mentioned in Chapter 5, there was support for IPv4 multipath routing cache, but it was removed in 2007 in kernel 2.6.23; in fact, it never did work very well, and never got out of the experimental state. Do not confuse the removal of the multipath routing cache with the removal of the routing cache; these are two different caches. The removal of the routing cache took place five years later, in kernel 3.6 (2012).

■ **NOTE** CONFIG_IP_ROUTE_MULTIPATH should be set for Multipath Routing Support.

Summary

This chapter covered advanced IPv4 routing topics, like Multicast Routing, the IGMP protocol, Policy Routing, and Multipath Routing. You learned about the fundamental structures of Multicast Routing, such as the multicast table (`mr_table`), the multicast forwarding cache (MFC), the Vif device, and more. You also learned what should be done to set a host to be a multicast router, and all about the use of the `ttl` field in Multicast Routing. Chapter 7 deals with the Linux neighbouring subsystem. The "Quick Reference" section that follows covers the top methods related to the topics discussed in this chapter, ordered by their context.

Quick Reference

I conclude this chapter with a short list of important routing subsystem methods (some of which were mentioned in this chapter), a list of macros, and `procfs` multicast entries and tables.

Methods

Let's start with the methods:

int ip_mroute_setsockopt(struct sock *sk, int optname, char __user *optval, unsigned int optlen);

This method handles `setsockopt()` calls from the multicast routing daemon. The supported socket options are: MRT_INIT, MRT_DONE, MRT_ADD_VIF, MRT_DEL_VIF, MRT_ADD_MFC, MRT_DEL_MFC, MRT_ADD_MFC_PROXY, MRT_DEL_MFC_PROXY, MRT_ASSERT, MRT_PIM (when PIM support is set), and MRT_TABLE (when Multicast Policy Routing is set).

int ip_mroute_getsockopt(struct sock *sk, int optname, char __user *optval, int __user *optlen);

This method handles `getsockopt()` calls from the multicast routing daemon. The supported socket options are MRT_VERSION, MRT_ASSERT and MRT_PIM.

struct mr_table *ipmr_new_table(struct net *net, u32 id);

This method creates a new multicast routing table. The id of the table will be the specified id.

void ipmr_free_table(struct mr_table *mrt);

This method frees the specified multicast routing table and the resources attached to it.

int ip_mc_join_group(struct sock *sk , struct ip_mreqn *imr);

This method is for joining a multicast group. The address of the multicast group to be joined is specified in the given ip_mreqn object. The method returns 0 on success.

static struct mfc_cache *ipmr_cache_find(struct mr_table *mrt, __be32 origin, __be32 mcastgrp);

This method performs a lookup in the IPv4 multicast routing cache. It returns NULL when no entry is found.

bool ipv4_is_multicast(__be32 addr);

This method returns true if the address is a multicast address.

int ip_mr_input(struct sk_buff *skb);

This method is the main IPv4 multicast Rx method (net/ipv4/ipmr.c).

struct mfc_cache *ipmr_cache_alloc(void);

This method allocates a multicast forwarding cache (mfc_cache) entry.

static struct mfc_cache *ipmr_cache_alloc_unres(void);

This method allocates a multicast routing cache (mfc_cache) entry for the unresolved cache and sets the expires field of the queue of unresolved entries.

void fib_select_multipath(struct fib_result *res);

This method is called to determine the nexthop when working with Multipath Routing.

int dev_set_allmulti(struct net_device *dev, int inc);

This method increments/decrements the allmulti counter of the specified network device according to the specified increment (the increment can be a positive number or a negative number).

int igmp_rcv(struct sk_buff *skb);

This method is the receive handler for IGMP packets.

static int ipmr_mfc_add(struct net *net, struct mr_table *mrt, struct mfcctl *mfc, int mrtsock, int parent);

This method adds a multicast cache entry; it is invoked by calling setsockopt() from userspace with MRT_ADD_MFC.

static int ipmr_mfc_delete(struct mr_table *mrt, struct mfcctl *mfc, int parent);

This method deletes a multicast cache entry; it is invoked by calling setsockopt() from userspace with MRT_DEL_MFC.

static int vif_add(struct net *net, struct mr_table *mrt, struct vifctl *vifc, int mrtsock);

This method adds a multicast virtual interface; it is invoked by calling setsockopt() from userspace with MRT_ADD_VIF.

static int vif_delete(struct mr_table *mrt, int vifi, int notify, struct list_head *head);

This method deletes a multicast virtual interface; it is invoked by calling setsockopt() from userspace with MRT_DEL_VIF.

static void ipmr_expire_process(unsigned long arg);

This method removes expired entries from the queue of unresolved entries.

static int ipmr_cache_report(struct mr_table *mrt, struct sk_buff *pkt, vifi_t vifi, int assert);

This method builds an IGMP packet, setting the type in the IGMP header to be the specified assert value and the code to be 0. This IGMP packet is delivered to the userspace multicast routing daemon by calling the sock_queue_rcv_skb() method. The assert parameter can be assigned one of these values: IGMPMSG_NOCACHE, when an unresolved cache entry is added to the queue of unresolved entries and wants to notify the userspace routing daemon that it should resolve it, IGMPMSG_WRONGVIF, and IGMPMSG_WHOLEPKT.

static int ipmr_device_event(struct notifier_block *this, unsigned long event, void *ptr);

This method is a notifier callback which is registered by the register_netdevice_notifier() method; when some network device is unregistered, a NETDEV_UNREGISTER event is generated; this callback receives this event and deletes the vif_device objects in the vif_table, whose device is the one that was unregistered.

static void mrtsock_destruct(struct sock *sk);

This method is called when the userspace routing daemon calls `setsockopt()` with MRT_DONE. This method nullifies the multicast routing socket (`mroute_sk` of the multicast routing table), decrements the `mc_forwarding` procfs entry, and calls the `mroute_clean_tables()` method to free resources.

Macros

This section describes our macros.

MFC_HASH(a,b)

This macro calculates the hash value for adding entries to the MFC cache. It takes the group multicast address and the source IPv4 address as parameters.

VIF_EXISTS(_mrt, _idx)

This macro checks the existence of an entry in the `vif_table`; it returns `true` if the array of multicast virtual devices (`vif_table`) of the specified multicast routing table (`mrt`) has an entry with the specified index (`_idx`).

Procfs Multicast Entries

The following is a description of two important `procfs` multicast entries:

/proc/net/ip_mr_vif

Lists all the multicast virtual interfaces; it displays all the `vif_device` objects in the multicast virtual device table (`vif_table`). Displaying the `/proc/net/ip_mr_vif` entry is handled by the `ipmr_vif_seq_show()` method.

/proc/net/ip_mr_cache

The state of the Multicast Forwarding Cache (MFC). This entry shows the following fields of all the cache entries: group multicast address (`mfc_mcastgrp`), source IP address (`mfc_origin`), input interface index (`mfc_parent`), forwarded packets (`mfc_un.res.pkt`), forwarded bytes (`mfc_un.res.bytes`), wrong interface index (`mfc_un.res.wrong_if`), the index of the forwarding interface (an index in the `vif_table`), and the entry in the `mfc_un.res.ttls` array corresponding to this index. Displaying the `/proc/net/ip_mr_cache` entry is handled by the `ipmr_mfc_seq_show()` method.

Table

And finally, here in Table 6-1, is the table of rule selectors.

Table 6-1. *IP Rule Selectors*

Linux Symbol	Selector	Member of fib_rule	fib4_rule
FRA_SRC	from	src	(fib4_rule)
FRA_DST	to	dst	(fib4_rule)
FRA_IIFNAME	iif	iifname	(fib_rule)
FRA_OIFNAME	oif	oifname	(fib_rule)
FRA_FWMARK	fwmark	mark	(fib_rule)
FRA_FWMASK	fwmark/fwmask	mark_mask	(fib_rule)
FRA_PRIORITY	preference,order,priority	pref	(fib_rule)
-	tos, dsfield	tos	(fib4_rule)

CHAPTER 7

■ ■ ■

Linux Neighbouring Subsystem

This chapter discusses the Linux neighbouring subsystem and its implementation in Linux. The neighbouring subsystem is responsible for the discovery of the presence of nodes on the same link and for translation of L3 (network layer) addresses to L2 (link layer) addresses. L2 addresses are needed to build the L2 header for outgoing packets, as described in the next section. The protocol that implements this translation is called the Address Resolution Protocol (ARP) in IPv4 and Neighbour Discovery protocol (NDISC or ND) in IPv6. The neighbouring subsystem provides a protocol-independent infrastructure for performing L3-to-L2 mappings. The discussion in this chapter, however, is restricted to the most common cases—namely, the neighbouring subsystem usage in IPv4 and in IPv6. Keep in mind that the ARP protocol, like the ICMP protocol discussed in Chapter 3, is subject to security threats—such as ARP poisoning attacks and ARP spoofing attacks (security aspects of the ARP protocol are beyond the scope of this book).

I first discuss the common neighbouring data structures in this chapter and some important API methods, which are used both in IPv4 and in IPv6. Then I discuss the particular implementations of the ARP protocol and NDISC protocol. You will see how a neighbour is created and how it is freed, and you will learn about the interaction between userspace and the neighbouring subsystem. You will also learn about ARP requests and ARP replies, about NDISC neighbour solicitation and NDISC neighbour advertisements, and about a mechanism called Duplicate Address Detection (DAD), which is used by the NDISC protocol to avoid duplicate IPv6 addresses.

The Neighbouring Subsystem Core

What is the neighbouring subsystem needed for? When a packet is sent over the L2 layer, the L2 destination address is needed to build an L2 header. Using the neighbouring subsystem solicitation requests and solicitation replies, the L2 address of a host can be found out given its L3 address (or the fact that such L3 address does not exist). In Ethernet, which is the most commonly used link layer (L2), the L2 address of a host is its MAC address. In IPv4, ARP is the neighbouring protocol, and solicitation requests and solicitation replies are called ARP requests and ARP replies, respectively. In IPv6, the neighbouring protocol is NDISC, and solicitation requests and solicitation replies are called neighbour solicitations and neighbour advertisements, respectively.

There are cases where the destination address can be found without any help from the neighbouring subsystem—for example, when a broadcast is sent. In this case, the destination L2 address is fixed (for example, it is FF:FF:FF:FF:FF:FF in Ethernet). Or when the destination address is a multicast address, there is a fixed mapping between the L3 multicast address to its L2 address. I discuss such cases in the course of this chapter.

The basic data structure of the Linux neighbouring subsystem is the neighbour. A *neighbour* represents a network node that is attached to the same link (L2). It is represented by the neighbour structure. This representation is not unique for a particular protocol. However, as mentioned, the discussion of the neighbour structure will be restricted to its use in the IPv4 and in the IPv6 protocols. Let's take a look in the neighbour structure:

```
struct neighbour {
        struct neighbour __rcu   *next;
        struct neigh_table       *tbl;
```

```
        struct neigh_parms      *parms;
        unsigned long           confirmed;
        unsigned long           updated;
        rwlock_t                lock;
        atomic_t                refcnt;
        struct sk_buff_head     arp_queue;
        unsigned int            arp_queue_len_bytes;
        struct timer_list       timer;
        unsigned long           used;
        atomic_t                probes;
        __u8                    flags;
        __u8                    nud_state;
        __u8                    type;
        __u8                    dead;
        seqlock_t               ha_lock;
        unsigned char           ha[ALIGN(MAX_ADDR_LEN, sizeof(unsigned long))];
        struct hh_cache         hh;
        int                     (*output)(struct neighbour *, struct sk_buff *);
        const struct neigh_ops  *ops;
        struct rcu_head         rcu;
        struct net_device       *dev;
        u8                      primary_key[0];
};
```

(include/net/neighbour.h)

The following is a description of some of the important members of the neighbour structure:

- next: A pointer to the next neighbour on the same bucket in the hash table.

- tbl: The neighbouring table associated to this neighbour.

- parms: The neigh_parms object associated to this neighbour. It is initialized by the constructor method of the associated neighbouring table. For example, in IPv4 the arp_constructor() method initializes parms to be the arp_parms of the associated network device. Do not confuse it with the neigh_parms object of the neighbouring table.

- confirmed: Confirmation timestamp (discussed later in this chapter).

- refcnt: Reference counter. Incremented by the neigh_hold() macro and decremented by the neigh_release() method. The neigh_release() method frees the neighbour object by calling the neigh_destroy() method only if after decrementing the reference counter its value is 0.

- arp_queue: A queue of unresolved SKBs. Despite the name, this member is not unique to ARP and is used by other protocols, such as the NDISC protocol.

- timer: Every neighbour object has a timer; the timer callback is the neigh_timer_handler() method. The neigh_timer_handler() method can change the Network Unreachability Detection (NUD) state of the neighbour. When sending solicitation requests, and the state of the neighbour is NUD_INCOMPLETE or NUD_PROBE, and the number of solicitation requests probes is higher or equal to neigh_max_probes(), then the state of the neighbour is set to be NUD_FAILED, and the neigh_invalidate() method is invoked.

- ha_lock: Provides access protection to the neighbour hardware address (ha).

- ha: The hardware address of the neighbour object; in the case of Ethernet, it is the MAC address of the neighbour.

- hh: A hardware header cache of the L2 header (An hh_cache object).

- output: A pointer to a transmit method, like the neigh_resolve_output() method or the neigh_direct_output() method. It is dependent on the NUD state and as a result can be assigned to different methods during a neighbour lifetime. When initializing the neighbour object in the neigh_alloc() method, it is set to be the neigh_blackhole() method, which discards the packet and returns -ENETDOWN.

  And here are the helper methods (methods which set the output callback):

  - void neigh_connect(struct neighbour *neigh)

    Sets the output() method of the specified neighbour to be neigh->ops->connected_output.

  - void neigh_suspect(struct neighbour *neigh)

    Sets the output() method of the specified neighbour to be neigh->ops->output.

- nud_state: The NUD state of the neighbour. The nud_state value can be changed dynamically during the lifetime of a neighbour object. Table 7-1 in the "Quick Reference" section at the end of this chapter describes the basic NUD states and their Linux symbols. The NUD state machine is very complex; I do not delve into all of its nuances in this book.

- dead: A flag that is set when the neighbour object is alive. It is initialized to 0 when creating a neighbour object, at the end of the __neigh_create() method. The neigh_destroy() method will fail for neighbour objects whose dead flag is not set. The neigh_flush_dev() method sets the dead flag to 1 but does not yet remove the neighbour entry. The removal of neighbours marked as dead (their dead flag is set) is done later, by the garbage collectors.

- primary_key: The IP address (L3) of the neighbour. A lookup in the neighbouring tables is done with the primary_key. The primary_key length is based on which protocol is used. For IPv4, for example, it should be 4 bytes. For IPv6 it should be sizeof(struct in6_addr), as the in6_addr structure represents an IPv6 address. Therefore, the primary_key is defined as an array of 0 bytes, and when allocating a neighbour it should be taken into account which protocol is used. See the explanation about entry_size and key_len later in this chapter, in the description of the neigh_table structure members.

To avoid sending solicitation requests for each new packet that is transmitted, the kernel keeps the mapping between L3 addresses and L2 addresses in a data structure called a neighbouring table; in the case of IPv4, it is the ARP table (sometimes also called the ARP cache, though they are the same)—in contrast to what you saw in the IPv4 routing subsystem in Chapter 5: the routing cache, before it was removed, and the routing table, were two different entities, which were represented by two different data structures. In the case of IPv6, the neighbouring table is the NDISC table (also known as the NDISC cache). Both the ARP table (arp_tbl) and the NDISC table (nd_tbl) are instances of the neigh_table structure. Let's take a look at the neigh_table structure:

```
struct neigh_table {
        struct neigh_table      *next;
        int                     family;
        int                     entry_size;
        int                     key_len;
        __u32                   (*hash)(const void *pkey,
                                        const struct net_device *dev,
                                        __u32 *hash_rnd);
```

```
int                    (*constructor)(struct neighbour *);
int                    (*pconstructor)(struct pneigh_entry *);
void                   (*pdestructor)(struct pneigh_entry *);
void                   (*proxy_redo)(struct sk_buff *skb);
char                   *id;
struct neigh_parms     parms;
/* HACK. gc_* should follow parms without a gap! */
int                    gc_interval;
int                    gc_thresh1;
int                    gc_thresh2;
int                    gc_thresh3;
unsigned long          last_flush;
struct delayed_work    gc_work;
struct timer_list      proxy_timer;
struct sk_buff_head    proxy_queue;
atomic_t               entries;
rwlock_t               lock;
unsigned long          last_rand;
struct neigh_statistics __percpu *stats;
struct neigh_hash_table __rcu *nht;
struct pneigh_entry    **phash_buckets;
};
```

(include/net/neighbour.h)

Here are some important members of the neigh_table structure:

- next: Each protocol creates its own neigh_table instance. There is a linked list of all the neighbouring tables in the system. The neigh_tables global variable is a pointer to the beginning of the list. The next variable points to the next item in this list.

- family: The protocol family: AF_INET for the IPv4 neighbouring table (arp_tbl), and AF_INET6 for the IPv6 neighbouring table (nd_tbl).

- entry_size: When allocating a neighbour entry by the neigh_alloc() method, the size for allocation is tbl->entry_size + dev->neigh_priv_len. Usually the neigh_priv_len value is 0. Before kernel 3.3, the entry_size was explicitly initialized to be sizeof(struct neighbour) + 4 for ARP, and sizeof(struct neighbour) + sizeof(struct in6_addr) for NDISC. The reason for this initialization was that when allocating a neighbour, you want to allocate space also for the primary_key[0] member. From kernel 3.3, the enrty_size was removed from the static initialization of arp_tbl and ndisc_tbl, and the entry_size initialization is done based on the key_len in the core neighbouring layer, by the neigh_table_init_no_netlink() method.

- key_len: The size of the lookup key; it is 4 bytes for IPv4, because the length of IPv4 address is 4 bytes, and it is sizeof(struct in6_addr) for IPv6. The in6_addr structure represents an IPv6 address.

- hash: The hash function for mapping a key (L3 address) to a specific hash value; for ARP it is the arp_hash() method. For NDISC it is the ndisc_hash() method.

- constructor: This method performs protocol-specific initialization when creating a neighbour object. For example, arp_constructor() for ARP in IPv4 and ndisc_constructor() for NDISC in IPv6. The constructor callback is invoked by the __neigh_create() method. It returns 0 on success.

- pconstructor: A method for creation of a neighbour proxy entry; it is not used by ARP, and it is pndisc_constructor for NDISC. This method should return 0 upon success. The pconstructor method is invoked from the pneigh_lookup() method if the lookup fails, on the condition that the pneigh_lookup() was invoked with creat = 1.

- pdestructor: A method for destroying a neighbour proxy entry. Like the pconstructor callback, the pdestructor is not used by ARP, and it is pndisc_destructor for NDISC. The pdestructor method is invoked from the pneigh_delete() method and from the pneigh_ifdown() method.

- id: The name of the table; it is arp_cache for IPv4 and ndisc_cache for IPv6.

- parms: A neigh_parms object: each neighbouring table has an associated neigh_parms object, which consists of various configuration settings, like reachability information, various timeouts, and more. The neigh_parms initialization is different in the ARP table and in the NDISC table.

- gc_interval: Not used directly by the neighbouring core.

- gc_thresh1, gc_thresh2, gc_thresh3: Thresholds of the number of neighbouring table entries. Used as criteria to activation of the synchronous garbage collector (neigh_forced_gc) and in the neigh_periodic_work() asynchronous garbage collector handler. See the explanation about allocating a neighbour object in the "Creating and Freeing a Neighbour" section later in this chapter. In the ARP table, the default values are: gc_thresh1 is 128, gc_thresh2 is 512, and gc_thresh3 is 1024. These values can be set by procfs. The same default values are also used in the NDISC table in IPv6. The IPv4 procfs entries are:

  - /proc/sys/net/ipv4/neigh/default/gc_thresh1

  - /proc/sys/net/ipv4/neigh/default/gc_thresh2

  - /proc/sys/net/ipv4/neigh/default/gc_thresh3

  and for IPv6, these are the procfs entries:

  - /proc/sys/net/ipv6/neigh/default/gc_thresh1

  - /proc/sys/net/ipv6/neigh/default/gc_thresh2

  - /proc/sys/net/ipv6/neigh/default/gc_thresh3

- last_flush: The most recent time when the neigh_forced_gc() method ran. It is initialized to be the current time (jiffies) in the neigh_table_init_no_netlink () method.

- gc_work: Asynchronous garbage collector handler. Set to be the neigh_periodic_work() timer by the neigh_table_init_no_netlink() method. The delayed_work struct is a type of a work queue. Before kernel 2.6.32, the neigh_periodic_timer() method was the asynchronous garbage collector handler; it processed only one bucket and not the entire neighbouring hash table. The neigh_periodic_work() method first checks whether the number of the entries in the table is less than gc_thresh1, and if so, it exits without doing anything; then it recomputes the reachable time (the reachable_time field of parms, which is the neigh_parms object associated with the neighbouring table). Then it scans the neighbouring hash table and removes entries which their state is not NUD_PERMANENT or NUD_IN_TIMER, and which their reference count is 1, and if one of these conditions is met: either they are in the NUD_FAILED state or the current time is after their used timestamp + gc_staletime (gc_staletime is a member of the neighbour parms object). Removal of the neighbour entry is done by setting the dead flag to 1 and calling the neigh_cleanup_and_release() method.

- proxy_timer: When a host is configured as an ARP proxy, it is possible to avoid immediate processing of solicitation requests and to process them with some delay. This is due to the fact that for an ARP proxy host, there can be a large number of solicitation requests (as opposed to the case when the host is not an ARP proxy, when you usually have a small amount of ARP requests). Sometimes you may prefer to delay the reply to such broadcasts so that you can give priority to hosts that own such IP addresses to be the first to get the request. This delay is a random value up to the proxy_delay parameter. The ARP proxy timer handler is the neigh_proxy_process() method. The proxy_timer is initialized by the neigh_table_init_no_netlink() method.

- proxy_queue: Proxy ARP queue of SKBs. SKBs are added with the pneigh_enqueue() method.

- stats: The neighbour statistics (neigh_statistics) object; consists of per CPU counters like allocs, which is the number of neighbour objects allocated by the neigh_alloc() method, or destroys, which is the number of neighbour objects which were freed by the neigh_destroy() method, and more. The neighbour statistics counters are incremented by the NEIGH_CACHE_STAT_INC macro. Note that because the statistics are per CPU counters, the macro this_cpu_inc() is used by this macro. You can display the ARP statistics and the NDISC statistics with cat /proc/net/stat/arp_cache and cat/proc/net/stat/ndisc_cache, respectively. In the "Quick Reference" section at the end of this chapter, there is a description of the neigh_statistics structure, specifying in which method each counter is incremented.

- nht: The neighbour hash table (neigh_hash_table object).

- phash_buckets: The neighbouring proxy hash table; allocated in the neigh_table_init_no_netlink() method.

The initialization of the neighbouring table is done with the neigh_table_init() method:

- In IPv4, the ARP module defines the ARP table (an instance of the neigh_table structure named arp_tbl) and passes it as an argument to the neigh_table_init() method (see the arp_init() method in net/ipv4/arp.c).

- In IPv6, the NDISC module defines the NDSIC table (which is also an instance of the neigh_table structure named nd_tbl) and passes it as an argument to the neigh_table_init() method (see the ndisc_init() method in net/ipv6/ndisc.c).

The neigh_table_init() method also creates the neighbouring hash table (the nht object) by calling the neigh_hash_alloc() method in the neigh_table_init_no_netlink() method, allocating space for eight hash entries:

```
static void neigh_table_init_no_netlink(struct neigh_table *tbl)
{
    . . .
    RCU_INIT_POINTER(tbl->nht, neigh_hash_alloc(3));
    . . .
}

static struct neigh_hash_table *neigh_hash_alloc(unsigned int shift)
{
```

The size of the hash table is 1<< shift (when size <= PAGE_SIZE):

```
size_t size = (1 << shift) * sizeof(struct neighbour *);
struct neigh_hash_table *ret;
struct neighbour __rcu **buckets;
int i;
```

```
    ret = kmalloc(sizeof(*ret), GFP_ATOMIC);
    if (!ret)
        return NULL;
    if (size <= PAGE_SIZE)
        buckets = kzalloc(size, GFP_ATOMIC);
    else
        buckets = (struct neighbour __rcu **)
                __get_free_pages(GFP_ATOMIC | __GFP_ZERO,
                        get_order(size));
    . . .

}
```

You may wonder why you need the neigh_table_init_no_netlink() method—why not perform all of the initialization in the neigh_table_init() method? The neigh_table_init_no_netlink() method performs all of the initializations of the neighbouring tables, except for linking it to the global linked list of neighbouring tables, neigh_tables. Originally such initialization, without linking to the neigh_tables linked list, was needed for ATM, and as a result the neigh_table_init() method was split, and the ATM clip module called the neigh_table_init_no_netlink() method instead of calling the neigh_table_init() method; however, over time, a different solution was found in ATM. Though the ATM clip module does not invoke the neigh_table_init_no_netlink() method anymore, the split of these methods remained, perhaps in case it is needed in the future.

I should mention that each L3 protocol that uses the neighbouring subsystem also registers a protocol handler: for IPv4, the handler for ARP packets (packets whose type in their Ethernet header is 0x0806) is the arp_rcv() method:

```
static struct packet_type arp_packet_type __read_mostly = {
        .type = cpu_to_be16(ETH_P_ARP),
        .func = arp_rcv,
};

void __init arp_init(void)
{
    . . .
        dev_add_pack(&arp_packet_type);
    . . .
}
```

(net/ipv4/arp.c)

For IPv6, the neighbouring messages are ICMPv6 messages, so they are handled by the icmpv6_rcv() method, which is the ICMPv6 handler. There are five ICMPv6 neighbouring messages; when each of them is received (by the icmpv6_rcv() method), the ndisc_rcv() method is invoked to handle them (see net/ipv6/icmp.c). The ndisc_rcv() method is discussed in a later section in this chapter. Each neighbour object defines a set of methods by the neigh_ops structure. This is done by its constructor method. The neigh_ops structure contains a protocol family member and four function pointers:

```
struct neigh_ops {
        int     family;
        void    (*solicit)(struct neighbour *, struct sk_buff *);
        void    (*error_report)(struct neighbour *, struct sk_buff *);
        int     (*output)(struct neighbour *, struct sk_buff *);
        int     (*connected_output)(struct neighbour *, struct sk_buff *);
};
```

(include/net/neighbour.h)

- `family`: AF_INET for IPv4 and AF_INET6 for IPv6.

- `solicit`: This method is responsible for sending the neighbour solicitation requests: in ARP it is the `arp_solicit()` method, and in NDISC it is the `ndisc_solicit()` method.

- `error_report`: This method is called from the `neigh_invalidate()` method when the neighbour state is NUD_FAILED. This happens, for example, after some timeout when a solicitation request is not replied.

- `output`: When the L3 address of the next hop is known, but the L2 address is not resolved, the output callback should be `neigh_resolve_output()`.

- `connected_output`: The output method of the neighbour is set to be `connected_output()` when the neighbour state is NUD_REACHABLE or NUD_CONNECTED. See the invocations of `neigh_connect()` in the `neigh_update()` method and in the `neigh_timer_handler()` method.

Creating and Freeing a Neighbour

A neighbour is created by the `__neigh_create()` method:

```
struct neighbour *__neigh_create(struct neigh_table *tbl, const void *pkey, struct
net_device *dev, bool want_ref)
```

First, the `__neigh_create()` method allocates a neighbour object by calling the `neigh_alloc()` method, which also performs various initializations. There are cases when the `neigh_alloc()` method calls the synchronous garbage collector (which is the `neigh_forced_gc()` method):

```
static struct neighbour *neigh_alloc(struct neigh_table *tbl, struct net_device *dev)
{
        struct neighbour *n = NULL;
        unsigned long now = jiffies;
        int entries;

        entries = atomic_inc_return(&tbl->entries) - 1;
```

If the number of table entries is greater than gc_thresh3 (1024 by default) or if the number of table entries is greater than gc_thresh2 (512 by default), and the time passed since the last flush is more than 5 Hz, the synchronous garbage collector method is invoked (the `neigh_forced_gc()` method). If after running the `neigh_forced_gc()` method, the number of table entries is greater than gc_thresh3 (1024), you do not allocate a neighbour object and return NULL:

```
        if (entries >= tbl->gc_thresh3 ||
            (entries >= tbl->gc_thresh2 &&
            time_after(now, tbl->last_flush + 5 * HZ))) {
                if (!neigh_forced_gc(tbl) &&
                    entries >= tbl->gc_thresh3)
                        goto out_entries;
        }
```

Then the `__neigh_create()` method performs the protocol-specific setup by calling the constructor method of the specified neighbouring table (`arp_constructor()` for ARP, `ndisc_constructor()` for NDISC). In the constructor method, special cases like multicast or loopback addresses are handled. In the arp_constructor() method, for example, you call the arp_mc_map() method to set the hardware address of the neighbour (ha) according to the neighbour IPv4 primary_key address, and you set the nud_state to be NUD_NOARP, because multicast addresses don't need ARP. In the ndisc_constructor() method, for example, you do something quite similar when handling multicast addresses: you call the ndisc_mc_map() to set the hardware address of the neighbour (ha) according to the neighbour IPv6 primary_key address, and you again set the nud_state to be NUD_NOARP. There's also special treatment for broadcast addresses: in the arp_constructor() method, for example, when the neighbour type is RTN_BROADCAST, you set the neighbour hardware address (ha) to be the network device broadcast address (the broadcast field of the net_device object), and you set the nud_state to be NUD_NOARP. Note that the IPv6 protocol does not implement traditional IP broadcast, so the notion of a broadcast address is irrelevant (there is a link-local all nodes multicast group at address ff02::1, though). There are two special cases when additional setup needs to be done:

- When the ndo_neigh_construct() callback of the netdev_ops is defined, it is invoked. In fact, this is done only in the classical IP over ATM code (clip); see net/atm/clip.c.

- When the neigh_setup() callback of the neigh_parms object is defined, it is invoked. This is used, for example, in the bonding driver; see drivers/net/bonding/bond_main.c.

When trying to create a neighbour object by the __neigh_create() method, and the number of the neighbour entries exceeds the hash table size, it must be enlarged. This is done by calling the neigh_hash_grow() method, like this:

```
struct neighbour *__neigh_create(struct neigh_table *tbl, const void *pkey,
                struct net_device *dev, bool want_ref)
{
    . . .
```

The hash table size is 1 << nht->hash_shift; the hash table must be enlarged if it is exceeded:

```
    if (atomic_read(&tbl->entries) > (1 << nht->hash_shift))
        nht = neigh_hash_grow(tbl, nht->hash_shift + 1);
    . . .
}
```

When the want_ref parameter is true, you will increment the neighbour reference count within this method. You also initialize the confirmed field of the neighbour object:

```
n->confirmed = jiffies - (n->parms->base_reachable_time << 1);
```

It is initialized to be a little less than the current time, jiffies (for the simple reason that you want reachability confirmation to be required sooner). At the end of the __neigh_create() method, the dead flag is initialized to be 0, and the neighbour object is added to the neighbour hash table.

The neigh_release() method decrements the reference counter of the neighbour and frees it when it reaches zero by calling the neigh_destroy() method. The neigh_destroy() method will verify that the neighbour is marked as dead: neighbours whose dead flag is 0 will not be removed.

In this section, you learned about the kernel methods to create and free a neighbour. Next you will learn how adding and deleting a neighbour entry can be triggered from userspace, as well as how to display the neighbouring table, with the arp command for IPv4 and the ip command for IPv4/IPv6.

Interaction Between Userspace and the Neighbouring Subsystem

Management of the ARP table is done with the `ip neigh` command of the `iproute2` package or with the `arp` command of the `net-tools` package. Thus, you can display the ARP table by running, from the command line, one of the following commands:

- arp: Handled by the `arp_seq_show()` method in `net/ipv4/arp.c`.

- ip neigh show (or ip neighbour show): Handled by the `neigh_dump_info()` method in `net/core/neighbour.c`.

Note that the `ip neigh show` command shows the NUD states of the neighbouring table entries (like NUD_REACHABLE or NUD_STALE). Note also that the `arp` command can display only the IPv4 neighbouring table (the ARP table), whereas with the `ip` command you can display both the IPv4 ARP table and the IPv6 neighbouring table. If you want to display only the IPv6 neighbouring table, you should run `ip -6 neigh show`.

The ARP and NDISC modules also export data via `procfs`. That means you can display the ARP table by running `cat /proc/net/arp` (this `procfs` entry is handled by the `arp_seq_show()` method, which is the same method that handles the `arp` command, as mentioned earlier). Or you can display ARP statistics by `cat /proc/net/stat/arp_cache`, and you can display the NDISC statistics by `cat /proc/net/stat/ndisc_cache` (both are handled by the `neigh_stat_seq_show()` method).

You can add an entry with `ip neigh add`, which is handled by the `neigh_add()` method. When running `ip neigh add`, you can specify the state of the entry which you are adding (like NUD_PERMANENT, NUD_STALE, NUD_REACHABLE and so on). For example:

```
ip neigh add 192.168.0.121 dev eth0 lladdr 00:30:48:5b:cc:45 nud permanent
```

Deleting an entry can be done by `ip neigh del`, and is handled by the `neigh_delete()` method. For example:

```
ip neigh del 192.168.0.121 dev eth0
```

Adding an entry to the proxy ARP table can be done with `ip neigh add proxy`. For example:

```
ip neigh add proxy 192.168.2.11 dev eth0
```

The addition is handled again by the `neigh_add()` method. In this case, the NTF_PROXY flag is set in the data passed from userspace (see the `ndm_flags` field of the `ndm` object), and therefore the `pneigh_lookup()` method is called to perform a lookup in the proxy neighbouring hash table (`phash_buckets`). In case the lookup failed, the `pneigh_lookup()` method adds an entry to the proxy neighbouring hash table.

Deleting an entry from the proxy ARP table can be done with `ip neigh del proxy`. For example:

```
ip neigh del proxy 192.168.2.11 dev eth0
```

The deletion is handled by the `neigh_delete()` method. Again, in this case the NTF_PROXY flag is set in the data passed from userspace (see the `ndm_flags` field of the `ndm` object), and therefore the `pneigh_delete()` method is called to delete the entry from the proxy neighbouring table.

With the `ip ntable` command, you can control the parameters for the neighbouring tables. For example:

- ip ntable show: Shows the parameters for all the neighbouring tables.

- ip ntable change: Change a value of a parameter of a neighbouring table. Handled by the `neightbl_set()` method. For example: `ip ntable change name arp_cache queue 20 dev eth0`.

You can also add entries to the ARP table by arp add. And it is possible to add static entries manually to the ARP table, like this: arp -s <IPAddress> <MacAddress>. The static ARP entries are not deleted by the neigbouring subsystem garbage collector, but they are not persistent over reboot.

The next section briefly describes how network events are handled in the neighbouring subsystem.

Handling Network Events

The neighbouring core does not register any events with the register_netdevice_notifier() method. On the other hand, the ARP module and the NDISC module do register network events. In ARP, the arp_netdev_event() method is registered as the callback for netdev events. It handles changes of MAC address events by calling the generic neigh_changeaddr() method and by calling the rt_cache_flush() method. From kernel 3.11, you handle a NETDEV_CHANGE event when there was a change of the IFF_NOARP flag by calling the neigh_changeaddr() method. A NETDEV_CHANGE event is triggered when a device changes its flags, by the __dev_notify_flags() method, or when a device changes its state, by the netdev_state_change() method. In NDISC, the ndisc_netdev_event() method is registered as the callback for netdev events; it handles the NETDEV_CHANGEADDR, NETDEV_DOWN, and NETDEV_NOTIFY_PEERS events.

After describing the fundamental data structures common to IPv4 and IPv6, like the neighbouring table (neigh_table) and the neighbour structure, and after discussing how a neighbour object is created and freed, it is time to describe the implementation of the first neighbouring protocol, the ARP protocol.

The ARP protocol (IPv4)

The ARP protocol is defined in RFC 826. When working with Ethernet, the addresses are called MAC addresses and are 48-bit values. MAC addresses should be unique, but you must take into account that you may encounter a non-unique MAC address. A common reason for this is that on most network interfaces, a system administrator can configure MAC addresses with userspace tools like ifconfig or ip.

When sending an IPv4 packet, you know the destination IPv4 address. You should build an Ethernet header, which should include a destination MAC address. Finding the MAC address based on a given IPv4 address is done by the ARP protocol as you will see shortly. If the MAC address is unknown, you send an ARP request as a broadcast. This ARP request contains the IPv4 address you are seeking. If there is a host with such an IPv4 address, this host sends a unicast ARP response as a reply. The ARP table (arp_tbl) is an instance of the neigh_table structure. The ARP header is represented by the arphdr structure:

```
struct arphdr {
    __be16          ar_hrd;         /* format of hardware address   */
    __be16          ar_pro;         /* format of protocol address   */
    unsigned char   ar_hln;         /* length of hardware address   */
    unsigned char   ar_pln;         /* length of protocol address   */
    __be16          ar_op;          /* ARP opcode (command)         */
#if 0
    *
    *       Ethernet looks like this : This bit is variable sized however...
    */
    unsigned char           ar_sha[ETH_ALEN];       /* sender hardware address  */
    unsigned char           ar_sip[4];              /* sender IP address        */
    unsigned char           ar_tha[ETH_ALEN];       /* target hardware address  */
    unsigned char           ar_tip[4];              /* target IP address        */
#endif
};
```

(include/uapi/linux/if_arp.h)

The following is a description of some of the important members of the arphdr structure:

- ar_hrd is the hardware type; for Ethernet it is 0x01. For the full list of available ARP header hardware identifiers, see ARPHRD_XXX definitions in include/uapi/linux/if_arp.h.

- ar_pro is the protocol ID; for IPv4 it is 0x80. For the full list of available protocols IDs, see ETH_P_XXX in include/uapi/linux/if_ether.h.

- ar_hln is the hardware address length in bytes, which is 6 bytes for Ethernet addresses.

- ar_pln is the length of the protocol address in bytes, which is 4 bytes for IPv4 addresses.

- ar_op is the opcode, ARPOP_REQUEST for an ARP request, and ARPOP_REPLY for an ARP reply. For the full list of available ARP header opcodes look in include/uapi/linux/if_arp.h.

Immediately after the ar_op are the sender hardware (MAC) address and IPv4 address, and the target hardware (MAC) address and IPv4 address. These addresses are not part of the ARP header (arphdr) structure. In the arp_process() method, they are extracted by reading the corresponding offsets of the ARP header, as you can see in the explanation about the arp_process() method in the section "ARP: Receiving Solicitation Requests and Replies" later in this chapter. Figure 7-1 shows an ARP header for an ARP Ethernet packet.

0		16	32
Hardware Type (0x01)		Protocol Type (0x80)	
Hardware Size (0x06)	Protocol Size (0x04)	Opcode	

Figure 7-1. *ARP header (for Ethernet)*

In ARP, four neigh_ops objects are defined: arp_direct_ops, arp_generic_ops, arp_hh_ops, and arp_broken_ops. The initialization of the ARP table neigh_ops object is done by the arp_constructor() method, based on the network device features:

- If the header_ops of the net_device object is NULL, the neigh_ops object will be set to be arp_direct_ops. In this case, sending the packet will be done with the neigh_direct_output() method, which is in fact a wrapper around dev_queue_xmit(). In most Ethernet network devices, however, the header_ops of the net_device object is initialized to be eth_header_ops by the generic ether_setup() method; see net/ethernet/eth.c.

- If the header_ops of the net_device object contains a NULL cache() callback, then the neigh_ops object will be set to be arp_generic_ops.

- If the header_ops of the net_device object contains a non-NULL cache() callback, then the neigh_ops object will be set to be arp_hh_ops. In the case of using the generic eth_header_ops object, the cache() callback is the eth_header_cache() callback.

- For three types of devices, the neigh_ops object will be set to be arp_broken_ops (when the type of the net_device object is ARPHRD_ROSE, ARPHRD_AX25, or ARPHRD_NETROM).

Now that I've covered the ARP protocol and the ARP header (arphdr) object, let's look at how ARP solicitation requests are sent.

ARP: Sending Solicitation Requests

Where are solicitation requests being sent? The most common case is in the Tx path, before actually leaving the network layer (L3) and moving to the link layer (L2). In the ip_finish_output2() method, you first perform a lookup for the next hop IPv4 address in the ARP table by calling the __ipv4_neigh_lookup_noref() method, and if you don't find any matching neighbour entry, you create one by calling the __neigh_create() method:

```
static inline int ip_finish_output2(struct sk_buff *skb)
{
        struct dst_entry *dst = skb_dst(skb);
        struct rtable *rt = (struct rtable *)dst;
        struct net_device *dev = dst->dev;
        unsigned int hh_len = LL_RESERVED_SPACE(dev);
        struct neighbour *neigh;
        u32 nexthop;
        . . .
        . . .
        nexthop = (__force u32) rt_nexthop(rt, ip_hdr(skb)->daddr);
        neigh = __ipv4_neigh_lookup_noref(dev, nexthop);
        if (unlikely(!neigh))
                neigh = __neigh_create(&arp_tbl, &nexthop, dev, false);
        if (!IS_ERR(neigh)) {
                int res = dst_neigh_output(dst, neigh, skb);
        . . .
}
```

Let's take a look in the dst_neigh_output() method:

```
static inline int dst_neigh_output(struct dst_entry *dst, struct neighbour *n,
                                   struct sk_buff *skb)
{
        const struct hh_cache *hh;

        if (dst->pending_confirm) {
                unsigned long now = jiffies;

                dst->pending_confirm = 0;
                /* avoid dirtying neighbour */
                if (n->confirmed != now)
                        n->confirmed = now;
        }
```

When you reach this method for the first time with this flow, nud_state is not NUD_CONNECTED, and the output callback is the neigh_resolve_output() method:

```
        hh = &n->hh;
        if ((n->nud_state & NUD_CONNECTED) && hh->hh_len)
                return neigh_hh_output(hh, skb);
        else
                return n->output(n, skb);
}
```

(include/net/dst.h)

In the neigh_resolve_output() method, you call the neigh_event_send() method, which eventually puts the SKB in the arp_queue of the neighbour by __skb_queue_tail(&neigh->arp_queue, skb); later, the neigh_probe() method, invoked from the neighbour timer handler, neigh_timer_handler(), will send the packet by invoking the solicit() method (neigh->ops->solicit is the arp_solicit() method in our case):

```
static void neigh_probe(struct neighbour *neigh)
        __releases(neigh->lock)
{
        struct sk_buff *skb = skb_peek(&neigh->arp_queue);
        . . .
        neigh->ops->solicit(neigh, skb);
        atomic_inc(&neigh->probes);
        kfree_skb(skb);
}
```

Let's take a look at the arp_solicit() method, which actually sends the ARP request:

```
static void arp_solicit(struct neighbour *neigh, struct sk_buff *skb)
{
        __be32 saddr = 0;
        u8 dst_ha[MAX_ADDR_LEN], *dst_hw = NULL;
        struct net_device *dev = neigh->dev;
        __be32 target = *(__be32 *)neigh->primary_key;
        int probes = atomic_read(&neigh->probes);
        struct in_device *in_dev;

        rcu_read_lock();
        in_dev = __in_dev_get_rcu(dev);
        if (!in_dev) {
                rcu_read_unlock();
                return;
        }
```

With the arp_announce procfs entry, you can set restrictions for which local source IP address to use for the ARP packet you want to send:

- *0:* Use any local address, configured on any interface. This is the default value.

- *1:* First try to use addresses that are on the target subnet. If there are no such addresses, use level 2.

- *2:* Use primary IP address.

Note that the max value of these two entries is used:

```
/proc/sys/net/ipv4/conf/all/arp_announce
/proc/sys/net/ipv4/conf/<netdeviceName>/arp_announce
```

See also the description of the IN_DEV_ARP_ANNOUNCE macro in the "Quick Reference" section at the end of this chapter.

```
switch (IN_DEV_ARP_ANNOUNCE(in_dev)) {
default:
case 0:            /* By default announce any local IP */
        if (skb && inet_addr_type(dev_net(dev),
                                  ip_hdr(skb)->saddr) == RTN_LOCAL)
            saddr = ip_hdr(skb)->saddr;
        break;
case 1:            /* Restrict announcements of saddr in same subnet */
        if (!skb)
        break;
        saddr = ip_hdr(skb)->saddr;
        if (inet_addr_type(dev_net(dev), saddr) == RTN_LOCAL) {
```

The inet_addr_onlink() method checks whether the specified target address and the specified source address are on the same subnet:

```
        /* saddr should be known to target */
        if (inet_addr_onlink(in_dev, target, saddr))
            break;
    }
    saddr = 0;
    break;
case 2:            /* Avoid secondary IPs, get a primary/preferred one */
    break;
}
rcu_read_unlock();

if (!saddr)
```

The inet_select_addr() method returns the address of the first primary interface of the specified device whose scope is smaller than the specified scope (RT_SCOPE_LINK in this case), and which is in the same subnet as the target:

```
saddr = inet_select_addr(dev, target, RT_SCOPE_LINK);

probes -= neigh->parms->ucast_probes;
if (probes < 0) {
        if (!(neigh->nud_state & NUD_VALID))
                pr_debug("trying to ucast probe in NUD_INVALID\n");
        neigh_ha_snapshot(dst_ha, neigh, dev);
        dst_hw = dst_ha;
} else {
        probes -= neigh->parms->app_probes;
        if (probes < 0) {
```

CONFIG_ARPD is set when working with the userspace ARP daemon; there are projects like OpenNHRP, which are based on ARPD. Next Hop Resolution Protocol (NHRP) is used to improve the efficiency of routing computer network traffic over Non-Broadcast, Multiple Access (NBMA) networks (I don't discuss the ARPD userspace daemon in this book):

```
#ifdef CONFIG_ARPD
                      neigh_app_ns(neigh);
#endif
                      return;
            }
       }
```

Now you call the arp_send() method to send an ARP request. Note that the last parameter, target_hw, is NULL. You do not yet know the target hardware (MAC) address. When calling arp_send() with target_hw as NULL, a broadcast ARP request is sent:

```
        arp_send(ARPOP_REQUEST, ETH_P_ARP, target, dev, saddr,
               dst_hw, dev->dev_addr, NULL);
}
```

Let's take a look at the arp_send() method, which is quite short:

```
void arp_send(int type, int ptype, __be32 dest_ip,
          struct net_device *dev, __be32 src_ip,
          const unsigned char *dest_hw, const unsigned char *src_hw,
          const unsigned char *target_hw)
{
       struct sk_buff *skb;

       /*
        *      No arp on this interface.
        */
```

You must check whether the IFF_NOARP is supported on this network device. There are cases in which ARP is disabled: an administrator can disable ARP, for example, by ifconfig eth1 -arp or by ip link set eth1 arp off. Some network devices set the IFF_NOARP flag upon creation—for example, IPv4 tunnel devices, or PPP devices, which do not need ARP. See the ipip_tunnel_setup() method in net/ipv4/ipip.c or the ppp_setup() method in drivers/net/ppp_generic.c.

```
        if (dev->flags&IFF_NOARP)
              return;
```

The arp_create() method creates an SKB with an ARP header and initializes it according to the specified parameters:

```
        skb = arp_create(type, ptype, dest_ip, dev, src_ip,
                    dest_hw, src_hw, target_hw);
        if (skb == NULL)
              return;
```

The only thing the arp_xmit() method does is call dev_queue_xmit() by the NF_HOOK() macro:

```
    arp_xmit(skb);
}
```

Now it is time to learn how these ARP requests are processed and how ARP replies are processed.

ARP: Receiving Solicitation Requests and Replies

In IPv4, the arp_rcv() method is responsible for handling ARP packets, as mentioned earlier. Let's take a look at the arp_rcv() method:

```
static int arp_rcv(struct sk_buff *skb, struct net_device *dev,
                   struct packet_type *pt, struct net_device *orig_dev)
{
        const struct arphdr *arp;
```

If the network device on which the ARP packet was received has the IFF_NOARP flag set, or if the packet is not destined for the local machine, or if it is for a loopback device, then the packet should be dropped. You continue and make some more sanity checks, and if everything is okay, you proceed to the arp_process() method, which performs the real work of processing an ARP packet:

```
        if (dev->flags & IFF_NOARP ||
            skb->pkt_type == PACKET_OTHERHOST ||
            skb->pkt_type == PACKET_LOOPBACK)
                goto freeskb;
```

If the SKB is shared, you must clone it because it might be changed by someone else while being processed by the arp_rcv() method. The skb_share_check() method creates a clone of the SKB if it is shared (see Appendix A).

```
        skb = skb_share_check(skb, GFP_ATOMIC);
        if (!skb)
                goto out_of_mem;

        /* ARP header, plus 2 device addresses, plus 2 IP addresses.  */
        if (!pskb_may_pull(skb, arp_hdr_len(dev)))
                goto freeskb;

        arp = arp_hdr(skb);
```

The ar_hln of the ARP header represents the length of a hardware address, which should be 6 bytes for Ethernet header, and should be equal to the addr_len of the net_device object. The ar_pln of the ARP header represents the length of the protocol address and should be equal to the length of an IPv4 address, which is 4 bytes:

```
        if (arp->ar_hln != dev->addr_len || arp->ar_pln != 4)
                goto freeskb;

        memset(NEIGH_CB(skb), 0, sizeof(struct neighbour_cb));
        return NF_HOOK(NFPROTO_ARP, NF_ARP_IN, skb, dev, NULL, arp_process);
```

```
freeskb:
        kfree_skb(skb);
out_of_mem:
        return 0;
}
```

Handling ARP requests is not restricted to packets that have the local host as their destination. When the local host is configured as a proxy ARP, or as a private VLAN proxy ARP (see RFC 3069), you also handle packets which have a destination that is not the local host. Support for private VLAN proxy ARP was added in kernel 2.6.34.

In the arp_process() method, you handle only ARP requests or ARP responses. For ARP requests you perform a lookup in the routing subsystem by the ip_route_input_noref() method. If the ARP packet is for the local host (the rt_type of the routing entry is RTN_LOCAL), you proceed to check some conditions (described shortly). If all these checks pass, an ARP reply is sent back with the arp_send() method. If the ARP packet is not for the local host but should be forwarded (the rt_type of the routing entry is RTN_UNICAST), then you check some conditions (also described shortly), and if they are fulfilled you perform a lookup in the proxy ARP table by calling the pneigh_lookup() method.

You will now see the implementation details of the main ARP method which handles ARP requests, the arp_process() method.

The arp_process() Method

Let's take a look at the arp_process() method, where the real work is done:

```
static int arp_process(struct sk_buff *skb)
{
        struct net_device *dev = skb->dev;
        struct in_device *in_dev = __in_dev_get_rcu(dev);
        struct arphdr *arp;
        unsigned char *arp_ptr;
        struct rtable *rt;
        unsigned char *sha;
        __be32 sip, tip;
        u16 dev_type = dev->type;
        int addr_type;
        struct neighbour *n;
        struct net *net = dev_net(dev);

        /* arp_rcv below verifies the ARP header and verifies the device
         * is ARP'able.
         */

        if (in_dev == NULL)
                goto out;
```

Fetch the ARP header from the SKB (it is the network header, see the arp_hdr() method):

```
        arp = arp_hdr(skb);

        switch (dev_type) {
        default:
                if (arp->ar_pro != htons(ETH_P_IP) ||
```

```
                    htons(dev_type) != arp->ar_hrd)
                         goto out;
            break;
    case ARPHRD_ETHER:
            . . .
            if ((arp->ar_hrd != htons(ARPHRD_ETHER) &&
                arp->ar_hrd != htons(ARPHRD_IEEE802)) ||
              arp->ar_pro != htons(ETH_P_IP))
                    goto out;
            break;
            . . .
```

You want to handle only ARP requests or ARP responses in the arp_process() method, and discard all other packets:

```
    /* Understand only these message types */

    if (arp->ar_op != htons(ARPOP_REPLY) &&
        arp->ar_op != htons(ARPOP_REQUEST))
            goto out;
```

```
/*
 *      Extract fields
 */
    arp_ptr = (unsigned char *)(arp + 1);
```

The arp_process() Method—Extracting Headers:

Immediately after the ARP header, there are the following fields (see the ARP header definition above):

- sha: The source hardware address (the MAC address, which is 6 bytes).

- sip: The source IPv4 address (4 bytes).

- tha: The target hardware address (the MAC address, which is 6 bytes).

- tip: The target IPv4 address (4 bytes).

Extract the sip and tip addresses:

```
    sha     = arp_ptr;
    arp_ptr += dev->addr_len;
```

Set sip to be the source IPv4 address after advancing arp_ptr with the corresponding offset:

```
    memcpy(&sip, arp_ptr, 4);
    arp_ptr += 4;
    switch (dev_type) {
    . . .
    default:
            arp_ptr += dev->addr_len;
    }
```

Set `tip` to be the target IPv4 address after advancing `arp_ptr` with the corresponding offset:

```
memcpy(&tip, arp_ptr, 4);
```

Discard these two types of packets:

- Multicast packets

- Packets for the loopback device if the use of local routing with loopback addresses is disabled; see also the description of the IN_DEV_ROUTE_LOCALNET macro in the "Quick Reference" section at the end of this chapter.

```
/*
 *      Check for bad requests for 127.x.x.x and requests for multicast
 *      addresses.  If this is one such, delete it.
 */
        if (ipv4_is_multicast(tip) ||
            (!IN_DEV_ROUTE_LOCALNET(in_dev) && ipv4_is_loopback(tip)))
                goto out;


        . . .
```

The source IP (`sip`) is 0 when you use Duplicate Address Detection (DAD). DAD lets you detect the existence of double L3 addresses on different hosts on a LAN. DAD is implemented in IPv6 as an integral part of the address configuration process, but not in IPv4. However, there is support for correctly handling DAD requests in IPv4, as you will soon see. The `arping` utility of the `iputils` package is an example for using DAD in IPv4. When sending ARP request with arping –D, you send an ARP request where the `sip` of the ARP header is 0. (The –D modifier tells `arping` to be in DAD mode); the `tip` is usually the sender IPv4 address (because you want to check whether there is another host on the same LAN with the same IPv4 address as yours); if there is a host with the same IP address as the `tip` of the DAD ARP request, it will send back an ARP reply (without adding the sender to its neighbouring table):

```
        /* Special case: IPv4 duplicate address detection packet (RFC2131) */
        if (sip == 0) {
                if (arp->ar_op == htons(ARPOP_REQUEST) &&
```

The arp_process() Method—arp_ignore() and arp_filter() Methods

The `arp_ignore` procfs entry provides support for different modes for sending ARP replies as a response for an ARP request. The value used is the max value of /proc/sys/net/ipv4/conf/all/arp_ignore and /proc/sys/net/ipv4/conf/<netDeviceName>/arp_ignore. By default, the value of the `arp_ignore` procfs entry is 0, and in such a case, the `arp_ignore()` method returns 0. You reply to the ARP request with `arp_send()`, as you can see in the next code snippet (assuming that inet_addr_type(net, tip) returned RTN_LOCAL). The `arp_ignore()` method checks the value of IN_DEV_ARP_IGNORE(in_dev); for more details, see the `arp_ignore()` implementation in net/ipv4/arp.c and the description of the IN_DEV_ARP_IGNORE macro in the "Quick Reference" section at the end of this chapter:

```
                    inet_addr_type(net, tip) == RTN_LOCAL &&
                    !arp_ignore(in_dev, sip, tip))
                    arp_send(ARPOP_REPLY, ETH_P_ARP, sip, dev, tip, sha,
                             dev->dev_addr, sha);
        goto out;
}
```

```
if (arp->ar_op == htons(ARPOP_REQUEST) &&
    ip_route_input_noref(skb, tip, sip, 0, dev) == 0) {

        rt = skb_rtable(skb);
        addr_type = rt->rt_type;
```

When addr_type equals RTN_LOCAL, the packet is for local delivery:

```
if (addr_type == RTN_LOCAL) {
        int dont_send;

        dont_send = arp_ignore(in_dev, sip, tip);
```

The arp_filter() method fails (returns 1) in two cases:

- When the lookup in the routing tables with the ip_route_output() method fails.

- When the outgoing network device of the routing entry is different than the network device on which the ARP request was received.

In case of success, the arp_filter() method returns 0 (see also the description of the IN_DEV_ARPFILTER macro in the "Quick Reference" section at the end of this chapter):

```
if (!dont_send && IN_DEV_ARPFILTER(in_dev))
        dont_send = arp_filter(sip, tip, dev);
if (!dont_send) {
```

Before sending the ARP reply, you want to add the sender to your neighbouring table or update it; this is done with the neigh_event_ns() method. The neigh_event_ns() method creates a new neighbouring table entry and sets its state to be NUD_STALE. If there is already such an entry, it updates its state to be NUD_STALE, with the neigh_update() method. Adding entries this way is termed *passive learning*:

```
n = neigh_event_ns(&arp_tbl, sha, &sip, dev);
if (n) {
        arp_send(ARPOP_REPLY, ETH_P_ARP, sip,
                dev, tip, sha, dev->dev_addr,
                sha);
        neigh_release(n);
}
}
goto out;
} else if (IN_DEV_FORWARD(in_dev)) {
```

The arp_fwd_proxy() method returns 1 when the device can be used as an ARP proxy; the arp_fwd_pvlan() method returns 1 when the device can be used as an ARP VLAN proxy:

```
if (addr_type == RTN_UNICAST  &&
    (arp_fwd_proxy(in_dev, dev, rt) ||
     arp_fwd_pvlan(in_dev, dev, rt, sip, tip) ||
     (rt->dst.dev != dev &&
      pneigh_lookup(&arp_tbl, net, &tip, dev, 0)))) {
```

Again, call the neigh_event_ns() method to create a neighbour entry of the sender with NUD_STALE, or if such an entry exists, update that entry state to be NUD_STALE:

```
                    n = neigh_event_ns(&arp_tbl, sha, &sip, dev);
                    if (n)
                            neigh_release(n);

                    if (NEIGH_CB(skb)->flags & LOCALLY_ENQUEUED ||
                        skb->pkt_type == PACKET_HOST ||
                        in_dev->arp_parms->proxy_delay == 0) {
                            arp_send(ARPOP_REPLY, ETH_P_ARP, sip,
                                        dev, tip, sha, dev->dev_addr,
                                        sha);
                    } else {
```

Delay sending an ARP reply by putting the SKB at the tail of the proxy_queue, by calling the pneigh_enqueue() method. Note that the delay is random and is a number between 0 and in_dev->arp_parms->proxy_delay:

```
                    pneigh_enqueue(&arp_tbl,
                                        in_dev->arp_parms, skb);
                    return 0;
                }
                goto out;
            }
        }
}
```

```
    /* Update our ARP tables */
```

Note that the last parameter of calling the __neigh_lookup() method is 0, which means that you only perform a lookup in the neighbouring table (and do not create a new neighbour if the lookup failed):

```
n = __neigh_lookup(&arp_tbl, &sip, dev, 0);
```

The IN_DEV_ARP_ACCEPT macro tells you whether the network device is set to accept ARP requests (see also the description of the IN_DEV_ARP_ACCEPT macro in the "Quick Reference" section at the end of this of this chapter):

```
if (IN_DEV_ARP_ACCEPT(in_dev)) {
        /* Unsolicited ARP is not accepted by default.
           It is possible, that this option should be enabled for some
           devices (strip is candidate)
        */
```

Unsolicited ARP requests are sent only to update the neighbouring table. In such requests, tip is equal to sip (the arping utility supports sending unsolicited ARP requests by arping –U):

```
if (n == NULL &&
    (arp->ar_op == htons(ARPOP_REPLY) ||
     (arp->ar_op == htons(ARPOP_REQUEST) && tip == sip)) &&
    inet_addr_type(net, sip) == RTN_UNICAST)
        n = __neigh_lookup(&arp_tbl, &sip, dev, 1);
}
```

```
if (n) {
        int state = NUD_REACHABLE;
        int override;

        /* If several different ARP replies follows back-to-back,
           use the FIRST one. It is possible, if several proxy
           agents are active. Taking the first reply prevents
           arp trashing and chooses the fastest router.
        */
        override = time_after(jiffies, n->updated + n->parms->locktime);

        /* Broadcast replies and request packets
           do not assert neighbour reachability.
         */
        if (arp->ar_op != htons(ARPOP_REPLY) ||
            skb->pkt_type != PACKET_HOST)
                state = NUD_STALE;
```

Call `neigh_update()` to update the neighbouring table:

```
        neigh_update(n, sha, state,
                          override ? NEIGH_UPDATE_F_OVERRIDE : 0);
        neigh_release(n);
    }

out:
        consume_skb(skb);
        return 0;
}
```

Now that you know about the IPv4 ARP protocol implementation, it is time to move on to IPv6 NDISC protocol implementation. You will soon notice some of the differences between the neighbouring subsystem implementation in IPv4 and in IPv6.

The NDISC Protocol (IPv6)

The Neighbour Discovery (NDISC) protocol is based on RFC 2461, "Neighbour Discovery for IP Version 6 (IPv6)," which was later obsoleted by RFC 4861 from 2007. IPv6 nodes (hosts or routers) on the same link use the Neighbour Discovery protocol to discover each other's presence, to discover routers, to determine each other's L2 addresses, and to maintain neighbour reachability information. Duplicate Address Detection (DAD) was added to avoid double L3 addresses on the same LAN. I discuss DAD and handling NDISC neighbour solicitation and neighbour advertisements shortly.

Next you learn how IPv6 neighbour discovery protocols avoid creating duplicate IPv6 addresses.

Duplicate Address Detection (DAD)

How can you be sure there is no other same IPv6 address on a LAN? The chances are low, but if such address does exist, it may cause trouble. DAD is a solution. When a host tries to configure an address, it first creates a Link Local address (a Link Local address starts with FE80). This address is tentative (IFA_F_TENTATIVE), which means that the host can communicate only with ND messages. Then the host starts the DAD process by calling the addrconf_dad_start() method (net/ipv6/addrconf.c). The host sends a Neighbour Solicitation DAD message. The target is its tentative address, the source is all zeros (the unspecified address). If there is no answer in a specified time interval, the state is changed to permanent (IFA_F_PERMANENT). When Optimistic DAD (CONFIG_IPV6_OPTIMISTIC_DAD) is set, you don't wait until DAD is completed, but allow hosts to communicate with peers before DAD has finished successfully. See RFC 4429, "Optimistic Duplicate Address Detection (DAD) for IPv6," from 2006.

The neighbouring table for IPv6 is called nd_tbl:

```
struct neigh_table nd_tbl = {
        .family =       AF_INET6,
        .key_len =      sizeof(struct in6_addr),
        .hash =         ndisc_hash,
        .constructor =  ndisc_constructor,
        .pconstructor = pndisc_constructor,
        .pdestructor =  pndisc_destructor,
        .proxy_redo =   pndisc_redo,
        .id =           "ndisc_cache",
        .parms = {
                .tbl                    = &nd_tbl,
                .base_reachable_time    = ND_REACHABLE_TIME,
                .retrans_time           = ND_RETRANS_TIMER,
                .gc_staletime           = 60 * HZ,
                .reachable_time         = ND_REACHABLE_TIME,
                .delay_probe_time       = 5 * HZ,
                .queue_len_bytes        = 64*1024,
                .ucast_probes           = 3,
                .mcast_probes           = 3,
                .anycast_delay          = 1 * HZ,
                .proxy_delay            = (8 * HZ) / 10,
                .proxy_qlen             = 64,
        },
        .gc_interval =  30 * HZ,
        .gc_thresh1 =   128,
        .gc_thresh2 =   512,
        .gc_thresh3 =   1024,
};
```
(net/ipv6/ndisc.c)

Note that some of the members of the NDISC table are equal to the parallel members in the ARP table—for example, the values of the garbage collector thresholds (gc_thresh1, gc_thresh2 and gc_thresh3).

The Linux IPv6 Neighbour Discovery implementation is based on ICMPv6 messages to manage the interaction between neighbouring nodes. The Neighbour Discovery protocol defines the following five ICMPv6 message types:

```
#define NDISC_ROUTER_SOLICITATION       133
#define NDISC_ROUTER_ADVERTISEMENT      134
#define NDISC_NEIGHBOUR_SOLICITATION    135
#define NDISC_NEIGHBOUR_ADVERTISEMENT   136
#define NDISC_REDIRECT                  137
```

(include/net/ndisc.h)

Note that these five ICMPv6 message types are informational messages. ICMPv6 message types whose values are in the range from 0 to 127 are error messages, and ICMPv6 message types whose values are from 128 to 255 are informational messages. For more on that, see Chapter 3, which discusses the ICMP protocol. This chapter discusses only the Neighbour Solicitation and the Neighbour Discovery messages.

As mentioned in the beginning of this chapter, because neighbouring discovery messages are ICMPv6 messages, they are handled by the icmpv6_rcv() method, which in turn invokes the ndisc_rcv() method for ICMPv6 packets whose message type is one of the five types mentioned earlier (see net/ipv6/icmp.c).

In NDISC, there are three neigh_ops objects: ndisc_generic_ops, ndisc_hh_ops, and ndisc_direct_ops:

- If the header_ops of the net_device object is NULL, the neigh_ops object will be set to be ndisc_direct_ops. As in the case of arp_direct_ops, sending the packet is done with the neigh_direct_output() method, which is in fact a wrapper around dev_queue_xmit(). Note that, as mentioned in the ARP section earlier, in most Ethernet network devices, the header_ops of the net_device object is not NULL.

- If the header_ops of the net_device object contains a NULL cache() callback, then the neigh_ops object is set to be ndisc_generic_ops.

- If the header_ops of the net_device object contains a non-NULL cache() callback, then the neigh_ops object is set to be ndisc_hh_ops.

This section discussed the DAD mechanism and how it helps to avoid duplicate addresses. The next section describes how solicitation requests are sent.

NIDSC: Sending Solicitation Requests

Similarly to what you saw in IPv6, you also perform a lookup and create an entry if you did not find any match:

```
static int ip6_finish_output2(struct sk_buff *skb)
{
        struct dst_entry *dst = skb_dst(skb);
        struct net_device *dev = dst->dev;
        struct neighbour *neigh;
        struct in6_addr *nexthop;
        int ret;
                . . .


                . . .

        nexthop = rt6_nexthop((struct rt6_info *)dst, &ipv6_hdr(skb)->daddr);
        neigh = __ipv6_neigh_lookup_noref(dst->dev, nexthop);
        if (unlikely(!neigh))
                neigh = __neigh_create(&nd_tbl, nexthop, dst->dev, false);
        if (!IS_ERR(neigh)) {
                ret = dst_neigh_output(dst, neigh, skb);
                . . .
```

Eventually, much like in the IPv4 Tx path, you call the solicit method neigh->ops->solicit(neigh, skb) from the neigh_probe() method. The neigh->ops->solicit in this case is the ndisc_solicit() method. The ndisc_solicit() is a very short method; it is in fact a wrapper around the ndisc_send_ns() method:

```
static void ndisc_solicit(struct neighbour *neigh, struct sk_buff *skb)
{
        struct in6_addr *saddr = NULL;
        struct in6_addr mcaddr;
```

```
        struct net_device *dev = neigh->dev;
        struct in6_addr *target = (struct in6_addr *)&neigh->primary_key;
        int probes = atomic_read(&neigh->probes);

        if (skb && ipv6_chk_addr(dev_net(dev), &ipv6_hdr(skb)->saddr, dev, 1))
                saddr = &ipv6_hdr(skb)->saddr;

        if ((probes -= neigh->parms->ucast_probes) < 0) {
                if (!(neigh->nud_state & NUD_VALID)) {
                        ND_PRINTK(1, dbg,
                                        "%s: trying to ucast probe in NUD_INVALID: %pI6\n",
                                        __func__, target);
                }
                ndisc_send_ns(dev, neigh, target, target, saddr);
        } else if ((probes -= neigh->parms->app_probes) < 0) {
#ifdef CONFIG_ARPD
                neigh_app_ns(neigh);
#endif
        } else {
                addrconf_addr_solict_mult(target, &mcaddr);
                ndisc_send_ns(dev, NULL, target, &mcaddr, saddr);
        }
}
```

In order to send the solicitation request, we need to build an nd_msg object:

```
struct nd_msg {
        struct icmp6hdr icmph;
        struct in6_addr target;
        __u8            opt[0];
};
```

(include/net/ndisc.h)

For a solicitation request, the ICMPv6 header type should be set to NDISC_NEIGHBOUR_SOLICITATION, and for solicitation reply, the ICMPv6 header type should be set to NDISC_NEIGHBOUR_ADVERTISEMENT. Note that with Neighbour Advertisement messages, there are cases when you need to set flags in the ICMPv6 header. The ICMPv6 header includes a structure named icmpv6_nd_advt, which includes the override, solicited, and router flags:

```
struct icmp6hdr {
        __u8            icmp6_type;
        __u8            icmp6_code;
        __sum16         icmp6_cksum;
        union {
                . . .
                . . .
                struct icmpv6_nd_advt {
#if defined(__LITTLE_ENDIAN_BITFIELD)
                        __u32           reserved:5,
                                        override:1,
                                        solicited:1,
```

```
                                        router:1,
                                        reserved2:24;
. . .
#endif

                } u_nd_advt;
        } icmp6_dataun;
. . .
#define icmp6_router            icmp6_dataun.u_nd_advt.router
#define icmp6_solicited         icmp6_dataun.u_nd_advt.solicited
#define icmp6_override          icmp6_dataun.u_nd_advt.override
. . .
```

(include/uapi/linux/icmpv6.h)

- When a message is sent in response to a Neighbour Solicitation, you set the solicited flag (icmp6_solicited).

- When you want to override a neighbouring cache entry (update the L2 address), you set the override flag (icmp6_override).

- When the host sending the Neighbour Advertisement message is a router, you set the router flag (icmp6_router).

You can see the use of these three flags in the ndisc_send_na() method that follows. Let's take a look at the ndisc_send_ns() method:

```
void ndisc_send_ns(struct net_device *dev, struct neighbour *neigh,
                const struct in6_addr *solicit,
                const struct in6_addr *daddr, const struct in6_addr *saddr)
{
        struct sk_buff *skb;
        struct in6_addr addr_buf;
        int inc_opt = dev->addr_len;
        int optlen = 0;
        struct nd_msg *msg;

        if (saddr == NULL) {
                if (ipv6_get_lladdr(dev, &addr_buf,
                                (IFA_F_TENTATIVE|IFA_F_OPTIMISTIC)))
                        return;
                saddr = &addr_buf;
        }

        if (ipv6_addr_any(saddr))
                inc_opt = 0;
        if (inc_opt)
                optlen += ndisc_opt_addr_space(dev);

        skb = ndisc_alloc_skb(dev, sizeof(*msg) + optlen);
        if (!skb)
                return;
```

Build the ICMPv6 header, which is embedded in the nd_msg object:

```
msg = (struct nd_msg *)skb_put(skb, sizeof(*msg));
*msg = (struct nd_msg) {
        .icmph = {
                .icmp6_type = NDISC_NEIGHBOUR_SOLICITATION,
        },
        .target = *solicit,
};

if (inc_opt)
        ndisc_fill_addr_option(skb, ND_OPT_SOURCE_LL_ADDR,
                               dev->dev_addr);

ndisc_send_skb(skb, daddr, saddr);
}
```

Let's take a look at the ndisc_send_na() method:

```
static void ndisc_send_na(struct net_device *dev, struct neighbour *neigh,
                    const struct in6_addr *daddr,
                    const struct in6_addr *solicited_addr,
                    bool router, bool solicited, bool override, bool inc_opt)
{
        struct sk_buff *skb;
        struct in6_addr tmpaddr;
        struct inet6_ifaddr *ifp;
        const struct in6_addr *src_addr;
        struct nd_msg *msg;
        int optlen = 0;

        . . .

        skb = ndisc_alloc_skb(dev, sizeof(*msg) + optlen);
        if (!skb)
                return;
```

Build the ICMPv6 header, which is embedded in the nd_msg object:

```
msg = (struct nd_msg *)skb_put(skb, sizeof(*msg));
*msg = (struct nd_msg) {
        .icmph = {
                .icmp6_type = NDISC_NEIGHBOUR_ADVERTISEMENT,
                .icmp6_router = router,
                .icmp6_solicited = solicited,
                .icmp6_override = override,
        },
        .target = *solicited_addr,
};
```

```
        if (inc_opt)
                ndisc_fill_addr_option(skb, ND_OPT_TARGET_LL_ADDR,
                                        dev->dev_addr);

        ndisc_send_skb(skb, daddr, src_addr);
}
```

This section described how solicitation requests are sent. The next section talks about how Neighbour Solicitations and Advertisements are handled.

NDISC: Receiving Neighbour Solicitations and Advertisements

As mentioned, the ndisc_rcv() method handles all five neighbour discovery message types; let's take a look at this method:

```
int ndisc_rcv(struct sk_buff *skb)
{
        struct nd_msg *msg;

        if (skb_linearize(skb))
                return 0;

        msg = (struct nd_msg *)skb_transport_header(skb);

        __skb_push(skb, skb->data - skb_transport_header(skb));
```

According to RFC 4861, the hop limit of neighbour messages should be 255; the hop limit length is 8 bits, so the maximum hop limit is 255. A value of 255 assures that the packet was not forwarded, and this assures you that you are not exposed to some security attack. Packets that do not fulfill this requirement are discarded:

```
        if (ipv6_hdr(skb)->hop_limit != 255) {
                ND_PRINTK(2, warn, "NDISC: invalid hop-limit: %d\n",
                        ipv6_hdr(skb)->hop_limit);
                return 0;
        }
```

According to RFC 4861, the ICMPv6 code of neighbour messages should be 0, so drop packets that do not fulfill this requirement:

```
        if (msg->icmph.icmp6_code != 0) {
                ND_PRINTK(2, warn, "NDISC: invalid ICMPv6 code: %d\n",
                        msg->icmph.icmp6_code);
        return 0;
        }

        memset(NEIGH_CB(skb), 0, sizeof(struct neighbour_cb));

        switch (msg->icmph.icmp6_type) {
        case NDISC_NEIGHBOUR_SOLICITATION:
                ndisc_recv_ns(skb);
                break;
```

```
        case NDISC_NEIGHBOUR_ADVERTISEMENT:
                ndisc_recv_na(skb);
                break;

        case NDISC_ROUTER_SOLICITATION:
                ndisc_recv_rs(skb);
                break;

        case NDISC_ROUTER_ADVERTISEMENT:
                ndisc_router_discovery(skb);
                break;

        case NDISC_REDIRECT:
                ndisc_redirect_rcv(skb);
                break;
        }

        return 0;
}
```

I do not discuss router solicitations and router advertisements in this chapter, since they are discussed in Chapter 8. Let's take a look at the ndisc_recv_ns() method:

```
static void ndisc_recv_ns(struct sk_buff *skb)
{
        struct nd_msg *msg = (struct nd_msg *)skb_transport_header(skb);
        const struct in6_addr *saddr = &ipv6_hdr(skb)->saddr;
        const struct in6_addr *daddr = &ipv6_hdr(skb)->daddr;
        u8 *lladdr = NULL;
        u32 ndoptlen = skb->tail - (skb->transport_header +
                                        offsetof(struct nd_msg, opt));
        struct ndisc_options ndopts;
        struct net_device *dev = skb->dev;
        struct inet6_ifaddr *ifp;
        struct inet6_dev *idev = NULL;
        struct neighbour *neigh;
```

The ipv6_addr_any() method returns 1 when saddr is the unspecified address of all zeroes (IPV6_ADDR_ANY). When the source address is the unspecified address (all zeroes), this means that the request is DAD:

```
        int dad = ipv6_addr_any(saddr);
        bool inc;
        int is_router = -1;
```

Perform some validity checks:

```
        if (skb->len < sizeof(struct nd_msg)) {
                ND_PRINTK(2, warn, "NS: packet too short\n");
                return;
        }
```

```
if (ipv6_addr_is_multicast(&msg->target)) {
        ND_PRINTK(2, warn, "NS: multicast target address\n");
        return;
}

/*
 * RFC2461 7.1.1:
 * DAD has to be destined for solicited node multicast address.
 */
if (dad && !ipv6_addr_is_solict_mult(daddr)) {
        ND_PRINTK(2, warn, "NS: bad DAD packet (wrong destination)\n");
        return;
}

if (!ndisc_parse_options(msg->opt, ndoptlen, &ndopts)) {
        ND_PRINTK(2, warn, "NS: invalid ND options\n");
        return;
}

if (ndopts.nd_opts_src_lladdr) {
        lladdr = ndisc_opt_addr_data(ndopts.nd_opts_src_lladdr, dev);
        if (!lladdr) {
                ND_PRINTK(2, warn,
                            "NS: invalid link-layer address length\n");
                return;
        }

        /* RFC2461 7.1.1:
         *      If the IP source address is the unspecified address,
         *      there MUST NOT be source link-layer address option
         *      in the message.
         */
        if (dad) {
                ND_PRINTK(2, warn,
                            "NS: bad DAD packet (link-layer address option)\n");
                return;
        }
}

inc = ipv6_addr_is_multicast(daddr);

ifp = ipv6_get_ifaddr(dev_net(dev), &msg->target, dev, 1);
if (ifp) {

        if (ifp->flags & (IFA_F_TENTATIVE|IFA_F_OPTIMISTIC)) {
                if (dad) {
                        /*
                         * We are colliding with another node
                         * who is doing DAD
                         * so fail our DAD process
                         */
```

```
                        addrconf_dad_failure(ifp);
                        return;
                } else {
                        /*
                         * This is not a dad solicitation.
                         * If we are an optimistic node,
                         * we should respond.
                         * Otherwise, we should ignore it.
                         */
                        if (!(ifp->flags & IFA_F_OPTIMISTIC))
                                goto out;
                }
        }

        idev = ifp->idev;
} else {
        struct net *net = dev_net(dev);

        idev = in6_dev_get(dev);
        if (!idev) {
                /* XXX: count this drop? */
                return;
        }

        if (ipv6_chk_acast_addr(net, dev, &msg->target) ||
            (idev->cnf.forwarding &&
             (net->ipv6.devconf_all->proxy_ndp || idev->cnf.proxy_ndp) &&
             (is_router = pndisc_is_router(&msg->target, dev)) >= 0)) {
                if (!(NEIGH_CB(skb)->flags & LOCALLY_ENQUEUED) &&
                    skb->pkt_type != PACKET_HOST &&
                    inc != 0 &&
                    idev->nd_parms->proxy_delay != 0) {
                        /*
                         * for anycast or proxy,
                         * sender should delay its response
                         * by a random time between 0 and
                         * MAX_ANYCAST_DELAY_TIME seconds.
                         * (RFC2461) -- yoshfuji
                         */
                        struct sk_buff *n = skb_clone(skb, GFP_ATOMIC);
                        if (n)
                                pneigh_enqueue(&nd_tbl, idev->nd_parms, n);
                        goto out;
                }
        } else
                goto out;
}
```

```
if (is_router < 0)
        is_router = idev->cnf.forwarding;

if (dad) {
```

Send a neighbour advertisement message:

```
        ndisc_send_na(dev, NULL, &in6addr_linklocal_allnodes, &msg->target,
                        !!is_router, false, (ifp != NULL), true);
        goto out;
}

if (inc)
        NEIGH_CACHE_STAT_INC(&nd_tbl, rcv_probes_mcast);
else
        NEIGH_CACHE_STAT_INC(&nd_tbl, rcv_probes_ucast);

/*
 *      update / create cache entry
 *      for the source address
 */
neigh = __neigh_lookup(&nd_tbl, saddr, dev,
                        !inc || lladdr || !dev->addr_len);
if (neigh)
```

Update your neighbouring table with the sender's L2 address; the nud_state will be set to be NUD_STALE:

```
        neigh_update(neigh, lladdr, NUD_STALE,
                        NEIGH_UPDATE_F_WEAK_OVERRIDE|
                        NEIGH_UPDATE_F_OVERRIDE);
if (neigh || !dev->header_ops) {
```

Send a Neighbour Advertisement message:

```
                ndisc_send_na(dev, neigh, saddr, &msg->target,
                                !!is_router,
                                true, (ifp != NULL && inc), inc);
                if (neigh)
                        neigh_release(neigh);
        }

out:
        if (ifp)
                in6_ifa_put(ifp);
        else
                in6_dev_put(idev);
}
```

Let's take a look at the method that handles Neighbour Advertisements, ndisc_recv_na():

```
static void ndisc_recv_na(struct sk_buff *skb)
{
        struct nd_msg *msg = (struct nd_msg *)skb_transport_header(skb);
        const struct in6_addr *saddr = &ipv6_hdr(skb)->saddr;
        const struct in6_addr *daddr = &ipv6_hdr(skb)->daddr;
        u8 *lladdr = NULL;
        u32 ndoptlen = skb->tail - (skb->transport_header +
                                    offsetof(struct nd_msg, opt));
        struct ndisc_options ndopts;
        struct net_device *dev = skb->dev;
        struct inet6_ifaddr *ifp;
        struct neighbour *neigh;

        if (skb->len < sizeof(struct nd_msg)) {
                ND_PRINTK(2, warn, "NA: packet too short\n");
                return;
        }

        if (ipv6_addr_is_multicast(&msg->target)) {
                ND_PRINTK(2, warn, "NA: target address is multicast\n");
                return;
        }

        if (ipv6_addr_is_multicast(daddr) &&
            msg->icmph.icmp6_solicited) {
                ND_PRINTK(2, warn, "NA: solicited NA is multicasted\n");
                return;
        }

        if (!ndisc_parse_options(msg->opt, ndoptlen, &ndopts)) {
                ND_PRINTK(2, warn, "NS: invalid ND option\n");
                return;
        }
        if (ndopts.nd_opts_tgt_lladdr) {
                lladdr = ndisc_opt_addr_data(ndopts.nd_opts_tgt_lladdr, dev);
                if (!lladdr) {
                        ND_PRINTK(2, warn,
                                  "NA: invalid link-layer address length\n");
                        return;
                }
        }
        ifp = ipv6_get_ifaddr(dev_net(dev), &msg->target, dev, 1);
        if (ifp) {
                if (skb->pkt_type != PACKET_LOOPBACK
                    && (ifp->flags & IFA_F_TENTATIVE)) {
                            addrconf_dad_failure(ifp);
                            return;
                }
                /* What should we make now? The advertisement
                   is invalid, but ndisc specs say nothing
```

```
                    about it. It could be misconfiguration, or
                    an smart proxy agent tries to help us :-)

                    We should not print the error if NA has been
                    received from loopback - it is just our own
                    unsolicited advertisement.
                 */
                if (skb->pkt_type != PACKET_LOOPBACK)
                        ND_PRINTK(1, warn,
                                    "NA: someone advertises our address %pI6 on %s!\n",
                                    &ifp->addr, ifp->idev->dev->name);
                in6_ifa_put(ifp);
                return;
        }
        neigh = neigh_lookup(&nd_tbl, &msg->target, dev);

        if (neigh) {
                u8 old_flags = neigh->flags;
                struct net *net = dev_net(dev);

                if (neigh->nud_state & NUD_FAILED)
                        goto out;

                /*
                 * Don't update the neighbour cache entry on a proxy NA from
                 * ourselves because either the proxied node is off link or it
                 * has already sent a NA to us.
                 */
                if (lladdr && !memcmp(lladdr, dev->dev_addr, dev->addr_len) &&
                    net->ipv6.devconf_all->forwarding &&
                    net->ipv6.devconf_all->proxy_ndp &&
                    pneigh_lookup(&nd_tbl, net, &msg->target, dev, 0)) {
                        /* XXX: idev->cnf.proxy_ndp */
                        goto out;
                }
```

Update the neighbouring table. When the received message is a Neighbour Solicitation, the `icmp6_solicited` is set, so you want to set the state to be NUD_REACHABLE. When the `icmp6_override` flag is set, you want the override flag to be set (this mean update the L2 address with the specified `lladdr`, if it is different):

```
                neigh_update(neigh, lladdr,
                            msg->icmph.icmp6_solicited ? NUD_REACHABLE : NUD_STALE,
                            NEIGH_UPDATE_F_WEAK_OVERRIDE|
                            (msg->icmph.icmp6_override ? NEIGH_UPDATE_F_OVERRIDE : 0)|
                            NEIGH_UPDATE_F_OVERRIDE_ISROUTER|
                            (msg->icmph.icmp6_router ? NEIGH_UPDATE_F_ISROUTER : 0));

                if ((old_flags & ~neigh->flags) & NTF_ROUTER) {
                        /*
                         * Change: router to host
                         */
```

```
                        struct rt6_info *rt;
                        rt = rt6_get_dflt_router(saddr, dev);
                        if (rt)
                                ip6_del_rt(rt);
                }

out:

                neigh_release(neigh);
        }
}
```

Summary

This chapter described the neighbouring subsystem in IPv4 and in IPv6. First you learned about the goals of the neighbouring subsystem. Then you learned about ARP requests and ARP replies in IPv4, and about NDISC Neighbour Solicitation and NDISC Neighbour Advertisements in IPv6. You also found out about how DAD implementation avoids duplicate IPv6 addresses, and you saw various methods for handling the neighbouring subsystem requests and replies. Chapter 8 discusses the IPv6 subsystem implementation. The "Quick Reference" section that follows covers the top methods and macros related to the topics discussed in this chapter, ordered by their context. I also show the neigh_statistics structure, which represents statistics collected by the neighbouring subsystem.

Quick Reference

The following are some important methods and macros of the neighbouring subsystem, and a description of the neigh_statistics structure.

■ **Note**   The core neighbouring code is in net/core/neighbour.c, include/net/neighbour.h and include/uapi/linux/neighbour.h.

The ARP code (IPv4) is in net/ipv4/arp.c, include/net/arp.h and in include/uapi/linux/if_arp.h.

The NDISC code (IPv6) is in net/ipv6/ndisc.c and include/net/ndisc.h.

Methods

Let's start by covering the methods.

void neigh_table_init(struct neigh_table *tbl)

This method invokes the neigh_table_init_no_netlink() method to perform the initialization of the neighbouring table, and links the table to the global neighbouring tables linked list (neigh_tables).

void neigh_table_init_no_netlink(struct neigh_table *tbl)

This method performs all the neighbour initialization apart from linking it to the global neighbouring table linked list, which is done by the neigh_table_init(), as mentioned earlier.

int neigh_table_clear(struct neigh_table *tbl)

This method frees the resources of the specified neighbouring table.

struct neighbour *neigh_alloc(struct neigh_table *tbl, struct net_device *dev)

This method allocates a neighbour object.

struct neigh_hash_table *neigh_hash_alloc(unsigned int shift)

This method allocates a neighbouring hash table.

struct neighbour *__neigh_create(struct neigh_table *tbl, const void *pkey, struct net_device *dev, bool want_ref)

This method creates a neighbour object.

int neigh_add(struct sk_buff *skb, struct nlmsghdr *nlh, void *arg)

This method adds a neighbour entry; it is the handler for netlink RTM_NEWNEIGH message.

int neigh_delete(struct sk_buff *skb, struct nlmsghdr *nlh, void *arg)

This method deletes a neighbour entry; it is the handler for netlink RTM_DELNEIGH message.

void neigh_probe(struct neighbour *neigh)

This method fetches an SKB from the neighbour arp_queue and calls the corresponding solicit() method to send it. In case of ARP, it will be arp_solicit(). It increments the neighbour probes counter and frees the packet.

int neigh_forced_gc(struct neigh_table *tbl)

This method is a synchronous garbage collection method. It removes neighbour entries that are not in the permanent state (NUD_PERMANENT) and whose reference count equals 1. The removal and cleanup of a neighbour is done by first setting the dead flag of the neighbour to be 1 and then calling the neigh_cleanup_and_release() method, which gets a neighbour object as a parameter. The neigh_forced_gc() method is invoked from the neigh_alloc() method under some conditions, as described in the "Creating and Freeing a Neighbour" section earlier in this chapter. The neigh_forced_gc() method returns 1 if at least one neighbour object was removed, and 0 otherwise.

void neigh_periodic_work(struct work_struct *work)

This method is the asynchronous garbage collector handler.

static void neigh_timer_handler(unsigned long arg)

This method is the per-neighbour periodic timer garbage collector handler.

struct neighbour *__neigh_lookup(struct neigh_table *tbl, const void *pkey, struct net_device *dev, int creat)

This method performs a lookup in the specified neighbouring table by the given key. If the creat parameter is 1, and the lookup fails, call the neigh_create() method to create a neighbour entry in the specified neighbouring table and return it.

neigh_hh_init(struct neighbour *n, struct dst_entry *dst)

This method initializes the L2 cache (hh_cache object) of the specified neighbour based on the specified routing cache entry.

void __init arp_init(void)

This method performs the setup for the ARP protocol: initialize the ARP table, register the arp_rcv() as a handler for receiving ARP packets, initialize procfs entries, register sysctl entries, and register the ARP netdev notifier callback, arp_netdev_event().

int arp_rcv(struct sk_buff *skb, struct net_device *dev, struct packet_type *pt, struct net_device *orig_dev)

This method is the Rx handler for ARP packets (Ethernet packets with type 0x0806).

int arp_constructor(struct neighbour *neigh)

This method performs ARP neighbour initialization.

int arp_process(struct sk_buff *skb)

This method, invoked by the arp_rcv() method, handles the main processing of ARP requests and ARP responses.

void arp_solicit(struct neighbour *neigh, struct sk_buff *skb)

This method sends the solicitation request (ARPOP_REQUEST) after some checks and initializations, by calling the arp_send() method.

void arp_send(int type, int ptype, __be32 dest_ip, struct net_device *dev, __be32 src_ip, const unsigned char *dest_hw, const unsigned char *src_hw, const unsigned char *target_hw)

This method creates an ARP packet and initializes it with the specified parameters, by calling the arp_create() method, and sends it by calling the arp_xmit() method.

void arp_xmit(struct sk_buff *skb)

This method actually sends the packet by calling the NF_HOOK macro with dev_queue_xmit().

struct arphdr *arp_hdr(const struct sk_buff *skb)

This method fetches the ARP header of the specified SKB.

int arp_mc_map(__be32 addr, u8 *haddr, struct net_device *dev, int dir)

This method translates an IPv4 address to L2 (link layer) address according to the network device type. When the device is an Ethernet device, for example, this is done with the ip_eth_mc_map() method; when the device is an Infiniband device, this is done with the ip_ib_mc_map() method.

static inline int arp_fwd_proxy(struct in_device *in_dev, struct net_device *dev, struct rtable *rt)

This method returns 1 if the specified device can use proxy ARP for the specified routing entry.

static inline int arp_fwd_pvlan(struct in_device *in_dev, struct net_device *dev, struct rtable *rt, __be32 sip, __be32 tip)

This method returns 1 if the specified device can use proxy ARP VLAN for the specified routing entry and specified IPv4 source and destination addresses.

int arp_netdev_event(struct notifier_block *this, unsigned long event, void *ptr)

This method is the ARP handler for netdev notification events.

int ndisc_netdev_event(struct notifier_block *this, unsigned long event, void *ptr)

This method is the NDISC handler for netdev notification events.

int ndisc_rcv(struct sk_buff *skb)

This method is the main NDISC handler for receiving one of the five types of solicitation packets.

static int neigh_blackhole(struct neighbour *neigh, struct sk_buff *skb)

This method discards the packet and returns -ENETDOWN error (network is down).

static void ndisc_recv_ns(struct sk_buff *skb) and static void ndisc_recv_na(struct sk_buff *skb)

These methods handle receiving Neighbour Solicitation and Neighbour Advertisement, respectively.

static void ndisc_recv_rs(struct sk_buff *skb) and static void ndisc_router_discovery(struct sk_buff *skb)

These methods handle receiving router solicitation and router advertisement, respectively.

int ndisc_mc_map(const struct in6_addr *addr, char *buf, struct net_device *dev, int dir)

This method translates an IPv4 address to a L2 (link layer) address according to the network device type. In Ethernet under IPv6, this is done by the `ipv6_eth_mc_map()` method.

int ndisc_constructor(struct neighbour *neigh)

This method performs NDISC neighbour initialization.

void ndisc_solicit(struct neighbour *neigh, struct sk_buff *skb)

This method sends the solicitation request after some checks and initializations, by calling the `ndisc_send_ns()` method.

int icmpv6_rcv(struct sk_buff *skb)

This method is a handler for receiving ICMPv6 messages.

bool ipv6_addr_any(const struct in6_addr *a)

This method returns 1 when the given IPv6 address is the unspecified address of all zeroes (IPV6_ADDR_ANY).

int inet_addr_onlink(struct in_device *in_dev, __be32 a, __be32 b)

This method checks whether the two specified addresses are on the same subnet.

Macros

Now, let's look at the macros.

IN_DEV_PROXY_ARP(in_dev)

This macro returns true if /proc/sys/net/ipv4/conf/<netDevice>/proxy_arp is set or if /proc/sys/net/ipv4/conf/all/proxy_arp is set, where netDevice is the network device associated with the specified in_dev.

IN_DEV_PROXY_ARP_PVLAN(in_dev)

This macro returns true if /proc/sys/net/ipv4/conf/<netDevice>/proxy_arp_pvlan is set, where netDevice is the network device associated with the specified in_dev.

IN_DEV_ARPFILTER(in_dev)

This macro returns true if /proc/sys/net/ipv4/conf/<netDevice>/arp_filter is set or if /proc/sys/net/ipv4/conf/all/arp_filter is set, where netDevice is the network device associated with the specified in_dev.

IN_DEV_ARP_ACCEPT(in_dev)

This macro returns true if /proc/sys/net/ipv4/conf/<netDevice>/arp_accept is set or if /proc/sys/net/ipv4/conf/all/arp_accept is set, where netDevice is the network device associated with the specified in_dev.

IN_DEV_ARP_ANNOUNCE(in_dev)

This macro returns the max value of /proc/sys/net/ipv4/conf/<netDevice>/arp_announce and /proc/sys/net/ipv4/conf/all/arp_announce, where netDevice is the network device associated with the specified in_dev.

IN_DEV_ARP_IGNORE(in_dev)

This macro returns the max value of /proc/sys/net/ipv4/conf/<netDevice>/arp_ignore and /proc/sys/net/ipv4/conf/all/arp_ignore, where netDevice is the network device associated with the specified in_dev.

IN_DEV_ARP_NOTIFY(in_dev)

This macro returns the max value of /proc/sys/net/ipv4/conf/<netDevice>/arp_notify and /proc/sys/net/ipv4/conf/all/arp_notify, where netDevice is the network device associated with the specified in_dev.

IN_DEV_SHARED_MEDIA(in_dev)

This macro returns true if /proc/sys/net/ipv4/conf/<netDevice>/shared_media is set or if /proc/sys/net/ipv4/conf/all/shared_media is set, where netDevice is the network device associated with the specified in_dev.

IN_DEV_ROUTE_LOCALNET(in_dev)

This macro returns true if /proc/sys/net/ipv4/conf/<netDevice>/route_localnet is set or if /proc/sys/net/ipv4/conf/all/route_localnet is set, where netDevice is the network device associated with the specified in_dev.

neigh_hold()

This macro increments the reference count of the specified neighbour.

The neigh_statistics Structure

The neigh_statistics structure is important for monitoring the neighbouring subsystem; as mentioned in the beginning of the chapter, both ARP and NDISC export this structure members via procfs (/proc/net/stat/arp_cache and /proc/net/stat/ndisc_cache, respectively). Following is a description of its members and pointing out where they are incremented:

```
struct neigh_statistics {
        unsigned long allocs;          /* number of allocated neighs     */
        unsigned long destroys;        /* number of destroyed neighs     */
        unsigned long hash_grows;      /* number of hash resizes         */
        unsigned long res_failed;      /* number of failed resolutions   */
        unsigned long lookups;         /* number of lookups              */
        unsigned long hits;            /* number of hits (among lookups) */
        unsigned long rcv_probes_mcast; /* number of received mcast ipv6 */
        unsigned long rcv_probes_ucast; /* number of received ucast ipv6 */
        unsigned long periodic_gc_runs; /* number of periodic GC runs    */
        unsigned long forced_gc_runs;  /* number of forced GC runs       */
        unsigned long unres_discards;  /* number of unresolved drops     */
};
```

Here is a description of the members of the neigh_statistics structure:

- allocs: The number of the allocated neighbours; incremented by the neigh_alloc() method.

- destroys: The number of the destroyed neighbours; incremented by the neigh_destroy() method.

- hash_grows: The number of times that hash resize was done; incremented by the neigh_hash_grow() method.

- res_failed: The number of failed resolutions; incremented by the neigh_invalidate() method.

- lookups: The number of neighbour lookups that were done; incremented by the neigh_lookup() method and by the neigh_lookup_nodev() method.

- hits: The number of hits when performing a neighbour lookup ; incremented by the neigh_lookup() method and by the neigh_lookup_nodev() method, when you have a hit.

- rcv_probes_mcast: The number of received multicast probes (IPv6 only); incremented by the ndisc_recv_ns() method.

- rcv_probes_ucast: The number of received unicast probes (IPv6 only); incremented by the ndisc_recv_ns() method.

- periodic_gc_runs: The number of periodic GC invocations; incremented by the neigh_periodic_work() method.

- `forced_gc_runs`: The number of forced GC invocations; incremented by the `neigh_forced_gc()` method.

- `unres_discards`: The number of unresolved drops; incremented by the `__neigh_event_send()` method when an unresolved packet is discarded.

Table

Here is the table that was covered.

Table 7-1. *Network Unreachability Detection States*

Linux	Symbol
NUD_INCOMPLETE	Address resolution is in progress and the link-layer address of the neighbour has not yet been determined. This means that a solicitation request was sent, and you are waiting for a solicitation reply or a timeout.
NUD_REACHABLE	The neighbour is known to have been reachable recently.
NUD_STALE	More than ReachableTime milliseconds have elapsed since the last positive confirmation that the forward path was functioning properly was received.
NUD_DELAY	The neighbour is no longer known to be reachable. Delay sending probes for a short while in order to give upper layer protocols a chance to provide reachability confirmation.
NUD_PROBE	The neighbour is no longer known to be reachable, and unicast Neighbour Solicitation probes are being sent to verify reachability.
NUD_FAILED	Set the neighbour to be unreachable. When you delete a neighbour, you set it to be in the NUD_FAILED state.

CHAPTER 8

IPv6

In Chapter 7, I dealt with the Linux Neighbouring Subsystem and its implementation. In this chapter, I will discuss the IPv6 protocol and its implementation in Linux. IPv6 is the next-generation network layer protocol of the TCP/IP protocol stack. It was developed by the Internet Engineering Task Force (IETF), and it is intended to replace IPv4, which still carries the vast majority of Internet traffic.

In the early '90s, the IETF started an effort to develop the next generation of the IP protocol, due to the anticipated Internet growth. The first IPv6 RFC is from 1995: RFC 1883, "Internet Protocol, Version 6 (IPv6) Specification." Later, in 1998, RFC 2460 replaced it. The main problem IPv6 solves is the shortage of addresses: the length of an IPv6 address is 128 bits. IPv6 sets a much larger address space. Instead of 2^{32} addresses in IPv4, we have 2^{128} addresses in IPv6. This indeed enlarges the address space significantly, probably far more than will be needed in the next few decades. But extended address space is not the only advantage of IPv6, as some might think. Based on the experience gained with IPv4, many changes were made in IPv6 to improve the IP protocol. We will discuss many of these changes in this chapter.

The IPv6 protocol is now gaining momentum as an improved network layer protocol. The growing popularity of the Internet all over the globe, and the growing markets for smart mobile devices and tablets, surely make the exhaustion of IPv4 addresses a more evident problem. This gives rise to the need for transitioning to the IPv4 successor, the IPv6 protocol.

IPv6 – Short Introduction

The IPv6 subsystem is undoubtedly a very broad subject, which is growing steadily. Exciting features were added during the last decade. Some of these new features are based on IPv4, like ICMPv6 sockets, IPv6 Multicast Routing, and IPv6 NAT. IPsec is mandatory in IPv6 and optional in IPv4, though most operating systems implemented IPsec also in IPv4. When we delve into the IPv6 kernel internals, we find many similarities. Sometime the names of the methods and even the names of some of the variables are similar, except for the addition of "v6" or "6." There are, however, some changes in the implementation in some places.

We chose to discuss in this chapter the important new features of IPv6, show some places where it differs from IPv4, and explain why a change was made. The extension headers, the Multicast Listener Discovery (MLD) protocol, and the Autoconfiguration process are some of the new features that we discuss and demonstrate with some userspace examples. We also discuss how receiving IPv6 packets works, how IPv6 forwarding works, and some points of difference when comparing them to IPv4. On the whole, it seems that the developers of IPv6 made a lot of improvements based on the past experience with IPv4, and the IPv6 implementation brings a lot of benefits not found in IPv4 and a lot of advantages over IPv4. We will discuss IPv6 addresses in the following section, including multicast addresses and special addresses.

IPv6 Addresses

The first step in learning IPv6 is to become familiar with the IPv6 Addressing Architecture, which is defined in RFC 4291. There are three types of IPv6 addresses:

- **Unicast:** This address uniquely identifies an interface. A packet sent to a unicast address is delivered to the interface identified by that address.

- **Anycast:** This address can be assigned for a set of interfaces (usually on different nodes). This type of address does not exist in IPv4. It is, in fact, a mixture of a unicast address and a multicast address. A packet sent to an anycast address is delivered to one of the interfaces identified by that address (the "nearest" one, according to the routing protocols).

- **Multicast:** This address can be assigned for a set of interfaces (usually on different nodes). A packet sent to a multicast address is delivered to all the interfaces identified by that address. An interface can belong to any number of multicast groups.

There is no broadcast address in IPv6. In IPv6, to get the same result as broadcast, you can send a packet to the group multicast address of all nodes (ff02::1). In IPv4, a large part of the functionality of the Address Resolution Protocol (ARP) protocol is based on broadcasts. The IPv6 subsystem uses neighbour discovery instead of ARP to map L3 addresses to L2 addresses. The IPv6 neighbour discovery protocol is based on ICMPv6, and it uses multicast addresses instead of broadcasts, as you saw in the previous chapter. You will see more examples of using multicast traffic later in this chapter.

An IPv6 address comprises of 8 blocks of 16 bits, which is 128 bits in total. An IPv6 address looks like this: xxxx:xxxx:xxxx:xxxx:xxxx:xxxx:xxxx:xxxx (where x is a hexadecimal digit.) Sometimes you will encounter "::" inside an IPv6 address; this is a shortcut for leading zeroes.

In IPv6, address prefixes are used. Prefixes are, in fact, the parallel of IPv4 subnet masks. IPv6 prefixes are described in RFC 4291, "IP Version 6 Addressing Architecture." An IPv6 address prefix is represented by the following notation: `ipv6-address/prefix-length`.

The prefix-length is a decimal value specifying how many of the leftmost contiguous bits of the address comprise the prefix. We use "/n" to denote a prefix n bits long. For example, for all IPv6 addresses that begin with the 32 bits 2001:0da7, the following prefix is used: 2001:da7::/32.

Now that you have learned about the types of IPv6 addresses, you will learn in the following section about some special IPv6 addresses and their usage.

Special Addresses

In this section, I describe some special IPv6 addresses and their usage. It is recommended that you be familiar with these special addresses because you will encounter some of them later in this chapter (like the unspecified address of all zeroes that is used in DAD, or Duplicate Address Detection) and while browsing the code. The following list contains special IPv6 addresses and explanations about their usage:

- There should be at least one **link-local** unicast address on each interface. The link-local address allows communication with other nodes in the same physical network; it is required for neighbour discovery, automatic address configuration, and more. Routers must not forward any packets with link-local source or destination addresses. Link-local addresses are assigned with the prefix fe80::/64.

- The Global Unicast Address general format is as follows: the first n bits are the global routing prefix, the next m bits are the subnet ID, and the rest of the 128-n-m bits are the interface ID.

- `global routing prefix`: A value assigned to a site. It represents the network ID or prefix of the address.

- `subnet ID`: An identifier of a subnet within the site.

- `interface ID`: An id; its value must be unique within the subnet. This is defined in RFC 3513, section 2.5.1.

The Global Unicast Address is described in RFC 3587, "IPv6 Global Unicast Address Format." The assignable Global Unicast Address space is defined in RFC 4291.

- The IPv6 loopback address is `0:0:0:0:0:0:0:1`, or `::1` in short notation.

- The address of all zeroes (`0:0:0:0:0:0:0:0`) is called the **unspecified address**. It is used in DAD (Duplicate Address Detection) as you saw in the previous chapter. It should not be used as a destination address. You cannot assign the unspecified address to an interface by using userspace tools like the `ip` command or the `ifconfig` command.

- **IPv4-mapped IPv6 addresses** are addresses that start with 80 bits of zero. The next 16 bits are one, and the remaining 32 bits are the IPv4 address. For example, `::ffff:192.0.2.128` represents the IPv4 address of 192.0.2.128. For usage of these addresses, see RFC 4038, "Application Aspects of IPv6 Transition."

- **The IPv4-compatible** format is deprecated; in this format, the IPv4 address is in the lower 32 bits of the IPv6 address and all remaining bits are 0; the address mentioned earlier should be `::192.0.2.128` in this format. See RFC 4291, section 2.5.5.1.

- **Site local addresses** were originally designed to be used for addressing inside of a site without the need for a global prefix, but they were deprecated in RFC 3879, "Deprecating Site Local Addresses," in 2004.

An IPv6 address is represented in Linux by the `in6_addr` structure; using a union with three arrays (with 8, 16, and 32 bit elements) in the `in6_addr` structure helps in bit-manipulation operations:

```
struct in6_addr {
        union {
                __u8            u6_addr8[16];
                __be16          u6_addr16[8];
                __be32          u6_addr32[4];
        } in6_u;
#define s6_addr                 in6_u.u6_addr8
#define s6_addr16               in6_u.u6_addr16
#define s6_addr32               in6_u.u6_addr32
};
```

(include/uapi/linux/in6.h)

Multicast plays an important role in IPv6, especially for ICMPv6-based protocols like NDISC (which I discussed in Chapter 7, which dealt with the Linux Neighbouring Subsystem) and MLD (which is discussed later in this chapter). I will now discuss multicast addresses in IPv6 in the next section.

Multicast Addresses

Multicast addresses provide a way to define a multicast group; a node can belong to one or more multicast groups. Packets whose destination is a multicast address should be delivered to every node that belongs to that multicast group. In IPv6, all multicast addresses start with FF (8 first bits). Following are 4 bits for flags and 4 bits for scope. Finally, the last 112 bits are the group ID. The 4 bits of the flags field have this meaning:

- **Bit 0:** Reserved for future use.

- **Bit 1:** A value of 1 indicates that a Rendezvous Point is embedded in the address. Discussion of Rendezvous Points is more related to userspace daemons and is not within the scope of this book. For more details, see RFC 3956, "Embedding the Rendezvous Point (RP) Address in an IPv6 Multicast Address." This bit is sometimes referred to as the R-flag (R for Rendezvous Point.)

- **Bit 2:** A value of 1 indicates a multicast address that is assigned based on the network prefix. (See RFC 3306.) This bit is sometimes referred to as the P-flag (P for Prefix information.)

- **Bit 3:** A value of 0 indicates a permanently-assigned ("well-known") multicast address, assigned by the Internet Assigned Numbers Authority (IANA). A value of 1 indicates a non-permanently-assigned ("transient") multicast address. This bit is sometimes referred to as the T-flag (T for Temporary.)

The scope can be one of the entries in Table 8-1, which shows the various IPv6 scopes by their Linux symbol and by their value.

Table 8-1. *IPv6 scopes*

Hex value	Description	Linux Symbol
0x01	node local	IPV6_ADDR_SCOPE_NODELOCAL
0x02	link local	IPV6_ADDR_SCOPE_LINKLOCAL
0x05	site local	IPV6_ADDR_SCOPE_SITELOCAL
0x08	organization	IPV6_ADDR_SCOPE_ORGLOCAL
0x0e	global	IPV6_ADDR_SCOPE_GLOBAL

Now that you've learned about IPv6 multicast addresses, you will learn about some special multicast addresses in the next section.

Special Multicast Addresses

There are some special multicast addresses that I will mention in this chapter. Section 2.7.1 of RFC 4291 defines these special multicast addresses:

- All Nodes Multicast Address group: ff01::1, ff02::1

- All Routers Multicast Address group: ff01::2, ff02::2, ff05::2

According to RFC 3810, there is this special address: All MLDv2-capable routers Multicast Group, which is ff02::16. Version 2 Multicast Listener Reports will be sent to this special address; I will discuss it in the "Multicast Listener Discovery (MLD)" section later in this chapter.

A node is required to compute and join (on the appropriate interface) the associated Solicited-Node multicast addresses for all unicast and anycast addresses that have been configured for the node's interfaces (manually or automatically). Solicited-Node multicast addresses are computed based on the node's unicast and anycast addresses. A Solicited-Node multicast address is formed by taking the low-order 24 bits of an address (unicast or anycast) and appending those bits to the prefix ff02:0:0:0:0:1:ff00::/104, resulting in a multicast address in the range ff02:0:0:0:0:1:ff00:0000 to ff02:0:0:0:0:1:ffff:ffff. See RFC 4291.

The method addrconf_addr_solict_mult() computes a link-local, solicited-node multicast address (include/net/addrconf.h). The method addrconf_join_solict() joins to a solicited address multicast group (net/ipv6/addrconf.c).

In the previous chapter, you saw that a neighbour advertisement message is sent by the ndisc_send_na() method to the link-local, all nodes address (ff02::1). You will see more examples of using special addresses like the all nodes multicast group address or all routers multicast group address in later subsections of this chapter. In this section, you have seen some multicast addresses, which you will encounter later in this chapter and while browsing the IPv6 source code. I will now discuss the IPv6 header in the following section.

IPv6 Header

Each IPv6 packet starts with an IPv6 header, and it is important to learn about its structure to understand fully the IPv6 Linux implementation. The IPv6 header has a fixed length of 40 bytes; for this reason, there is no field specifying the IPv6 header length (as opposed to IPv4, where the ihl member of the IPv4 header represents the header length). Note that there is also no checksum field in the IPv6 header, and this will be explained later in this chapter. In IPv6, there is no IP options mechanism as in IPv4. The IP options processing mechanism in IPv4 has a performance cost. Instead, IPV6 has a much more efficient mechanism of extension headers, which will be discussed in the next section, "extension headers." Figure 8-1 shows the IPv6 header and its fields.

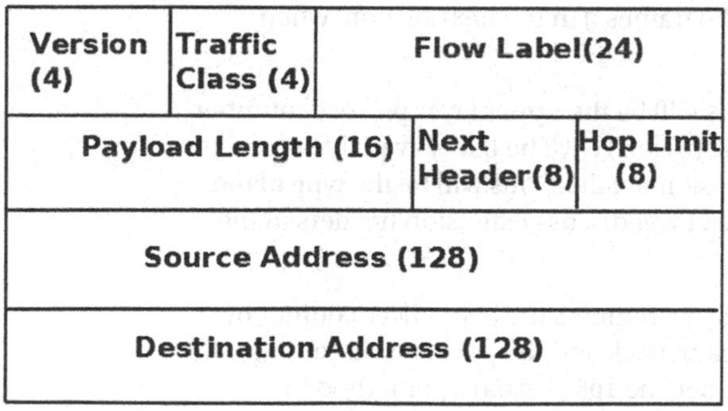

Figure 8-1. *IPv6 header*

Note that in the original IPv6 standard, RFC 2460, the priority (Traffic Class) is 8 bits and the flow label is 20 bits. In the definition of the ipv6hdr structure, the priority (Traffic Class) field size is 4 bits. In fact, in the Linux IPv6 implementation, the first 4 bits of flow_lbl are glued to the priority (Traffic Class) field in order to form a "class." Figure 8-1 reflects the Linux definition of the ipv6hdr structure, which is shown here:

```
struct ipv6hdr {
#if defined(__LITTLE_ENDIAN_BITFIELD)
        __u8                    priority:4,
                                version:4;
#elif defined(__BIG_ENDIAN_BITFIELD)
        __u8                    version:4,
```

```
                                    priority:4;
#else
#error   "Please fix <asm/byteorder.h>"
#endif
         __u8                       flow_lbl[3];

         __be16                     payload_len;
         __u8                       nexthdr;
         __u8                       hop_limit;

         struct   in6_addr          saddr;
         struct   in6_addr          daddr;
};
```

(include/uapi/linux/ipv6.h)

The following is a description of the members of the ipv6hdr structure:

- version: A 4-bit field. It should be set to 6.

- priority: Indicates the traffic class or priority of the IPv6 packet. RFC 2460, the base of IPv6, does not define specific traffic class or priority values.

- flow_lbl: The flow labeling field was regarded as experimental when the base IPv6 standard was written (RFC 2460). It provides a way to label sequences of packets of a particular flow; this labeling can be used by upper layers for various purposes. RFC 6437, "IPv6 Flow Label Specification," from 2011, suggests using flow labeling to detect address spoofing.

- payload_len: A 16-bit field. The size of the packet, without the IPv6 header, can be up to 65,535 bytes. I will discuss larger packets ("jumbo frames") in the next section, when presenting the Hop-by-Hop Options header.

- nexthdr: When there are no extension headers, this will be the upper layer protocol number, like IPPROTO_UDP (17) for UDP or IPPROTO_TCP (6) for TCP. The list of available protocols is in include/uapi/linux/in.h. When using extension headers, this will be the type of the next header immediately following the IPv6 header. I will discuss extension headers in the next section.

- hop_limit: One byte field. Every forwarding device decrements the hop_limit counter by one. When it reaches zero, an ICMPv6 message is sent back and the packet is discarded. This parallels the TTL member in the IPv4 header. See the ip6_forward() method in net/ipv6/ip6_output.c.

- saddr: IPv6 source address (128 bit).

- daddr: IPv6 destination address (128 bit). This is possibly not the final packet destination if a Routing Header is used.

Note that, as opposed to the IPv4 header, there is no checksum in the IPv6 header. Checksumming is assumed to be assured by both Layer 2 and Layer 4. UDP in IPv4 permits having a checksum of 0, indicating no checksum; UDP in IPV6 requires having its own checksum normally. There are some special cases in IPv6 where zero UDP checksum is allowed for IPv6 UDP tunnels; see RFC 6935, "IPv6 and UDP Checksums for Tunneled Packets." In Chapter 4, which deals with the IPv4 subsystem, you saw that when forwarding a packet the ip_decrease_ttl() method is invoked. This method recomputes the checksum of the IPv4 header because the value of the ttl was changed. In IPv6, there is no such a need for recomputation of the checksum when forwarding a packet, because there is no checksum at all in the IPv6 header. This results in a performance improvement in software-based routers.

In this section, you have seen how the IPv6 header is built. You saw some differences between the IPv4 header and the IPv6 header—for example, in the IPv6 header there is no checksum and no header length. The next section discusses the IPv6 extension headers, which are the counterpart of IPv4 options.

Extension Headers

The IPv4 header can include IP options, which can extend the IPv4 header from a minimum size of 20 bytes to 60 bytes. In IPv6, we have optional extension headers instead. With one exception (Hop-by-Hop Options header), extension headers are not processed by any node along a packet's delivery path until the packet reaches its final destination; this improves the performance of the forwarding process significantly. The base IPv6 standard defines extension headers. An IPv6 packet can include 0, 1 or more extension headers. These headers can be placed between the IPv6 header and the upper-layer header in a packet. The nexthdr field of the IPv6 header is the number of the next header immediately after the IPv6 header. These extension headers are chained; every extension header has a Next Header field. In the last extension header, the Next Header indicates the upper-layer protocol (such as TCP, UDP, or ICMPv6). Another advantage of extension headers is that adding new extension headers in the future is easy and does not require any changes in the IPv6 header.

Extension headers must be processed strictly in the order they appear in the packet. Each extension header should occur at most once, except for the Destination Options header, which should occur at most twice. (See more detail later in this section in the description of the Destination Options header.) The Hop-by-Hop Options header must appear immediately after the IPv6 header; all other options can appear in any order. Section 4.1 of RFC 2460 ("Extension Header Order") states a recommended order in which extension headers should appear, but this is not mandatory. When an unknown Next Header number is encountered while processing a packet, an ICMPv6 "Parameter Problem" message with a code of "unknown Next Header" (ICMPV6_UNK_NEXTHDR) will be sent back to the sender by calling the icmpv6_param_prob() method. A description of the available ICMPv6 "Parameter Problem Codes" appears in Table 8-4 in the "Quick Reference" section at the end of this chapter.

Each extension header must be aligned on an 8-byte boundary. For extension headers of variable size, there is a Header Extension Length field, and they use padding if needed to ensure that they are aligned on an 8-byte boundary. The numbers of all Linux IPv6 extension headers and their Linux Kernel symbol representation are displayed in Table 8-2, "IPv6 extension headers," in the "Quick Reference" section at the end of this chapter.

A protocol handler is registered for each of the extension headers (except the Hop-by-Hop Options header) with the inet6_add_protocol() method. The reason for not registering a protocol handler for the Hop-by-Hop Options header is that there is a special method for parsing the Hop-by-Hop Options header, the ipv6_parse_hopopts() method. This method is invoked before calling the protocol handlers. (See the ipv6_rcv() method, net/ipv6/ip6_input.c). As mentioned before, the Hop-by-Hop Options header must be the first one, immediately following the IPv6 header. In this way, for example, the protocol handler for the Fragment extension header is registered:

```
static const struct inet6_protocol frag_protocol =
{
    .handler    =    ipv6_frag_rcv,
    .flags      =    INET6_PROTO_NOPOLICY,
};


int __init ipv6_frag_init(void)
{
    int ret;

    ret = inet6_add_protocol(&frag_protocol, IPPROTO_FRAGMENT);
```

(net/ipv6/reassembly.c)

Here is a description of all IPv6 Extension headers:

- **Hop-by-Hop Options header:** The Hop-by-Hop Options header must be processed on each node. It is parsed by the `ipv6_parse_hopopts()` method (`net/ipv6/exthdrs.c`).

- The Hop-by-Hop Options header must be immediately after the IPv6 header. It is used, for example, by the Multicast Listener Discovery protocol, as you will see in the "Multicast Listener Discovery (MLD)" section later in this chapter. The Hop-by-Hop Options header includes a variable-length option field. Its first byte is its type, which can be one of the following:

  - Router Alert (Linux Kernel symbol: IPV6_TLV_ROUTERALERT, value: 5). See RFC 6398, "IP Router Alert Considerations and Usage."

  - Jumbo (Linux Kernel symbol: IPV6_TLV_JUMBO, value: 194). The IPv6 packet payload normally can be up to 65,535 bytes long. With the jumbo option, it can be up to 2^{32} bytes. See RFC 2675, "IPv6 Jumbograms."

  - Pad1 (Linux Kernel symbol: IPV6_TLV_PAD1, value: 0). The Pad1 option is used to insert one byte of padding. When more than one padding byte is needed, the PadN option (see next) should be used (and not multiple Pad1 options). See section 4.2 of RFC 2460.

  - PadN (Linux Kernel symbol: IPV6_TLV_PADN, value: 1). The PadN option is used to insert two or more octets of padding into the Options area of a header.

- **Routing Options header:** This parallels the IPv4 Loose Source Record Route (IPOPT_LSRR), which is discussed in the "IP Options" section in Chapter 4. It provides the ability to specify one or more routers that should be visited along the packet's traversal route to its final destination.

- **Fragment Options header:** As opposed to IPv4, fragmentation in IPv6 can occur only on the host that sends the packet, not on any of the intermediate nodes. Fragmentation is implemented by the `ip6_fragment()` method, which is invoked from the `ip6_finish_output()` method. In the `ip6_fragment()` method, there is a slow path and a fast path, much the same as in IPv4 fragmentation. The implementation of IPv6 fragmentation is in `net/ipv6/ip6_output.c`, and the implementation of IPv6 defragmentation is in `net/ipv6/reassembly.c`.

- **Authentication Header:** The Authentication header (AH) provides data authentication, data integrity, and anti-replay protection. It is described in RFC 4302, "IP Authentication Header," which makes RFC 2402 obsolete.

- **Encapsulating Security Payload Options header:** It is described in RFC 4303, "IP Encapsulating Security Payload (ESP)," which makes RFC 2406 obsolete. Note: The Encapsulating Security Payload (ESP) protocol is discussed in Chapter 10, which discusses the IPsec subsystem.

- **Destination Options header:** The Destination Options header can appear twice in a packet; before a Routing Options header, and after it. When it is before the Routing Options header, it includes information that should be processed by the routers that are specified by the Router Options header. When it is after the Router Options header, it includes information that should be processed by the final destination.

In the next section, you will see how the IPv6 protocol handler, which is the `ipv6_rcv()` method, is associated with IPv6 packets.

IPv6 Initialization

The inet6_init() method performs various IPv6 initializations (like procfs initializations, registration of protocol handlers for TCPv6, UDPv6 and other protocols), initialization of IPv6 subsystems (like IPv6 neighbour discovery, IPv6 Multicast Routing, and IPv6 routing subsystem) and more. For more details, look in net/ipv6/af_inet6.c. The ipv6_rcv() method is registered as a protocol handler for IPv6 packets by defining a packet_type object for IPv6 and registering it with the dev_add_pack() method, quite similarly to what is done in IPv4:

```
static struct packet_type ipv6_packet_type __read_mostly = {
        .type = cpu_to_be16(ETH_P_IPV6),
        .func = ipv6_rcv,
};

static int __init ipv6_packet_init(void)
{
        dev_add_pack(&ipv6_packet_type);
        return 0;
}
```

(net/ipv6/af_inet6.c)

As a result of the registration just shown, each Ethernet packet whose ethertype is ETH_P_IPV6 (0x86DD) will be handled by the ipv6_rcv() method. Next, I will discuss the IPv6 Autoconfiguration mechanism for setting IPv6 addresses.

Autoconfiguration

Autoconfiguration is a mechanism that allows a host to obtain or create a unique address for each of its interfaces. The IPv6 autoconfiguration process is initiated at system startup; nodes (both hosts and routers) generate a link-local address for their interfaces. This address is regarded as "tentative" (the interface flag IFA_F_TENTATIVE is set); this means that it can communicate only with neighbour discovery messages. It should be verified that this address is not already in use by another node on the link. This is done with the DAD (Duplicate Address Detection) mechanism, which was described in the previous chapter which deals with the Linux Neighbouring Subsystem. If the node is not unique, the autoconfiguration process will stop and manual configuration will be needed. In cases where the address is unique, the autoconfiguration process will continue. The next phase of autoconfiguration of hosts involves sending one or more Router Solicitations to the all routers multicast group address (ff02::2). This is done by calling the ndisc_send_rs() method from the addrconf_dad_completed() method. Routers reply with a Router Advertisement message, which is sent to the all hosts address, ff02::1. Both the Router Solicitation and the Router Advertisement use the Neighbour Discovery Protocol via ICMPv6 messages. The router solicitation ICMPv6 type is NDISC_ROUTER_SOLICITATION (133), and the router advertisement ICMPv6 type is NDISC_ROUTER_ADVERTISEMENT (134).

The radvd daemon is an example of an open source Router Advertisement daemon that is used for stateless autoconfiguration (http://www.litech.org/radvd/). You can set a prefix in the radvd configuration file, which will be sent in Router Advertisement messages. The radvd daemon sends Router Advertisements periodically. Apart from that, it also listens to Router Solicitations (RS) requests and answers with Router Advertisement (RA) reply messages. These Router Advertisement (RA) messages include a prefix field, which plays an important role in the autoconfiguration process, as you will immediately see. The prefix must be 64 bits long. When a host receives the Router Advertisement (RA) message, it configures its IP address based on this prefix and its own MAC address. If the Privacy Extensions feature (CONFIG_IPV6_PRIVACY) was set, there is also an element of randomness added in the IPv6 address creation. The Privacy Extensions mechanism avoids getting details about the identity of a machine from its IPv6 address, which is generated normally using its MAC address and a prefix, by adding randomness as was mentioned earlier. For more details on Privacy Extensions, see RFC 4941, "Privacy Extensions for Stateless Address Autoconfiguration in IPv6."

When a host receives a Router Advertisement message, it can automatically configure its address and some other parameters. It can also choose a default router based on these advertisements. It is also possible to set a **preferred lifetime** and a **valid lifetime** for the addresses that are configured automatically on the hosts. The preferred lifetime value specifies the length of time in seconds that the address, which was generated from the prefix via stateless address autoconfiguration, remains in a preferred state. When the preferred time is over, this address will stop communicating (will not answer ping6, etc.). The valid lifetime value specifies the length of time in seconds that the address is valid (i.e., that applications already using it can keep using it); when this time is over, the address is removed. The preferred lifetime and the valid lifetime are represented in the kernel by the prefered_lft and the valid_lft fields of the inet6_ifaddr object, respectively (include/net/if_inet6.h).

Renumbering is the process of replacing an old prefix with a new prefix, and changing the IPv6 addresses of hosts according to a new prefix. Renumbering can also be done quite easily with radvd, by adding a new prefix to its configuration settings, setting a preferred lifetime and a valid lifetime, and restarting the radvd daemon. See also RFC 4192, "Procedures for Renumbering an IPv6 Network without a Flag Day," and RFCs 5887, 6866, and 6879.

The Dynamic Host Configuration Protocol version 6 (DHCPv6) is an example of stateful address configuration; in the stateful autoconfiguration model, hosts obtain interface addresses and/or configuration information and parameters from a server. Servers maintain a database that keeps track of which addresses have been assigned to which hosts. I will not delve into the details of the DHCPv6 protocol in this book. The DHCPv6 protocol is specified by RFC 3315, "Dynamic Host Configuration Protocol for IPv6 (DHCPv6)." The IPv6 Stateless Autoconfiguration standard is described in RFC 4862, "IPv6 Stateless Address Autoconfiguration."

You have learned in this section about the Autoconfiguration process, and you saw how easy it is to replace an old prefix with a new prefix by configuring and restarting radvd. The next section discusses how the ipv6_rcv() method, which is the IPv6 protocol handler, handles the reception of IPv6 packets in a somewhat similar way to what you saw in IPv4.

Receiving IPv6 Packets

The main IPv6 receive method is the ipv6_rcv() method, which is the handler for all IPv6 packets (including multicasts; there are no broadcasts in IPv6 as mentioned before). There are many similarities between the Rx path in IPv4 and in IPv6. As in IPv4, we first make some sanity checks, like checking that the version of the IPv6 header is 6 and that the source address is not a multicast address. (According to section 2.7 of RFC 4291, this is forbidden.) If there is a Hop-by-Hop Options header, it must be the first one. If the value of the nexthdr of the IPV6 header is 0, this indicates a Hop-by-Hop Options header, and it is parsed by calling the ipv6_parse_hopopts() method. The real work is done by the ip6_rcv_finish() method, which is invoked by calling the NF_HOOK() macro. If there is a netfilter callback that is registered at this point (NF_INET_PRE_ROUTING), it will be invoked. I will discuss netfilter hooks in the next chapter. Let's take a look at the ipv6_rcv() method:

```
int ipv6_rcv(struct sk_buff *skb, struct net_device *dev, struct packet_type *pt,
        struct net_device *orig_dev)
{
        const struct ipv6hdr *hdr;
        u32             pkt_len;
        struct inet6_dev *idev;
```

Fetch the network namespace from the network device that is associated with the Socket Buffer (SKB):

```
struct net *net = dev_net(skb->dev);


        . . .
```

Fetch the IPv6 header from the SKB:

```
hdr = ipv6_hdr(skb);
```

Perform some sanity checks, and discard the SKB if necessary:

```
if (hdr->version != 6)
        goto err;

/*
 * RFC4291 2.5.3
 * A packet received on an interface with a destination address
 * of loopback must be dropped.
 */
if (!(dev->flags & IFF_LOOPBACK) &&
    ipv6_addr_loopback(&hdr->daddr))
        goto err;

. . .

/*
 * RFC4291 2.7
 * Multicast addresses must not be used as source addresses in IPv6
 * packets or appear in any Routing header.
 */
if (ipv6_addr_is_multicast(&hdr->saddr))
        goto err;

. . .

if (hdr->nexthdr == NEXTHDR_HOP) {
        if (ipv6_parse_hopopts(skb) < 0) {
                IP6_INC_STATS_BH(net, idev, IPSTATS_MIB_INHDRERRORS);
                rcu_read_unlock();
                return NET_RX_DROP;
        }
}
. . .

return NF_HOOK(NFPROTO_IPV6, NF_INET_PRE_ROUTING, skb, dev, NULL,
                ip6_rcv_finish);
err:
        IP6_INC_STATS_BH(net, idev, IPSTATS_MIB_INHDRERRORS);
drop:
        rcu_read_unlock();
        kfree_skb(skb);
        return NET_RX_DROP;
}
```

(net/ipv6/ip6_input.c)

The `ip6_rcv_finish()` method first performs a lookup in the routing subsystem by calling the `ip6_route_input()` method, in case there is no `dst` attached to the SKB. The `ip6_route_input()` method eventually invokes the `fib6_rule_lookup()`.

```
int ip6_rcv_finish(struct sk_buff *skb)
{
    . . .
    if (!skb_dst(skb))
            ip6_route_input(skb);
```

Invoke the `input` callback of the `dst` attached to the SKB:

```
    return dst_input(skb);
}
```

(net/ipv6/ip6_input.c)

■ **Note** There are two different implementations of the `fib6_rule_lookup()` method: one when Policy Routing (CONFIG_IPV6_MULTIPLE_TABLES) is set, in `net/ipv6/fib6_rules.c`, and one when Policy Routing is not set, in `net/ipv6/ip6_fib.c`.

As you saw in Chapter 5, which dealt with advanced topics of the IPv4 Routing Subsystem, the lookup in the routing subsystem builds a `dst` object and sets its `input` and `output` callbacks; in IPv6, similar tasks are performed. After the `ip6_rcv_finish()` method performs the lookup in the routing subsystem, it calls the `dst_input()` method, which in fact invokes the `input` callback of the `dst` object that is associated with the packet.

Figure 8-2 shows the receive path (Rx) of a packet that is received by the network driver. This packet can either be delivered to the local machine or be forwarded to another host. It is the result of the lookup in the routing tables that determines which of these two options will take place.

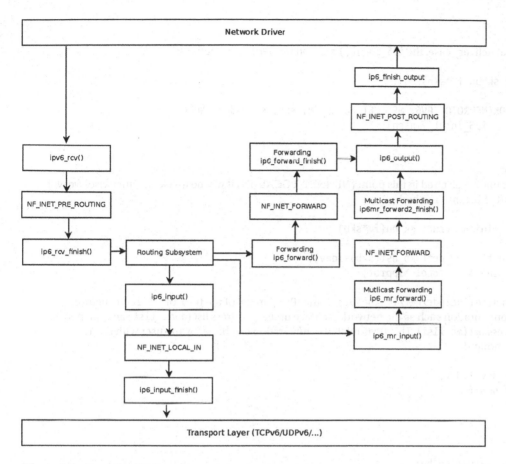

Figure 8-2. *Receiving IPv6 packets*

■ **Note**   For simplicity, the diagram does not include the fragmentation/defragmentation/ parsing of extension headers /IPsec methods.

The lookup in the IPv6 routing subsystem will set the input callback of the destination cache (dst) to be:

- ip6_input() when the packet is destined to the local machine.

- ip6_forward() when the packet is to be forwarded.

- ip6_mc_input() when the packet is destined to a multicast address.

- ip6_pkt_discard() when the packet is to be discarded. The ip6_pkt_discard()
  method drops the packet and replies to the sender with a destination unreachable
  (ICMPV6_DEST_UNREACH) ICMPv6 message.

Incoming IPv6 packets can be locally delivered or forwarded; in the next section, you will learn about local delivery of IPv6 packets.

Local Delivery

Let's look first at the local delivery case: the ip6_input() method is a very short method:

```
int ip6_input(struct sk_buff *skb)
{
        return NF_HOOK(NFPROTO_IPV6, NF_INET_LOCAL_IN, skb, skb->dev, NULL,
                        ip6_input_finish);
}
```

(net/ipv6/ip6_input.c)

If there is a netfilter hook registered in this point (NF_INET_LOCAL_IN) it will be invoked. Otherwise, we will proceed to the ip6_input_finish() method:

```
static int ip6_input_finish(struct sk_buff *skb)
{
        struct net *net = dev_net(skb_dst(skb)->dev);
        const struct inet6_protocol *ipprot;
```

The inet6_dev structure (include/net/if_inet6.h) is the IPv6 parallel of the IPv4 in_device structure. It contains IPv6-related configuration such as the network interface unicast address list (addr_list) and the network interface multicast address list (mc_list). This IPv6-related configuration can be set by the user with the ip command or with the ifconfig command.

```
        struct inet6_dev *idev;
        unsigned int nhoff;
        int nexthdr;
        bool raw;

        /*
         *      Parse extension headers
         */

        rcu_read_lock();
resubmit:
        idev = ip6_dst_idev(skb_dst(skb));
        if (!pskb_pull(skb, skb_transport_offset(skb)))
                goto discard;
        nhoff = IP6CB(skb)->nhoff;
```

Fetch the next header number from the SKB:

```
nexthdr = skb_network_header(skb)[nhoff];
```

First in case of a raw socket packet, we try to deliver it to a raw socket:

```
raw = raw6_local_deliver(skb, nexthdr);
```

Every extension header (except the Hop by Hop extension header) has a protocol handler which was registered by the inet6_add_protocol() method; this method in fact adds an entry to the global inet6_protos array (see net/ipv6/protocol.c).

```
if ((ipprot = rcu_dereference(inet6_protos[nexthdr])) != NULL) {
        int ret;

        if (ipprot->flags & INET6_PROTO_FINAL) {
                const struct ipv6hdr *hdr;

                /* Free reference early: we don't need it any more,
                   and it may hold ip_conntrack module loaded
                   indefinitely. */
                nf_reset(skb);

                skb_postpull_rcsum(skb, skb_network_header(skb),
                                        skb_network_header_len(skb));
                hdr = ipv6_hdr(skb);
```

RFC 3810, which is the MLDv2 specification, says: "Note that MLDv2 messages are not subject to source filtering and must always be processed by hosts and routers." We do not want to discard MLD multicast packets due to source filtering, since these MLD packets should be always processed according to the RFC. Therefore, before discarding the packet we make sure that if the destination address of the packet is a multicast address, the packet is not an MLD packet. This is done by calling the ipv6_is_mld() method before discarding it. If this method indicates that the packet is an MLD packet, it is not discarded. You can also see more about this in the "Multicast Listener Discovery (MLD)" section later in this chapter.

```
                if (ipv6_addr_is_multicast(&hdr->daddr) &&
                    !ipv6_chk_mcast_addr(skb->dev, &hdr->daddr,
                    &hdr->saddr) &&
                    !ipv6_is_mld(skb, nexthdr, skb_network_header_len(skb)))
                        goto discard;
}
```

When the INET6_PROTO_NOPOLICY flag is set, this indicates that there is no need to perform IPsec policy checks for this protocol:

```
        if (!(ipprot->flags & INET6_PROTO_NOPOLICY) &&
            !xfrm6_policy_check(NULL, XFRM_POLICY_IN, skb))
                goto discard;
        ret = ipprot->handler(skb);
        if (ret > 0)
                goto resubmit;
        else if (ret == 0)
                IP6_INC_STATS_BH(net, idev, IPSTATS_MIB_INDELIVERS);
} else {
        if (!raw) {
                if (xfrm6_policy_check(NULL, XFRM_POLICY_IN, skb)) {
                        IP6_INC_STATS_BH(net, idev,
                                            IPSTATS_MIB_INUNKNOWNPROTOS);
                        icmpv6_send(skb, ICMPV6_PARAMPROB,
                                        ICMPV6_UNK_NEXTHDR, nhoff);
                }
                kfree_skb(skb);
        } else {
```

Everything went fine, so increment the INDELIVERS SNMP MIB counter (/proc/net/snmp6/Ip6InDelivers) and free the packet with the consume_skb() method:

```
                    IP6_INC_STATS_BH(net, idev, IPSTATS_MIB_INDELIVERS);
                    consume_skb(skb);
            }
    }
    rcu_read_unlock();
    return 0;

discard:
    IP6_INC_STATS_BH(net, idev, IPSTATS_MIB_INDISCARDS);
    rcu_read_unlock();
    kfree_skb(skb);
    return 0;
}
```

(net/ipv6/ip6_input.c)

You have seen the implementation details of local delivery, which is performed by the ip6_input() and ip6_input_finish() methods. Now is the time to turn to the implementation details of forwarding in IPv6. Also here, there are many similarities between forwarding in IPv4 and forwarding in IPv6.

Forwarding

Forwarding in IPv6 is very similar to forwarding in IPv4. There are some slight changes, though. For example, in IPv6, a checksum is not calculated when forwarding a packet. (There is no checksum field at all in an IPv6 header, as was mentioned before.) Let's take a look at the ip6_forward() method:

```
int ip6_forward(struct sk_buff *skb)
{
    struct dst_entry *dst = skb_dst(skb);
    struct ipv6hdr *hdr = ipv6_hdr(skb);
    struct inet6_skb_parm *opt = IP6CB(skb);
    struct net *net = dev_net(dst->dev);
    u32 mtu;
```

The IPv6 procfs forwarding entry (/proc/sys/net/ipv6/conf/all/forwarding) should be set:

```
if (net->ipv6.devconf_all->forwarding == 0)
    goto error;
```

When working with Large Receive Offload (LRO), the packet length will exceed the Maximum transmission unit (MTU). As in IPv4, when LRO is enabled, the SKB is freed and an error of –EINVAL is returned:

```
if (skb_warn_if_lro(skb))
    goto drop;

if (!xfrm6_policy_check(NULL, XFRM_POLICY_FWD, skb)) {
    IP6_INC_STATS(net, ip6_dst_idev(dst), IPSTATS_MIB_INDISCARDS);
    goto drop;
}
```

Drop packets that are not destined to go to the local host. The pkt_type associated with an SKB is determined according to the destination MAC address in the Ethernet header of an incoming packet. This is done by the eth_type_trans() method, which is typically called in the network device driver when handling an incoming packet. See the eth_type_trans() method, net/ethernet/eth.c.

```
if (skb->pkt_type != PACKET_HOST)
        goto drop;

skb_forward_csum(skb);

/*
 *      We DO NOT make any processing on
 *      RA packets, pushing them to user level AS IS
 *      without any WARRANTY that application will be able
 *      to interpret them. The reason is that we
 *      cannot make anything clever here.
 *
 *      We are not end-node, so that if packet contains
 *      AH/ESP, we cannot make anything.
 *      Defragmentation also would be mistake, RA packets
 *      cannot be fragmented, because there is no warranty
 *      that different fragments will go along one path. --ANK
 */
if (opt->ra) {
        u8 *ptr = skb_network_header(skb) + opt->ra;
```

We should try to deliver the packet to sockets that had the IPV6_ROUTER_ALERT socket option set by setsockopt(). This is done by calling the ip6_call_ra_chain() method; if the delivery in ip6_call_ra_chain() succeeded, the ip6_forward() method returns 0 and the packet is not forwarded. See the implementation of the ip6_call_ra_chain() method in net/ipv6/ip6_output.c.

```
        if (ip6_call_ra_chain(skb, (ptr[2]<<8) + ptr[3]))
                return 0;
}

/*
 *      check and decrement ttl
 */
if (hdr->hop_limit <= 1) {
        /* Force OUTPUT device used as source address */
        skb->dev = dst->dev;
```

Send back an ICMP error message when the Hop Limit is 1 (or less), much like what we have in IPv4 when forwarding a packet and the TTL reaches 0. In this case, the packet is discarded:

```
        icmpv6_send(skb, ICMPV6_TIME_EXCEED, ICMPV6_EXC_HOPLIMIT, 0);
        IP6_INC_STATS_BH(net,
                        ip6_dst_idev(dst), IPSTATS_MIB_INHDRERRORS);

        kfree_skb(skb);
        return -ETIMEDOUT;
}
```

```
/* XXX: idev->cnf.proxy_ndp? */
if (net->ipv6.devconf_all->proxy_ndp &&
    pneigh_lookup(&nd_tbl, net, &hdr->daddr, skb->dev, 0)) {
        int proxied = ip6_forward_proxy_check(skb);
        if (proxied > 0)
                return ip6_input(skb);
        else if (proxied < 0) {
                IP6_INC_STATS(net, ip6_dst_idev(dst),
                                IPSTATS_MIB_INDISCARDS);
                goto drop;
        }
}

if (!xfrm6_route_forward(skb)) {
        IP6_INC_STATS(net, ip6_dst_idev(dst), IPSTATS_MIB_INDISCARDS);
        goto drop;
}
dst = skb_dst(skb);

/* IPv6 specs say nothing about it, but it is clear that we cannot
   send redirects to source routed frames.
   We don't send redirects to frames decapsulated from IPsec.
 */
if (skb->dev == dst->dev && opt->srcrt == 0 && !skb_sec_path(skb)) {
        struct in6_addr *target = NULL;
        struct inet_peer *peer;
        struct rt6_info *rt;

        /*
         *      incoming and outgoing devices are the same
         *      send a redirect.
         */

        rt = (struct rt6_info *) dst;
        if (rt->rt6i_flags & RTF_GATEWAY)
                target = &rt->rt6i_gateway;
        else
                target = &hdr->daddr;

        peer = inet_getpeer_v6(net->ipv6.peers, &rt->rt6i_dst.addr, 1);

        /* Limit redirects both by destination (here)
           and by source (inside ndisc_send_redirect)
         */
        if (inet_peer_xrlim_allow(peer, 1*HZ))
        ndisc_send_redirect(skb, target);
        if (peer)
        inet_putpeer(peer);
} else {
        int addrtype = ipv6_addr_type(&hdr->saddr);
```

```
        /* This check is security critical. */
        if (addrtype == IPV6_ADDR_ANY ||
            addrtype & (IPV6_ADDR_MULTICAST | IPV6_ADDR_LOOPBACK))
        goto error;
        if (addrtype & IPV6_ADDR_LINKLOCAL) {
                icmpv6_send(skb, ICMPV6_DEST_UNREACH,
                            ICMPV6_NOT_NEIGHBOUR, 0);
                goto error;
        }
}
```

Note that the IPv6 IPV6_MIN_MTU is 1280 bytes, according to section 5, "Packet Size Issues," of the base IPv6 standard, RFC 2460.

```
mtu = dst_mtu(dst);
if (mtu < IPV6_MIN_MTU)
        mtu = IPV6_MIN_MTU;

if ((!skb->local_df && skb->len > mtu && !skb_is_gso(skb)) ||
    (IP6CB(skb)->frag_max_size && IP6CB(skb)->frag_max_size > mtu)) {
        /* Again, force OUTPUT device used as source address */
        skb->dev = dst->dev;
```

Reply back to the sender with an ICMPv6 message of "Packet Too Big," and free the SKB; the ip6_forward() method returns –EMSGSIZ in this case:

```
        icmpv6_send(skb, ICMPV6_PKT_TOOBIG, 0, mtu);
        IP6_INC_STATS_BH(net,
                            ip6_dst_idev(dst), IPSTATS_MIB_INTOOBIGERRORS);
        IP6_INC_STATS_BH(net,
                            ip6_dst_idev(dst), IPSTATS_MIB_FRAGFAILS);
        kfree_skb(skb);
        return -EMSGSIZE;
}
if (skb_cow(skb, dst->dev->hard_header_len)) {
        IP6_INC_STATS(net, ip6_dst_idev(dst), IPSTATS_MIB_OUTDISCARDS);
        goto drop;
}
```

```
hdr = ipv6_hdr(skb);
```

The packet is to be forwarded, so decrement the hop_limit of the IPv6 header.

```
/* Mangling hops number delayed to point after skb COW */
hdr->hop_limit--;

IP6_INC_STATS_BH(net, ip6_dst_idev(dst), IPSTATS_MIB_OUTFORWDATAGRAMS);
IP6_ADD_STATS_BH(net, ip6_dst_idev(dst), IPSTATS_MIB_OUTOCTETS, skb->len);
return NF_HOOK(NFPROTO_IPV6, NF_INET_FORWARD, skb, skb->dev, dst->dev,
                ip6_forward_finish);
```

```
error:
        IP6_INC_STATS_BH(net, ip6_dst_idev(dst), IPSTATS_MIB_INADDRERRORS);
drop:
        kfree_skb(skb);
        return -EINVAL;
}
```

(net/ipv6/ip6_output.c)

The ip6_forward_finish() method is a one-line method, which simply invokes the destination cache (dst) output callback:

```
static inline int ip6_forward_finish(struct sk_buff *skb)
{
return dst_output(skb);
}
```

(net/ipv6/ip6_output.c)

You have seen in this section how the reception of IPv6 packets is handled, either by local delivery or by forwarding. You have also seen some differences between receiving IPv6 packets and receiving IPv4 packets. In the next section, I will discuss the Rx path for multicast traffic.

Receiving IPv6 Multicast Packets

The ipv6_rcv() method is the IPv6 handler for both unicast packets and multicast packets. As mentioned above, after some sanity checks, it invokes the ip6_rcv_finish() method, which performs a lookup in the routing subsystem by calling the ip6_route_input() method. In the ip6_route_input() method, the input callback is set to be the ip6_mc_input method in cases of receiving a multicast packet. Let's take a look at the ip6_mc_input() method:

```
int ip6_mc_input(struct sk_buff *skb)
{       const struct ipv6hdr *hdr;
        bool deliver;

        IP6_UPD_PO_STATS_BH(dev_net(skb_dst(skb)->dev),
                            ip6_dst_idev(skb_dst(skb)), IPSTATS_MIB_INMCAST,
                            skb->len);

        hdr = ipv6_hdr(skb);
```

The ipv6_chk_mcast_addr() method (net/ipv6/mcast.c) checks whether the multicast address list (mc_list) of the specified network device contains the specified multicast address (which is the destination address in the IPv6 header in this case, hdr->daddr). Note that because the third parameter is NULL, we do not check in this invocation whether there are any source filters for the source address; handling source filtering is discussed later in this chapter.

```
deliver = ipv6_chk_mcast_addr(skb->dev, &hdr->daddr, NULL);
```

If the local machine is a multicast router (that is, CONFIG_IPV6_MROUTE is set), we continue after some checks to the ip6_mr_input() method. The IPv6 multicast routing implementation is very similar to the IPv4 multicast routing implementation, which was discussed in Chapter 6, so I will not discuss it in this book. The IPv6 multicast routing implementation is in net/ipv6/ip6mr.c. Support for IPv6 Multicast Routing was added in kernel 2.6.26 (2008), based on a patch by Mickael Hoerdt.

```
#ifdef CONFIG_IPV6_MROUTE
. . .
        if (dev_net(skb->dev)->ipv6.devconf_all->mc_forwarding &&
            !(ipv6_addr_type(&hdr->daddr) &
             (IPV6_ADDR_LOOPBACK|IPV6_ADDR_LINKLOCAL)) &&
            likely(!(IP6CB(skb)->flags & IP6SKB_FORWARDED))) {
                /*
                 * Okay, we try to forward - split and duplicate
                 * packets.
                 */
                struct sk_buff *skb2;

                if (deliver)
                        skb2 = skb_clone(skb, GFP_ATOMIC);
                else {
                        skb2 = skb;
                        skb = NULL;
                }
```

Continue to the IPv6 Multicast Routing code, via the ip6_mr_input() method (net/ipv6/ip6mr.c):

```
                        ip6_mr_input(skb2);
                }

        }
#endif
        if (likely(deliver))
                ip6_input(skb);
        else {
                /* discard */
                kfree_skb(skb);
        }

        return 0;
}
```

(net/ipv6/ip6_input.c)

When the multicast packet is not destined to be forwarded by multicast routing (for example, when CONFIG_IPV6_MROUTE is not set), we will continue to the ip6_input() method, which is in fact a wrapper around the ip6_input_finish() method as you already saw. In the ip6_input_finish() method, we again call the ipv6_chk_mcast_addr() method, but this time the third parameter is not NULL, it is the source address from the IPv6 header. This time we do check in the ipv6_chk_mcast_addr() method whether source filtering is set, and we handle the packet accordingly. Source filtering is discussed in the "Multicast Source Filtering (MSF)" section later in this chapter. Next, I will describe the Multicast Listener Discovery protocol, which parallels the IPv4 IGMPv3 protocol.

Multicast Listener Discovery (MLD)

The MLD protocol is used to exchange group information between multicast hosts and routers. The MLD protocol is an asymmetric protocol; it specifies different behavior to Multicast Routers and to Multicast Listeners. In IPv4, multicast group management is handled by the Internet Group Management Protocol (IGMP) protocol, as you saw in Chapter 6. In IPv6, multicast group management is handled by the MLDv2 protocol, which is specified in RFC 3810, from 2004. The MLDv2 protocol is derived from the IGMPv3 protocol, which is used by IPv4. However, as opposed to the IGMPv3 protocol, MLDv2 is part of the ICMPv6 protocol, while IGMPv3 is a standalone protocol that does not use any of the ICMPv4 services; this is the main reason why the IGMPv3 protocol is not used in IPv6. Note that you might encounter the term GMP (Group Management Protocol), which is used to refer to both IGMP and MLD.

The former version of the Multicast Listener Discovery protocol is MLDv1, and it is specified in RFC 2710; it is derived from IGMPv2. MLDv1 is based on the Any-Source Multicast (ASM) model; this means that you do not specify interest in receiving multicast traffic from a single source address or from a set of addresses. MLDv2 extends MLDv1 by adding support for Source Specific Multicast (SSM); this means the ability of a node to specify interest in including or excluding listening to packets from specific unicast source addresses. This feature is referred to as **source filtering**. Later in this section, I will show a short, detailed userspace example of how to use source filtering. See more in RFC 4604, "Using Internet Group Management Protocol Version 3 (IGMPv3) and Multicast Listener Discovery Protocol Version 2 (MLDv2) for Source-Specific Multicast."

The MLDv2 protocol is based on Multicast Listener Reports and Multicast Listener Queries. An MLDv2 Router (which is also sometimes termed "Querier") sends periodically Multicast Listener Queries in order to learn about the state of multicast groups of nodes. If there are several MLDv2 Routers on the same link, only one of them is selected to be the Querier, and all the other routers are set to be in a Non-Querier state. This is done by a Querier Election mechanism, as described in section 7.6.2 of RFC 3810. Nodes respond to these queries with Multicast Listener Reports, in which they provide information about multicast groups to which they belong. When a listener wants to stop listening on some multicast group, it informs the Querier about it, and the Querier must query for other listeners of that multicast group address before deleting it from its Multicast Address Listener state. An MLDv2 router can provide state information about listeners to multicast routing protocols.

Now that you have learned generally what the MLD protocol is, I will turn your attention in the following section to how joining and leaving a multicast group is handled.

Joining and Leaving a Multicast Group

There are two ways to join or leave a multicast group in IPv6. The first one is from within the kernel, by calling the `ipv6_dev_mc_inc()` method, which gets as a parameter a network device object and a multicast group address. For example, when registering a network device, the `ipv6_add_dev()` method is invoked; each device should join the interface-local all nodes multicast group (`ff01::1`) and the link-local all nodes multicast group (`ff02::1`).

```
static struct inet6_dev *ipv6_add_dev(struct net_device *dev) {

. . .

        /* Join interface-local all-node multicast group */
        ipv6_dev_mc_inc(dev, &in6addr_interfacelocal_allnodes);

        /* Join all-node multicast group */
        ipv6_dev_mc_inc(dev, &in6addr_linklocal_allnodes);

. . .

}
```

(net/ipv6/addrconf.c)

Routers are devices that have their procfs forwarding entry, /proc/sys/net/ipv6/conf/all/forwarding, set. Routers join three multicast address groups, in addition to the two multicast group that each host joins and that were mentioned earlier. These are the link-local all-routers multicast group (ff02::2), interface-local all routers multicast group (ff01::2), and site-local all routers multicast group (ff05::2).

Note that setting the IPv6 procfs forwarding entry value is handled by the addrconf_fixup_forwarding() method, which eventually calls the dev_forward_change() method, which causes the specified network interface to join or leave these three multicast address groups according to the value of the procfs entry (which is represented by idev->cnf.forwarding, as you can see in the following code snippet):

```
static void dev_forward_change(struct inet6_dev *idev)
{
        struct net_device *dev;
        struct inet6_ifaddr *ifa;
    . . .
        dev = idev->dev;
    . . .
        if (dev->flags & IFF_MULTICAST) {
                if (idev->cnf.forwarding) {
                        ipv6_dev_mc_inc(dev, &in6addr_linklocal_allrouters);
                        ipv6_dev_mc_inc(dev, &in6addr_interfacelocal_allrouters);
                        ipv6_dev_mc_inc(dev, &in6addr_sitelocal_allrouters);
                } else {
                        ipv6_dev_mc_dec(dev, &in6addr_linklocal_allrouters);
                        ipv6_dev_mc_dec(dev, &in6addr_interfacelocal_allrouters);
                        ipv6_dev_mc_dec(dev, &in6addr_sitelocal_allrouters);
                }
        }
    . . .
}
```

(net/ipv6/addrconf.c)

To leave a multicast group from within the kernel, you should call the ipv6_dev_mc_dec() method. The second way of joining a multicast group is by opening an IPv6 socket in userspace, creating a multicast request (ipv6_mreq object) and setting the ipv6mr_multiaddr of the request to be the multicast group address to which this host wants to join, and setting the ipv6mr_interface to the ifindex of the network interface it wants to set. Then it should call setsockopt() with the IPV6_JOIN_GROUP socket option:

```
int             sockd;
struct ipv6_mreq  mcgroup;
struct addrinfo   *results;
. . .

/* read an IPv6 multicast group address to which we want to join */
/* into the address info object (results) */
. . .
```

Set the network interface that we want to use (by its ifindex value):

```
mcgroup.ipv6mr_interface=3;
```

Set the multicast group address for the group that we want to join in the request (ipv6mr_multiaddr):

```
memcpy( &(mcgroup.ipv6mr_multiaddr),
        &(((struct sockaddr_in6 *) results->ai_addr)->sin6_addr),
        sizeof(struct in6_addr));

sockd  = socket(AF_INET6, SOCK_DGRAM,0);
```

Call setsockopt() with IPV6_JOIN_GROUP to join the multicast group; this call is handled in the kernel by the ipv6_sock_mc_join() method (net/ipv6/mcast.c).

```
status = setsockopt(sockd, IPPROTO_IPV6, IPV6_JOIN_GROUP,
                    &mcgroup, sizeof(mcgroup));
```
. . .

The IPV6_ADD_MEMBERSHIP socket option can be used instead of IPV6_JOIN_GROUP. (They are equivalent.) Note that we can set the same multicast group address on more than one network device by setting different values of network interfaces to mcgroup.ipv6mr_interface. The value of mcgroup.ipv6mr_interface is passed as the ifindex parameter to the ipv6_sock_mc_join() method. In such a case, the kernel builds and sends an MLDv2 Multicast Listener Report packet (ICMPV6_MLD2_REPORT), where the destination address is ff02::16 (the all MLDv2-capable routers Multicast Group Address). According to section 5.2.14 in RFC 3810, all MLDv2-capable multicast routers should listen to this multicast address. The number of Multicast Address Records in the MLDv2 header (shown in Figure 8-3) will be 1, because only one Multicast Address Record is used, containing the address of the multicast group that we want to join. The multicast group address that a host wants to join is part of the ICMPv6 header. The Hop-by-Hop Options header with Router Alert is set in this packet. MLD packets contain a Hop-by-Hop Options header, which in turn contains a Router Alert options header; the next header of the Hop-by-Hop extension header is IPPROTO_ICMPV6 (58), because following the Hop-by-Hop header is the ICMPv6 packet, which contains the MLDv2 message.

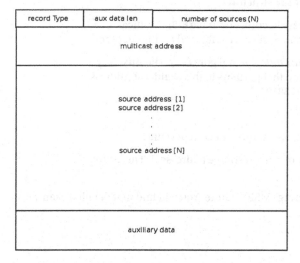

**Multicast Listener
Report Message (MLDv2)**

**Multicast
Address
Record**

Figure 8-3. *MLDv2 Multicast Listener Report*

A host can leave a multicast group by calling setsockopt() with the IPV6_DROP_MEMBERSHIP socket option, which is handled in the kernel by calling the ipv6_sock_mc_drop() method or by closing the socket. Note that IPV6_LEAVE_GROUP is equivalent to IPV6_DROP_MEMBERSHIP.

After talking about how joining and leaving a multicast group is handled, it is time to see what an MLDv2 Multicast Listener Report is.

MLDv2 Multicast Listener Report

The MLDv2 Multicast Listener Report is represented in the kernel by the mld2_report structure:

```
struct mld2_report {
        struct icmp6hdr         mld2r_hdr;
        struct mld2_grec        mld2r_grec[0];
};
```

(include/net/mld.h)

The first member of the mld2_report structure is the mld2r_hdr, which is an ICMPv6 header; its icmp6_type should be set to ICMPV6_MLD2_REPORT (143). The second member of the mld2_report structure is the mld2r_grec[0], an instance of the mld2_grec structure, which represents the MLDv2 group record. (This is the Multicast Address Record in Figure 8-3.) Following is the definition of the mld2_grec structure:

```
struct mld2_grec {
        __u8            grec_type;
        __u8            grec_auxwords;
        __be16          grec_nsrcs;
        struct in6_addr grec_mca;
        struct in6_addr grec_src[0];
};
```

(include/net/mld.h)

The following is a description of the members of the mld2_grec structure:

- grec_type: Specifies the type of the Multicast Address Record. See Table 8-3, "Multicast Address Record (record types)" in the "Quick Reference" section at the end of this chapter.

- grec_auxwords: The length of the Auxiliary Data (*aux data len* in Figure 8-3). The Auxiliary Data field, if present, contains additional information that pertains to this Multicast Address Record. Usually it is 0. See also section 5.2.10 in RFC 3810.

- grec_nsrcs: The number of source addresses.

- grec_mca: The multicast address to which this Multicast Address Record pertains.

- grec_src[0]: A unicast source address (or an array of unicast source addresses). These are addresses that we want to filter (block or allow).

In the next section, I will discuss the Multicast Source Filtering (MSF) feature. You will find in it detailed examples of how a Multicast Address Record is used in source filtering.

Multicast Source Filtering (MSF)

With Multicast Source Filtering, the kernel will drop the multicast traffic from sources other than the expected ones. This feature, which is also known as Source-Specific Multicast (SSM) was not part of MLDv1. It was introduced in MLDv2; see RFC 3810. It is the opposite of Any-Source Multicast (ASM), where a receiver expresses interest in a destination multicast address. To understand better what Multicast Source Filtering is all about, I will show here an example of a userspace application demonstrating how to join and leave a multicast group with source filtering.

Joining and Leaving a Multicast Group with Source Filtering

A host can join a multicast group with source filtering by opening an IPv6 socket in userspace, creating a multicast group source request (group_source_req object), and setting three parameters in the request:

- gsr_group: The multicast group address that this host wants to join

- gsr_source: The multicast group source address that it wants to allow

- ipv6mr_interface: The *ifindex* of the network interface it wants to set

Then it should call setsockopt() with the MCAST_JOIN_SOURCE_GROUP socket option. Following here is a code snippet of a userspace application demonstrating this (checking the success of the system calls was removed, for brevity):

```
int                    sockd;
struct group_source_req   mreq;
struct addrinfo        *results1;
struct addrinfo        *results2;

/* read an IPv6 multicast group address that we want to join into results1 */
/* read an IPv6 multicast group address which we want to allow into results2 */
memcpy(&(mreq.gsr_group),  results1->ai_addr,  sizeof(struct sockaddr_in6));
memcpy(&(mreq.gsr_source), results2->ai_addr,  sizeof(struct sockaddr_in6));

mreq.gsr_interface = 3;

sockd = socket(AF_INET6, SOCK_DGRAM, 0);
setsockopt(sockd, IPPROTO_IPV6, MCAST_JOIN_SOURCE_GROUP, &mreq, sizeof(mreq));
```

This request is handled in the kernel first by the ipv6_sock_mc_join() method, and then by the ip6_mc_source() method. To leave the group, you should call setsockopt() with the MCAST_LEAVE_SOURCE_GROUP socket option or close the socket that you opened.

You can set another address that you want to allow and again call setsockopt() with this socket with the MCAST_UNBLOCK_SOURCE socket option. This will add additional addresses to the source filter list. Each such call to setsockopt() will trigger sending an MLDv2 Multicast Listener Report message with one Multicast Address Record; the Record Type will be 5 ("Allow new sources"), and the number of sources will be 1 (the unicast address that you want to unblock). I will show now an example of using the MCAST_MSFILTER socket option for source filtering.

Example: Using MCAST_MSFILTER for Source Filtering

You can also block or permit multicast traffic from several multicast addresses in one setsockopt() call using MCAST_MSFILTER and a group_filter object. First, let's take a look at the definition of the group_filter structure definition in userspace, which is quite self-explanatory:

```
struct group_filter
  {
    /* Interface index.  */
    uint32_t gf_interface;

    /* Group address.  */
    struct sockaddr_storage gf_group;

    /* Filter mode.  */
    uint32_t gf_fmode;

    /* Number of source addresses.  */
    uint32_t gf_numsrc;
    /* Source addresses.  */
    struct sockaddr_storage gf_slist[1];
};
```

(include/netinet/in.h)

The Filter mode (gf_fmode) can be MCAST_INCLUDE (when you want to allow multicast traffic from some unicast address) or MCAST_EXCLUDE (when you want to disallow multicast traffic from some unicast address). Following are two examples for this; the first will allow multicast traffic from three resources, and the second will disallow multicast traffic from two resources:

```
struct ipv6_mreq        mcgroup;
struct group_filter     filter;
struct sockaddr_in6     *psin6;

int                     sockd[2];
```

Set the multicast group address that we want to join, ffff::9.

```
inet_pton(AF_INET6,"ffff::9", &mcgroup.ipv6mr_multiaddr);
```

Set the network interface that we want to use by its ifindex (here, we use eth0, which has an ifindex value of 2):

```
mcgroup.ipv6mr_interface=2;
```

Set the filter parameters: use the same ifindex (2), use MCAST_INCLUDE to set the filter to allow traffic from the sources that are specified by the filter, and set gf_numsrc to 3, because we want to prepare a filter of 3 unicast addresses:

```
filter.gf_interface = 2;
```

We want to prepare two filters: the first one will allow traffic from a set of three multicast addresses, and the second one will permit traffic from a set of two multicast addresses. First set the filter mode to MCAST_INCLUDE, which means to allow traffic from this filter:

```
filter.gf_fmode = MCAST_INCLUDE;
```

Set the number of source addresses of the filter (gf_numsrc) to be 3:

```
filter.gf_numsrc = 3;
```

Set the group address of the filter (gf_group) to be the same one that we use for the mcgrouop earlier, ffff::9:

```
psin6 = (struct sockaddr_in6 *)&filter.gf_group;
psin6->sin6_family = AF_INET6;
inet_pton(PF_INET6, "ffff::9", &psin6->sin6_addr);
```

The three unicast addresses that we want to allow are 2000::1, 2000::2, and 2000::3.
Set filter.gf_slist[0], filter.gf_slist[1], and filter.gf_slist[2] accordingly:

```
psin6 = (struct sockaddr_in6 *)&filter.gf_slist[0];
psin6->sin6_family = AF_INET6;
inet_pton(PF_INET6, "2000::1", &psin6->sin6_addr);
```

```
psin6 = (struct sockaddr_in6 *)&filter.gf_slist[1];
psin6->sin6_family = AF_INET6;
inet_pton(PF_INET6, "2000::2", &psin6->sin6_addr);

psin6 = (struct sockaddr_in6 *)&filter.gf_slist[2];
psin6->sin6_family = AF_INET6;
inet_pton(PF_INET6, "2000::3",&psin6->sin6_addr);
```

Create a socket, and join a multicast group:

```
sockd[0] = socket(AF_INET6, SOCK_DGRAM,0);
status = setsockopt(sockd[0], IPPROTO_IPV6, IPV6_JOIN_GROUP,
        &mcgroup, sizeof(mcgroup));
```

Activate the filter we created:

```
status=setsockopt(sockd[0], IPPROTO_IPV6, MCAST_MSFILTER, &filter,
   GROUP_FILTER_SIZE(filter.gf_numsrc));
```

This will trigger sending of an MLDv2 Multicast Listener Report (ICMPV6_MLD2_REPORT) to all MLDv2 routers (ff02::16) with a Multicast Address Record object (mld2_grec) embedded in it. (See the description of the mld2_report structure and Figure 8-3 earlier.) The values of the fields of mld2_grec will be as follows:

- grec_type will be MLD2_CHANGE_TO_INCLUDE (3).

- grec_auxwords will be 0. (We do not use Auxiliary Data.)

- grec_nsrcs is 3 (because we want to use a filter with 3 source addresses and we set gf_numsrc to 3).

- grec_mca will be ffff::9; this is the multicast group address that the Multicast Address Record pertains to.

The following three unicast source addresses:

- grec_src[0] is 2000::1

- grec_src[1] is 2000::2

- grec_src[2] is 2000::3

Now we want to create a filter of 2 unicast source addresses that we want to exclude. So first create a new userspace socket:

```
sockd[1] = socket(AF_INET6, SOCK_DGRAM,0);
```

Set the filter mode to EXCLUDE, and set the number of sources of the filter to be 2:

```
filter.gf_fmode = MCAST_EXCLUDE;
filter.gf_numsrc = 2;
```

Set the two addresses we want to exclude, 2001::1 and 2001::2:

```
psin6 = (struct sockaddr_in6 *)&filter.gf_slist[0];
psin6->sin6_family = AF_INET6;
inet_pton(PF_INET6, "2001::1", &psin6->sin6_addr);

psin6 = (struct sockaddr_in6 *)&filter.gf_slist[1];
psin6->sin6_family = AF_INET6;
inet_pton(PF_INET6, "2001::2", &psin6->sin6_addr);
```

Create a socket, and join a multicast group:

```
status = setsockopt(sockd[1], IPPROTO_IPV6, IPV6_JOIN_GROUP,
        &mcgroup, sizeof(mcgroup));
```

Activate the filter:

```
status=setsockopt(sockd[1], IPPROTO_IPV6, MCAST_MSFILTER, &filter,
        GROUP_FILTER_SIZE(filter.gf_numsrc));
```

This again will trigger the sending of an MLDv2 Multicast Listener Report (ICMPV6_MLD2_REPORT) to all MLDv2 routers (ff02::16). This time the content of the Multicast Address Record object (mld2_grec) will be different:

- grec_type will be MLD2_CHANGE_TO_EXCLUDE (4).

- grec_auxwords will be 0. (We do not use Auxiliary Data.)

- grec_nsrcs is 2 (because we want to use 2 source addresses and we set gf_numsrc to 2).

- grec_mca will be ffff::9, as before; this is the multicast group address that the Multicast Address Record pertains to.

- The following two unicast source addresses:

  - grec_src[0] is 2001::1

  - grec_src[1] is 2002::2

■ **Note**   We can display the source filtering mapping that we created by cat/proc/net/mcfilter6; this is handled in the kernel by the igmp6_mcf_seq_show() method.

For example, the first three entries in this mapping will show that for the ffff::9 multicast address, we permit (INCLUDE) multicast traffic from 2000::1, 2000::2, and 2000::3. Note that for the first three entries the value in the INC (Include) column is 1. For the fourth and fifth entries, we disallow traffic from 2001::1 and 2001::2. Note that the value in the EX (Exclude) column is 1 for the fourth and fifth entries.

```
cat  /proc/net/mcfilter6
Idx Device Multicast Address                Source Address                   INC   EXC
  2    eth0 ffff0000000000000000000000000009 20000000000000000000000000000001 1     0
  2    eth0 ffff0000000000000000000000000009 20000000000000000000000000000002 1     0
  2    eth0 ffff0000000000000000000000000009 20000000000000000000000000000003 1     0
  2    eth0 ffff0000000000000000000000000009 20010000000000000000000000000001 0     1
  2    eth0 ffff0000000000000000000000000009 20010000000000000000000000000002 0     1
```

■ **Note** Creating filters by calling the setsockopt() method with MCAST_MSFILTER is handled in the kernel by the ip6_mc_msfilter() method, in net/ipv6/mcast.c.

An MLD router (which is also sometimes known as the "Querier") joins the all MLDv2-capable routers Multicast Group (ff02::16) when it is started. It periodically sends Multicast Listener Query packets in order to know which hosts belong to a Multicast group, and to which Multicast group they belong. These are ICMPv6 packets whose type is ICMPV6_MGM_QUERY. The destination address of these query packets is the all-hosts multicast group (ff02::1). When a host receives an ICMPv6 Multicast Listener Query packet, the ICMPv6 Rx handler (the icmpv6_rcv() method) calls the igmp6_event_query() method to handle that query. Note that the igmp6_event_query() method handles both MLDv2 queries and MLDv1 queries (because both use ICMPV6_MGM_QUERY as the ICMPv6 type). The igmp6_event_query() method finds out whether the message is MLDv1 or MLDv2 by checking its length; in MLDv1 the length is 24 bytes, and in MLDv2 it is 28 bytes at least. Handling MLDv1 and MLDv2 messages is different; for MLDv2, we should support source filtering, as was mentioned before in this section, while this feature is not available in MLDv1. The host sends back a Multicast Listener Report by calling the igmp6_send() method. The Multicast Listener Report packet is an ICMPv6 packet.

An example of an IPv6 MLD router is the mld6igmp daemon of the open source XORP project: http://www.xorp.org. The MLD router keeps information about the multicast address groups of network nodes (MLD listeners) and updates this information dynamically. This information can be provided to Multicast Routing daemons. Delving into the implementation of MLDv2 routing daemons like the mld6igmp daemon, or into the implementation of other Multicast Routing daemons, is beyond the scope of this book because it is implemented in userspace.

According to RFC 3810, MLDv2 should be interoperable with nodes that implement MLDv1; an implementation of MLDv2 must support the following two MLDv1 message types:

- MLDv1 Multicast Listener Report (ICMPV6_MGM_REPORT, decimal 131)

- MLDv1 Multicast Listener Done (ICMPV6_MGM_REDUCTION, decimal 132)

We can use the MLDv1 protocol for Multicast Listener messages instead of MLDv2; this can be done by using the following:

```
echo 1 > /proc/sys/net/ipv6/conf/all/force_mld_version
```

In such a case, when a host joins a multicast group, a Multicast Listener Report message will be sent by the igmp6_send() method. This message will use ICMPV6_MGM_REPORT (131) of MLDv1 as the ICMPv6 type, not ICMPV6_MLD2_REPORT(143) as in MLDv2. Note that in this case you cannot use source filtering request for this message, as MLDv1 does not support it. We will join the multicast group by calling the igmp6_join_group() method. When you leave the multicast group, a Multicast Listener Done message will be sent. In this message, the ICMPv6 type is ICMPV6_MGM_REDUCTION (132).

In the next section, I will very briefly talk about the IPv6 Tx path, which is quite similar to the IPv4 Tx path, and which I do not cover in depth in this chapter.

Sending IPv6 Packets

The IPv6 Tx path is very similar to the IPv4 Tx path; even the names of the methods are very similar. Also in IPv6, there are two main methods for sending IPv6 packets from Layer 4, the transport layer: the first is the ip6_xmit() method, which is used by the TCP, Stream Control Transmission Protocol (SCTP), and Datagram Congestion Control Protocol (DCCP) protocols. The second method is the ip6_append_data() method, which is used, for example, by UDP and Raw sockets. Packets that are created on the local host are sent out by the ip6_local_out() method. The ip6_output() method is set to be the output callback of the protocol-independent dst_entry; it first calls the NF_HOOK() macro for the NF_INET_POST_ROUTING hook, and then it calls the ip6_finish_output() method. If fragmentation is needed, the ip6_finish_output() method calls the ip6_fragment() method to handle it; otherwise, it calls the ip6_finish_output2() method, which eventually sends the packet. For implementation details, look in the IPv6 Tx path code; it is mostly in net/ipv6/ip6_output.c.

In the next section, I will very briefly talk about IPv6 routing, which is, again, quite similar to the IPv4 routing, and which I do not cover in depth in this chapter.

IPv6 Routing

The implementation of IPv6 routing is very similar to the IPv4 routing implementation that was discussed in Chapter 5, which dealt with the IPv4 routing subsystem. Like in the IPv4 routing subsystem, Policy routing is also supported in IPv6 (when CONFIG_IPV6_MULTIPLE_TABLES is set). A routing entry is represented in IPv6 by the rt6_info structure (include/net/ip6_fib.h). The rt6_info object parallels the IPv4 rtable structure, and the flowi6 structure (include/net/flow.h) parallels the IPv4 flowi4 structure. (In fact, they both have as their first member the same flowi_common object.) For implementation details, look in the IPv6 routing modules: net/ipv6/route.c, net/ipv6/ip6_fib.c, and the policy routing module, net/ipv6/fib6_rules.c.

Summary

I dealt with the IPv6 subsystem and its implementation in this chapter. I discussed various IPv6 topics, like IPv6 addresses (including Special Addresses and Multicast Addresses), how the IPv6 header is built, what the IPv6 extension headers are, the autoconfiguration process, the Rx path in IPv6, and the MLD protocol. In the next chapter, we will continue our journey into the kernel networking internals and discuss the netfilter subsystem and its implementation. In the "Quick Reference" section that follows, we will cover the top methods related to the topics we discussed in this chapter, ordered by their context.

Quick Reference

I conclude this chapter with a short list of important methods of the IPv6 subsystem. Some of them were mentioned in this chapter. Subsequently, there are three tables and two short sections about IPv6 Special Addresses and about the management of routing tables in IPv6.

Methods

Let's start with the methods.

bool ipv6_addr_any(const struct in6_addr *a);

This method returns true if the specified address is the all-zeroes address ("unspecified address").

bool ipv6_addr_equal(const struct in6_addr *a1, const struct in6_addr *a2);

This method returns true if the two specified IPv6 addresses are equal.

static inline void ipv6_addr_set(struct in6_addr *addr, __be32 w1, __be32 w2, __be32 w3, __be32 w4);

This method sets the IPv6 address according to the four 32-bit input parameters.

bool ipv6_addr_is_multicast(const struct in6_addr *addr);

This method returns true if the specified address is a multicast address.

bool ipv6_ext_hdr(u8 nexthdr);

This method returns true if the specified nexthdr is a well-known extension header.

struct ipv6hdr *ipv6_hdr(const struct sk_buff *skb);

This method returns the IPv6 header (ipv6hdr) of the specified skb.

struct inet6_dev *in6_dev_get(const struct net_device *dev);

This method returns the inet6_dev object associated with the specified device.

bool ipv6_is_mld(struct sk_buff *skb, int nexthdr, int offset);

This method returns true if the specified nexthdr is ICMPv6 (IPPROTO_ICMPV6) and the type of the ICMPv6 header located at the specified offset is an MLD type. It should be one of the following:

- ICMPV6_MGM_QUERY
- ICMPV6_MGM_REPORT
- ICMPV6_MGM_REDUCTION
- ICMPV6_MLD2_REPORT

bool raw6_local_deliver(struct sk_buff *, int);

This method tries to deliver the packet to a raw socket. It returns true on success.

int ipv6_rcv(struct sk_buff *skb, struct net_device *dev, struct packet_type *pt, struct net_device *orig_dev);

This method is the main Rx handler for IPv6 packets.

bool ipv6_accept_ra(struct inet6_dev *idev);

This method returns true if a host is configured to accept Router Advertisements, in these cases:

- If forwarding is enabled, the special hybrid mode should be set, which means that /proc/sys/net/ipv6/conf/<deviceName>/accept_ra is 2.

- If forwarding is not enabled, /proc/sys/net/ipv6/conf/<deviceName>/accept_ra should be 1.

void ip6_route_input(struct sk_buff *skb);

This method is the main IPv6 routing subsystem lookup method in the Rx path. It sets the dst entry of the specified skb according to the results of the lookup in the routing subsystem.

int ip6_forward(struct sk_buff *skb);

This method is the main forwarding method.

struct dst_entry *ip6_route_output(struct net *net, const struct sock *sk, struct flowi6 *fl6);

This method is the main IPv6 routing subsystem lookup method in the Tx path. The return value is the destination cache entry (dst).

■ **Note** Both the ip6_route_input() method and the ip6_route_output() method eventually perform the lookup by calling the fib6_lookup() method.

---

void in6_dev_hold(struct inet6_dev *idev); and void __in6_dev_put(struct inet6_dev *idev);

This method increments and decrements the reference counter of the specified idev object, respectively.

int ip6_mc_msfilter(struct sock *sk, struct group_filter *gsf);

This method handles a setsockopt() call with MCAST_MSFILTER.

int ip6_mc_input(struct sk_buff *skb);

This method is the main Rx handler for multicast packets.

int ip6_mr_input(struct sk_buff *skb);

This method is the main Rx handler for multicast packets that are to be forwarded.

int ipv6_dev_mc_inc(struct net_device *dev, const struct in6_addr *addr);

This method adds the specified device to a multicast group specified by addr, or creates such a group if not found.

int __ipv6_dev_mc_dec(struct inet6_dev *idev, const struct in6_addr *addr);

This method removes the specified device from the specified address group.

bool ipv6_chk_mcast_addr(struct net_device *dev, const struct in6_addr *group, const struct in6_addr *src_addr);

This method checks if the specified network device belongs to the specified multicast address group. If the third parameter is not NULL, it will also check whether source filtering permits receiving multicast traffic from the specified address (src_addr) that is destined to the specified multicast address group.

inline void addrconf_addr_solict_mult(const struct in6_addr *addr, struct in6_addr *sollcited)

This method computes link-local solicited-node multicast addresses.

void addrconf_join_solict(struct net_device *dev, const struct in6_addr *addr);

This method joins to a solicited address multicast group.

int ipv6_sock_mc_join(struct sock *sk, int ifindex, const struct in6_addr *addr);

This method handles socket join on a multicast group.

int ipv6_sock_mc_drop(struct sock *sk, int ifindex, const struct in6_addr *addr);

This method handles socket leave on a multicast group.

int inet6_add_protocol(const struct inet6_protocol *prot, unsigned char protocol);

This method registers an IPv6 protocol handler. It's used with L4 protocol registration (UDPv6, TCPv6, and more) and also with extension headers (like the Fragment Extension Header).

int ipv6_parse_hopopts(struct sk_buff *skb);

This method parses the Hop-by-Hop Options header, which must be the first extension header immediately after the IPv6 header.

int ip6_local_out(struct sk_buff *skb);

This method sends out packets that were generated on the local host.

int ip6_fragment(struct sk_buff *skb, int (*output)(struct sk_buff *));

This method handles IPv6 fragmentation. It is called from the ip6_finish_output() method.

void icmpv6_param_prob(struct sk_buff *skb, u8 code, int pos);

This method sends an ICMPv6 parameter problem (ICMPV6_PARAMPROB) error. It is called when there is some problem in parsing extension headers or in the defragmentation process.

int do_ipv6_setsockopt(struct sock *sk, int level, int optname, char __user *optval, unsigned int optlen); static int do_ipv6_getsockopt(struct sock *sk, int level, int optname, char __user *optval, int __user *optlen, unsigned int flags);

These methods are the generic IPv6 handlers for calling the setsockopt() and getsockopt() methods on IPv6 sockets, respectively (net/ipv6/ipv6_sockglue.c).

int igmp6_event_query(struct sk_buff *skb);

This method handles MLDv2 and MLDv1 queries.

void ip6_route_input(struct sk_buff *skb);

This method performs a routing lookup by building a flow6 object, based on the specified skb and invoking the ip6_route_input_lookup() method.

Macros

And here are the macros.

IPV6_ADDR_MC_SCOPE()

This macro returns the scope of the specified IPv6 Multicast address, which is located in bits 11-14 of the multicast address.

IPV6_ADDR_MC_FLAG_TRANSIENT()

This macro returns 1 if the T bit of the flags of the specified multicast address is set.

IPV6_ADDR_MC_FLAG_PREFIX()

This macro returns 1 if the P bit of the flags of the specified multicast address is set.

IPV6_ADDR_MC_FLAG_RENDEZVOUS()

This macro returns 1 if the R bit of the flags of the specified multicast address is set.

Tables

Here are the tables.

Table 8-2 shows the IPv6 extension headers by their Linux symbol, value and description. You can find more details in the "extension headers" section of this chapter.

Table 8-2. *IPv6 extension headers*

Linux Symbol	Value	Description
NEXTHDR_HOP	0	Hop-by-Hop Options header.
NEXTHDR_TCP	6	TCP segment.
NEXTHDR_UDP	17	UDP message.
NEXTHDR_IPV6	41	IPv6 in IPv6.
NEXTHDR_ROUTING	43	Routing header.
NEXTHDR_FRAGMENT	44	Fragmentation/reassembly header.
NEXTHDR_GRE	47	GRE header.
NEXTHDR_ESP	50	Encapsulating security payload.
NEXTHDR_AUTH	51	Authentication header.
NEXTHDR_ICMP	58	ICMP for IPv6.
NEXTHDR_NONE	59	No next header.
NEXTHDR_DEST	60	Destination options header.
NEXTHDR_MOBILITY	135	Mobility header.

Table 8-3 shows the Multicast Address Record types by their Linux symbol and value. For more details see the "MLDv2 Multicast Listener Report" section in this chapter.

Table 8-3. *Multicast Address Record (record types)*

Linux Symbol	Value
MLD2_MODE_IS_INCLUDE	1
MLD2_MODE_IS_EXCLUDE	2
MLD2_CHANGE_TO_INCLUDE	3
MLD2_CHANGE_TO_EXCLUDE	4
MLD2_ALLOW_NEW_SOURCES	5
MLD2_BLOCK_OLD_SOURCES	6

(include/uapi/linux/icmpv6.h)

Table 8-4 shows the codes of ICMPv6 "Parameter Problem" message by their Linux symbol and value. These codes gives more information about the type of problem which occurred.

Table 8-4. *ICMPv6 Parameter Problem codes*

Linux Symbol	Value
ICMPV6_HDR_FIELD	0 Erroneous header field encountered
ICMPV6_UNK_NEXTHDR	1 Unknown header field encountered
ICMPV6_UNK_OPTION	2 Unknown IPv6 option encountered

Special Addresses

All of the following variables are instances of the in6_addr structure:

- in6addr_any: Represents the unspecified device of all zeroes (::).

- in6addr_loopback: Represents the loopback device (::1).

- in6addr_linklocal_allnodes: Represents the link-local all nodes multicast address (ff02::1).

- in6addr_linklocal_allrouters: Represents the link-local all routers multicast address (ff02::2).

- in6addr_interfacelocal_allnodes: Represents the interface-local all nodes (ff01::1).

- in6addr_interfacelocal_allrouters: Represents the interface-local all routers (ff01::2).

- in6addr_sitelocal_allrouters: Represents the site-local all routers address (ff05::2).

(include/linux/in6.h)

Routing Tables Management in IPv6

Like in IPv4, we can manage adding and deleting routing entries and displaying the routing tables with the ip route command of iproute2 and with the route command of net-tools:

- Adding a route by ip -6 route add is handled by the inet6_rtm_newroute() method by invoking the ip6_route_add() method.

- Deleting a route by ip -6 route del is handled by the inet6_rtm_delroute() method by invoking the ip6_route_del() method.

- Displaying the routing table by ip -6 route show is handled by the inet6_dump_fib() method.

- Adding a route by route -A inet6 add is implemented by sending SIOCADDRT IOCTL, which is handled by the ipv6_route_ioctl() method, by invoking the ip6_route_add() method.

- Deleting a route by route -A inet6 del is implemented by sending SIOCDELRT IOCTL, which is handled by the ipv6_route_ioctl() method by invoking the ip6_route_del() method.

CHAPTER 9

■ ■ ■

Netfilter

Chapter 8 discusses the IPv6 subsystem implementation. This chapter discusses the netfilter subsystem. The netfilter framework was started in 1998 by Rusty Russell, one of the most widely known Linux kernel developers, as an improvement of the older implementations of ipchains (Linux 2.2.x) and ipfwadm (Linux 2.0.x). The netfilter subsystem provides a framework that enables registering callbacks in various points (netfilter hooks) in the packet traversal in the network stack and performing various operations on packets, such as changing addresses or ports, dropping packets, logging, and more. These netfilter hooks provide the infrastructure to netfilter kernel modules that register callbacks in order to perform various tasks of the netfilter subsystem.

Netfilter Frameworks

The netfilter subsystem provides the following functionalities, discussed in this chapter:

- Packet selection (iptables)

- Packet filtering

- Network Address Translation (NAT)

- Packet mangling (modifying the contents of packet headers before or after routing)

- Connection tracking

- Gathering network statistics

Here are some common frameworks that are based on the Linux kernel netfilter subsystem:

- **IPVS (IP Virtual Server):** A transport layer load-balancing solution (net/netfilter/ipvs). There is support for IPv4 IPVS from very early kernels, and support for IPVS in IPv6 is included since kernel 2.6.28. The IPv6 kernel support for IPVS was developed by Julius Volz and Vince Busam from Google. For more details, see the IPVS official website, www.linuxvirtualserver.org.

- **IP sets:** A framework which consists of a userspace tool called ipset and a kernel part (net/netfilter/ipset). An IP set is basically a set of IP addresses. The IP sets framework was developed by Jozsef Kadlecsik. For more details, see http://ipset.netfilter.org.

- **iptables:** Probably the most popular Linux firewall, **iptables** is the front end of netfilter, and it provides a management layer for netfilter: for example, adding and deleting netfilter rules, displaying statistics, adding a table, zeroing the counters of a table, and more.

There are different iptables implementations in the kernel, according to the protocol:

- **iptables** for IPv4: (net/ipv4/netfilter/ip_tables.c)

- **ip6tables** for IPv6: (net/ipv6/netfilter/ip6_tables.c)

- **arptables** for ARP: (net/ipv4/netfilter/arp_tables.c)

- **ebtables** for Ethernet: (net/bridge/netfilter/ebtables.c)

In userspace, you have the iptables and the ip6tables command-line tools, which are used to set up, maintain, and inspect the IPv4 and IPv6 tables, respectively. See man 8 iptables and man 8 ip6tables. Both iptables and ip6tables use the setsockopt()/getsockopt() system calls to communicate with the kernel from userspace. I should mention here two interesting ongoing netfilter projects. The xtables2 project—being developed primarily by Jan Engelhardt, a work in progress as of this writing—uses a netlink-based interface to communicate with the kernel netfilter subsystem. See more details on the project website, http://xtables.de. The second project, the nftables project, is a new packet filtering engine that is a candidate to replace iptables. The nftables solution is based on using a virtual machine and a single unified implementation instead of the four iptables objects mentioned earlier (iptables, ip6tables, arptables, and ebtables). The nftables project was first presented in a netfilter workshop in 2008, by Patrick McHardy. The kernel infrastructure and userspace utility have been developed by Patrick McHardy and Pablo Neira Ayuso. For more details, see http://netfilter.org/projects/nftables, and "Nftables: a new packet filtering engine" at http://lwn.net/Articles/324989/.

There are a lot of netfilter modules that extend the core functionality of the core netfilter subsystem; apart from some examples, I do not describe these modules here in depth. There are a lot of information resources about these netfilter extensions from the administration perspective on the web and in various administration guides. See also the official netfilter project website: www.netfilter.org.

Netfilter Hooks

There are five points in the network stack where you have netfilter hooks: you have encountered these points in previous chapters' discussions of the Rx and Tx paths in IPv4 and in IPv6. Note that the names of the hooks are common to IPv4 and IPv6:

- NF_INET_PRE_ROUTING: This hook is in the ip_rcv() method in IPv4, and in the ipv6_rcv() method in IPv6. The ip_rcv() method is the protocol handler of IPv4, and the ipv6_rcv() method is the protocol handler of IPv6. It is the first hook point that all incoming packets reach, before performing a lookup in the routing subsystem.

- NF_INET_LOCAL_IN: This hook is in the ip_local_deliver() method in IPv4, and in the ip6_input() method in IPv6. All incoming packets addressed to the local host reach this hook point after first passing via the NF_INET_PRE_ROUTING hook point and after performing a lookup in the routing subsystem.

- NF_INET_FORWARD: This hook is in the ip_forward() method in IPv4, and in the ip6_forward() method in IPv6. All forwarded packets reach this hook point after first passing via the NF_INET_PRE_ROUTING hook point and after performing a lookup in the routing subsystem.

- NF_INET_POST_ROUTING: This hook is in the ip_output() method in IPv4, and in the ip6_finish_output2() method in IPv6. Packets that are forwarded reach this hook point after passing the NF_INET_FORWARD hook point. Also packets that are created in the local machine and sent out arrive to NF_INET_POST_ROUTING after passing the NF_INET_LOCAL_OUT hook point.

- NF_INET_LOCAL_OUT: This hook is in the __ip_local_out() method in IPv4, and in the __ip6_local_out() method in IPv6. All outgoing packets that were created on the local host reach this point before reaching the NF_INET_POST_ROUTING hook point.

(include/uapi/linux/netfilter.h)

The NF_HOOK macro, mentioned in previous chapters, is called in some distinct points along the packet traversal in the kernel network stack; it is defined in include/linux/netfilter.h:

```
static inline int NF_HOOK(uint8_t pf, unsigned int hook, struct sk_buff *skb,
                struct net_device *in, struct net_device *out,
                int (*okfn)(struct sk_buff *))
{
    return NF_HOOK_THRESH(pf, hook, skb, in, out, okfn, INT_MIN);
}
```

The parameters of the NF_HOOK() are as follows:

- pf: Protocol family. NFPROTO_IPV4 for IPv4 and NFPROTO_IPV6 for IPv6.

- hook: One of the five netfilter hooks mentioned earlier (for example, NF_INET_PRE_ROUTING or NF_INET_LOCAL_OUT).

- skb: The SKB object represents the packet that is being processed.

- in: The input network device (net_device object).

- out: The output network device (net_device object). There are cases when the output device is NULL, as it is yet unknown; for example, in the ip_rcv() method, net/ipv4/ip_input.c, which is called before a routing lookup is performed, and you don't know yet which is the output device; the NF_HOOK() macro is invoked in this method with a NULL output device.

- okfn: A pointer to a continuation function which will be called when the hook will terminate. It gets one argument, the SKB.

The return value from a netfilter hook must be one of the following values (which are also termed *netfilter verdicts*):

- NF_DROP (0): Discard the packet silently.

- NF_ACCEPT (1): The packet continues its traversal in the kernel network stack as usual.

- NF_STOLEN (2): Do not continue traversal. The packet is processed by the hook method.

- NF_QUEUE (3): Queue the packet for user space.

- NF_REPEAT (4): The hook function should be called again.

(include/uapi/linux/netfilter.h)

Now that you know about the various netfilter hooks, the next section covers how netfilter hooks are registered.

Registration of Netfilter Hooks

To register a hook callback at one of the five hook points mentioned earlier, you first define an nf_hook_ops object (or an array of nf_hook_ops objects) and then register it; the nf_hook_ops structure is defined in include/linux/netfilter.h:

```
struct nf_hook_ops {
    struct list_head list;
```

```
/* User fills in from here down. */
nf_hookfn       *hook;
struct module *owner;
u_int8_t        pf;
unsigned int  hooknum;
/* Hooks are ordered in ascending priority. */
int             priority;
};
```

The following introduces some of the important members of the nf_hook_ops structure:

- hook: The hook callback you want to register. Its prototype is:

```
unsigned int nf_hookfn(unsigned int hooknum,
                       struct sk_buff *skb,
                       const struct net_device *in,
                       const struct net_device *out,
                       int (*okfn)(struct sk_buff *));
```

- pf: The protocol family (NFPROTO_IPV4 for IPv4 and NFPROTO_IPV6 for IPv6).

- hooknum: One of the five netfilter hooks mentioned earlier.

- priority: More than one hook callback can be registered on the same hook. Hook callbacks with lower priorities are called first. The nf_ip_hook_priorities enum defines possible values for IPv4 hook priorities (include/uapi/linux/netfilter_ipv4.h). See also Table 9-4 in the "Quick Reference" section at the end of this chapter.

There are two methods to register netfilter hooks:

- int nf_register_hook(struct nf_hook_ops *reg): Registers a single nf_hook_ops object.

- int nf_register_hooks(struct nf_hook_ops *reg, unsigned int n): Registers an array of n nf_hook_ops objects; the second parameter is the number of the elements in the array.

You will see two examples of registration of an array of nf_hook_ops objects in the next two sections. Figure 9-1 in the next section illustrates the use of priorities when registering more than one hook callback on the same hook point.

Connection Tracking

It is not enough to filter traffic only according to the L4 and L3 headers in modern networks. You should also take into account cases when the traffic is based on sessions, such as an FTP session or a SIP session. By FTP session, I mean this sequence of events, for example: the client first creates a TCP control connection on TCP port 21, which is the default FTP port. Commands sent from the FTP client (such as listing the contents of a directory) to the server are sent on this control port. The FTP server opens a data socket on port 20, where the destination port on the client side is dynamically allocated. Traffic should be filtered according to other parameters, such as the state of a connection or timeout. This is one of the main reasons for using the Connection Tracking layer.

Connection Tracking allows the kernel to keep track of sessions. The Connection Tracking layer's primary goal is to serve as the basis of NAT. The IPv4 NAT module (net/ipv4/netfilter/iptable_nat.c) cannot be built if CONFIG_NF_CONNTRACK_IPV4 is not set. Similarly, the IPv6 NAT module (net/ipv6/netfilter/ip6table_nat.c) cannot be built if the CONFIG_NF_CONNTRACK_IPV6 is not set. However, Connection Tracking does not depend on NAT; you can run the Connection Tracking module without activating any NAT rule. The IPv4 and IPv6 NAT modules are discussed later in this chapter.

> ■ **Note** There are some userspace tools (conntrack-tools) for Connection Tracking administration mentioned in the "Quick Reference" section at the end of this chapter. These tools may help you to better understand the Connection Tracking layer.

Connection Tracking Initialization

An array of nf_hook_ops objects, called ipv4_conntrack_ops, is defined as follows:

```
static struct nf_hook_ops ipv4_conntrack_ops[] __read_mostly = {
        {
                .hook           = ipv4_conntrack_in,
                .owner          = THIS_MODULE,
                .pf             = NFPROTO_IPV4,
                .hooknum        = NF_INET_PRE_ROUTING,
                .priority       = NF_IP_PRI_CONNTRACK,
        },
        {
                .hook           = ipv4_conntrack_local,
                .owner          = THIS_MODULE,
                .pf             = NFPROTO_IPV4,
                .hooknum        = NF_INET_LOCAL_OUT,
                .priority       = NF_IP_PRI_CONNTRACK,
        },
        {
                .hook           = ipv4_helper,
                .owner          = THIS_MODULE,
                .pf             = NFPROTO_IPV4,
                .hooknum        = NF_INET_POST_ROUTING,
                .priority       = NF_IP_PRI_CONNTRACK_HELPER,
        },
        {
                .hook           = ipv4_confirm,
                .owner          = THIS_MODULE,
                .pf             = NFPROTO_IPV4,
                .hooknum        = NF_INET_POST_ROUTING,
                .priority       = NF_IP_PRI_CONNTRACK_CONFIRM,
        },
        {
                .hook           = ipv4_helper,
                .owner          = THIS_MODULE,
                .pf             = NFPROTO_IPV4,
                .hooknum        = NF_INET_LOCAL_IN,
                .priority       = NF_IP_PRI_CONNTRACK_HELPER,
        },
        {
                .hook           = ipv4_confirm,
                .owner          = THIS_MODULE,
                .pf             = NFPROTO_IPV4,
```

```
        .hooknum        = NF_INET_LOCAL_IN,
        .priority       = NF_IP_PRI_CONNTRACK_CONFIRM,
    },
};
```

(net/ipv4/netfilter/nf_conntrack_l3proto_ipv4.c)

The two most important Connection Tracking hooks you register are the NF_INET_PRE_ROUTING hook, handled by the ipv4_conntrack_in() method, and the NF_INET_LOCAL_OUT hook, handled by the ipv4_conntrack_local() method. These two hooks have a priority of NF_IP_PRI_CONNTRACK (-200). The other hooks in the ipv4_conntrack_ops array have an NF_IP_PRI_CONNTRACK_HELPER (300) priority and an NF_IP_PRI_CONNTRACK_CONFIRM (INT_MAX, which is $2^{31}-1$) priority. In netfilter hooks, a callback with a lower-priority value is executed first. (The enum nf_ip_hook_priorities in include/uapi/linux/netfilter_ipv4.h represents the possible priority values for IPv4 hooks). Both the ipv4_conntrack_local() method and the ipv4_conntrack_in() method invoke the nf_conntrack_in() method, passing the corresponding hooknum as a parameter. The nf_conntrack_in() method belongs to the protocol-independent NAT core, and is used both in IPv4 Connection Tracking and in IPv6 Connection Tracking; its second parameter is the protocol family, specifying whether it is IPv4 (PF_INET) or IPv6 (PF_INET6). I start the discussion with the nf_conntrack_in() callback. The other hook callbacks, ipv4_confirm() and ipv4_help(), are discussed later in this section.

■ **Note** When the kernel is built with Connection Tracking support (CONFIG_NF_CONNTRACK is set), the Connection Tracking hook callbacks are called even if there are no iptables rules that are activated. Naturally, this has some performance cost. If the performance is very important, and you know beforehand that the device will not use the netfilter subsystem, consider building the kernel without Connection Tracking support or building Connection Tracking as a kernel module and not loading it.

Registration of IPv4 Connection Tracking hooks is done by calling the nf_register_hooks() method in the nf_conntrack_l3proto_ipv4_init() method (net/ipv4/netfilter/nf_conntrack_l3proto_ipv4.c):

```
in nf_conntrack_l3proto_ipv4_init(void) {
    . . .
    ret = nf_register_hooks(ipv4_conntrack_ops,
                            ARRAY_SIZE(ipv4_conntrack_ops))
    . . .
}
```

In Figure 9-1, you can see the Connection Tracking callbacks (ipv4_conntrack_in(), ipv4_conntrack_local(), ipv4_helper() and ipv4_confirm()), according to the hook points where they are registered.

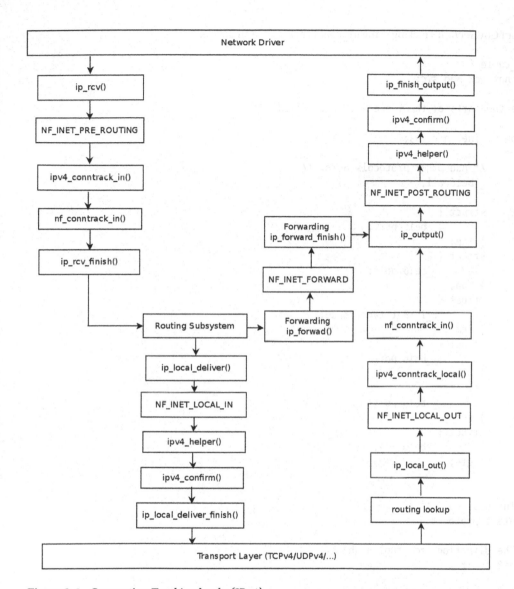

Figure 9-1. *Connection Tracking hooks (IPv4)*

■ **Note** For the sake of simplicity, Figure 9-1 does not include more complex scenarios, such as when using IPsec or fragmentation or multicasting. It also omits the functions that are called for packets generated on the local host and sent out (like the ip_queue_xmit() method or the ip_build_and_send_pkt() method) for the sake of simplicity.

The basic element of Connection Tracking is the nf_conntrack_tuple structure:

```c
struct nf_conntrack_tuple {
        struct nf_conntrack_man src;

        /* These are the parts of the tuple which are fixed. */
        struct {
                union nf_inet_addr u3;
                union {
                        /* Add other protocols here. */
                        __be16 all;

                        struct {
                                __be16 port;
                        } tcp;
                        struct {
                                __be16 port;
                        } udp;
                        struct {
                                u_int8_t type, code;
                        } icmp;
                        struct {
                                __be16 port;
                        } dccp;
                        struct {
                                __be16 port;
                        } sctp;
                        struct {
                                __be16 key;
                        } gre;
                } u;

                /* The protocol. */
                u_int8_t protonum;

                /* The direction (for tuplehash) */
                u_int8_t dir;
        } dst;
};
```

(include/net/netfilter/nf_conntrack_tuple.h)

The nf_conntrack_tuple structure represents a flow in one direction. The union inside the dst structure includes various protocol objects (like TCP, UDP, ICMP, and more). For each transport layer (L4) protocol, there is a Connection Tracking module, which implements the protocol-specific part. Thus, for example, you have net/netfilter/nf_conntrack_proto_tcp.c for the TCP protocol, net/netfilter/nf_conntrack_proto_udp.c for the UDP protocol, net/netfilter/nf_conntrack_ftp.c for the FTP protocol, and more; these modules support both IPv4 and IPv6. You will see examples of how protocol-specific implementations of Connection Tracking modules differ later in this section.

Connection Tracking Entries

The nf_conn structure represents the Connection Tracking entry:

```
struct nf_conn {
        /* Usage count in here is 1 for hash table/destruct timer, 1 per skb,
           plus 1 for any connection(s) we are `master' for */
        struct nf_conntrack ct_general;

        spinlock_t lock;

        /* XXX should I move this to the tail ? - Y.K */
        /* These are my tuples; original and reply */
        struct nf_conntrack_tuple_hash tuplehash[IP_CT_DIR_MAX];

        /* Have we seen traffic both ways yet? (bitset) */
        unsigned long status;

        /* If we were expected by an expectation, this will be it */
        struct nf_conn *master;

        /* Timer function; drops refcnt when it goes off. */
        struct timer_list timeout;



        /* Extensions */
        struct nf_ct_ext *ext;
#ifdef CONFIG_NET_NS
        struct net *ct_net;
#endif

        /* Storage reserved for other modules, must be the last member */
        union nf_conntrack_proto proto;
};
```

(include/net/netfilter/nf_conntrack.h)

The following is a description of some of the important members of the nf_conn structure :

- ct_general: A reference count.

- tuplehash: There are two tuplehash objects: tuplehash[0] is the original direction, and tuplehash[1] is the reply. They are usually referred to as tuplehash[IP_CT_DIR_ORIGINAL] and tuplehash[IP_CT_DIR_REPLY], respectively.

- status: The status of the entry. When you start to track a connection entry, it is IP_CT_NEW; later on, when the connection is established, it becomes IP_CT_ESTABLISHED. See the ip_conntrack_info enum in include/uapi/linux/netfilter/nf_conntrack_common.h.

- master: An expected connection. Set by the init_conntrack() method, when an expected packet arrives (this means that the nf_ct_find_expectation() method, which is invoked by the init_conntrack() method, finds an expectation). See also the "Connection Tracking Helpers and Expectations" section later in this chapter.

- timeout: Timer of the connection entry. Each connection entry is expired after some time interval when there is no traffic. The time interval is determined according to the protocol. When allocating an nf_conn object with the __nf_conntrack_alloc() method, the timeout timer is set to be the death_by_timeout() method.

Now that you know about the nf_conn struct and some of its members, let's take a look at the nf_conntrack_in() method:

```
unsigned int nf_conntrack_in(struct net *net, u_int8_t pf, unsigned int hooknum,
                        struct sk_buff *skb)
{
        struct nf_conn *ct, *tmpl = NULL;
        enum ip_conntrack_info ctinfo;
        struct nf_conntrack_l3proto *l3proto;
        struct nf_conntrack_l4proto *l4proto;
        unsigned int *timeouts;
        unsigned int dataoff;
        u_int8_t protonum;
        int set_reply = 0;
        int ret;

        if (skb->nfct) {
                /* Previously seen (loopback or untracked)?  Ignore. */
                tmpl = (struct nf_conn *)skb->nfct;
                if (!nf_ct_is_template(tmpl)) {
                        NF_CT_STAT_INC_ATOMIC(net, ignore);
                        return NF_ACCEPT;
                }
                skb->nfct = NULL;
        }
```

First you try to find whether the network layer (L3) protocol can be tracked:

```
        l3proto = __nf_ct_l3proto_find(pf);
```

Now you try to find if the transport layer (L4) protocol can be tracked. For IPv4, it is done by the ipv4_get_l4proto() method (net/ipv4/netfilter/nf_conntrack_l3proto_ipv4):

```
        ret = l3proto->get_l4proto(skb, skb_network_offset(skb),
                        &dataoff, &protonum);
        if (ret <= 0) {
           . . .
                ret = -ret;
                goto out;
        }
```

```
l4proto = __nf_ct_l4proto_find(pf, protonum);

/* It may be an special packet, error, unclean...
 * inverse of the return code tells to the netfilter
 * core what to do with the packet. */
```

Now you check protocol-specific error conditions (see, for example, the udp_error() method in net/netfilter/nf_conntrack_proto_udp.c, which checks for malformed packets, packets with invalid checksum, and more, or the tcp_error() method, in net/netfilter/nf_conntrack_proto_tcp.c):

```
if (l4proto->error != NULL) {
        ret = l4proto->error(net, tmpl, skb, dataoff, &ctinfo,
                                 pf, hooknum);
        if (ret <= 0) {
                NF_CT_STAT_INC_ATOMIC(net, error);
                NF_CT_STAT_INC_ATOMIC(net, invalid);
                ret = -ret;
                goto out;
        }
        /* ICMP[v6] protocol trackers may assign one conntrack. */
        if (skb->nfct)
                goto out;
}
```

The resolve_normal_ct() method, which is invoked hereafter immediately, performs the following:

- Calculates the hash of the tuple by calling the hash_conntrack_raw() method.

- Performs a lookup for a tuple match by calling the __nf_conntrack_find_get() method, passing the hash as a parameter.

- If no match is found, it creates a new nf_conntrack_tuple_hash object by calling the init_conntrack() method. This nf_conntrack_tuple_hash object is added to the list of unconfirmed tuplehash objects. This list is embedded in the network namespace object; the net structure contains a netns_ct object, which consists of network namespace specific Connection Tracking information. One of its members is unconfirmed, which is a list of unconfirmed tuplehash objects (see include/net/netns/conntrack.h). Later on, in the __nf_conntrack_confirm() method, it will be removed from the unconfirmed list. I discuss the __nf_conntrack_confirm() method later in this section.

- Each SKB has a member called nfctinfo, which represents the connection state (for example, it is IP_CT_NEW for new connections), and also a member called nfct (an instance of the nf_conntrack struct) which is in fact a reference counter. The resolve_normal_ct() method initializes both of them.

```
ct = resolve_normal_ct(net, tmpl, skb, dataoff, pf, protonum,
                       l3proto, l4proto, &set_reply, &ctinfo);
if (!ct) {
        /* Not valid part of a connection */
        NF_CT_STAT_INC_ATOMIC(net, invalid);
        ret = NF_ACCEPT;
        goto out;
}
```

```
if (IS_ERR(ct)) {
        /* Too stressed to deal. */
        NF_CT_STAT_INC_ATOMIC(net, drop);
        ret = NF_DROP;
        goto out;
}

NF_CT_ASSERT(skb->nfct);
```

You now call the nf_ct_timeout_lookup() method to decide what timeout policy you want to apply to this flow. For example, for UDP, the timeout is 30 seconds for unidirectional connections and 180 seconds for bidirectional connections; see the definition of the udp_timeouts array in net/netfilter/nf_conntrack_proto_udp.c. For TCP, which is a much more complex protocol, there are 11 entries in tcp_timeouts array (net/netfilter/nf_conntrack_proto_tcp.c):

```
/* Decide what timeout policy we want to apply to this flow. */
timeouts = nf_ct_timeout_lookup(net, ct, l4proto);
```

You now call the protocol-specific packet() method (for example, the udp_packet() for UDP or the tcp_packet() method for TCP). The udp_packet() method extends the timeout according to the status of the connection by calling the nf_ct_refresh_acct() method. For unreplied connections (where the IPS_SEEN_REPLY_BIT flag is not set), it will be set to 30 seconds, and for replied connections, it will be set to 180. Again, in the case of TCP, the tcp_packet() method is much more complex, due to the TCP advanced state machine. Moreover, the udp_packet() method always returns a verdict of NF_ACCEPT, whereas the tcp_packet() method may sometimes fail:

```
ret = l4proto->packet(ct, skb, dataoff, ctinfo, pf, hooknum, timeouts);
if (ret <= 0) {
        /* Invalid: inverse of the return code tells
         * the netfilter core what to do */
        pr_debug("nf_conntrack_in: Can't track with proto module\n");
        nf_conntrack_put(skb->nfct);
        skb->nfct = NULL;
        NF_CT_STAT_INC_ATOMIC(net, invalid);
        if (ret == -NF_DROP)
                NF_CT_STAT_INC_ATOMIC(net, drop);
        ret = -ret;
        goto out;
}

if (set_reply && !test_and_set_bit(IPS_SEEN_REPLY_BIT, &ct->status))
        nf_conntrack_event_cache(IPCT_REPLY, ct);
out:
if (tmpl) {
        /* Special case: we have to repeat this hook, assign the
         * template again to this packet. We assume that this packet
         * has no conntrack assigned. This is used by nf_ct_tcp. */
        if (ret == NF_REPEAT)
                skb->nfct = (struct nf_conntrack *)tmpl;
        else
                nf_ct_put(tmpl);
}

return ret;
}
```

The ipv4_confirm() method, which is called in the NF_INET_POST_ROUTING hook and in the NF_INET_LOCAL_IN hook, will normally call the __nf_conntrack_confirm() method, which will remove the tuple from the unconfirmed list.

Connection Tracking Helpers and Expectations

Some protocols have different flows for data and for control—for example, FTP, the File Transfer Protocol, and SIP, the Session Initiation Protocol, which is a VoIP protocol. Usually in these protocols, the control channel negotiates some configuration setup with the other side and agrees with it on which parameters to use for the data flow. These protocols are more difficult to handle by the netfilter subsystem, because the netfilter subsystem needs to be aware that flows are related to each other. In order to support these types of protocols, the netfilter subsystem provides the Connection Tracking Helpers, which extend the Connection Tracking basic functionality. These modules create expectations (nf_conntrack_expect objects), and these expectations tell the kernel that it should expect some traffic on a specified connection and that two connections are related. Knowing that two connections are related lets you define rules on the master connection that pertain also to the related connections. You can use a simple iptables rule based on the Connection Tracking state to accept packets whose Connection Tracking state is RELATED:

```
iptables -A INPUT -m conntrack --ctstate RELATED -j ACCEPT
```

■ **Note**   Connections can be related not only as a result of expectation. For example, an ICMPv4 error packet such as "ICMP fragmentation needed" will be related if netfilter finds a conntrack entry that matches the tuple in the ICMP-embedded L3/L4 header. See the icmp_error_message() method for more details, net/ipv4/netfilter/nf_conntrack_proto_icmp.c.

The Connection Tracking Helpers are represented by the nf_conntrack_helper structure (include/net/netfilter/nf_conntrack_helper.h). They are registered and unregistered by the nf_conntrack_helper_register() method and the nf_conntrack_helper_unregister() method, respectively. Thus, for example, the nf_conntrack_helper_register() method is invoked by nf_conntrack_ftp_init() (net/netfilter/nf_conntrack_ftp.c) in order to register the FTP Connection Tracking Helpers. The Connection Tracking Helpers are kept in a hash table (nf_ct_helper_hash). The ipv4_helper() hook callback is registered in two hook points, NF_INET_POST_ROUTING and NF_INET_LOCAL_IN (see the definition of ipv4_conntrack_ops array in the "Connection Tracking Initialization" section earlier). Because of this, when the FTP packet reaches the NF_INET_POST_ROUTING callback, ip_output(), or the NF_INET_LOCAL_IN callback, ip_local_deliver(), the ipv4_helper() method is invoked, and this method eventually calls the callbacks of the registered Connection Tracking Helpers. In the case of FTP, the registered helper method is the help() method, net/netfilter/nf_conntrack_ftp.c. This method looks for FTP-specific patterns, like the "PORT" FTP command; see the invocation of the find_pattern() method in the help() method, in the following code snippet (net/netfilter/nf_conntrack_ftp.c). If there is a match, an nf_conntrack_expect object is created by calling the nf_ct_expect_init() method:

```
static int help(struct sk_buff *skb,
        unsigned int protoff,
        struct nf_conn *ct,
        enum ip_conntrack_info ctinfo)
{
    struct nf_conntrack_expect *exp;
    . . .
```

```
        for (i = 0; i < ARRAY_SIZE(search[dir]); i++) {
            found = find_pattern(fb_ptr, datalen,
                            search[dir][i].pattern,
                            search[dir][i].plen,
                            search[dir][i].skip,
                            search[dir][i].term,
                            &matchoff, &matchlen,
                            &cmd,
                            search[dir][i].getnum);
                if (found) break;
        }

        if (found == -1) {
                /* We don't usually drop packets.  After all, this is
                   connection tracking, not packet filtering.
                   However, it is necessary for accurate tracking in
                   this case. */
                nf_ct_helper_log(skb, ct, "partial matching of `%s'",
                            search[dir][i].pattern);
```

───

■ **Note** Normally, Connection Tracking does not drop packets. There are some cases when, due to some error or abnormal situation, packets are dropped. The following is an example of such a case: the invocation of find_pattern() earlier returned −1, which means that there is only a partial match; and the packet is dropped due to not finding a full pattern match.

───

```
            ret = NF_DROP;
            goto out;
        } else if (found == 0) { /* No match */
                ret = NF_ACCEPT;
                goto out_update_nl;
        }

        pr_debug("conntrack_ftp: match `%.*s' (%u bytes at %u)\n",
                matchlen, fb_ptr + matchoff,
                matchlen, ntohl(th->seq) + matchoff);

        exp = nf_ct_expect_alloc(ct);
. . .
        nf_ct_expect_init(exp, NF_CT_EXPECT_CLASS_DEFAULT, cmd.l3num,
                        &ct->tuplehash[!dir].tuple.src.u3, daddr,
                        IPPROTO_TCP, NULL, &cmd.u.tcp.port);

. . .
}
(net/netfilter/nf_conntrack_ftp.c)
```

Later on, when a new connection is created by the init_conntrack() method, you check whether it has expectations, and if it does, you set the IPS_EXPECTED_BIT flag and set the master of the connection (ct->master) to refer to the connection that created the expectation:

```
static struct nf_conntrack_tuple_hash *
init_conntrack(struct net *net, struct nf_conn *tmpl,
               const struct nf_conntrack_tuple *tuple,
               struct nf_conntrack_l3proto *l3proto,
               struct nf_conntrack_l4proto *l4proto,
               struct sk_buff *skb,
               unsigned int dataoff, u32 hash)
{
        struct nf_conn *ct;
        struct nf_conn_help *help;
        struct nf_conntrack_tuple repl_tuple;
        struct nf_conntrack_ecache *ecache;
        struct nf_conntrack_expect *exp;
        u16 zone = tmpl ? nf_ct_zone(tmpl) : NF_CT_DEFAULT_ZONE;
        struct nf_conn_timeout *timeout_ext;
        unsigned int *timeouts;

        . . .
        ct = __nf_conntrack_alloc(net, zone, tuple, &repl_tuple, GFP_ATOMIC,
                                  hash);
    . . .

        exp = nf_ct_find_expectation(net, zone, tuple);
        if (exp) {
                pr_debug("conntrack: expectation arrives ct=%p exp=%p\n",
                        ct, exp);
                /* Welcome, Mr. Bond.  We've been expecting you... */
                __set_bit(IPS_EXPECTED_BIT, &ct->status);
                ct->master = exp->master;
                if (exp->helper) {
                        help = nf_ct_helper_ext_add(ct, exp->helper,
                                                    GFP_ATOMIC);
                        if (help)
                                rcu_assign_pointer(help->helper, exp->helper);
                }
        . . .
```

Note that helpers listen on a predefined port. For example, the FTP Connection Tracking Helper listens on port 21 (see FTP_PORT definition in include/linux/netfilter/nf_conntrack_ftp.h). You can set a different port (or ports) in one of two ways: the first way is by a module parameter—you can override the default port value by supplying a single port or a comma-separated list of ports to the modprobe command:

```
modprobe nf_conntrack_ftp ports=2121
modprobe nf_conntrack_ftp ports=2022,2023,2024
```

The second way is by using the CT target:

```
iptables -A PREROUTING -t raw -p tcp --dport 8888 -j CT --helper ftp
```

Note that the CT target (net/netfilter/xt_CT.c) was added in kernel 2.6.34.

■ **Note** Xtables target extensions are represented by the xt_target structure and are registered by the xt_register_target() method for a single target, or by the xt_register_targets() method for an array of targets. Xtables match extensions are represented by the xt_match structure and are registered by the xt_register_match() method, or by the xt_register_matches() for an array of matches. The match extensions inspect a packet according to some criterion defined by the match extension module; thus, for example, the xt_length match module (net/netfilter/xt_length.c) inspects packets according to their length (the tot_len of the SKB in case of IPv4 packet), and the xt_connlimit module (net/netfilter/xt_connlimit.c) limits the number of parallel TCP connections per IP address.

This section detailed the Connection Tracking initialization. The next section deals with iptables, which is probably the most known part of the netfilter framework.

IPTables

There are two parts to iptables. The kernel part—the core is in net/ipv4/netfilter/ip_tables.c for IPv4, and in net/ipv6/netfilter/ip6_tables.c for IPv6. And there is the userspace part, which provides a front end for accessing the kernel iptables layer (for example, adding and deleting rules with the iptables command). Each table is represented by the xt_table structure (defined in include/linux/netfilter/x_tables.h). Registration and unregistration of a table is done by the ipt_register_table() and the ipt_unregister_table() methods, respectively. These methods are implemented in net/ipv4/netfilter/ip_tables.c. In IPv6, you also use the xt_table structure for creating tables, but registration and unregistration of a table is done by the ip6t_register_table() method and the ip6t_unregister_table() method, respectively.

The network namespace object contains IPv4- and IPv6-specific objects (netns_ipv4 and netns_ipv6, respectively). The netns_ipv4 and netns_ipv6 objects, in turn, contain pointers to xt_table objects. For IPv4, in struct netns_ipv4 you have, for example, iptable_filter, iptable_mangle, nat_table, and more (include/net/netns/ipv4.h). In struct netns_ipv6 you have, for example, ip6table_filter, ip6table_mangle, ip6table_nat, and more (include/net/netns/ipv6.h). For a full list of the IPv4 and of the IPv6 network namespace netfilter tables and the corresponding kernel modules, see Tables 9-2 and 9-3 in the "Quick Reference" section at the end of this chapter.

To understand how iptables work, let's take a look at a real example with the filter table. For the sake of simplicity, let's assume that the filter table is the only one that is built, and also that the LOG target is supported; the only rule I am using is for logging, as you will shortly see. First, let's take a look at the definition of the filter table:

```
#define FILTER_VALID_HOOKS ((1 << NF_INET_LOCAL_IN) | \
                            (1 << NF_INET_FORWARD) | \
                            (1 << NF_INET_LOCAL_OUT))

static const struct xt_table packet_filter = {
        .name           = "filter",
        .valid_hooks    = FILTER_VALID_HOOKS,
        .me             = THIS_MODULE,
        .af             = NFPROTO_IPV4,
        .priority       = NF_IP_PRI_FILTER,
};

(net/ipv4/netfilter/iptable_filter.c)
```

Initialization of the table is done first by calling the xt_hook_link() method, which sets the iptable_filter_hook() method as the hook callback of the nf_hook_ops object of the packet_filter table:

```
static struct nf_hook_ops *filter_ops __read_mostly;
static int __init iptable_filter_init(void)
{
    . . .
        filter_ops = xt_hook_link(&packet_filter, iptable_filter_hook);
    . . .
}
```

Then you call the ipt_register_table() method (note that the IPv4 netns object, net->ipv4, keeps a pointer to the filter table, iptable_filter):

```
static int __net_init iptable_filter_net_init(struct net *nct)
{
    . . .
      net->ipv4.iptable_filter =
                ipt_register_table(net, &packet_filter, repl);
    . . .

      return PTR_RET(net->ipv4.iptable_filter);
}
```

(net/ipv4/netfilter/iptable_filter.c)

Note that there are three hooks in the filter table:

- NF_INET_LOCAL_IN

- NF_INET_FORWARD

- NF_INET_LOCAL_OUT

For this example, you set the following rule, using the iptable command line:

```
iptables -A INPUT -p udp --dport=5001 -j LOG --log-level 1
```

The meaning of this rule is that you will dump into the syslog incoming UDP packets with destination port 5001. The log-level modifier is the standard syslog level in the range 0 through 7; 0 is emergency and 7 is debug. Note that when running an iptables command, you should specify the table you want to use with the –t modifier; for example, iptables -t nat -A POSTROUTING -o eth0 -j MASQUERADE will add a rule to the NAT table. When not specifying a table name with the –t modifier, you use the filter table by default. So by running iptables -A INPUT -p udp --dport=5001 -j LOG --log-level 1, you add a rule to the filter table.

■ **Note** You can set targets to iptables rules; usually these can be targets from the Linux netfilter subsystems (see the earlier example for using the LOG target). You can also write your own targets and extend the iptables userspace code to support them. See "Writing Netfilter modules," by Jan Engelhardt and Nicolas Bouliane: http://inai.de/documents/ Netfilter_Modules.pdf.

Note that CONFIG_NETFILTER_XT_TARGET_LOG must be set in order to use the LOG target in an iptables rule, as shown in the earlier example. You can refer to the code of net/netfilter/xt_LOG.c as an example of an iptables target module.

When a UDP packet with destination port 5001 reaches the network driver and goes up to the network layer (L3), the first hook it encounters is the NF_INET_PRE_ROUTING hook; the filter table callback does not register a hook in NF_INET_PRE_ROUTING. It has only three hooks: NF_INET_LOCAL_IN, NF_INET_FORWARD, and NF_INET_LOCAL_OUT, as mentioned earlier. So you continue to the ip_rcv_finish() method and perform a lookup in the routing subsystem. Now there are two cases: the packet is intended to be delivered to the local host or intended to be forwarded (let's ignore cases when the packet is to be discarded). In Figure 9-2, you can see the packet traversal in both cases.

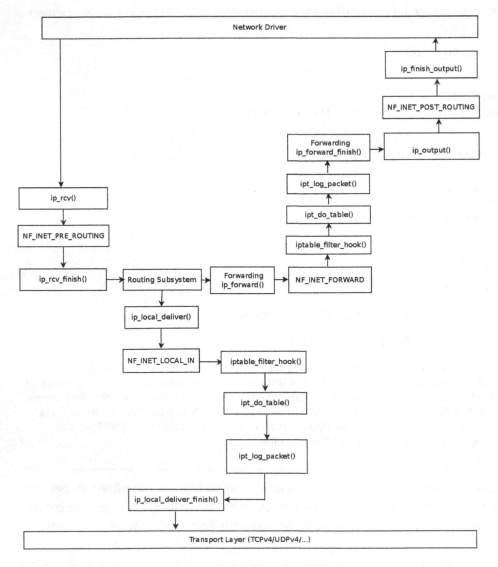

Figure 9-2. *Traffic for me and Forwarded Traffic with a Filter table rule*

Delivery to the Local Host

First you reach the ip_local_deliver() method; take a short look at this method:

```
int ip_local_deliver(struct sk_buff *skb)
{
    . . .
        return NF_HOOK(NFPROTO_IPV4, NF_INET_LOCAL_IN, skb, skb->dev, NULL,
                        ip_local_deliver_finish);
}
```

As you can see, you have the NF_INET_LOCAL_IN hook in this method, and as mentioned earlier, NF_INET_LOCAL_IN is one of the filter table hooks; so the NF_HOOK() macro will invoke the iptable_filter_hook() method. Now take a look in the iptable_filter_hook() method:

```
static unsigned int iptable_filter_hook(unsigned int hook, struct sk_buff *skb,
                                        const struct net_device *in,
                        const struct net_device *out,
                                int (*okfn)(struct sk_buff *))
{
        const struct net *net;
        . . .
        net = dev_net((in != NULL) ? in : out);
        . . .

        return ipt_do_table(skb, hook, in, out, net->ipv4.iptable_filter);
}
```
(net/ipv4/netfilter/iptable_filter.c)

The ipt_do_table() method, in fact, invokes the LOG target callback, ipt_log_packet(), which writes the packet headers into the syslog. If there were more rules, they would have been called at this point. Because there are no more rules, you continue to the ip_local_deliver_finish() method, and the packet continues its traversal to the transport layer (L4) to be handled by a corresponding socket.

Forwarding the Packet

The second case is that after a lookup in the routing subsystem, you found that the packet is to be forwarded, so the ip_forward() method is called:

```
int ip_forward(struct sk_buff *skb)
  {
  . . .
    return NF_HOOK(NFPROTO_IPV4, NF_INET_FORWARD, skb, skb->dev,
                        rt->dst.dev, ip_forward_finish);
  . . .
```

Because the filter table has a registered hook callback in NF_INET_FORWARD, as mentioned, you again invoke the iptable_filter_hook() method. And consequently, as before, you again call the ipt_do_table() method, which will in turn again call the ipt_log_packet() method. You will continue to the ip_forward_finish() method (note that ip_forward_finish is the last argument of the NF_HOOK macro above, which represents the continuation method). Then call the ip_output() method, and because the filter table has no NF_INET_POST_ROUTING hook, you continue to the ip_finish_output() method.

■ **Note** You can filter packets according to their Connection Tracking state. The next rule will dump into syslog packets whose Connection Tracking state is ESTABLISHED:

iptables -A INPUT -p tcp -m conntrack --ctstate ESTABLISHED -j LOG --log-level 1

Network Address Translation (NAT)

The Network Address Translation (NAT) module deals mostly with IP address translation, as the name implies, or port manipulation. One of the most common uses of NAT is to enable a group of hosts with a private IP address on a Local Area Network to access the Internet via some residential gateway. You can do that, for example, by setting a NAT rule. The NAT, which is installed on the gateway, can use such a rule and provide the hosts the ability to access the Web. The netfilter subsystem has NAT implementation for IPv4 and for IPv6. The IPv6 NAT implementation is mainly based on the IPv4 implementation and provides, from a user perspective, an interface similar to IPv4. IPv6 NAT support was merged in kernel 3.7. It provides some features like an easy solution to load balancing (by setting a DNAT on incoming traffic) and more. The IPv6 NAT module is in net/ipv6/netfilter/ip6table_nat.c. There are many types of NAT setups, and there is a lot of documentation on the Web about NAT administration. I talk about two common configurations: SNAT is source NAT, where the source IP address is changed, and DNAT is a destination NAT, where the destination IP address is changed. You can use the -j flag to select SNAT or DNAT. The implementation of both DNAT and SNAT is in net/netfilter/xt_nat.c. The next section discusses NAT initialization.

NAT initialization

The NAT table, like the filter table in the previous section, is also an xt_table object. It is registered on all hook points, except for the NF_INET_FORWARD hook:

```
static const struct xt_table nf_nat_ipv4_table = {
        .name          = "nat",
        .valid_hooks   = (1 << NF_INET_PRE_ROUTING) |
                         (1 << NF_INET_POST_ROUTING) |
                         (1 << NF_INET_LOCAL_OUT) |
                         (1 << NF_INET_LOCAL_IN),
        .me            = THIS_MODULE,
        .af            = NFPROTO_IPV4,
};
```

(net/ipv4/netfilter/iptable_nat.c)

Registration and unregistration of the NAT table is done by calling the ipt_register_table() and the ipt_unregister_table(), respectively (net/ipv4/netfilter/iptable_nat.c). The network namespace (struct net) includes an IPv4 specific object (netns_ipv4), which includes a pointer to the IPv4 NAT table (nat_table), as mentioned in the earlier "IP tables" section. This xt_table object, which is created by the ipt_register_table() method, is assigned to this nat_table pointer. You also define an array of nf_hook_ops objects and register it:

```
static struct nf_hook_ops nf_nat_ipv4_ops[] __read_mostly = {
        /* Before packet filtering, change destination */
        {
                .hook           = nf_nat_ipv4_in,
                .owner          = THIS_MODULE,
                .pf             = NFPROTO_IPV4,
                .hooknum        = NF_INET_PRF_ROUTING,
                .priority       = NF_IP_PRI_NAT_DST,
        },
        /* After packet filtering, change source */
        {
                .hook           = nf_nat_ipv4_out,
                .owner          = THIS_MODULE,
                .pf             = NFPROTO_IPV4,
                .hooknum        = NF_INET_POST_ROUTING,
                .priority       = NF_IP_PRI_NAT_SRC,
        },
        /* Before packet filtering, change destination */
        {
                .hook           = nf_nat_ipv4_local_fn,
                .owner          = THIS_MODULE,
                .pf             = NFPROTO_IPV4,
                .hooknum        = NF_INET_LOCAL_OUT,
                .priority       = NF_IP_PRI_NAT_DST,
        },
        /* After packet filtering, change source */
        {
                .hook           = nf_nat_ipv4_fn,
                .owner          = THIS_MODULE,
                .pf             = NFPROTO_IPV4,
                .hooknum        = NF_INET_LOCAL_IN,
                .priority       = NF_IP_PRI_NAT_SRC,
        },
};
```

Registration of the nf_nat_ipv4_ops array is done in the iptable_nat_init() method:

```
static int __init iptable_nat_init(void)
{
        int err;
        ...
        err = nf_register_hooks(nf_nat_ipv4_ops, ARRAY_SIZE(nf_nat_ipv4_ops));
        if (err < 0)
                goto err2;
        return 0;
        ...
}
```

(net/ipv4/netfilter/iptable_nat.c)

NAT Hook Callbacks and Connection Tracking Hook Callbacks

There are some hooks on which both NAT callbacks and Connection Tracking callbacks are registered. For example, on the NF_INET_PRE_ROUTING hook (the first hook an incoming packet arrives at), there are two registered callbacks: the Connection Tracking callback, ipv4_conntrack_in(), and the NAT callback, nf_nat_ipv4_in(). The priority of the Connection Tracking callback, ipv4_conntrack_in(), is NF_IP_PRI_CONNTRACK (-200), and the priority of the NAT callback, nf_nat_ipv4_in(), is NF_IP_PRI_NAT_DST (-100). Because callbacks of the same hook with lower priorities are invoked first, the Connection Tracking ipv4_conntrack_in() callback, which has a priority of –200, will be invoked before the NAT nf_nat_ipv4_in() callback, which has a priority of –100. See Figure 9-1 for the location of the ipv4_conntrack_in() method and Figure 9-4 for the location of the nf_nat_ipv4_in(); both are in the same place, in the NF_INET_PRE_ROUTING point. The reason behind this is that NAT performs a lookup in the Connection Tracking layer, and if it does not find an entry, NAT does not perform any address translation action:

```
static unsigned int nf_nat_ipv4_fn(unsigned int hooknum,
                         struct sk_buff *skb,
                         const struct net_device *in,
                         const struct net_device *out,
                         int (*okfn)(struct sk_buff *))
{
        struct nf_conn *ct;
        . . .
        /* Don't try to NAT if this packet is not conntracked */
        if (nf_ct_is_untracked(ct))
                return NF_ACCEPT;
        . . .
}

(net/ipv4/netfilter/iptable_nat.c)
```

■ **Note**   The nf_nat_ipv4_fn () method is called from the NAT PRE_ROUTING callback, nf_nat_ipv4_in().

On the NF_INET_POST_ROUTING hook, you have two registered Connection Tracking callbacks: the ipv4_helper() callback (with priority of NF_IP_PRI_CONNTRACK_HELPER, which is 300) and the ipv4_confirm() callback with priority of NF_IP_PRI_CONNTRACK_CONFIRM (INT_MAX, which is the highest integer value for a priority). You also have a registered NAT hook callback, nf_nat_ipv4_out(), with a priority of NF_IP_PRI_NAT_SRC, which is 100. As a result, when reaching the NF_INET_POST_ROUTING hook, first the NAT callback, nf_nat_ipv4_out(), will be called, and then the ipv4_helper() method will be called, and the ipv4_confirm() will be the last to be called. See Figure 9-4.

Let's take a look in a simple DNAT rule and see the traversal of a forwarded packet and the order in which the Connection Tracking callbacks and the NAT callbacks are called (for the sake of simplicity, assume that the filter table is not built in this kernel image). In the setup shown in Figure 9-3, the middle host (the AMD server) runs this DNAT rule:

```
iptables -t nat -A PREROUTING -j DNAT -p udp --dport 9999 --to-destination 192.168.1.8
```

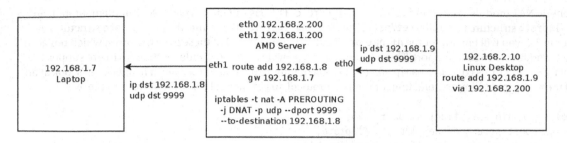

Figure 9-3. *A simple setup with a DNAT rule*

The meaning of this DNAT rule is that incoming UDP packets that are sent on UDP destination port 9999 will change their destination IP address to 192.168.1.8. The right side machine (the Linux desktop) sends UDP packets to 192.168.1.9 with UDP destination port of 9999. In the AMD server, the destination IPv4 address is changed to 192.168.1.8 by the DNAT rule, and the packets are sent to the laptop on the left.

In Figure 9-4, you can see the traversal of a first UDP packet, which is sent according to the setup mentioned earlier.

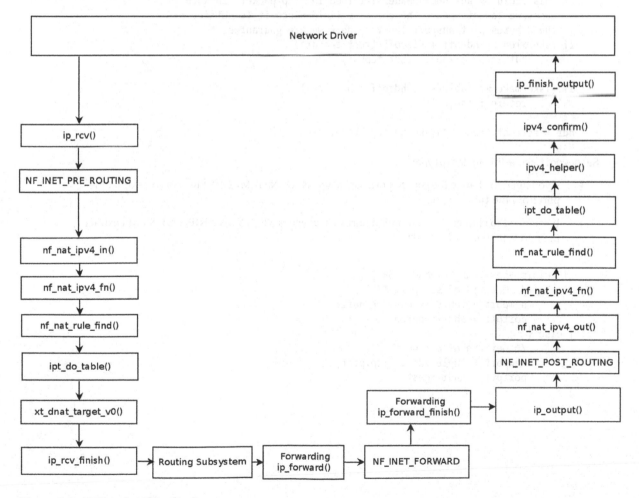

Figure 9-4. *NAT and netfilter hooks*

The generic NAT module is net/netfilter/nf_nat_core.c. The basic elements of the NAT implementation are the nf_nat_l4proto structure (include/net/netfilter/nf_nat_l4proto.h) and the nf_nat_l3proto structure. In kernels prior to 3.7, you will encounter the nf_nat_protocol structure instead of these two structures, which replaced them as part of adding IPv6 NAT support. These two structures provide a protocol-independent NAT core support.

Both of these structures contain a manip_pkt() function pointer that changes the packet headers. Let's look at an example of the manip_pkt() implementation for the TCP protocol, in net/netfilter/nf_nat_proto_tcp.c:

```
static bool tcp_manip_pkt(struct sk_buff *skb,
            const struct nf_nat_l3proto *l3proto,
            unsigned int iphdroff, unsigned int hdroff,
            const struct nf_conntrack_tuple *tuple,
            enum nf_nat_manip_type maniptype)
{
        struct tcphdr *hdr;
        __be16 *portptr, newport, oldport;
        int hdrsize = 8; /* TCP connection tracking guarantees this much */

        /* this could be an inner header returned in icmp packet; in such
           cases we cannot update the checksum field since it is outside of
           the 8 bytes of transport layer headers we are guaranteed */
        if (skb->len >= hdroff + sizeof(struct tcphdr))
                hdrsize = sizeof(struct tcphdr);

        if (!skb_make_writable(skb, hdroff + hdrsize))
                return false;

        hdr = (struct tcphdr *)(skb->data + hdroff);
```

Set newport according to maniptype:

- If you need to change the source port, maniptype is NF_NAT_MANIP_SRC. So you extract the port from the tuple->src.

- If you need to change the destination port, maniptype is NF_NAT_MANIP_DST. So you extract the port from the tuple->dst:

```
        if (maniptype == NF_NAT_MANIP_SRC) {
                /* Get rid of src port */
                newport = tuple->src.u.tcp.port;
                portptr = &hdr->source;
        } else {
                /* Get rid of dst port */
                newport = tuple->dst.u.tcp.port;
                portptr = &hdr->dest;
        }
```

You are going to change the source port (when maniptype is NF_NAT_MANIP_SRC) or the destination port (when maniptype is NF_NAT_MANIP_DST) of the TCP header, so you need to recalculate the checksum. You must keep the old port for the checksum recalculation, which will be immediately done by calling the csum_update() method and the inet_proto_csum_replace2() method:

```
oldport = *portptr;
*portptr = newport;

if (hdrsize < sizeof(*hdr))
        return true;
```

Recalculate the checksum:

```
l3proto->csum_update(skb, iphdroff, &hdr->check, tuple, maniptype);
inet_proto_csum_replace2(&hdr->check, skb, oldport, newport, 0);
return true;
}
```

NAT Hook Callbacks

The protocol-specific NAT module is net/ipv4/netfilter/iptable_nat.c for the IPv4 protocol, and net/ipv6/netfilter/ip6table_nat.c for the IPv6 protocol. These two NAT modules have four hooks callbacks each, shown in Table 9-1.

Table 9-1. *IPv4 and IPv6 NAT Callbacks*

Hook	Hook Callback (IPv4)	Hook Callback (IPv6)
NF_INET_PRE_ROUTING	nf_nat_ipv4_in	nf_nat_ipv6_in
NF_INET_POST_ROUTING	nf_nat_ipv4_out	nf_nat_ipv6_out
NF_INET_LOCAL_OUT	nf_nat_ipv4_local_fn	nf_nat_ipv6_local_fn
NF_INET_LOCAL_IN	nf_nat_ipv4_fn	nf_nat_ipv6_fn

The nf_nat_ipv4_fn() is the most important of these methods (for IPv4). The other three methods, nf_nat_ipv4_in(), nf_nat_ipv4_out(), and nf_nat_ipv4_local_fn(), all invoke the nf_nat_ipv4_fn() method. Let's take a look at the nf_nat_ipv4_fn() method:

```
static unsigned int nf_nat_ipv4_fn(unsigned int hooknum,
                        struct sk_buff *skb,
                        const struct net_device *in,
                        const struct net_device *out,
                        int (*okfn)(struct sk_buff *))
{
        struct nf_conn *ct;
        enum ip_conntrack_info ctinfo;
        struct nf_conn_nat *nat;
        /* maniptype == SRC for postrouting. */
        enum nf_nat_manip_type maniptype = HOOK2MANIP(hooknum);
```

```
        /* We never see fragments: conntrack defrags on pre-routing
         * and local-out, and nf_nat_out protects post-routing.
         */
        NF_CT_ASSERT(!ip_is_fragment(ip_hdr(skb)));

        ct = nf_ct_get(skb, &ctinfo);
        /* Can't track?  It's not due to stress, or conntrack would
         * have dropped it.  Hence it's the user's responsibilty to
         * packet filter it out, or implement conntrack/NAT for that
         * protocol. 8) --RR
         */
        if (!ct)
                return NF_ACCEPT;

        /* Don't try to NAT if this packet is not conntracked */
        if (nf_ct_is_untracked(ct))
                return NF_ACCEPT;

        nat = nfct_nat(ct);
        if (!nat) {
                /* NAT module was loaded late. */
                if (nf_ct_is_confirmed(ct))
                        return NF_ACCEPT;
                nat = nf_ct_ext_add(ct, NF_CT_EXT_NAT, GFP_ATOMIC);
                if (nat == NULL) {
                        pr_debug("failed to add NAT extension\n");
                        return NF_ACCEPT;
                }
        }

        switch (ctinfo) {
        case IP_CT_RELATED:
        case IP_CT_RELATED_REPLY:
                if (ip_hdr(skb)->protocol == IPPROTO_ICMP) {
                        if (!nf_nat_icmp_reply_translation(skb, ct, ctinfo,
                                                                hooknum))

                                return NF_DROP;
                        else
                                return NF_ACCEPT;
                }
                /* Fall thru... (Only ICMPs can be IP_CT_IS_REPLY) */
        case IP_CT_NEW:
                /* Seen it before?  This can happen for loopback, retrans,
                 * or local packets.
                 */
                if (!nf_nat_initialized(ct, maniptype)) {
                        unsigned int ret;
```

The nf_nat_rule_find() method calls the ipt_do_table() method, which iterates through all the matches of an entry in a specified table, and if there is a match, calls the target callback:

```
                ret = nf_nat_rule_find(skb, hooknum, in, out, ct);
                if (ret != NF_ACCEPT)
                        return ret;
        } else {
                pr_debug("Already setup manip %s for ct %p\n",
                        maniptype == NF_NAT_MANIP_SRC ? "SRC" : "DST",
                        ct);
                if (nf_nat_oif_changed(hooknum, ctinfo, nat, out))
                        goto oif_changed;
        }
        break;

default:
        /* ESTABLISHED */
        NF_CT_ASSERT(ctinfo == IP_CT_ESTABLISHED ||
                        ctinfo == IP_CT_ESTABLISHED_REPLY);
        if (nf_nat_oif_changed(hooknum, ctinfo, nat, out))
                goto oif_changed;
}

        return nf_nat_packet(ct, ctinfo, hooknum, skb);

oif_changed:
        nf_ct_kill_acct(ct, ctinfo, skb);
        return NF_DROP;
}
```

Connection Tracking Extensions

Connection Tracking (CT) Extensions were added in kernel 2.6.23. The main point of Connection Tracking Extensions is to allocate only what is required—for example, if the NAT module is not loaded, the extra memory needed for NAT in the Connection Tracking layer will not be allocated. Some extensions are enabled by sysctls or even depending on certain iptables rules (for example, -m connlabel). Each Connection Tracking Extension module should define an nf_ct_ext_type object and perform registration by the nf_ct_extend_register() method (unregistration is done by the nf_ct_extend_unregister() method). Each extension should define a method to attach its Connection Tracking Extension to a connection (nf_conn) object, which should be called from the init_conntrack() method. Thus, for example, you have the nf_ct_tstamp_ext_add() method for the timestamp CT Extension and nf_ct_labels_ext_add() for the labels CT Extension. The Connection Tracking Extensions infrastructure is implemented in net/netfilter/nf_conntrack_extend.c. These are the Connection Tracking Extensions modules as of this writing (all under net/netfilter):

- nf_conntrack_timestamp.c

- nf_conntrack_timeout.c

- nf_conntrack_acct.c

- nf_conntrack_ecache.c

- nf_conntrack_labels.c

- nf_conntrack_helper.c

Summary

This chapter described the netfilter subsystem implementation. I covered the netfilter hooks and how they are registered. I also discussed important subjects such as the Connection Tracking mechanism, iptables, and NAT. Chapter 10 deals with the IPsec subsystem and its implementation.

Quick Reference

This section covers the top methods that are related to the topics discussed in this chapter, ordered by their context, followed by three tables and a short section about tools and libraries.

Methods

The following is a short list of important methods of the netfilter subsystem. Some of them were mentioned in this chapter.

struct xt_table *ipt_register_table(struct net *net, const struct xt_table *table, const struct ipt_replace *repl);

This method registers a table in the netfilter subsystem.

void ipt_unregister_table(struct net *net, struct xt_table *table);

This method unregisters a table in the netfilter subsystem.

int nf_register_hook(struct nf_hook_ops *reg);

This method registers a single nf_hook_ops object.

int nf_register_hooks(struct nf_hook_ops *reg, unsigned int n);

This method registers an array of *n* nf_hook_ops objects; the second parameter is the number of the elements in the array.

void nf_unregister_hook(struct nf_hook_ops *reg);

This method unregisters a single nf_hook_ops object.

void nf_unregister_hooks(struct nf_hook_ops *reg, unsigned int n);

This method unregisters an array of *n* nf_hook_ops objects; the second parameter is the number of the elements in the array.

static inline void nf_conntrack_get(struct nf_conntrack *nfct);

This method increments the reference count of the associated nf_conntrack object.

static inline void nf_conntrack_put(struct nf_conntrack *nfct);

This method decrements the reference count of the associated nf_conntrack object. If it reaches 0, the nf_conntrack_destroy() method is called.

int nf_conntrack_helper_register(struct nf_conntrack_helper *me);

This method registers an nf_conntrack_helper object.

static inline struct nf_conn *resolve_normal_ct(struct net *net, struct nf_conn *tmpl, struct sk_buff *skb, unsigned int dataoff, u_int16_t l3num, u_int8_t protonum, struct nf_conntrack_l3proto *l3proto, struct nf_conntrack_l4proto *l4proto, int *set_reply, enum ip_conntrack_info *ctinfo);

This method tries to find an nf_conntrack_tuple_hash object according to the specified SKB by calling the __nf_conntrack_find_get() method, and if it does not find such an entry, it creates one by calling the init_conntrack() method. The resolve_normal_ct() method is called from the nf_conntrack_in() method (net/netfilter/nf_conntrack_core.c).

struct nf_conntrack_tuple_hash *init_conntrack(struct net *net, struct nf_conn *tmpl, const struct nf_conntrack_tuple *tuple, struct nf_conntrack_l3proto *l3proto, struct nf_conntrack_l4proto *l4proto, struct sk_buff *skb, unsigned int dataoff, u32 hash);

This method allocates a Connection Tracking nf_conntrack_tuple_hash object. Invoked from the resolve_normal_ct() method, it tries to find an expectation for this connection by calling the nf_ct_find_expectation() method.

static struct nf_conn *__nf_conntrack_alloc(struct net *net, u16 zone, const struct nf_conntrack_tuple *orig, const struct nf_conntrack_tuple *repl, gfp_t gfp, u32 hash);

This method allocates an nf_conn object. Sets the timeout timer of the nf_conn object to be the death_by_timeout() method.

int xt_register_target(struct xt_target *target);

This method registers an Xtable target extension.

void xt_unregister_target(struct xt_target *target);

This method unregisters an Xtable target extension.

int xt_register_targets(struct xt_target *target, unsigned int n);

This method registers an array of Xtable target extensions; n is the number of targets.

void xt_unregister_targets(struct xt_target *target, unsigned int n);

This method unregisters an array of Xtable target extensions; *n* is the number of targets.

int xt_register_match(struct xt_match *target);

This method registers an Xtable match extension.

void xt_unregister_match(struct xt_match *target);

This method unregisters an Xtable match extension.

int xt_register_matches(struct xt_match *match, unsigned int n);

This method registers an array of Xtable match extensions; *n* is the number of matches.

void xt_unregister_matches(struct xt_match *match, unsigned int n);

This method unregisters an array of Xtable match extensions; *n* is the number of matches.

int nf_ct_extend_register(struct nf_ct_ext_type *type);

This method registers a Connection Tracking Extension object.

void nf_ct_extend_unregister(struct nf_ct_ext_type *type);

This method unregisters a Connection Tracking Extension object.

int __init iptable_nat_init(void);

This method initializes the IPv4 NAT table.

int __init nf_conntrack_ftp_init(void);

This method initializes the Connection Tracking FTP Helper. Calls the nf_conntrack_helper_register() method to register the FTP helpers.

MACRO

Let's look at the macro used in this chapter.

NF_CT_DIRECTION(hash)

This is a macro that gets an nf_conntrack_tuple_hash object as a parameter and returns the direction (IP_CT_DIR_ORIGINAL, which is 0, or IP_CT_DIR_REPLY, which is 1) of the destination (dst object) of the associated tuple (include/net/netfilter/nf_conntrack_tuple.h).

Tables

And here are the tables, showing netfilter tables in IPv4 network namespace and in IPv6 network namespace and netfilter hook priorities.

Table 9-2. *IPv4 Network Namespace (netns_ipv4) Tables (xt_table Objects)*

Linux Symbol (netns_ipv4)	Linux Module
iptable_filter	net/ipv4/netfilter/iptable_filter.c
iptable_mangle	net/ipv4/netfilter/iptable_mangle.c
iptable_raw	net/ipv4/netfilter/iptable_raw.c
arptable_filter	net/ipv4/netfilter/arp_tables.c
nat_table	net/ipv4/netfilter/iptable_nat.c
iptable_security	net/ipv4/netfilter/iptable_security.c (Note: CONFIG_SECURITY should be set).

Table 9-3. *IPv6 Network Namespace (netns_ipv6) Tables (xt_table Objects)*

Linux Symbol (netns_ipv6)	Linux Module
ip6table_filter	net/ipv6/netfilter/ip6table_filter.c
ip6table_mangle	net/ipv6/netfilter/ip6table_mangle.c
ip6table_raw	net/ipv6/netfilter/ip6table_raw.c
ip6table_nat	net/ipv6/netfilter/ip6table_nat.c
ip6table_security	net/ipv6/netfilter/ip6table_security.c (Note: CONFIG_SECURITY should be set).

Table 9-4. *Netfilter Hook Priorities*

Linux Symbol	value
NF_IP_PRI_FIRST	INT_MIN
NF_IP_PRI_CONNTRACK_DEFRAG	-400
NF_IP_PRI_RAW	-300
NF_IP_PRI_SELINUX_FIRST	-225
NF_IP_PRI_CONNTRACK	-200
NF_IP_PRI_MANGLE	-150
NF_IP_PRI_NAT_DST	-100
NF_IP_PRI_FILTER	0
NF_IP_PRI_SECURITY	50
NF_IP_PRI_NAT_SRC	100
NF_IP_PRI_SELINUX_LAST	225
NF_IP_PRI_CONNTRACK_HELPER	300
NF_IP_PRI_CONNTRACK_CONFIRM	INT_MAX
NF_IP_PRI_LAST	INT_MAX

See the nf_ip_hook_priorities enum definition in include/uapi/linux/netfilter_ipv4.h.

Tools and Libraries

The conntrack-tools consist of a userspace daemon, conntrackd, and a command line tool, conntrack. It provides a tool with which system administrators can interact with the netfilter Connection Tracking layer. See: http://conntrack-tools.netfilter.org/.

Some libraries are developed by the netfilter project and allow you to perform various userspace tasks; these libraries are prefixed with "libnetfilter"; for example, libnetfilter_conntrack, libnetfilter_log, and libnetfilter_queue. For more details, see the netfilter official website, www.netfilter.org.

CHAPTER 10

■ ■ ■

IPsec

Chapter 9 deals with the netfilter subsystem and with its kernel implementation. This chapter discusses the Internet Protocol Security (IPsec) subsystem. IPsec is a group of protocols for securing IP traffic by authenticating and encrypting each IP packet in a communication session. Most security services are provided by two major IPsec protocols: the Authentication Header (AH) protocol and the Encapsulating Security Payload (ESP) protocol. Moreover, IPsec provides protection against trying to eavesdrop and send again packets (replay attacks). IPsec is mandatory according to IPv6 specification and optional in IPv4. Nevertheless, most modern operating systems, including Linux, have support for IPsec both in IPv4 and in IPv6. The first IPsec protocols were defined in 1995 (RFCs 1825–1829). In 1998, these RFCs were deprecated by RFCs 2401–2412. Then again in 2005, these RFCs were updated by RFCs 4301–4309.

The IPsec subsystem is very complex—perhaps the most complex part of the Linux kernel network stack. Its importance is paramount when considering the growing security requirements of organizations and of private citizens. This chapter gives you a basis for delving into this complex subsystem.

General

IPsec has become a standard for most of the IP Virtual Private Network (VPN) technology in the world. That said, there are also VPNs based on different technologies, such as Secure Sockets Layer (SSL) and pptp (tunneling a PPP connection over the GRE protocol). Among IPsec's several modes of operation, the most important are transport mode and tunnel mode. In transport mode, only the payload of the IP packet is encrypted, whereas in tunnel mode, the entire IP packet is encrypted and inserted into a new IP packet with a new IP header. When using a VPN with IPsec, you usually work in tunnel mode, although there are cases in which you work in transport mode (L2TP/IPsec, for example).

I start with a short discussion about the Internet Key Exchange (IKE) userspace daemon and cryptography in IPsec. These are topics that are mostly not a part of the kernel networking stack but that are related to IPsec operation and are needed to get a better understanding of the kernel IPsec subsystem. I follow that with a discussion of the XFRM framework, which is the configuration and monitoring interface between the IPsec userspace part and IPsec kernel components, and explain the traversal of IPsec packets in the Tx and Rx paths. I conclude the chapter with a short section about NAT traversal in IPsec, which is an important and interesting feature, and a "Quick Reference" section. The next section begins the discussion with the IKE protocol.

IKE (Internet Key Exchange)

The most popular open source userspace Linux IPsec solutions are Openswan (and libreswan, which forked from Openswan), strongSwan, and racoon (of ipsec-tools). Racoon is part of the Kame project, which aimed to provide a free IPv6 and IPsec protocol stack implementation for variants of BSD.

To establish an IPsec connection, you need to set up a Security Association (SA). You do that with the help of the already mentioned userspace projects. An SA is defined by two parameters: a source address and a 32-bit Security Parameter Index (SPI). Both sides (called *initiator* and *responder* in IPsec terminology) should agree on parameters such as a key (or more than one key), authentication, encryption, data integrity and key exchange algorithms, and other parameters such as key lifetime (IKEv1 only). This can be done in two different ways of key distribution: by manual key exchange, which is rarely used since it is less secure, or by the IKE protocol. Openswan and strongSwan implementations provide an IKE daemon (pluto in Openswan and charon in strongSwan) that uses UDP port 500 (both source and destination) to send and receive IKE messages. Both use the XFRM Netlink interface to communicate with the native IPsec stack of the Linux kernel. The strongSwan project is the only complete open source implementation of RFC 5996, "Internet Key Exchange Protocol Version 2 (IKEv2)," whereas the Openswan project only implements a small mandatory subset.

You can use IKEv1 Aggressive Mode in Openswan and in strongSwan 5.x (for strongSwan, it should be explicitly configured, and the name of the charon daemon changes to be weakSwan in this case); but this option is regarded unsafe. IKEv1 is still used by Apple operating systems (iOS and Mac OS X) because of the built-in racoon legacy client. Though many implementations use IKEv1, there are many improvements and advantages when using IKEv2. I'll mention some of them very briefly: in IKEv1, more messages are needed to establish an SA than in IKEv2. IKEv1 is very complex, whereas IKEv2 is considerably simpler and more robust, mainly because each IKEv2 request message must be acknowledged by an IKEv2 response message. In IKEv1, there are no acknowledgements, but there is a backoff algorithm which, in case of packet loss, keeps trying forever. However, in IKEv1 there can be a race when the two sides perform retransmission, whereas in IKEv2 that can't happen because the responsibility for retransmission is on the initiator only. Among the other important IKEv2 features are that IKEv2 has integrated NAT traversal support, automatic narrowing of Traffic Selectors (left|rightsubnet on both sides don't have to match exactly, but one proposal can be a subset of the other proposal), an IKEv2 configuration payload allowing to assign virtual IPv4/IPv6 addresses and internal DNS information (replacement for IKEv1 Mode Config), and finally IKEv2 EAP authentication (replacement for the dangerous IKEv1 XAUTH protocol), which solves the problem of potentially weak PSKs by requesting a VPN server certificate and digital signature first, before the client uses a potentially weak EAP authentication algorithm (for example, EAP-MSCHAPv2).

There are two phases in IKE: the first is called Main Mode. In this stage, each side verifies the identity of the other side, and a common session key is established using the Diffie-Hellman key exchange algorithm. This mutual authentication is based on RSA or ECDSA certificates or pre-shared secrets (pre-shared key, PSKs), which are password based and assumed to be weaker. Other parameters like the Encryption algorithm and the Authentication method to be used are also negotiated. If this phase completes successfully, the two peers are said to establish an ISAKMP SA (Internet Security Association Key Management Protocol Security Association). The second phase is called Quick Mode. In this phase, both sides agree on the cryptographic algorithms to use. The IKEv2 protocol does not differentiate between phase 1 and 2 but establishes the first CHILD_SA as part of the IKE_AUTH message exchange. THE CHILD_SA_CREATE message exchange is used only to establish additional CHILD_SAs or for the periodic rekeying of the IKE and IPsec SAs. This is why IKEv1 needs nine messages to establish a single IPsec SA, whereas IKEv2 does the same in just four messages.

The next section briefly discusses cryptography in the context of IPsec (a fuller treatment of the subject would be beyond the scope of this book).

IPsec and Cryptography

There are two widely used IPsec stacks for Linux: the native Netkey stack (developed by Alexey Kuznetsov and David S. Miller) introduced with the 2.6 kernel, and the KLIPS stack, originally written for 2.0 kernel (it predates netfilter!). Netkey uses the Linux kernel Crypto API, whereas KLIPS might support more crypto hardware through Open Cryptography Framework (OCF). OCF's advantage is that it enables using asynchronous calls to encrypt/decrypt data. In the Linux kernel, most of the Crypto API performs synchronous calls. I should mention the acrypto kernel code, which is the asynchronous crypto layer of the Linux kernel. There are asynchronous implementations for all algorithm types. A lot of hardware crypto accelerators use the asynchronous crypto interface for crypto request offloading. That is simply because they can't block until the crypto job is done. They have to use the asynchronous API.

It is also possible to use software-implemented algorithms with the asynchronous API. For example, the cryptd crypto template can run arbitrary algorithms in asynchronous mode. And you can use the pcrypt crypto template when working in multicore environment. This template parallelizes the crypto layer by sending incoming crypto requests to a configurable set of CPUs. It also takes care of the order of the crypto requests, so it does not introduce packet reorder when used with IPsec. The use of pcrypt can speed up IPsec by magnitudes in some situations. The crypto layer has a user management API which is used by the crconf (http://sourceforge.net/projects/crconf/) tool to configure the crypto layer, so asynchronous crypto algorithms can be configured whenever needed. With the Linux 2.6.25 kernel, released in 2008, the XFRM framework started to offer support for the very efficient AEAD (Authenticated Encryption with Associated Data) algorithms (for example, AES-GCM), especially when the Intel AES-NI instruction set is available and data integrity comes nearly for free. Delving deeply into the details of cryptography in IPsec is beyond the scope of this book. For further information, I suggest reading the relevant chapters in *Network Security Essentials,* Fifth Edition by William Stallings (Prentice Hall, 2013).

The next section discusses the XFRM framework, which is the infrastructure of IPsec.

The XFRM Framework

IPsec is implemented by the XFRM (pronounced "transform") framework, originated in the USAGI project, which aimed at providing a production quality IPv6 and IPsec protocol stack. The term *transform* refers to an incoming packet or an outgoing packet being transformed in the kernel stack according to some IPsec rule. The XFRM framework was introduced in kernel 2.5. The XFRM infrastructure is protocol-family independent, which means that there is a generic part common to both IPv4 and IPv6, located under net/xfrm. Both IPv4 and IPv6 have their own implementation of ESP, AH, and IPCOMP. For example, the IPv4 ESP module is net/ipv4/esp4.c, and the IPv6 ESP module is net/ipv6/esp6.c. Apart from it, IPv4 and IPv6 implement some protocol-specific modules for supporting the XFRM infrastructure, such as net/ipv4/xfrm4_policy.c or net/ipv6/xfrm6_policy.c.

The XFRM framework supports network namespaces, which is a form of lightweight process virtualization that enables a single process or a group of processes to have their own network stack (I discuss network namespaces in Chapter 14). Each network namespace (instance of struct net) includes a member called xfrm, which is an instance of the netns_xfrm structure. This object includes many data structures and variables that you will encounter in this chapter, such as the hash tables of XFRM policies and the hash tables of XFRM states, sysctl parameters, XFRM state garbage collector, counters, and more:

```
struct netns_xfrm {
        struct hlist_head       *state_bydst;
        struct hlist_head       *state_bysrc;
        struct hlist_head       *state_byspi;
        . . .
        unsigned int            state_num;
        . . .

        struct work_struct      state_gc_work;


        . . .

        u32                     sysctl_aevent_etime;
        u32                     sysctl_aevent_rseqth;
        int                     sysctl_larval_drop;
        u32                     sysctl_acq_expires;
};
```

(include/net/netns/xfrm.h)

XFRM Initialization

In IPv4, XFRM initialization is done by calling the xfrm_init() method and the xfrm4_init() method from the ip_rt_init() method in net/ipv4/route.c. In IPv6, the xfrm6_init() method is invoked from the ip6_route_init() method for performing XFRM initialization. Communication between the userspace and the kernel is done by creating a NETLINK_XFRM netlink socket and sending and receiving netlink messages. The netlink NETLINK_XFRM kernel socket is created in the following method:

```
static int __net_init xfrm_user_net_init(struct net *net)
{
        struct sock *nlsk;
        struct netlink_kernel_cfg cfg = {
                .groups = XFRMNLGRP_MAX,
                .input  = xfrm_netlink_rcv,
        };

        nlsk = netlink_kernel_create(net, NETLINK_XFRM, &cfg);
        . . .
        return 0;
}
```

Messages sent from userspace (like XFRM_MSG_NEWPOLICY for creating a new Security Policy or XFRM_MSG_NEWSA for creating a new Security Association) are handled by the xfrm_netlink_rcv() method (net/xfrm/xfrm_user.c), which in turn calls the xfrm_user_rcv_msg() method (I discuss netlink sockets in Chapter 2).

The XFRM policy and the XFRM state are the fundamental data structures of the XFRM framework. I start by describing what XFRM policy is, and subsequently I describe what XFRM state is.

XFRM Policies

A Security Policy is a rule that tells IPsec whether a certain flow should be processed or whether it can bypass IPsec processing. The xfrm_policy structure represents an IPsec policy. A policy includes a selector (an xfrm_selector object). A policy is applied when its selector matches a flow. The XFRM selector consists of fields like source and destination addresses, source and destination ports, protocol, and more, which can identify a flow:

```
struct xfrm_selector {
        xfrm_address_t  daddr;
        xfrm_address_t  saddr;
        __be16  dport;
        __be16  dport_mask;
        __be16  sport;
        __be16  sport_mask;
        __u16   family;
        __u8    prefixlen_d;
        __u8    prefixlen_s;
        __u8    proto;
        int     ifindex;
        __kernel_uid32_t        user;
};
```

(include/uapi/linux/xfrm.h)

The xfrm_selector_match() method, which gets an XFRM selector, a flow, and a family (AF_INET for IPv4 or AF_INET6 for IPv6) as parameters, returns true when the specified flow matches the specified XFRM selector. Note that the xfrm_selector structure is also used in XFRM states, as you will see hereafter in this section. A Security Policy is represented by the xfrm_policy structure:

```
struct xfrm_policy {
        . . .
        struct hlist_node               bydst;
        struct hlist_node               byidx;

        /* This lock only affects elements except for entry. */
        rwlock_t                        lock;
        atomic_t                        refcnt;
        struct timer_list               timer;

        struct flow_cache_object        flo;
        atomic_t                        genid;
        u32                             priority;
        u32                             index;
        struct xfrm_mark                mark;
        struct xfrm_selector            selector;
        struct xfrm_lifetime_cfg        lft;
        struct xfrm_lifetime_cur        curlft;
        struct xfrm_policy_walk_entry   walk;
        struct xfrm_policy_queue        polq;
        u8                              type;
        u8                              action;
        u8                              flags;
        u8                              xfrm_nr;
        u16                             family;
        struct xfrm_sec_ctx             *security;
        struct xfrm_tmpl                xfrm_vec[XFRM_MAX_DEPTH];
};
```

(include/net/xfrm.h)

The following description covers the important members of the xfrm_policy structure:

- refcnt: The XFRM policy reference counter; initialized to 1 in the xfrm_policy_alloc( ) method, incremented by the xfrm_pol_hold() method, and decremented by the xfrm_pol_put() method.

- timer: Per-policy timer; the timer callback is set to be xfrm_policy_timer() in the xfrm_policy_alloc() method. The xfrm_policy_timer() method handles policy expiration: it is responsible for deleting a policy when it is expired by calling the xfrm_policy_delete() method, and sending an event (XFRM_MSG_POLEXPIRE) to all registered Key Managers by calling the km_policy_expired() method.

- lft: The XFRM policy lifetime (xfrm_lifetime_cfg object). Every XFRM policy has a lifetime, which is a time interval (expressed as a time or byte count).

You can set XFRM policy lifetime values with the `ip` command and the `limit` parameter—for example:

```
ip xfrm policy add src 172.16.2.0/24 dst 172.16.1.0/24 limit byte-soft 6000 ...
```

- sets the `soft_byte_limit` of the XFRM policy lifetime (`lft`) to be 6000; see `man 8 ip xfrm`.

You can display the lifetime (`lft`) of an XFRM policy by inspecting the lifetime configuration entry when running `ip -stat xfrm policy show`.

- `curlft`: The XFRM policy current lifetime, which reflects the current status of the policy in context of lifetime. The `curlft` is an `xfrm_lifetime_cur` object. It consists of four members (all of them are fields of 64 bits, unsigned):

  - `bytes`: The number of bytes which were processed by the IPsec subsystem, incremented in the Tx path by the `xfrm_output_one()` method and in the Rx path by the `xfrm_input()` method.

  - `packets`: The number of packets that were processed by the IPsec subsystem, incremented in the Tx path by the `xfrm_output_one()` method, and in the Rx path by the `xfrm_input()` method.

  - `add_time`: The timestamp of adding the policy, initialized when adding a policy, in the `xfrm_policy_insert()` method and in the `xfrm_sk_policy_insert()` method.

  - `use_time`: The timestamp of last access to the policy. The `use_time` timestamp is updated, for example, in the `xfrm_lookup()` method or in the `__xfrm_policy_check()` method. Initialized to 0 when adding the XFRM policy, in the `xfrm_policy_insert()` method and in the `xfrm_sk_policy_insert()` method.

■ **Note**   You can display the current lifetime (`curlft`) object of an XFRM policy by inspecting the lifetime current entry when running `ip -stat xfrm policy show`.

- `polq`: A queue to hold packets that are sent while there are still no XFRM states associated with the policy. As a default, such packets are discarded by calling the `make_blackhole()` method. When setting the `xfrm_larval_drop` sysctl entry to 0 (/proc/sys/net/core/xfrm_larval_drop), these packets are kept in a queue (`polq.hold_queue`) of SKBs; up to 100 packets (XFRM_MAX_QUEUE_LEN) can be kept in this queue. This is done by creating a dummy XFRM bundle, by the `xfrm_create_dummy_bundle()` method (see more in the "XFRM lookup" section later in this chapter). By default, the `xfrm_larval_drop` sysctl entry is set to 1 (see the `__xfrm_sysctl_init()` method in net/xfrm/xfrm_sysctl.c).

- `type`: Usually the type is XFRM_POLICY_TYPE_MAIN (0). When the kernel has support for subpolicy (CONFIG_XFRM_SUB_POLICY is set), two policies can be applied to the same packet, and you can use the XFRM_POLICY_TYPE_SUB (1) type. Policy that lives a shorter time in kernel should be a subpolicy. This feature is usually needed only for developers/debugging and for mobile IPv6, because you might apply one policy for IPsec and one for mobile IPv6. The IPsec policy is usually the main policy with a longer lifetime than the mobile IPv6 (sub) policy.

- `action`: Can have one of these two values:

  - XFRM_POLICY_ALLOW (0): Permit the traffic.

  - XFRM_POLICY_BLOCK(1): Disallow the traffic (for example, when using `type=reject` or `type=drop` in /etc/ipsec.conf).

- `xfrm_nr`: Number of templates associated with the policy—can be up to six templates (XFRM_MAX_DEPTH). The `xfrm_tmpl` structure is an intermediate structure between the XFRM state and the XFRM policy. It is initialized in the `copy_templates()` method, `net/xfrm/xfrm_user.c`.

- `family`: IPv4 or IPv6.

- `security`: A security context (`xfrm_sec_ctx` object) that allows the XFRM subsystem to restrict the sockets that can send or receive packets via Security Associations (XFRM states). For more details, see `http://lwn.net/Articles/156604/`.

- `xfrm_vec`: An array of XFRM templates (`xfrm_tmpl` objects).

The kernel stores the IPsec Security Policies in the Security Policy Database (SPD). Management of the SPD is done by sending messages from a userspace socket. For example:

- Adding an XFRM policy (XFRM_MSG_NEWPOLICY) is handled by the `xfrm_add_policy()` method.

- Deleting an XFRM policy (XFRM_MSG_DELPOLICY) is handled by the `xfrm_get_policy()` method.

- Displaying the SPD (XFRM_MSG_GETPOLICY) is handled by the `xfrm_dump_policy()` method.

- Flushing the SPD (XFRM_MSG_FLUSHPOLICY) is handled by the `xfrm_flush_policy()` method.

The next section describes what XFRM state is.

XFRM States (Security Associations)

The `xfrm_state` structure represents an IPsec Security Association (SA) (`include/net/xfrm.h`). It represents unidirectional traffic and includes information such as cryptographic keys, flags, request id, statistics, replay parameters, and more. You add XFRM states by sending a request (XFRM_MSG_NEWSA) from a userspace socket; it is handled in the kernel by the `xfrm_state_add()` method (`net/xfrm/xfrm_user.c`). Likewise, you delete a state by sending an XFRM_MSG_DELSA message, and it is handled in the kernel by the `xfrm_del_sa()` method:

```
struct xfrm_state {
        . . .
        union {
                struct hlist_node       gclist;
                struct hlist_node       bydst;
        };
        struct hlist_node       bysrc;
        struct hlist_node       byspi;

        atomic_t                refcnt;
        spinlock_t              lock;

        struct xfrm_id          id;
        struct xfrm_selector    sel;
        struct xfrm_mark        mark;
        u32                     tfcpad;
```

```
        u32                     genid;

/* Key manager bits */
struct xfrm_state_walk  km;

/* Parameters of this state. */
struct {
        u32             reqid;
        u8              mode;
        u8              replay_window;
        u8              aalgo, ealgo, calgo;
        u8              flags;
        u16             family;
        xfrm_address_t  saddr;
        int             header_len;
        int             trailer_len;
} props;

struct xfrm_lifetime_cfg lft;

/* Data for transformer */
struct xfrm_algo_auth   *aalg;
struct xfrm_algo        *ealg;
struct xfrm_algo        *calg;
struct xfrm_algo_aead   *aead;

/* Data for encapsulator */
struct xfrm_encap_tmpl  *encap;

/* Data for care-of address */
xfrm_address_t  *coaddr;

/* IPComp needs an IPIP tunnel for handling uncompressed packets */
struct xfrm_state       *tunnel;

/* If a tunnel, number of users + 1 */
atomic_t                tunnel_users;

/* State for replay detection */
struct xfrm_replay_state replay;
struct xfrm_replay_state_esn *replay_esn;

/* Replay detection state at the time we sent the last notification */
struct xfrm_replay_state preplay;
struct xfrm_replay_state_esn *preplay_esn;

/* The functions for replay detection. */
struct xfrm_replay      *reply;
```

```
    /* internal flag that only holds state for delayed aevent at the
     * moment
     */
    u32                     xflags;

    /* Replay detection notification settings */
    u32                     replay_maxage;
    u32                     replay_maxdiff;

    /* Replay detection notification timer */
    struct timer_list       rtimer;

    /* Statistics */
    struct xfrm_stats       stats;

    struct xfrm_lifetime_cur curlft;
    struct tasklet_hrtimer  mtimer;

    /* used to fix curlft->add_time when changing date */
    long            saved_tmo;

    /* Last used time */
    unsigned long           lastused;

    /* Reference to data common to all the instances of this
     * transformer. */
    const struct xfrm_type  *type;
    struct xfrm_mode        *inner_mode;
    struct xfrm_mode        *inner_mode_iaf;
    struct xfrm_mode        *outer_mode;

    /* Security context */
    struct xfrm_sec_ctx     *security;

    /* Private data of this transformer, format is opaque,
     * interpreted by xfrm_type methods. */
    void                    *data;
};
```

(include/net/xfrm.h)

The following description details some of the important members of the xfrm_state structure:

- refcnt: A reference counter, incremented by the xfrm_state_hold() method and decremented by the __xfrm_state_put() method or by the xfrm_state_put() method (the latter also releases the XFRM state by calling the __xfrm_state_destroy() method when the reference counter reaches 0).

- id: The id (xfrm_id object) consists of three fields, which uniquely define it: destination address, spi, and security protocol (AH, ESP, or IPCOMP).

- props: The properties of the XFRM state. For example:

  - mode: Can be one of five modes (for example, XFRM_MODE_TRANSPORT for transport mode or XFRM_MODE_TUNNEL for tunnel mode; see include/uapi/linux/xfrm.h).

  - flag: For example, XFRM_STATE_ICMP. These flags are available in include/uapi/linux/xfrm.h. These flags can be set from userspace, for example, with the ip command and the flag option: ip xfrm add state flag icmp …

  - family: IPv4 of IPv6.

  - saddr: The source address of the XFRM state.

  - lft: The XFRM state lifetime (xfrm_lifetime_cfg object).

  - stats: An xfrm_stats object, representing XFRM state statistics. You can display the XFRM state statistics by ip -stat xfrm show.

The kernel stores the IPsec Security Associations in the Security Associations Database (SAD). The xfrm_state objects are stored in three hash tables in netns_xfrm (the XFRM namespace, discussed earlier): state_bydst, state_bysrc, state_byspi. The keys to these tables are computed by the xfrm_dst_hash(), xfrm_src_hash(), and xfrm_spi_hash() methods, respectively. When an xfrm_state object is added, it is inserted into these three hash tables. If the value of the spi is 0 (the value 0 is not normally to be used for spi—I will shortly mention when it is 0), the xfrm_state object is not added to the state_byspi hash table (see the __xfrm_state_insert() method in net/xfrm/xfrm_state.c).

■ **Note** An spi with value of 0 is only used for acquire states. The kernel sends an acquire message to the key manager and adds a temporary acquire state with spi 0 if traffic matches a policy, but the state is not yet resolved. The kernel does not bother to send a further acquire as long as the acquire state exists; the lifetime can be configured at net->xfrm.sysctl_acq_expires. If the state gets resolved, this acquire state is replaced by the actual state.

Lookup in the SAD can be done by the following:

- xfrm_state_lookup() method: In the state_byspi hash table.

- xfrm_state_lookup_byaddr() method: In the state_bysrc hash table.

- xfrm_state_find() method: In the state_bydst hash table.

The ESP protocol is the most commonly used IPsec protocol; it supports both encryption and authentication. The next section discusses the IPv4 ESP implementation.

ESP Implementation (IPv4)

The ESP protocol is specified in RFC 4303; it supports both encryption and authentication. Though it also supports encryption-only and authentication-only modes, it is usually used with both encryption and authentication because it is safer. I should also mention here the new Authenticated Encryption (AEAD) methods like AES-GCM, which can do the encryption and data integrity computations in a single pass and can be highly parallelized on multiple cores, so that with the Intel AES-NI instruction set, an IPsec throughput of several Gbit/s can be achieved. The ESP protocol supports both tunnel mode and transport mode; the protocol identifier is 50 (IPPROTO_ESP). The ESP adds a new header and a trailer to each packet. According to the ESP format, illustrated in Figure 10-1, there are the following fields:

- *SPI:* A 32-bit Security Parameter Index. Together with the source address, it identities an SA.

- *Sequence Number:* 32 bits, incremented by 1 for each transmitted packet in order to protect against replay attacks.

- *Payload Data:* A variable size encrypted data block.

- *Padding:* Padding for the encrypted data block in order to satisfy alignment requirements (0–255 bytes).

- *Pad Length:* The size of padding in bytes (1 byte).

- *Next Header:* The type of the next header (1 byte).

- *Authentication Data:* The Integrity Check Value (ICV).

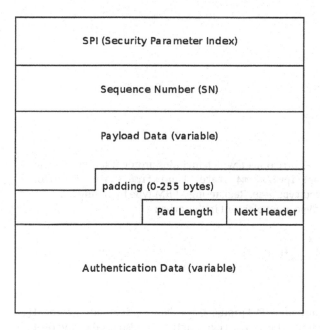

Figure 10-1. *ESP format*

The next section discusses IPv4 ESP initialization.

IPv4 ESP Initialization

We first define an esp_type (xfrm_type object) and esp4_protocol (net_protocol object) and register them thus:

```
static const struct xfrm_type esp_type =
{
        .description    = "ESP4",
        .owner          = THIS_MODULE,
        .proto          = IPPROTO_ESP,
        .flags          = XFRM_TYPE_REPLAY_PROT,
        .init_state     = esp_init_state,
        .destructor     = esp_destroy,
        .get_mtu        = esp4_get_mtu,
        .input          = esp_input,
        .output         = esp_output
};

static const struct net_protocol esp4_protocol = {
        .handler        =       xfrm4_rcv,
        .err_handler    =       esp4_err,
        .no_policy      =       1,
        .netns_ok       =       1,
};

static int __init esp4_init(void)
{
```

Each protocol family has an instance of an xfrm_state_afinfo object, which includes protocol-family specific state methods; thus there is xfrm4_state_afinfo for IPv4 (net/ipv4/xfrm4_state.c) and xfrm6_state_afinfo for IPv6. This object includes an array of xfrm_type objects called type_map. Registering XFRM type by calling the xfrm_register_type() method will set the specified xfrm_type as an element in this array:

```
        if (xfrm_register_type(&esp_type, AF_INET) < 0) {
                pr_info("%s: can't add xfrm type\n", __func__);
                return -EAGAIN;
        }
```

Registering the IPv4 ESP protocol is done like registering any other IPv4 protocol, by calling the inet_add_protocol() method. Note that the protocol handler used by IPv4 ESP, namely the xfrm4_rcv() method, is also used by the IPv4 AH protocol (net/ipv4/ah4.c) and by the IPv4 IPCOMP (IP Payload Compression Protocol) protocol (net/ipv4/ipcomp.c).

```
        if (inet_add_protocol(&esp4_protocol, IPPROTO_ESP) < 0) {
                pr_info("%s: can't add protocol\n", __func__);
                xfrm_unregister_type(&esp_type, AF_INET);
                return -EAGAIN;
        }
        return 0;
}
```

(net/ipv4/esp4.c)

Receiving an IPsec Packet (Transport Mode)

Suppose you work in transport mode in IPv4, and you receive an ESP packet that is destined to the local host. ESP in transport mode does not encrypt the IP header, only the IP payload. Figure 10-2 shows the traversal of an incoming IPv4 ESP packet, and its stages are described in this section. We will pass all the usual stages of local delivery, starting with the ip_rcv() method, and we will reach the ip_local_deliver_finish() method. Because the value of the protocol field in the IPv4 header is ESP (50), we invoke its handler, which is the xfrm4_rcv() method, as you saw earlier. The xfrm4_rcv() method further calls the generic xfrm_input() method, which performs a lookup in the SAD by calling the xfrm_state_lookup() method. If the lookup fails, the packet is dropped. In case of a lookup hit, the input callback method of the corresponding IPsec protocol is invoked:

```
int xfrm_input(struct sk_buff *skb, int nexthdr, __be32 spi, int encap_type)
{
        struct xfrm_state *x;
        do {
                . . .
```

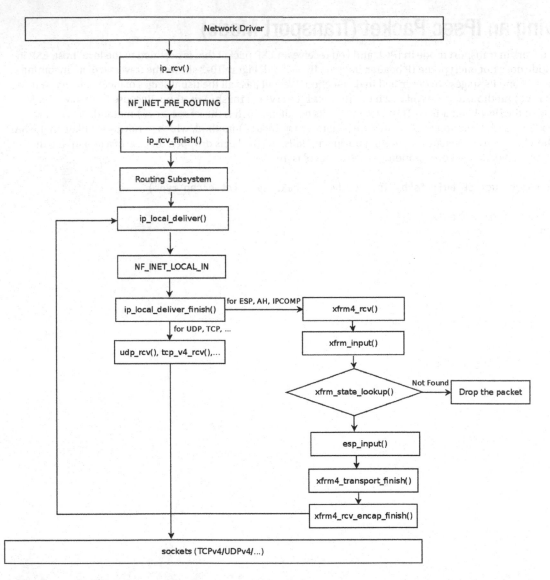

Figure 10-2. *Receiving IPv4 ESP packet, local delivery, transport mode. Note: The figure describes an IPv4 ESP packet.*
For IPv4 AH packets, the ah_input() method is invoked instead of the esp_input() method; likewise, for IPv4 IPCOMP
packets, the ipcomp_input() method is invoked instead of the esp_input() method

Perform a lookup in the state_byspi hash table:

```
x = xfrm_state_lookup(net, skb->mark, daddr, spi, nexthdr, family);
```

Drop the packet silently if the lookup failed:

```
if (x == NULL) {
        XFRM_INC_STATS(net, LINUX_MIB_XFRMINNOSTATES);
        xfrm_audit_state_notfound(skb, family, spi, seq);
        goto drop;
}
```

In this case, of IPv4 ESP incoming traffic, the XFRM type associated with the state (x->type) is the ESP XFRM Type (esp_type); its input callback was set to esp_input(), as mentioned earlier in the "IPv4 ESP initialization" section.

By calling x->type->input(), in the following line the esp_input() method is invoked; this method returns the protocol number of the original packet, before it was encrypted by ESP:

```
nexthdr = x->type->input(x, skb);
. . .
```

The original protocol number is kept in the control buffer (cb) of the SKB by using the XFRM_MODE_SKB_CB macro; it will be used later for modifying the IPv4 header of the packet, as you will see:

```
XFRM_MODE_SKB_CB(skb)->protocol = nexthdr;
```

After the esp_input() method terminates, the xfrm4_transport_finish() method is invoked. This method modifies various fields of the IPv4 header. Take a look at the xfrm4_transport_finish() method:

```
int xfrm4_transport_finish(struct sk_buff *skb, int async)
{
        struct iphdr *iph = ip_hdr(skb);
```

The protocol of the IPv4 header (iph->protocol) is 50 (ESP) at this point; you should set it to be the protocol number of the original packet (before it was encrypted by ESP) so that it will be processed by L4 sockets. The protocol number of the original packet was kept in XFRM_MODE_SKB_CB(skb)->protocol, as you saw earlier in this section:

```
iph->protocol = XFRM_MODE_SKB_CB(skb)->protocol;

. . .
__skb_push(skb, skb->data - skb_network_header(skb));
iph->tot_len = htons(skb->len);
```

Recalculate the checksum, since the IPv4 header was modified:

```
ip_send_check(iph);
```

Invoke any netfilter NF_INET_PRE_ROUTING hook callback and then call the xfrm4_rcv_encap_finish() method:

```
NF_HOOK(NFPROTO_IPV4, NF_INET_PRE_ROUTING, skb, skb->dev, NULL,
            xfrm4_rcv_encap_finish);
    return 0;
}
```

The xfrm4_rcv_encap_finish() method calls the ip_local_deliver() method. Now the value of the protocol member in the IPv4 header is the original transport protocol (UDPv4, TCPv4, and so on), so from now on you proceed in the usual packet traversal, and the packet is passed to the transport layer (L4).

Sending an IPsec Packet (Transport Mode)

Figure 10-3 shows the Tx path of an outgoing packet sent via IPv4 ESP in transport mode. The first step after performing a lookup in the routing subsystem (by calling the ip_route_output_flow() method), is to perform a lookup for an XFRM policy, which can be applied on this flow. You do that by calling the xfrm_lookup() method (I discuss the internals of this method later in this section). If there is a lookup hit, continue to the ip_local_out() method, and then, after calling several methods as you can see in Figure 10-3, you eventually reach the esp_output() method, which encrypts the packet and then sends it out by calling the ip_output() method.

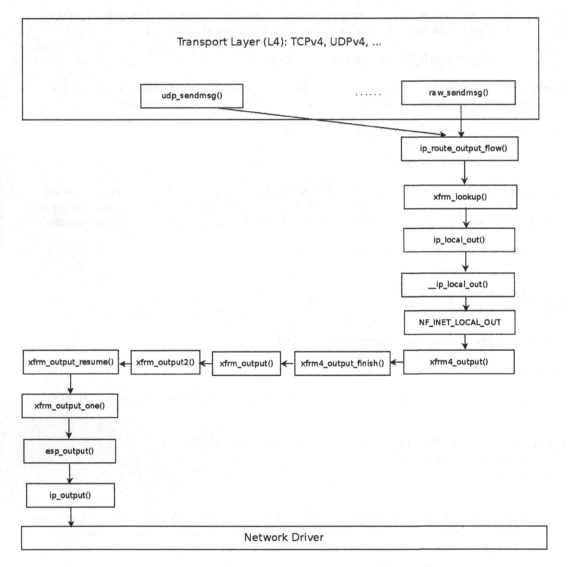

Figure 10-3. *Transmitting IPv4 ESP packet, transport mode. For the sake of simplicity, the case of creating a dummy bundle (when there are no XFRM states) and some other details are omitted*

The following section talks about how a lookup is performed in XFRM.

XFRM Lookup

The xfrm_lookup() method is called for each packet that is sent out of the system. You want this lookup to be as efficient as possible. To achieve this goal, bundles are used. Bundles let you cache important information such as the route, the policies, the number of policies, and more; these bundles, which are instances of the xfrm_dst structure, are stored by using the flow cache. When the first packet of some flow arrives, you create an entry in the generic flow cache and subsequently create a bundle (xfrm_dst object). The bundle creation is done after a lookup for this bundle fails, because it is the first packet of this flow. When subsequent packets of this flow arrive, you will get a hit when performing a flow cache lookup:

```
struct xfrm_dst {
        union {
                struct dst_entry        dst;
                struct rtable           rt;
                struct rt6_info         rt6;
        } u;
        struct dst_entry *route;
        struct flow_cache_object flo;
        struct xfrm_policy *pols[XFRM_POLICY_TYPE_MAX];
        int num_pols, num_xfrms;
#ifdef CONFIG_XFRM_SUB_POLICY
        struct flowi *origin;
        struct xfrm_selector *partner;
#endif
        u32 xfrm_genid;
        u32 policy_genid;
        u32 route_mtu_cached;
        u32 child_mtu_cached;
        u32 route_cookie;
        u32 path_cookie;
};
```

(include/net/xfrm.h)

The xfrm_lookup() method is a very complex method. I discuss its important parts but I don't delve into all its nuances. Figure 10-4 shows a block diagram of the internals of the xfrm_lookup() method.

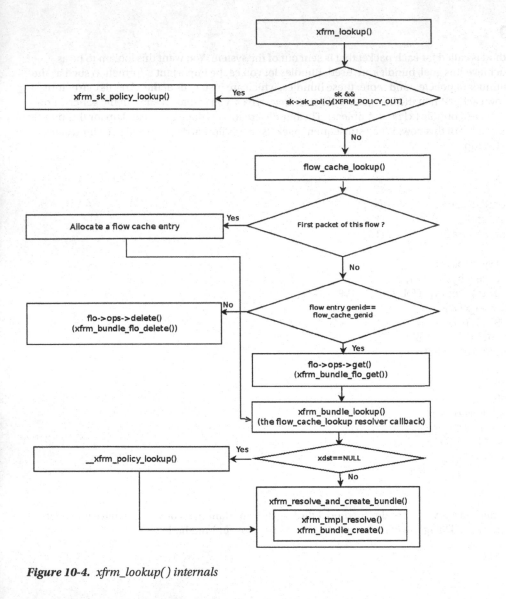

Figure 10-4. *xfrm_lookup() internals*

Let's take a look at the xfrm_lookup() method:

```
struct dst_entry *xfrm_lookup(struct net *net, struct dst_entry *dst_orig,
                              const struct flowi *fl, struct sock *sk, int flags)
{
```

The xfrm_lookup() method handles only the Tx path; so you set the flow direction (dir) to be FLOW_DIR_OUT by:

```
    u8 dir = policy_to_flow_dir(XFRM_POLICY_OUT);
```

If a policy is associated with this socket, you perform a lookup by the xfrm_sk_policy_lookup() method, which checks whether the packet flow matches the policy selector. Note that if the packet is to be forwarded, the xfrm_lookup() method was invoked from the __xfrm_route_forward() method, and there is no socket associated with the packet, because it was not generated on the local host; in this case, the specified sk argument is NULL:

```
if (sk && sk->sk_policy[XFRM_POLICY_OUT]) {
        num_pols = 1;
        pols[0] = xfrm_sk_policy_lookup(sk, XFRM_POLICY_OUT, fl);

        . . .

}
```

If there is no policy associated with this socket, you perform a lookup in the generic flow cache by calling the flow_cache_lookup() method, passing as an argument a function pointer to the xfrm_bundle_lookup method (the resolver callback). The key to the lookup is the flow object (the specified fl parameter). If you don't find an entry in the flow cache, allocate a new flow cache entry. If you find an entry with the same genid, call the xfrm_bundle_flo_get() method by invoking flo->ops->get(flo). Eventually, you call the xfrm_bundle_lookup() method by invoking the resolver callback, which gets the flow object as a parameter (oldflo). See the flow_cache_lookup() method implementation in net/core/flow.c:

```
flo = flow_cache_lookup(net, fl, family, dir, xfrm_bundle_lookup, dst_orig);
```

Fetch the bundle (xfrm_dst object) that contains the flow cache object as a member:

```
xdst = container_of(flo, struct xfrm_dst, flo);
```

Fetch cached data, like the number of policies, number of templates, the policies and the route:

```
num_pols = xdst->num_pols;
num_xfrms = xdst->num_xfrms;
memcpy(pols, xdst->pols, sizeof(struct xfrm_policy*) * num_pols);
route = xdst->route;
}
```

```
dst = &xdst->u.dst;
```

Next comes handling a dummy bundle. A *dummy bundle* is a bundle where the route member is NULL. It is created in the XFRM bundle lookup process (by the xfrm_bundle_lookup() method) when no XFRM states were found, by calling the xfrm_create_dummy_bundle() method. In such a case, either one of the two options are available, according to the value of sysctl_larval_drop (/proc/sys/net/core/xfrm_larval_drop):

- If sysctl_larval_drop is set (which means its value is 1—it is so by default, as mentioned earlier in this chapter), the packet should be discarded.

- If sysctl_larval_drop is not set (its value is 0), the packets are kept in a per-policy queue (polq.hold_queue), which can contain up to 100 (XFRM_MAX_QUEUE_LEN) SKBs; this is implemented by the xdst_queue_output() method. These packets are kept until the XFRM states are resolved or until some timeout elapses. Once the states are resolved, the packets are sent out of the queue. If the XFRM states are not resolved after some time interval (the timeout of the xfrm_policy_queue object), the queue is flushed by the xfrm_queue_purge() method:

```
if (route == NULL && num_xfrms > 0) {
        /* The only case when xfrm_bundle_lookup() returns a
         * bundle with null route, is when the template could
         * not be resolved. It means policies are there, but
         * bundle could not be created, since we don't yet
         * have the xfrm_state's. We need to wait for KM to
         * negotiate new SA's or bail out with error.*/
        if (net->xfrm.sysctl_larval_drop) {
```

For IPv4, the make_blackhole() method calls the ipv4_blackhole_route() method. For IPv6, it calls the ip6_blackhole_route() method:

```
        return make_blackhole(net, family, dst_orig);
}
```

The next section covers one of the most important features of IPsec—NAT traversal—and explains what it is and why it is needed.

NAT Traversal in IPsec

Why don't NAT devices allow IPsec traffic to pass? NAT changes the IP addresses and sometimes also the port numbers of the packet. As a result, it recalculates the checksum of the TCP or the UDP header. The transport layer checksum calculation takes into account the source and destination of the IP addresses. So even if only the IP addresses were changed, the TCP or UDP checksum should be recalculated. However, with ESP encryption in transport mode, the NAT device can't update the checksum because the TCP or UDP headers are encrypted with ESP. There are protocols where the checksum does not cover the IP header (like SCTP), so this problem does not occur there. To solve these problems, the NAT traversal standard for IPsec was developed (or, as officially termed in RFC 3948, "UDP Encapsulation of IPsec ESP Packets"). UDP Encapsulation can be applied to IPv4 packets as well as to IPv6 packets. NAT traversal solutions are not limited to IPsec traffic; these techniques are typically required for client-to-client networking applications, especially for peer-to-peer and Voice over Internet Protocol (VoIP) applications.

There are some partial solutions for VoIP NAT-traversal, such as STUN, TURN, ICE, and more. I should mention here that strongSwan implements the IKEv2 Mediation Extension service (http://tools.ietf.org/html/draft-brunner-ikev2-mediation-00), which allows two VPN endpoints located behind a NAT router each to establish a direct peer-to-peer IPsec tunnel using a mechanism similar to TURN and ICE. STUN, for example, is used in the VoIP open source Ekiga client (formerly gnomemeeting). The problem with these solutions is NAT devices they don't cope with. Devices called SBCs (session border controllers) provide a full solution for NAT traversal in VoIP. SBCs can be implemented in hardware (Juniper Networks, for example, provides a router-integrated SBC solution) or in software. These SBC solutions perform NAT traversal of the media traffic—which is sent by Real Time Protocol (RTP)—and sometimes also for the signaling traffic—which is sent by Session Initiation Protocol (SIP). NAT traversal is optional in IKEv2. Openswan, strongSwan, and racoon support NAT traversal, but Openswan and racoon support NAT-T only with IKEv1, whereas strongSwan supports NAT traversal in both IKEv1 and IKEv2.

NAT-T Mode of Operation

How does NAT traversal work? First, keep in mind that NAT-T is a good solution only for ESP traffic and not for AH. Another restriction is that NAT-T can't be used with manual keying, but only with IKEv1 and IKEv2. This is because NAT-T is tied with exchanging IKEv1/IKEv2 messages. First, you must tell the userspace daemon (pluto) that you want to use the NAT traversal feature, because it is not activated by default. You do that in Openswan by adding nat_traversal=yes to the connection parameters in /etc/ipsec.conf. Clients not behind a NAT are not affected by the addition of this entry. In strongSwan, the IKEv2 charon daemon always supports NAT traversal, and this feature cannot be deactivated. In the first phase of IKE (Main Mode), you check whether both peers support NAT-T. In IKEv1, when a peer supports NAT-T, one of the ISAKAMP header members (vendor ID) tells whether it supports NAT-T. In IKEv2, NAT-T is part of the standard and does not have to be announced. If this condition is met, you check whether there is one or more NAT devices in the path between the two IPsec peers by sending NAT-D payload messages. If this condition is also met, NAT-T protects the original IPsec encoded packet by inserting in it a UDP header between the IP header and the ESP header. Both the source and destination ports in the UDP header are 4500. Besides, NAT-T sends keep-alive messages every 20 seconds so that the NAT retains its mapping. Keep alive messages are also sent on UDP port 4500 and are recognized by their content and value (which is one byte, 0xFF). When this packet reaches the IPsec peer, after going through the NAT, the kernel strips the UDP header and decrypts the ESP payload. See the xfrm4_udp_encap_rcv() method in net/ipv4/xfrm4_input.c.

Summary

This chapter covered IPsec and the XFRM framework, which is the infrastructure of IPsec, and XFRM policies and states, which are the fundamental data structures of the XFRM framework. I also discussed IKE, the ESP4 implementation, the Rx/Tx path of ESP4 in transport mode, and NAT traversal in IPsec. Chapter 11 deals with the following transport Layer (L4) protocols: UDP, TCP, SCTP, and DCCP. The "Quick Reference" section that follows covers the top methods related to the topics discussed in this chapter, ordered by their context.

Quick Reference

I conclude this chapter with a short list of important methods of IPsec. Some of them were mentioned in this chapter. Afterward, I include a table of XFRM SNMP MIB counters.

Methods

Let's start with the methods.

bool xfrm_selector_match(const struct xfrm_selector *sel, const struct flowi *fl, unsigned short family);

This method returns true when the specified flow matches the specified XFRM selector. Invokes the __xfrm4_selector_match() method for IPv4 or the __xfrm6_selector_match() method for IPv6.

int xfrm_policy_match(const struct xfrm_policy *pol, const struct flowi *fl, u8 type, u16 family, int dir);

This method returns 0 if the specified policy can be applied to the specified flow, otherwise it returns an –errno.

struct xfrm_policy *xfrm_policy_alloc(struct net *net, gfp_t gfp);

This method allocates and initializes an XFRM policy. It sets its reference counter to 1, initializes the read-write lock, assigns the policy namespace (xp_net) to be the specified network namespace, sets its timer callback to be xfrm_policy_timer(), and sets its state resolution packet queue timer (policy->polq.hold_timer) callback to be xfrm_policy_queue_process().

void xfrm_policy_destroy(struct xfrm_policy *policy);

This method removes the timer of specified XFRM policy object and releases the specified XFRM policy memory.

void xfrm_pol_hold(struct xfrm_policy *policy);

This method increments by 1 the reference count of the specified XFRM policy.

static inline void xfrm_pol_put(struct xfrm_policy *policy);

This method decrements by 1 the reference count of the specified XFRM policy. If the reference count reaches 0, call the xfrm_policy_destroy() method.

struct xfrm_state_afinfo *xfrm_state_get_afinfo(unsigned int family);

This method returns the xfrm_state_afinfo object associated with the specified protocol family.

struct dst_entry *xfrm_bundle_create(struct xfrm_policy *policy, struct xfrm_state **xfrm, int nx, const struct flowi *fl, struct dst_entry *dst);

This method creates an XFRM bundle. Called from the xfrm_resolve_and_create_bundle() method.

int policy_to_flow_dir(int dir);

This method returns the flow direction according to the specified policy direction. For example, return FLOW_DIR_IN when the specified direction is XFRM_POLICY_IN, and so on.

static struct xfrm_dst *xfrm_create_dummy_bundle(struct net *net, struct dst_entry *dst, const struct flowi *fl, int num_xfrms, u16 family);

This method creates a dummy bundle. Called from the xfrm_bundle_lookup() method when policies were found but there are no matching states.

struct xfrm_dst *xfrm_alloc_dst(struct net *net, int family);

This method allocates an XFRM bundle object. Called from the xfrm_bundle_create() method and from the xfrm_create_dummy_bundle() method.

int xfrm_policy_insert(int dir, struct xfrm_policy *policy, int excl);

This method adds an XFRM policy to the SPD. Invoked from the xfrm_add_policy() method (net/xfrm/xfrm_user.c), or from the pfkey_spdadd() method (net/key/af_key.c).

int xfrm_policy_delete(struct xfrm_policy *pol, int dir);

This method releases the resources of the specified XFRM policy object. The direction argument (dir) is needed to decrement by 1 the corresponding XFRM policy counter in the policy_count in the per namespace netns_xfrm object.

int xfrm_state_add(struct xfrm_state *x);

This method adds the specified XFRM state to the SAD.

int xfrm_state_delete(struct xfrm_state *x);

This method deletes the specified XFRM state from the SAD.

void __xfrm_state_destroy(struct xfrm_state *x);

This method releases the resources of an XFRM state by adding it to the XFRM states garbage list and activating the XFRM state garbage collector.

int xfrm_state_walk(struct net *net, struct xfrm_state_walk *walk, int (*func)(struct xfrm_state *, int, void*), void *data);

This method iterates over all XFRM states (net->xfrm.state_all) and invokes the specified func callback.

struct xfrm_state *xfrm_state_alloc(struct net *net);

This method allocates and initializes an XFRM state.

void xfrm_queue_purge(struct sk_buff_head *list);

This method flushes the state resolution per-policy queue (polq.hold_queue).

int xfrm_input(struct sk_buff *skb, int nexthdr, __be32 spi, int encap_type);

This method is the main Rx IPsec handler.

static struct dst_entry *make_blackhole(struct net *net, u16 family, struct dst_entry *dst_orig);

This method is invoked from the xfrm_lookup() method when there are no resolved states and sysctl_larval_drop is set. For IPv4, the make_blackhole() method calls the ipv4_blackhole_route() method; for IPv6, it calls the ip6_blackhole_route() method.

int xdst_queue_output(struct sk_buff *skb);

This method handles adding packets to the per-policy state resolution packet queue (pq->hold_queue). This queue can contain up to 100 (XFRM_MAX_QUEUE_LEN) packets.

struct net *xs_net(struct xfrm_state *x);

This method returns the namespace object (xs_net) associated with the specified xfrm_state object.

struct net *xp_net(const struct xfrm_policy *xp);

This method returns the namespace object (xp_net) associated with the specified xfrm_policy object.

int xfrm_policy_id2dir(u32 index);

This method returns the direction of the policy according to the specified index.

int esp_input(struct xfrm_state *x, struct sk_buff *skb);

This method is the main IPv4 ESP protocol handler.

struct ip_esp_hdr *ip_esp_hdr(const struct sk_buff *skb);

This method returns the ESP header associated with the specified SKB.

int verify_newpolicy_info(struct xfrm_userpolicy_info *p);

This method verifies that the specified xfrm_userpolicy_info object contains valid values. (xfrm_userpolicy_info is the object which is passed from userspace). It returns 0 if it is a valid object, and -EINVAL or -EAFNOSUPPORT if not.

Table

Table 10-1 lists XFRM SNMP MIB counters.

Table 10-1. *XFRM SNMP MIB counters*

Linux Symbol	SNMP (procfs) Symbol	Methods in Which the Counter Might Be Incremented
LINUX_MIB_XFRMINERROR	XfrmInError	xfrm_input()
LINUX_MIB_XFRMINBUFFERERROR	XfrmInBufferError	xfrm_input(),__xfrm_policy_check()
LINUX_MIB_XFRMINHDRERROR	XfrmInHdrError	xfrm_input(),__xfrm_policy_check()
LINUX_MIB_XFRMINNOSTATES	XfrmInNoStates	xfrm_input()
LINUX_MIB_XFRMINSTATEPROTOERROR	XfrmInStateProtoError	xfrm_input()
LINUX_MIB_XFRMINSTATEMODEERROR	XfrmInStateModeError	xfrm_input()
LINUX_MIB_XFRMINSTATESEQERROR	XfrmInStateSeqError	xfrm_input()
LINUX_MIB_XFRMINSTATEEXPIRED	XfrmInStateExpired	xfrm_input()
LINUX_MIB_XFRMINSTATEMISMATCH	XfrmInStateMismatch	xfrm_input(), __xfrm_policy_check()
LINUX_MIB_XFRMINSTATEINVALID	XfrmInStateInvalid	xfrm_input()
LINUX_MIB_XFRMINTMPLMISMATCH	XfrmInTmplMismatch	__xfrm_policy_check()
LINUX_MIB_XFRMINNOPOLS	XfrmInNoPols	__xfrm_policy_check()
LINUX_MIB_XFRMINPOLBLOCK	XfrmInPolBlock	__xfrm_policy_check()
LINUX_MIB_XFRMINPOLERROR	XfrmInPolError	__xfrm_policy_check()
LINUX_MIB_XFRMOUTERROR	XfrmOutError	xfrm_output_one(),xfrm_output()
LINUX_MIB_ XFRMOUTBUNDLEGENERROR	XfrmOutBundleGenError	xfrm_resolve_and_create_bundle()
LINUX_MIB_ XFRMOUTBUNDLECHECKERROR	XfrmOutBundleCheckError	xfrm_resolve_and_create_bundle()
LINUX_MIB_XFRMOUTNOSTATES	XfrmOutNoStates	xfrm_lookup()
LINUX_MIB_ XFRMOUTSTATEPROTOERROR	XfrmOutStateProtoError	xfrm_output_one()
LINUX_MIB_ XFRMOUTSTATEMODEERROR	XfrmOutStateModeError	xfrm_output_one()
LINUX_MIB_XFRMOUTSTATESEQERROR	XfrmOutStateSeqError	xfrm_output_one()
LINUX_MIB_XFRMOUTSTATEEXPIRED	XfrmOutStateExpired	xfrm_output_one()
LINUX_MIB_XFRMOUTPOLBLOCK	XfrmOutPolBlock	xfrm_lookup()
LINUX_MIB_XFRMOUTPOLDEAD	XfrmOutPolDead	n/a
LINUX_MIB_XFRMOUTPOLERROR	XfrmOutPolError	xfrm_bundle_lookup(), xfrm_resolve_and_create_bundle()
LINUX_MIB_XFRMFWDHDRERROR	XfrmFwdHdrError	__xfrm_route_forward()
LINUX_MIB_XFRMOUTSTATEINVALID	XfrmOutStateInvalid	xfrm_output_one()

■ **Note** The IPsec git tree: `git://git.kernel.org/pub/scm/linux/kernel/git/klassert/ipsec.git`.

The ipsec git tree is for fixes for the IPsec networking subsystem; the development in this tree is done against David Miller's net git tree.

The ipsec-next git tree: `git://git.kernel.org/pub/scm/linux/kernel/git/klassert/ipsec-next.git`.

The ipsec-next tree is for changes for IPsec with linux-next as target; the development in this tree is done against David Miller's net-next git tree.

The IPsec subsystem maintainers are Steffen Klassert, Herbert Xu, and David S. Miller.

CHAPTER 11

■ ■ ■

Layer 4 Protocols

Chapter 10 discussed the Linux IPsec subsystem and its implementation. In this chapter, I will discuss four transport layer (L4) protocols. I will start our discussion with the two most commonly used transport layer (L4) protocols, the User Datagram Protocol (UDP) and the Transmission Control Protocol (TCP), which are used for many years. Subsequently, I will discuss the newer Stream Control Transmission Protocol (SCTP) and Datagram Congestion Control Protocol (DCCP) protocols, which combine features of TCP and UDP. I will start the chapter with describing the sockets API, which is the interface between the transport layer (L4) and the userspace. I will discuss how sockets are implemented in the kernel and how data flows from the userspace to the transport layer and from the transport layer to the userspace. I will also deal with passing packets from the network layer (L3) to the transport layer (L4) when working with these protocols. I will discuss here mainly the IPv4 implementation of these four protocols, though some of the code is common to IPv4 and IPv6.

Sockets

Every operating system has to provide an entry point and an API to its networking subsystems. The Linux kernel networking subsystem provides an interface to the userspace by the standard POSIX socket API, which was specified by the IEEE (IEEE Std 1003.1g-2000, describing networking APIs, also known as POSIX.1g). This API is based on Berkeley sockets API (also known as BSD sockets), which originated from the 4.2BSD Unix operating system and is an industry standard in several operating systems. In Linux, everything above the transport layer belongs to the userspace. Conforming to the Unix paradigm that "everything is a file," sockets are associated with files, as you will see later in this chapter. Using the uniform sockets API makes porting applications easier. These are the available socket types:

- **Stream sockets (SOCK_STREAM):** Provides a reliable, byte-stream communication channel. TCP sockets are an example of stream sockets.

- **Datagram sockets (SOCK_DGRAM):** Provides for exchanging of messages (called *datagrams*). Datagram sockets provide an unreliable communication channel, because packets can be discarded, arrive out of order, or be duplicated. UDP sockets are an example of datagram sockets.

- **Raw sockets (SOCK_RAW):** Uses direct access to the IP layer, and allows sending or receiving traffic without any protocol-specific, transport-layer formatting.

- **Reliably delivered message (SOCK_RDM):** Used by the Transparent Inter-Process Communication (TIPC), which was originally developed at Ericsson from 1996–2005 and was used in cluster applications. See http://tipc.sourceforge.net.

- **Sequenced packet stream (SOCK_SEQPACKET):** This socket type is similar to the SOCK_STREAM type and is also connection-oriented. The only difference between these types is that record boundaries are maintained using the SOCK_SEQPACKET type. Record boundaries are visible to the receiver via the MSG_EOR (End of record) flag. The Sequenced packet stream type is not discussed in this chapter.

- **DCCP sockets (SOCK_DCCP):** The Datagram Congestion Control Protocol is a transport protocol that provides a congestion-controlled flow of unreliable datagrams. It combines features of both TCP and UDP. It is discussed in a later section of this chapter.

- **Data links sockets (SOCK_PACKET):** The SOCK_PACKET is considered obsolete in the AF_INET family. See the __sock_create() method in net/socket.c.

The following is a description of some methods that the sockets API provides (all the kernel methods that appear in the following list are implemented in net/socket.c):

- socket(): Creates a new socket; will be discussed in the subsection "Creating Sockets."

- bind(): Associates a socket with a local port and an IP address; implemented in the kernel by the sys_bind() method.

- send(): Sends a message; implemented in the kernel by the sys_send() method.

- recv(): Receives a message; implemented in the kernel by the sys_recv() method.

- listen(): Allows a socket to receive connections from other sockets; implemented in the kernel by the sys_listen() method. Not relevant to datagram sockets.

- accept(): Accepts a connection on a socket; implemented in the kernel by the sys_accept() method. Relevant only with connection-based socket types (SOCK_STREAM, SOCK_SEQPACKET).

- connect(): Establishes a connection to a peer socket; implemented in the kernel by the sys_connect() method. Relevant to connection-based socket types (SOCK_STREAM or SOCK_SEQPACKET) as well as to connectionless socket types (SOCK_DGRAM).

This book focuses on the kernel network implementation, so I will not delve into the details of the userspace socket API. If you want more information, I recommend the following books:

- *Unix Network Programming, Volume 1: The Sockets Networking API (3rd Edition)* by W. Richard Stevens, Bill Fenner, and Andrew M. Rudoff (Addison-Wesley Professional, 2003).

- *The Linux Programming Interface* by Michael Kerrisk (No Starch Press, 2010).

■ **Note** All the socket API calls are handled by the socketcall() method, in net/socket.c.

Now that you have learned about some socket types, you will learn what happens in the kernel when a socket is created. In the next section, I will introduce the two structures that implement sockets: struct socket and struct sock. I will also describe the difference between them and I will describe the msghdr struct and its members.

Creating Sockets

There are two structures that represent a socket in the kernel: the first is struct socket, which provides an interface to the userspace and is created by the sys_socket() method. I will discuss the sys_socket() method later in this section. The second is struct sock, which provides an interface to the network layer (L3). Since the sock structure resides in the network layer, it is a protocol agnostic structure. I will discuss the sock structure also later in this section. The socket structure is short:

```
struct socket {
        socket_state            state;

        kmemcheck_bitfield_begin(type);
        short                   type;
        kmemcheck_bitfield_end(type);

        unsigned long           flags;

        . . .

        struct file             *file;
        struct sock             *sk;
        const struct proto_ops  *ops;
};
```

(include/linux/net.h)

The following is a description of the members of the socket structure:

- state: A socket can be in one of several states, like SS_UNCONNECTED, SS_CONNECTED, and more. When an INET socket is created, its state is SS_UNCONNECTED; see the inet_create() method. After a stream socket connects successfully to another host, its state is SS_CONNECTED. See the socket_state enum in include/uapi/linux/net.h.

- type: The type of the socket, like SOCK_STREAM or SOCK_RAW; see the enum sock_type in include/linux/net.h.

- flags: The socket flags; for example, the SOCK_EXTERNALLY_ALLOCATED flag is set in the TUN device when allocating a socket, not by the socket() system call. See the tun_chr_open() method in drivers/net/tun.c. The socket flags are defined in include/linux/net.h.

- file: The file associated with the socket.

- sk: The sock object associated with the socket. The sock object represents the interface to the network layer (L3). When creating a socket, the associated sk object is created. For example, in IPv4, the inet_create() method, which is invoked when creating a socket, allocates a sock object, sk, and associates it with the specified socket object.

- ops: This object (an instance of the proto_ops object) consists mostly of callbacks for this socket, like connect(), listen(), sendmsg(), recvmsg(), and more. These callbacks are the interface to the userspace. The sendmsg() callback implements several library-level routines, such as write(), send(), sendto(), and sendmsg(). Quite similarly, the recvmsg() callback implements several library-level routines, such as read(), recv(), recvfrom(), and recvmsg(). Each protocol defines a proto_ops object of its own according to the protocol requirements. Thus, for TCP, its proto_ops object includes a listen callback, inet_listen(), and an accept callback, inet_accept(). On the other hand, the UDP protocol, which does not work in the client-server model, defines the listen() callback to be the sock_no_listen() method, and it defines the accept() callback to be the sock_no_accept() method. The only thing that both these methods do is return an error of –EOPNOTSUPP. See Table 11-1 in the "Quick Reference" section at the end of this chapter for the definitions of the TCP and UDP proto_ops objects. The proto_ops structure is defined in include/linux/net.h.

The sock structure is the network-layer representation of sockets; it is quite long, and following here are only some of its fields that are important for our discussion:

```
struct sock {

        struct sk_buff_head     sk_receive_queue;
        int                     sk_rcvbuf;

        unsigned long           sk_flags;

        int                     sk_sndbuf;
        struct sk_buff_head     sk_write_queue;
        . . .
        unsigned int            sk_shutdown  : 2,
                                sk_no_check  : 2,
                                sk_protocol  : 8,
                                sk_type      : 16;

        . . .

        void                    (*sk_data_ready)(struct sock *sk, int bytes);
        void                    (*sk_write_space)(struct sock *sk);
};
```

(include/net/sock.h)

The following is a description of the members of the sock structure:

- sk_receive_queue: A queue for incoming packets.

- sk_rcvbuf: The size of the receive buffer in bytes.

- sk_flags: Various flags, like SOCK_DEAD or SOCK_DBG; see the sock_flags enum definition in include/net/sock.h.

- sk_sndbuf: The size of the send buffer in bytes.

- sk_write_queue: A queue for outgoing packets.

■ **Note**   You will see later, in the "TCP Socket Initialization" section, how the sk_rcvbuf and the sk_sndbuf are initialized, and how this can be changed by writing to procfs entries.

- sk_no_check: Disable checksum flag. Can be set with the SO_NO_CHECK socket option.

- sk_protocol: This is the protocol identifier, which is set according to the third parameter (protocol) of the socket() system call.

- sk_type: The type of the socket, like SOCK_STREAM or SOCK_RAW; see the enum sock_type in include/linux/net.h.

- sk_data_ready: A callback to notify the socket that new data has arrived.

- sk_write_space: A callback to indicate that there is free memory available to proceed with data transmission.

Creating sockets is done by calling the socket() system call from userspace:

```
sockfd = socket(int socket_family, int socket_type, int protocol);
```

The following is a description of the parameters of the socket() system call:

- socket_family: Can be, for example, AF_INET for IPv4, AF_INET6 for IPv6, or AF_UNIX for UNIX domain sockets, and so on. (UNIX domain sockets is a form of Inter Process Communication (IPC), which allows communication between processes that are running on the same host.)

- socket_type: Can be, for example, SOCK_STREAM for stream sockets, SOCK_DGRAM for datagram sockets, or SOCK_RAW for raw sockets, and so on.

- protocol: Can be any of the following:

  - 0 or IPPROTO_TCP for TCP sockets.

  - 0 or IPPROTO_UDP for UDP sockets.

  - A valid IP protocol identifier (like IPPROTO_TCP or IPPROTO_ICMP) for raw sockets; see RFC 1700, "Assigned Numbers."

The return value of the socket() system call (sockfd) is the file descriptor that should be passed as a parameter to subsequent calls with this socket. The socket() system call is handled in the kernel by the sys_socket() method. Let's take a look at the implementation of the socket() system call:

```
SYSCALL_DEFINE3(socket, int, family, int, type, int, protocol)
{
        int retval;
        struct socket *sock;
        int flags;

        . . .
        retval = sock_create(family, type, protocol, &sock);
        if (retval < 0)
                goto out;
        . . .
        retval = sock_map_fd(sock, flags & (O_CLOEXEC | O_NONBLOCK));
        if (retval < 0)
                goto out_release;
out:
        . . .
        return retval;

}
```

(net/socket.c)

The sock_create() method calls the address-family specific socket creation method, create(); in the case of IPv4, it is the inet_create() method. (See the inet_family_ops definition in net/ipv4/af_inet.c.) The inet_create() method creates the sock object (sk) that is associated with the socket; the sock object represents the network layer socket interface. The sock_map_fd() method returns an fd (file descriptor) that is associated with the socket; normally, the socket() system call returns this fd.

Sending data from a userspace socket, or receiving data in a userspace socket from the transport layer, is handled in the kernel by the sendmsg() and recvmsg() methods, respectively, which get a msghdr object as a parameter. The msghdr object includes the data blocks to send or to fill, as well as some other parameters.

```
struct msghdr {
        void            *msg_name;       /* Socket name                                  */
        int             msg_namelen;     /* Length of name                               */
        struct iovec    *msg_iov;        /* Data blocks                                  */
        __kernel_size_t msg_iovlen;      /* Number of blocks                             */
        void            *msg_control;    /* Per protocol magic (eg BSD file descriptor passing) */
        __kernel_size_t msg_controllen;  /* Length of cmsg list                          */
        unsigned int    msg_flags;
};
```

(include/linux/socket.h)

The following is a description of some of the important members of the msghdr structure:

- msg_name: The destination socket address. To get the destination socket, you usually cast the msg_name opaque pointer to a struct sockaddr_in pointer. See, for example, the udp_sendmsg() method.

- msg_namelen: The length of the address.

- iovec: A vector of data blocks.

- msg_iovlen: The number of blocks in the iovec vector.

- msg_control: Control information (also known as *ancillary data*).

- msg_controllen: The length of the control information.

- msg_flags: Flags of received messages, like MSG_MORE. (See, for example, the section "Sending Packets with UDP" later in this chapter.)

Note that the maximum control buffer length that the kernel can process is limited per socket by the value in sysctl_optmem_max (/proc/sys/net/core/optmem_max).

In this section, I described the kernel implementation of the socket and the msghdr struct, which is used when sending and receiving packets. In the next section, I will start my discussion about transport layer protocols (L4) by describing the UDP protocol, which is the simplest among the protocols to be discussed in this chapter.

UDP (User Datagram Protocol)

The UDP protocol is described in RFC 768 from 1980. The UDP protocol is a thin layer around the IP layer, adding only port, length, and checksum information. It dates back as early as 1980 and provides unreliable, message-oriented transport without congestion control. Many protocols use UDP. I will mention, for example, the RTP protocol (Real-time Transport Protocol), which is used for delivery of audio and video over IP networks. Such a type of traffic can tolerate some packet loss. The RTP is commonly used in VoIP applications, usually in conjunction with SIP (Session Initiation Protocol) based clients.(It should be mentioned here that, in fact, the RTP protocol can also use TCP, as specified in RFC 4571, but this is not used much.) I should mention here UDP-Lite, which is an extension of the UDP protocol to support variable-length checksums (RFC 3828). Most of UDP-Lite is implemented in net/ipv4/udplite.c, but you will encounter it also in the main UDP module, net/ipv4/udp.c. The UDP header length is 8 bytes:

```
struct udphdr {
        __be16  source;
        __be16  dest;
        __be16  len;
        __sum16 check;
};
```
(include/uapi/linux/udp.h)

The following is a description of the members of the UDP header:

- source: The source port (16 bit), in the range 1-65535.

- dest: The destination port (16 bit), in the range 1-65535.

- len: The length in bytes (the payload length and the UDP header length).

- checksum: The checksum of the packet.

Figure 11-1 shows a UDP header.

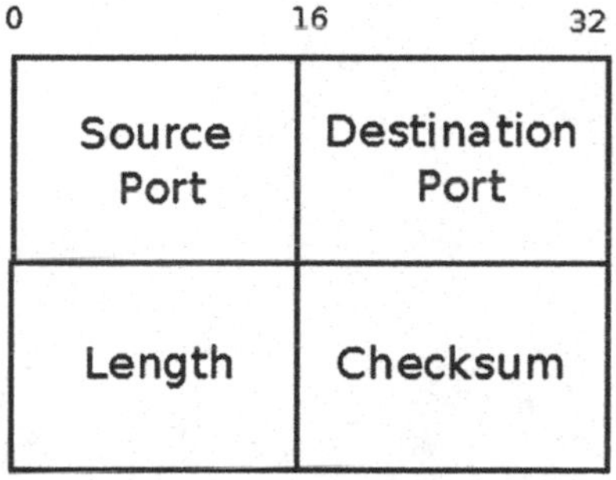

```
0                16               32
┌───────────────┬─────────────────┐
│   Source      │  Destination    │
│   Port        │     Port        │
├───────────────┼─────────────────┤
│               │                 │
│   Length      │   Checksum      │
└───────────────┴─────────────────┘
```

Figure 11-1. *A UDP header (IPv4)*

In this section, you learned about the UDP header and its members. To understand how the userspace applications, which use the sockets API, communicate with the kernel (sending and receiving packets), you should know about how UDP initialization is done, which is described in the next section.

UDP Initialization

We define the udp_protocol object (net_protocol object) and add it with the inet_add_protocol() method. This sets the udp_protocol object to be an element in the global protocols array (inet_protos).

```
static const struct net_protocol udp_protocol = {
        .handler =      udp_rcv,
        .err_handler =  udp_err,
        .no_policy =    1,
        .netns_ok =     1,
};
```
(net/ipv4/af_inet.c)

```
static int __init inet_init(void)
{
        . . .
        if (inet_add_protocol(&udp_protocol, IPPROTO_UDP) < 0)
                pr_crit("%s: Cannot add UDP protocol\n", __func__);
        . . .
}
(net/ipv4/af_inet.c)
```

We further define a udp_prot object and register it by calling the proto_register() method. This object contains mostly callbacks; these callbacks are invoked when opening a UDP socket in userspace and using the socket API. For example, calling the setsockopt() system call on a UDP socket will invoke the udp_setsockopt() callback.

```
struct proto udp_prot = {
        .name                   = "UDP",
        .owner                  = THIS_MODULE,
        .close                  = udp_lib_close,
        .connect                = ip4_datagram_connect,
        .disconnect             = udp_disconnect,
        .ioctl                  = udp_ioctl,
        . . .
        .setsockopt             = udp_setsockopt,
        .getsockopt             = udp_getsockopt,
        .sendmsg                = udp_sendmsg,
        .recvmsg                = udp_recvmsg,
        .sendpage               = udp_sendpage,
        . . .
};

(net/ipv4/udp.c)
int __init inet_init(void)
{
    int rc = -EINVAL;
    . . .
    rc = proto_register(&udp_prot, 1);
    . . .

}
(net/ipv4/af_inet.c)
```

■ **Note**   The UDP protocol, along with other core protocols, is initialized via the inet_init() method at boot-time.

Now that you know about UDP initialization and its callback for sending packets, which is the udp_sendmsg() callback of the udp_prot object that was shown in this section, it is time to learn how packets are sent by UDP in IPV4.

Sending Packets with UDP

Sending data from a UDP userspace socket can be done by several system calls: send(), sendto(), sendmsg(), and write(); eventually all of them are handled by the udp_sendmsg() method in the kernel. The userspace application builds a msghdr object that contains the data blocks and passes this msghdr object to the kernel. Let's take a look at this method:

```
int udp_sendmsg(struct kiocb *iocb, struct sock *sk, struct msghdr *msg,
                size_t len)
{
```

In general, UDP packets are sent immediately. This behavior can be changed with the UDP_CORK socket option (introduced in kernel 2.5.44), which causes packet data passed to the udp_sendmsg() method to be accumulated until the final packet is released by unsetting the option. The same result can be achieved by setting the MSG_MORE flag:

```
int corkreq = up->corkflag || msg->msg_flags&MSG_MORE;
struct inet_sock *inet = inet_sk(sk);
    . . .
```

First we make some sanity checks. The specified len, for example, cannot be greater than 65535 (remember that the len field in the UDP header is 16 bits):

```
if (len > 0xFFFF)
            return -EMSGSIZE;
```

We need to know the destination address and the destination port in order to build a flowi4 object, which is needed for sending the SKB with the udp_send_skb() method or with the ip_append_data() method. The destination port should not be 0. There are two cases here: the destination is specified in the msg_name of the msghdr, or the socket is connected and its state is TCP_ESTABLISHED. Note that UDP (in contrast to TCP) is almost a fully stateless protocol. The notion of TCP_ESTABLISHED in UDP mostly means that the socket has passed some sanity checks.

```
if (msg->msg_name) {
        struct sockaddr_in *usin = (struct sockaddr_in *)msg->msg_name;
        if (msg->msg_namelen < sizeof(*usin))
                return -EINVAL;
        if (usin->sin_family != AF_INET) {
                if (usin->sin_family != AF_UNSPEC)
                        return -EAFNOSUPPORT;
        }

        daddr = usin->sin_addr.s_addr;
        dport = usin->sin_port;
```

Linux code honors the fact that zero UDP/TCP ports are reserved by the IANA. The reservation of port 0 in TCP and UDP dates back to RFC 1010, "Assigned Numbers" (1987), and it was still present in RFC 1700, which was obsoleted by the online database (see RFC 3232), where they are still present. See www.iana.org/assignments/service-names-port-numbers/service-names-port-numbers.xhtml.

```
            if (dport == 0)
                    return -EINVAL;
    } else {
            if (sk->sk_state != TCP_ESTABLISHED)
                    return -EDESTADDRREQ;
```

```
                    daddr = inet->inet_daddr;
                    dport = inet->inet_dport;
                    /* Open fast path for connected socket.
                       Route will not be used, if at least one option is set.
                     */
                    connected = 1;
}
```

. . .

A userspace application can send control information (also known as *ancillary data*) by setting msg_control and msg_controllen in the msghdr object. Ancillary data is, in fact, a sequence of cmsghdr objects with appended data. (For more details, see man 3 cmsg.) You can send and receive ancillary data by calling the sendmsg() and recvmsg() methods, respectively. For example, you can create an IP_PKTINFO ancillary message to set a source route to an unconnected UDP socket. (See man 7 ip.) When msg_controllen is not 0, this is a control information message, which is handled by the ip_cmsg_send() method. The ip_cmsg_send() method builds an ipcm_cookie (IP Control Message Cookie) object by parsing the specified msghdr object. The ipcm_cookie structure includes information that is used further when processing the packet. For example, when using an IP_PKTINFO ancillary message, you can set the source address by setting an address field in the control messages, which eventually sets the addr in the ipcm_cookie object. The ipcm_cookie is a short structure:

```
struct ipcm_cookie {
        __be32                  addr;
        int                     oif;
        struct ip_options_rcu   *opt;
        __u8                    tx_flags;
};
(include/net/ip.h)
```

Let's continue our discussion of the udp_sendmsg() method:

```
        if (msg->msg_controllen) {
                err = ip_cmsg_send(sock_net(sk), msg, &ipc);
                if (err)
                        return err;
                if (ipc.opt)
                        free = 1;
                connected = 0;
        }
        . . .
        if (connected)
                rt = (struct rtable *)sk_dst_check(sk, 0);
        . . .
```

If the routing entry is NULL, a routing lookup should be performed:

```
        if (rt == NULL) {
                struct net *net = sock_net(sk);

                fl4 = &fl4_stack;
                flowi4_init_output(fl4, ipc.oif, sk->sk_mark, tos,
                                   RT_SCOPE_UNIVERSE, sk->sk_protocol,
                                   inet_sk_flowi_flags(sk)|FLOWI_FLAG_CAN_SLEEP,
                                   faddr, saddr, dport, inet->inet_sport);
```

```
                security_sk_classify_flow(sk, flowi4_to_flowi(fl4));
                rt = ip_route_output_flow(net, fl4, sk);
                if (IS_ERR(rt)) {
                        err = PTR_ERR(rt);
                        rt = NULL;
                        if (err == -ENETUNREACH)
                                IP_INC_STATS_BH(net, IPSTATS_MIB_OUTNOROUTES);
                        goto out;
                }

        . . .
```

In kernel 2.6.39, a lockless transmit fast path was added. This means that when the corking feature is not set, we do not hold the socket lock and we call the udp_send_skb() method, and when the corking feature is set, we hold the socket lock by calling the lock_sock() method and then send the packet:

```
        /* Lockless fast path for the non-corking case. */
        if (!corkreq) {
                skb = ip_make_skb(sk, fl4, getfrag, msg->msg_iov, ulen,
                                  sizeof(struct udphdr), &ipc, &rt,
                                  msg->msg_flags);
                err = PTR_ERR(skb);
                if (!IS_ERR_OR_NULL(skb))
                        err = udp_send_skb(skb, fl4);
                 goto out;
        }
```

Now we handle the case when the corking feature is set:

```
        lock_sock(sk);
do_append_data:
        up->len += ulen;
```

The ip_append_data() method buffers the data for transmission but does not transmit it yet. Subsequently calling the udp_push_pending_frames() method will actually perform the transmission. Note that the udp_push_pending_frames() method also handles fragmentation by the specified getfrag callback:

```
        err = ip_append_data(sk, fl4, getfrag, msg->msg_iov, ulen,
                             sizeof(struct udphdr), &ipc, &rt,
                             corkreq ? msg->msg_flags|MSG_MORE : msg->msg_flags);
```

If the method failed, we should flush all pending SKBs. This is achieved by calling the udp_flush_pending_frames() method, which will free all the SKBs in the write queue of the socket (sk_write_queue) by the ip_flush_pending_frames() method:

```
        if (err)
                udp_flush_pending_frames(sk);
        else if (!corkreq)
                err = udp_push_pending_frames(sk);
        else if (unlikely(skb_queue_empty(&sk->sk_write_queue)))
                up->pending = 0;
        release_sock(sk);
```

You learned in this section about sending packets with UDP. Now, to complete our discussion about UDP in IPv4, it's time to learn about how packets from the network layer (L3) are received with UDP in IPv4.

Receiving Packets from the Network Layer (L3) with UDP

The main handler for receiving UDP packets from the network layer (L3) is the udp_rcv() method. All it does is invoke the __udp4_lib_rcv() method (net/ipv4/udp.c):

```
int udp_rcv(struct sk_buff *skb)
{
        return __udp4_lib_rcv(skb, &udp_table, IPPROTO_UDP);
}
```

Let's take a look at the __udp4_lib_rcv() method:

```
int __udp4_lib_rcv(struct sk_buff *skb, struct udp_table *udptable,
                   int proto)
{
        struct sock *sk;
        struct udphdr *uh;
        unsigned short ulen;
        struct rtable *rt = skb_rtable(skb);
        __be32 saddr, daddr;
        struct net *net = dev_net(skb->dev);
        . . .
```

We fetch the UDP header, header length, and source and destination addresses from the SKB:

```
        uh   = udp_hdr(skb);
        ulen = ntohs(uh->len);
        saddr = ip_hdr(skb)->saddr;
        daddr = ip_hdr(skb)->daddr;
```

We will skip some sanity checks that are being performed, like making sure that the UDP header length is not greater than the length of the packet and that the specified proto is the UDP protocol identifier (IPPROTO_UDP). If the packet is a broadcast or a multicast packet, it will be handled by the __udp4_lib_mcast_deliver() method:

```
        if (rt->rt_flags & (RTCF_BROADCAST|RTCF_MULTICAST))
            return __udp4_lib_mcast_deliver(net, skb, uh,
                                            saddr, daddr, udptable);
```

Next we perform a lookup in the UDP sockets hash table:

```
        sk = __udp4_lib_lookup_skb(skb, uh->source, uh->dest, udptable);
            if (sk != NULL) {
```

We arrive here because the lookup we performed found a matching socket. So process the SKB further by calling the udp_queue_rcv_skb() method, which invokes the generic sock_queue_rcv_skb() method, which in turn adds the specified SKB to the tail of sk->sk_receive_queue (by calling the __skb_queue_tail() method):

```
int ret = udp_queue_rcv_skb(sk, skb);
sock_put(sk);

/* a return value > 0 means to resubmit the input, but
* it wants the return to be -protocol, or 0
*/
if (ret > 0)
    return -ret;
```

Everything is fine; return 0 to denote success:

```
    return 0;
}
. . .
```

We arrived here because the lookup for a socket failed. This means that we should not handle the packet. This can occur, for example, when there is no listening UDP socket on the destination port. If the checksum is incorrect, we should drop the packet silently. If it is correct, we should send an ICMP reply back to the sender. This should be an ICMP message of "Destination Unreachable" with code of "Port Unreachable." Further on, we should free the packet and update an SNMP MIB counter:

```
/* No socket. Drop packet silently, if checksum is wrong */
if (udp_lib_checksum_complete(skb))
    goto csum_error;
```

The next command increments the UDP_MIB_NOPORTS (NoPorts) MIB counter. Note that you can query various UDP MIB counters by cat /proc/net/snmp or by netstat -s.

```
UDP_INC_STATS_BH(net, UDP_MIB_NOPORTS, proto == IPPROTO_UDPLITE);
icmp_send(skb, ICMP_DEST_UNREACH, ICMP_PORT_UNREACH, 0);

/*
* Hmm.  We got an UDP packet to a port to which we
* don't wanna listen.  Ignore it.
*/
kfree_skb(skb);
return 0;
```

Figure 11-2 illustrates our discussion in this section about receiving UDP packets.

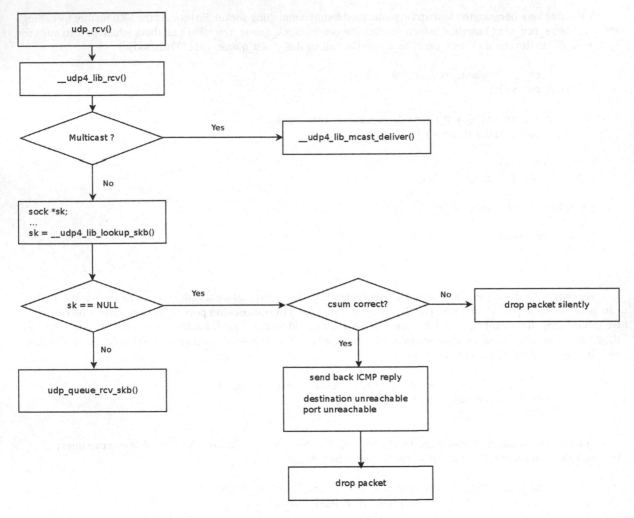

Figure 11-2. *Receiving UDP packets*

Our discussion about UDP is now finished. The next section describes the TCP protocol, which is the most complex among the protocols discussed in this chapter.

TCP (Transmission Control Protocol)

The TCP protocol is described in RFC 793 from 1981. During the years since then, there have been many updates, variations, and additions to the base TCP protocol. Some additions were for specific types of networks (high-speed, satellite), whereas others were for performance improvements.

The TCP protocol is the most commonly used transport protocol on the Internet today. Many well-known protocols are based upon TCP. The most well-known protocol is probably HTTP, and we should also mention here some other well-known protocols such as ftp, ssh, telnet, smtp, and ssl. The TCP protocol provides a reliable and connection-oriented transport, as opposed to UDP. Transmission is made reliable by using sequence numbers and acknowledgments.

TCP is a very complex protocol; we will not discuss all the details, optimizations, and nuances of the TCP implementation in this chapter, as this requires a separate book in itself. TCP functionality consists of two ingredients: management of connections, and transmitting and receiving data. We will focus in this section on TCP initialization and TCP connection setup, which pertains to the first ingredient, connections management, and on receiving and sending packets, which pertains to the second ingredient. These are the important basics that enable further delving into the TCP protocol implementation. We should note that the TCP protocol self-regulates the byte-stream flow via congestion control. Many different congestion-control algorithms have been specified, and Linux provides a pluggable and configurable architecture to support a wide variety of algorithms. Delving into the details of the individual congestion-control algorithms is beyond the scope of this book.

Every TCP packet starts with a TCP header. You must learn about the TCP header in order to understand the operation of TCP. The next section describes the IPv4 TCP header.

TCP Header

The TCP header length is 20 bytes, but it is scalable up to 60 bytes when using TCP options:

```
struct tcphdr {
        __be16  source;
        __be16  dest;
        __be32  seq;
        __be32  ack_seq;
#if defined(__LITTLE_ENDIAN_BITFIELD)
        __u16   res1:4,
                doff:4,
                fin:1,
                syn:1,
                rst:1,
                psh:1,
                ack:1,
                urg:1,
                ece:1,
                cwr:1;
#elif defined(__BIG_ENDIAN_BITFIELD)
        __u16   doff:4,
                res1:4,
                cwr:1,
                ece:1,
                urg:1,
                ack:1,
                psh:1,
                rst:1,
                syn:1,
                fin:1;
#else
#error  "Adjust your <asm/byteorder.h> defines"
```

```
#endif
        __be16  window;
        __sum16 check;
        __be16  urg_ptr;
};
```

(include/uapi/linux/tcp.h)

The following is a description of the members of the `tcphdr` structure:

- `source`: The source port (16 bit), in the range 1-65535.

- `dest`: The destination port (16 bit), in the range 1-65535.

- `seq`: The Sequence number (32 bits).

- `ack_seq`: Acknowledgment number (32 bits). If the ACK flag is set, the value of this field is the next sequence number that the receiver is expecting.

- `res1`: Reserved for future use (4 bits). It should always be set to 0.

- `doff`: Data offset (4 bits). The size of the TCP header in multiplies of 4 bytes; the minimum is 5 (20 bytes) and the maximum is 15 (60 bytes).

The following are the TCP flags; each is 1 bit:

- `fin`: No more data from sender (when one of the endpoints wants to close the connection).

- `syn`: The SYN flag is initially sent when establishing the 3-way handshake between two endpoints.

- `rst`: The Reset flag is used when a segment that is not intended for the current connection arrives.

- `psh`: The data should be passed to userspace as soon as possible.

- `ack`: Signifies that the acknowledgment number (`ack_seq`) value in the TCP header is meaningful.

- `urg`: Signifies that the urgent pointer is meaningful.

- `ece`: ECN - Echo flag. *ECN* stands for "Explicit Congestion Notification." ECN provides a mechanism that sends end-to-end notification about network congestion without dropping packets. It was added by RFC 3168, "The Addition of Explicit Congestion Notification (ECN) to IP," from 2001.

- `cwr`: Congestion Window Reduced flag.

- `window`: TCP receive window size in bytes (16 bit).

- `check`: Checksum of the TCP header and TCP data.

- `urg_ptr`: Has significance only when the `urg` flag is set. It represents an offset from the sequence number indicating the last urgent data byte (16 bit).

Figure 11-3 shows a diagram of a TCP header.

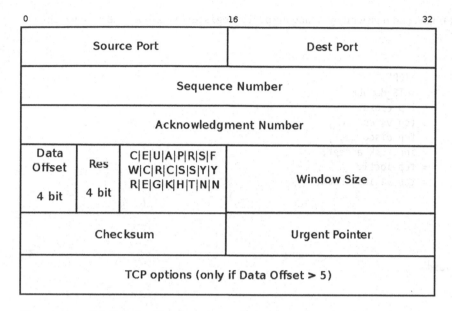

Figure 11-3. *TCP header (IPv4)*

In this section, I described the IPv4 TCP header and its members. You saw that, as opposed to the UDP header, which has only 4 members, the TCP header has a lot more members, since TCP is a much more complex protocol. In the following section, I will describe how TCP initialization is done so that you will learn how and where the initialization of the callbacks for receiving and sending TCP packets takes place.

TCP Initialization

We define the tcp_protocol object (net_protocol object) and add it with the inet_add_protocol() method:

```
static const struct net_protocol tcp_protocol = {
        .early_demux    =       tcp_v4_early_demux,
        .handler        =       tcp_v4_rcv,
        .err_handler    =       tcp_v4_err,
        .no_policy      =       1,
        .netns_ok       =       1,
};

(net/ipv4/af_inet.c)

static int __init inet_init(void)
  {
        . . .
        if (inet_add_protocol(&tcp_protocol, IPPROTO_TCP) < 0)
            pr_crit("%s: Cannot add TCP protocol\n", __func__);
        . . .
}

(net/ipv4/af_inet.c)
```

We further define a tcp_prot object and register it by calling the proto_register() method, like what we did with UDP:

```
struct proto tcp_prot = {
        .name                   = "TCP",
        .owner                  = THIS_MODULE,
        .close                  = tcp_close,
        .connect                = tcp_v4_connect,
        .disconnect             = tcp_disconnect,
        .accept                 = inet_csk_accept,
        .ioctl                  = tcp_ioctl,
        .init                   = tcp_v4_init_sock,
        . . .
};
```

(net/ipv4/tcp_ipv4.c)

```
static int __init inet_init(void)
{
        int rc;
        . . .
        rc = proto_register(&tcp_prot, 1);
        . . .
}
```

(net/ipv4/af_inet.c)

Note that in the tcp_prot definition, the init function pointer is defined to be the tcp_v4_init_sock() callback, which performs various initializations, like setting the timers by calling the tcp_init_xmit_timers() method, setting the socket state, and more. Conversely, in UDP, which is a much simpler protocol, the init function pointer was not defined at all because there are no special initializations to perform in UDP. We will discuss the tcp_v4_init_sock() callback later in this section.

In the next section, I will describe briefly the timers used by the TCP protocol.

TCP Timers

TCP timers are handled in net/ipv4/tcp_timer.c. There are four timers used by TCP:

- **Retransmit timer:** Responsible for resending packets that were not acknowledged in a specified time interval. This can happen when a packet gets lost or corrupted. This timer is started after each segment is sent; if an ACK arrives before the timer expires, the timer is canceled.

- **Delayed ACK timer:** Delays sending ACK packets. It is set when TCP receives data that must be acknowledged but does not need to be acknowledged immediately.

- **Keep Alive timer:** Checks whether the connection is down. There are cases when sessions are idle for a long time and one side goes down. The Keep Alive timer detects such cases and calls the tcp_send_active_reset() method to reset the connection.

- **Zero window probe timer (also known as the *persistent timer*):** When the receive buffer is full, the receiver advertises a zero window and the sender stops sending. Now, when a receiver sends a segment with a new window size and this segment is lost, the sender will keep waiting forever. The solution is this: when the sender gets a zero window, it uses a persistent timer to probe the receiver for its window size; when getting a non-zero window size, the persistent timer is stopped.

TCP Socket Initialization

To use a TCP socket, a userspace application should create a SOCK_STREAM socket and call the socket() system call. This is handled in the kernel by the tcp_v4_init_sock() callback, which invokes the tcp_init_sock() method to do the real work. Note that the tcp_init_sock() method performs address-family independent initializations, and it is invoked also from the tcp_v6_init_sock() method. The important tasks of the tcp_init_sock() method are the following:

- Set the state of the socket to be TCP_CLOSE.

- Initialize TCP timers by calling the tcp_init_xmit_timers() method.

- Initialize the socket send buffer (sk_sndbuf) and receive buffer (sk_rcvbuf); sk_sndbuf is set to be to sysctl_tcp_wmem[1], which is by default 16384 bytes, and sk_rcvbuf is set to be sysctl_tcp_rmem[1], which is by default 87380 bytes. These default values are set in the tcp_init() method; the sysctl_tcp_wmem and sysctl_tcp_rmem arrays default values can be overridden by writing to /proc/sys/net/ipv4/tcp_wmem and to /proc/sys/net/ipv4/tcp_rmem, respectively. See the "TCP Variables" section in Documentation/networking/ip-sysctl.txt.

- Initialize the out-of-order queue and the prequeue.

- Initialize various parameters. For example, the TCP initial congestion window is initialized to 10 segments (TCP_INIT_CWND), according to RFC 6928, "Increasing TCP's Initial Window," from 2013.

Now that you have learned how a TCP socket is initialized, I will discuss how to set up a TCP connection.

TCP Connection Setup

TCP connection setup and teardown and TCP connection properties are described as transitions in a state machine. At each given moment, a TCP socket can be in one specified state; for example, the socket enters the TCP_LISTEN state when the listen() system call is invoked. The state of the sock object is represented by its sk_state member. For a list of all available states, refer to include/net/tcp_states.h.

A three way handshake is used to set up a TCP connection between a TCP client and a TCP server:

- First, the client sends a SYN request to the server. Its state changes to TCP_SYN_SENT.

- The server socket, which is listening (its state is TCP_LISTEN), creates a request socket to represent the new connection in the TCP_SYN_RECV state and sends back a SYN ACK.

- The client that receives the SYN ACK changes its state to TCP_ESTABLISHED and sends an ACK to the server.

- The server receives the ACK and changes the request socket into a child socket in the TCP_ESTABLISHED state, as the connection is now established and data can be sent.

■ **Note** to further look into the TCP state machine details, refer to the tcp_rcv_state_process() method (net/ipv4/tcp_input.c), which is the state machine engine, both for IPv4 and for IPv6. (It is called both from the tcp_v4_do_rcv() method and from the tcp_v6_do_rcv() method.)

The next section describes how packets are received from the network layer (L3) with TCP in IPv4.

Receiving Packets from the Network Layer (L3) with TCP

The main handler for receiving TCP packets from the network layer (L3) is the `tcp_v4_rcv()` method (net/ipv4/tcp_ipv4.c). Let's take a look at this function:

```
int tcp_v4_rcv(struct sk_buff *skb)
{
        struct sock *sk;
        . . .
```

First we make some sanity checks (for example, checking to see if the packet type is not PACKET_HOST or if the packet size is shorter than the TCP header) and discard the packet if there are any problems; then some initializations are made and also a lookup for a corresponding socket is performed by calling the __inet_lookup_skb() method, which first performs a lookup in the established sockets hash table by calling the __inet_lookup_established() method. In the case of a lookup miss, it performs a lookup in the listening sockets hash table by calling the __inet_lookup_listener() method. If no socket is found, the packet is discarded at this stage.

```
        sk = __inet_lookup_skb(&tcp_hashinfo, skb, th->source, th->dest);
        . . .
        if (!sk)
                goto no_tcp_socket;
```

Now we check whether the socket is owned by some application. The `sock_owned_by_user()` macro returns 1 when there is currently an application that owns the socket, and it returns a value of 0 when there is no application that owns the socket:

```
        if (!sock_owned_by_user(sk)) {
        . . .
                {
```

We arrive here if no application owns the socket, so it can accept packets. First we try to put the packet in the prequeue by calling the `tcp_prequeue()` method, as packets in the prequeue are processed more efficiently. The `tcp_prequeue()` will return `false` if processing in the prequeue is not possible (for example, when the queue has no space); in such a case, we will call the `tcp_v4_do_rcv()` method, which we will discuss shortly:

```
                if (!tcp_prequeue(sk, skb))
                        ret = tcp_v4_do_rcv(sk, skb);
        }
```

When an application owns the socket, it means that it is in a locked state, so it cannot accept packets. In such a case, we add the packet to the backlog by calling the sk_add_backlog() method:

```
        } else if (unlikely(sk_add_backlog(sk, skb,
                                        sk->sk_rcvbuf + sk->sk_sndbuf))) {
                bh_unlock_sock(sk);
                NET_INC_STATS_BH(net, LINUX_MIB_TCPBACKLOGDROP);
                goto discard_and_relse;
        }
}
```

Let's take a look at the tcp_v4_do_rcv() method:

```
int tcp_v4_do_rcv(struct sock *sk, struct sk_buff *skb)
{
```

If the socket is in the TCP_ESTABLISHED state, we call the tcp_rcv_established() method:

```
    if (sk->sk_state == TCP_ESTABLISHED) { /* Fast path */
    . . .
            if (tcp_rcv_established(sk, skb, tcp_hdr(skb), skb->len)) {
                    rsk = sk;
                    goto reset;
            }
            return 0;
```

If the socket is in the TCP_LISTEN state, we call the tcp_v4_hnd_req() method:

```
    if (sk->sk_state == TCP_LISTEN) {
            struct sock *nsk = tcp_v4_hnd_req(sk, skb);

    }
```

If we are not in the TCP_LISTEN state, we invoke the tcp_rcv_state_process() method:

```
    if (tcp_rcv_state_process(sk, skb, tcp_hdr(skb), skb->len)) {
            rsk = sk;
            goto reset;
    }
    return 0;

reset:
        tcp_v4_send_reset(rsk, skb);

}
```

In this section, you learned about the reception of a TCP packet. In the next section, we conclude the TCP part of this chapter by describing how packets are sent with TCP in IPv4.

Sending Packets with TCP

As with UDP, sending packets from TCP sockets that were created in userspace can be done by several system calls: send(), sendto(), sendmsg(), and write(). Eventually all of them are handled by the tcp_sendmsg() method (net/ipv4/tcp.c). This method copies the payload from the userspace to the kernel and sends it as TCP segments. It is much more complicated than the udp_sendmsg() method.

```
int tcp_sendmsg(struct kiocb *iocb, struct sock *sk, struct msghdr *msg,
                size_t size)
{
        struct iovec *iov;
        struct tcp_sock *tp = tcp_sk(sk);
        struct sk_buff *skb;
```

```
        int iovlen, flags, err, copied = 0;
        int mss_now = 0, size_goal, copied_syn = 0, offset = 0;
        bool sg;
        long timeo;
        . . .
```

I will not delve into all the details of copying the data from the userspace to the SKB in this method. Once the SKB is built, it is sent with the tcp_push_one() method that calls the tcp_write_xmit() method, which in turn invokes the tcp_transmit_skb() method:

```
static int tcp_transmit_skb(struct sock *sk, struct sk_buff *skb, int clone_it,
                            gfp_t gfp_mask)
{
```

The icsk_af_ops object (INET Connection Socket ops) is an address-family specific object. In the case of IPv4 TCP, it is set to be an inet_connection_sock_af_ops object named ipv4_specific in the tcp_v4_init_sock() method. The queue_xmit() callback is set to be the generic ip_queue_xmit() method. See net/ipv4/tcp_ipv4.c.

```
        . . .
        err = icsk->icsk_af_ops->queue_xmit(skb, &inet->cork.fl);
        . . .
}
(net/ipv4/tcp_output.c)
```

Now that you learned about TCP and UDP, you are ready to proceed to the next section which deals with the SCTP (Stream Control Transmission Protocol) protocol. The SCTP protocol combines features of both UDP and TCP, and it is newer than both of them.

SCTP (Stream Control Transmission Protocol)

The SCTP protocol is specified in RFC 4960 from 2007. It was first specified in 2000. It is designed for Public Switched Telephone Network (PSTN) signaling over IP networks, but it can be used with other applications. The IETF SIGTRAN (Signaling Transport) working group originally developed the SCTP protocol and later handed the protocol over to the Transport Area working group (TSVWG) for the continued evolvement of SCTP as a general-purpose transport protocol. LTE (Long Term Evolution) uses SCTP; one of the main reasons for this is that the SCTP protocol is able to detect when a link goes down or when packets are dropped very quickly, whereas TCP does not have this feature. SCTP flow-control and congestion-control algorithms are very similar in TCP and SCTP. The SCTP protocol uses a variable for the advertised receiver window size (a_rwnd); this variable represents the current available space in the receiver buffer. The sender cannot send any new data if the receiver indicates that a_rwnd is 0 (no receive space available). The important features of SCTP are the following ones:

- SCTP combines the features of TCP and UDP. It is a reliable transport protocol with congestion control like TCP; it is a message-oriented protocol like UDP, whereas TCP is stream-oriented.

- The SCTP protocol provides improved security with its 4-way handshake (compared to the TCP 3-way handshake) to protect against SYN flooding attacks. I will discuss the 4-way handshake later in this chapter in the "Setting Up an SCTP Association" section.

- SCTP supports multihoming—that is, multiple IP addresses on both endpoints. This provides a network-level, fault-tolerance capability. I will discuss SCTP chunks later in this section.

- SCTP supports multistreaming, which means that it can send in parallel streams of data chunks. This can reduce the latency of streaming multimedia in some environments. I will discuss SCTP chunks later in this section.

- SCTP uses a heartbeat mechanism to detect idle/unreachable peers in the case of multihoming. I will discuss the SCTP heartbeat mechanism later in this chapter.

After this short description of the SCTP protocol, we will now discuss how SCTP initialization is done. The sctp_init() method allocates memory for various structures, initializes some sysctl variables, and registers the SCTP protocol in IPv4 and in IPv6:

```
int sctp_init(void)
{
        int status = -EINVAL;
         . . .
         status = sctp_v4_add_protocol();

        if (status)
                goto err_add_protocol;

        /* Register SCTP with inet6 layer.  */
        status = sctp_v6_add_protocol();
        if (status)
                goto err_v6_add_protocol;
         . . .
}
```

(net/sctp/protocol.c)

The registration of the SCTP protocol is done by defining an instance of net_protocol (named sctp_protocol for IPv4 and sctpv6_protocol for IPv6) and calling the inet_add_protocol() method, quite similarly to what you saw in other transport protocols, like the UDP protocol. We also call the register_inetaddr_notifier() to receive notifications about adding or deleting a network address. These events will be handled by the sctp_inetaddr_event() method, which will update the SCTP global address list (sctp_local_addr_list) accordingly.

```
  static const struct net_protocol sctp_protocol = {
        .handler     = sctp_rcv,
        .err_handler = sctp_v4_err,
        .no_policy   = 1,
};
```

(net/sctp/protocol.c)

```
static int sctp_v4_add_protocol(void)
{
        /* Register notifier for inet address additions/deletions. */
        register_inetaddr_notifier(&sctp_inetaddr_notifier);

        /* Register SCTP with inet layer.  */
        if (inet_add_protocol(&sctp_protocol, IPPROTO_SCTP) < 0)
                return -EAGAIN;

        return 0;
}
```

(net/sctp/protocol.c)

■ **Note** The `sctp_v6_add_protocol()` method (`net/sctp/ipv6.c`) is very similar, so we will not show it here.

Each SCTP packet starts with an SCTP header. I will now describe the structure of an SCTP header. I will start the discussion with SCTP chunks in the next section.

SCTP Packets and Chunks

Each SCTP packet has an SCTP common header, which is followed by one or more chunks. Each chunk can contain either data or SCTP control information. Several chunks can be bundled into one SCTP packet (except for three chunks that are used when establishing and terminating a connection: INIT, INIT_ACK, and SHUTDOWN_COMPLETE). These chunks use the Type-Length-Value (TLV) format that you first encountered in Chapter 2.

SCTP Common Header

```
typedef struct sctphdr {
        __be16 source;
        __be16 dest;
        __be32 vtag;
        __le32 checksum;
} __attribute__((packed)) sctp_sctphdr_t;
```

(include/linux/sctp.h)

Following is a description of the members of the `sctphdr` structure:

- `source`: SCTP source port.

- `dest`: SCTP destination port.

- `vtag`: Verification Tag, which is a 32 bit random value.

- `checksum`: Checksum of SCTP common header and all chunks.

SCTP Chunk Header

The SCTP chunk header is represented by struct `sctp_chunkhdr`:

```
typedef struct sctp_chunkhdr {
        __u8 type;
        __u8 flags;
        __be16 length;
} __packed sctp_chunkhdr_t;
```

(include/linux/sctp.h)

The following is a description of the members of the `sctp_chunkhdr` structure:

- `type`: The SCTP type. For example, the type of data chunks is SCTP_CID_DATA. See Table 11-2, Chunk types, in the "Quick Reference" section at the end of this chapter, and also see the chunk ID enum definition (`sctp_cid_t`) in include/linux/sctp.h.

- flags: Usually, all 8 bits in it should be set to 0 by the sender and ignored by the receiver. There are cases when different values are used. For example, in ABORT chunk, we use the T bit (the LSB) thus: it is set to 0 if the sender filled in the Verification Tag, and it is set to 1 if the Verification Tag is reflected.

- length: The length of the SCTP chunk.

SCTP Chunk

The SCTP chunk is represented by struct sctp_chunk. Each chunk object contains the source and destination address for this chunk and a subheader (member of the subh union) according to its type. For example, for data packets we have the sctp_datahdr subheader, and for the INIT type we have the sctp_inithdr subtype:

```
struct sctp_chunk {
    . . . . . .
    atomic_t refcnt;

    union {
            __u8 *v;
            struct sctp_datahdr        *data_hdr;
            struct sctp_inithdr        *init_hdr;
            struct sctp_sackhdr        *sack_hdr;
            struct sctp_heartbeathdr   *hb_hdr;
            struct sctp_sender_hb_info *hbs_hdr;
            struct sctp_shutdownhdr    *shutdown_hdr;
            struct sctp_signed_cookie  *cookie_hdr;
            struct sctp_ecnehdr        *ecne_hdr;
            struct sctp_cwrhdr         *ecn_cwr_hdr;
            struct sctp_errhdr         *err_hdr;
            struct sctp_addiphdr       *addip_hdr;
            struct sctp_fwdtsn_hdr     *fwdtsn_hdr;
            struct sctp_authhdr        *auth_hdr;
    } subh;

    struct sctp_chunkhdr    *chunk_hdr;
    struct sctphdr          *sctp_hdr;

    struct sctp_association *asoc;

    /* What endpoint received this chunk? */
    struct sctp_ep_common   *rcvr;

    . . .

    /* What is the origin IP address for this chunk?  */
    union sctp_addr source;
    /* Destination address for this chunk. */
    union sctp_addr dest;

    . . .
```

```
        /* For an inbound chunk, this tells us where it came from.
         * For an outbound chunk, it tells us where we'd like it to
         * go.  It is NULL if we have no preference.
         */
        struct sctp_transport *transport;

};
```

(include/net/sctp/structs.h)

We will now describe an SCTP association (which is the counterpart of a TCP connection).

SCTP Associations

In SCTP, we use the term *association* instead of a *connection*; a connection refers to communication between two IP addresses, whereas association refers to communication between two endpoints that might have multiple IP addresses. An SCTP association is represented by struct sctp_association:

```
struct sctp_association {
        ...

        sctp_assoc_t assoc_id;

        /* These are those association elements needed in the cookie.  */
        struct sctp_cookie c;

        /* This is all information about our peer.  */
        struct {
                struct list_head transport_addr_list;

                . . .
                __u16 transport_count;
                __u16 port;
                . . .

                struct sctp_transport *primary_path;
                struct sctp_transport *active_path;

        } peer;

        sctp_state_t state;
        . . .
        struct sctp_priv_assoc_stats stats;
};
```

(include/net/sctp/structs.h).

The following is a description of some of the important members of the sctp_association structure:

- assoc_id: The association unique id. It's set by the sctp_assoc_set_id() method.
- c: The state cookie (sctp_cookie object) that is attached to the association.

- peer: An inner structure representing the peer endpoint of the association. Adding a peer is done by the sctp_assoc_add_peer() method; removing a peer is done by the sctp_assoc_rm_peer() method. Following is a description of some of the peer structure important members:

  - transport_addr_list: Represents one or more addresses of the peer. We can add addresses to this list or remove addresses from it by using the sctp_connectx() method when an association is established.

  - transport_count: The counter of the peer addresses in the peer address list (transport_addr_list).

  - primary_path: Represents the address to which the initial connection was made (INIT <--> INIT_ACK exchange). The association will attempt to always use the primary path if it is active.

  - active_path: The address of the peer that is currently used when sending data.

  - state: The state that the association is in, like SCTP_STATE_CLOSED or SCTP_STATE_ESTABLISHED. Various SCTP states are discussed later in this section.

Adding multiple local addresses to an SCTP association or removing multiple addresses from one can be done, for example, with the sctp_bindx() system call, in order to support the multihoming feature mentioned earlier. Every SCTP association includes a peer object, which represents the remote endpoint; the peer object includes a list of one or more addresses of the remote endpoint (transport_addr_list). We can add one or more addresses to this list by calling the sctp_connectx() system call when establishing an association. An SCTP association is created by the sctp_association_new() method and initialized by the sctp_association_init() method. At any given moment, an SCTP association can be in one of 8 states; thus, for example, when it is created, its state is SCTP_STATE_CLOSED. Later on, these states can change; see, for example, the "Setting Up an SCTP Association" section later in this chapter. These states are represented by the sctp_state_t enum (include/net/sctp/constants.h).

To send data between two endpoints, an initialization process must be completed. In this process, an SCTP association between these two endpoints is set; a cookie mechanism is used to provide protection against synchronization attacks. This process is discussed in the following section.

Setting Up an SCTP Association

The initialization process is a 4-way handshake that consists of the following steps:

- One endpoint ("A") sends an INIT chunk to the endpoint it wants to communicate with ("Z"). This chunk will include a locally generated Tag in the Initiate Tag field of the INIT chunk, and it will also include a verification tag (vtag in the SCTP header) with a value of 0 (zero).

- After sending the INIT chunk, the association enters the SCTP_STATE_COOKIE_WAIT state.

- The other endpoint ("Z") sends to "A" an INIT-ACK chunk as a reply. This chunk will include a locally generated Tag in the Initiate Tag field of the INIT-ACK chunk and the remote Initiate Tag as the verification tag (vtag in the SCTP header). "Z" should also generate a state cookie and send it with the INIT-ACK reply.

- When "A" receives the INIT-ACK chunk, it leaves the SCTP_STATE_COOKIE_WAIT state. "A" will use the remote Initiate Tag as the verification tag (vtag in the SCTP header) in all transmitted packets from now on. "A" will send the state cookie it received in a COOKIE ECHO chunk. "A" will enter the SCTP_STATE_COOKIE_ECHOED state.

- When "Z" receives the COOKIE ECHO chunk, it will build a TCB (Transmission Control Block). The TCB is a data structure containing connection information on either side of an SCTP connection. "Z" will further change its state to SCTP_STATE_ESTABLISHED and reply with a COOKIE ACK chunk. This is where the association is finally established on "Z" and, at this point, this association will use the saved tags.

- When "A" receives the COOKIE ACK, it will move from the SCTP_STATE_COOKIE_ECHOED state to the SCTP_STATE_ESTABLISHED state.

■ **Note**   An endpoint might respond to an INIT, INIT ACK, or COOKIE ECHO chunk with an ABORT chunk when some mandatory parameters are missing, or when receiving invalid parameter values. The cause of the ABORT chunk should be specified in the reply.

Now that you have learned about SCTP associations and how they are created, you will see how SCTP packets are received with SCTP and how SCTP packets are sent.

Receiving Packets with SCTP

The main handler for receiving SCTP packets is the sctp_rcv() method, which gets an SKB as a single parameter (net/sctp/input.c). First some sanity checks are made (size, checksum, and so on). If everything is fine, we proceed to check whether this packet is an "Out of the Blue" (OOTB) packet. A packet is an OOTB packet if it is correctly formed (that is, no checksum error), but the receiver is not able to identify the SCTP association to which this packet belongs. (See section 8.4 in RFC 4960.) The OOTB packets are handled by the sctp_rcv_ootb() method, which iterates over all the chunks of the packet and takes an action according to the chunk type, as specified in the RFC. Thus, for example, an ABORT chunk is discarded. If this packet is not an OOTB packet, it is put into an SCTP inqueue by calling the sctp_inq_push() method and proceeds on its journey with the sctp_assoc_bh_rcv() method or with the sctp_endpoint_bh_rcv() method.

Sending Packets with SCTP

Writing to a userspace SCTP socket reaches the sctp_sendmsg() method (net/sctp/socket.c). The packet is passed to the lower layers by calling the sctp_primitive_SEND() method, which in turn calls the state machine callback, sctp_do_sm() (net/sctp/sm_sideeffect.c), with SCTP_ST_PRIMITIVE_SEND. The next stage is to call sctp_side_effects(), and eventually call the sctp_packet_transmit() method.

SCTP HEARTBEAT

The HEARTBEAT mechanism tests the connectivity of a transport or path by exchanging HEARTBEAT and HEARTBEAT-ACK SCTP packets. It declares the transport IP address to be down once it reaches the threshold of a nonreturned heartbeat acknowledgment. A HEARTBEAT chunk is sent every 30 seconds by default to monitor the reachability of an idle destination transport address. This time interval is configurable by setting /proc/sys/net/sctp/hb_interval. The default is 30000 milliseconds (30 seconds). Sending heartbeat chunks is performed by the sctp_sf_sendbeat_8_3() method. The reason for the 8_3 in the method name is that it refers to section 8.3 (Path Heartbeat) in RFC 4960. When an endpoint receives a HEARTBEAT chunk, it replies with a HEARTBEAT-ECHO chunk if it is in the SCTP_STATE_COOKIE_ECHOED state or the SCTP_STATE_ESTABLISHED state.

SCTP Multistreaming

Streams are unidirectional data flows within a single association. The number of Outbound Streams and the number of Inbound Streams are declared during the association setup (by the INIT chunk), and the streams are valid during the entire association lifetime. A userspace application can set the number of streams by creating an `sctp_initmsg` object and initializing its `sinit_num_ostreams` and `sinit_max_instreams`, and then calling the `setsockopt()` method with SCTP_INITMSG. Initialization of the number of streams can also be done with the `sendmsg()` system call. This, in turn, sets the corresponding fields in the `initmsg` object of the `sctp_sock` object. One of the biggest reasons streams were added was to remove the Head-of-Line blocking (HoL Blocking) condition. Head-of-line blocking is a performance-limiting phenomenon that occurs when a line of packets is held up by the first packet—for example, in multiple requests in HTTP pipelining. When working with SCTP Multistreaming, this problem does not exist because each stream is sequenced separately and guaranteed to be delivered in order. Thus, once one of the streams is blocked due to loss/congestion, the other streams might not be blocked and data will continue to be delivered. This is due to that one stream can be blocked while the other streams are not blocked,

---

■ **Note**   Regarding using sockets for SCTP, I should mention the `lksctp-tools` project (`http://lksctp.sourceforge.net/`). This project provides a Linux userspace library for SCTP (`libsctp`), including C language header files (`netinet/sctp.h`), for accessing SCTP-specific application programming interfaces not provided by the standard sockets, and also some helper utilities around SCTP. I should also mention RFC 6458, "Sockets API Extensions for Stream Control Transmission Protocol (SCTP)," which describes a mapping of the Stream Control Transmission Protocol (SCTP) into the sockets API.

SCTP Multihoming

SCTP multihoming refers to having multiple IP addresses on both endpoints. One of the really nice features of SCTP is that endpoints are multihomed by default if the local ip address was specified as a wildcard. Also, there has been a lot of confusion about the multihoming feature because people expect that simply by binding to multiple addresses, the associations will end up being multihomed. This is not true because we implement only destination multihoming. In other words, both connected endpoints have to be multihomed for it to have true failover capability. If the local association knows about only a single destination address, there will be only one path and thus no multihoming.

With describing SCTP multihoming in this section, the SCTP part of this chapter has ended. In the next section, I will describe the DCCP protocol, which is the last transport protocol to be discussed in this chapter.

DCCP: The Datagram Congestion Control Protocol

DCCP is an unreliable, congestion-controlled transport layer protocol and, as such, it borrows from both UDP and TCP while adding new features. Like UDP, it is message-oriented and unreliable. Like TCP, it is a connection-oriented protocol and it also uses a 3-way handshake to set up the connection. Development of DCCP was helped by ideas from academia, through participation of several research institutes, but it has not been tested so far in larger-scale Internet setups. The use of DCCP would make sense, for instance, in applications that require minor delays and where a small degree of data loss is permitted, like in telephony and in streaming media applications.

Congestion control in DCCP differs from that in TCP in that the congestion-control algorithm (called CCID) can be negotiated between endpoints and congestion control can be applied on both the forward and reverse paths of a connection (called half-connections in DCCP). Two classes of pluggable congestion control have been specified so far. The first type is a rate-based, smooth "TCP-friendly" algorithm (CCID-3, RFC 4342 and 5348), for which there is an experimental small-packet variation called CCID-4 (RFC 5622, RFC 4828). The second type of congestion control,

"TCP-like" (RFC 4341) applies a basic TCP congestion-control algorithm with selective acknowledgments (SACK, RFC 2018) to DCCP flows. At least one CCID needs to be implemented by endpoints in order to function. The first DCCP Linux implementation was released in Linux kernel 2.6.14 (2005). This chapter describes the implementation principles of the DCCPv4 (IPv4). Delving into the implementation details of individual DCCP congestion-control algorithms is beyond the scope of this book.

Now that I've introduced the DCCP protocol in general, I will describe the DCCP header.

DCCP Header

Every DCCP packet starts with a DCCP header. The minimum DCCP header length is 12 bytes. DCCP uses a variable-length header, which can range from 12 to 1020 bytes, depending on whether short sequence numbers are used and which TLV packet options are used. DCCP sequence numbers are incremented for each packet (not per each byte as in TCP) and can be shortened from 6 to 3 bytes.

```
struct dccp_hdr {
        __be16   dccph_sport,
                 dccph_dport;
        __u8     dccph_doff;
#if defined(__LITTLE_ENDIAN_BITFIELD)
        __u8     dccph_cscov:4,
                 dccph_ccval:4;
#elif defined(__BIG_ENDIAN_BITFIELD)
        __u8     dccph_ccval:4,
                 dccph_cscov:4;
#else
#error   "Adjust your <asm/byteorder.h> defines"
#endif
        __sum16 dccph_checksum;
#if defined(__LITTLE_ENDIAN_BITFIELD)
        __u8     dccph_x:1,
                 dccph_type:4,
                 dccph_reserved:3;
#elif defined(__BIG_ENDIAN_BITFIELD)
        __u8     dccph_reserved:3,
                 dccph_type:4,
                 dccph_x:1;
#else
#error   "Adjust your <asm/byteorder.h> defines"
#endif
        __u8     dccph_seq2;
        __be16   dccph_seq;
};
```

(include/uapi/linux/dccp.h)

The following is a description of the important members of the dccp_hdr structure:

- dccph_sport: Source port (16 bit).

- dccph_dport: Destination port (16 bit).

- dccph_doff: Data offset (8 bits). The size of the DCCP header is in multiples of 4 bytes.

- dccph_cscov: Determines which part of the packet is covered in the checksum. Using partial checksumming might improve performance when it is used with applications that can tolerate corruption of some low percentage.

- dccph_ccval: CCID-specific information from sender to receiver (not always used).

- dccph_x: Extended Sequence Numbers bit (1 bit). This flag is set when using 48-bit Extended Sequence and Acknowledgment Numbers.

- dccph_type: The DCCP header type (4 bits). This can be, for example, DCCP_PKT_DATA for a data packet or DCCP_PKT_ACK for an ACK. See Table 11-3, "DCCP packet types," in the "Quick Reference" section at the end of this chapter.

- dccph_reserved: Reserved for future use (1 bit).

- dccph_checksum: The checksum (16 bit). The Internet checksum of the DCCP header and data, computed similarly to UDP and TCP. If partial checksums are used, only the length specified by dccph_cscov of the application data is checksummed.

- dccph_seq2: Sequence number. This is used when working with Extended Sequence Numbers (8 bit).

- dccph_seq: Sequence number. It is incremented by 1 for each packet (16 bit).

■ **Note** DCCP sequence numbers depend on dccph_x. (For details, refer to the dccp_hdr_seq() method, include/linux/dccp.h).

Figure 11-4 shows a DCCP header. The dccph_x flag is set, so we use 48-bit Extended Sequence numbers.

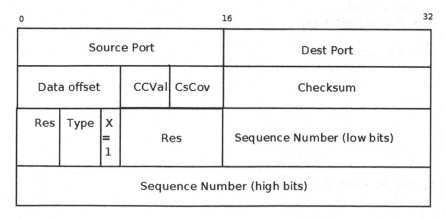

Figure 11-4. *DCCP header (the Extended Sequence Numbers bit is set, dccph_x=1)*

Figure 11-5 shows a DCCP header. The dccph_x flag is not set, so we use 24-bit Sequence numbers.

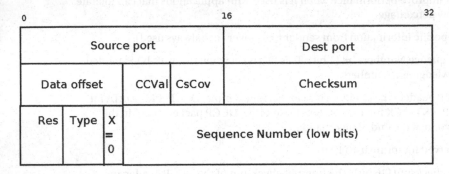

Figure 11-5. *DCCP header (the Extended Sequence Numbers bit is not set, dccph_x=0)*

DCCP Initialization

DCCP initialization happens much like in TCP and UDP. Considering the DCCPv4 case (net/dccp/ipv4.c), first a proto object is defined (dccp_v4_prot) and its DCCP specific callbacks are set; we also define a net_protocol object (dccp_v4_protocol) and initialize it:

```
static struct proto dccp_v4_prot = {
        .name                   = "DCCP",
        .owner                  = THIS_MODULE,
        .close                  = dccp_close,
        .connect                = dccp_v4_connect,
        .disconnect             = dccp_disconnect,
        .ioctl                  = dccp_ioctl,
        .init                   = dccp_v4_init_sock,
        . . .
        .sendmsg                = dccp_sendmsg,
        .recvmsg                = dccp_recvmsg,
        . . .

}

(net/dccp/ipv4.c)


static const struct net_protocol dccp_v4_protocol = {
        .handler        = dccp_v4_rcv,
        .err_handler    = dccp_v4_err,
        .no_policy      = 1,
        .netns_ok       = 1,
};

(net/dccp/ipv4.c)
```

We register the dccp_v4_prot object and the dccp_v4_protocol object in the dccp_v4_init() method:

```
static int __init dccp_v4_init(void)
{
        int err = proto_register(&dccp_v4_prot, 1);

        if (err != 0)
                goto out;

        err = inet_add_protocol(&dccp_v4_protocol, IPPROTO_DCCP);
        if (err != 0)
                goto out_proto_unregister;
```
(net/dccp/ipv4.c)

DCCP Socket Initialization

Socket creation in DCCP from userspace uses the socket() system call, where the domain argument (SOCK_DCCP) indicates that a DCCP socket is to be created. Within the kernel, this causes DCCP socket initialization via the dccp_v4_init_sock() callback, which relies on the dccp_init_sock() method to perform the actual work:

```
static int dccp_v4_init_sock(struct sock *sk)
{
        static __u8 dccp_v4_ctl_sock_initialized;
        int err = dccp_init_sock(sk, dccp_v4_ctl_sock_initialized);

        if (err == 0) {
                if (unlikely(!dccp_v4_ctl_sock_initialized))
                        dccp_v4_ctl_sock_initialized = 1;
                inet_csk(sk)->icsk_af_ops = &dccp_ipv4_af_ops;
        }

        return err;
}
```

(net/dccp/ipv4.c)

The most important tasks of the dccp_init_sock() method are these:

- Initialization of the DCCP socket fields with sane default values (for example, the socket state is set to be DCCP_CLOSED)

- Initialization of the DCCP timers (via the dccp_init_xmit_timers() method)

- Initialization of the feature-negotiation part via calling the dccp_feat_init() method. Feature negotiation is a distinguishing feature of DCCP by which endpoints can mutually agree on properties of each side of the connection. It extends TCP feature negotiation and is described further in RFC 4340, sec. 6.

Receiving Packets from the Network Layer (L3) with DCCP

The main handler for receiving DCCP packets from the network layer (L3) is the dccp_v4_rcv () method:

```
static int dccp_v4_rcv(struct sk_buff *skb)
{
        const struct dccp_hdr *dh;
        const struct iphdr *iph;
        struct sock *sk;
        int min_cov;
```

First we discard invalid packets. For example, if the packet is not for this host (the packet type is not PACKET_HOST), or if the packet size is shorter than the DCCP header (which is 12 bytes):

```
        if (dccp_invalid_packet(skb))
                goto discard_it;
```

Then we perform a lookup according to the flow:

```
        sk = __inet_lookup_skb(&dccp_hashinfo, skb,
                                dh->dccph_sport, dh->dccph_dport);
```

If no socket was found, the packet is dropped:

```
        if (sk == NULL) {
                . . .
                goto no_dccp_socket;
        }
```

We make some more checks relating to Minimum Checksum Coverage, and if everything is fine, we proceed to the generic sk_receive_skb() method to pass the packet to the transport layer (L4). Note that the dccp_v4_rcv() method is very similar in structure and function to the tcp_v4_rcv() method. This is because the original author of DCCP in Linux, Arnaldo Carvalho de Melo, has worked quite hard to make the similarities between TCP and DCCP obvious and clear in the code.

```
        . . .
        return sk_receive_skb(sk, skb, 1);
        }
```

(net/dccp/ipv4.c)

Sending Packets with DCCP

Sending data from a DCCP userspace socket is eventually handled by the dccp_sendmsg() method in the kernel (net/dccp/proto.c). This parallels the TCP case, where the tcp_sendmsg() kernel method handles sending data from a TCP userspace socket. Let's take a look at the dccp_sendmsg() method:

```
int dccp_sendmsg(struct kiocb *iocb, struct sock *sk, struct msghdr *msg,
                size_t len)
{
        const struct dccp_sock *dp = dccp_sk(sk);
        const int flags = msg->msg_flags;
```

```
        const int noblock = flags & MSG_DONTWAIT;
        struct sk_buff *skb;
        int rc, size;
        long timeo;
```

Allocate an SKB:

```
        skb = sock_alloc_send_skb(sk, size, noblock, &rc);
        lock_sock(sk);
        if (skb == NULL)
                goto out_release;

        skb_reserve(skb, sk->sk_prot->max_header);
```

Copy the data blocks from the msghdr object to the SKB:

```
        rc = memcpy_fromiovec(skb_put(skb, len), msg->msg_iov, len);
        if (rc != 0)
                goto out_discard;

        if (!timer_pending(&dp->dccps_xmit_timer))
                dccp_write_xmit(sk);
```

Depending upon the type of congestion control (window-based or rate-based) chosen for the connection, the dccp_write_xmit() method will cause a packet to be sent later (via dccps_xmit_timer() expiry) or passed on for immediate sending by the dccp_xmit_packet() method. This, in turn, relies on the dccp_transmit_skb() method to initialize the outgoing DCCP header and pass it to the L3-specific queue_xmit sending callback (using the ip_queue_xmit() method for IPv4, and the inet6_csk_xmit() method for IPv6). I will conclude our discussion about DCCP with a short section about DCCP and NAT.

DCCP and NAT

Some NAT devices do not let DCCP through (usually because their firmware is typically small, and hence does not support "exotic" IP protocols such as DCCP). RFC 5597 (September 2009) has suggested behavioral requirements for NATs to support NAT-ed DCCP communications. However, it is not clear to what extent the recommendations are put into consumer devices. One of the motivations for DCCP-UDP was the absence of NAT devices that would let DCCP through (RFC 6773, sec. 1). There is a detail that might be interesting in the comparison with TCP. The latter, by default, supports simultaneous open (RFC 793, section 3.4), whereas the initial specification of DCCP in RFC 4340, section 4.6 disallowed the use of simultaneous-open. To support NAPT traversal, RFC 5596 updated RFC 4340 in September 2009 with a "near simultaneous open" technique, which added one packet type (DCCP-LISTEN, RFC 5596, section 2.2.1) to the list and changed the state machine to support two more states (2.2.2) to support near-simultaneous open. The motivation was a NAT "hole punching" technique, which would require, however, that NATs with DCCP existed (same problem as above). As a result of this chicken-and-egg problem, DCCP has not seen much exposure over the Internet. Perhaps the UDP encapsulation will change that. But then it would no longer really be considered as a transport layer protocol.

Summary

This chapter discussed four transport protocols: UDP and TCP, which are the most commonly used, and SCTP and DCCP, which are newer protocols. You learned the basic differences between these protocols. You learned that TCP is a much more complex protocol than UDP, as its uses a state machine and several timers and requires acknowledgments. You learned about the header of each of these protocols and about sending and receiving packets with these protocols. I discussed some unique features of the SCTP protocol, like multihoming and multistreaming.

The next chapter will deal with the Wireless subsystem and its implementation in Linux. In the "Quick Reference" section that follows, I will cover the top methods related to the topics discussed in this chapter, ordered by their context, and also I will present the two tables that were mentioned in this chapter.

Quick Reference

I will conclude this chapter with a short list of important methods of sockets and transport-layer protocols that we discussed in this chapter. Some of them were mentioned in this chapter. Afterward, there is one macro and three tables.

Methods

Here are the methods.

int ip_cmsg_send(struct net *net, struct msghdr *msg, struct ipcm_cookie *ipc);

This method builds an `ipcm_cookie` object by parsing the specified `msghdr` object.

void sock_put(struct sock *sk);

This method decrements the reference count of the specified `sock` object.

void sock_hold(struct sock *sk);

This method increments the reference count of the specified `sock` object.

int sock_create(int family, int type, int protocol, struct socket **res);

This method performs some sanity checks, and if everything is fine, it allocates a socket by calling the `sock_alloc()` method, and then calling `net_families[family]->create`. (In the case of IPv4, it is the `inet_create()` method.)

int sock_map_fd(struct socket *sock, int flags);

This method allocates a file descriptor and fills in the file entry.

bool sock_flag(const struct sock *sk, enum sock_flags flag);

This method returns `true` if the specified `flag` is set in the specified `sock` object.

int tcp_v4_rcv(struct sk_buff *skb);

This method is the main handler to process incoming TCP packets arriving from the network layer (L3).

void tcp_init_sock(struct sock *sk);

This method performs address-family independent socket initializations.

struct tcphdr *tcp_hdr(const struct sk_buff *skb);

This method returns the TCP header associated with the specified skb.

int tcp_sendmsg(struct kiocb *locb, struct sock *sk, struct msghdr *msg, size_t size);

This method handles sending TCP packets that are sent from userspace.

struct tcp_sock *tcp_sk(const struct sock *sk);

This method returns the tcp_sock object associated with the specified sock object (sk).

int udp_rcv(struct sk_buff *skb);

This method is the main handler to process incoming UDP packets arriving from the network layer (L3).

struct udphdr *udp_hdr(const struct sk_buff *skb);

This method returns the UDP header associated with the specified skb.

int udp_sendmsg(struct kiocb *iocb, struct sock *sk, struct msghdr *msg, size_t len);

This method handles UDP packets that are sent from the userspace.

struct sctphdr *sctp_hdr(const struct sk_buff *skb);

This method returns the SCTP header associated with the specified skb.

struct sctp_sock *sctp_sk(const struct sock *sk);

This method returns the SCTP socket (sctp_sock object) associated with the specified sock object.

int sctp_sendmsg(struct kiocb *iocb, struct sock *sk, struct msghdr *msg, size_t msg_len);

This method handles SCTP packets that are sent from userspace.

struct sctp_association *sctp_association_new(const struct sctp_endpoint *ep, const struct sock *sk, sctp_scope_t scope, gfp_t gfp);

This method allocates and initializes a new SCTP association.

void sctp_association_free(struct sctp_association *asoc);

This method frees the resources of an SCTP association.

void sctp_chunk_hold(struct sctp_chunk *ch);

This method increments the reference count of the specified SCTP chunk.

void sctp_chunk_put(struct sctp_chunk *ch);

This method decrements the reference count of the specified SCTP chunk. If the reference count reaches 0, it frees it by calling the sctp_chunk_destroy() method.

int sctp_rcv(struct sk_buff *skb);

This method is the main input handler for input SCTP packets.

static int dccp_v4_rcv(struct sk_buff *skb);

This method is the main Rx handler for processing incoming DCCP packets that arrive from the network layer (L3).

int dccp_sendmsg(struct kiocb *iocb, struct sock *sk, struct msghdr *msg, size_t len);

This method handles DCCP packets that are sent from the userspace.

Macros

And here is the macro.

sctp_chunk_is_data()

This macro returns 1 if the specified chunk is a data chunk; otherwise, it returns 0.

Tables

Take a look at the tables used in this chapter.

Table 11-1. *TCP and UDP prot_ops objects*

prot_ops callback	TCP	UDP
release	inet_release	inet_release
bind	inet_bind	inet_bind
connect	inet_stream_connect	inet_dgram_connect
socketpair	sock_no_socketpair	sock_no_socketpair
accept	inet_accept	sock_no_accept
getname	inet_getname	inet_getname
poll	tcp_poll	udp_poll
ioctl	inet_ioctl	inet_ioctl
listen	inet_listen	sock_no_listen
shutdown	inet_shutdown	inet_shutdown
setsockopt	sock_common_setsockopt	sock_common_setsockopt
getsockopt	sock_common_getsockopt	sock_common_getsockopt
sendmsg	inet_sendmsg	inet_sendmsg
recvmsg	inet_recvmsg	inet_recvmsg
mmap	sock_no_mmap	sock_no_mmap
sendpage	inet_sendpage	inet_sendpage
splice_read	tcp_splice_read	-
compat_setsockopt	compat_sock_common_setsockopt	compat_sock_common_setsockopt
compat_getsockopt	compat_sock_common_getsockopt	compat_sock_common_getsockopt
compat_ioctl	inet_compat_ioctl	inet_compat_ioctl

■ **Note** See the inet_stream_ops and the inet_dgram_ops definitions in net/ipv4/af_inet.c.

Table 11-2. *Chunk types*

Chunk Type	Linux Symbol	Value
Payload Data	SCTP_CID_DATA	0
Initiation	SCTP_CID_INIT	1
Initiation Acknowledgment	SCTP_CID_INIT_ACK	2
Selective Acknowledgment	SCTP_CID_SACK	3
Heartbeat Request	SCTP_CID_HEARTBEAT	4

(continued)

Table 11-2. (*continued*)

Chunk Type	Linux Symbol	Value
Heartbeat Acknowledgment	SCTP_CID_HEARTBEAT_ACK	5
Abort	SCTP_CID_ABORT	6
Shutdown	SCTP_CID_SHUTDOWN	7
Shutdown Acknowledgment	SCTP_CID_SHUTDOWN_ACK	8
Operation Error	SCTP_CID_ERROR	9
State Cookie	SCTP_CID_COOKIE_ECHO	10
Cookie Acknowledgment	SCTP_CID_COOKIE_ACK	11
Explicit Congestion Notification Echo (ECNE)	SCTP_CID_ECN_ECNE	12
Congestion Window Reduced (CWR)	SCTP_CID_ECN_CWR	13
Shutdown Complete	SCTP_CID_SHUTDOWN_COMPLETE	14
SCTP Authentication Chunk (RFC 4895)	SCTP_CID_AUTH	0x0F
Transmission Sequence Numbers	SCTP_CID_FWD_TSN	0xC0
Address Configuration Change Chunk	SCTP_CID_ASCONF	0xC1
Address Configuration Acknowledgment Chunk	SCTP_CID_ASCONF_ACK	0x80

Table 11-3. *DCCP packet types*

Linux Symbol	Description
DCCP_PKT_REQUEST	Sent by the client to initiate a connection (the first part of the three-way initiation handshake).
DCCP_PKT_RESPONSE	Sent by the server in response to a DCCP-Request (the second part of the three-way initiation handshake).
DCCP_PKT_DATA	Used to transmit application data.
DCCP_PKT_ACK	Used to transmit pure acknowledgments.
DCCP_PKT_DATAACK	Used to transmit application data with piggybacked acknowledgment information.
DCCP_PKT_CLOSEREQ	Sent by the server to request that the client close the connection.
DCCP_PKT_CLOSE	Used by the client or the server to close the connection; elicits a DCCP-Reset packet in response.
DCCP_PKT_RESET	Used to terminate the connection, either normally or abnormally.
DCCP_PKT_SYNC	Used to resynchronize sequence numbers after large bursts of packet loss.
DCCP_PKT_SYNCACK	Acknowledge a DCCP_PKT_SYNC.

CHAPTER 12

■ ■ ■

Wireless in Linux

Chapter 11 deals with Layer 4 protocols, which enable us to communicate with userspace. This chapter deals with the wireless stack in the Linux kernel. I describe the Linux wireless stack (mac80211 subsystem) and discuss some implementation details of important mechanisms in it, such as packet aggregation and block acknowledgement, used in IEEE 802.11n, and power save mode. Becoming familiar with the 802.11 MAC header is essential in order to understand the wireless subsystem implementation. The 802.11 MAC header, its members, and their usage are described in depth in this chapter. I also discuss some common wireless topologies, like infrastructure BSS, independent BSS, and Mesh networking.

Mac80211 Subsystem

At the end of the 1990s, there were discussions in IEEE regarding a protocol for wireless local area networks (WLANS). The original version of the IEEE 802.11 spec for WLANS was released in 1997 and revised in 1999. In the following years, some extensions were added, formally termed 802.11 amendments. These extensions can be divided into PHY (Physical) layer extensions, MAC (Medium Access Control) layer extensions, Regulatory extensions, and others. PHY layer extensions are, for example, 802.11b from 1999, 802.11a (also from 1999), and 802.11g from 2003. MAC layer extensions are, for example, 802.11e for QoS and 802.11s for Mesh networking. The "Mesh Networking" section of this chapter deals with the Linux kernel implementation of the IEEE802.11s amendment. The IEEE802.11 spec was revised, and in 2007 a second version of 1,232 pages was released. In 2012, a spec of 2,793 pages was released, available from `http://standards.ieee.org/findstds/standard/802.11-2012.html`. I refer to this spec as IEEE 802.11-2012 in this chapter. Following is a partial list of important 802.11 amendments:

- *IEEE 802.11d:* International (country-to-country) roaming extensions (2001).

- *IEEE 802.11e:* Enhancements: QoS, including packet bursting (2005).

- *IEEE 802.11h:* Spectrum Managed 802.11a for European compatibility (2004).

- *IEEE 802.11i:* Enhanced security (2004).

- *IEEE 802.11j:* Extensions for Japan (2004).

- *IEEE 802.11k:* Radio resource measurement enhancements (2008).

- *IEEE 802.11n:* Higher throughput improvements using MIMO (multiple input, multiple output antennas) (2009).

- *IEEE 802.11p:* WAVE: Wireless Access for the Vehicular Environment (such as ambulances and passenger cars). It has some peculiarities such as not using the BSS concept and narrower (5/10 MHz) channels. Note that IEEE 802.11p isn't supported in Linux as of this writing.

- *IEEE 802.11v:* Wireless network management.

- *IEEE 802.11w:* Protected Management Frames.

- *IEEE 802.11y:* 3650–3700 MHz operation in the U.S. (2008)

- *IEEE 802.11z:* Extensions to Direct Link Setup (DLS) (Aug 2007–Dec 2011).

It was only in about 2001, about four years after the IEEE 802.11 first spec was approved, that laptops became very popular; many of these laptops were sold with wireless network interfaces. Today every laptop includes WiFi as standard equipment. It was important to the Linux community at that time to provide Linux drivers to these wireless network interfaces and to provide a Linux network wireless stack, in order to stay competitive with other OSes (such as Windows, Mac OS, and others). Less effort has been done regarding architecture and design. "They just want their hardware to work," as Jeff Garzik, the Linux Kernel Wireless maintainer at that time, put it. When the first wireless drivers for Linux were developed, there was no general wireless API. As a result, there were many cases of duplication of code between drivers, when developers implemented their drivers from scratch. Some drivers were based on FullMAC, which means that most of the management layer (MLME) is managed in hardware. In the years since, a new 802.11 wireless stack called mac80211 was developed. It was integrated into the Linux kernel in July 2007, for the 2.6.22 Linux kernel. The mac80211 stack is based on the d80211 stack, which is an open source, GPL-licensed stack by a company named Devicescape.

I cannot delve into the details of the PHY layer, because that subject is very wide and deserves a book of its own. However, I must note that there are many differences between 802.11 and 802.3 wired Ethernet. Here are two major differences:

- Ethernet works with CSMA/CD, whereas 802.11 works with CSMA/CA. CSMA/CA stands for carrier sense multiple access/collision avoidance, and CSMA/CD stands for carrier sense multiple access/collision detection. The difference, as you might guess, is the collision detection. With Ethernet, a station starts to transmit when the medium is idle; if a collision is detected during transmission, it stops, and a random backoff period starts. Wireless stations cannot detect collisions while transmitting, whereas wired stations can. With CSMA/CA, the wireless station waits for a free medium and only then transmits the frame. In case of a collision, the station will not notice it, but because no acknowledgment frame should be sent for this packet, it is retransmitted after a timeout has elapsed if an acknowledgment is not received.

- Wireless traffic is sensitive to interferences. As a result, the 802.11 spec requires that every frame, except for broadcast and multicast, be acknowledged when it is received. Packets that are not acknowledged in time should be retransmitted. Note that since IEEE 802.11e, there is a mode which does not require acknowledgement—the QoSNoAck mode—but it's rarely used in practice.

The 802.11 MAC Header

Each MAC frame consists of a MAC header, a frame body of variable length, and an FCS (Frame Check Sequence) of 32 bit CRC. Figure 12-1 shows the 802.11 header.

Frame Control 2 bytes	Duration/ID 2 bytes	Address 1 6 bytes	Address 2 6 bytes	Address 3 6 bytes	Sequence Control 2 bytes	Address 4 6 bytes	QoS Control 2 bytes	HT Control 4 bytes

Figure 12-1. IEEE 802.11 header. Note that all members are not always used, as this section will shortly explain

The 802.11 header is represented in mac80211 by the `ieee80211_hdr` structure:

```
struct ieee80211_hdr {
        __le16 frame_control;
        __le16 duration_id;
        u8 addr1[6];
        u8 addr2[6];
        u8 addr3[6];
        __le16 seq_ctrl;
        u8 addr4[6];
} __packed;
```

(include/linux/ieee80211.h)

In contrast to an Ethernet header (`struct ethhdr`), which contains only three fields (source MAC address, destination MAC address, and Ethertype), the 802.11 header contains up to six addresses and some other fields. For a typical data frame, though, only three addresses are used (for example, Access Point or AP/client communication). With an ACK frame, only the receiver address is used. Note that Figure 12-1 shows only four addresses, but when working with Mesh networking, a Mesh extension header with two additional addresses is used.

I now turn to a description of the 802.11 header fields, starting with the first field in the 802.11 header, called the *frame control*. This is an important field, and in many cases its contents determine the meaning of other fields of the 802.11 MAC header (especially addresses).

The Frame Control

The frame control length is 16 bits. Figure 12-2 shows its fields and the size of each field.

Protocol Version	Type	SubType	ToDS	FromDS	More Frag	Retry	Pwr Mgmt	More Data	Protected Frame	Order
2 bits	2 bits	4 bits	1 bit	1 bit	1 bit	1 bit	1 bit	1 bit	1 bit	1 bit

Figure 12-2. Frame control fields

The following is a description of the frame control members:

- `Protocol version`: The version of the MAC 802.11 we use. Currently there is only one version of MAC, so this field is always 0.

- Type: There are three types of packets in 802.11—management, control, and data:

  - Management packets (IEEE80211_FTYPE_MGMT) are for management actions like association, authentication, scanning, and more.

  - Control packets (IEEE80211_FTYPE_CTL) usually have some relevance to data packets; for example, a PS-Poll packet is for retrieving packets from an AP buffer. Another example: a station that wants to transmit first sends a control packet named RTS (request to send); if the medium is free, the destination station will send back a control packet named CTS (clear to send).

  - Data packets (IEEE80211_FTYPE_DATA) are the raw data packets. Null packets are a special case of raw packets, carrying no data and used mostly for power management control purposes. I discuss null packets in the "Power Save Mode" section later in this chapter.

- Subtype: For all the aforementioned three types of packets (management, control, and data), there is a sub-type field which identifies the character of the packet used. For example:

    - A value of 0100 for the sub-type field in a management frame denotes that the packet is a Probe Request (IEEE80211_STYPE_PROBE_REQ) management packet, which is used in a scan operation.

    - A value of 1011 for the sub-type field in a control packet denotes that this is a request to send (IEEE80211_STYPE_RTS) control packet. A value of 0100 for the sub-type field of a data packet denotes that this is a null data (IEEE80211_STYPE_NULLFUNC) packet, which is used for power management control.

    - A value of 1000 (IEEE80211_STYPE_QOS_DATA) for the sub-type of a data packet means that this is a QoS data packet; this sub-type was added by the IEEE802.11e amendment, which dealt with QoS enhancements.

- ToDS: When this bit is set, it means the packet is for the distribution system.

- FromDS: When this bit is set, it means the packet is from the distribution system.

- More Frag: When you use fragmentation, this bit is set to 1.

- Retry: When a packet is retransmitted, this bit is set to 1. A typical case of retransmission is when a packet that was sent did not receive an acknowledgment in time. The acknowledgments are usually sent by the firmware of the wireless driver.

- Pwr Mgmt: When the power management bit is set, it means that the station will enter power save mode. I discuss power save mode in the "Power Save Mode" section later in this chapter.

- More Data: When an AP sends packets that it buffered for a sleeping station, it sets the More Data bit to 1 when the buffer is not empty. Thus the station knows that there are more packets it should retrieve. When the buffer has been emptied, this bit is set to 0.

- Protected Frame: This bit is set to 1 when the frame body is encrypted; only data frames and authentication frames can be encrypted.

- Order: With the MAC service called strict ordering, the order of frames is important. When this service is in use, the order bit is set to 1. It is rarely used.

■ **Note**   The action frame (IEEE80211_STYPE_ACTION) was introduced with the 802.11h amendment, which dealt with spectrum and transmit power management. However, because of a lack of space for management packets sub-types, action frames are used also in various newer amendments to the standard—for example, HT action frames in 802.11n.

The Other 802.11 MAC Header Members

The following describes the other members of the mac802.11 header, after the frame control:

- Duration/ID: The duration holds values for the Network Allocation Vector (NAV) in microseconds, and it consists of 15 bits of the Duration/ID field. The sixteenth field is 0. When working in power save mode, it is the AID (association id) of a station for PS-Poll frames (see 8.2.4.2 (a) in IEEE 802.11-2012). The Network Allocation Vector (NAV) is a virtual carrier sensing mechanism. I do not delve into NAV internals because that is beyond the scope of this chapter.

- Sequence Control: This is a 2-byte field specifying the sequence control. In 802.11, it is possible that a packet will be received more than once, most commonly when an acknowledgment is not received for some reason. The sequence control field consists of a fragment number (4 bits) and a sequence number (12 bits). The sequence number is generated by the transmitting station, in the ieee80211_tx_h_sequence() method. In the case of a duplicate frame in a retransmission, it is dropped, and a counter of the dropped duplicate frames (dot11FrameDuplicateCount) is incremented by 1; this is done in the ieee80211_rx_h_check() method. The Sequence Control field is not present in control packets.

- Address1 - Address4: There are four addresses, but you don't always use all of them. Address 1 is the Receive Address (RA), and is used in all packets. Address 2 is the Transmit Address (TA), and it exists in all packets except ACK and CTS packets. Address 3 is used only for management and data packets. Address 4 is used when ToDS and FromDS bits of the frame control are set; this happens when operating in a Wireless Distribution System.

- QoS Control: The QoS control field was added by the 802.11e amendment and is only present in QoS data packets. Because it is not part of the original 802.11 spec, it is not part of the original mac80211 implementation, so it is not a member of the IEEE802.11 header (ieee80211_hdr struct). In fact, it was added at the end of the IEEE802.11 header and can be accessed by the ieee80211_get_qos_ctl() method. The QoS control field includes the tid (Traffic Identification), the ACK Policy, and a field called A-MSDU present, which tells whether an A-MSDU is present. I discuss A-MSDU later in this chapter, in the "High Throughput (ieee802.11n)" section.

- HT Control Field: HT (high throughput) control field was added by the 802.11n amendment (see 7.1.3.5(a) of the 802.11n-2009 spec).

This section covered the 802.11 MAC header, with a description of its members and their use. Becoming familiar with the 802.11 MAC header is essential for understanding the mac802.11 stack.

Network Topologies

There are two popular network topologies in 802.11 wireless networks. The first topology I discuss is *Infrastructure BSS* mode, which is the most popular. You encounter Infrastructure BSS wireless networks in home wireless networks and offices. Later I discuss the IBSS (Ad Hoc) mode. Note that IBSS is *not* Infrastructure BSS; IBSS is *Independent BSS*, which is an ad hoc network, discussed later in this section.

Infrastructure BSS

When working in Infrastructure BSS mode, there is a central device, called an Access Point (AP), and some client stations. Together they form a BSS (Basic Service Set). These client stations must first perform association and authentication against the AP to be able to transmit packets via the AP. On many occasions, client stations perform scanning prior to authentication and association, in order to get details about the AP. Association is exclusive: a client can be associated with only one AP in a given moment. When a client associates with an AP successfully, it gets an AID (association id), which is a unique number (to this BSS) in the range 1–2007. An AP is in fact a wireless network device with some hardware additions (like Ethernet ports, LEDs, a button to reset to manufacturer defaults, and more). A management daemon runs on the AP device. An example of such software is the hostapd daemon. This software handles some of the management tasks of the MLME layer, such as authentication and association requests. It achieves this by registering itself to receive the relevant management frames via nl80211. The hostapd project is an open source project which enables several wireless network devices to operate as an AP.

Clients can communicate with other clients (or to stations in a different network which is bridged to the AP) by sending packets to the AP, which are relayed by the AP to their final destination. To cover a large area, you can deploy multiple APs and connect them by wire. This type of deployment is called Extended Service Set (ESS). Within ESS deployment, there are two or more BSSs. Multicasts and broadcasts sent in one BSS, which may arrive on a nearby BSS, are rejected in the nearby BSS stations (the bssid in the 802.11 header does not match). Within such a deployment, each AP usually uses a different channel to minimize interference.

IBSS, or Ad Hoc Mode

IBSS network is often formed without preplanning, for only as long as the WLAN is needed. An IBSS network is also called ad hoc network. Creating an IBSS is a simple procedure. You can set an IBSS by running from a command line this iw command (note that the 2412 parameter is for using channel 1):

```
iw wlan0 ibss join AdHocNetworkName 2412
```

Or when using the iwconfig tool, with these two commands:

```
iwconfig wlan0 mode ad-hoc
iwconfig wlan0 essid AdHocNetworkrName
```

This triggers IBSS creation by calling the ieee80211_sta_create_ibss() method (net/mac80211/ibss.c). Then the ssid (AdHocNetworkName in this case) has to be distributed manually (or otherwise) to everyone who wants to connect to the ad hoc network. When working with IBSS, you do not have an AP. The bssid of the IBSS is a random 48-bit address (based on calling the get_random_bytes() method). Power management in Ad Hoc mode is a bit more complex than power management in Infrastructure BSS; it uses Announcement Traffic Indication Map (ATIM) messages. ATIM is not supported by mac802.11 and is not discussed in this chapter.

The next section describes power save mode, which is one of the most important mechanisms of the mac80211 network stack.

Power Save Mode

Apart from relaying packets, there is another important function for the AP: buffering packets for client stations that enter power save mode. Clients are usually battery-powered devices. From time to time, the wireless network interface enters power save mode.

Entering Power Save Mode

When a client station enters power save mode, it informs the AP about it by sending usually a null data packet. In fact, technically speaking, it does not have to be a null data packet; it is enough that it is a packet with PM=1 (PM is the Power Management flag in the frame control). An AP that gets such a null packet starts keeping unicast packets which are destined to that station in a special buffer called ps_tx_buf; there is such a buffer for every station. This buffer is in fact a linked list of packets, and it can hold up to 128 packets (STA_MAX_TX_BUFFER) for each station. If the buffer is filled, it will start discarding the packets that were received first (FIFO). Apart from this, there is a single buffer called bc_buf, for multicast and broadcast packets (in the 802.11 stack, multicast packets should be received and processed by all the stations in the same BSS). The bc_buf buffer can also hold up to 128 packets (AP_MAX_BC_BUFFER). When a wireless network interface is in power save mode, it cannot receive or send packets.

Exiting Power Save Mode

From time to time, an associated station is awakened by itself (by some timer); it then checks for special management packets, called *beacons*, which the AP sends periodically. Typically, an AP sends 10 beacons in a second; on most APs, this is a configurable parameter. These beacons contain data in *information elements*, which constitute the data in the management packet. The station that awoke checks a specific information element called TIM (Traffic Indication Map), by calling the ieee80211_check_tim() method (include/linux/ieee80211.h). The TIM is an array of 2008 entries. Because the TIM size is 251 bytes (2008 bits), you are allowed to send a partial virtual bitmap, which is smaller in size. If the entry in the TIM for that station is set, it means that the AP saved unicast packets for this station, so that station should empty the buffer of packets that the AP kept for it. The station starts sending null packets (or, more rarely, special control packets, called PS-Poll packets) to retrieve these buffered packets from the AP. Usually after the buffer has been emptied, the station goes to sleep (however, this is not mandatory according to the spec).

Handling the Multicast/Broadcast Buffer

The AP buffers multicast and broadcast packets whenever at least one station is in sleeping mode. The AID for multicast/broadcast stations is 0; so, in such a case, you set TIM[0] to true. The Delivery Team (DTIM), which is a special type of TIM, is sent not in every beacon, but once for a predefined number of beacon intervals (the DTIM period). After a DTIM is sent, the AP sends its buffered broadcast and multicast packets. You retrieve packets from the multicast/broadcast buffer (bc_buf) by calling the ieee80211_get_buffered_bc() method. In Figure 12-3 you can see an AP that contains a linked list of stations (sta_info objects), each of them with a unicast buffer (ps_tx_buf) of its own, and a single bc_buf buffer, for storing multicast and broadcast packets.

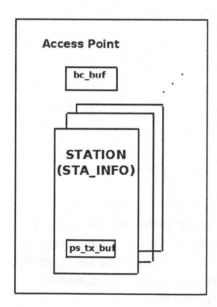

Figure 12-3. Buffering packets in an AP

The AP is implemented as an ieee80211_if_ap object in mac80211. Each such ieee80211_if_ap object has a member called ps (an instance of ps_data), where power save data is stored. One of the members of the ps_data structure is the broadcast/multicast buffer, bc_buf.

In Figure 12-4 you can see a flow of PS-Poll packets that a client sends in order to retrieve packets from the AP unicast buffer, ps_tx_buf. Note that the AP sends all the packets with the IEEE80211_FCTL_MOREDATA flag, except for the last one. Thus, the client knows that it should keep on sending PS-Poll packets until the buffer is emptied. For the sake of simplicity, the ACK traffic in this diagram is not included, but it should be mentioned here that the packets should be acknowledged.

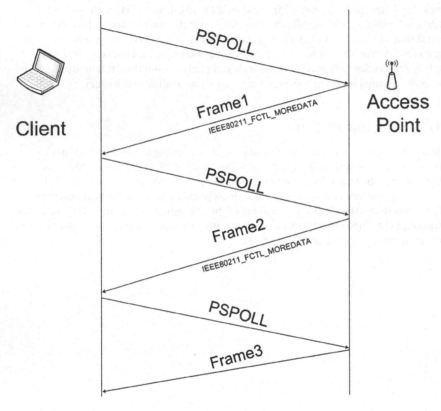

Figure 12-4. *Sending PSPOLL packets from a client to retrieve packets from the* ps_tx_buf *buffer within an AP*

■ **Note** *Power management* and *power save mode* are two different topics. Power management deals with handling machines that perform suspend (whether it is suspend to RAM or suspend to disk, aka hibernate, or in some cases, both suspend to RAM and suspend to disk, aka hybrid suspend), and is handled in net/mac80211/pm.c. In the drivers, power management is handled by the resume/suspend methods. Power save mode, on the other hand, deals with handling stations that enter sleep mode and wake up; it has nothing to do with suspend and hibernation.

This section described power save mode and the buffering mechanism. The next section discusses the management layer and the different tasks it handles.

The Management Layer (MLME)

There are three components in the 802.11 management architecture:

- The Physical Layer Management Entity (PLME).

- The System Management Entity (SME).

- The MAC Layer Management Entity (MLME).

Scanning

There are two types of scanning: passive scanning and active scanning. Passive scanning means to listen passively for beacons, without transmitting any packets for scanning. When performing passive scanning (the flags of the scan channel contain IEEE80211_CHAN_PASSIVE_SCAN), the station moves from channel to channel, trying to receive beacons. Passive scanning is needed in some higher 802.11a frequency bands, because you're not allowed to transmit anything at all until you've heard an AP beacon. With active scanning, each station sends a Probe Request packet; this is a management packet, with sub-type Probe Request (IEEE80211_STYPE_PROBE_REQ). Also with active scanning, the station moves from channel to channel, sending a Probe Request management packet on each channel (by calling the ieee80211_send_probe_req() method). This is done by calling the ieee80211_request_scan() method. Changing channels is done via a call to the ieee80211_hw_config() method, passing IEEE80211_CONF_CHANGE_CHANNEL as a parameter. Note that there is a one-to-one correspondence between a channel in which a station operates and the frequency in which it operates; the ieee80211_channel_to_frequency() method (net/wireless/util.c) returns the frequency in which a station operates, given its channel.

Authentication

Authentication is done by calling the ieee80211_send_auth() method (net/mac80211/util.c). It sends a management frame with authentication sub-type (IEEE80211_STYPE_AUTH). There are many authentications types; the original IEEE802.11 spec talked about only two forms: open-system authentication and shared key authentication. The only mandatory authentication method required by the IEEE802.11 spec is the open-system authentication (WLAN_AUTH_OPEN). This is a very simple authentication algorithm—in fact, it is a null authentication algorithm. Any client that requests authentication with this algorithm will become authenticated. An example of another option for an authentication algorithm is the shared key authentication (WLAN_AUTH_SHARED_KEY). In shared key authentication, the station should authenticate using a Wired Equivalent Privacy (WEP) key.

Association

In order to associate, a station sends a management frame with association sub-type (IEEE80211_STYPE_ASSOC_REQ). Association is done by calling the ieee80211_send_assoc() method (net/mac80211/mlme.c).

Reassociation

When a station moves between APs within an ESS, it is said to be *roaming*. The roaming station sends a reassociation request to a new AP by sending a management frame with reassociation sub-type (IEEE80211_STYPE_REASSOC_REQ). Reassociation is done by calling the ieee80211_send_assoc() method; there are many similarities between association and reassociation, so this method handles both. In addition, with reassociation, the AP returns an AID (association id) to the client in case of success.

This section talked about the management layer (MLME) and some of the operations it supports, like scanning, authentication, association, and more. In the next section I describe some mac80211 implementation details that are important in order to understand the wireless stack.

Mac80211 Implementation

Mac80211 has an API for interfacing with the low level device drivers. The implementation of mac80211 is complex and full of many small details. I cannot give an exhaustive description of the mac80211 API and implementation; I do discuss some important points that can give a good starting point to those who want to delve into the code. A fundamental structure of mac80211 API is the ieee80211_hw struct (include/net/mac80211.h); it represents hardware information. The priv (pointer to a private area) pointer of ieee80211_hw is of an opaque type (void *). Most wireless device drivers define a private structure for this private area, like lbtf_private (Marvell wireless driver) or iwl_priv (iwlwifi from Intel). Memory allocation and initialziation for the ieee80211_hw struct is done by the ieee80211_alloc_hw() method. Here are some methods related to the ieee80211_hw struct:

- int ieee80211_register_hw(struct ieee80211_hw *hw): Called by wireless drivers for registering the specified ieee80211_hw object.

- void ieee80211_unregister_hw(struct ieee80211_hw *hw): Unregisters the specified 802.11 hardware device.

- struct ieee80211_hw *ieee80211_alloc_hw(size_t priv_data_len, const struct ieee80211_ops *ops): Allocates an ieee80211_hw object and initializes it.

- ieee80211_rx_irqsafe(): This method is for receiving a packet. It is implemented in net/mac80211/rx.c and called from low level wireless drivers.

The ieee80211_ops object, which is passed to the ieee80211_alloc_hw() method as you saw earlier, consists of pointers to callbacks to the driver. Not all of these callbacks must be implemented by the drivers. The following is a short description of these methods:

- tx(): The transmit handler called for each transmitted packet. It usually returns NETDEV_TX_OK (except for under certain limited conditions).

- start(): Activates the hardware device and is called before the first hardware device is enabled. It turns on frame reception.

- stop(): Turns off frame reception and usually turns off the hardware.

- add_interface(): Called when a network device attached to the hardware is enabled.

- remove_interface(): Informs a driver that the interface is going down.

- config(): Handles configuration requests, such as hardware channel configuration.

- configure_filter(): Configures the device's Rx filter.

Figure 12-5 shows a block diagram of the architecture of the Linux wireless subsystem. You can see that the interface between wireless device drivers layer and the mac80211 layer is the ieee80211_ops object and its callbacks.

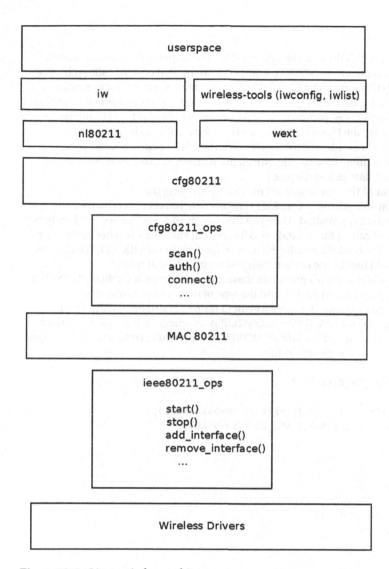

Figure 12-5. *Linux wireless architecture*

Another important structure is the sta_info struct (net/mac80211/sta_info.h), which represents a station. Among the members of this structure are various statistics counters, various flags, debugfs entries, the ps_tx_buf array for buffering unicast packets, and more. Stations are organized in a hash table (sta_hash) and a list (sta_list). The important methods related to sta_info are as follows:

- int sta_info_insert(struct sta_info *sta): Adds a station.

- int sta_info_destroy_addr(struct ieee80211_sub_if_data *sdata, const u8 *addr): Removes a station (by calling the __sta_info_destroy() method).

- struct sta_info *sta_info_get(struct ieee80211_sub_if_data *sdata, const u8 *addr): Fetches a station; the address of the station (it's bssid) is passed as a parameter.

Rx Path

The ieee80211_rx() function (net/mac80211/rx.c) is the main receive handler. The status of the received packet (ieee80211_rx_status) is passed by the wireless driver to mac80211, embedded in the SKB control buffer (cb). The IEEE80211_SKB_RXCB() macro is used to fetch this status. The flag field of the Rx status specifies, for example, whether the FCS check failed on the packet (RX_FLAG_FAILED_FCS_CRC). The various values possible for the flag field are presented in Table 12-1 in the "Quick Reference" section of this chapter. In the ieee80211_rx() method, the ieee80211_rx_monitor() is invoked to remove the FCS (checksum) and remove a radiotap header (struct ieee80211_radiotap_header) which might have been added if the wireless interface is in monitor mode. (You use a network interface in monitor mode in case of sniffing, for example. Not all the wireless network interfaces support monitor mode, see the section "Wireless Modes" later in this chapter.)

If you work with HT (802.11n), you perform AMPDU reordering if needed by invoking the ieee80211_rx_reorder_ampdu() method. Then you call the __ieee80211_rx_handle_packet() method, which eventually calls the ieee80211_invoke_rx_handlers() method. Then you call, one by one, various receive handlers (using a macro named CALL_RXH). The order of calling these handlers is important. Each handler checks whether it should handle the packet or not. If it decides it should not handle the packet, then you return RX_CONTINUE and proceed to the next handler. If it decides it should handle the packet, then you return RX_QUEUED.

There are certain cases when a handler decides to drop a packet; in these cases, it returns RX_DROP_MONITOR or RX_DROP_UNUSABLE. For example, if you get a PS-Poll packet, and the type of the receiver shows that it is not an AP, you return RX_DROP_UNUSABLE. Another example: for a management frame, if the length of the SKB is less than the minimum (24), the packet is discarded and RX_DROP_MONITOR is returned. Or if the packet is not a management packet, then also the packet is discarded and RX_DROP_MONITOR is returned. Here is the code snippet from the ieee80211_rx_h_mgmt_check() method that implements this:

```
ieee80211_rx_h_mgmt_check(struct ieee80211_rx_data *rx)
{
        struct ieee80211_mgmt *mgmt = (struct ieee80211_mgmt *) rx->skb->data;
        struct ieee80211_rx_status *status = IEEE80211_SKB_RXCB(rx->skb);

        . . .
        if (rx->skb->len < 24)
                return RX_DROP_MONITOR;

        if (!ieee80211_is_mgmt(mgmt->frame_control))
                return RX_DROP_MONITOR;
                . . .
}
```

(net/mac80211/rx.c)

Tx Path

The ieee80211_tx() method is the main handler for transmission (net/mac80211/tx.c). First it invokes the __ieee80211_tx_prepare() method, which performs some checks and sets certain flags. Then it calls the invoke_tx_handlers() method, which calls, one by one, various transmit handlers (using a macro named CALL_TXH). If a transmit handler finds that it should do nothing with the packet, it returns TX_CONTINUE and you proceed to the next handler. If it decides it should handle a certain packet, it returns TX_QUEUED, and if it decides it should drop the packet, it returns TX_DROP. The invoke_tx_handlers() method returns 0 upon success. Let's take a short look in the implementation of the ieee80211_tx() method:

```
static bool ieee80211_tx(struct ieee80211_sub_if_data *sdata,
                         struct sk_buff *skb, bool txpending,
                         enum ieee80211_band band)
{
        struct ieee80211_local *local = sdata->local;
        struct ieee80211_tx_data tx;
        ieee80211_tx_result res_prepare;
        struct ieee80211_tx_info *info = IEEE80211_SKB_CB(skb);
        bool result = true;
        int led_len;
```

Perform a sanity check, drop the SKB if its length is less than 10:

```
if (unlikely(skb->len < 10)) {
        dev_kfree_skb(skb);
        return true;
}

/* initialises tx */
led_len = skb->len;

res_prepare = ieee80211_tx_prepare(sdata, &tx, skb);

if (unlikely(res_prepare == TX_DROP)) {
        ieee80211_free_txskb(&local->hw, skb);
        return true;
} else if (unlikely(res_prepare == TX_QUEUED)) {
        return true;
}
```

Invoke the Tx handlers; if everything is fine, continue with invoking the __ieee80211_tx() method:

```
        . . .
        if (!invoke_tx_handlers(&tx))
                result = __ieee80211_tx(local, &tx.skbs, led_len,
                                        tx.sta, txpending);

        return result;
}
```

(net/mac80211/tx.c)

Fragmentation

Fragmentation in 802.11 is done only for unicast packets. Each station is assigned a fragmentation threshold size (in bytes). Packets that are bigger than this threshold should be fragmented. You can lower the number of collisions by reducing the fragmentation threshold size, making the packets smaller. You can inspect the fragmentation threshold of a station by running iwconfig or by inspecting the corresponding debugfs entry (see the "Mac80211 debugfs" section later in this chapter). You can set the fragmentation threshold with the iwconfig command; thus, for example, you can set the fragmentation threshold to 512 bytes by:

```
iwconfig wlan0 frag 512
```

Each fragment is acknowledged. The more fragment field in the fragment header is set to 1 if there are more fragments. Each fragment has a fragment number (a subfield in the sequence control field of the frame control). Reassembling of the fragments on the receiver is done according to the fragments numbers. Fragmentation in the transmitter side is done by the ieee80211_tx_h_fragment() method (net/mac80211/tx.c). Reassembly on the receiver side is done by the ieee80211_rx_h_defragment() method (net/mac80211/rx.c). Fragmentation is incompatible with aggregation (used for higher throughput), and given the high rates and thus short (in time) packets it is very rarely used nowadays.

Mac80211 debugfs

debugfs is a technique that enables exporting debugging information to userspace. It creates entries under the sysfs filesystem. debugfs is a virtual filesystem devoted to debugging information. For mac80211, handling mac80211 debugfs is mostly in net/mac80211/debugfs.c. After mounting debugfs, various mac802.11 statistics and information entries can be inspected. Mounting debugfs is performed like this:

```
mount -t debugfs none_debugs /sys/kernel/debug
```

■ **Note** CONFIG_DEBUG_FS must be set when building the kernel to be able to mount and work with debugfs.

For example, let's say your phy is phy0; the following is a discussion about some of the entries under /sys/kernel/debug/ieee80211/phy0:

- total_ps_buffered: This is the total number of packets (unicast and multicasts/broadcasts) which the AP buffered for the station. The total_ps_buffered counter is incremented by ieee80211_tx_h_unicast_ps_buf() for unicasts, and by ieee80211_tx_h_multicast_ps_buf() for multicasts or broadcasts.

- Under /sys/kernel/debug/ieee80211/phy0/statistics, you have various statistical information—for example:

  - frame_duplicate_count denotes the number of duplicate frames. This debugfs entry represents the duplicate frames counter, dot11FrameDuplicateCount, which is incremented by the ieee80211_rx_h_check() method.

  - transmitted_frame_count denotes the number of transmitted packets. This debugfs entry represents dot11TransmittedFrameCount; it is incremented by the ieee80211_tx_status() method.

  - retry_count denotes number of retransmissions. This debugfs entry represents dot11RetryCount; it is incremented also by the ieee80211_tx_status() method.

  - fragmentation_threshold: The size of the fragmentation threshold, in bytes. See the "Fragmentation" section earlier.

- Under /sys/kernel/debug/ieee80211/phy0/netdev:wlan0, you have some entries that give information about the interface; for example, if the interface is in station mode, you will have aid for the association id of the station, assoc_tries for the number of times the stations tried to perform association, bssid is for the bssid of the station, and so on.

- Every station uses a rate control algorithm. Its name is exported by the following debugfs entry: /sys/kernel/debug/ieee80211/phy1/rc/name.

Wireless Modes

You can set a wireless network interface to operate in several modes, depending on its intended use and the topology of the network in which it is deployed. In some cases, you can set the mode with the iwconfig command, and in some cases you must use a tool like hostapd for this. Note that not all devices support all modes. See www.linuxwireless.org/en/users/Drivers for a list of Linux drivers that support different modes. Alternatively, you can also check to which values the interface_modes field of the wiphy member (in the ieee80211_hw object) is initialized in the driver code. The interface_modes are initialized to one or more modes of the nl80211_iftype enum, like NL80211_IFTYPE_STATION or NL80211_IFTYPE_ADHOC (see: include/uapi/linux/nl80211.h). The following is a detailed description of these wireless modes:

- *AP mode:* In this mode, the device acts as an AP (NL80211_IFTYPE_AP). The AP maintains and manages a list of associated stations. The network (BSS) name is the MAC address of the AP (bssid). There is also a human-readable name for the BSS, called the SSID.

- *Station infrastructure mode:* A managed station in an infrastructure mode (NL80211_IFTYPE_STATION).

- *Monitor mode:* All incoming packets are handed unfiltered in monitor mode (NL80211_IFTYPE_MONITOR). This is useful for sniffing. It is usually possible to transmit packets in monitor mode. This is termed *packet injection*; these packets are marked with a special flag (IEEE80211_TX_CTL_INJECTED).

- *Ad Hoc (IBSS) mode:* A station in an ad hoc (IBSS) network (NL80211_IFTYPE_ADHOC). With Ad Hoc mode, there is no AP device in the network.

- *Wireless Distribution System (WDS) mode:* A station in a WDS network (NL80211_IFTYPE_WDS).

- *Mesh mode:* A station in a Mesh network (NL80211_IFTYPE_MESH_POINT), discussed in the "Mesh Networking (802.11s)" section later in this chapter.

The next section discusses the ieee802.11n technology, which provides higher performance, and how it is implemented in the Linux wireless stack. You will learn also about block acknowledgment and packet aggregation in 802.11n and how these techniques are used to improve performance.

High Throughput (ieee802.11n)

A little after 802.11g was approved, a new task group was created in IEEE, called High Throughput Task Group (TGn). IEEE 802.11n became a final spec at the end of 2009. The IEEE 802.11n protocol allows coexistence with legacy devices. There were some vendors who already sold 802.11n pre-standard devices based on the 802.11n draft before the official approval. Broadcom set a precedent for releasing wireless interfaces based on a draft. In 2003, it released a chipset of a wireless device based on a draft of 802.11g. Following this precedent, as early as 2005 some vendors released products based on the 802.11n draft. For example, Intel Santa Rose processor has Intel Next-Gen Wireless-N (Intel WiFi Link 5000 series), supports 802.11n. Other Intel wireless network interfaces, like 4965AGN, also supported 802.11n. Other vendors, including Atheros and Ralink, also released 802.11n draft-based wireless devices. The WiFi alliance started certification of 802.11n draft devices in June 2007. A long list of vendors released products which comply with Wi-Fi CERTIFIED 802.11n draft 2.0.

802.11n can operate on the 2.4 GHz and/or 5 GHz bands, whereas 802.11g and 802.11b operate only in the 2.4 GHz radio frequency band, and 802.11a operates only in the 5 GHz radio frequency band. The 802.11n MIMO (Multiple Input, Multiple Output) technology increases the range and reliability of traffic over the wireless coverage area. MIMO technology uses multiple transmitter and receiver antennas on both APs and clients, to allow for simultaneous data streams. The result is increased range and increased throughput. With 802.11n you can achieve a theoretical PHY rate of up to 600 Mbps (actual throughput will be much lower due to medium access rules, and so on).

802.11n added many improvements for the 802.11 MAC layer. The most well known is packet aggregation, which concatenates multiple packets of application data into a single transmission frame. A block acknowledgment (BA) mechanism was added (discussed in the next section). BA permits multiple packets to be acknowledged by a single packet instead of sending an ACK for each received packet. The wait time between two consecutive packets is cut. This enables sending multiple data packets with a fixed overhead cost of a single packet. The BA protocol was introduced in the 802.11e amendment from 2005.

Packet Aggregation

There are two types of packet aggregation:

- *AMSDU*: Aggregated Mac Service Data Unit

- *AMPDU*: Aggregated Mac Protocol Data Unit

Note that the AMSDU is only supported on Rx, and not on Tx, and is wholly independent from the Block Ack mechanism described in this section; so the discussion in this section only pertains to AMPDU.

There are two sides to a Block Ack session: *originator* and *recipient*. Each block session has a different Traffic Identifier (TID). The originator starts the block acknowledgement session by calling the ieee80211_start_tx_ba_session() method. This is done typically from a rate control algorithm method in the driver. For example, with the ath9k wireless driver, the ath_tx_status() function (drivers/net/wireless/ath/ath9k/rc.c), which is a rate control callback, invokes the ieee80211_start_tx_ba_session() method. The ieee80211_start_tx_ba_session() method sets the state to HT_ADDBA_REQUESTED_MSK and sends an ADDBA request packet, by invoking the ieee80211_send_addba_request() method. The call to ieee80211_send_addba_request() passes parameters for the session, such as the wanted reorder buffer size and the TID of the session.

The reorder buffer size is limited to 64K (see the definition of ieee80211_max_ampdu_length_exp in include/linux/ieee80211.h). These parameters are part of the capability member (capab) in the struct addba_req. The response to the ADDBA request should be received within 1 Hz, which is one second in x86_64 machines (ADDBA_RESP_INTERVAL). If you do not get a response in time, the sta_addba_resp_timer_expired() method will stop the BA session by calling the ___ieee80211_stop_tx_ba_session() method. When the other side (the recipient) receives the ADDBA request, it first sends an ACK (every packet in ieee802.11 should be acknowledged, as mentioned before). Then it processes the ADDBA request by calling the ieee80211_process_addba_request() method; if everything is okay, it sets the aggregation state of this machine to operational (HT_AGG_STATE_OPERATIONAL) and sends an ADDBA response by calling the ieee80211_send_addba_resp() method. It also stops the response timer (the timer which has as its callback the sta_addba_resp_timer_expired() method) by calling del_timer_sync() on this timer. After a session is started, a data block containing multiple MPDU packets is sent. Consequently, the originator sends a Block Ack Request (BAR) packet by calling the ieee80211_send_bar() method.

Block Ack Request (BAR)

The BAR is a control packet with Block Ack Request sub-type (IEEE80211_STYPE_BACK_REQ). The BAR packet includes the SSN (start sequence number), which is the sequence number of the oldest MSDU in the block that should be acknowledged. The recipient receives the BAR and reorders the ampdu buffer accordingly, if needed. Figure 12-6 shows a BAR request.

Frame Control	Duration	RA	TA	Control	Start Sequence Number
2 bytes	2 bytes	6 bytes	6 bytes	2 bytes	2 bytes

Figure 12-6. *BAR request*

When sending a BAR, the type subfield in the frame control is control (IEEE80211_FTYPE_CTL), and the subtype subfield is Block Ack request (IEEE80211_STYPE_BACK_REQ). The BAR is represented by the ieee80211_bar struct:

```
struct ieee80211_bar {
        __le16 frame_control;
        __le16 duration;
        __u8 ra[6];
        __u8 ta[6];
        __le16 control;
        __le16 start_seq_num;
} __packed;
```

(include/linux/ieee80211.h)

The RA is the recipient address, and the TA is the transmitter (originator) address. The control field of the BAR request includes the TID.

Block Ack

There are two types of Block Ack: Immediate Block Ack and Delayed Block Ack. Figure 12-7 shows Immediate Block Ack.

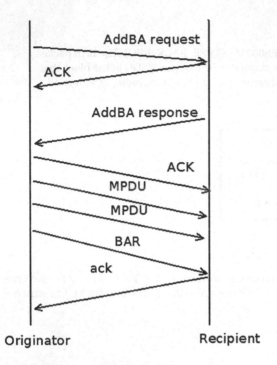

Figure 12-7. *Immediate Block Ack*

The difference between Immediate Block Ack and Delayed Block Ack is that with Delayed Block Ack, the BAR request itself is answered first with an ACK, and then after some delay, with a BA (Block Ack). When using Delayed Block Ack, there is more time to process the BAR, and this is sometime needed when working with software based processing. Using Immediate Block Ack is better in terms of performance. The BA itself is also acknowledged. When the originator has no more data to send, it can terminate the Block Ack session by calling the ieee80211_send_delba() method; this function sends a DELBA request packet to the other side. The DELBA request is handled by the ieee80211_process_delba() method. The DELBA message, which causes a Block Ack session tear down, can be sent either from the originator or recipient of the Block Ack session. The AMPDU maximum length is 65535 octets. Note that packet aggregation is only implemented for APs and managed stations; packet aggregation for IBSS is not supported by the spec.

Mesh Networking (802.11s)

The IEEE 802.11s protocol started as a Study Group of IEEE in September 2003, and became a Task Group named TGs in 2004. In 2006, 2 proposals, out of 15 (the "SEEMesh" and "Wi-Mesh" proposals) were merged into one, which resulted in draft D0.01. 802.11s was ratified in July 2011 and is now part of IEEE 802.11-2012. Mesh networks allow the creation of an 802.11 Basic Service Set over fully and partially connected Mesh topology. This can be seen as an improvement over 802.11 ad hoc network, which requires a fully-connected Mesh topology. Figures 12-8 and 12-9 illustrate the difference between the two types of Mesh topologies.

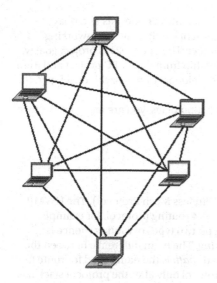

Figure 12-8. *Full Mesh*

In a partially-connected Mesh, nodes are connected to only some of the other nodes, but not to all of them. This topology is much more common in wireless Mesh networks. Figure 12-9 shows an example of a partial mesh.

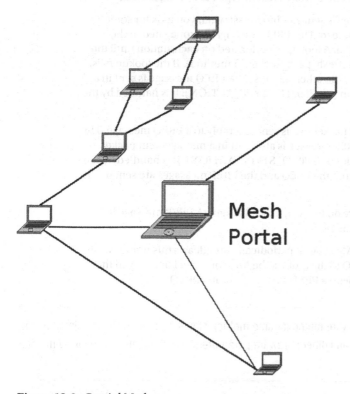

Mesh
Portal

Figure 12-9. *Partial Mesh*

Wireless mesh networks forward data packets over multiple wireless hops. Each mesh node acts as a relay point/router for the other mesh nodes. In kernel 2.6.26 (2008), support for the draft of wireless mesh networking (802.11s) was added to the network wireless stack, thanks to the open80211s project. The open80211s project goal was to create the first open implementation of 802.11s. The project got some sponsorship from the OLPC project and from some commercial companies. Luis Carlos Cobo and Javier Cardona and other developers from Cozybit developed the Linux mac80211 Mesh code.

Now that you have learned a bit about Mesh networking and Mesh network topologies, you are ready for the next section, which covers the HWMP routing protocol for Mesh networks.

HWMP Protocol

The 802.11s protocol defines a default routing protocol called HWMP (Hybrid Wireless Mesh Protocol). The HWMP protocol works with Layer 2 and deals with MAC addresses, as opposed to the IPV4 routing protocol, for example, which works with Layer 3 and deals with IP addresses. HWMP routing is based on two types of routing (hence it is called *hybrid*). The first is *on-demand* routing, and the second is *proactive routing*. The main difference between the two mechanisms has to do with the time in which path establishment is initiated (*path* is the name used for route in Layer 2). In on-demand routing, a path to a destination is established by the protocol only after the protocol stack has received frames for such a destination. This minimizes the amount of management traffic required to maintain the Mesh network at the expense of introducing additional latency in data traffic. Proactive routing can be used if a Mesh node is known to be the recipient of a lot of mesh traffic. In that case, the node will periodically announce itself over the Mesh network and trigger path establishments to itself from all the Mesh nodes in the network. Both on-demand and proactive routing are implemented in the Linux kernel. There are four types of routing messages:

- *PREQ (Path Request):* This type of message is sent as a broadcast when you look for some destination that you still do not have a route to. This PREQ message is propagated in the Mesh network until it gets to its destination. A lookup is performed on each station until the final destination is reached (by calling the mesh_path_lookup() method). If the lookup fails, the PREQ is forwarded (as a broadcast) to the other stations. The PREQ message is sent in a management packet; its sub-type is action (IEEE80211_STYPE_ACTION). It is handled by the hwmp_preq_frame_process() method.

- *PREP (Path Reply):* This type is a unicast packet that is sent as a reply to a PREQ message. This packet is sent in the reverse path. The PREP message is also sent in a management packet and its subtype is also the action sub-type (IEEE80211_STYPE_ACTION). It is handled by the hwmp_prep_frame_process() method. Both the PREQ and the PREP messages are sent by the mesh_path_sel_frame_tx() method.

- *PERR (Path Error):* If there is some failure on the way, a PERR is sent. A PERR message is handled by the mesh_path_error_tx() method.

- *RANN (Root Announcement):* The Root Mesh point periodically broadcasts this frame. Mesh points that receive it send a unicast RREQ to the root via the MP from which it received the RANN. In response, the Root Mesh will send a PREP response to each PREQ.

■ **Note** The route takes into consideration a radio-aware metric (airtime metric). The airtime metric is calculated by the airtime_link_metric_get() method (based on rate and other hardware parameters). Mesh points continuously monitor their links and update metric values with neighbours.

The station that sent the PREQ may try to send packets to the final destination while still not knowing the route to that destination; these packets are kept in a buffer of SKBs named frame_queue, which is a member of the mesh_path object (net/mac80211/mesh.h). In such a case, when a PREP finally arrives, the pending packets of this buffer are sent to the final destination (by calling the mesh_path_tx_pending() method). The maximum number of frames buffered per destination for unresolved destinations is 10 (MESH_FRAME_QUEUE_LEN). The advantages of Mesh networking are as follows:

- Rapid deployment

- Minimal configuration, inexpensive

- Easy to deploy in hard-to-wire environments

- Connectivity while nodes are in motion

- Higher reliability: no single point of failure and the ability to heal itself

The disadvantages are as follows:

- Many broadcasts limit network performance.

- Not all wireless drivers support Mesh mode at the moment.

Setting Up a Mesh Network

There are two sets of userspace tools for managing wireless devices and networks in Linux: one is the older Wireless Tools for Linux, an open source project based on IOCTLs. Examples of command line utilities of the wireless tools are iwconfig, iwlist, ifrename, and more. The newer tool is iw, based on generic netlink sockets (described in Chapter 2). However, there are some tasks that only the newer tool, iw, can perform. You can set a wireless device to work in Mesh mode only with the iw command.

Example: setting a wireless network interface (wlan0) to work in Mesh mode can be done like this:

```
iw wlan0 set type mesh
```

■ **Note** Setting a wireless network interface (wlan0) to work in mesh mode can be done also like this:

```
iw wlan0 set type mp
```

mp stands for Mesh Point. See "Adding interfaces with iw" in http://wireless.kernel.org/en/users/Documentation/iw

---

Joining the mesh is done by: iw wlan0 mesh join "my-mesh-ID"
You can display statistics about a station by the following:

- iw wlan0 station dump

- iw wlan0 mpath dump

I should mention here also the authsae and the wpa_supplicant tools, which can be used to create secure Mesh networks and do not depend upon iw.

Linux Wireless Development Process

Most development is done using the `git` distributed version control system, as with many other Linux subsystems. There are three main `git` trees; the bleeding edge is the wireless-testing tree. There are also the regular wireless tree and the wireless-next tree. The following are the links to the `git` repositories for the development trees:

- wireless-testing development tree:

  `git://git.kernel.org/pub/scm/linux/kernel/git/linville/wireless-testing.git`

- wireless development tree:

  `git://git.kernel.org/pub/scm/linux/kernel/git/linville/wireless-2.6.git`

- wireless-next development tree:

  `git://git.kernel.org/pub/scm/linux/kernel/git/linville/wireless-next-2.6.git`

Patches are sent and discussed in the wireless mailing list: `linux-wireless@vger.kernel.org`. From time to time a pull request is sent to the kernel networking mailing list, `netdev`, mentioned in Chapter 1.

As mentioned in the "Mac80211 subsystem" section, which dealt with the mac80211 subsystem, some wireless network interface vendors maintain their own development trees for their Linux drivers on their own sites. In some cases, the code they are using does not use the mac80211 API; for example, some Ralink and Realtek wireless device drivers. Since January 2006, the maintainer of the Linux wireless subsystem is John W. Linville, who replaced Jeff Garzik. The maintainer of mac80211 is Johannes Berg, from October 2007. There were some annual Linux wireless summits; the first took place in 2006 in Beaverton (OR). A very detailed wiki page is here: `http://wireless.kernel.org/`. This web site includes a lot of important documentation. For example, a table specifies the modes each wireless network interface supports. There is a lot of information in this wiki page regarding many wireless device drivers, hardware, and various tools (such as CRDA, the central regulatory domain agent, `hostapd`, `iw`, and more).

Summary

A lot of development has been done in Linux wireless stack in recent years. The most significant change is the integration of the mac80211 stack and porting wireless drivers to use the mac80211 API, making the code much more organized. The situation is much better than before; many more wireless devices are supported in Linux. Mesh networking got a boost recently thanks to the open802.11s project. It was integrated in the Linux 2.6.26 kernel. The future will probably see more drivers that support the new standard, IEEE802.11ac, a 5 GHz-only technology that can reach maximum throughputs well above a gigabit per second, and more drivers that support P2P.

Chapter 13 discusses InfiniBand and RDMA in the Linux kernel. The "Quick Reference" section covers the top methods that are related to the topics discussed in this chapter, ordered by their context.

Quick Reference

I conclude this chapter with a short list of important methods of the Linux wireless subsystem, some of which are mentioned in this chapter. Table 12-1 shows the various possible values for the `flag` member of the `ieee80211_rx_status` object.

Methods

This section discusses the methods.

void ieee80211_send_bar(struct ieee80211_vif *vif, u8 *ra, u16 tid, u16 ssn);

This method sends a block acknowledgment request.

int ieee80211_start_tx_ba_session(struct ieee80211_sta *pubsta, u16 tid, u16 timeout);

This method starts a Block Ack session by calling the wireless driver ampdu_action() callback, passing IEEE80211_AMPDU_TX_START. As a result, the driver will later call the ieee80211_start_tx_ba_cb() callback or the ieee80211_start_tx_ba_cb_irqsafe() callback, which will start the aggregation session.

int ieee80211_stop_tx_ba_session(struct ieee80211_sta *pubsta, u16 tid);

This method stops a Block Ack session by calling the wireless driver ampdu_action() function, passing IEEE80211_AMPDU_TX_STOP. The driver must later call the ieee80211_stop_tx_ba_cb() callback or the ieee80211_stop_tx_ba_cb_irqsafe() callback.

static void ieee80211_send_addba_request(struct ieee80211_sub_if_data *sdata, const u8 *da, u16 tid, u8 dialog_token, u16 start_seq_num, u16 agg_size, u16 timeout);

This method sends an ADDBA message. An ADDBA message is a management action message.

void ieee80211_process_addba_request(struct ieee80211_local *local, struct sta_info *sta, struct ieee80211_mgmt *mgmt, size_t len);

This method handles an ADDBA message.

static void ieee80211_send_addba_resp(struct ieee80211_sub_if_data *sdata, u8 *da, u16 tid, u8 dialog_token, u16 status, u16 policy, u16 buf_size, u16 timeout);

This method sends an ADDBA response. An ADDBA response is a management packet, with subtype of action (IEEE80211_STYPE_ACTION).

static ieee80211_rx_result debug_noinline ieee80211_rx_h_amsdu(struct ieee80211_rx_data *rx);

This method handles AMSDU aggregation (Rx path).

void ieee80211_process_delba(struct ieee80211_sub_if_data *sdata, struct sta_info *sta, struct ieee80211_mgmt *mgmt, size_t len);

This method handles a DELBA message.

void ieee80211_send_delba(struct ieee80211_sub_if_data *sdata, const u8 *da, u16 tid, u16 initiator, u16 reason_code);

This method sends a DELBA message.

void ieee80211_rx_irqsafe(struct ieee80211_hw *hw, struct sk_buff *skb);

This method receives a packet. The ieee80211_rx_irqsafe() method can be called in hardware interrupt context.

static void ieee80211_rx_reorder_ampdu(struct ieee80211_rx_data *rx, struct sk_buff_head *frames);

This method handles the A-MPDU reorder buffer.

static bool ieee80211_sta_manage_reorder_buf(struct ieee80211_sub_if_data *sdata, struct tid_ampdu_rx *tid_agg_rx, struct sk_buff_head *frames);

This method handles the A-MPDU reorder buffer.

static ieee80211_rx_result debug_noinline ieee80211_rx_h_check(struct ieee80211_rx_data *rx);

This method drops duplicate frames of a retransmission and increment dot11FrameDuplicateCount and the station num_duplicates counter.

void ieee80211_send_nullfunc(struct ieee80211_local *local, struct ieee80211_sub_if_data *sdata, int powersave);

This method sends a special NULL data frame.

void ieee80211_send_pspoll(struct ieee80211_local *local, struct ieee80211_sub_if_data *sdata);

This method sends a PS-Poll control packet to an AP.

static void ieee80211_send_assoc(struct ieee80211_sub_if_data *sdata);

This method performs association or reassociation by sending a management packet with association sub-type of IEEE80211_STYPE_ASSOC_REQ or IEEE80211_STYPE_REASSOC_REQ, respectively. The ieee80211_send_assoc() method is invoked from the ieee80211_do_assoc() method.

void ieee80211_send_auth(struct ieee80211_sub_if_data *sdata, u16 transaction, u16 auth_alg, u16 status, const u8 *extra, size_t extra_len, const u8 *da, const u8 *bssid, const u8 *key, u8 key_len, u8 key_idx, u32 tx_flags);

This method performs authentication by sending a management packet with authentication sub-type (IEEE80211_STYPE_AUTH).

static inline bool ieee80211_check_tim(const struct ieee80211_tim_ie *tim, u8 tim_len, u16 aid);

This method checks whether the tim[aid] is set; the aid is passed as a parameter, and it represents the association id of the station.

int ieee80211_request_scan(struct ieee80211_sub_if_data *sdata, struct cfg80211_scan_request *req);

This method starts active scanning.

void mesh_path_tx_pending(struct mesh_path *mpath);

This method send packets from the frame_queue.

struct mesh_path *mesh_path_lookup(struct ieee80211_sub_if_data *sdata, const u8 *dst);

This method performs a lookup in a Mesh path table (routing table) of a Mesh point. The second parameter to the mesh_path_lookup() method is the hardware address of the destination. It returns NULL if there is no entry in the table, otherwise it returns a pointer to the mesh path structure which was found.

static void ieee80211_sta_create_ibss(struct ieee80211_sub_if_data *sdata);

This method creates an IBSS.

int ieee80211_hw_config(struct ieee80211_local *local, u32 changed);

This method is called for various configurations by the driver; in most cases, it delegates the call to the driver config() method, if implemented. The second parameter specifies which action to take (for instance, IEEE80211_CONF_CHANGE_CHANNEL to change channel, or IEEE80211_CONF_CHANGE_PS to change the power save mode of the driver).

struct ieee80211_hw *ieee80211_alloc_hw(size_t priv_data_len, const struct ieee80211_ops *ops);

This method allocates a new 802.11 hardware device.

int ieee80211_register_hw(struct ieee80211_hw *hw);

This method registers a 802.11 hardware device.

void ieee80211_unregister_hw(struct ieee80211_hw *hw);

This method unregisters a 802.11 hardware device and frees its allocated resources.

int sta_info_insert(struct sta_info *sta);

This method adds a station to the hash table of stations and to the list of stations.

int sta_info_destroy_addr(struct ieee80211_sub_if_data *sdata, const u8 *addr);

This method removes a station and frees its resources.

struct sta_info *sta_info_get(struct ieee80211_sub_if_data *sdata, const u8 *addr);

This method returns a pointer to a station by performing a lookup in the hash table of stations.

void ieee80211_send_probe_req(struct ieee80211_sub_if_data *sdata, u8 *dst, const u8 *ssid, size_t ssid_len, const u8 *ie, size_t ie_len, u32 ratemask, bool directed, u32 tx_flags, struct ieee80211_channel *channel, bool scan);

This method sends a probe request management packet.

static inline void ieee80211_tx_skb(struct ieee80211_sub_if_data *sdata, struct sk_buff *skb);

This method transmits an SKB.

int ieee80211_channel_to_frequency(int chan, enum ieee80211_band band);

This method returns the frequency in which a station operates, given its channel. There is a one-to-one correspondence between a channel and a frequency.

static int mesh_path_sel_frame_tx(enum mpath_frame_type action, u8 flags, const u8 *orig_addr, __le32 orig_sn, u8 target_flags, const u8 *target, __le32 target_sn, const u8 *da, u8 hop_count, u8 ttl, __le32 lifetime, __le32 metric, __le32 preq_id, struct ieee80211_sub_if_data *sdata);

This method sends a PREQ or PREP management packet.

static void hwmp_preq_frame_process(struct ieee80211_sub_if_data *sdata, struct ieee80211_mgmt *mgmt, const u8 *preq_elem, u32 metric);

This method handles a PREQ message.

struct ieee80211_rx_status *IEEE80211_SKB_RXCB(struct sk_buff *skb);

This method returns the `ieee80211_rx_status` object associated with the control buffer (cb), which is associated with the specified SKB.

static bool ieee80211_tx(struct ieee80211_sub_if_data *sdata, struct sk_buff *skb, bool txpending, enum ieee80211_band band);

This method is the main handler for transmission.

Table

Table 12-1 shows the bits of the flag member (a 32-bit field) of the `ieee80211_rx_status` structure and the corresponding Linux symbol.

Table 12-1. *Rx Flags: Various Possible Values for the Flag Field of the* `ieee80211_rx_status` *Object*

Linux Symbol	Bit	Description
RX_FLAG_MMIC_ERROR	0	Michael MIC error was reported on this frame.
RX_FLAG_DECRYPTED	1	This frame was decrypted in hardware.
RX_FLAG_MMIC_STRIPPED	3	The Michael MIC is stripped off this frame, verification has been done by the hardware.
RX_FLAG_IV_STRIPPED	4	The IV/ICV are stripped from this frame.
RX_FLAG_FAILED_FCS_CRC	5	The FCS check failed on the frame.
RX_FLAG_FAILED_PLCP_CRC	6	The PCLP check failed on the frame.
RX_FLAG_MACTIME_START	7	The timestamp passed in the RX status is valid and contains the time the first symbol of the MPDU was received.

(continued)

Table 12-1. (*continued*)

Linux Symbol	Bit	Description
RX_FLAG_SHORTPRE	8	Short preamble was used for this frame.
RX_FLAG_HT	9	HT MCS was used and rate_idx is MCS index
RX_FLAG_40MHZ	10	HT40 (40 MHz) was used.
RX_FLAG_SHORT_GI	11	Short guard interval was used.
RX_FLAG_NO_SIGNAL_VAL	12	The signal strength value is not present.
RX_FLAG_HT_GF	13	This frame was received in a HT-greenfield transmission
RX_FLAG_AMPDU_DETAILS	14	A-MPDU details are known, in particular the reference number must be populated and be a distinct number for each A-MPDU.
RX_FLAG_AMPDU_REPORT_ZEROLEN	15	Driver reports 0-length subframes.
RX_FLAG_AMPDU_IS_ZEROLEN	16	This is a zero-length subframe, for monitoring purposes only.
RX_FLAG_AMPDU_LAST_KNOWN	17	Last subframe is known, should be set on all subframes of a single A-MPDU.
RX_FLAG_AMPDU_IS_LAST	18	This subframe is the last subframe of the A-MPDU.
RX_FLAG_AMPDU_DELIM_CRC_ERROR	19	A delimiter CRC error has been detected on this subframe.
RX_FLAG_AMPDU_DELIM_CRC_KNOWN	20	The delimiter CRC field is known (the CRC is stored in the ampdu_delimiter_crc field of the ieee80211_rx_status)
RX_FLAG_MACTIME_END	21	The timestamp passed in the RX status is valid and contains the time the last symbol of the MPDU (including FCS) was received.
RX_FLAG_VHT	22	VHT MCS was used and rate_index is MCS index
RX_FLAG_80MHZ	23	80 MHz was used
RX_FLAG_80P80MHZ	24	80+80 MHz was used
RX_FLAG_160MHZ	25	160 MHz was used

CHAPTER 13

■ ■ ■

InfiniBand

This chapter was written by Dotan Barak, an InfiniBand Expert. Dotan is a Senior Software Manager at Mellanox Technologies working on RDMA Technologies. Dotan has been working at Mellanox for more than 10 years in various roles, both as a developer and a manager. Additionally, Dotan maintains a blog about the RDMA technology: `http://www.rdmamojo.com`.

Chapter 12 dealt with the wireless subsystem and its implementation in Linux. In this chapter, I will discuss the InfiniBand subsystem and its implementation in Linux. Though the InfiniBand technology might be perceived as a very complex technology for those who are unfamiliar with it, the concepts behind it are surprisingly straightforward, as you will see in this chapter. I will start our discussion with Remote Direct Memory Access (RDMA), and discuss its main data structures and its API. I will give some examples illustrating how to work with RDMA, and conclude this chapter with a short discussion about using RDMA API from the kernel level and userspace.

RDMA and InfiniBand—General

Remote Direct Memory Access (RDMA) is the ability for one machine to access—that is, to read or write to—memory on a remote machine. There are several main network protocols that support RDMA: InfiniBand, RDMA over Converged Ethernet (RoCE) and internet Wide Area RDMA Protocol (iWARP), and all of them share the same API. InfiniBand is a completely new networking protocol, and its specifications can be found in the document "InfiniBand Architecture specifications," which is maintained by the InfiniBand Trade Association (IBTA). RoCE allows you to have RDMA over an Ethernet network, and its specification can be found as an Annex to the InfiniBand specifications. iWARP is a protocol that allows using RDMA over TCP/IP, and its specifications can be found in the document, "An RDMA Protocol Specification," which is being maintained by the RDMA Consortium. **Verbs** is the description of the API to use RDMA from a client code. The RDMA API implementation was introduced to the Linux kernel in version 2.6.11. At the beginning, it supported only InfiniBand, and after several kernel versions, iWARP and RoCE support were added to it as well. When describing the API, I mention only one of them, but the following text refers to all. All of the definitions to this API can be found in `include/rdma/ib_verbs.h`. Here are some notes about the API and the implementation of the RDMA stack:

- Some of the functions are inline functions, and some of them aren't. Future implementation might change this behavior.

- Most of the APIs have the prefix "ib"; however, this API supports InfiniBand, iWARP and RoCE.

- The header `ib_verbs.h` contains functions and structures to be used by:

  - The RDMA stack itself

  - Low-level drivers for RDMA devices

  - Kernel modules that use the stack as consumers

I will concentrate on functions and structures that are relevant only for kernel modules that use the stack as consumers (the third case). The following section discusses the RDMA stack organization in the kernel tree.

The RDMA Stack Organization

Almost all of the kernel RDMA stack code is under `drivers/infiniband` in the kernel tree. The following are some of its important modules (this is not an exhaustive list, as I do not cover the entire RDMA stack in this chapter):

- **CM:** Communication manager (`drivers/infiniband/core/cm.c`)

- **IPoIB:** IP over InfiniBand (`drivers/infiniband/ulp/ipoib/`)

- **iSER:** iSCSI extension for RDMA (`drivers/infiniband/ulp/iser/`)

- **RDS:** Reliable Datagram Socket (`net/rds/`)

- **SRP:** SCSI RDMA protocol (`drivers/infiniband/ulp/srp/`)

- Hardware low-level drivers of different vendors (`drivers/infiniband/hw`)

- **verbs:** Kernel verbs (`drivers/infiniband/core/verbs.c`)

- **uverbs:** User verbs (`drivers/infiniband/core/uverbs_*.c`)

- **MAD:** Management datagram (`drivers/infiniband/core/mad.c`)

Figure 13-1 shows the Linux InfiniBand stack architecture.

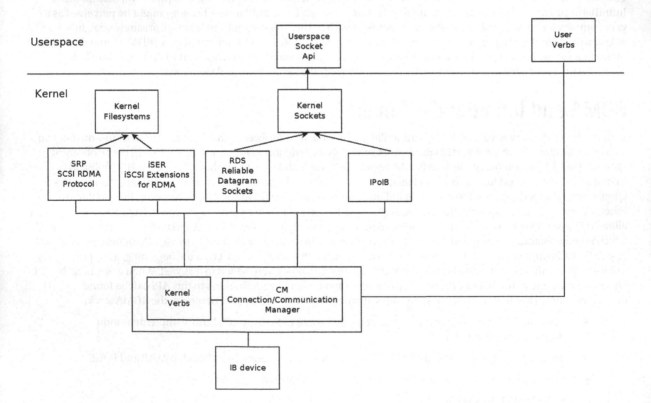

Figure 13-1. *Linux Infiniband stack architecture*

In this section, I covered the RDMA stack organization and the kernel modules that are part of it in the Linux kernel.

RDMA Technology Advantages

Here I will cover the advantages of the RDMA technology and explain the features that make it popular in many markets:

- **Zero copy:** The ability to directly write data to and read data from remote memory allows you to access remote buffers directly without the need to copy it between different software layers.

- **Kernel bypass:** Sending and receiving data from the same context of the code (that is, userspace or kernel level) saves the context switches time.

- **CPU offload:** The ability to send or receive data using dedicated hardware without any CPU intervention allows for decreasing the usage of the CPU on the remote side, because it doesn't perform any active operations.

- **Low latency:** RDMA technologies allow you to reach a very low latency for short messages. (In current hardware and on current servers, the latency for sending up to tens of bytes can be a couple of hundred nanoseconds.)

- **High Bandwidth:** In an Ethernet device, the maximum bandwidth is limited by the technology (that is, 10 or 40 Gbits/sec). In InfiniBand, the same protocol and equipment can be used from 2.5 Gbits/sec up to 120 Gbits/sec. (In current hardware and on current servers, the BW can be upto 56 Gbits/sec.)

InfiniBand Hardware Components

Like in any other interconnect technologies, in InfiniBand several hardware components are described in the spec, some of them are endpoints to the packets (generating packets and the target of the packet), and some of them forward packets in the same subnet or between different subnets. Here I will cover the most common ones:

- **Host Channel Adapter (HCA):** The network adapter that can be placed at a host or at any other system (for example, storage device). This component initiates or is the target of packets.

- **Switch:** A component that knows how to receive a packet from one port and send it to another port. If needed, it can duplicate multicast messages. (Broadcast isn't supported in InfiniBand.) Unlike other technologies, every switch is a very simple device with forwarding tables that are configured by the Subnet Manager (SM), which is an entity that configures and manages the subnet (later on in this section, I will discuss its role in more detail). The switch doesn't learn anything by itself or parse and analyze packets; it forwards packets only within the same subnet.

- **Router:** A component that connects several different InfiniBand subnets.

A subnet is a set of HCAs, switches, and router ports that are connected together. In this section, I described the various hardware components in InfiniBand, and now I will discuss the addressing of the devices, system, and ports in InfiniBand.

Addressing in InfiniBand

Here are some rules about InfiniBand addressing and an example:

- In InfiniBand, the unique identifier of components is the Globally Unique Identifier (GUID), which is a 64-bit value that is unique in the world.

- Every node in the subnet has a Node GUID. This is the identifier of the node and a constant attribute of it.

- Every port in the subnet, including in HCAs and in switches, has a port GUID. This is the identifier of the port and a constant attribute of it.

- In systems that are made from several components, there can be a system GUID. All of the components in that system have the same system GUID.

Here is an example that demonstrates all the aforementioned GUIDs: a big switch system that is combined from several switch chips. Every switch chip has a unique Node GUID. Every port in every switch has a unique port GUID. All of the chips in that system have the same system GUID.

- Global IDentifier (GID) is used to identify an end port or a multicast group. Every port has at least one valid GID at the GID table in index 0. It is based on the port GUID plus the subnet identifier that this port is part of.

- Local IDentifier (LID) is a 16-bit value that is assigned to every subnet port by the Subnet Manager. A switch is an exception, and the switch management port has the LID assignment, and not all of its ports. Every port can be assigned only one LID, or a contiguous range of LIDs, in order to have several paths to this port. Each LID is unique at a specific point of time in the same subnet, and it is used by the switches when forwarding the packets to know which egress port to use. The unicast LID's range is 0x001 to 0xbfff. The multicast LIDs range is 0xc000 to 0xfffe.

InfiniBand Features

Here we will cover some of the InfiniBand protocol features:

- InfiniBand allows you to configure partitions of ports of HCAs, switches, and routers and allows you to provide virtual isolation over the same physical subnet. Every Partition Key (P_Key) is a 16-bit value that is combined from the following: 15 lsbs are the key value, and the msb is the membership level; 0 is limited membership; and 1 is full membership. Every port has a P_Key table that is being configured by the SM, and every Queue Pair (QP), the actual object in InfiniBand that sends and receives data, is associated with one P_Key index in this table. One QP can send or receive packets from a remote QP only if, in the P_Keys that each of them is associated with, the following is true:

  - The key value is equal.

  - At least one of them has full membership.

- **Queue Key (Q_Key):** An Unreliable Datagram (UD) QP will get unicast or multicast messages from a remote UD QP only if the Q_Key of the message is equal to the Q_Key value of this UD QP.

- **Virtual Lanes (VL):** This is a mechanism for creating multiple virtual links over a single physical link. Every virtual lane represents an autonomic set of buffers for send and receive packets in each port. The number of supported VLs is an attribute of a port.

- **Service Level (SL):** InfiniBand supports up to 16 service levels. The protocol doesn't specify the policy of each level. In InfiniBand, the QoS is implemented using the SL-to-VL mapping and the resources for each VL.

- **Failover:** Connected QPs are QPs that can send packets to or receive packets from only one remote QP. InfiniBand allows defining a primary path and an alternate path for connected QPs. If there is a problem with the primary path, instead of reporting an error, the alternate path will be used automatically.

In the next section, we will look at what packets in InfiniBand look like. This is very useful when you debug problems in InfiniBand.

InfiniBand Packets

Every packet in InfiniBand is a combination of several headers and, in many cases, a payload, which is the data of the messages that the clients want to send. Messages that contain only an ACK or messages with zero bytes (for example, if only immediate data is being sent) won't contain a payload. Those headers describe from where the packet was sent, what the target of the packet is, the used operation, the information needed to separate the packets into messages, and enough information to detect packet loss errors.

Figure 13-2 presents the InfiniBand packet headers.

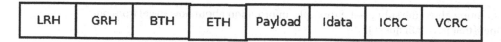

Figure 13-2. InfiniBand packet headers

Here are the headers in InfiniBand:

- **Local Routing Header (LRH):** 8 bytes. Always present. It identifies the local source and destination ports of the packet. It also specifies the requested QoS attributes (SL and VL) of the message.

- **Global Routing Header (GRH):** 40 bytes. Optional. Present for multicast packets or packets that travel in multiple subnets. It describes the source and destination ports using GIDs. Its format is identical to the IPv6 header.

- **Base Transport Header (BTH):** 12 bytes. Always present. It specifies the source and destination QPs, the operation, packet sequence number, and partition.

- **Extended Transport Header (ETH):** from 4 to 28 bytes. Optional. Extra family of headers that might be present, depending on the class of the service and the operation used.

- **Payload:** Optional. The data that the client wants to send.

- **Immediate data:** 4 bytes. Optional. Out-of-band, 32-bit value that can be added to Send and RDMA Write operations.

- **Invariant CRC (ICRC):** 4 bytes. Always present. It covers all fields that should not be changed as the packet travels in the subnet.

- **Variant CRC (VCRC):** 2 bytes. Always present. It covers all of the fields of the packet.

Management Entities

The SM is the entity in the subnet that is responsible for analyzing the subnet and configuring it. These are some of its missions:

- Discover the physical topology of the subnet.

- Assign the LIDs and other attributes—such as active MTU, active speeds, and more—to each port in the subnet.

- Configure the forwarding table in the subnet switches.

- Detect any changes in the topology (for example, if new nodes were added or removed from the subnet).

- Handle various errors in the subnet.

Subnet Manager is usually a software entity that can be running in a switch (which is called a *managed switch*) or in any node in the subnet.

Several SMs can be running in a subnet, but only one of them will be active and the rest of them will be in standby mode. There is an internal protocol that performs master election and decides which SM will be active. If the active SM is going down, one of the standby SMs will become the active SM. Every port in the subnet has a Subnet Management Agent (SMA), which is an agent that knows how to receive management messages sent by the SM, handle them, and return a response. Subnet Administrator (SA) is a service that is part of the SM. These are some of its missions:

- Provide information about the subnet—for example, information about how to get from one port to another (that is, a path query).

- Allow you to register to get notifications about events.

- Provide services for management of the subnet, such as joining or leaving a multicast. Those services might cause the SM to (re)configure the subnet.

Communication Manager (CM) is an entity that is capable of running on each port, if the port supports it, to establish, maintain, and tear down QP connections.

RDMA Resources

In the RDMA API, a lot of resources need to be created and handled before any data can be sent or received. All of the resources are in the scope of a specific RDMA device, those resources cannot be shared or used across more than one local device, even if there are multiple devices in the same machine. Figure 13-3 presents the RDMA resource creation hierarchy.

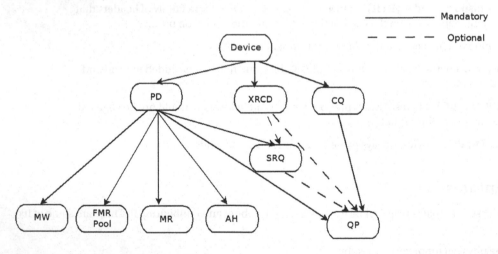

Figure 13-3. RDMA resource creation hierarchy

RDMA Device

The client needs to register with the RDMA stack in order to be notified about any RDMA device that is being added to the system or removed from it. After the initial registration, the client is notified for all existing RDMA devices. A callback will be invoked for every RDMA device, and the client can start working with these devices in the following ways:

- Query the device for various attributes

- Modify the device attributes

- Create, work with and destroy resources

The ib_register_client() method registers a kernel client that wants to use the RDMA stack. The specified callbacks will be invoked for every new InfiniBand device that currently exists in the system and that will be added to or removed from (using hot-plug functionality) the system. The ib_unregister_client() method unregisters a kernel client that wants to stop using the RDMA stack. Usually, it is called when the driver is being unloaded. Here is an sample code that shows how to register the RDMA stack in a kernel client:

```c
static void my_add_one(struct ib_device *device)
{
...
}

static void my_remove_one(struct ib_device *device)
{
...
}

static struct ib_client my_client = {
    .name    = "my RDMA module",
    .add     = my_add_one,
    .remove  = my_remove_one
};

static int __init my_init_module(void)
{
    int ret;

    ret = ib_register_client(&my_client);
    if (ret) {
        printk(KERN_ERR "Failed to register IB client\n");
        return ret;
    }

    return 0;
}

static void __exit my_cleanup_module(void)
{
    ib_unregister_client(&my_client);
}

module_init(my_init_module);
module_exit(my_cleanup_module);
```

Following here is a description of several more methods for handling an InfiniBand device.

- The ib_set_client_data() method sets a client context to be associated with an InfiniBand device.

- The ib_get_client_data() method returns the client context that was associated with an InfiniBand device using the ib_set_client_data() method.

- The ib_register_event_handler() method registers a callback to be called for every asynchronous event that will occur to the InfiniBand device. The callback structure must be initialized with the INIT_IB_EVENT_HANDLER macro.

- The ib_unregister_event_handler() method unregisters the event handler.

- The ib_query_device() method queries the InfiniBand device for its attributes. Those attributes are constant and won't be changed in subsequent calls of this method.

- The ib_query_port() method queries the InfiniBand device port for its attributes. Some of those attributes are constant, and some of them might be changed in subsequent calls of this method—for example, the port LID, state, and some other attributes.

- The rdma_port_get_link_layer() method returns the link layer of the device port.

- The ib_query_gid() method queries the InfiniBand device port's GID table in a specific index. The ib_find_gid() method returns the index of a specific GID value in a port's GID table.

- The ib_query_pkey() method queries the InfiniBand device port's P_Key table in a specific index. The ib_find_pkey() method returns the index of a specific P_Key value in a port's P_Key table.

Protection Domain (PD)

A PD allows associating itself with several other RDMA resources—such as SRQ, QP, AH, or MR—in order to provide a means of protection among them. RDMA resources that are associated with PDx cannot work with RDMA resources that were associated with PDy. Trying to mix those resources will end with an error. Typically, every module will have one PD. However, if a specific module wants to increase its security, it will use one PD for each remote QP or service that it uses. Allocation and deallocation of a PD is done like this:

- The ib_alloc_pd() method allocates a PD. It takes as an argument the pointer of the device object that was returned when the driver callback was called after its registration.

- The ib_dealloc_pd() method deallocates a PD. It is usually called when the driver is being unloaded or when the resources that are associated with the PD are being destroyed.

Address Handle (AH)

An AH is used in the Send Request of a UD QP to describe the path of the message from the local port to the remote port. The same AH can be used for several QPs if all of them send messages to the same remote port using the same attributes. Following is a description of four methods related to the AH:

- The ib_create_ah() method creates an AH. It takes as an argument a PD and attributes for the AH. The AH attributes of the AH can be filled directly or by calling the ib_init_ah_from_wc() method, which gets as a parameter a received Work Completion (ib_wc object) that includes the attributes of a successfully completed incoming message, and the port it was received from. Instead of calling the ib_init_ah_from_wc() method and then the ib_create_ah() method, one can call the ib_create_ah_from_wc() method.

- The ib_modify_ah() method modifies the attributes of an existing AH.

- The ib_query_ah() method queries for the attributes of an existing AH.

- The ib_destroy_ah() method destroys an AH. It is called when there isn't a need to send any further messages to the node that the AH describes the path to.

Memory Region (MR)

Every memory buffer that is accessed by the RDMA device needs to be registered. During the registration process, the following tasks are performed on the memory buffer:

- Separate the contiguous memory buffer to memory pages.

- The mapping of the virtual-to-physical translation will be done.

- The memory pages permission is checked to ensure that the requested permissions for the MR is supported by them.

- The memory pages are pinned, to prevent them from being swapped out. This keeps the virtual-to-physical mapping unchanged.

After a successful memory registration is completed, it has two keys:

- **Local key (lkey):** A key for accessing this memory by local Work Requests.

- **Remote key (rkey):** A key for accessing this memory by a remote machine using RDMA operations.

Those keys will be used in Work Requests when referring to those memory buffers. The same memory buffers can be registered several times, even with different permissions. The following is a description of some methods related to the MR:

- The ib_get_dma_mr() method returns a Memory Region for system memory that is usable for DMA. It takes a PD and the requested access permission for the MR as arguments.

- The ib_dma_map_single() method maps a kernel virtual address, that was allocated by the kmalloc() method family, to a DMA address. This DMA address will be used to access local and remote memory. The ib_dma_mapping_error() method should be used to check whether the mapping was successful.

- The ib_dma_unmap_single() method unmaps a DMA mapping that was done using ib_dma_map_single(). It should be called when this memory isn't needed anymore.

■ **Note**   There are some more flavors of ib_dma_map_single() that allow the mapping of pages, mapping according to DMA attributes, mapping using a scatter/gather list, or mapping using a scatter/gather list with DMA attributes: ib_dma_map_page(), ib_dma_map_single_attrs(), ib_dma_map_sg(), and ib_dma_map_sg_attrs(). All of them have corresponding unmap functions.

Before accessing a DMA mapped memory, the following methods should be called:

- ib_dma_sync_single_for_cpu() if the DMA region is going to be accessed by the CPU, or ib_dma_sync_single_for_device() if the DMA region is going to be accessed by the InfiniBand device.

- The ib_dma_alloc_coherent() method allocates a memory block that can be accessed by the CPU and maps it for DMA.

- The ib_dma_free_coherent() method frees a memory block that was allocated using ib_dma_alloc_coherent().

- The ib_reg_phys_mr() method takes a set of physical pages, registers them, and prepares a virtual address that can be accessed by an RDMA device. If you want to change it after it was created, you should call the ib_rereg_phys_mr() method.

- The ib_query_mr() method retrieves the attributes of a specific MR. Note that most low-level drivers do not implement this method.

- The ib_dereg_mr() method deregisters an MR.

Fast Memory Region (FMR) Pool

Registration of a Memory Region is a "heavy" procedure that might take some time to complete, and the context that performs it even might sleep if required resources aren't available when it is called. This behavior might be problematic when performed in certain contexts—for example, in the interrupt handler. Working with an FMR pool allows you to work with FMRs with registrations that are "lightweight" and can be registered in any context. The API of the FMR pool can be found in include/rdma/ib_fmr_pool.h.

Memory Window (MW)

Enabling a remote access to a memory can be done in two ways:

- Register a memory buffer with remote permissions enabled.

- Register a Memory Region and then bind a Memory Window to it.

Both of those ways will create a remote key (rkey) that can be used to access this memory with the specified permissions. However, if you wish to invalidate the rkey to prevent remote access to this memory, performing Memory Region deregistration might be a heavy procedure. Working with Memory Window on this Memory Region and binding or unbinding it when needed might provide a "lightweight" procedure for enabling and disabling remote access to memory. Following is a description of three methods related to the MW:

- The ib_alloc_mw() method allocates a Memory Window. It takes a PD and the MW type as arguments.

- The ib_bind_mw() method binds a Memory Window to a specified Memory Region with a specific address, size, and remote permissions by posting a special Work Request to a QP. It is called when you want to allow temporary remote access to its memory. A Work Completion in the Send Queue of the QP will be generated to describe the status of this operation. If ib_bind_mw() was called to a Memory Windows that is already bounded, to the same Memory Region or a different one, the previous binding will be invalidated.

- The ib_dealloc_mw() method deallocates the specified MW object.

Completion Queue (CQ)

Every posted Work Request, to either Send or Receive Queue, is considered outstanding until there is a corresponding Work Completion for it or for any Work Request that was posted after it. While the Work Request is outstanding, the content of the memory buffers that it points to is undetermined:

- If the RDMA device reads this memory and sends its content over the wire, the client cannot know if this buffer can be (re)used or released. If this is a reliable QP, a successful Work Completion means that the message was received by the remote side. If this is an unreliable QP, a successful Work Completion means that the message was sent.

- If the RDMA device writes a message to this memory, the client cannot know if this buffer contains the incoming message.

A Work Completion specifies that the corresponding Work Request was completed and provides some information about it: its status, the used opcode, its size, and so on. A CQ is an object that contains the Work Completions. The client needs to poll the CQ in order to read the Work Completions that it has. The CQ works on a first-in, first-out (FIFO) basis: the order of Work Completions that will be de-queued from it by the client will be according to the order that they were enqueued to the CQ by the RDMA device. The client can read the Work Completions in polling mode or request to get a notification when a new Work Completion is added to the CQ. A CQ cannot hold more Work Completions than its size. If more Work Completions than its capacity are added to it, a Work Completion with an error will be added, a CQ error asynchronous event will be generated, and all the Work Queues associated with it will get an error. Here are some methods related to the CQ:

- The ib_create_cq() method creates a CQ. It takes the following as its arguments: the pointer of the device object that was returned when the driver callback was called after its registration and the attributes for the CQ, including its size and the callbacks that will be called when there is an asynchronous event on this CQ or a Work Completion is added to it.

- The ib_resize_cq() method changes the size of a CQ. The new number of entries cannot be less than the number of the Work Completions that currently populate the CQ.

- The ib_modify_cq() method changes the moderation parameter for a CQ. A Completion event will be generated if at least a specific number of Work Completions enter the CQ or a timeout will expire. Using it might help reduce the number of interrupts that happen in an RDMA device.

- The ib_peek_cq() method returns the number of available Work Completions in a CQ.

- The ib_req_notify_cq() method requests that a Completion event notification be generated when the next Work Completion, or Work Completion that includes a solicited event indication, is added to the CQ. If no Work Completion is added to the CQ after the ib_req_notify_cq() method was called, no Completion event notification will occur.

- The ib_req_ncomp_notif() method requests that a Completion event notification be created when a specific number of Work Completions exists in the CQ. Unlike the ib_req_notify_cq() method, when calling the ib_req_ncomp_notif() method, a Completion event notification will be generated even if the CQ currently holds this number of Work Completions.

- The ib_poll_cq() method polls for Work Completions from a CQ. It reads the Work Completions from the CQ in the order they were added to it and removes them from it.

Here is an example of a code that empties a CQ—that is, reads all the Work Completions from a CQ, and checks their status:

```
struct ib_wc wc;
int num_comp = 0;

while (ib_poll_cq(cq, 1, &wc) > 0) {
    if (wc.status != IB_WC_SUCCESS) {
        printk(KERN_ERR "The Work Completion[%d] has a bad status %d\n",
                        num_comp, wc.status);
        return -EINVAL;
    }
    num_comp ++;
}
```

eXtended Reliable Connected (XRC) Domain

An XRC Domain is an object that is used to limit the XRC SRQs an incoming message can target. That XRC domain can be associated with several other RDMA resources that work with XRC, such as SRQ and QP.

Shared Receive Queue (SRQ)

An SRQ is a way for the RDMA architecture to be more scalable on the receive side. Instead of having a separate Receive Queue for every Queue Pair, there is a shared Receive Queue that all of the QPs are connected to. When they need to consume a Receive Request, they fetch it from the SRQ. Figure 13-4 presents QPs that are associated with an SRQ.

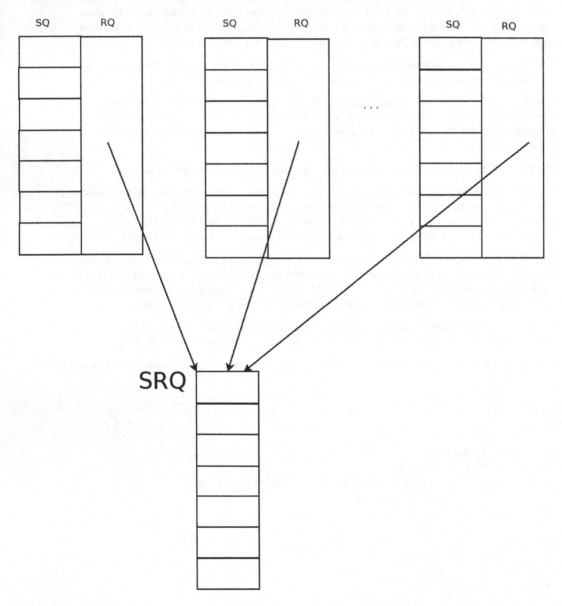

Figure 13-4. QPs that are associated with an SRQ

Here's what you do if you have *N* QPs, and each of them might receive a burst of *M* messages at a random time:

- Without using an SRQ, you post N*M Receive Requests.

- With SRQs, you post K*M (where K << N) Receive Requests.

Unlike a QP, which doesn't have any mechanism to determine the number of outstanding Work Requests in it, with an SRQ you can set a watermark limit. When the number of Receive Requests drops below this limit, an SRQ limit asynchronous event will be created for this SRQ. The downside of using an SRQ is that you cannot predict which QP will consume every posted Receive Request from the SRQ, so the message size that each posted Receive Request will be able to hold must be the maximum incoming message size that any of the QPs might get. This limitation can be handled by creating several SRQs, one for each different maximum message size, and associating them with the relevant QPs according to their expected message sizes.

Here is a description of some methods related to the SRQ and an example:

- The ib_create_srq() method creates an SRQ. It takes a PD and attributes for the SRQ.

- The ib_modify_srq() method modifies the attributes of the SRQ. It is used to set a new watermark value for the SRQ's limit event or to resize the SRQ for devices that support it.

Here is an example for setting the value of the watermark to get an asynchronous event when the number of RRs in the SRQ drops below 5:

```
struct ib_srq_attr srq_attr;
int ret;

memset(&srq_attr, 0, sizeof(srq_attr));
srq_attr.srq_limit = 5;

ret = ib_modify_srq(srq, &srq_attr, IB_SRQ_LIMIT);
if (ret) {
    printk(KERN_ERR "Failed to set the SRQ's limit value\n");
    return ret;
}
```

Following here is a description of several more methods for handling an SRQ.

- The ib_query_srq() method queries for the current SRQ attributes. This method is usually used to check the content of the SRQ's limit value. The value 0 in the srq_limit member in the ib_srq_attr object means that there isn't any SRQ limit watermark set.

- The ib_destroy_srq() method destroys an SRQ.

- The ib_post_srq_recv() method takes a linked list of Receive Requests as an argument and adds them to a specified Shared Receive Queue for future processing.

Here is an example for posting a single Receive Request to an SRQ. It saves an incoming message in a memory buffer, using its registered DMA address in a single gather entry:

```
struct ib_recv_wr wr, *bad_wr;
struct ib_sge sg;
int ret;

memset(&sg, 0, sizeof(sg));
sg.addr   = dma_addr;
sg.length = len;
sg.lkey   = mr->lkey;
```

```
memset(&wr, 0, sizeof(wr));
wr.next     = NULL;
wr.wr_id    = (uintptr_t)dma_addr;
wr.sg_list  = &sg;
wr.num_sge  = 1;

ret = ib_post_srq_recv(srq, &wr, &bad_wr);
if (ret) {
    printk(KERN_ERR "Failed to post Receive Request to an SRQ\n");
    return ret;
}
```

Queue Pair (QP)

Queue Pair is the actual object used to send and receive data in InfiniBand. It has two separate Work Queues: Send and Receive Queues. Every Work Queue has a specific number of Work Requests (WR) that can be posted to it, a number of scatter/gather elements that are supported for each WR, and a CQ to which the Work Requests whose processing has ended will add Work Completion. Those Work Queues can be created with similar or different attributes—for example, the number of WRs that can be posted to each Work Queue. The order in each Work Queue is guaranteed—that is, the processing of a Work Request in the Send Queue will start according to the order of the Send Requests submission. And the same behavior applies to the Receive Queue. However, there isn't any relation between them—that is, an outstanding Send Request can be processed even if it was posted after posting a Receive Request to the Receive Queue. Figure 13-5 presents a QP.

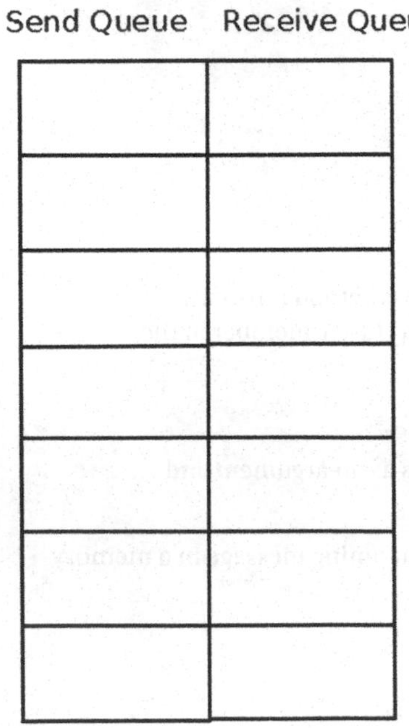

Send Queue   Receive Queue

Figure 13-5. *QP (Queue Pair)*

Upon creation, every QP has a unique number across the RDMA device at a specific point in time.

QP Transport Types

There are several QP transport types supported in InfiniBand:

- **Reliable Connected (RC):** One RC QP is connected to a single remote RC QP, and reliability is guaranteed—that is, the arrival of all packets according to their order with the same content that they were sent with is guaranteed. Every message is fragmented to packets with the size of the path MTU at the sender side and defragmented at the receiver side. This QP supports Send, RDMA Write, RDMA Read, and Atomic operations.

- **Unreliable Connected (UC):** One UC QP is connected to a single remote UC QP, and reliability isn't guaranteed. Also, if a packet in a message is lost, the whole message is lost. Every message is fragmented to packets with the size of the path MTU at the sender side and defragmented at the receiver side. This QP supports Send and RDMA Write operations.

- **Unreliable Datagram (UD):** One UD QP can send a unicast message to any UD QP in the subnet. Multicast messages are supported. Reliability isn't guaranteed. Every message is limited to one packet message, with its size limited to the path MTU size. This QP supports only Send operations.

- **eXtended Reliable Connected (XRC):** Several QPs from the same node can send messages to a remote SRQ in a specific node. This is useful for decreasing the number of QPs between two nodes from the order of the number of CPU cores—that is, QP in a process per core, to one QP. This QP supports all operations that are supported by RC QP. This type is relevant only for userspace applications.

- **Raw packet:** Allows the client to build a complete packet, including the L2 headers, and send it as is. At the receiver side, no header will be stripped by the RDMA device.

- **Raw IPv6/Raw Ethertype:** QPs that allow sending raw packets that aren't interpreted by the IB device. Currently, both of these types aren't supported by any RDMA device.

There are special QP transport types that are used for subnet management and special services:

- **SMI/QP0:** QP used for subnet managements packets.

- **GSI/QP1:** QP used for general services packets.

The ib_create_qp() method creates a QP. It takes a PD and the requested attributes that this QP will be created with as arguments. Here is an example for creating an RC QP using a PD that was created, with two different CQs: one for the Send Queue and one for the Receive Queue.

```
struct ib_qp_init_attr init_attr;
struct ib_qp *qp;

memset(&init_attr, 0, sizeof(init_attr));
init_attr.event_handler     = my_qp_event;
init_attr.cap.max_send_wr   = 2;
init_attr.cap.max_recv_wr   = 2;
init_attr.cap.max_recv_sge  = 1;
init_attr.cap.max_send_sge  = 1;
init_attr.sq_sig_type       = IB_SIGNAL_ALL_WR;
init_attr.qp_type           = IB_QPT_RC;
init_attr.send_cq           = send_cq;
init_attr.recv_cq           = recv_cq;
```

```
qp = ib_create_qp(pd, &init_attr);
if (IS_ERR(qp)) {
    printk(KERN_ERR "Failed to create a QP\n");
    return PTR_ERR(qp);
}
```

QP State Machine

A QP has a state machine that defines what the QP is capable of doing at each state:

- **Reset state:** Each QP is generated at this state. At this state, no Send Requests or Receive Requests can be posted to it. All incoming messages are silently dropped.

- **Initialized state:** At this state, no Send Requests can be posted to it. However, Receive Requests can be posted, but they won't be processed. All incoming messages are silently dropped. It is a good practice to post a Receive Request to a QP at this state before moving it to RTR (Ready To Receive). Doing this prevents a case where remote QP sends messages need to consume a Receive Request but such were not posted yet.

- **Ready To Receive (RTR) state:** At this state, no Send Requests can be posted to it, but Receive Requests can be posted and processed. All incoming messages will be handled. The first incoming message that is received at this state will generate the communication-established asynchronous event. A QP that only receives messages can stay at this state.

- **Ready To Send (RTS) state:** At this state, both Send Requests and Receive Requests can be posted and processed. All incoming messages will be handled. This is the common state for QPs.

- **Send Queue Drained (SQD) state:** At this state, the QP completes the processing of all the Send Requests that their processing has started. Only when there aren't any messages that can be sent, you can change some of the QP attributes. This state is separated into two internal states:

  - **Draining:** Messages are still being sent.

  - **Drained:** The sending of the messages was completed.

- **Send Queue Error (SQE) state:** The RDMA device automatically moves a QP to this state when there is an error in the Send Queue for unreliable transport types. The Send Request that caused the error will be completed with the error reason, and all of the consecutive Send Requests will be flushed. The Receive Queue will still work—that is, Receive Requests can be posted, and incoming messages will be handled. The client can recover from this state and modify the QP state back to RTS.

- **Error state:** At this state, all of the outstanding Work Requests will be flushed. The RDMA device can move the QP to this state if this is a reliable transport type and there was an error with a Send Request, or if there was an error in the Receive Queue regardless of which transport type was used. All incoming messages are silently dropped.

A QP can be transitioned by ib_modify_qp() from any state to the Reset state and to the Error state. Moving the QP to the Error state will flush all of the outstanding Work Requests. Moving the QP to the Reset state will clear all previously configured attributes and remove all of the outstanding Work Request and Work Completions that were ended on this QP in the Completion Queues that this QP is working with. Figure 13-6 presents a QP state machine diagram.

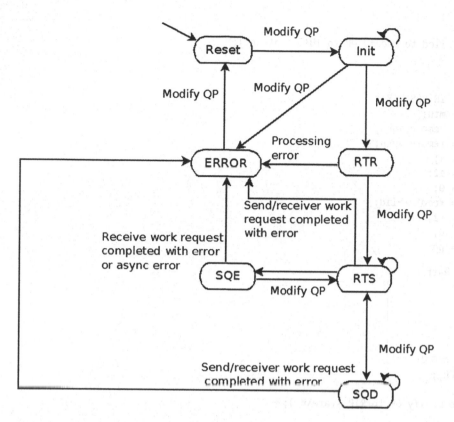

Figure 13-6. QP state machine

The ib_modify_qp() method modifies the attributes of a QP. It takes as an argument the QP to modify and the attributes of the QP that will be modified. The state machine of the QP can be changed according to the diagram shown in Figure 13-6. Every QP transport type requires different attributes to be set in each QP state transition.

Here is an example for modifying a newly created RC QP to the RTS state, in which it can send and receive packets. The local attributes are the outgoing port, the used SL, and the starting Packet Serial Number for the Send Queue. The remote attributes needed are the Receive PSN, the QP number, and the LID of the port that it uses.

```
struct ib_qp_attr attr = {
    .qp_state       = IB_QPS_INIT,
    .pkey_index     = 0,
    .port_num       = port,
    .qp_access_flags = 0
};

ret = ib_modify_qp(qp, &attr,
        IB_QP_STATE        |
        IB_QP_PKEY_INDEX   |
        IB_QP_PORT         |
        IB_QP_ACCESS_FLAGS);
```

```
if (ret) {
          printk(KERN_ERR "Failed to modify QP to INIT state\n");
          return ret;
}

attr.qp_state            = IB_QPS_RTR;
attr.path_mtu            = mtu;
attr.dest_qp_num         = remote->qpn;
attr.rq_psn              = remote->psn;
attr.max_dest_rd_atomic  = 1;
attr.min_rnr_timer       = 12;
attr.ah_attr.is_global   = 0;
attr.ah_attr.dlid        = remote->lid;
attr.ah_attr.sl          = sl;
attr.ah_attr.src_path_bits = 0,
attr.ah_attr.port_num    = port

ret = ib_modify_qp(ctx->qp, &attr,
          IB_QP_STATE              |
          IB_QP_AV                 |
          IB_QP_PATH_MTU           |
          IB_QP_DEST_QPN           |
          IB_QP_RQ_PSN             |
          IB_QP_MAX_DEST_RD_ATOMIC |
          IB_QP_MIN_RNR_TIMER);
if (ret) {
  printk(KERN_ERR "Failed to modify QP to RTR state\n");
  return ret;
}

attr.qp_state      = IB_QPS_RTS;
attr.timeout       = 14;
attr.retry_cnt     = 7;
attr.rnr_retry     = 6;
attr.sq_psn        = my_psn;
attr.max_rd_atomic = 1;
ret = ib_modify_qp(ctx->qp, &attr,
          IB_QP_STATE            |
          IB_QP_TIMEOUT          |
          IB_QP_RETRY_CNT        |
          IB_QP_RNR_RETRY        |
          IB_QP_SQ_PSN           |
          IB_QP_MAX_QP_RD_ATOMIC);
if (ret) {
  printk(KERN_ERR "Failed to modify QP to RTS state\n");
  return ret;
}
```

Following here is a description of several more methods for handling a QP:

- The ib_query_qp() method queries for the current QP attributes. Some of the attributes are constant (the values that the client specifies), and some of them can be changed (for example, the state).

- The ib_destroy_qp() method destroys a QP. It is called when the QP isn't needed anymore.

Work Request Processing

Every posted Work Request, to either the Send or Receive Queue, is considered outstanding until there is a Work Completion, which was polled from the CQ which is associated with this Work Queue for this Work Request or for Work Requests in the same Work Queue that were posted after it. Every outstanding Work Request in the Receive Queue will end with a Work Completion. A Work Request processing flow in a Work Queue is according to the diagram shown in Figure 13-7.

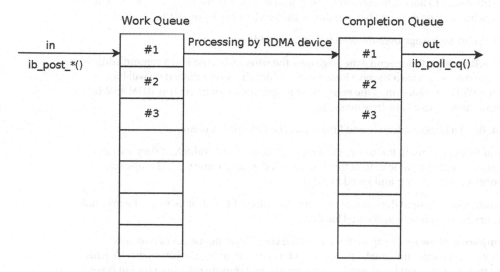

Figure 13-7. *Work Request processing flow*

In the Send Queue, you can choose (when creating a QP) whether you want every Send Request to end with a Work Completion or whether you want to select the Send Requests that will end with Work Completions—that is, selective signaling. You might encounter an error for an unsignaled Send Request; nevertheless, a Work Completion with bad status will be generated for it.

When a Work Request is outstanding one cannot (re)use or free the resources that were specified in it when posting this Work Request. For example:

- When posting a Send Request for a UD QP, the AH cannot be freed.

- When posting a Receive Request, the memory buffers that were referred to in a scatter/gather (s/g) list cannot be read, because it is unknown if the RDMA device already wrote the data in them.

"Fencing" is the ability to prevent the processing of a specific Send Request until the processing of the previous RDMA Read and Atomic operations ends. Adding the Fence indication to a Send Request can be useful, for example, when using RDMA Read from a remote address and sending the data, or part of it, in the same Send Queue. Without fencing, the send operation might start before the data is retrieved and available in local memory. When posting a Send Request to a UC or RC QP, the path to the target is known, because it was provided when moving the QP to the RTR state. However, when posting a Send Request to a UD QP, you need to add an AH to describe the path to the target(s) of this message. If there is an error related to the Send Queue, and if this is an Unreliable transport type, the Send Queue will move to the Error state (that is, the SQE state) but the Receive Queue will still be fully functional. The client can recover from this state and change the QP state back to RTS. If there is an error related to the Receive Queue, the QP will be moved to the Error state because this is an unrecoverable error. When a Work Queue is moved to the Error state, the Work Request that caused the error is ended with a status that indicates the nature of the error and the rest of the Work Requests in this Queue are flushed with error.

Supported Operations in the RDMA Architecture

There are several operation types supported in InfiniBand:

- **Send:** Send a message over the wire. The remote side needs to have a Receive Request available, and the message will be written in its buffers.

- **Send with Immediate:** Send a message over the wire with an extra 32 bits of out-of-band data. The remote side needs to have a Receive Request available, and the message will be written in its buffers. This immediate data will be available in the Work Completion of the receiver.

- **RDMA Write:** Send a message over the wire to a remote address.

- **RDMA Write with Immediate:** Send a message over the wire, and write it to a remote address. The remote side needs to have a Receive Request available. This immediate data will be available in the Work Completion of the receiver. This operation can be seen as RDMA Write + Send with immediate with a zero-byte message.

- **RDMA Read:** Read a remote address, and fill the local buffer with its content.

- **Compare and Swap:** Compare the content of a remote address with valueX; if they are equal, replace its content with the valueY. All of this is performed in an atomic way. The original remote memory content is sent and saved locally.

- **Fetch and Add:** Add a value to the content of a remote address in an atomic way. The original remote memory content is sent and saved locally.

- **Masked Compare and Swap:** Compare the part of the content using maskX of a remote address with valueX; if they are equal, replace part of its content using the bits in maskY with valueY. All of this is performed in an atomic way. The original remote memory content is sent and saved locally.

- **Masked Fetch and Add:** Add a value to the content of a remote address in an atomic way, and change only the bits that are specified in the mask. The original remote memory content is sent and saved locally.

- **Bind Memory Window:** Binds a Memory Windows to a specific Memory Region.

- **Fast registration:** Registers a Fast Memory Region using a Work Request.

- **Local invalidate:** Invalidates a Fast Memory Region using a Work Request. If someone uses its old lkey/rkey, it will be considered an error. It can be combined with send/RDMA read; in such a case, first the send/read will be performed, and only then this Fast Memory Region will be invalidated.

The Receive Request specifies where the incoming message will be saved for operations that consume a Receive Request. The total size of the memory buffers specified in the scatter list must be equal to or greater than the size of the incoming message.

For UD QP, because the origin of the message is unknown in advance (same subnet or another subnet, unicast or multicast message), an extra 40 bytes, which is the GRH header size, must be added to the Receive Request buffers. The first 40 bytes will be filled with the GRH of the message, if such is available. This GRH information describes how to send a message back to the sender. The message itself will start at offset 40 in the memory buffers that were described in the scatter list.

The ib_post_recv() method takes a linked list of Receive Requests and adds them to the Receive Queue of a specific QP for future processing. Here is an example for posting a single Receive Request for a QP. It saves an incoming message in a memory buffer using its registered DMA address in a single gather entry. qp is a pointer to a QP that was created using ib_create_qp(). The memory buffer is a block that was allocated using kmalloc() and mapped for DMA using ib_dma_map_single(). The used lkey is from the MR that was registered using ib_get_dma_mr().

```
struct ib_recv_wr wr, *bad_wr;
struct ib_sge sg;
int ret;

memset(&sg, 0, sizeof(sg));
sg.addr   = dma_addr;
sg.length = len;
sg.lkey   = mr->lkey;

memset(&wr, 0, sizeof(wr));
wr.next   = NULL;
wr.wr_id  = (uintptr_t)dma_addr;
wr.sg_list = &sg;
wr.num_sge = 1;

ret = ib_post_recv(qp, &wr, &bad_wr);

if (ret) {
    printk(KERN_ERR "Failed to post Receive Request to a QP\n");
    return ret;
}
```

The ib_post_send() method takes as an argument a linked list of Send Requests and adds them to the Send Queue of a specific QP for future processing. Here is an example for posting a single Send Request of a Send operation for a QP. It sends the content of a memory buffer using its registered DMA address in a single gather entry.

```
struct ib_sge sg;
struct ib_send_wr wr, *bad_wr;
int ret;

memset(&sg, 0, sizeof(sg));
sg.addr   = dma_addr;
sg.length = len;
sg.lkey   = mr->lkey;

memset(&wr, 0, sizeof(wr));
wr.next       = NULL;
wr.wr_id      = (uintptr_t)dma_addr;
wr.sg_list    = &sg;
wr.num_sge    = 1;
wr.opcode     = IB_WR_SEND;
wr.send_flags = IB_SEND_SIGNALED;

ret = ib_post_send(qp, &wr, &bad_wr);
```

```
if (ret) {
    printk(KERN_ERR "Failed to post Send Request to a QP\n");
    return ret;
}
```

Work Completion Status

Every Work Completion can be ended successfully or with an error. If it ends successfully, the operation was finished and the data was sent according to the transport type reliability level. If this Work Completion contains an error, the content of the memory buffers is unknown. There can be many reasons that the Work Request status indicates that there is an error: protection violation, bad address, and so on. The violation errors won't perform any retransmission. However, there are two special retry flows that are worth mentioning. Both of them are done automatically by the RDMA device, which retransmit packets, until the problem is solved or it exceeds the number of retransmissions. If the issue was solved, the client code won't be aware that this even happened, besides a temporary performance hiccup. This is relevant only for Reliable transport types.

Retry Flow

If the receiver side didn't return any ACK or NACK to the sender side within the expected timeout, the sender might send the message again, according to the timeout and the retry count attributes that were configured in the QP attributes. There might be several reasons for having such a problem:

- The attributes of the remote QP or the path to it aren't correct.

- The remote QP state didn't get to (at least) the RTR state.

- The remote QP state moved to the Error state.

- The message itself was dropped on the way from the sender to the receiver (for example, a CRC error).

- The ACK or NACK of messages was dropped on the way from the receiver to the sender (for example, a CRC error).

Figure 13-8 presents the retry flow becasue of a packet loss that overcame a packet drop.

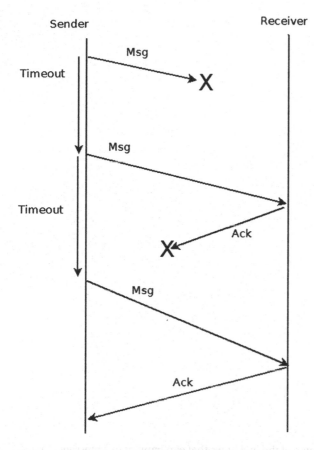

Figure 13-8. *A retry flow (on reliable transport types)*

If eventually the ACK/NACK is received by the sender QP successfully, it will continue to send the rest of the messages. If any message in the future has this problem too, the retry flow will be done again for this message as well, without any history that this was done before. If even after retrying several times the receiver side still doesn't respond, there will be a Work Completion with Retry Error on the sender side.

Receiver Not Ready (RNR) Flow

If the receiver side got a message that needs to consume a Receive Request from the Receiver Queue, but there isn't any outstanding Receive Request, the receiver will send back to the sender an RNR NACK. After a while, according to the time that was specified in the RNR NACK, the sender will try to send the message again.

If eventually the receiver side posts a Receiver Request in time, and the incoming message consumes it, an ACK will be sent to the sender side to indicate that the message was saved successfully. If any message in the future has this problem too, the RNR retry flow will be done again for this message as well, without any history that this was done before. If even after retrying several times the receiver side still didn't post a Receiver Request and an RNR NACK was sent to the sender for each sent message, a Work Completion with RNR Retry Error will be generated on the sender side. Figure 13-9 presents the RNR retry flow of retry that overcome a missing Receive Request in he receiver side.

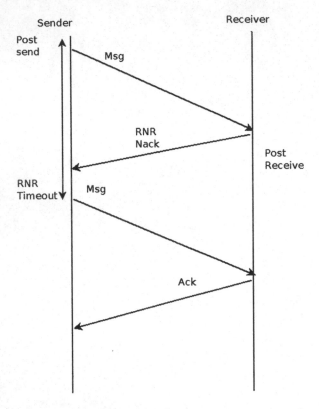

Figure 13-9. *RNR retry flow (on reliable transport types)*

In this section, I covered the Work Request status and some of the bad flows that can happen to a message. In the next section, I will discuss the multicast groups.

Multicast Groups

Multicast groups are a means to send a message from one UD QP to many UD QPs. Every UD QP that wants to get this message needs to be attached to the multicast group. When a device gets a multicast packet, it duplicates it to all of the QPs that are attached to that group. Following is a description of two methods related to multicast groups:

- The ib_attach_mcast() method attaches a UD QP to a multicast group within an InfiniBand device. It accepts the QP to be attached and the multicast group attributes.

- The ib_detach_mcast() method detaches a UD QP from a multicast group.

Difference Between the Userspace and the Kernel-Level RDMA API

The userspace and the kernel level of the RDMA stack API are quite similar, because they cover the same technology and need to be able to provide the same functionality. When the userspace is calling a method of the control path from the RDMA API, it performs a context switch to the kernel level to protect privileged resources and to synchronize objects that need to be synchronized (for example, the same QP number cannot be assigned to more than one QP at the same time).

However, there are some differences between the userspace and the kernel-level RDMA API and functionality:

- The prefix of all the APIs in the kernel level is "ib_", while in the userspace the prefix is "ibv_".

- There are enumerations and macros that exist only in the RDMA API in the kernel level.

- There are QP types that are available only in the kernel (for example, the SMI and GSI QPs).

- There are privileged operations that can be performed only in the kernel level—for example, registration of a physical memory, registration of an MR using a WR, and FMRs.

- Some functionality isn't available in the RDMA API in the userspace—for example, Request for N notification.

- The kernel API is asynchronous. There are callbacks that are called when there is an asynchronous event or Completion event. In the userspace, everything is synchronous and the user needs to explicitly check if there is an asynchronous event or Completion event in its running context (that is, thread).

- XRC isn't relevant for kernel-level clients.

- There are new features that were introduced to the kernel level, but they are not available (yet) in the userspace.

The userspace API is supplied by the userspace library "libibverbs." And although some of the RDMA functionality in the user level is less than the kernel-level one, it is enough to enjoy the benefits of the InfiniBand technology.

Summary

You have learned in this chapter about the advantages of the InfiniBand technology. I reviewed the RDMA stack organization. I discussed the resource-creation hierarchy and all of the important objects and their API, which is needed in order to write client code that uses InfiniBand. You also saw some examples that use this API. The next chapter will deal with advanced topics like network namespaces and the Bluetooth subsystem.

Quick Reference

I will conclude this chapter with a short list of important methods of the RDMA API. Some of them were mentioned in this chapter.

Methods

Here are the methods.

int ib_register_client(struct ib_client *client);

Register a kernel client that wants to use the RDMA stack.

void ib_unregister_client(struct ib_client *client);

Unregister a kernel client that wants to stop using the RDMA stack.

void ib_set_client_data(struct ib_device *device, struct ib_client *client, void *data);

Set a client context to be associated with an InfiniBand device.

void *ib_get_client_data(struct ib_device *device, struct ib_client *client);

Read the client context that was associated with an InfiniBand device.

int ib_register_event_handler(struct ib_event_handler *event_handler);

Register a callback to be called for every asynchronous event that occurs to the InfiniBand device.

int ib_unregister_event_handler(struct ib_event_handler *event_handler);

Unregister a callback to be called for every asynchronous event that occurs to the InfiniBand device.

int ib_query_device(struct ib_device *device, struct ib_device_attr *device_attr);

Query an InfiniBand device for its attributes.

int ib_query_port(struct ib_device *device, u8 port_num, struct ib_port_attr *port_attr);

Query an InfiniBand device port for its attributes.

enum rdma_link_layer rdma_port_get_link_layer(struct ib_device *device, u8 port_num);

Query for the link layer of the InfiniBand device's port.

int ib_query_gid(struct ib_device *device, u8 port_num, int index, union ib_gid *gid);

Query for the GID in a specific index in the InfiniBand device's port GID table.

int ib_query_pkey(struct ib_device *device, u8 port_num, u16 index, u16 *pkey);

Query for the P_Key-specific index in the InfiniBand device's port P_Key table.

int ib_find_gid(struct ib_device *device, union ib_gid *gid, u8 *port_num, u16 *index);

Find the index of a specific GID value in the InfiniBand device's port GID table.

int ib_find_pkey(struct ib_device *device, u8 port_num, u16 pkey, u16 *index);

Find the index of a specific P_Key value in the InfiniBand device's port P_Key table.

struct ib_pd *ib_alloc_pd(struct ib_device *device);

Allocate a PD to be used later to create other InfiniBand resources.

int ib_dealloc_pd(struct ib_pd *pd);

Deallocate a PD.

struct ib_ah *ib_create_ah(struct ib_pd *pd, struct ib_ah_attr *ah_attr);

Create an AH that will be used when posting a Send Request in a UD QP.

int ib_init_ah_from_wc(struct ib_device *device, u8 port_num, struct ib_wc *wc, struct ib_grh *grh, struct ib_ah_attr *ah_attr);

Initializes an AH attribute from a Work Completion of a received message and a GRH buffer. Those AH attributes can be used when calling the ib_create_ah() method.

struct ib_ah *ib_create_ah_from_wc(struct ib_pd *pd, struct ib_wc *wc, struct ib_grh *grh, u8 port_num);

Create an AH from a Work Completion of a received message and a GRH buffer.

int ib_modify_ah(struct ib_ah *ah, struct ib_ah_attr *ah_attr);

Modify the attributes of an existing AH.

int ib_query_ah(struct ib_ah *ah, struct ib_ah_attr *ah_attr);

Query the attributes of an existing AH.

int ib_destroy_ah(struct ib_ah *ah);

Destroy an AH.

struct ib_mr *ib_get_dma_mr(struct ib_pd *pd, int mr_access_flags);

Return an MR system memory that is usable for DMA.

static inline int ib_dma_mapping_error(struct ib_device *dev, u64 dma_addr);

Check if the DMA memory points to an invalid address—that is, check whether the DMA mapping operation failed.

static inline u64 ib_dma_map_single(struct ib_device *dev, void *cpu_addr, size_t size, enum dma_data_direction direction);

Map a kernel virtual address to a DMA address.

static inline void ib_dma_unmap_single(struct ib_device *dev, u64 addr, size_t size, enum dma_data_direction direction);

Unmap a DMA mapping of a virtual address.

static inline u64 ib_dma_map_single_attrs(struct ib_device *dev, void *cpu_addr, size_t size, enum dma_data_direction direction, struct dma_attrs *attrs)

Map a kernel virtual memory to a DMA address according to DMA attributes.

static inline void ib_dma_unmap_single_attrs(struct ib_device *dev, u64 addr, size_t size, enum dma_data_direction direction, struct dma_attrs *attrs);

Unmap a DMA mapping of a virtual address that was mapped according to DMA attributes.

static inline u64 ib_dma_map_page(struct ib_device *dev, struct page *page, unsigned long offset, size_t size, enum dma_data_direction direction);

Maps a physical page to a DMA address.

static inline void ib_dma_unmap_page(struct ib_device *dev, u64 addr, size_t size, enum dma_data_direction direction);

Unmap a DMA mapping of a physical page.

static inline int ib_dma_map_sg(struct ib_device *dev, struct scatterlist *sg, int nents, enum dma_data_direction direction);

Map a scatter/gather list to a DMA address.

static inline void ib_dma_unmap_sg(struct ib_device *dev, struct scatterlist *sg, int nents, enum dma_data_direction direction);

Unmap a DMA mapping of a scatter/gather list.

```
static inline int ib_dma_map_sg_attrs(struct ib_device *dev, struct scatterlist *sg,
int nents, enum dma_data_direction direction, struct dma_attrs *attrs);
```

Map a scatter/gather list to a DMA address according to DMA attributes.

```
static inline void ib_dma_unmap_sg_attrs(struct ib_device *dev, struct scatterlist
*sg, int nents, enum dma_data_direction direction, struct dma_attrs *attrs);
```

Unmap a DMA mapping of a scatter/gather list according to DMA attributes.

```
static inline u64 ib_sg_dma_address(struct ib_device *dev, struct scatterlist *sg);
```

Return the address attribute of a scatter/gather entry.

```
static inline unsigned int ib_sg_dma_len(struct ib_device *dev, struct
scatterlist *sg);
```

Return the length attribute of a scatter/gather entry.

```
static inline void ib_dma_sync_single_for_cpu(struct ib_device *dev, u64 addr,
size_t size, enum dma_data_direction dir);
```

Transfer a DMA region ownership to the CPU. It should be called before the CPU accesses a DMA mapped region whose ownership was previously transferred to the device.

```
static inline void ib_dma_sync_single_for_device(struct ib_device *dev, u64 addr,
size_t size, enum dma_data_direction dir);
```

Transfer a DMA region ownership to the device. It should be called before the device accesses a DMA mapped region whose ownership was previously transferred to the CPU.

```
static inline void *ib_dma_alloc_coherent(struct ib_device *dev, size_t size,
u64 *dma_handle, gfp_t flag);
```

Allocate a memory block that can be accessed by the CPU, and map it for DMA.

```
static inline void ib_dma_free_coherent(struct ib_device *dev, size_t size,
void *cpu_addr, u64 dma_handle);
```

Free a memory block that was allocated using ib_dma_alloc_coherent().

struct ib_mr *ib_reg_phys_mr(struct ib_pd *pd, struct ib_phys_buf *phys_buf_array, int num_phys_buf, int mr_access_flags, u64 *iova_start);

Take a physical page list, and prepare it for being accessed by the InfiniBand device.

int ib_rereg_phys_mr(struct ib_mr *mr, int mr_rereg_mask, struct ib_pd *pd, struct ib_phys_buf *phys_buf_array, int num_phys_buf, int mr_access_flags, u64 *iova_start);

Change the attributes of an MR.

int ib_query_mr(struct ib_mr *mr, struct ib_mr_attr *mr_attr);

Query for the attributes of an MR.

int ib_dereg_mr(struct ib_mr *mr);

Deregister an MR.

struct ib_mw *ib_alloc_mw(struct ib_pd *pd, enum ib_mw_type type);

Allocate an MW. This MW will be used to allow remote access to an MR.

static inline int ib_bind_mw(struct ib_qp *qp, struct ib_mw *mw, struct ib_mw_bind *mw_bind);

Bind an MW to an MR to allow a remote access to local memory with specific permissions.

int ib_dealloc_mw(struct ib_mw *mw);

Deallocates an MW.

struct ib_cq *ib_create_cq(struct ib_device *device, ib_comp_handler comp_handler, void (*event_handler)(struct ib_event *, void *), void *cq_context, int cqe, int comp_vector);

Create a CQ. This CQ will be used to indicate the status of ended Work Requests for Send or Receive Queues.

int ib_resize_cq(struct ib_cq *cq, int cqe);

Change the number of entries in a CQ.

int ib_modify_cq(structib_cq *cq, u16 cq_count, u16 cq_period);

Modify the moderation attributes of a CQ. This method is used to decrease the number of interrupts of an InfiniBand device.

int ib_peek_cq(structib_cq *cq, intwc_cnt);

Return the number of available Work Completions in a CQ.

static inline int ib_req_notify_cq(struct ib_cq *cq, enum ib_cq_notify_flags flags);

Request a Completion notification event to be generated when the next Work Completion is added to the CQ.

static inline int ib_req_ncomp_notif(struct ib_cq *cq, int wc_cnt);

Request a Completion notification event to be generated when there is a specific number of Work Completions in a CQ.

static inline int ib_poll_cq(struct ib_cq *cq, int num_entries, struct ib_wc *wc);

Read and remove one or more Work Completions from a CQ. They are read in the order that they were added to the CQ.

struct ib_srq *ib_create_srq(struct ib_pd *pd, struct ib_srq_init_attr *srq_init_attr);

Create an SRQ that will be used as a shared Receive Queue for several QPs.

int ib_modify_srq(struct ib_srq *srq, struct ib_srq_attr *srq_attr, enum ib_srq_attr_mask srq_attr_mask);

Modify the attributes of an SRQ.

int ib_query_srq(struct ib_srq *srq, struct ib_srq_attr *srq_attr);

Query for the attributes of an SRQ. The SRQ limit value might be changed in subsequent calls to this method.

int ib_destroy_srq(struct ib_srq *srq);

Destroy an SRQ.

struct ib_qp *ib_create_qp(struct ib_pd *pd, struct ib_qp_init_attr *qp_init_attr);

Create a QP. Every new QP is assigned with a QP number that isn't in use by other QPs at the same time.

int ib_modify_qp(struct ib_qp *qp, struct ib_qp_attr *qp_attr, int qp_attr_mask);

Modify the attributes of a QP, which includes Send and Receive Queue attributes and the QP state.

int ib_query_qp(struct ib_qp *qp, struct ib_qp_attr *qp_attr, int qp_attr_mask, struct ib_qp_init_attr *qp_init_attr);

Query for the attributes of a QP. Some of the attributes might be changed in subsequent calls to this method.

int ib_destroy_qp(struct ib_qp *qp);

Destroy a QP.

static inline int ib_post_srq_recv(struct ib_srq *srq, struct ib_recv_wr *recv_wr, struct ib_recv_wr **bad_recv_wr);

Adds a linked list of Receive Requests to an SRQ.

static inline int ib_post_recv(struct ib_qp *qp, struct ib_recv_wr *recv_wr, struct ib_recv_wr **bad_recv_wr);

Adds a linked list of Receive Requests to the Receive Queue of a QP.

static inline int ib_post_send(struct ib_qp *qp, struct ib_send_wr *send_wr, struct ib_send_wr **bad_send_wr);

Adds a linked list of Send Requests to the Send Queue of a QP.

int ib_attach_mcast(struct ib_qp *qp, union ib_gid *gid, u16 lid);

Attaches a UD QP to a multicast group.

int ib_detach_mcast(struct ib_qp *qp, union ib_gid *gid, u16 lid);

Detaches a UD QP from a multicast group.

CHAPTER 14

■ ■ ■

Advanced Topics

Chapter 13 dealt with the InfiniBand subsystem and its implementation in Linux. This chapter deals with several advanced topics and some topics that didn't fit logically into other chapters. The chapter starts with a discussion about network namespaces, a type of lightweight process virtualization mechanism that was added to Linux in recent years. I will discuss the namespaces implementation in general and network namespaces in particular. You will learn that only two new system calls are needed in order to implement namespaces. You will also see several examples of how simple it is to create and manage network namespaces with the `ip` command of `iproute2`, and how simple it is to move one network device from one network namespace to another and to attach a specified process to a specified network namespace. The cgroups subsystem also provides resource management solution, which is different from namespaces. I will describe the cgroups subsystem and its two network modules, `net_prio` and `cls_cgroup`, and give two examples of using these cgroup network modules.

Later on in this chapter, you will learn about Busy Poll Sockets and how to tune them. The Busy Poll Sockets feature provides an interesting performance optimization technique for sockets that need low latency and are willing to pay a cost of higher CPU utilization. The Busy Poll Sockets feature is available from kernel 3.11. I will also cover the Bluetooth subsystem, the IEEE 802.15.4 subsystem and the Near Field Communication (NFC) subsystem; these three subsystems typically work in short range networks, and the development of new features for these subsystem is progressing at a rapid pace. I will also discuss Notification Chains, which is an important mechanism that you may encounter while developing or debugging kernel networking code and the PCI subsystem, as many network devices are PCI devices. I will not delve deep into the PCI subsystem details, as this book is not about device drivers. I will conclude the chapter with three short sections, one about the teaming network driver (which is the new kernel link aggregation solution), one about the Point-to-Point over Ethernet (PPPoE) Protocol, and finally one about Android.

Network Namespaces

This section covers Linux namespaces, what they are for and how they are implemented. It includes an in-depth discussion of network namespaces, giving some examples that will demonstrate their usage. Linux namespaces are essentially a virtualization solution. Operating system virtualization was implemented in mainframes many years before solutions like Xen or KVM hit the market. Also with Linux namespaces, which are a form of process virtualization, the idea is not new at all. It was tried in the Plan 9 operating system (see this article from 1992: "The Use of Name Spaces in Plan 9", `www.cs.bell-labs.com/sys/doc/names.html`).

Namespaces is a form of lightweight process virtualization, and it provides resource isolation. As opposed to virtualization solutions like KVM or Xen, with namespaces you do not create additional instances of the operating system on the same host, but use only a single operating system instance. I should mention in this context that the Solaris operating system has a virtualization solution named Solaris Zones, which also uses a single operating system instance, but the scheme of resource partitioning is somewhat different than that of Linux namespaces (for example, in Solaris Zones there is a global zone which is the primary zone, and which has more capabilities). In the FreeBSD operating system there is a mechanism called `jails,` which also provides resource partitioning without running more than one instance of the kernel.

The main idea of Linux namespaces is to partition resources among groups of processes to enable a process (or several processes) to have a different view of the system than processes in other groups of processes. This feature is used, for example, to provide resource isolation in the Linux containers project (http://lxc.sourceforge.net/). The Linux containers project also uses another resource management mechanism that is provided by the cgroups subsystem, which will be described later in this chapter. With containers, you can run different Linux distributions on the same host using one instance of the operating systems. Namespaces are also needed for the checkpoint/restore feature, which is used in high performance computing (HPC). For example, it is used in CRIU (http://criu.org/Main_Page), a software tool of OpenVZ (http://openvz.org/Main_Page), which implements checkpoint/restore functionality for Linux processes mostly in userspace, though there are very few places when CRIU kernel patches were merged. I should mention that there were some projects to implement checkpoint/restore in the kernel, but these projects were not accepted in mainline because they were too complex. For example, take the CKPT project: https://ckpt.wiki.kernel.org/index.php/Main_Page. The checkpoint/restore feature (sometimes referred to as checkpoint/restart) enables stopping and saving several processes on a filesystem, and at a later time restores those processes (possibly on a different host) from the filesystem and resumes its execution from where it was stopped. Without namespaces, checkpoint/restore has very limited use cases, in particular live migration is only possible with them. Another use case for network namespaces is when you need to set up an environment that needs to simulate different network stacks for testing, debugging, etc. For readers who want to learn more about checkpoint/restart, I suggest reading the article "Virtual Servers and Checkpoint/Restart in Mainstream Linux," by Sukadev Bhattiprolu, Eric W. Biederman, Serge Hallyn, and Daniel Lezcano.

Mount namespaces were the first type of Linux namespaces to be merged in 2002, for kernel 2.4.19. User namespaces were the last to be implemented, in kernel 3.8, for almost all filesystems types. It could be that additional namespaces will be developed, as is discussed later in this section. For creating a namespace you should have the CAP_SYS_ADMIN capability for all namespaces, except for the user namespace. Trying to create a namespace without the CAP_SYS_ADMIN capability for all namespaces, except for the user namespace, will result with an –EPRM error ("Operation not permitted"). Many developers took part in the development of namespaces, among them are Eric W. Biederman, Pavel Emelyanov, Al Viro, Cyrill Gorcunov, Andrew Vagin, and more.

After getting some background about process virtualization and Linux namespaces, and how they are used, you are now ready to dive in into the gory implementation details.

Namespaces Implementation

As of this writing, six namespaces are implemented in the Linux kernel. Here is a description of the main additions and changes that were needed in order to implement namespaces in the Linux kernel and to support namespaces in userspace packages:

- A structure called nsproxy (namespace proxy) was added. This structure contains pointers to five namespaces out of the six namespaces that are implemented. There is no pointer to the user namespace in the nsproxy structure; however, all the other five namespace objects contain a pointer to the user namespace object that owns them, and in each of these five namespaces, the user namespace pointer is called user_ns. The user namespace is a special case; it is a member of the credentials structure (cred), called user_ns. The cred structure represents the security context of a process. Each process descriptor (task_struct) contains two cred objects, for effective and objective process descriptor credentials. I will not delve into all the details and nuances of user namespaces implementation, since this is not in the scope of this book. An nsproxy object is created by the create_nsproxy() method and it is released by the free_nsproxy() method. A pointer to nsproxy object, which is also called nsproxy, was added to the process descriptor (a process descriptor is represented by the `task_struct` structure, `include/linux/sched.h`.) Let's take a look at the `nsproxy` structure, as it's quite short and should be quite self-explanatory:

```
struct nsproxy {
    atomic_t count;
    struct uts_namespace *uts_ns;
    struct ipc_namespace *ipc_ns;
    struct mnt_namespace *mnt_ns;
    struct pid_namespace *pid_ns;
    struct net           *net_ns;
};
(include/linux/nsproxy.h)
```

- You can see in the `nsproxy` structure five pointers of namespaces (there is no user namespace pointer). Using the `nsproxy` object in the process descriptor (`task_struct` object) instead of five namespace objects is an optimization. When performing `fork()`, a new child is likely to live in the same set of namespaces as its parent. So instead of five reference counter increments (one per each namespace), only one reference counter increment would happen (of the `nsproxy` object). The `nsproxy` `count` member is a reference counter, which is initialized to 1 when the `nsproxy` object is created by the `create_nsproxy()` method, and which is decremented by the `put_nsproxy()` method and incremented by the `get_nsproxy()` method. Note that the `pid_ns` member of the `nsproxy` object was renamed to `pid_ns_for_children` in kernel 3.11.

- A new system call, `unshare()`, was added. This system call gets a single parameter that is a bitmask of CLONE* flags. When the flags argument consists of one or more namespace CLONE_NEW* flags, the `unshare()` system call performs the following steps:

  - First, it creates a new namespace (or several namespaces) according to the specified flag. This is done by calling the `unshare_nsproxy_namespaces()` method, which in turn creates a new `nsproxy` object and one or more namespaces by calling the `create_new_namespaces()` method. The type of the new namespace (or namespaces) is determined according to the specified CLONE_NEW* flag. The `create_new_namespaces()` method returns a new `nsproxy` object that contains the new created namespace (or namespaces).

  - Then it attaches the calling process to that newly created `nsproxy` object by calling the `switch_task_namespaces()` method.

  When CLONE_NEWPID is the flag of the `unshare()` system call, it works differently than with the other flags; it's an implicit argument to `fork()`; only the child task will happen in a new PID namespace, not the one calling the `unshare()` system call. Other CLONE_NEW* flags immediately put the calling process into a new namespace.

  The six CLONE_NEW* flags, which were added to support the creation of namespaces, are described later in this section. The implementation of the `unshare()` system call is in `kernel/fork.c`.

- A new system call, setns(), was added. It attaches the calling thread to an existing namespace. Its prototype is int setns(int fd, int nstype); the parameters are:

  - fd: A file descriptor which refers to a namespace. These are obtained by opening links from the /proc/<pid>/ns/ directory.

  - nstype: An optional parameter. When it is one of the new CLONE_NEW* namespaces flags, the specified file descriptor must refer to a namespace which matches the type of the specified CLONE_NEW* flag. When the nstype is not set (its value is 0) the fd argument can refer to a namespace of any type. If the nstype does not correspond to the namespace type associated with the specified fd, a value of –EINVAL is returned.

You can find the implementation of the setns() system call in kernel/nsproxy.c.

- The following six new clone flags were added in order to support namespaces:

  - CLONE_NEWNS (for mount namespaces)

  - CLONE_NEWUTS (for UTS namespaces)

  - CLONE_NEWIPC (for IPC namespaces)

  - CLONE_NEWPID (for PID namespaces)

  - CLONE_NEWNET (for network namespaces)

  - CLONE_NEWUSER (for user namespaces)

  The clone() system call is used traditionally to create a new process. It was adjusted to support these new flags so that it will create a new process attached to a new namespace (or namespaces). Note that you will encounter usage of the CLONE_NEWNET flag, for creating a new network namespace, in some of the examples later in this chapter.

- Each subsystem, from the six for which there is a namespace support, had implemented a unique namespace of its own. For example, the mount namespace is represented by a structure called mnt_namespace, and the network namespace is represented by a structure called net, which is discussed later in this section. I will mention the other namespaces later in this chapter.

- For namespaces creation, a method named create_new_namespaces() was added (kernel/nsproxy.c). This method gets as a first parameter a CLONE_NEW* flag or a bitmap of CLONE_NEW* flags. It first creates an nsproxy object by calling the create_nsproxy() method, and then it associates a namespace according to the specified flag; since the flag can be a bitmask of flags, the create_new_namespaces() method can associate more than one namespace. Let's take a look at the create_new_namespaces() method:

```
static struct nsproxy *create_new_namespaces(unsigned long flags,
        struct task_struct *tsk, struct user_namespace *user_ns,
        struct fs_struct *new_fs)
{
        struct nsproxy *new_nsp;
        int err;
```

Allocate an nsproxy object and initialize its reference counter to 1:

```
new_nsp = create_nsproxy();
if (!new_nsp)
        return ERR_PTR(-ENOMEM);
. . .
```

After creating successfully an nsproxy object, we should create namespaces according to the specified flags, or associate an existing namespace to the new nsproxy object we created. We start by calling copy_mnt_ns(), for the mount namespaces, and then we call copy_utsname(), for the UTS namespace. I will describe here shortly the copy_utsname() method, because the UTS namespace is discussed in the "UTS Namespaces Implementation" section later in this chapter. If the CLONE_NEWUTS is not set in the specified flags of the copy_utsname() method, the copy_utsname() method does not create a new UTS namespace; it returns the UTS namespace that was passed by tsk->nsproxy->uts_ns as the last parameter to the copy_utsname() method. In case the CLONE_NEWUTS is set, the copy_utsname() method clones the specified UTS namespace by calling the clone_uts_ns() method. The clone_uts_ns() method, in turn, allocates a new UTS namespace object, copies the new_utsname object of the specified UTS namespace (tsk->nsproxy->uts_ns) into the new_utsname object of the newly created UTS namespace object, and returns the newly created UTS namespace. You will learn more about the new_utsname structure in the "UTS Namespaces Implementation" section later in this chapter:

```
new_nsp->uts_ns = copy_utsname(flags, user_ns, tsk->nsproxy->uts_ns);
if (IS_ERR(new_nsp->uts_ns)) {
        err = PTR_ERR(new_nsp->uts_ns);
        goto out_uts;
}
. . .
```

After handling the UTS namespace, we continue with calling the copy_ipcs() method to handle the IPC namespace, copy_pid_ns() to handle the PID namespace, and copy_net_ns() to handle the network namespace. Note that there is no call to the copy_user_ns() method, as the nsproxy does not contain a pointer to user namespace, as was mentioned earlier. I will describe here shortly the copy_net_ns() method. If the CLONE_NEWNET is not set in the specified flags of the create_new_namespaces() method, the copy_net_ns() method returns the network namespace that was passed as the third parameter to the copy_net_ns() method, tsk->nsproxy->net_ns, much like the copy_utsname() did, as you saw earlier in this section. If the CLONE_NEWNET is set, the copy_net_ns() method allocates a new network namespace by calling the net_alloc() method, initializes it by calling the setup_net() method, and adds it to the global list of all network namespaces, net_namespace_list:

```
new_nsp->net_ns = copy_net_ns(flags, user_ns, tsk->nsproxy->net_ns);
if (IS_ERR(new_nsp->net_ns)) {
        err = PTR_ERR(new_nsp->net_ns);
        goto out_net;
}
return new_nsp;
}
```

Note that the setns() system call, which does not create a new namespace but only attaches the calling thread to a specified namespace, also calls create_new_namespaces(), but it passes 0 as a first parameter; this implies that only an nsproxy is created by calling the create_nsproxy() method, but no new namespace is created, but the calling thread is associated with an existing network namespace which is identified by the specified fd argument of the setns() system call. Later in the setns() system call implementation, the switch_task_namespaces() method is invoked, and it assigns the new nsproxy which was just created to the calling thread (see kernel/nsproxy.c).

- A method named exit_task_namespaces() was added in kernel/nsproxy.c. It is called when a process is terminated, by the do_exit() method (kernel/exit.c). The exit_task_namespaces() method gets the process descriptor (task_struct object) as a single parameter. In fact the only thing it does is call the switch_task_namespaces() method, passing the specified process descriptor and a NULL nsproxy object as arguments. The switch_task_namespaces() method, in turn, nullifies the nsproxy object of the process descriptor of the process which is being terminated. If there are no other processes that use that nsproxy, it is freed.

- A method named get_net_ns_by_fd() was added. This method gets a file descriptor as its single parameter, and returns the network namespace associated with the inode that corresponds to the specified file descriptor. For readers who are not familiar with filesystems and with inode semantics, I suggest reading the "Inode Objects" section of Chapter 12, "The Virtual Filesystem," in *Understanding the Linux Kernel* by Daniel P. Bovet and Marco Cesati (O'Reilly, 2005).

- A method named get_net_ns_by_pid() was added. This method gets a PID number as a single argument, and it returns the network namespace object to which this process is attached.

- Six entries were added under /proc/<pid>/ns, one for each namespace. These files, when opened, should be fed into the setns() system call. You can use ls -al or readlink to display the unique proc inode number which is associated with a namespace. This unique proc inode is created by the proc_alloc_inum() method when the namespace is created, and is freed by the proc_free_inum() method when the namespace is released. See, for example, in the create_pid_namespace() method in kernel/pid_namespace.c. In the following example, the number in square brackets on the right is the unique proc inode number of each namespace:

```
ls -al /proc/1/ns/
total 0
dr-x--x--x 2 root root 0 Nov  3 13:32 .
dr-xr-xr-x 8 root root 0 Nov  3 12:17 ..
lrwxrwxrwx 1 root root 0 Nov  3 13:32 ipc -> ipc:[4026531839]
lrwxrwxrwx 1 root root 0 Nov  3 13:32 mnt -> mnt:[4026531840]
lrwxrwxrwx 1 root root 0 Nov  3 13:32 net -> net:[4026531956]
lrwxrwxrwx 1 root root 0 Nov  3 13:32 pid -> pid:[4026531836]
lrwxrwxrwx 1 root root 0 Nov  3 13:32 user -> user:[4026531837]
lrwxrwxrwx 1 root root 0 Nov  3 13:32 uts -> uts:[4026531838]
```

- A namespace can stay alive if either one of the following conditions is met:

  - The namespace file under /proc/<pid>/ns/ descriptor is held.

  - bind mounting the namespace proc file somewhere else, for example, for PID namespace, by: mount --bind /proc/self/ns/pid /some/filesystem/path

- For each of the six namespaces, a proc namespace operations object (an instance of proc_ns_operations structure) is defined. This object consists of callbacks, such as inum, to return the unique proc inode number associated with the namespace or install, for namespace installation (in the install callback, namespace specific actions are performed, such as attaching the specific namespace object to the nsproxy object, and more; the install callback is invoked by the setns system call). The proc_ns_operations structure in defined in include/linux/proc_fs.h. Following is the list of the six proc_ns_operations objects:

- utsns_operations for UTS namespace (kernel/utsname.c)

- ipcns_operations for IPC namespace (ipc/namespace.c)

- mntns_operations for mount namespaces (fs/namespace.c)

- pidns_operations for PID namespaces (kernel/pid_namespace.c)

- userns_operations for user namespace (kernel/user_namespace.c)

- netns_operations for network namespace (net/core/net_namespace.c)

- For each namespace, except the mount namespace, there is an **initial namespace**:

  - init_uts_ns: For UTS namespace (init/version.c).

  - init_ipc_ns: For IPC namespace (ipc/msgutil.c).

  - init_pid_ns: For PID namespace (kernel/pid.c).

  - init_net: For network namespace (net/core/net_namespace.c).

  - init_user_ns: For user namespace (kernel/user.c).

- An initial, default nsproxy object is defined: it is called init_nsproxy and it contains pointers to five initial namespaces; they are all initialized to be the corresponding specific initial namespace except for the mount namespace, which is initialized to be NULL:

```
struct nsproxy init_nsproxy = {
        .count  = ATOMIC_INIT(1),
        .uts_ns = &init_uts_ns,
#if defined(CONFIG_POSIX_MQUEUE) || defined(CONFIG_SYSVIPC)
        .ipc_ns = &init_ipc_ns,
#endif
        .mnt_ns = NULL,
        .pid_ns = &init_pid_ns,
#ifdef CONFIG_NET
        .net_ns = &init_net,
#endif
};
(kernel/nsproxy.c)
```

- A method named task_nsproxy() was added; it gets as a single parameter a process descriptor (task_struct object), and it returns the nsproxy associated with the specified task_struct object. See include/linux/nsproxy.h.

These are the six namespaces available in the Linux kernel as of this writing:

- **Mount namespaces:** The mount namespaces allows a process to see its own view of the filesystem and of its mount points. Mounting a filesystem in one mount namespace does not propagate to the other mount namespaces. Mount namespaces are created by setting the CLONE_NEWNS flag when calling the clone() or unshare() system calls. In order to implement mount namespaces, a structure called mnt_namespace was added (fs/mount.h), and nsproxy holds a pointer to an mnt_namespace object called mnt_ns. Mount namespaces are available from kernel 2.4.19. Mount namespaces are implemented primarily in fs/namespace.c. When creating a new mount namespace, the following rules apply:

- All previous mounts will be visible in the new mount namespace.

- Mounts/unmounts in the new mount namespace are invisible to the rest of the system.

- Mounts/unmounts in the global mount namespace are visible in the new mount namespace.

Mount namespaces use a VFS enhancement called *shared subtrees*, which was introduced in the Linux 2.6.15 kernel; the shared subtrees feature introduced new flags: MS_PRIVATE, MS_SHARED, MS_SLAVE and MS_UNBINDABLE . (See http://lwn.net/Articles/159077/ and Documentation/filesystems/sharedsubtree.txt.) I will not discuss the internals of mount namespaces implementation. For readers who want to learn more about mount namespaces usage, I suggest reading the following article: "Applying Mount Namespaces," by Serge E. Hallyn and Ram Pai (http://www.ibm.com/developerworks/linux/library/l-mount-namespaces/index.html).

- **PID namespaces:** The PID namespaces provides the ability for different processes in different PID namespaces to have the same PID. This feature is a building block for Linux containers. It is important for checkpoint/restore of a process, because a process checkpointed on one host can be restored on a different host even if there is a process with the same PID on that host. When creating the first process in a new PID namespace, its PID is 1. The behavior of this process is somewhat like the behavior of the init process. This means that when a process dies, all its orphaned children will now have the process with PID 1 as their parent (child reaping). Sending SIGKILL signal to a process with PID 1 does not kill the process, regardless of in which namespace the SIGKILL signal was sent, in the initial PID namespace or in any other PID namespace. But killing init of one PID namespace from another (parent one) will work. In this case, all of the tasks living in the former namespace will be killed and the PID namespace will be stopped. PID namespaces are created by setting the CLONE_NEWPID flag when calling the clone() or unshare() system calls. In order to implement PID namespaces, a structure called pid_namespace was added (include/linux/pid_namespace.h), and nsproxy holds a pointer to a pid_namespace object called pid_ns. In order to have PID namespaces support, CONFIG_PID_NS should be set. PID namespaces are available from kernel 2.6.24. PID namespaces are implemented primarily in kernel/pid_namespace.c.

- **Network namespaces:** The network namespace allows creating what appears to be multiple instances of the kernel network stack. Network namespaces are created by setting the CLONE_NEWNET flag when calling the clone() or unshare() system calls. In order to implement network namespaces, a structure called net was added (include/net/net_namespace.h), and nsproxy holds a pointer to a net object called net_ns. In order to have network namespaces support, CONFIG_NET_NS should be set. I will discuss network namespaces later in this section. Network namespaces are available from kernel 2.6.29. Network namespaces are implemented primarily in net/core/net_namespace.c.

- **IPC namespaces:** The IPC namespace allows a process to have its own System V IPC resources and POSIX message queues resources. IPC namespaces are created by setting the CLONE_NEWIPC flag when calling the clone() or unshare() system calls. In order to implement IPC namespaces, a structure called ipc_namespace was added (include/linux/ipc_namespace.h), and nsproxy holds a pointer to an ipc_namespace object called ipc_ns.

In order to have IPC namespaces support, CONFIG_IPC_NS should be set. Support for System V IPC resources is available in IPC namespaces from kernel 2.6.19. Support for POSIX message queues resources in IPC namespaces was added later, in kernel 2.6.30. IPC namespaces are implemented primarily in `ipc/namespace.c`.

- **UTS namespaces:** The UTS namespace provides the ability for different UTS namespaces to have different host name or domain name (or other information returned by the `uname()` system call). UTS namespaces are created by setting the CLONE_NEWUTS flag when calling the `clone()` or `unshare()` system calls. UTS namespace implementation is the simplest among the six namespaces that were implemented. In order to implement the UTS namespace, a structure called `uts_namespace` was added (`include/linux/utsname.h`), and `nsproxy` holds a pointer to a `uts_namespace` object called `uts_ns`. In order to have UTS namespaces support, CONFIG_UTS_NS should be set. UTS namespaces are available from kernel 2.6.19. UTS namespaces are implemented primarily in `kernel/utsname.c`.

- **User namespaces:** The user namespace allows mapping of user and group IDs. This mapping is done by writing to two `procfs` entries that were added for supporting user namespaces: `/proc/sys/kernel/overflowuid` and `/proc/sys/kernel/overflowgid`. A process attached to a user namespace can have a different set of capabilities then the host. User namespaces are created by setting the CLONE_NEWUSER flag when calling the `clone()` or `unshare()` system calls. In order to implement user namespaces, a structure called `user_namespace` was added (`include/linux/user_namespace.h`). The `user_namespace` object contains a pointer to the user namespace object that created it (`parent`). As opposed to the other five namespaces, `nsproxy` does not hold a pointer to a `user_namespace` object. I will not delve into more implementation details of user namespaces, as it is probably the most complex namespace and as it is beyond the scope of the book. In order to have user namespaces support, CONFIG_USER_NS should be set. User namespaces are available from kernel 3.8 for almost all filesystem types. User namespaces are implemented primarily in `kernel/user_namespace.c`.

Support to namespaces was added in four userspace packages:

- In `util-linux`:
  - The `unshare` utility can create any of the six namespaces, available since version 2.17.
  - The `nsenter` utility (which is in fact a light wrapper around the `setns` system call), available since version 2.23.

- In `iproute2`, management of network namespaces is done with the `ip netns` command, and you will see several examples for this later in this chapter. Moreover, you can move a network interface to a different network namespace with the `ip link` command as you will see in the "Moving a Network Interface to a different Network Namespace" section later in this chapter.

- In `ethtool`, support was added to enable to find out whether the NETIF_F_NETNS_LOCAL feature is set for a specified network interface. When the NETIF_F_NETNS_LOCAL feature is set, this indicates that the network interface is local to that network namespace, and you cannot move it to a different network namespace. The NETIF_F_NETNS_LOCAL feature will be discussed later in this section.

- In the wireless `iw` package, an option was added to enable moving a wireless interface to a different namespace.

■ **Note** In a presentation in Ottawa Linux Symposium (OLS) in 2006, "Multiple Instances of the Global Linux Namespaces," Eric W. Biederman (one of the main developers of Linux namespaces) mentioned ten namespaces; the other four namespaces that he mentioned in this presentation and that are not implemented yet are: device namespace, security namespace, security keys namespace, and time namespace. (See `https://www.kernel.org/doc/ols/2006/ols2006v1-pages-101-112.pdf`.) For more information about namespaces, I suggest reading a series of six articles about it by Michael Kerrisk (`https://lwn.net/Articles/531114/`). Mobile OS virtualization projects triggered a development effort to support device namespaces; for more information about device namespaces, which are not yet part of the kernel, see "Device Namespaces" By Jake Edge (`http://lwn.net/Articles/564854/`) and also (`http://lwn.net/Articles/564977/`). There was also some work for implementing a new syslog namespace (see the article "Stepping Closer to Practical Containers: "syslog" namespaces", `http://lwn.net/Articles/527342/`).

The following three system calls can be used with namespaces:

- `clone()`: Creates a new process attached to a new namespace (or namespaces). The type of the namespace is specified by a CLONE_NEW* flag which is passed as a parameter. Note that you can also use a bitmask of these CLONE_NEW* flags. The implementation of the `clone()` system call is in `kernel/fork.c`.

- `unshare()`: Discussed earlier in this section.

- `setns()`: Discussed earlier in this section.

■ **Note** Namespaces do not have names inside the kernel that userspace processes can use to talk with them. If namespaces would have names, this would require keeping them globally, in yet another special namespace. This would complicate the implementation and can raise problems in checkpoint/restore for example. Instead, userspace processes should open namespace files under `/proc/<pid>/ns/` and their file descriptors can be used to talk to a specific namespace, in order to keep that namespace alive. Namespaces are identified by a unique proc inode number generated when they are created and freed when they are released. Each of the six namespace structures contains an integer member called `proc_inum`, which is the namespace unique proc inode number and is assigned by calling the `proc_alloc_inum()` method. Each of the six namespaces has also a `proc_ns_operations` object, which includes namespace-specific callbacks; one of these callbacks, called `inum`, returns the `proc_inum` of the associated namespace (for the definition of `proc_ns_operations` structure, refer to `include/linux/proc_fs.h`).

Before discussing network namespaces, let's describe how the simplest namespace, the UTS namespace, is implemented. This is a good starting point to understand the other, more complex namespaces.

UTS Namespaces Implementation

In order to implement UTS namespaces, a struct called `uts_namespace` was added:

```
struct uts_namespace {
        struct kref kref;
        struct new_utsname name;
```

```
        struct user_namespace *user_ns;
        unsigned int proc_inum;
};
(include/linux/utsname.h)
```

Here is a short description of the members of the `uts_namespace` structure:

- `kref`: A reference counter. It is a generic kernel reference counter, incremented by the `kref_get()` method and decremented by the `kref_put()` method. Besides the UTS namespace, also the PID namespace has a `kref` object as a reference counter; all the other four namespaces use an atomic counter for reference counting. For more info about the `kref` API look in `Documentation/kref.txt`.

- `name`: A `new_utsname` object, contains fields like `domainname` and `nodename` (will be discussed shortly).

- `user_ns`: The user namespace associated with the UTS namespace.

- `proc_inum`: The unique proc inode number of the UTS namespace.

The `nsproxy` structure contains a pointer to the `uts_namespace`:

```
struct nsproxy {
        . . .
        struct uts_namespace *uts_ns;
        . . .
};
(include/linux/nsproxy.h)
```

As you saw earlier, the `uts_namespace` object contains an instance of the `new_utsname` structure. Let's take a look at the `new_utsname` structure, which is the essence of the UTS namespace:

```
struct new_utsname {
        char sysname[__NEW_UTS_LEN + 1];
        char nodename[__NEW_UTS_LEN + 1];
        char release[__NEW_UTS_LEN + 1];
        char version[__NEW_UTS_LEN + 1];
        char machine[__NEW_UTS_LEN + 1];
        char domainname[__NEW_UTS_LEN + 1];
};
(include/uapi/linux/utsname.h)
```

The `nodename` member of the `new_utsname` is the host name, and `domainname` is the domain name. A method named `utsname()` was added; this method simply returns the `new_utsname` object which is associated with the process that currently runs (`current`):

```
static inline struct new_utsname *utsname(void)
{
        return &current->nsproxy->uts_ns->name;
}
(include/linux/utsname.h)
```

Now, the new gethostname() system call implementation is the following:

```
SYSCALL_DEFINE2(gethostname, char __user *, name, int, len)
{
        int i, errno;
        struct new_utsname *u;

        if (len < 0)
                return -EINVAL;
        down_read(&uts_sem);
```

Invoke the utsname() method, which accesses the new_utsname object of the UTS namespace associated with the current process:

```
        u = utsname();
        i = 1 + strlen(u->nodename);
        if (i > len)
                i = len;
        errno = 0;
```

Copy to userspace the nodename of the new_utsname object that the utsname() method returned:

```
        if (copy_to_user(name, u->nodename, i))
                errno = -EFAULT;
        up_read(&uts_sem);
        return errno;
}
```
(kernel/sys.c)

You can find a similar approach in the sethostbyname() and in the uname() system calls, which are also defined in kernel/sys.c. I should note that UTS namespaces implementation also handles UTS procfs entries. There are only two UTS procfs entries, /proc/sys/kernel/domainname and /proc/sys/kernel/hostname, which are writable (this means that you can change them from userspace). There are other UTS procfs entries which are not writable, like /proc/sys/kernel/ostype and /proc/sys/kernel/osrelease. If you will look at the table of the UTS procfs entries, uts_kern_table (kernel/utsname_sysctl.c), you will see that some entries, like ostype and osrelease, have mode of "0444", which means they are not writable, and only two of them, hostname and domainname, have mode of "0644", which means they are writable. Reading and writing the UTS procfs entries is handled by the proc_do_uts_string() method. Readers who want to learn more about how UTS procfs entries are handled should look into the proc_do_uts_string() method and into the get_uts() method; both are in kernel/utsname_sysctl.c.

Now that you learned about how the simplest namespace, the UTS namespace, is implemented, it is time to learn about network namespaces and their implementation.

Network Namespaces Implementation

A network namespace is logically another copy of the network stack, with its own network devices, routing tables, neighbouring tables, netfilter tables, network sockets, network procfs entries, network sysfs entries, and other network resources. A practical feature of network namespaces is that network applications running in a given namespace (let's say ns1) will first look for configuration files under /etc/netns/ns1, and only afterward under /etc. So, for example, if you created a namespace called ns1 and you have created /etc/netns/ns1/hosts, every userspace application that tries to access the hosts file will first access /etc/netns/ns1/hosts and only then (if the entry being looked for does not exist) will it read /etc/hosts. This feature is implemented using bind mounts and is available only for network namespaces created with the ip netns add command.

The Network Namespace Object (struct net)

Let's turn now to the definition of the net structure, which is the fundamental data structure that represents a network namespace:

```
struct net {
        . . .
        struct user_namespace    *user_ns;       /* Owning user namespace */
        unsigned int             proc_inum;
        struct proc_dir_entry    *proc_net;
        struct proc_dir_entry    *proc_net_stat;
        . . .
        struct list_head         dev_base_head;
        struct hlist_head        *dev_name_head;
        struct hlist_head        *dev_index_head;
        . . .
        int                      ifindex;
        . . .
        struct net_device        *loopback_dev;  /* The loopback */
        . . .
        atomic_t                 count;          /* To decided when the network
                                                 *  namespace should be shut down.
                                                 */

        struct netns_ipv4        ipv4;
#if IS_ENABLED(CONFIG_IPV6)
        struct netns_ipv6        ipv6;
#endif
#if defined(CONFIG_IP_SCTP) || defined(CONFIG_IP_SCTP_MODULE)
        struct netns_sctp        sctp;
#endif
        . . .

#if defined(CONFIG_NF_CONNTRACK) || defined(CONFIG_NF_CONNTRACK_MODULE)
        struct netns_ct          ct;
#endif
#if IS_ENABLED(CONFIG_NF_DEFRAG_IPV6)
        struct netns_nf_frag     nf_frag;
#endif
        . . .
        struct net_generic __rcu *gen;
#ifdef CONFIG_XFRM
        struct netns_xfrm        xfrm;
#endif
        . . .
};
(include/net/net_namespace.h)
```

Here is a short description of several members of the net structure:

- user_ns represents the user namespace that created the network namespace; it owns the network namespace and all its resources. It is assigned in the setup_net() method. For the initial network namespace object (init_net), the user namespace that created it is the initial user namespace, init_user_ns.

- proc_inum is the unique proc inode number associated to the network namespace. This unique proc inode is created by the proc_alloc_inum() method, which also assigns proc_inum to be the proc inode number. The proc_alloc_inum() method is invoked by the network namespace initialization method, net_ns_net_init(), and it is freed by calling the proc_free_inum() method in the network namespace cleanup method, net_ns_net_exit().

- proc_net represents the network namespace procfs entry (/proc/net) as each network namespace maintains its own procfs entry.

- proc_net_stat represents the network namespace procfs statistics entry (/proc/net/stat) as each network namespace maintains its own procfs statistics entry.

- dev_base_head points to a linked list of all network devices.

- dev_name_head points to a hashtable of network devices, where the key is the network device name.

- dev_index_head points to a hashtable of network devices, where the key is the network device index.

- ifindex is the last device index assigned inside a network namespace. Indices are virtualized in network namespaces; this means that loopback devices would always have index of 1 in all network namespaces, and other network devices may have coinciding indices when living in different network namespaces.

- loopback_dev is the loopback device. Every new network namespace is created with only one network device, the loopback device. The loopback_dev object of a network namespace is assigned in the loopback_net_init() method, drivers/net/loopback.c. You cannot move the loopback device from one network namespace to another.

- count is the network namespace reference counter. It is initialized to 1 when the network namespace is created by the by the setup_net() method. It is incremented by the get_net() method and decremented by the put_net() method. If the count reference counter reaches 0 in the put_net() method, the __put_net() method is called. The __put_net() method, in turn, adds the network namespace to a global list of network namespaces to be removed, cleanup_list, and later removes it.

- ipv4 (an instance of the netns_ipv4 structure) for the IPv4 subsystem. The netns_ipv4 structure contains IPv4 specific fields which are different for different namespaces. For example, in chapter 6 you saw that the multicast routing table of a specified network namespace called net is stored in net->ipv4.mrt. I will discuss the netns_ipv4 later in this section.

- ipv6 (an instance of the netns_ipv6 structure) for the IPv6 subsystem.

- sctp (an instance of the netns_sctp structure) for SCTP sockets.

- ct (an instance of the netns_ct structure, which is discussed in chapter 9) for the netfilter connection tracking subsystem.

- gen (an instance of the net_generic structure, defined in include/net/netns/generic.h) is a set of generic pointers on structures describing a network namespace context of optional subsystems. For example, the sit module (Simple Internet Transition, an IPv6 tunnel, implemented in net/ipv6/sit.c) puts its private data on struct net using this engine. This was introduced in order not to flood the struct net with pointers for every single network subsystem that is willing to have per network namespace context.

- xfrm (an instance of the netns_xfrm structure, which is mentioned several times in chapter 10) for the IPsec subsystem.

Let's take a look at the IPv4 specific namespace, the netns_ipv4 structure:

```
struct netns_ipv4 {
. . .
#ifdef CONFIG_IP_MULTIPLE_TABLES
        struct fib_rules_ops    *rules_ops;
        bool                    fib_has_custom_rules;
        struct fib_table        *fib_local;
        struct fib_table        *fib_main;
        struct fib_table        *fib_default;
#endif
. . .
        struct hlist_head       *fib_table_hash;
        struct sock             *fibnl;

        struct sock             **icmp_sk;
. . .
#ifdef CONFIG_NETFILTER
        struct xt_table         *iptable_filter;
        struct xt_table         *iptable_mangle;
        struct xt_table         *iptable_raw;
        struct xt_table         *arptable_filter;
#ifdef CONFIG_SECURITY
        struct xt_table         *iptable_security;
#endif
        struct xt_table         *nat_table;
#endif

        int sysctl_icmp_echo_ignore_all;
        int sysctl_icmp_echo_ignore_broadcasts;
        int sysctl_icmp_ignore_bogus_error_responses;
        int sysctl_icmp_ratelimit;
        int sysctl_icmp_ratemask;
        int sysctl_icmp_errors_use_inbound_ifaddr;

        int sysctl_tcp_ecn;

        kgid_t sysctl_ping_group_range[2];
        long sysctl_tcp_mem[3];

        atomic_t dev_addr_genid;
```

```
#ifdef CONFIG_IP_MROUTE
#ifndef CONFIG_IP_MROUTE_MULTIPLE_TABLES
        struct mr_table          *mrt;
#else
        struct list_head         mr_tables;
        struct fib_rules_ops     *mr_rules_ops;
#endif
#endif
};
(net/netns/ipv4.h)
```

You can see in the netns_ipv4 structure many IPv4-specific tables and variables, like the routing tables, the netfilter tables, the multicast routing tables, and more.

Network Namespaces Implementation: Other Data Structures

In order to support network namespaces, a member called nd_net, which is a pointer to a network namespace, was added to the network device object (struct net_device). Setting the network namespace for a network device is done by calling the dev_net_set() method, and getting the network namespace associated to a network device is done by calling the dev_net() method. Note that a network device can belong to only a single network namespace at a given moment. The nd_net is set typically when a network device is registered or when a network device is moved to a different network namespace. For example, when registering a VLAN device, both these methods just mentioned are used:

```
static int register_vlan_device(struct net_device *real_dev, u16 vlan_id)
{
    struct net_device *new_dev;
```

The network namespace to be assigned to the new VLAN device is the network namespace associated with the real device, which is passed as a parameter to the register_vlan_device() method; we get this namespace by calling dev_net(real_dev):

```
    struct net *net = dev_net(real_dev);
    . . .
    new_dev = alloc_netdev(sizeof(struct vlan_dev_priv), name, vlan_setup);

    if (new_dev == NULL)
        return -ENOBUFS;
```

Switch the network namespace by calling the dev_net_set() method:

```
    dev_net_set(new_dev, net);

    . . .
}
```

A member called sk_net, a pointer to a network namespace, was added to struct sock, which represents a socket. Setting the network namespace for a sock object is done by calling the sock_net_set() method, and getting the network namespace associated to a sock object is done by calling the sock_net() method. Like in the case of the nd_net object, also a sock object can belong to only a single network namespace at a given moment.

When the system boots, a default network namespace, init_net, is created. After the boot, all physical network devices and all sockets belong to that initial namespace, as well as the network loopback device.

Some network devices and some network subsystems should have network namespaces specific data. In order to enable this, a structure named pernet_operations was added; this structure includes an init and exit callbacks:

```
struct pernet_operations {
        . . .
        int (*init)(struct net *net);
        void (*exit)(struct net *net);
        . . .
        int *id;
        size_t size;
};
(include/net/net_namespace.h)
```

Network devices that need network namespaces specific data should define a pernet_operations object, and define its init() and exit() callbacks for device specific initialization and cleanup, respectively, and call the register_pernet_device() method in their module initialization and the unregister_pernet_device() method when the module is removed, passing the pernet_operations object as a single parameter in both cases. For example, the PPPoE module exports information about PPPoE session by a procfs entry, /proc/net/pppoe. The information exported by this procfs entry depends on the network namespace to which this PPPoE device belongs (since different PPPoE devices can belong to different network namespaces). So the PPPoE module defines a pernet_operations object called pppoe_net_ops:

```
static struct pernet_operations pppoe_net_ops = {
        .init = pppoe_init_net,
        .exit = pppoe_exit_net,
        .id   = &pppoe_net_id,
        .size = sizeof(struct pppoe_net),
}
(net/ppp/pppoe.c)
```

In the init callback, pppoe_init_net(), it only creates the PPPoE procfs entry, /proc/net/pppoe, by calling the proc_create() method:

```
static __net_init int pppoe_init_net(struct net *net)
{
        struct pppoe_net *pn = pppoe_pernet(net);
        struct proc_dir_entry *pde;

        rwlock_init(&pn->hash_lock);

        pde = proc_create("pppoe", S_IRUGO, net->proc_net, &pppoe_seq_fops);
#ifdef CONFIG_PROC_FS
        if (!pde)
                return -ENOMEM;
#endif

        return 0;
}
(net/ppp/pppoe.c)
```

And in the exit callback, pppoe_exit_net(), it only removes the PPPoE procfs entry, /proc/net/pppoe, by calling the remove_proc_entry() method:

```
static __net_exit void pppoe_exit_net(struct net *net)
{
        remove_proc_entry("pppoe", net->proc_net);
}
(net/ppp/pppoe.c)
```

Network subsystems that need network-namespace-specific data should call register_pernet_subsys() when the subsystem is initialized and unregister_pernet_subsys() when the subsystem is removed. You can look for examples in net/ipv4/route.c, and there are many other examples of reviewing these methods. The network namespace module itself also defines a net_ns_ops object and registers it in the boot phase:

```
static struct pernet_operations __net_initdata net_ns_ops = {
        .init = net_ns_net_init,
        .exit = net_ns_net_exit,
};

static int __init net_ns_init(void)
{
    . . .
    register_pernet_subsys(&net_ns_ops);
    . . .
}
(net/core/net_namespace.c)
```

Each time a new network namespace is created, the init callback (net_ns_net_init) is called, and each time a network namespace is removed, the exit callback (net_ns_net_exit) is called. The only thing that the net_ns_net_init() does is to allocate a unique proc inode for the newly created namespace by calling the proc_alloc_inum() method; the newly created unique proc inode number is assigned to net->proc_inum:

```
static __net_init int net_ns_net_init(struct net *net)
{
        return proc_alloc_inum(&net->proc_inum);
}
```

And the only thing that the net_ns_net_exit() method does is to remove that unique proc inode by calling the proc_free_inum() method:

```
static __net_exit void net_ns_net_exit(struct net *net)
{
        proc_free_inum(net->proc_inum);
}
```

When you create a new network namespace, it has only the network loopback device. The most common ways to create a network namespace are:

- By a userspace application which will create a network namespace with the clone() system call or with the unshare() system call, setting the CLONE_NEWNET flag in both cases.

- Using ip netns command of iproute2 (you will shortly see an example).

- Using the unshare utility of util-linux, with the --net flag.

Network Namespaces Management

Next you will see some examples of using the `ip netns` command of the `iproute2` package to perform actions such as creating a network namespace, deleting a network namespace, showing all the network namespaces, and more.

- Creating a network namespace named `ns1` is done by:

```
ip netns add ns1
```

Running this command triggers first the creation of a file called /var/run/netns/ns1, and then the creation of the network namespace by the `unshare()` system call, passing it a CLONE_NEWNET flag. Then /var/run/netns/ns1 is attached to the network namespace (/proc/self/ns/net) by a bind mount (calling the `mount()` system call with MS_BIND). Note that network namespaces can be nested, which means that from within `ns1` you can also create a new network namespace, and so on.

- Deleting a network namespace named `ns1` is done by:

```
ip netns del ns1
```

Note that this will not delete a network namespace if there is one or more processes attached to it. In case there are no such processes, the /var/run/netns/ns1 file is deleted. Note also that when deleting a namespace, all its network devices are moved to the initial, default network namespace, init_net, except for network namespace local devices, which are network devices whose NETIF_F_NETNS_LOCAL feature is set; such network devices are deleted. See more in the "Moving a Network Interface to a Network Namespace" section later in this chapter and in Appendix A.

- Showing all the network namespaces in the system that were added by `ip netns add` is done by:

```
ip netns list
```

In fact, running `ip netns list` simply shows the names of files under /var/run/netns. Note that network namespaces not added by `ip netns add` will not be displayed by `ip netns list`, because creating such network namespaces did not trigger creation of any file under /var/run/netns. So, for example, a network namespace created by `unshare --net bash` will not appear when running `ip netns list`.

- Monitoring creation and removal of a network namespace is done by:

```
ip netns monitor
```

After running `ip netns monitor`, when you add a new namespace by `ip netns add ns2` you will see on screen the following message: "add ns2", and after you delete that namespace by `ip netns delete ns2` you will see on screen the following message: "delete ns2". Note that adding and removing network namespaces not by running `ip netns add` and `ip netns delete`, respectively, does not trigger displaying any messages on screen by `ip netns monitor`. The `ip netns monitor` command is implemented by setting an inotify watch on /var/run/netns. Note that in case you will run `ip netns monitor` before adding at least one network namespace with `ip netns add` you will get the following error: inotify_add_watch failed: No such file or directory. The reason is that trying to set a watch on /var/run/netns, which does not exist yet, fails. See man `inotify_init()` and man `inotify_add_watch()`.

- Start a shell in a specified namespace (ns1 in this example) is done by:

  `ip netns exec ns1 bash`

  Note that with `ip netns exec` you can run **any** command in a specified network namespace. For example, the following command will display all network interfaces in the network namespace called ns1:

  `ip netns exec ns1 ifconfig -a`

In recent versions of `iproute2` (since version 3.8), you have these two additional helpful commands:

- Show the network namespace associated with the specified pid:

  `ip netns identify #pid`

  This is implemented by reading /proc/<pid>/ns/net and iterating over the files under /var/run/netns to find a match (using the `stat()` system call).

- Show the PID of a process (or list of processes) attached to a network namespace called ns1 by:

  `ip netns pids ns1`

  This is implemented by reading /var/run/netns/ns1, and then iterating over /proc/<pid> entries to find a matching /proc/pid/ns/net entry (using the `stat()` system call).

■ **Note** For more information about the various ip netns command options see man `ip netns`.

Moving a Network Interface to a Different Network Namespace

Moving a network interface to a network namespace named ns1 can be done with the `ip` command. For example, by: `ip link set eth0 netns ns1`. As part of implementing network namespaces, a new feature named NETIF_F_NETNS_LOCAL was added to the features of the net_device object (The net_device structure represents a network interface. For more information about the net_device structure and its features see Appendix A). You can find out whether the NETIF_F_NETNS_LOCAL feature is set for a specified network device by looking at the netns-local flag in the output of `ethtool -k eth0` or in the output of `ethtool --show-features eth0` (both commands are equivalent.) Note that you cannot set the NETIF_F_NETNS_LOCAL feature with `ethtool`. This feature, when set, denotes that the network device is a network namespace local device. For example, the loopback, the bridge, the VXLAN and the PPP devices are network namespace local devices. Trying to move a network device whose NETIF_F_NETNS_LOCAL feature is set to a different namespace will fail with an error of –EINVAL, as you will shortly see in the following code snippet. The dev_change_net_namespace() method is invoked when trying to move a network interface to a different network namespace, for example by: `ip link set eth0 netns ns1`. Let's take a look at the dev_change_net_namespace() method:

```
int dev_change_net_namespace(struct net_device *dev, struct net *net, const char *pat)
{
        int err;
```

```
        ASSERT_RTNL();

        /* Don't allow namespace local devices to be moved. */
        err = -EINVAL;
```

Return –EINVAL in case that the device is a local device (The NETIF_F_NETNS_LOCAL flag in the features of net_device object is set)

```
        if (dev->features & NETIF_F_NETNS_LOCAL)
                goto out;
        . . .
```

Actually switch the network namespace by setting nd_net of the net_device object to the new specified namespace:

```
        dev_net_set(dev, net)
        . . .
out:
        return err;
}
(net/core/dev.c)
```

■ **Note** You can move a network interface to a network namespace named ns1 also by specifying a PID of a process that is attached to that namespace, without specifying the namespace name explicitly. For example, if you know that a process whose PID is <pidNumber> is attached to ns1, running ip link set eth1 netns <pidNumber> will move eth1 to the ns1 namespace. Implementation details: getting the network namespace object when specifying one of the PIDs of its attached processes is implemented by the get_net_ns_by_pid() method, whereas getting the network namespace object when specifying the network namespace name is implemented by the get_net_ns_by_fd() method; both methods are in net/core/net_namespace.c. In order to move a wireless network interface to a different network namespace you should use the iw command. For example, if you want to move wlan0 to a network namespace and you know that a process whose PID is <pidNumber> is attached to that namespace, you can run iw phy phy0 set netns <pidNumber> to move it to that network namespace. For the implementation details, refer to the nl80211_wiphy_netns() method in net/wireless/nl80211.c.

Communicating Between Two Network Namespaces

I will end the network namespaces section with a short example of how two network namespaces can communicate with each other. It can be done either by using Unix sockets or by using the Virtual Ethernet (VETH) network driver to create a pair of virtual network devices and moving one of them to another network namespace. For example, here are the first two namespaces, ns1 and ns2:

```
ip netns add ns1
ip netns add ns2
```

Start a shell in ns1:

```
ip netns exec ns1 bash
```

Create a virtual Ethernet device (its type is veth):

```
ip link add name if_one type veth peer name if_one_peer
```

Move if_one_peer to ns2:

```
ip link set dev if_one_peer netns ns2
```

You can now set addresses on if_one and on if_one_peer as usual, with the ifconfig command or with the ip command, and send packets from one network namespace to the other.

■ **Note** Network namespaces are not mandatory for a kernel image. By default, network namespaces are enabled (CONFIG_NET_NS is set) in most distributions. However, you can build and boot a kernel where network namespaces are disabled.

I have discussed in this section what namespaces are, and in particular what are network namespaces. I mentioned some of the major changes that were required in order to implement namespaces in general, like adding 6 new CLONE_NEW* flags, adding two new systems calls, adding an nsproxy object to the process descriptor, and more. I also described the implementation of UTS namespaces, which are the most simple among all namespaces, and the implementation of network namespaces. Several examples were given showing how simple it is to manipulate network namespaces with the ip netns command of the iproute2 package. Next I will describe the cgroups subsystem, which provides another solution of resource management, and two network modules that belong to it.

Cgroups

The cgroups subsystem is a project started by Paul Menage, Rohit Seth, and other Google developers in 2006. It was initially called "process containers," but later it was renamed to "Control Groups." It provides resource management and resource accounting for groups of processes. It has been part of the mainline kernel since kernel 2.6.24, and it's used in several projects: for example by systemd (a service manager which replaced SysV init scripts; used, for example, by Fedora and by openSUSE), by the Linux Containers project, which was mentioned earlier in this chapter, by Google containers (https://github.com/google/lmctfy/), by libvirt (http://libvirt.org/cgroups.html) and more. Cgroups kernel implementation is mostly in non-critical paths in terms of performance. The cgroups subsystem implements a new Virtual File System (VFS) type named "cgroups". All cgroups actions are done by filesystem actions, like creating cgroups directories in a cgroup filesystem, writing or reading to entries in these directories, mounting cgroup filesystems, etc. There is a library called libcgroup (a.k.a. libcg), which provides a set of userspace utilities for cgroups management: for example, cgcreate to create a new cgroup, cgdelete to delete a cgroup, cgexec to run a task in a specified control group, and more. In fact this is done by calling the cgroup filesystem operations from the libcg library. The libcg library is likely to see reduced usage in the future because it doesn't provide any coordination among multiple parties trying to use the cgroup controllers. It could be that in the future all the cgroup file operations will be performed by a library or by a daemon and not directly. The cgroups subsystem, as currently implemented, needs some form of coordination, because there is only a single controller for each resource type. When multiple actors modify it, this necessarily leads to conflicts. The cgroups controllers can be used by many projects like libvirt, systemd, lxc and more, simultaneously. When working only via cgroups filesystem operations, and when all the projects try to impose their own policy through cgroups at too low a level, without knowing about each other, they may accidently walk over each other. When each will talk to a daemon, for example, such a clash will be avoided. For more information about libcg see http://libcg.sourceforge.net/.

As opposed to namespaces, no new system calls were added for implementing the cgroup subsystem. As in namespaces, several cgroups can be nested. There were code additions in the boot phase, mainly for the initialization of the cgroups subsystem, and in various subsystems, like the memory subsystem or security subsystem. Following here is a short, partial list of tasks that you can perform with cgroups:

- Assign a set of CPUs to a set of processes, with the cpusets cgroup controller. You can also control the NUMA node memory is allocated from with the cpusets cgroup controller.

- Manipulate the out of memory (oom) killer operation or create a process with a limited amount of memory with the memory cgroup controller (memcg). You will see an example later in this chapter.

- Assign permissions to devices under /dev, with the devices cgroup. You will see later an example of using the devices cgroup in the "Cgroup Devices – A Simple Example" section.

- Assign priority to traffic (see the section "The net_prio Module" later in this chapter).

- Freeze processes with the freezer cgroup.

- Report CPU resource usage of tasks of a cgroup with the cpuacct cgroup. Note that there is also the cpu controller, which can provision CPU cycles either by priority or by absolute bandwidth and provides the same or a superset of statistics.

- Tag network traffic with a class identifier (classid); see the section "The cls_cgroup Classifier" later in this chapter.

Next I will describe very briefly some changes that were done for supporting cgroups.

Cgroups Implementation

The cgroup subsystem is very complex. Here are several implementation details about the cgroup subsystem that should give you a good starting point to delve into its internals:

- A new structure called cgroup_subsys was added (include/linux/cgroup.h). It represents a cgroup subsystem (also known as a cgroup controller). The following cgroup subsystems are implemented:

  - mem_cgroup_subsys: mm/memcontrol.c

  - blkio_subsys: block/blk-cgroup.c

  - cpuset_subsys: kernel/cpuset.c

  - devices_subsys: security/device_cgroup.c

  - freezer_subsys: kernel/cgroup_freezer.c

  - net_cls_subsys: net/sched/cls_cgroup.c

  - net_prio_subsys: net/core/netprio_cgroup.c

  - perf_subsys: kernel/events/core.c

  - cpu_cgroup_subsys: kernel/sched/core.c

  - cpuacct_subsys: kernel/sched/core.c

  - hugetlb_subsys: mm/hugetlb_cgroup.c

- A new structure called cgroup was added; it represents a control group (linux/cgroup.h)

- A new virtual file system was added; this was done by defining the cgroup_fs_type object and a cgroup_ops object (instance of super_operations):

```
static struct file_system_type cgroup_fs_type = {
        .name = "cgroup",
        .mount = cgroup_mount,
        .kill_sb = cgroup_kill_sb,
};
static const struct super_operations cgroup_ops = {
        .statfs = simple_statfs,
        .drop_inode = generic_delete_inode,
        .show_options = cgroup_show_options,
        .remount_fs = cgroup_remount,
};
(kernel/cgroup.c)
```

  And registering it is done like any other filesystem with the register_filesystem() method in the cgroup_init() method; see kernel/cgroup.c.

- The following sysfs entry, /sys/fs/cgroup, is created by default when the cgroup subsystem is initialized; this is done by calling kobject_create_and_add("cgroup", fs_kobj) in the cgroup_init() method. Note that cgroup controllers can be mounted also on other directories.

- There is a global array of cgroup_subsys objects named subsys, defined in kernel/cgroup.c (note that from kernel 3.11, the array name was changed from subsys to cgroup_subsys). There are CGROUP_SUBSYS_COUNT elements in this array. A procfs entry called /proc/cgroups is exported by the cgroup subsystem. You can display the elements of the global subsys array in two ways:

  - By running cat /proc/cgroups.

  - By the lssubsys utility of libcgroup-tools.

- Creating a new cgroup entails generating these four control files always under that cgroup VFS:

  - notify_on_release: Its initial value is inherited from its parent. It's represents a boolean variable, and its usage is related to the release_agent topmost-only control file, which will be explained shortly.

  - cgroup.event_control: This file enables getting notification from a cgroup, using the eventfd() system call. See man 2 eventfd, and fs/eventfd.c.

  - tasks: A list of the PIDs which are attached to this group. Attaching a process to a cgroup is done by writing the value of its PID to the tasks control file and is handled by the cgroup_attach_task() method, kernel/cgroup.c. Displaying the cgroups to which a process is attached is done by cat /proc/<processPid>/cgroup. This is handled in the kernel by the proc_cgroup_show() method, in kernel/cgroup.c.

- cgroup.procs: A list of the thread group ids which are attached to this cgroup. The tasks entry allows attaching threads of the same process to different cgroup controllers, whereas cgroup.procs has a process-level granularity (all threads of a single process are moved together and belong to the same cgroup).

- In addition to these four control files, a control file named release_agent is created for the topmost cgroup root object only. The value of this file is a path of an executable that will be executed when the last process of a cgroup is terminated; the notify_on_release mentioned earlier should be set so that the release_agent feature will be enabled. The release_agent can be assigned as a cgroup mount option; this is the case, for example, in systemd in Fedora. The release_agent mechanism is based on a user-mode helper: the call_usermodehelper() method is invoked and a new userspace process is created each time that the release_agent is activated, which is costly in terms of performance. See: "The past, present, and future of control groups", lwn.net/Articles/574317/. For the release_agent implementation details see the cgroup_release_agent() method in kernel/cgroup.c.

- Apart from these four default control files and the release_agent topmost-only control file, each subsystem can create its own specific control files. This is done by defining an array of cftype (Control File type) objects and assigning this array to the base_cftypes member of the cgroup_subsys object. For example, for the memory cgroup controller, we have this definition for the usage_in_bytes control file:

```
static struct cftype mem_cgroup_files[] = {
        {
                .name = "usage_in_bytes",
                .private = MEMFILE_PRIVATE(_MEM, RES_USAGE),
                .read = mem_cgroup_read,
                .register_event = mem_cgroup_usage_register_event,
                .unregister_event = mem_cgroup_usage_unregister_event,
        },
        . . .

struct cgroup_subsys mem_cgroup_subsys = {
        .name = "memory",
        . . .
        .base_cftypes = mem_cgroup_files,
};
(mm/memcontrol.c)
```

- A member called cgroups, which is a pointer to a css_set object, was added to the process descriptor, task_struct. The css_set object contains an array of pointers to cgroup_subsys_state objects (one such pointer for each cgroup subsystem). The process descriptor itself (task_struct) does not contain a direct pointer to a cgroup subsystem it is associated to, but this could be determined from this array of cgroup_subsys_state pointers.

Two cgroups networking modules were added. They will be discussed later in this section:

- net_prio (net/core/netprio_cgroup.c).

- cls_cgroup (net/sched/cls_cgroup.c).

■ **Note**   The cgroup subsystem is still in its early days and likely to see a fair amount of development in its features and interface.

Next you will see a short example that illustrates how the devices cgroup controller can be used to change the write permission of a device file.

Cgroup Devices Controller: A Simple Example

Let's look at a simple example of using the devices cgroup. Running the following command will create a devices cgroup:

```
mkdir   /sys/fs/cgroup/devices/0
```

Three control files will be created under /sys/fs/cgroup/devices/0:

- devices.deny: Devices for which access is denied.
- devices.allow: Devices for which access is allowed.
- devices.list: Available devices.

Each such control file consists of four fields:

- type: possible values are: 'a' is all, 'c' is char device and 'b' is block device.
- The device major number.
- The device minor number.
- Access permission: 'r' is permission to read, 'w' is permission to write, and 'm' is permission to perform mknod.

By default, when creating a new devices cgroup, it has all the permissions:

```
cat /sys/fs/cgroup/devices/0/devices.list
a *:* rwm
```

The following command adds the current shell to the devices cgroup that you created earlier:

```
echo $$ > /sys/fs/cgroup/devices/0/tasks
```

The following command will deny access from all devices:

```
echo a > /sys/fs/cgroup/devices/0/devices.deny
echo "test" > /dev/null
-bash: /dev/null: Operation not permitted
```

The following command will return the access permission for all devices:

```
echo a >  /sys/fs/cgroup/devices/0/devices.allow
```

Running the following command, which previously failed, will succeed now:

```
echo "test" > /dev/null
```

Cgroup Memory Controller: A Simple Example

You can disable the out of memory (OOM) killer thus, for example:

```
mkdir /sys/fs/cgroup/memory/0
echo $$ > /sys/fs/cgroup/memory/0/tasks
echo 1 > /sys/fs/cgroup/memory/0/memory.oom_control
```

Now if you will run some memory-hogging userspace program, the OOM killer will not be invoked. Enabling the OOM killer can be done by:

```
echo 0 > /sys/fs/cgroup/memory/0/memory.oom_control
```

You can use the eventfd() system call the get notifications in a userspace application about a change in the status of a cgroup. See man 2 eventfd.

■ **Note** You can limit the memory a process in a cgroup can have up to 20M, for example, by:

echo 20M > /sys/fs/cgroup/memory/0/memory.limit_in_bytes

The net_prio Module

The network priority control group (net_prio) provides an interface for setting the priority of network traffic that is generated by various userspace applications. Usually this can be done by setting the SO_PRIORITY socket option, which sets the priority of the SKB, but it is not always wanted to use this socket option. To support the net_prio module, an object called priomap, an instance of netprio_map structure, was added to the net_device object. Let's take a look at the netprio_map structure:

```
struct netprio_map {
        struct rcu_head rcu;
        u32 priomap_len;
        u32 priomap[];
};
(include/net/netprio_cgroup.h)
```

The priomap array is using the net_prio sysfs entries, as you will see shortly. The net_prio module exports two entries to cgroup sysfs: net_prio.ifpriomap and net_prio.prioidx. The net_prio.ifpriomap is used to set the priomap object of a specified network device, as you will see in the example immediately following. In the Tx path, the dev_queue_xmit() method invokes the skb_update_prio() method to set skb->priority according to the priomap which is associated with the outgoing network device (skb->dev). The net_prio.prioidx is a read-only entry, which shows the id of the cgroup. The net_prio module is a good example of how simple it is to develop a cgroup kernel module in less than 400 lines of code. The net_prio module was developed by Neil Horman and is available from kernel 3.3. For more information see Documentation/cgroups/net_prio.txt. The following is an example of how to use the network priority cgroup module (note that you must load the netprio_cgroup.ko kernel module in case CONFIG_NETPRIO_CGROUP is set as a module and not as a built-in):

```
mkdir /sys/fs/cgroup/net_prio
mount -t cgroup -onet_prio none /sys/fs/cgroup/net_prio
mkdir /sys/fs/cgroup/net_prio/0
echo "eth1 4" > /sys/fs/cgroup/net_prio/0/net_prio.ifpriomap
```

This sequence of commands would set any traffic originating from processes belonging to the netprio "0" group and outgoing on interface eth1 to have the priority of four. The last command triggers writing an entry to a field in the net_device object called priomap.

■ **Note**   In order to work with net_prio, CONFIG_NETPRIO_CGROUP should be set.

The cls_cgroup Classifier

The cls_cgroup classifier provides an interface to tag network packets with a class identifier (classid). You can use it in conjunction with the tc tool to assign different priorities to packets from different cgroups, as the example that you will soon see demonstrates. The cls_cgroup module exports one entry to cgroup sysfs, net_cls.classid. The control group classifier (cls_cgroup) was merged in kernel 2.6.29 and was developed by Thomas Graf. Like the net_prio module which was discussed in the previous section, also this cgroup kernel module is less than 400 lines of code, which proves again that adding a cgroup controller by a kernel module is not a heavy task. Here is an example of using the control group classifier (note that you must load the cls_cgroup.ko kernel module in case that CONFIG_NETPRIO_CGROUP is set as a module and not as a built-in):

```
mkdir /sys/fs/cgroup/net_cls
mount -t cgroup -onet_cls none /sys/fs/cgroup/net_cls
mkdir /sys/fs/cgroup/net_cls/0
echo 0x100001 > /sys/fs/cgroup/net_cls/0/net_cls.classid
```

The last command assigns classid 10:1 to group 0. The iproute2 package contains a utility named tc for managing traffic control settings. You can use the tc tool with this class id, for example:

```
tc qdisc add dev eth0 root handle 10: htb
tc class add dev eth0 parent 10: classid 10:1 htb rate 40mbit
tc filter add dev eth0 parent 10: protocol ip prio 10 handle 1: cgroup
```

For more information see Documentation/cgroups/net_cls.txt (only from kernel 3.10.)

■ **Note**   In order to work with cls_cgroup, CONFIG_NET_CLS_CGROUP should be set.

I will conclude the discussion about the cgroup subsystem with a short section about mounting cgroups.

Mounting cgroup Subsystems

Mounting a cgroup subsystem can be done also in other mount points than /sys/fs/cgroup, which is created by default. For example, you can mount the memory controller on /mycgroup/mymemtest by the following sequence:

```
mkdir -p /mycgroup/mymemtest
mount -t cgroup -o memory mymemtest /mycgroup/mymemtest
```

Here are some of the mount options when mounting cgroup subsystems:

- all: Mount all cgroup controllers.
- none: Do not mount any controller.
- release_agent: A path to an executable which will be executed when the last process of a cgroup is terminated. Systemd uses the release_agent cgroup mount option.

- noprefix: Avoid prefix in control files. Each cgroup controller has its own prefix for its own control files; for example, the cpuset controller entry mem_exclusive appears as cpuset.mem_exclusive. The noprefix mount option avoids adding the controller prefix. For example,

```
mkdir /cgroup
mount -t tmpfs xxx /cgroup/
mount -t cgroup -o noprefix,cpuset xxx /cgroup/
ls /cgroup/
cgroup.clone_children  mem_hardwall            mems
cgroup.event_control   memory_migrate          notify_on_release
cgroup.procs           memory_pressure         release_agent
cpu_exclusive          memory_pressure_enabled sched_load_balance
cpus                   memory_spread_page      sched_relax_domain_level
mem_exclusive          memory_spread_slab      tasks
```

■ **Note**   Readers who want to delve into how parsing of the cgroups mount options is implemented should look into the parse_cgroupfs_options() method, kernel/cgroup.c.

For more information about cgroups, see the following resources:

- Documentation/cgroups

- cgroups mailing list: cgroups@vger.kernel.org

- cgroups mailing list archives: http://news.gmane.org/gmane.linux.kernel.cgroups

- git repository: git://git.kernel.org/pub/scm/linux/kernel/git/tj/cgroup.git

■ **Note**   Linux namespaces and cgroups are orthogonal and are not related technically. You can build a kernel with namespaces support and without cgroups support, and vice versa. In the past there were experiments with a cgroups namespace subsystem, called "ns", but the code was eventually removed.

You have seen what cgroups are and you learned about its two network modules, net_prio and cls_cgroup. You also saw short examples demonstrating how the devices, memory, and the networking cgroups controllers can be used. The Busy Poll Sockets feature, which was added in kernel 3.11 and above, provides lower latency for sockets. Let's take a look at how it is implemented and how it is configured and used.

Busy Poll Sockets

The traditional way the networking stack operates when the socket queue runs dry, is that it will sleep waiting for the driver to put more data on the socket queue, or returns if it is a non-blocking operation. This causes additional latency due to interrupts and context switches. For sockets applications that need the lowest possible latency and are willing to pay a cost of higher CPU utilization, Linux has added a capability for Busy Polling on Sockets from kernel 3.11 and above (in the beginning this technique was called Low Latency Sockets Poll, but it was changed to Busy Poll Sockets according to Linus suggestion). Busy Polling takes a more aggressive approach toward moving data to the application. When the application asks for more data and there is none in the socket queue, the networking stack actively calls into the device driver. The driver checks for newly arrived data and pushes it through the network layer (L3) to the socket. The driver may find data for other sockets and will push that data as well. When the poll call returns to the networking stack, the socket code checks whether new data is pending on the socket receive queue.

In order that a network driver will support busy polling, it should supply its busy polling method and add it as the ndo_busy_poll callback of the net_device_ops object. This driver ndo_busy_poll callback should move the packets into the network stack; see for example, the ixgbe_low_latency_recv() method, drivers/net/ethernet/intel/ixgbe/ixgbe_main.c. This ndo_busy_poll callback should return the number of packets that were moved to the stack or 0 if there were no such packets, and LL_FLUSH_FAILED or LL_FLUSH_BUSY in case of some problem. An unmodified driver that does not fill in the ndo_busy_poll callback will continue to work as usual and will not be busy polled.

An important component to providing low latency is busy polling. Sometimes when the driver polling routine returns with no data, more data is arriving and just misses being returned to the networking stack. This is where busy polling comes in to play. The networking stack polls the driver for a configurable period of time so new packets can be picked up as soon as they arrive.

The active and busy polling of the device driver can provide reduced latency very close to that of the hardware. Busy polling can be used for large numbers of sockets at the same time but will not yield the best results, since busy polling on some sockets will slow down other sockets when using the same CPU core. Figure 14-1 contrasts the traditional receive flow with that of a socket that has been enabled for Busy Polling.

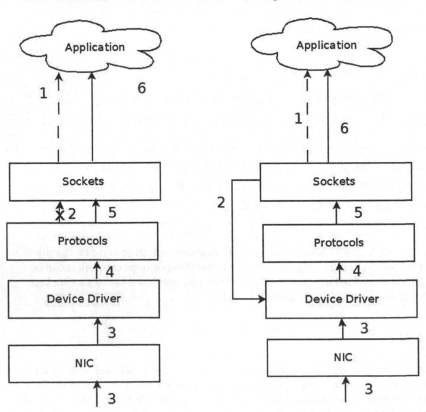

Figure 14-1. *Traditional receive flow versus Busy Poll Sockets receive flow*

1. Application checks for receive.
2. No immediate receive - thus block.
3. Packet Received.
4. Driver passes packet to the protocol layer.
5. Protocol/socket wakes application.
   - Bypass context switch and interrupt.
6. Application receives data through sockets.
   Repeat.

1. Application checks for receive
2. Check device driver for pending packet (poll starts).
3. Meanwhile, packet received to NIC.
4. Driver processes pending packet
5. Driver passes to the protocol layer
6. Application receives data through sockets.
   Repeat.

Enabling Globally

Busy Polling on Sockets can be turned on globally for all sockets via procfs parameters or it can be turned on for individual sockets by setting the SO_BUSY_POLL socket option. For global enabling, there are two parameters: net.core.busy_poll and net.core.busy_read, which are exported to procfs by /proc/sys/net/core/busy_poll and /proc/sys/net/core/busy_read, respectively. Both are zero by default, which means that Busy Polling is off. Setting these values will enable Busy Polling globally. A value of 50 will usually yield good results, but some experimentation might help find a better value for some applications.

- busy_read controls the time limit when busy polling on blocking read operations. For a non-blocking read, if busy polling is enabled for the socket, the stack code polls just once before returning control to the user.

- busy_poll controls how long select and poll will busy poll waiting for new events on any of the sockets that are enabled for Busy Polling. Only sockets with the busy read socket operation enabled are busy polled.

For more information, see: Documentation/sysctl/net.txt.

Enabling Per Socket

A better way to enable Busy Polling is to modify the application to use the SO_BUSY_POLL socket option, which sets the sk_ll_usec of the socket object (an instance of the sock structure). By using this socket option, an application can specify which sockets are Busy Polled so CPU utilization is increased only for those sockets. Sockets from other applications and services will continue to use the traditional receive path. The recommended starting value for SO_BUSY_POLL is 50. The sysctl.net.busy_read value must be set to 0 and the sysctl.net.busy_poll value should be set as described in Documentation/sysctl/net.txt.

Tuning and Configuration

Here are several ways in which you can tune and configure Busy Poll sockets:

- The interrupt coalescing (ethtool -C setting for rx-usecs) on the network device should be on the order of 100 to lower the interrupt rate. This limits the number of context switches caused by interrupts.

- Disabling GRO and LRO by using ethtool -K on the network device may avoid out of order packets on the receive queue. This should only be an issue when mixed bulk and low latency traffic arrive on the same queue. Generally, keeping GRO and LRO enabled usually gives best results.

- Application threads and the network device IRQs should be bound to separate CPU cores. Both sets of cores should be on the same CPU NUMA node as the network device. When the application and the IRQ run on the same core, there is a small penalty. If interrupt coalescing is set to a low value this penalty can be very large.

- For lowest latency, it may help to turn off the I/O Memory Management Unit (IOMMU) support. This may already be disabled by default on some systems.

Performance

Many applications that use Busy Polling Sockets should show reduced latency and jitter as well as improved transactions per second. However, overloading the system with too many sockets that are busy polling can hurt performance as CPU contention increases. The parameters net.core.busy_poll, net.core.busy_read and the SO_BUSY_POLL socket option are all tunable. Experimenting with these values may give better results for various applications.

I will now start a discussion of three wireless subsystems, which typically serve short range and low power devices: the Bluetooth subsystem, IEEE 802.15.4 and NFC. There is a growing interest in these three subsystems as new exciting features are added quite steadily. I will start the discussion with the Bluetooth subsystem.

The Linux Bluetooth Subsystem

The Bluetooth protocol is one of the major transport protocols mainly for small and embedded devices. Bluetooth network interfaces are included nowadays in almost every new laptop or tablet and in every mobile phone, and in many electronic gadgets. The Bluetooth protocol was created by the mobile vendor Ericsson in 1994. In the beginning, it was intended to be a cable-replacement for point-to-point connections. Later, it evolved to enable wireless Personal Area Networks (PANs). Bluetooth operates in the 2.4 GHz Industrial, Scientific and Medical (ISM) radio-frequency band, which is license-free for low-power transmissions. The Bluetooth specifications are formalized by the Bluetooth Special Interest Group (SIG), which was founded in 1998; see https://www.bluetooth.org. The SIG is responsible for development of Bluetooth specification and for the qualification process that helps to ensure interoperability between Bluetooth devices from different vendors. The Bluetooth core specification is freely available. There were several specifications for Bluetooth over the years, I will mention the most recent:

- Bluetooth v2.0 + Enhanced Data Rate (EDR) from 2004.

- Bluetooth v2.1 + EDR 2007; included improvement of the pairing process by secure simple pairing (SSP).

- Bluetooth v3.0 + HS (High Speed) from 2009; the main new feature is AMP (Alternate MAC/PHY), the addition of 802.11 as a high-speed transport.

- Bluetooth v4.0 + BLE (Bluetooth Low Energy, which was formerly known as WiBree) from 2010.

There is a variety of uses for the Bluetooth protocol, like file transfer, audio streaming, health-care devices, networking, and more. Bluetooth is designed for short distance data exchange, in a range that typically extends up to 10 meters. There are three classes of Bluetooth devices, with the following ranges:

- Class 1 – about 100 m.

- Class 2 – about 10 m.

- Class 3 – about 1 m.

The Linux Bluetooth protocol stack is called BlueZ. Originally it was a project started by Qualcomm. It was officially integrated in kernel 2.4.6 (2001). Figure 14-2 shows the Bluetooth stack.

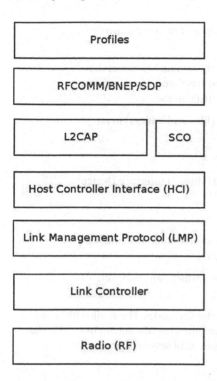

Figure 14-2. *Bluetooth stack. Note: In the layer above L2CAP there can be other Bluetooth protocols that are not discussed in this chapter, like AVDTP (Audio/Video Distribution Transport Protocol), HFP (Hands-Free Profile), Audio/video control transport protocol (AVCTP), and more*

- The lower three layers (The RADIO layer, Link controller and Link Management Protocol) are implemented in hardware or firmware.

- The Host Controller Interface (HCI) specifies how the host interacts and communicates with a local Bluetooth device (the controller). I will discuss it in the "HCI Layer" section, later in this chapter.

- The L2CAP (Logical link control and adaptation protocol) provides the ability to transmit and to receive packets from other Bluetooth devices. An application can use the L2CAP protocol as a message-based, unreliable data-delivery transport protocol similarly to the UDP protocol. Access to the L2CAP protocol from userspace is done by BSD sockets API, which was discussed in Chapter 11. Note that in L2CAP, packets are always delivered in the order they were sent, as opposed to UDP. In Figure 14-2, I showed three protocols that are located on top of L2CAP (there are other protocols on top of L2CAP that are not discussed in this chapter, as mentioned earlier).

  - BNEP: Bluetooth Network Encapsulation Protocol. I will present an example of using the BNEP protocol later in this chapter.

  - RFCOMM: The Radio Frequency Communications (RFCOMM) protocol is a reliable streams-based protocol. RFCOMM allows operation over only 30 ports. RFCOMM is used for emulating communication over a serial port and for sending unframed data.

- SDP: Service Discovery Protocol. Enables an application to register a description and a port number in an SDP server it runs. Clients can perform a lookup in the SDP server providing the description.

- The SCO (Synchronous Connection-Oriented) Layer: for sending audio; I do not delve into its details in this chapter as it falls outside the scope of this book.

- Bluetooth profiles are definitions of possible applications and specify general behaviors that Bluetooth- enabled devices use to communicate with other Bluetooth devices. There are many Bluetooth profiles, and I will mention some of the most commonly used ones:

  - File Transfer Profile (FTP): Manipulates and transfers objects (files and folders) in an object store (file system) of another system.

  - Health Device Profile (HDP): Handles medical data.

  - Human Interface Device Profile (HID): A wrapper of USB HID (Human Interface Device) that provides support for devices like mice and keyboards.

  - Object Push Profile (OPP) – Push objects profile.

  - Personal Area Networking Profile (PAN): Provides networking over a Bluetooth link; you will see an example of it in the BNEP section later in this chapter.

  - Headset Profile (HSP): Provides support for Bluetooth headsets, which are used with mobile phones.

The seven layers in this diagram are roughly parallel to the seven layers of the OS model. The Radio (RF) layer is parallel to the Physical layer, the Link Controller is parallel to the Data Link Layer, the Link Management Protocol is parallel to the Network Protocol, and so on. The Linux Bluetooth subsystem consists of several ingredients:

- Bluetooth Core

  - HCI device and connection manager, scheduler; files: `net/bluetooth/hci*.c`, `net/bluetooth/mgmt.c`.

  - Bluetooth Address Family sockets; file: `net/bluetooth/af_bluetooth.c`.

  - SCO audio links; file: `net/bluetooth/sco.c`.

  - L2CAP (Logical Link Control and Adaptation Protocol); files: `net/bluetooth/l2cap*.c`.

  - SMP (Security Manager Protocol) on LE (Low Energy) links; file: `net/bluetooth/smp.c`

  - AMP manager - Alternate MAC/PHY management; file: `net/bluetooth/a2mp.c`.

- HCI Device drivers (Interface to the hardware); files: `drivers/bluetooth/*`. Includes vendor specific drivers as well as generic drivers, like the Bluetooth USB generic driver, `btusb`.

- RFCOMM Module (RFCOMM Protocol); files: `net/bluetooth/rfcomm/*`.

- BNEP Module (Bluetooth Network Encapsulation Protocol); files: `net/bluetooth/bnep/*`.

- CMTP Module (CAPI Message Transport Protocol), used by the ISDN protocol. CMTP is in fact obsolete; files: `net/bluetooth/cmtp/*`.

- HIDP Module (Human Interface Device Protocol); files: `net/bluetooth/hidp/*`.

I discussed briefly the Bluetooth protocol, the architecture of the Bluetooth stack and the Linux Bluetooth subsystem tree, and Bluetooth profiles. In the next section I will describe the HCI layer, which is the first layer above the LMP (see Figure 14-2 earlier in this section).

HCI Layer

I will start the discussion of the HCI layer with describing the HCI device, which represents a Bluetooth controller. Later in this section I will describe the interface between the HCI layer and the layer below it, the Link Controller layer, and the interface between the HCI and the layers above it, L2CAP and SCO.

HCI Device

A Bluetooth device is represented by struct hci_dev. This structure is quite big (over 100 members), and will partially be shown here:

```
struct hci_dev {
        char            name[8];
        unsigned long   flags;
        __u8            bus;
        bdaddr_t        bdaddr;
        __u8            dev_type;
        . . .
        struct work_struct      rx_work;
        struct work_struct      cmd_work;
        . . .
        struct sk_buff_head     rx_q;
        struct sk_buff_head     raw_q;
        struct sk_buff_head     cmd_q;
        . . .
        int (*open)(struct hci_dev *hdev);
        int (*close)(struct hci_dev *hdev);
        int (*flush)(struct hci_dev *hdev);
        int (*send)(struct sk_buff *skb);
        void (*notify)(struct hci_dev *hdev, unsigned int evt);
        int (*ioctl)(struct hci_dev *hdev, unsigned int cmd, unsigned long arg);
}
(include/net/bluetooth/hci_core.h)
```

Here is a description of some of the important members of the hci_dev structure:

- flags: Represents the state of a device, like HCI_UP or HCI_INIT.

- bus: The bus associated with the device, like USB (HCI_USB), UART (HCI_UART), PCI (HCI_PCI), etc. (see include/net/bluetooth/hci.h).

- bdaddr: Each HCI device has a unique address of 48 bits. It is exported to sysfs by: /sys/class/bluetooth/<hciDeviceName>/address

- dev_type: There are two types of Bluetooth devices:

  - Basic Rate devices (HCI_BREDR).

  - Alternate MAC and PHY devices (HCI_AMP).

- rx_work: Handles receiving packets that are kept in the rx_q queue of the HCI device, by the hci_rx_work() callback.

- cmd_work: Handles sending command packets which are kept in the cmd_q queue of the HCI device, by the hci_cmd_work() callback.

- rx_q: Receive queue of SKBs. SKBs are added to the rx_q by calling the skb_queue_tail() method when receiving an SKB, in the hci_recv_frame() method.

- raw_q: SKBs are added to the raw_q by calling the skb_queue_tail() method in the hci_sock_sendmsg() method.

- cmd_q: Command queue. SKBs are added to the cmd_q by calling the skb_queue_tail() method in the hci_sock_sendmsg() method.

The hci_dev callbacks (like open(), close(), send(), etc) are typically assigned in the probe() method of a Bluetooth device driver (for example, refer to the generic USB Bluetooth driver, drivers/bluetooth/btusb.c).

The HCI layer exports methods for registering/unregistering an HCI device (by the hci_register_dev() and the hci_unregister_dev() methods, respectively). Both methods get an hci_dev object as a single parameter. The registration will fail if the open() or close() callbacks of the specified hci_dev object are not defined.

There are five types of HCI packets:

- HCI_COMMAND_PKT: Commands sent from the host to the Bluetooth device.

- HCI_ACLDATA_PKT: Asynchronous data which is sent or received from a Bluetooth device. ACL stands for Asynchronous Connection-oriented Link (ACL) protocol.

- HCI_SCODATA_PKT: Synchronous data which is sent or received from a Bluetooth device (usually audio). SCO stands for Synchronous Connection-Oriented (SCO).

- HCI_EVENT_PKT: Sent when an event (such as connection establishment) occurs.

- HCI_VENDOR_PKT: Used in some Bluetooth device drivers for vendor specific needs.

HCI and the Layer Below It (Link Controller)

The HCI communicates with the layer below it, the Link Controller, by:

- Sending data packets (HCI_ACLDATA_PKT or HCI_SCODATA_PKT) by calling the hci_send_frame() method, which delegates the call to the send() callback of the hci_dev object. The hci_send_frame() method gets an SKB as a single parameter.

- Sending command packets (HCI_COMMAND_PKT), by calling the hci_send_cmd() method. For example, sending a scan command.

- Receiving data packets, by calling the hci_acldata_packet() method or by calling the hci_scodata_packet() method.

- Receiving event packets, by calling the hci_event_packet() method. Handling HCI commands is asynchronous; so some time after sending a command packet (HCI_COMMAND_PKT), a single event or several events are received as a response by the HCI rx_work work_queue (the hci_rx_work() method). There are more than 45 different events (see HCI_EV_* in include/net/bluetooth/hci.h). For example, when performing a scan for nearby Bluetooth devices using the command-line hcitool, by hcitool scan, a command packet (HCI_OP_INQUIRY) is sent. As a result, three event packets are returned asynchronously to be handled by the hci_event_packet() method: HCI_EV_CMD_STATUS, HCI_EV_EXTENDED_INQUIRY_RESULT, and HCI_EV_INQUIRY_COMPLETE.

HCI and the Layers Above It (L2CAP/SCO)

Let's take a look at the methods by which the HCI layer communicates with the layers above it, the L2CAP layer and the SCO layer:

- HCI communicates with the L2CAP layer above it when receiving data packets by calling the `hci_acldata_packet()` method, which invokes the `l2cap_recv_acldata()` method of the L2CAP protocol.

- HCI communicates with the SCO layer above it when receiving SCO packets by calling the `hci_scodata_packet()` method, which invokes the `sco_recv_scodata()` method of the SCO protocol.

HCI Connection

The HCI connection is represented by the `hci_conn` structure:

```
struct hci_conn {
        struct list_head list;
        atomic_t          refcnt;
        bdaddr_t          dst;
        . . .
        __u8              type;

}
(include/net/bluetooth/hci_core.h)
```

The following is a description of some of the members of the `hci_conn` structure:

- `refcnt`: A reference counter.

- `dst`: The Bluetooth destination address.

- `type`: Represents the type of the connection:

  - SCO_LINK for SCO connection.

  - ACL_LINK for ACL connection.

  - ESCO_LINK for Extended Synchronous connection.

  - LE_LINK – represents LE (Low Energy) connection; was added in kernel v2.6.39 to support Bluetooth V4.0, which added the LE feature.

  - AMP_LINK – Added in v3.6 to support Bluetooth AMP controllers.

An HCI connection is created by calling the `hci_connect()` method. There are three types of connections: SCO, ACL, and LE connection.

L2CAP

In order to provide several data streams, L2CAP uses channels, which are represented by the `l2cap_chan` structure (include/net/bluetooth/l2cap.h). There is a global linked list of channels, named `chan_list`. Access to this list is serialized by a global read-write lock, `chan_list_lock`.

The l2cap_recv_acldata() method, which I described in the section "HCI and the layers above it (L2CAP/SCO)" earlier in this chapter, is called when HCI passes data packets to the L2CAP layer. The l2cap_recv_acldata() method first performs some sanity checks and drops the packet if something is wrong, then it invokes the l2cap_recv_frame() method in case a complete packet was received. Each received packet starts with an L2CAP header:

```
struct l2cap_hdr {
        __le16     len;
        __le16     cid;
} __attribute__ ((packed));
(include/net/bluetooth/l2cap.h)
```

The l2cap_recv_frame() method checks the channel id of the received packet by inspecting the cid of the l2cap_hdr object. In case it is an L2CAP command (the cid is 0x0001) the l2cap_sig_channel() method is invoked to handle it. For example, when another Bluetooth device wants to connect to our device, an L2CAP_CONN_REQ request is received on the L2CAP signal channel, which will be handled by the l2cap_connect_req() method, net/bluetooth/l2cap_core.c. In the l2cap_connect_req() method, an L2CAP channel is created by calling the l2cap_chan_create() method, via pchan->ops->new_connection(). The L2CAP channel state is set to be BT_OPEN, and the configuration state is set to be CONF_NOT_COMPLETE. This means that the channel should be configured in order to work with it.

BNEP

The BNEP protocol enables IP over Bluetooth, which means in practical terms running TCP/IP applications on top of L2CAP Bluetooth channels. You can also run TCP/IP applications with PPP over Bluetooth RFCOMM, but networking over serial PPP link is less efficient. The BNEP protocol uses a PAN profile. I will show a short example of using the BNEP protocol to setup Bluetooth over IP, and subsequently I will describe the kernel methods which implement such communication. Delving into the details of BNEP is beyond the scope of this book. If you want to learn more, see the BNEP spec, which can be found in: http://grouper.ieee.org/groups/802/15/Bluetooth/BNEP.pdf. A very simple way to create a PAN is by running:

- On the server side:
  - pand --listen --role=NAP
  - Note: NAP stands for: Network Access Point (NAP)
- On the client side
  - pand --connect btAddressOfTheServer

On both endpoints, a virtual interface (bnep0) is created. Afterward, you can assign an IP addresses on bnep0 for both endpoints with the ifconfig command (or with the ip command), just like with Ethernet devices, and you will have a network connection over Bluetooth between these endpoints. See more in http://bluez.sourceforge.net/contrib/HOWTO-PAN.

The pand --listen command creates an L2CAP server socket, and calls the accept() system call, whereas the pand --connect btAddressOfTheServer creates an L2CAP client socket and calls the connect() system call. When the connect request is received in the server side, it sends an IOCTL of BNEPCONNADD, which is handled in the kernel by the bnep_add_connection() method (net/bluetooth/bnep/core.c), which performs the following tasks:

- Creates a BNEP session (bnep_session object).
- Adds the BNEP session object to the BNEP session list (bnep_session_list) by calling the __bnep_link_session() method.

- Creates a network device named bnepX (for the first BNEP device X is 0, for the second X is 1, and so on).

- Registers the network device by calling the register_netdev() method.

- Creates a kernel thread named "kbnepd btDeviceName". This kernel thread runs the bnep_session() method which contains an endless loop, to receive or transmit packets. This endless loop terminates only when a userspace application sends an IOCTL of BNEPCONNDEL, which calls the method bnep_del_connection() to set the terminate flag of the BNEP session, or when the state of the socket is changed and it is not connected anymore.

- The bnep_session() method invokes the bnep_rx_frame() method to receive incoming packets and to pass them to the network stack, and it invokes the bnep_tx_frame() method to send outgoing packets.

Receiving Bluetooth Packets: Diagram

Figure 14-3 shows the path of a received Bluetooth ACL packet (as opposed to SCO, which is for handling audio and is handled differently). The first layer where the packet is handled is the HCI layer, by the hci_acldata_packet() method. It then proceeds to the higher L2CAP layer by calling the l2cap_recv_acldata() method.

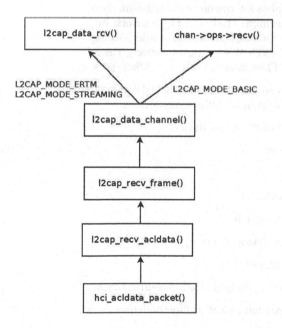

Figure 14-3. Receiving an ACL packet

The l2cap_recv_acldata() method calls the l2cap_recv_frame() method, which fetches the L2CAP header (the l2cap_hdr object was described earlier) from the SKB.

An action is being taken according to the channel ID of the L2CAP header.

L2CAP Extended Features

Support for L2CAP Extended Features (also called eL2CAP) was added in kernel 2.6.36. These extended features include:

- Enhanced Retransmission Mode (ERTM), a reliable protocol with error and flow control.

- Streaming Mode (SM), an unreliable protocol for streaming purposes.

- Frame Check Sequence (FCS), a checksum for each received packet.

- Segmentation and Reassembly (SAR) of L2CAP packets that make retransmission easier.

Some of these extensions were required for new profiles, like the Bluetooth Health Device Profile (HDP). Note that these features were available also before, but they were considered experimental and were disabled by default, and you should have set CONFIG_BT_L2CAP_EXT_FEATURES to enable them.

Bluetooth Tools

Accessing the kernel from userspace is done with sockets with minor changes: instead of using AF_INET sockets, we use AF_BLUTOOTH sockets. Here is a short description of some important and useful Bluetooth tools:

- `hciconfig`: A tool for configuring Bluetooth devices. Displays information such as the interface type (BR/EDR or AMP), its Bluetooth address, its flags, and more. The `hciconfig` tool works by opening a raw HCI socket (BTPROTO_HCI) and sending IOCTLs; for example, in order to bring up or bring down the HCI device, an HCIDEVUP or HCIDEVDOWN is sent, respectively. These IOCTLs are handled in the kernel by the `hci_sock_ioctl()` method, net/bluetooth/hci_sock.c.

- `hcitool`: A tool for configuring Bluetooth connections and sending some special command to Bluetooth devices. For example `hcitool scan` will scan for nearby Bluetooth devices.

- `hcidump`: Dump raw HCI data coming from and going to a Bluetooth device.

- `l2ping`: Send an L2CAP echo request and receive answer.

- `btmon`: A friendlier version of `hcidump`.

- `bluetoothctl`: A friendlier version of `hciconfig`/`hcitool`.

You can find more information about the Linux Bluetooth subsystem in:

- Linux BlueZ, the official Linux Bluetooth website: `http://www.bluez.org`.

- Linux Bluetooth mailing list: `linux-bluetooth@vger.kernel.org`.

- Linux Bluetooth mailing list archives: `http://www.spinics.net/lists/linux-bluetooth/`.

  - Note that this mailing list is for Bluetooth kernel patches as well as Bluetooth userspace patches.

- IRC channels on `freenode.net`:

  - `#bluez` (development related topics)

  - `#bluez-users` (non-development related topics)

In this section I described the Linux Bluetooth subsystem, focusing on the networking aspects of this subsystem. You learned about the layers of the Bluetooth stack and how they are implemented in the Linux kernel. You also learned about the important Bluetooth kernel structures like HCI device and HCI connection. Next, I will describe the second wireless subsystem, the IEEE 802.15.4 subsystem, and its implementation.

IEEE 802.15.4 and 6LoWPAN

The IEEE 802.15.4 standard (IEEE Std 802.15.4-2011) specifies the Medium Access Control (MAC) layer and Physical (PHY) layer for Low-Rate Wireless Personal Area Networks (LR-WPANs). It is intended for low-cost and low-power consumption devices in a short-range network. Several bands are supported, among which the most common are the 2.4 GHz ISM band, 915 MHz, and 868 MHz. IEEE 802.15.4 devices can be used for example in wireless sensor networks (WSNs), security systems, industry automation systems, and more. It was designed to organize networks of sensors, switches, automation devices, etc. The maximum allowed bit rate is 250 kb/s. The standard also supports a 1000 kb/s bit rate for the 2.4 GHz band, but it is less common. Typical personal operating space is around 10m. The IEEE 802.15.4 standard is maintained by the IEEE 802.15 working group (`http://www.ieee802.org/15/`). There are several protocols which sit on top of IEEE 802.15.4; the most known are ZigBee and 6LoWPAN.

The ZigBee Alliance (ZA) has published non GPL specifications for IEEE802.15.4, but also the ZigBee IP (Z-IP) open standard (`http://www.zigbee.org/Specifications/ZigBeeIP/Overview.aspx`). It is based on Internet protocols such as IPv6, TCP, UDP, 6LoWPAN, and more. Using the IPv6 protocol for IEEE 802.15.4 is a good option because there is a huge address space of IPv6 addresses, which makes it possible to assign a unique routable address to each IPv6 node. The IPv6 header is simpler than the IPv4 header, and processing its extension headers is simpler than processing IPv4 header options. Using IPv6 with LR-WPANs is termed IPv6 over Low-power Wireless Personal Area Networks (6LoWPAN). IPv6 is not adapted for its use on an LR-WPAN and therefore requires an adaptation layer, as will be explained later in this section. There are five RFCs related to 6LoWPAN:

- RFC 4944: "Transmission of IPv6 Packets over IEEE 802.15.4 Networks."

- RFC 4919: "IPv6 over Low-Power Wireless Personal Area Networks (6LoWPANs): Overview, Assumptions, Problem Statement, and Goals."

- RFC 6282: "Compression Format for IPv6 Datagrams over IEEE 802.15.4-Based Networks." This RFC introduced a new encoding format, the LOWPAN_IPHC Encoding Format, instead of LOWPAN_HC1 and LOWPAN_HC2.

- RFC 6775: "Neighbor Discovery Optimization for IPv6 over Low-Power Wireless Personal Area Networks (6LoWPANs)."

- RFC 6550: "RPL: IPv6 Routing Protocol for Low-Power and Lossy Networks."

The main challenges for implementing 6LoWPAN are:

- Different packet sizes: IPv6 has MTU of 1280 whereas IEEE802.15.4 has an MTU of 127 (IEEE802154_MTU). In order to support packets larger than 127 bytes, an adaptation layer between IPv6 and IEEE 802.15.4 should be defined. This adaptation layer is responsible for the transparent fragmentation/defragmentation of IPv6 packets.

- Different addresses: IPv6 address is 128 bit whereas IEEE802.15.4 are IEEE 64-bit extended (IEEE802154_ADDR_LONG) or, after association and after a PAN id is assigned, a 16 bit short addresses (IEEE802154_ADDR_SHORT) which are unique in that PAN. The main challenge is that we need compression mechanisms to reduce the size of a 6LoWPAN packet, largely made up of the IPv6 addresses. 6LoWPAN can for example leverage the fact that IEEE802.15.4 supports 16 bits short addresses to avoid the need of a 64-bit IID.

- Multicast is not supported natively in IEEE 802.15.4 whereas IPv6 uses multicast for ICMPv6 and for protocols that rely on ICMPv6 like the Neighbour Discovery protocol.

IEEE 802.15.4 defines four types of frames:

- Beacon frames (IEEE802154_FC_TYPE_BEACON)

- MAC command frames (IEEE802154_FC_TYPE_MAC_CMD)

- Acknowledgement frames (IEEE802154_FC_TYPE_ACK)

- Data frames (IEEE802154_FC_TYPE_DATA)

IPv6 packets must be carried on the fourth type, data frames. Acknowledgment for data packets is not mandatory, although it is recommended. As with 802.11, there are device drivers that implement most parts of the protocol by themselves (HardMAC device drivers), and device drivers that handle most of the protocol in software (SoftMAC device drivers). There are three types of nodes in 6LoWPAN:

- 6LoWPAN Node (6LN): Either a host or a router.

- 6LoWPAN Router (6LR): can send and receive Router Advertisements (RA) and Router Solicitations (RS) messages as well as forward and route IPv6 packets. These nodes are more complex than simple 6LoWPAN nodes and may need more memory and processing capacity.

- 6LoWPAN Border Router (6LBR): A border router located at the junction of separate 6LoWPAN networks or between a 6LoWPAN network and another IP network. The 6LBR is responsible for Forwarding between the IP network and the 6LoWPAN network and for the IPv6 configuration of the 6LoWPAN nodes. A 6LBR requires much more memory and processing capacity than a 6LN. They share context for the nodes in the LoWPAN, keep track of registered nodes with 6LoWPAN-ND and RPL. Generally 6LBR is always-on in contrast to 6LN who sleep most of their times. Figure 14-4 shows a simple setup with 6LBR, which connects between an IP network and a Wireless Sensor Network based on 6LoWPAN.

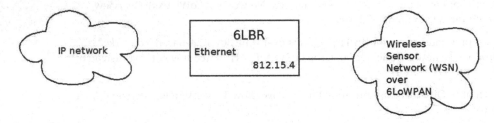

Figure 14-4. *6LBR connecting an IP network to WSN which runs over 6LoWPAN*

Neighbor Discovery Optimization

There are two reasons we should have optimizations and extensions for the IPv6 Neighboring protocol:

- IEEE 802.15.4 link layer does not have multicast support, although it supports broadcast (it uses 0xFFFF short address for message broadcasting).

- The Neighbor Discovery protocol is designed for sufficiently powered devices, and IEEE 802.15.4 devices can sleep in order to preserve energy; moreover, they operate in a lossy network environment, as the RFC puts it.

RFC 6775, which deals with Neighbor Discovery Optimization, added new optimizations such as:

- Host-initiated refresh of Router Advertisement information. In IPv6, routers usually send periodically Router Advertisements. This feature removes the need for periodic or unsolicited Router Advertisements sent from routers to hosts.

- EUI-64-based IPv6 addresses are considered to be globally unique. When such addresses are used, DAD (Duplicate Address Detection) is not needed.

- Three options were added:

  - Address Registration Option (ARO): The ARO option (33) can be a part of unicast NS message that a host sends as part of NUD (Neighbor Unreachability Detection) to determine that it can still reach a default router. When a host has a non-link-local address, it sends periodically NS messages to its default routers with the ARO options in order to register its address. Unregistration is done by sending an NS with an ARO containing a lifetime of 0.

  - 6LoWPAN Context Option (6CO): The 6CO option (34) carries prefix information for LoWPAN header compression, and is similar to Prefix Information option (PIO) which is specified in RFC 4861.

  - Authoritative Border Router Option (ABRO): The ABRO option (35) enables disseminating prefixes and context information across a route-over topology.

- Two new DAD messages were added:

  - Duplicate Address Request (DAR). New ICMPv6 type of 157.

  - Duplicate Address Confirmation (DAC). New ICMPv6 type of 158.

Linux Kernel 6LoWPAN

The 6LoWPAN basic implementation was integrated into v3.2 Linux. It was contributed by the Embedded Systems Open Platform Group, from Siemens Corporate Technology. It has three layers:

- Network layer - net/ieee802154 (includes the 6lowpan module, Raw IEEE 802.15.4 sockets, the netlink interface, and more).

- MAC layer - net/mac802154. Implements a partial MAC layer for SoftMAC device drivers.

- PHY layer - drivers/net/ieee802154 – the IEEE802154 device drivers.

- There are currently two 802.15.4 devices which are supported:

  - AT86RF230/231 transceiver driver

  - Microchip MRF24J40

- There is the Fakelb driver (IEEE 802.15.4 loopback interface).

- These two devices, as well as many other 802.15.4 transceivers, are connected via SPI. There is also a serial driver, although it is not included in the mainline kernel and still experimental. There are devices like atusb, which are based on an AT86RF231 BN but are not in mainline as of this writing.

6LoWPAN Initialization

In the lowpan_init_module() method, initialization of 6LoWPAN netlink sockets is done by calling the lowpan_netlink_init() method, and a protocol handler is registered for 6LoWPAN packets by calling the dev_add_pack() method:

```
. . .
static struct packet_type lowpan_packet_type = {
        .type = __constant_htons(ETH_P_IEEE802154),
        .func = lowpan_rcv,
};
```

```
. . .
static int __init lowpan_init_module(void)
{
        . . .
        dev_add_pack(&lowpan_packet_type);
        . . .
}
```
(net/ieee802154/6lowpan.c)

The lowpan_rcv() method is the main Rx handler for 6LoWPAN packets, which has an ethertype of 0x00F6 (ETH_P_IEEE802154). It handles two cases:

- Reception of uncompressed packets (dispatch type is IPv6.)

- Reception of compressed packets.

You use a virtual link to ensure the translation between 6LoWPAN and IPv6 packets. One endpoint of this virtual link speaks IPv6 and has an MTU of 1280, this is the 6LoWPAN interface. The other one speaks 6LoWPAN and has an MTU of 127, this is the WPAN interface. Compressed 6LoWPAN packets are processed by the lowpan_process_data() method, which calls the lowpan_uncompress_addr() to uncompress addresses and the lowpan_uncompress_udp_header() to uncompress the UDP header accordingly to the IPHC header. The uncompressed IPv6 packet is then delivered to the 6LoWPAN interface with the lowpan_skb_deliver() method (net/ieee802154/6lowpan.c).

Figure 14-5 shows the 6LoWPAN Adaptation layer.

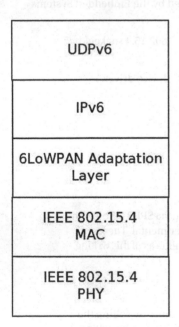

Figure 14-5. *6LoWPAN Adaptation layer*

Figure 14-6 shows the path of a packet from the PHY layer (the driver) via the MAC layer to the 6LoWPAN adaptation layer.

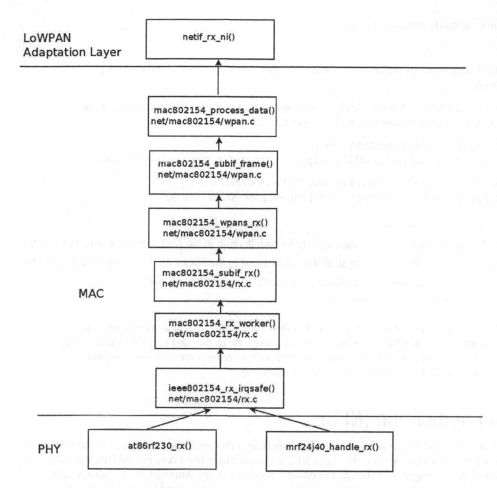

LoWPAN Adaptation Layer — netif_rx_ni()

MAC
- mac802154_process_data() net/mac802154/wpan.c
- mac802154_subif_frame() net/mac802154/wpan.c
- mac802154_wpans_rx() net/mac802154/wpan.c
- mac802154_subif_rx() net/mac802154/rx.c
- mac802154_rx_worker() net/mac802154/rx.c
- ieee802154_rx_irqsafe() net/mac802154/rx.c

PHY — at86rf230_rx()   mrf24j40_handle_rx()

Figure 14-6. Receiving a packet

I will not delve into the details of the device drivers implementation, as this is out of our scope. I will mention that each device driver should create an ieee802154_dev object by calling the ieee802154_alloc_device() method, passing as a parameter an ieee802154_ops object. Every driver should define some ieee802154_ops object callbacks, like xmit, start, stop, and more. This applies for SoftMAC drivers only.

I will mention here that an Internet-Draft was submitted for applying 6LoWPAN technology over Bluetooth Low-Energy devices (these devices are part of the Bluetooth 4.0 specification, as was mentioned in the previous chapter). See "Transmission of IPv6 Packets over Bluetooth Low Energy," http://tools.ietf.org/html/draft-ietf-6lowpan-btle-12.

■ **Note**   Contiki is an open source Operating System implementing the Internet of Things (IoT) concept; some patches of the Linux IEEE802.15.4 6LoWPAN are derived from it, like the UDP header compression and decompression. It implements 6LoWPAN, and RPL. It was developed by Adam Dunkels. See http://www.contiki-os.org/

For additional resources about 6LoWPAN and 802.15.4:

- Books:

  - "6LoWPAN: The Wireless Embedded Internet", by Zach Shelby and Carsten Bormann, Wiley, 2009.

  - "Interconnecting Smart Objects with IP: The Next Internet," by Jean-Philippe Vasseur and Adam Dunkels (the Contiki developer), Morgan Kaufmann, 2010.

- An article about IPv6 Neighbor Discovery Optimization: `http://www.internetsociety.org/articles/ipv6-neighbor-discovery-optimization`.

The `lowpan-tools` is a set of utilities to manage the Linux LoWPAN stack. See: `http://sourceforge.net/projects/linux-zigbee/files/linux-zigbee-sources/0.3/`

■ **Note** The IEEE802.15.4 does not maintain a `git` repository of its own (though in the past there was one). Patches are sent to the `netdev` mailing list; some of the developers send the patches first to the linux zigbee developer mailing list to get some feedback: `https://lists.sourceforge.net/lists/listinfo/linux-zigbee-devel`

I described the IEEE 802.15.4 and the 6LoWPAN protocol in this section and the challenges it poses for integration in the Linux kernel, like adding Neighboring Discovery messages. In the next section I will describe the third wireless subsystem, which is intended for the most shortest ranges among the three wireless subsystems described in this chapter: the Near Field Communication (NFC) subsystem.

Near Field Communication (NFC)

Near Field Communication is a very short range wireless technology (less than two inches) designed to transfer small amount of data over a very low latency link at up to 424 kb/s. NFC payloads range from very simple URLs or raw texts to more complex out of band data to trigger connection handover. Through its very short range and latency, NFC implements a tap and share concept by linking proximity to an immediate action triggered by the NFC data payload. Touch an NFC tag with your NFC enabled mobile phone and this will, for example, immediately fire up a web browser.

NFC runs on the 13.65MHz band and is based on the Radio Frequency ID (RFID) ISO14443 and FeliCa standards. The NFC Forum (`http://www.nfc-forum.org/`) is a consortium responsible for standardizing the technology through a set of specifications, ranging from the NFC Digital layer up to high-level services definitions like the NFC Connection Handover or the Personal Health Device Communication (PHDC) ones. All adopted NFC Forum specifications are available free of charge. See `http://www.nfc-forum.org/specs/`.

At the heart of the NFC Forum specification is the NFC Data Exchange Format (NDEF) definition. It defines the NFC data structure used to exchange NFC payloads from NFC tags or between NFC peers. All NDEFs contain one or more NDEF Records that embed the actual payload. NDEF record header contains metadata that allow applications to build the semantic link between the NFC payload and an action to trigger on the reader side.

NFC Tags

NFC tags are cheap, mostly static and battery less data containers. They're typically made of an inductive antenna connected to a very small amount of flash memory, packaged in many different form factors (labels, key rings, stickers, etc.). As per the NFC Forum definitions, NFC tags are passive devices, i.e., they're unable to generate any radio field. Instead they're powered by NFC active devices initiated RF fields. The NFC Forum defines four different tag types, each of them carrying a strong RFID and smart card legacy:

- Type 1 specifications derive from Innovision/Broadcom Topaz and Jewel card specifications. They can expose from 96 up to 2 KBytes of data at 106 kb/s.

- Type 2 tags are based on NXP Mifare Ultralight specifications. They're very similar to Type 1 tags.

- Type 3 tags are built on top of the non-secure parts of Sony FeliCa tags. They're more expensive than Type 1 and 2 tags, but can carry up to 1 MBytes at 212 or 424 kb/s.

- Type 4 specifications are based on NXP DESFire cards, support up to 32 KBytes and three transmission speeds: 106, 212, or 424 kb/s.

NFC Devices

As opposed to NFC tags, NFC devices can generate their own magnetic field to initiate NFC communications. NFC-enabled mobile phones and NFC readers are the most common kinds of NFC devices. They support a larger feature set than NFC tags. They can read from or write to NFC tags, but they can also pretend to be a card and be seen as simple NFC tags from any reader. But one of the key advantages of the NFC technology over RFID is the possibility to have two NFC devices talking to each other in an NFC specific peer-to-peer mode. The link between two NFC devices is kept alive as long as the two devices are in magnetic range. In practice this means two NFC devices can maintain a peer-to-peer link while they physically touch each other. This introduces a whole new range of mobile use cases where one can exchange data, context, or credentials by touching someone else NFC device.

Communication and Operation Modes

The NFC Forum defines two communication and three operation modes. An active NFC communication is established when two NFC devices can talk to one another by alternatively generating the magnetic field. This implies that both devices have their own power supply as they don't rely on any inductively generated power. Active communications can only be established in NFC peer-to-peer mode. On the other hand, only one NFC device generates the radio field on a passive NFC communication, and the other device replies by using that field.

There are three NFC operation modes:

- Reader/Writer: An NFC device (e.g., an NFC-enabled mobile phone) read from or write to an NFC tag.

- Peer-to-peer: Two NFC devices establish a Logical Link Control Protocol (LLCP) over which several NFC services can be multiplexed: Simple NDEF Exchange Protocol (SNEP) for exchanging NDEF formatted data, Connection Handover for initiating a carrier (Bluetooth or WiFi) handover, or any proprietary protocol.

- Card Emulation: An NFC device replies to a reader poll by pretending to be an NFC tag. Payment and transaction issuers rely on this mode to implement contactless payments on top of NFC. In card emulation mode, payment applets running on a trusted execution environment (also known as "secure elements") take control of the NFC radio and expose themselves as a legacy payment card that can be read from an NFC-enabled point-of-sale terminal.

Host-Controller Interfaces

Communication between hardware controllers and host stacks must follow a precisely defined interface: the host-controller one (HCI). The NFC hardware ecosystem is quite fragmented in that regard, as most of the initial NFC controllers implement an ETSI specified HCI originally designed for communication between SIM cards and contactless front-ends. (See http://www.etsi.org/deliver/etsi_ts/102600_102699/102622/07.00.00_60/ ts_102622v070000p.pdf). This HCI was not tailored for NFC specific use cases, and so each and every manufacturer defined a large number of proprietary extensions to support their features. The NFC Forum tries to address that situation by defining its own interface, much more NFC oriented, the NFC Controller Interface (NCI). The industry trend is clearly showing that manufacturers abandon ETSI HCI in favor of NCI, building a more standardized hardware ecosystem.

Linux NFC support

Unlike the Android operating system NFC stack, which is described later in this section, the standard Linux one is partly implemented by the kernel itself. Since the 3.1 Linux kernel release, Linux based application will find an NFC specific socket domain, along with a generic netlink family for NFC. (See http://git.kernel.org/?p=linux/kernel/git/ sameo/nfc-next.git;a=shortlog;h=refs/heads/master.) The NFC generic netlink family is intended to be an NFC out of band channel for controlling and monitoring NFC adapters. The NFC socket domain supports two families:

- Raw sockets for sending NFC frames that will arrive unmodified to the drivers

- LLCP sockets for implementing NFC peer-to-peer services

The hardware abstraction is implemented in NFC kernel drivers that register against various parts of the stack, mostly depending on the host-controller interface used by the controllers they support. As a consequence, Linux applications can work on top of a hardware agnostic and fully POSIX compatible NFC kernel APIs. The Linux NFC stack is split between kernel and userspace. The kernel NFC sockets allow userspace applications to implement NFC tags support by sending tag types specific commands through the raw protocol. NFC peer-to-peer protocols (SNEP, Connection Handover, PHDC, etc.) can be implemented by transmitting their specific payloads through NFC sockets as well. Finally, card emulation mode is built on top of the secure element parts of the kernel NFC netlink API. The Linux NFC daemon, neard, sits on top of the kernel and implements all three NFC modes, regardless of the NFC controller physically wired to the host platform. (See https://01.org/linux-nfc/.)

Figure 14-7 shows an overview of the NFC system.

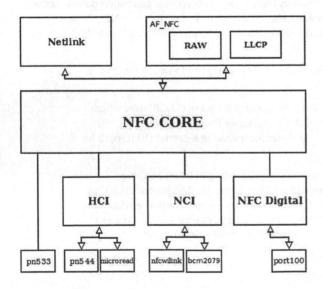

Figure 14-7. NFC overview

NFC Sockets

NFC sockets are of two kinds: raw and LLCP. Raw NFC sockets were designed with reader mode support in mind, as they provide a way to transmit tag specific commands and receive the tag replies back. The neard daemon uses NFC Raw sockets to implement all four tag types support, in both reader and writer modes. LLCP sockets implement the NFC peer-to-peer logical link control protocol on top of which neard implements all NFC Forum specified peer-to-peer services (SNEP, Connection Handover, and PHDC).

Depending on the selected protocol, NFC socket semantics differ.

Raw Sockets

- connect: Select and enable a detected NFC tag

- bind: Not supported

- send/recv: Send and receive raw NFC payloads. The NFC core implementation does not modify those payloads.

LLCP Sockets

- connect: Connect to a specific LLCP service on a detected peer device, like the SNEP or Connection Handover services.

- bind: Link a device to a specific LLCP service. The service will be exported through the LLCP service name lookup (SNL) protocol for any NFC peer device to attempt a connection to it.

- send/recv: Transmit LLCP service payloads to and from an NFC peer device. The kernel will handle the LLCP specific link layer encapsulation and fragmentation.

- LLCP transport can be connected or connectionless, and this is handled through the UNIX standard SOCK_STREAM and SOCK_DGRAM socket types. NFC LLCP sockets also support the SOCK_RAW type for monitoring and sniffing purposes.

NFC Netlink API

The NFC generic netlink API is designed to implement out of band NFC specific operations. It also handles any discoverable secure element from an NFC controller. Through NFC netlink commands, you can:

- List all available NFC controllers.

- Power NFC controllers up and down.

- Start (and stop) NFC polls for discovering NFC tags and devices.

- Enable NFC peer-to-peer (a.k.a. LLCP) links between the local controller and remote NFC peers.

- Send LLCP service name lookup requests, in order to discover the available LLCP services on a remote peer.

- Enable and disable NFC discoverable secure elements (typically SIM card based or embedded secure elements).

- Send ISO7816 frames to enabled secure elements.

- Trigger NFC controller firmware downloads.

The netlink API is not only about sending synchronous commands from NFC applications, but also about receiving asynchronous NFC-related events. Applications listening for broadcast NFC events on an NFC netlink socket will get notified about:

- Detected NFC tags and devices

- Discovered secure elements

- Secure element transaction status

- LLCP service name lookup replies

The entire netlink API (both commands and events) along with the socket one are exported through the kernel headers, and installed at /usr/include/linux/nfc.h on standard Linux distributions.

NFC Initialization

NFC initialization is done by the nfc_init() method:

```
static int __init nfc_init(void)
{
        int rc;
        . . .
```

Register the generic netlink NFC family and the NFC notifier callback, the nfc_genl_rcv_nl_event() method:

```
        rc = nfc_genl_init();
        if (rc)
                goto err_genl;

        /* the first generation must not be 0 */
        nfc_devlist_generation = 1;
```

Initialize NFC Raw sockets:

```
        rc = rawsock_init();
        if (rc)
                goto err_rawsock;
```

Initialize NFC LLCP sockets:

```
        rc = nfc_llcp_init();
        if (rc)
                goto err_llcp_sock;
```

Initialize the AF_NFC protocol:

```
        rc = af_nfc_init();
        if (rc)
                goto err_af_nfc;
```

```
    return 0;
    . . .
}
(net/nfc/core.c)
```

Drivers API

As explained earlier, most NFC controllers nowadays either use HCI or NCI as their host-controller interface. Others define their proprietary interface over USB, like most PC-compatible NFC readers, for example. There are also some "Soft" NFC controllers that expect the host platform to implement the NFC Forum Digital layer and talk to an analog-only capable firmware. In order to support this variety of hardware controllers, the NFC kernel implements NFC NCI, HCI, and Digital layers. Depending on the NFC hardware they intend to support, device driver developers will need to register at module probing time against one of these stacks, or directly against the NFC core implementation for purely proprietary protocols. When registering, they typically provide a stack operands implementation, which is the actual hardware abstraction layer between NFC kernel drivers and the core parts of the NFC stack. The NFC driver registration APIs and operand prototypes are defined in the kernel include/net/nfc/ directory.

Figure 14-8 shows a block diagram of the NFC Linux Architecture.

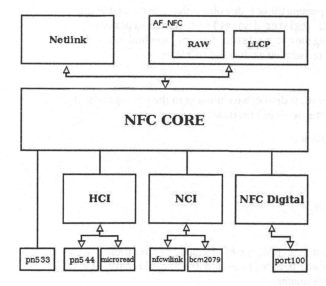

Figure 14-8. *NFC Linux Kernel Architecture. (Note that the NFC Digital layer is not in kernel 3.9. It is to be integrated into kernel 3.13.)*

The hierarchy shown in this figure can be understood better by looking into the implementation details of the registration of NFC device drivers directly to the NFC core and against the HCI and the NCI layer:

- Registration directly against the NFC core is done typically in the driver probe() callback. The registration is done using these steps:

    - Create an nfc_dev object by calling the nfc_allocate_device() method.

    - Call the nfc_register_device() method, passing the nfc_dev object which was created in the previous step as a single parameter.

    - See: drivers/nfc/pn533.c.

- Registration against the HCI layer is done typically also in the probe() callback of the driver; in the case of the pn544 and microread NFC device drivers, which are the only HCI drivers in kernel 3.9, this probe() method is invoked by the I2C subsystem. The registration is done using these steps:

    - Create an nfc_hci_dev object by calling the nfc_hci_allocate_device() method.

    - The nfc_hci_dev structure is defined in include/net/nfc/hci.h.

    - Call the nfc_hci_register_device() method, passing the nfc_hci_dev object which was created in the previous step as a single parameter. The nfc_hci_register_device() method in turn performs a registration against the NFC core by calling the nfc_register_device() method.

    - See drivers/nfc/pn544/pn544.c and drivers/nfc/microread/microread.c.

- Registration against the NCI layer is done typically also in the probe() callback of the driver, for example in the nfcwilink driver. The registration is done using these steps:

    - Create an nci_dev object by calling the nci_allocate_device() method.

    - The nci_dev structure is defined in include/net/nfc/nci_core.h.

    - Call the nci_register_device() method, passing the nci_dev object that was created in the previous step as a single parameter. The nci_register_device() method in turn performs a registration against the NFC core by calling the nfc_register_device() method, similarly to what you saw earlier in this section with registration against the HCI layer.

    - See drivers/nfc/nfcwilink.c.

When working directly against the NFC core, the driver must define five callbacks in the nfs_ops object (this object is passed as a first parameter of the nfc_allocate_device() method):

- start_poll: Set the driver to work in polling mode.

- stop_poll: Stop polling.

- activate_target: Activate a chosen target.

- deactivate_target: Deactivate a chosen target.

- im_transceive: Transceive operation.

When working with HCI , the hci_nfc_ops object, which is an instance of nfs_ops, defines these five callbacks, and when allocating an HCI object with the nfc_hci_allocate_device() method, the nfc_allocate_device() method is invoked with this hci_nfc_ops object as a first parameter.

With NCI, there is something quite similar, with the nci_nfc_ops object; see: net/nfc/nci/core.c.

Userspace Architecture

neard (http://git.kernel.org/?p=network/nfc/neard.git;a=summary) is the Linux NFC daemon that runs on top of the kernel NFC APIs. It is a single threaded, GLib based process that implements the higher layers of the NFC peer-to-peer stack along with the four tag types specific commands for reading from and writing to NFC tags. The NDEF Push Protocol (NPP), SNEP, PHDC, and Connection Handover specifications are implemented through neard plugins. One of neard's main design goals is to provide a small, simple, and uniform NFC API for Linux based applications willing to provide high-level NFC services. This is achieved through a small D-Bus API that abstracts tags and devices interfaces and methods, hiding the NFC complexity away from application developers. This API is compatible with the freedesktop D-Bus ObjectManager one and provides the following interfaces:

- `org.neard.Adapter`: For detecting new NFC controllers, turning them on and off, and starting NFC polls.

- `org.neard.Device`, `org.neard.Tag`: For representing detected NFC tags and devices. Calling the Device.Push method will send NDEFs to the peer device while Tag.Write will write them to the selected tag.

- `org.neard.Record`: Represents human readable and understandable NDEF record payload and properties. Registering agents against the `org.neard.NDEFAgent` interface will give application access to the NDEF raw payloads.

You can find more information about the neard userspace daemon here: `http://git.kernel.org/cgit/network/nfc/neard.git/tree/doc`.

NFC on Android

The initial NFC support was added to the Android operating system on December 2010, with the official 2.3 (Gingerbread) release. Android 2.3 only supported the reader/writer mode, but things have improved significantly since then, and the latest Android releases (Jelly Bean 4.3) come with a fully featured NFC support. For more information, see the Android NFC page: `http://developer.android.com/guide/topics/connectivity/nfc/index.html`. Following the classic Android architecture, a Java specific NFC API is available for applications to provide NFC services and operations. It is left to integrators to implement these APIs through native hardware abstraction layers (HAL). Google ships a Broadcom NFC HAL that currently only supports Broadcom NFC hardware. Here again, it is left to Android OEMs and integrators to either adapt the Broadcom NFC HAL to their selected NFC chipset or to implement their own HAL. It is important to note that since the Broadcom stack implements the NFC Controller Interface (NCI) specification, it is relatively easy to adapt it to support any NCI compatible NFC controller. The Android NFC architecture is what one could call a userspace NFC stack. In fact the entire NFC implementation is done in userspace through the HAL. NFC frames are then pushed down to the NFC controller through a kernel driver stub. The driver simply encapsulates those frames into buffers that are ready to be sent to the physical link (e.g., I2C, SPI, UART) between the host platform and the NFC controller.

■ **Note** Pull requests of the `nfc-next` git tree are sent to the `wireless-next` tree (Apart from the NFC subsystem, also the Bluetooth subsystem and the mac802.11 subsystem pull requests are handled by the wireless maintainer). From the `wireless-next` tree, pull requests are sent to `net-next` tree, and from there to Linus `linux-next` tree. The `nfc-next` tree is available in: `git://git.kernel.org/pub/scm/linux/kernel/git/sameo/nfc-next.git`

There is also an `nfc-fixes` git repository, which contains urgent and critical fixes for the current release(-rc*). The git tree of `nfc-fixes` is available in: `git://git.kernel.org/pub/scm/linux/kernel/git/sameo/nfc-fixes.git/`

NFC mailing list: `linux-nfc@lists.01.org`.

NFC mailing list archives: `https://lists.01.org/pipermail/linux-nfc/`.

In this section you learned about what NFC is in general, and about the Linux NFC subsystem implementation and about the Android NFC subsystem implementation. In the next section I will discuss the notification chains mechanism, which is an important mechanism to inform network devices about various events.

Notifications Chains

Network devices state can change dynamically; from time to time, the user/administrator can register/unregister network devices, change their MAC address, change their MTU, etc. The network stack and other subsystems and modules should be able to be notified about these events and handle them properly. The network notifications chains provide a mechanism for handling such events, and I will describe its API and the possible network events it handles in this section. For a full list of the events, see Table 14-1 later in this section. Every subsystem and every module can register itself to notification chains. This is done by defining a `notifier_block` and registering it. The core methods of notification chain registration and unregistration is the `notifier_chain_register()` and the `notifier_chain_unregister()` method, respectively. Generation of notification events is done by calling the `notifier_call_chain()` method. These three methods are not used directly (they are not exported; see `kernel/notifier.c`), and they do not use any locking mechanism. The following methods are wrappers around `notifier_chain_register()`, all of them implemented in `kernel/notifier.c`:

- `atomic_notifier_chain_register()`
- `blocking_notifier_chain_register()`
- `raw_notifier_chain_register()`
- `srcu_notifier_chain_register()`
- `register_die_notifier()`

Table 14-1. *Network Device Events:*

Event	Meaning
NETDEV_UP	device up event
NETDEV_DOWN	device down event
NETDEV_REBOOT	detected a hardware crash and restarted the device
NETDEV_CHANGE	device state change
NETDEV_REGISTER	device registration event
NETDEV_UNREGISTER	device unregistration event
NETDEV_CHANGEMTU	device MTU changed
NETDEV_CHANGEADDR	device MAC address changed
NETDEV_GOING_DOWN	device is going down
NETDEV_CHANGENAME	device has changed its name
NETDEV_FEAT_CHANGE	device features changed
NETDEV_BONDING_FAILOVER	bonding failover event
NETDEV_PRE_UP	this event enables to veto changing the device state to UP; for example, in cfg80211, denying interfaces to be set UP if the device is known to be rfkill'ed. see `cfg80211_netdev_notifier_call()`
NETDEV_PRE_TYPE_CHANGE	The device is about to change its type. This is a generalization of the NETDEV_BONDING_OLDTYPE flag, which was replaced by NETDEV_PRE_TYPE_CHANGE

(continued)

Table 14-1. (*continued*)

Event	Meaning
NETDEV_POST_TYPE_CHANGE	device changed its type. This is a generalization of the NETDEV_BONDING_NEWTYPE flag, which was replaced by NETDEV_POST_TYPE_CHANGE
NETDEV_POST_INIT	This event is generated in device registration (`register_netdevice()`), before creating the network device kobjects by `netdev_register_kobject()`; used in cfg80211 (`net/wireless/core.c`)
NETDEV_UNREGISTER_FINAL	An event which is generated to finalize the device unregistration.
NETDEV_RELEASE	the last slave of a bond is released (when working with netconsole over bonding) (This flag was also once used for bridges, in `br_if.c`).
NETDEV_NOTIFY_PEERS	notify network peers event (i.e., a device wants to inform the rest of the network about some sort of reconfiguration such as a failover event or a virtual machine migration)
NETDEV_JOIN	The device added a slave. Used for example in the bonding driver, in the `bond_enslave()` method, where we add a slave; see `drivers/net/bonding/bond_main.c`

There are also corresponding wrapper methods for unregistering notification chains and for generating notification events for each of these wrappers. For example, for the notification chain registered with the `atomic_notifier_chain_register()` method, the `atomic_notifier_chain_unregister()` is for unregistering the notification chain, and the `__atomic_notifier_call_chain()` method is for generating notification events. Each of these wrappers has also a corresponding macro to define a notification chain; for the `atomic_notifier_chain_register()` wrapper it is the `ATOMIC_NOTIFIER_HEAD` macro (`include/linux/notifier.h`).

After registering a `notifier_block` object, when every one of the events shown in Table 14-1 occurs, the callback specified in a `notifier_block` is invoked. The fundamental data structure of notification chains is the `notifier_block` structure; let's take a look:

```
struct notifier_block {
        int (*notifier_call)(struct notifier_block *, unsigned long, void *);
        struct notifier_block __rcu *next;
        int priority;
};
(include/linux/notifier.h)
```

- `notifier_call`: The callback to be invoked.

- `priority`: callbacks of `notifier_block` objects with higher priority are performed first.

There are many chains in the networking subsystem and in other subsystems. Let's mention some of the important ones:

- `netdev_chain`: Registered by the `register_netdevice_notifier()` method and unregistered by the `unregister_netdevice_notifier()` method (`net/core/dev.c`).

- `inet6addr_chain`: Registered by the `register_inet6addr_notifier()` method and unregistered by the `unregister_inet6addr_notifier ()` method. Notifications are generated by the `inet6addr_notifier_call_chain ()` method (`net/ipv6/addrconf_core.c`).

- netevent_notif_chain: Registered by the register_netevent_notifier() method and unregistered by the unregister_netevent_notifier() method. Notifications are generated by the call_netevent_notifiers() method (net/core/netevent.c).

- inetaddr_chain: Registered by the register_inetaddr_notifier() method and unregistered by the unregister_inetaddr_notifier() method. Notifications are generated by calling the blocking_notifier_call_chain() method.

Let's take a look at an example of using the netdev_chain; you saw earlier that with netdev_chain, registration is done with the register_netdevice_notifier() method, which is a wrapper around the raw_notifier_chain_register() method. Following is an example of registering a callback named br_device_event; First, a notifier_block object is defined, and then it is registered by calling the register_netdevice_notifier() method:

```
struct notifier_block br_device_notifier = {
        .notifier_call = br_device_event
};
(net/bridge/br_notify.c)
static int __init br_init(void)
{
        ...
        register_netdevice_notifier(&br_device_notifier);
        ...
}
(net/bridge/br.c)
```

Notifications of the netdev_chain are generated by invoking the call_netdevice_notifiers() method. The first parameter of this method is the event. The call_netdevice_notifiers() method :is in fact a wrapper around raw_notifier_call_chain().

So, when a network notification is generated, all callbacks which were registered are invoked; in this example, the br_device_event() callback will be called, regardless of which network event occurred; the callback will decide how to handle the notification, or maybe it will ignore it. Let's take a look at the callback method, br_device_event():

```
static int br_device_event(struct notifier_block *unused, unsigned long event, void *ptr)
{
        struct net_device *dev = ptr;
        struct net_bridge_port *p;
        struct net_bridge *br;
        bool changed_addr;
        int err;
        . . .
```

The second parameter for the br_device_event() method is the event (all the events are defined in include/linux/netdevice.h):

```
        switch (event) {
        case NETDEV_CHANGEMTU:
                dev_set_mtu(br->dev, br_min_mtu(br));
                break;
        . . .
}
```

■ **Note**   Registration of notification chains is not limited only to the networking subsystem. Thus, for example, the clockevents subsystem defines a chain called clockevents_chain and registers it by calling the raw_notifier_chain_register() method, and the hung_task module defines a chain named panic_notifier_list and registers it by calling the atomic_notifier_chain_register() method.

Beside the notifications that are discussed in this section, there is another type or notifications, named RTNetlink notifications; these notifications are sent with the rtmsg_ifinfo() method. :This type of notifications was discussed in Chapter 2, which dealt with Netlink Sockets.

These are the event types supported for networking (Note: the event types mentioned in the following table are defined in include/linux/netdevice.h):

We have now covered notification events, a mechanism that enables network devices to get notifications about events such as change of MTU, change of MAC address and more. The next section will discuss shortly the PCI subsystem, describing some of its main data structures.

The PCI Subsystem

Many network interfaces cards are Peripheral Component Interconnect (PCI) devices and should work in conjunction with the Linux PCI subsystem. Not all network interfaces are PCI devices; there are many embedded devices where the network interface is not on a PCI bus; the initialization and handling of these devices is done in a different way, and the following discussion is not relevant for these non-PCI devices. The new PCI devices are PCI Express (PCIe or PCIE) devices; the standard was created in 2004. They have a serial interface instead of a parallel interface, and as a result they have higher maximum system bus throughput. Each PCI device has a read-only configuration space; it is at least 256 bytes. The extended configuration space, available in PCI-X 2.0 and PCI Express buses, is 4096 bytes. You can read the PCI configuration space and the extended PCI configuration space by lspci (the lspci utility belongs to the pciutils package):

- lspci   -xxx: Shows a hexadecimal dump of the PCI configuration space.

- lspci –xxxx: Shows a hexadecimal dump of the extended PCI configuration space.

The Linux PCI API provides three methods for reading the configuration space, for handling 8-, 16-, and 32-bit granularity:

- static inline int pci_read_config_byte(const struct pci_dev *dev, int where, u8 *val)

- static inline int pci_read_config_word(const struct pci_dev *dev, int where, u16 *val)

- static inline int pci_read_config_dword(const struct pci_dev *dev, int where, u32 *val)

There are also three methods for writing the configuration space; likewise, 8-, 16-, and 32-bit granularities are handled:

- static inline int pci_write_config_byte(const struct pci_dev *dev, int where, u8 val)

- static inline int pci_write_config_word(const struct pci_dev *dev, int where, u16 val)

- static inline int pci_write_config_dword(const struct pci_dev *dev, int where, u32 val)

Every PCI manufacturer assigns values to at least the vendor, device, and class fields in the configuration space of the PCI device. A PCI device is identified by the Linux PCI subsystem by a pci_device_id object. The pci_device_id struct is defined in include/linux/mod_devicetable.h:

```
struct pci_device_id {
        __u32 vendor, device;          /* Vendor and device ID or PCI_ANY_ID*/
        __u32 subvendor, subdevice;    /* Subsystem ID's or PCI_ANY_ID */
        __u32 class, class_mask;       /* (class,subclass,prog-if) triplet */
        kernel_ulong_t driver_data;    /* Data private to the driver */
};
(include/linux/mod_devicetable.h)
```

The vendor, device, and class fields in pci_device_id identify a PCI device; most drivers do not need to specify the class as vendor/device is normally sufficient.

Each PCI device driver declares a pci_driver object. Let's take a look at the pci_driver structure:

```
struct pci_driver {
    . . .
    const char *name;
    const struct pci_device_id *id_table;   /* must be non-NULL for probe to be called */
    int  (*probe)  (struct pci_dev *dev, const struct pci_device_id *id);   /* New device inserted */
    void (*remove) (struct pci_dev *dev);   /* Device removed (NULL if not a hot-plug capable driver) */
    int  (*suspend) (struct pci_dev *dev, pm_message_t state);       /* Device suspended */
    . . .
    int  (*resume) (struct pci_dev *dev);                            /* Device woken up */
    . . .
};
(include/linux/pci.h)
```

Here are short descriptions of the members of the pci_driver structure:

- name: Name of the PCI device.

- id_table: An array of pci_device_id objects which it supports. Initializing id_table is done usually with the DEFINE_PCI_DEVICE_TABLE macro.

- probe: A method for device initialization.

- remove: A method for freeing the device. The remove() method usually frees all the resources that were assigned in the probe() method.

- suspend: A power management callback which puts the device to be in low power state, for devices that support power management.

- resume: A power management callback that wakes the device from low power state, for devices that support power management.

A PCI device is represented by struct pci_dev. It is a large structure; let's take a look at some of its members (they are self-explanatory):

```
struct pci_dev {
        . . .
        unsigned short  vendor;
        unsigned short  device;
```

```
        unsigned short  subsystem_vendor;
        unsigned short  subsystem_device;
        . . .
        struct pci_driver *driver;      /* which driver has allocated this device */
        . . .
        pci_power_t     current_state;  /* Current operating state. In ACPI-speak,
                                           this is D0-D3, D0 being fully functional,
                                           and D3 being off. */
        struct  device  dev;            /* Generic device interface */

        int             cfg_size;       /* Size of configuration space */

        unsigned int    irq;
};
(include/linux/pci.h)
```

Registering of a PCI network device against the PCI subsystem is done by defining a `pci_driver` object and calling the `pci_register_driver()` macro, which gets as its single argument a `pci_driver` object. In order to initialize the PCI device before it's being used, a driver should call the `pci_enable_device()` method. This method wakes up the device if it was suspended, and allocates the required I/O resources and memory resources. Unregistering the PCI driver is done by the `pci_unregister_driver()` method. Usually the `pci_register_driver()` macro is called in the driver `module_init()` method and the `pci_unregister_driver()` method is called in the driver `module_exit()` method. Each driver should call the `request_irq()` method specifying the IRQ handler when the device is brought up, and call `free_irq()` when the device is brought down.

Allocation and freeing of DMA (Direct Memory Access) memory is usually done with `dma_alloc_coherent()`/`dma_free_coherent()` when working with uncached memory buffer. With `dma_alloc_coherent()` we don't need to worry about cache coherency, as the mappings of this method are cache-coherent. See for example in `e1000_alloc_ring_dma()`, `drivers/net/ethernet/intel/e1000e/netdev.c`. The Linux DMA API is described in *Documentation/DMA-API.txt*.

■ **Note** Single Root I/O Virtualization (SR-IOV) is a PCI feature that makes one physical device appear as several virtual devices. The SR-IOV specification was created by the PCI SIG. See `http://www.pcisig.com/specifications/iov/single_root/`. For more information see `Documentation/PCI/pci-iov-howto.txt`.

More information about PCI can be found in the third edition of "Linux Device Drivers" by Jonathan Corbet, Alessandro Rubini, and Greg Kroah-Hartman, which is available (under Creative Commons License) in this URL: *http://lwn.net/Kernel/LDD3/*.

Wake-On-LAN (WOL)

Wake-On-LAN is a standard that allows a device that had been soft-powered-down to be powered up or awakened by a network packet. Wake-On-LAN is disabled by default. There are some network device drivers which let the sysadmin enable the Wake-On-LAN feature, usually by running from userspace the `ethtool` command. In order to support this, the network device driver should define a `set_wol()` callback in the `ethtool_ops` object. See for example, the 8139cp driver of RealTek (`net/ethernet/realtek/8139cp.c`). Running `ethtool` `<networkDeviceName>` shows whether the network device supports Wake-On-LAN. The `ethtool` also lets the sysadmin define which packets should wake the device; for example, `ethtool -s eth1 wol g` will enable Wake-On-LAN for MagicPacket frames (MagicPacket is a standard of AMD). You can use the `ether-wake` utility of the net-tools package to send Wake-On-LAN MagicPacket frames.

Teaming Network Device

The virtual teaming network device driver is intended to be a replacement for the bonding network device (`drivers/net/bonding`). The bonding network device provides a link aggregation solution (also known as: "link bundling" or "trunking"). See `Documentation/networking/bonding.txt`. The bonding driver is implemented fully in the kernel, and is known to be very large and prone to problems. The teaming network driver is controlled by userspace, as opposed to the bonding network driver. The userspace daemon is called `teamd` and it communicates with the kernel teaming driver by a library name `libteam`. The libteam library is based on generic netlink sockets (see Chapter 2).

There are four modes for the teaming driver:

- **loadbalance:** Used in Link Aggregation Control Protocol (LACP), which is part of the 802.3ad standard.

  `net/team/team_mode_loadbalance.c`

- **activebackup:** Only one port is active at a given time. This port can transmit and receive SKBs. The other ports are backup ports. A userspace application can specify which port to use as the active port.

  `net/team/team_mode_activebackup.c`

- **broadcast:** All packets are sent by all ports.

  `net/team/team_mode_broadcast.c`

- **roundrobin:** Selection of ports is done by a round robin algorithm. No need for interaction with userspace for this mode.

  `net/team/team_mode_roundrobin.c`

■ **Note** The teaming network driver resides under `drivers/net/team` and is developed by Jiri Pirko.

For more information see `http://libteam.org/`.

`libteam` site: `https://github.com/jpirko/libteam`.

Our brief overview about the teaming driver is over. Many of the readers use PPPoE services when they are surfing the Internet. The following short section covers the PPPoE protocol.

The PPPoE Protocol

PPPoE is a specification for connecting multiple clients to a remote site. PPPoE is typically used by DSL providers to handle IP addresses and authenticate users. The PPPoE protocol provides the ability to use PPP encapsulation for Ethernet packets. The PPPoE protocol is specified in RFC 2516 from 1999, and the PPP protocol is specified in RFC 1661 from 1994. There are two stages in PPPoE:

- PPPoE discovery stage. The discovery is done in a client-server session. The server is called an Access Concentrator, and there can be more than one. These Access Concentrators are often deployed by an Internet Server Provider (ISP). These are the four steps in the Discovery stage:

    - The PPPoE Active Discovery Initiation (PADI). A broadcast packet is sent from a host. The code in the PPPoE header is 0x09 (PADI_CODE), and the session id (sid) in the PPPoE header must be 0.

    - The PPPoE Active Discovery Offer (PADO). An Access Concentrator replies to a PADI request with a PADO reply. The destination address is the address of the host that sent the PADI. The code in the PPPoE header is 0x07 (PADO_CODE). The session id (sid) in the PPPoE header must again be 0.

    - PPPoE Active Discovery Request (PADR). A host sends a PADR packet to an Access Concentrator after it receives a PADO reply. The code in the PPPoE header is 0x19 (PADR_CODE). The session id (sid) in the PPPoE header must again be 0.

    - PPPoE Active Discovery Session-confirmation (PADS). When the Access Concentrator gets a PADR request, it generates a unique session id, and sends a PADS packet as a reply. The code in the PPPoE header is 0x65 (PADS_CODE). The session id (sid) in the PPPoE header is the session id that it generated. The destination of the packet is the IP address of the host that sent the PADR request.

    - A session is terminated by sending PPPoE Active Discovery Terminate (PADT) packet. The code in the PPPoE header is 0xa7 (PADT_CODE). A PADT can be sent either by an Access Concentrator or a host, and it can be sent any time after the session was established. The destination address is a unicast address. The ethertype of the Ethernet header of all the five discovery packets (PADI, PADO, PADR, PADS and PADT) is 0x8863 (ETH_P_PPP_DISC).

- PPPoE Session stage. Once the PPPoE discovery stage completed successfully, packets are sent using PPP encapsulation, which means adding a PPP header of two bytes. Using PPP enables registration and authentication using PPP subprotocols like Password Authentication Protocol (PAP) or Challenge Handshake Authentication Protocol (CHAP), and also PPP subprotocol called the Link Control Protocol (LCP), which is responsible for establishing and testing the data-link connection. The ethertype of the Ethernet header is 0x8864 (ETH_P_PPP_SES).

Every PPPoE packet starts with a 6-byte of PPPoE header, and you must learn about the PPPoE header in order to understand better the PPPoE protocol.

PPPoE Header

I will start by showing the PPPoE header definition in the Linux kernel:

```
struct pppoe_hdr {
#if defined(__LITTLE_ENDIAN_BITFIELD)
        __u8 ver : 4;
        __u8 type : 4;
```

```
#elif defined(__BIG_ENDIAN_BITFIELD)
        __u8 type : 4;
        __u8 ver : 4;
#else
#error  "Please fix <asm/byteorder.h>"
#endif
        __u8 code;
        __be16 sid;
        __be16 length;
        struct pppoe_tag tag[0];
} __packed;
(include/uapi/linux/if_pppox.h)
```

The following is a description of the members of the pppoe_hdr structure:

- ver: The ver field is a 4-bit field and it must be set to 0x1 according to section 4 in RFC 2516.

- type: The type field is a 4-bit field and it must also be set to 0x1 according to section 4 in RFC 2516.

- code: The code field is a 8-bit field and it can be one of the constants mentioned earlier: PADI_CODE, PADO_CODE, PADR_CODE, PADS_CODE and PADT_CODE.

- sid: Session ID (16-bit).

- length: The length is a 16-bit field, and it represents the length of the PPPoE payload, without the length of the PPPoE header or the length of the Ethernet header.

- tag[0]: The PPPoE payload can contains zero or more tags, in a type-length-value (TLV) format. A tag consists of 3 fields:

  - TAG_TYPE: 16-bit (for example, AC-Name, Service-Name, Generic-Error and more).

  - TAG_LENGTH: 16-bit.

  - TAG_VALUE: variable in length.

- Appendix A of RFC 2516 lists the various TAG_TYPEs and TAG_VALUEs.

Figure 14-9 shows a PPPoE header:

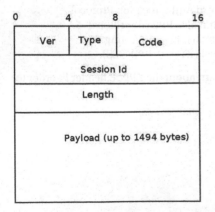

Figure 14-9. *PPPoE header*

PPPoE Initialization

PPPoE Initialization is done by the pppoe_init() method, drivers/net/ppp/pppoe.c. Two PPPoE protocol handlers are registered, one for PPPoE discovery packets, and one for PPPoE session packets. Let's take a look at the PPPoE protocol handler registration:

```
static struct packet_type pppoes_ptype __read_mostly = {
        .type   = cpu_to_be16(ETH_P_PPP_SES),
        .func   = pppoe_rcv,
};

static struct packet_type pppoed_ptype __read_mostly = {
        .type   = cpu_to_be16(ETH_P_PPP_DISC),
        .func   = pppoe_disc_rcv,
};

static int __init pppoe_init(void)
{
        int err;

        dev_add_pack(&pppoes_ptype);
        dev_add_pack(&pppoed_ptype);
        . . .

        return 0;

}
```

The dev_add_pack() method is the generic method for registering protocol handlers, and you encountered in previous chapters. The protocol handlers which are registered by the pppoe_init() method are:

- The pppoe_disc_rcv() method is the handler for PPPoE discovery packets.

- The pppoe_rcv() method is the handler for PPPoE session packets.

The PPPoE module exports an entry to procfs, /proc/net/pppoe. This entry consists of the session id, the MAC address, and the device of the current PPPoE sessions. Running cat /proc/net/pppoe is handled by the pppoe_seq_show() method. A notifier chain is registered by the pppoe_init() method by calling the register_netdevice_notifier(&pppoe_notifier).

PPPoX Sockets

PPPoX sockets are represented by the pppox_sock structure (include/linux/if_pppox.h) and are implemented in net/ppp/pppox.c. These sockets implement a Generic PPP encapsulation socket family. Apart from PPPoE, they are used also by Layer 2 Tunneling Protocol (L2TP) over PPP. PPPoX sockets are registered by calling register_pppox_proto(PX_PROTO_OE, &pppoe_proto) in the pppoe_init() method. Let's take a look at the definition of the pppox_sock structure:

```
struct pppox_sock {
        /* struct sock must be the first member of pppox_sock */
        struct sock sk;
        struct ppp_channel chan;
        struct pppox_sock       *next;    /* for hash table */
```

```
        union {
                struct pppoe_opt pppoe;
                struct pptp_opt  pptp;
        } proto;
        __be16                     num;
};
(include/linux/if_pppox.h)
```

When the PPPoX socket is used by PPPoE, the pppoe_opt of the proto union of the pppox_sock object is used. The pppoe_opt structure includes a member called pa, which is an instance of the pppoe_addr structure. The pppoe_addr structure represents the parameters of the PPPoE session: session id, remote MAC address of the peer, and the name of the network device that is used:

```
struct pppoe_addr {
        sid_t          sid;               /* Session identifier */
        unsigned char remote[ETH_ALEN];   /* Remote address */
        char           dev[IFNAMSIZ];     /* Local device to use */
};
(include/uapi/linux/if_pppox.h)
```

■ **Note**   Access to the pa member of the pppoe_opt structure which is embedded in the proto union is done in most cases in the PPPoE module using the pppoe_pa macro:

```
#define pppoe_pa        proto.pppoe.pa
```

(include/linux/if_pppox.h)

Sending and Receiving Packets with PPPoE

Once the discovery stage is completed, the PPP protocol must be used in order to enable traffic between the two peers, as was mentioned earlier. When starting a PPP connection by running, for example, pppd eth0 (see the example later in this section), the userspace pppd daemon creates a PPPoE socket by calling socket(AF_PPPOX, SOCK_STREAM, PX_PROTO_OE); this is done in the rp-pppoe plugin of the pppd daemon, in the PPPOEConnectDevice() method of pppd/plugins/rp-pppoe/plugin.c. This socket() system call creates a PPPoE socket by the pppoe_create() method of the PPPoE kernel module. Releasing the socket after the PPPoE session completed is done by the pppoe_release() method of the PPPoE kernel module. Let's take a look at the pppoe_create() method:

```
static const struct proto_ops pppoe_ops = {
        .family        = AF_PPPOX,
        .owner         = THIS_MODULE,
        .release       = pppoe_release,
        .bind          = sock_no_bind,
        .connect       = pppoe_connect,
        . . .
        .sendmsg       = pppoe_sendmsg,
        .recvmsg       = pppoe_recvmsg,
        . . .
        .ioctl         = pppox_ioctl,
};
```

```
static int pppoe_create(struct net *net, struct socket *sock)
{
        struct sock *sk;

        sk = sk_alloc(net, PF_PPPOX, GFP_KERNEL, &pppoe_sk_proto);
        if (!sk)
                return -ENOMEM;

        sock_init_data(sock, sk);

        sock->state     = SS_UNCONNECTED;
        sock->ops       = &pppoe_ops;

        sk->sk_backlog_rcv      = pppoe_rcv_core;
        sk->sk_state            = PPPOX_NONE;
        sk->sk_type             = SOCK_STREAM;
        sk->sk_family           = PF_PPPOX;
        sk->sk_protocol         = PX_PROTO_OE;

        return 0;
}
(drivers/net/ppp/pppoe.c)
```

By defining pppoe_ops we set callbacks for this socket. So calling from userspace the connect() system call on an AF_PPPOX socket will be handled by the pppoe_connect() method of the PPPoE module in the kernel. After creating a PPPoE socket, the PPPOEConnectDevice() method calls connect(). Let's take a look at the pppoe_connect() method:

```
static int pppoe_connect(struct socket *sock, struct sockaddr *uservaddr,
                int sockaddr_len, int flags)
{
        struct sock *sk = sock->sk;
        struct sockaddr_pppox *sp = (struct sockaddr_pppox *)uservaddr;
        struct pppox_sock *po = pppox_sk(sk);
        struct net_device *dev = NULL;
        struct pppoe_net *pn;
        struct net *net = NULL;
        int error;

        lock_sock(sk);

        error = -EINVAL;
        if (sp->sa_protocol != PX_PROTO_OE)
                goto end;

        /* Check for already bound sockets */
        error = -EBUSY;
```

The stage_session() method returns true when the session id is not 0 (as mentioned earlier, the session id is 0 in the discovery stage only). In case the socket is connected and it is in the session stage, the socket is already bound, so we exit:

```
if ((sk->sk_state & PPPOX_CONNECTED) &&
      stage_session(sp->sa_addr.pppoe.sid))
          goto end;
```

Reaching here means that the socket is not connected (it's sk_state is not PPPOX_CONNECTED) and we need to register a PPP channel:

```
. . .
/* Re-bind in session stage only */
if (stage_session(sp->sa_addr.pppoe.sid)) {
        error = -ENODEV;
        net = sock_net(sk);
        dev = dev_get_by_name(net, sp->sa_addr.pppoe.dev);
        if (!dev)
                goto err_put;

        po->pppoe_dev = dev;
        po->pppoe_ifindex = dev->ifindex;
        pn = pppoe_pernet(net);
```

The network device must be up:

```
        if (!(dev->flags & IFF_UP)) {
                goto err_put;
        }

        memcpy(&po->pppoe_pa,
                &sp->sa_addr.pppoe,
                sizeof(struct pppoe_addr));

        write_lock_bh(&pn->hash_lock);
```

The __set_item() method inserts the pppox_sock object, po, into the PPPoE socket hashtable; the hash key is generated according to the session id and the remote peer MAC address by the hash_item() method. The remote peer MAC address is po->pppoe_pa.remote. If there is an entry in the hash table with the same session id and the same remote MAC address and the same ifindex of the network device, the __set_item() method will return an error of –EALREADY:

```
        error = __set_item(pn, po);
        write_unlock_bh(&pn->hash_lock);

        if (error < 0)
                goto err_put;
```

po->chan is a ppp_channel object, see earlier in the pppox_sock structure definition. Before registering it by the ppp_register_net_channel() method, some of its members should be initialized:

```
po->chan.hdrlen = (sizeof(struct pppoe_hdr) +
                   dev->hard_header_len);

po->chan.mtu = dev->mtu - sizeof(struct pppoe_hdr);
po->chan.private = sk;
po->chan.ops = &pppoe_chan_ops;

error = ppp_register_net_channel(dev_net(dev), &po->chan);
if (error) {
```

The delete_item() method deletes a pppox_sock object from the PPPoE socket hashtable.

```
delete_item(pn, po->pppoe_pa.sid,
            po->pppoe_pa.remote, po->pppoe_ifindex);
    goto err_put;
}
```

Set the socket state to be connected:

```
    sk->sk_state = PPPOX_CONNECTED;
}

po->num = sp->sa_addr.pppoe.sid;
end:
    release_sock(sk);
    return error;
err_put:
    if (po->pppoe_dev) {
        dev_put(po->pppoe_dev);
        po->pppoe_dev = NULL;
    }
    goto end;
}
```

By registration of a PPP channel we are allowed to use PPP services. We are able to process PPPoE session packets by calling the generic PPP method, ppp_input(), from the pppoe_rcv_core() method. Transmission of PPPoE session packets is done with the generic ppp_start_xmit() method.

RP-PPPoE is an open source project which provides a PPPoE client and a PPPoE server for Linux: http://www.roaringpenguin.com/products/pppoe. A simple example of running a PPPoE server is:

```
pppoe-server -I  p3p1 -R 192.168.3.101  -L 192.168.3.210 -N 200
```

The options that are used in this example are:

- -I: The interface name (p3p1)

- -L: Set local IP address (192.168.3.210)

- -R: Set the starting remote IP address (192.168.3.101)

- -N: Max number of concurrent PPPoE sessions (200 in this case)

For other options, see man 8 pppoe-server.

Clients on the same LAN can create a PPPoE connection to this server by a pppd daemon, using the rp-pppoe plugin.

Android popularity as a mobile Operating System for smartphones and tablets is growing steadily. I will conclude the book with a short section about Android, discussing briefly the Android development model and showing four examples about Android networking.

Android

In the recent years, the Android operating system proved to be a very reliable and successful mobile OS. The Android operating system is based on a Linux kernel, with changes by Google developers. Android runs on hundreds of types of mobile devices, which are mostly based on the ARM processor. (I should mention that there is a project of porting Android to Intel x86 processors, http://www.android-x86.org/). The first generation of Google TV devices is based on x86 processors by Intel, but the second generation of Google TV devices are based on ARM. Originally Android was developed by "Android Inc.", a company that was founded in California in 2003 by Andy Rubin and others. Google bought this company in 2005. The Open Handset Alliance (OHA), a consortium of over 80 companies, announced Android in 2007. Android is an open source operating system, and its source code is released under the Apache License. Unlike Linux, most of the development is done by Google employees behind closed doors. As opposed to Linux, there is no public mailing list where developers are sending and discussing patches. One can, however, send patches to public Gerrit (see http://source.android.com/source/submit-patches.html). But it is up to Google only to decide whether or not they will be included in the Android tree.

Google developers had contributed a lot to the Linux kernel. You had learned earlier in this chapter that the cgroup subsystem was started by Google developers. I will mention also two Linux kernel networking patches, the Receive Packet Steering (RPS) patch, and the Receive flow steering (RFS) patch by Tom Herbert from Google (see http://lwn.net/Articles/362339/ and http://lwn.net/Articles/382428/), which were integrated into kernel 2.6.35. When working with multicore platforms, RPS and RFS let you steer packets according to the hash of the payload to a specific CPU. And there are a lot of other examples of contributions from Google to the Linux kernel, and it seems that also in the future you will encounter many important contributions to the Linux kernel from Google. One can find a lot of code from Android kernel in the staging tree of the Linux kernel. However, it is difficult to say whether the Android kernel will be merged fully into the Linux kernel; probably a very large part of it will find its way into the Linux kernel. For more information about Mainlining Android see this wiki: http://elinux.org/Android_Mainlining_Project. In the past there were many obstacles in the way, as Google implemented unique mechanisms, like wakelocks, alternative power management, its own IPC (called Binder), which is based on a Lightweight Remote Procedure Call (RPC), Android shared memory driver (Ashmem), Low Memory Killer and more. In fact, the Kernel community rejected the Google power management wakelocks patches in 2010. But since then, some of these features were merged and the situation changed. (See "Autosleep and Wake Locks," https://lwn.net/Articles/479841/, and "The LPC Android microconference", https://lwn.net/Articles/570406/). Linaro (www.linaro.org/) is a non-profit organization that was established in 2010 by leading big companies such as ARM, Freescale, IBM, Samsung, ST-Ericsson, and Texas Instruments (TI). Its engineering teams develop Linux ARM kernel and also optimizations for GCC toolchain. Linaro teams are doing an amazing job of coordinating and pushing/tweaking changes upstream. Delving into the details of Android kernel implementation and mainlining is beyond the scope of this book.

Android Networking

The main networking issue with Android is, however, not due to Linux kernel but to Android userspace. Android heavily relies on HAL even for networking, as well as for system framework. Originally (i.e., up to 4.2), there's no Ethernet support at all at framework level. If drivers are compiled in the kernel, the TCP/IP stack still allows basic Ethernet connectivity for Android Debug Bridge (ADB) debugging, but that's all. Starting with 4.0, Android-x86 project fork added an early implementation (badly designed but somehow working) of Ethernet at framework level. Starting with 4.2, official upstream sources support Ethernet, but there is no way to actually configure it (it detects Ethernet plug in/out, and if a DHCP server is there, it provides an IP address to the interface). Applications can actually make use of this interface through framework, but mostly no one does this. If you require real Ethernet support (i.e., being able to configure your interface, static/DHCP configure it, set proxy, ensure that all apps are using the interface, then a lot of hacks are still required (see `www.slideshare.net/gxben/abs-2013-dive-into-android-networking-adding-ethernet-connectivity`). In all cases, only one interface is being supported at a time (`eth0` only, even if you have `eth0` and `eth1`, so don't expect to act as a router of any kind). I will show here four short examples of how Android networking differs from Linux kernel networking:

- Security privileges and networking: Android added a security feature (named "paranoid network") to the Linux kernel, which restricts access to some networking features, depending on the group of the calling process. As opposed to the standard Linux kernel, where any application can open a socket and transmit/receive with it, in Android access to network resources is filtered by GID (group ID). The part of network security will be probably very difficult to merge into the mainline kernel, as it includes many features that are unique to Android. For more information about Android network security, see `http://elinux.org/Android_Security#Paranoid_network-ing`.

- Bluetooth: Bluedroid is a Bluetooth stack based on code that was developed by Broadcom. It replaced the BlueZ based stack in Android 4.2. Support for Bluetooth Low Energy (BLE, or Bluetooth LE) devices, also known as Bluetooth Smart and Smart Ready devices, was introduced in Android 4.3 (API Level 18), July 2013. Prior to this, Android Open Source Project (AOSP) did not have support for BLE devices, but there were some vendors who provided an API to BLE.

- Netfilter: There is an interesting project from Google that provides better network statistics on Android. This is implemented by `xt_qtaguid`, a netfilter module, which enables userspace applications to tag their sockets. This project required some changes in the Linux kernel netfilter subsystem. Patches of these changes were also sent to the Linux Kernel Mailing List (LKML); see `http://lwn.net/Articles/517358/`. For details, see "Android netfilter changes" `http://www.linuxplumbersconf.org/2013/ocw/sessions/1491`.

- NFC: As was described in the Near Field Communication (NFC) section earlier in this chapter, the Android NFC architecture is a userspace NFC stack: the implementation is done in userspace through the HAL which is supplied by Broadcom or by Android OEMs.

Android internals: Resources

Although there are many resources about developing applications for Android (whether in books, mailing list, forums, courses, etc.), there are very few resources about the internals of Android. For those readers who are interested to learn more, I suggest these resources:

- The book *Embedded Android: Porting, Extending, and Customizing,* by Karim Yaghmour (O'Reilly Media, 2013)

- Slides: Android System Development by Maxime Ripard, Alexandre Belloni (over 400 slides); `http://free-electrons.com/doc/training/android/`.

- Slides: Android Platform Anatomy by Benjamin Zores (59 slides); `http://www.slideshare.net/gxben/droidcon-2013-france-android-platform-anatomy`.

- Slides: Jelly Bean Device Porting by Benjamin Zores (127 slides); `http://www.slideshare.net/gxben/as-2013-jelly-bean-device-porting-walkthrough`.

- Website: `http://developer.android.com/index.html`.

- Android platform internals forum - archives:
  `http://news.gmane.org/gmane.comp.handhelds.android.platform`

- Once a year, an Android Builders Summit (ABS) is held. The first ABS was held in 2011 in San Francisco. It is recommended to read slides, watch videos, or attend.

- XDA Developers Conference: `http://xda-devcon.com/`; Slides and videos in
  `http://xda-devcon.com/presentations/`

- Slides: Android Internals, Marko Gargenta:
  `http://www.scandevconf.se/db/Marakana-Android-Internals.pdf`

■ **Note**   Android git repositories are available in `https://android.googlesource.com/`

Note that Android uses a special tool based on `python` called `repo` for management of hundreds of `git` repositories, which makes working with `git` easier.

Summary

I have dealt in this chapter with namespaces in Linux, focusing on network namespaces. I also described the cgroups subsystem and its implementation; furthermore, I described its two network modules, `net_prio` and `cls_cgroup`. The Linux Bluetooth subsystem and its implementation, the IEEE 802.15.4 Linux subsystem and 6LoWPAN, and the NFC subsystem were all covered. The optimization achieved by Low Latency Sockets Poll was also discussed in this chapter, along with the Notification Chains mechanism, which is widely used in the kernel networking stack (and you will encounter it when browsing the source code). Another topic that was briefly discussed was the PCI subsystem, in order to give some background about PCI devices, as many network devices are PCI devices. The chapter was concluded with three short sections about the network teaming driver (which is intended to replace the bonding driver), the PPPoE implementation, and Android.

   Although we've come to the end of the book, there is much more to learn about Linux Kernel networking, as it is a vast ocean of details, and it is progressing dynamically and at such a fast pace. New features and new patches are added constantly. I hope you enjoyed the book and that you learned a thing or two!

Quick Reference

I will conclude with a list of methods and macros that were mentioned in this chapter.

Methods

The following list contains the prototypes and descriptions of several methods covered in this chapter.

void switch_task_namespaces(struct task_struct *p, struct nsproxy *new);

This method assigns the specified `nsproxy` object to the specified process descriptor (`task_struct` object).

struct nsproxy *create_nsproxy(void);

This method allocates an nsproxy object and initializes its reference counter to 1.

void free_nsproxy(struct nsproxy *ns);

This method released the resources of the specified nsproxy object.

struct net *dev_net(const struct net_device *dev);

This method returns the network namespace object (nd_net) associated with the specified network device.

void dev_net_set(struct net_device *dev, struct net *net);

This method associates the specified network namespace to the specified network device by setting the nd_net member of the net_device object.

void sock_net_set(struct sock *sk, struct net *net);

This method associates the specified network namespace to the specified sock object.

struct net *sock_net(const struct sock *sk);

This method returns the network namespace object (sk_net) associated with the specified sock object.

int net_eq(const struct net *net1, const struct net *net2);

This method returns 1 if the first specified network namespace pointer equals the second specified network namespace pointer and 0 otherwise.

struct net *net_alloc(void);

This method allocates a network namespace. It is invoked from the copy_net_ns() method.

struct net *copy_net_ns(unsigned long flags, struct user_namespace *user_ns, struct net *old_net);

This method creates a new network namespace if the CLONE_NEWNET flag is set in its first parameter, flags. It creates the new network namespace by first calling the net_alloc() method to allocate it, then it initializes it by calling the setup_net() method, and finally adds it to the global list of all namespaces, net_namespace_list. In case the CLONE_NEWNET flag is set in its first parameter, flags, there is no need to create a new namespace and the specified old network namespace, old_net, is returned. Note that this description of the copy_net_ns() method refers to the case when CONFIG_NET_NS is set. When CONFIG_NET_NS is not set, there is a second implementation of copy_net_ns(), which the only thing it does is first verify that CLONE_NEWNET is set in the specified flags, and in case it is, returns the specified old network namespace (old_net); see include/net/net_namespace.h.

int setup_net(struct net *net, struct user_namespace *user_ns);

This method initializes the specified network namespace object. It assigns the network namespace user_ns member to be the specified user_ns, it initializes the reference counter (count) of the specified network namespace to be 1, and performs more initializations. It is invoked from the copy_net_ns() method and from the net_ns_init() method.

int proc_alloc_inum(unsigned int *inum);

This method allocates a proc inode and sets *inum to be the generated proc inode number (an integer between 0xf0000000 and 0xffffffff). It returns 0 on success.

struct nsproxy *task_nsproxy(struct task_struct *tsk);

This method returns the nsproxy object which is attached to the specified process descriptor (tsk).

struct new_utsname *utsname(void);

This method returns the new_utsname object which is associated with the process which currently runs (current).

struct uts_namespace *clone_uts_ns(struct user_namespace *user_ns, struct uts_namespace *old_ns);

This method creates a new UTS namespace object by calling the create_uts_ns() method, and copies the new_utsname object of the specified old_ns UTS namespace into the new_utsname of the newly created UTS namespace.

struct uts_namespace *copy_utsname(unsigned long flags, struct user_namespace *user_ns, struct uts_namespace *old_ns);

This method creates a new UTS namespace if the CLONE_NEWUTS flag is set in its first parameter, flags. It creates the new UTS namespace by calling the clone_uts_ns() method, and returns the newly created UTS namespace. In case the CLONE_NEWUTS flag is set in its first parameter, there is no need to create a new namespace and the specified old UTS namespace (old_ns) is returned.

struct net *sock_net(const struct sock *sk);

This method returns the network namespace object (sk_net) associated with the specified sock object.

void sock_net_set(struct sock *sk, struct net *net);

This method assigns the specified network namespace to the specified sock object.

int dev_change_net_namespace(struct net_device *dev, struct net *net, const char *pat);

This method changes the network namespace of the specified network device to be the specified network namespace. It returns 0 on success or -errno on failure. Callers must hold the rtnl semaphore. If the NETIF_F_NETNS_LOCAL flag is set in the features of the network device, an error of -EINVAL is returned.

void put_net(struct net *net);

This method decrements the reference counter of the specified network namespace. In case it reaches zero, it calls the __put_net() method to free its resources.

struct net *get_net(struct net *net);

This method returns the specified network namespace object after incrementing its reference counter.

void get_nsproxy(struct nsproxy *ns);

This method increments the reference counter of the specified nsproxy object.

struct net *get_net_ns_by_pid(pid_t pid);

This method gets a process id (PID) as an argument, and returns the network namespace object to which this process is attached.

struct net *get_net_ns_by_fd(int fd);

This method gets a file descriptor as an argument, and returns the network namespace associated with the inode that corresponds to the specified file descriptor.

struct pid_namespace *ns_of_pid(struct pid *pid);

This method returns the PID namespace in which the specified pid was created.

void put_nsproxy(struct nsproxy *ns);

This method decrements the reference counter of the specified nsproxy object; in case it reaches 0, the specified nsproxy is freed by calling the free_nsproxy() method.

int register_pernet_device(struct pernet_operations *ops);

This method registers a network namespace device.

void unregister_pernet_device(struct pernet_operations *ops);

This method unregisters a network namespace device.

int register_pernet_subsys(struct pernet_operations *ops);

This method registers a network namespace subsystem.

void unregister_pernet_subsys(struct pernet_operations *ops);

This method unregisters a network namespace subsystem.

static int register_vlan_device(struct net_device *real_dev, u16 vlan_id);

This method registers a VLAN device associated with the specified physical device (real_dev).

void cgroup_release_agent(struct work_struct *work);

This method is called when a cgroup is released. It creates a userspace process by invoking the call_usermodehelper() method.

int call_usermodehelper(char * path, char ** argv, char ** envp, int wait);

This method prepares and starts a userspace application.

int bacmp(bdaddr_t *ba1, bdaddr_t *ba2);

This method compares two Bluetooth addresses. It returns 0 if they are equal.

void bacpy(bdaddr_t *dst, bdaddr_t *src);

This method copies the specified source Bluetooth address (src) to the specified destination Bluetooth address (dst).

int hci_send_frame(struct sk_buff *skb);

This method is the main Bluetooth method for transmitting SKBs (commands and data).

int hci_register_dev(struct hci_dev *hdev);

This method registers the specified HCI device. It is invoked from Bluetooth device drivers. If the open() or close() callbacks of the specified hci_dev object are not defined, the method will fail and return –EINVAL. This method sets the HCI_SETUP flag in the dev_flags member of the specified HCI device; it also creates a sysfs entry for the device.

void hci_unregister_dev(struct hci_dev *hdev);

This method unregisters the specified HCI device. It is invoked from Bluetooth device drivers. It sets the HCI_UNREGISTER flag in the dev_flags member of the specified HCI device; it also removes the sysfs entry of the device.

void hci_event_packet(struct hci_dev *hdev, struct sk_buff *skb);

This method handles events that are received from the HCI layer by the hci_rx_work() method.

int lowpan_rcv(struct sk_buff *skb, struct net_device *dev, struct packet_type *pt, struct net_device *orig_dev);

This method is the main Rx handler for 6LoWPAN packets. 6LoWPAN packets have an ethertype of 0x00F6.

void pci_unregister_driver(struct pci_driver *dev);

This method unregisters a PCI driver. It is usually called in the network driver module_exit() method.

int pci_enable_device(struct pci_dev *dev);

This method initializes the PCI device before it is used by driver.

int request_irq(unsigned int irq, irq_handler_t handler, unsigned long flags, const char *name, void *dev);

This method registers the specified handler as the interrupt service routine for the specified irq.

void free_irq(unsigned int irq, void *dev_id);

This method frees an interrupt which was allocated with the request_irq() method.

int nfc_init(void);

This method performs initialization of the NFC subsystem by registering the generic netlink NFC family, initializing NFC Raw sockets and NFC LLCP sockets, and initializing the AF_NFC protocol.

int nfc_register_device(struct nfc_dev *dev);

This method registers an NFC device (an nfc_dev object) against the NFC core.

int nfc_hci_register_device(struct nfc_hci_dev *hdev);

This method registers an NFC HCI device (an nfc_hci_dev object) against the NFC HCI layer.

int nci_register_device(struct nci_dev *ndev);

This method registers an NFC NCI device (an nci_dev object) against the NFC NCI layer.

static int __init pppoe_init(void);

This method initializes the PPPoE layer (PPPoE protocol handlers, the sockets used by PPPoE, the network notification handler, the PPPoE procfs entry, and more).

struct pppoe_hdr *pppoe_hdr(const struct sk_buff *skb);

This method returns the PPPoE header associated with the specified skb.

static int pppoe_create(struct net *net, struct socket *sock);

This method creates a PPPoE socket. Return 0 on success or –ENOMEM if allocation of a socket by the sk_alloc() method failed.

int __set_item(struct pppoe_net *pn, struct pppox_sock *po);

This method inserts the specified pppox_sock object into the PPPoE socket hashtable. The hash key is calculated according to the session id and the remote peer MAC address by the hash_item() method.

void delete_item(struct pppoe_net *pn, __be16 sid, char *addr, int ifindex);

This method removes the PPPoE socket hashtable entry which has the specified session id, the specified MAC address, and the specified network interface index (ifindex).

bool stage_session(__be16 sid);

This method returns true when the specified session id is not 0.

int notifier_chain_register(struct notifier_block **nl, struct notifier_block *n);

This method registers the specified notifier_block object (n) to the specified notifier chain (nl). Note that this method is not used directly, there are several wrappers around it.

int notifier_chain_unregister(struct notifier_block **nl, struct notifier_block *n);

This method unregistered the specified notifier_block object (n) from the specified notifier chain (nl). Note that also this method is not used directly, there are several wrappers around it.

int register_netdevice_notifier(struct notifier_block *nb);

This method registers the specified notifier_block object to netdev_chain by calling the raw_notifier_chain_register() method.

int unregister_netdevice_notifier(struct notifier_block *nb);

This method unregisters the specified notifier_block object from netdev_chain by calling the raw_notifier_chain_unregister() method.

int register_inet6addr_notifier(struct notifier_block *nb);

This method registers the specified notifier_block object to inet6addr_chain by calling the atomic_notifier_chain_register() method.

int unregister_inet6addr_notifier(struct notifier_block *nb);

This method unregisters the specified notifier_block object from inet6addr_chain by calling the atomic_notifier_chain_unregister() method.

int register_netevent_notifier(struct notifier_block *nb);

This method registers the specified notifier_block object to netevent_notif_chain by calling the atomic_notifier_chain_register() method.

int unregister_netevent_notifier(struct notifier_block *nb);

This method unregisters the specified notifier_block object from netevent_notif_chain by calling the atomic_notifier_chain_unregister() method.

int __kprobes notifier_call_chain(struct notifier_block **nl, unsigned long val, void *v, int nr_to_call, int *nr_calls);

This method is for generating notification events. Note that also this method is not used directly, there are several wrappers around it.

int call_netdevice_notifiers(unsigned long val, struct net_device *dev);

This method is for generating notification events on the netdev_chain, by calling the raw_notifier_call_chain() method.

int blocking_notifier_call_chain(struct blocking_notifier_head *nh, unsigned long val, void *v);

This method is for generating notification events; eventually, after using locking mechanism, it invokes the notifier_call_chain() method.

int __atomic_notifier_call_chain(struct atomic_notifier_head *nh,unsigned long val, void *v, int nr_to_call, int *nr_calls);

This method is for generating notification events. Eventually, after using locking mechanism, it invokes the `notifier_call_chain()` method.

Macros

Here you'll find a description of the macro that was covered in this chapter.

pci_register_driver()

This macro registers a PCI driver in the PCI subsystem. It gets a `pci_driver` object as a parameter. It is usually called in the network driver `module_init()` method.

APPENDIX A

∎ ∎ ∎

Linux API

In this appendix I cover the two most fundamental data structures in the Linux Kernel Networking stack: the sk_buff and the net_device. This is reference material that can help when reading the rest of this book, as you will probably encounter these two structures in almost every chapter. Becoming familiar with and learning about these two data structures is essential for understanding the Linux Kernel Networking stack. Subsequently, there is a section about remote DMA (RDMA), which is further reference material for Chapter 13. It describes in detail the main methods and the main data structures that are used by RDMA. This appendix is a good place to always return to, especially when looking for definitions of the basic terms.

The sk_buff Structure

The sk_buff structure represents a packet. SKB stands for *socket buffer*. A packet can be generated by a local socket in the local machine, which was created by a userspace application; the packet can be sent outside or to another socket in the same machine. A packet can also be created by a kernel socket; and you can receive a physical frame from a network device (Layer 2) and attach it to an sk_buff and pass it on to Layer 3. When the packet destination is your local machine, it will continue to Layer 4. If the packet is not for your machine, it will be forwarded according to your routing tables rules, if your machine supports forwarding. If the packet is damaged for any reason, it will be dropped. The sk_buff is a very large structure; I mention most of its members in this section. The sk_buff structure is defined in include/linux/skbuff.h. Here is a description of most of its members:

- ktime_t tstamp

  Timestamp of the arrival of the packet. Timestamps are stored in the SKB as offsets to a base timestamp. Note: do not confuse tstamp of the SKB with hardware timestamping, which is implemented with the hwtstamps of skb_shared_info. I describe the skb_shared_info object later in this appenidx.

  Helper methods:

  - skb_get_ktime(const struct sk_buff *skb): Returns the tstamp of the specified skb.

  - skb_get_timestamp(const struct sk_buff *skb, struct timeval *stamp): Converts the offset back to a struct timeval.

  - net_timestamp_set(struct sk_buff *skb): Sets the timestamp for the specified skb. The timestamp calculation is done with the ktime_get_real() method, which returns the time in ktime_t format.

  - net_enable_timestamp(): This method should be called to enable SKB timestamping.

  - net_disable_timestamp(): This method should be called to disable SKB timestamping.

- struct sock *sk

The socket that owns the SKB, for local generated traffic and for traffic that is destined for the local host. For packets that are being forwarded, sk is NULL. Usually when talking about sockets you deal with sockets which are created by calling the socket() system call from userspace. It should be mentioned that there are also kernel sockets, which are created by calling the sock_create_kern() method. See for example in vxlan_init_net() in the VXLAN driver, drivers/net/vxlan.c.

Helper method:

- skb_orphan(struct sk_buff *skb): If the specified skb has a destructor, call this destructor; set the sock object (sk) of the specified skb to NULL, and set the destructor of the specified skb to NULL.

- struct net_device *dev

The dev member is a net_device object which represents the network interface device associated to the SKB; you will sometimes encounter the term NIC (Network Interface Card) for such a network device. It can be the network device on which the packet arrives, or the network device on which the packet will be sent. The net_device structure will be discussed in depth in the next section.

- char cb[48]

This is the control buffer. It is free to use by any layer. This is an opaque area used to store private information. For example, the TCP protocol uses it for the TCP control buffer:

```
#define TCP_SKB_CB(__skb) ((struct tcp_skb_cb *)&((__skb)->cb[0]))
(include/net/tcp.h)
```

The Bluetooth protocol also uses the control block:

```
#define bt_cb(skb) ((struct bt_skb_cb *)((skb)->cb))
    (include/net/bluetooth/bluetooth.h)
```

- unsigned long _skb_refdst

The destination entry (dst_entry) address. The dst_entry struct represents the routing entry for a given destination. For each packet, incoming or outgoing, you perform a lookup in the routing tables. Sometimes this lookup is called FIB lookup. The result of this lookup determines how you should handle this packet; for example, whether it should be forwarded, and if so, on which interface it should be transmitted; or should it be thrown, should an ICMP error message be sent, and so on. The dst_entry object has a reference counter (the __refcnt field). There are cases when you use this reference count, and there are cases when you do not use it. The dst_entry object and the lookup in the FIB is discussed in more detail in Chapter 4.

Helper methods:

- skb_dst_set(struct sk_buff *skb, struct dst_entry *dst): Sets the skb dst, assuming a reference was taken on dst and should be released by the dst_release() method (which is invoked by the skb_dst_drop() method).

- skb_dst_set_noref(struct sk_buff *skb, struct dst_entry *dst): Sets the skb dst, assuming a reference was not taken on dst. In this case, the skb_dst_drop() method will not call the dst_release() method for the dst.

■ **Note**   The SKB might have a dst_entry pointer attached to it; it can be reference counted or not. The low order bit of _skb_refdst is set if the reference counter was not taken.

- struct sec_path *sp

  The security path pointer. It includes an array of IPsec XFRM transformations states (xfrm_state objects). IPsec (IP Security) is a Layer 3 protocol which is used mostly in VPNs. It is mandatory in IPv6 and optional in IPv4. Linux, like many other operating systems, implements IPsec both for IPv4 and IPv6. The sec_path structure is defined in include/net/xfrm.h. See more in Chapter 10, which deals with the IPsec subsystem.

  Helper method:

  - struct sec_path *skb_sec_path(struct sk_buff *skb): Returns the sec_path object (sp) associated with the specified skb.

- unsigned int len

  The total number of packet bytes.

- unsigned int data_len

  The data length. This field is used only when the packet has nonlinear data (paged data).

  Helper method:

  - skb_is_nonlinear(const struct sk_buff *skb): Returns true when the data_len of the specified skb is larger than 0.

- __u16 mac_len

  The length of the MAC (Layer 2) header.

- __wsum csum

  The checksum.

- __u32 priority

  The queuing priority of the packet. In the Tx path, the priority of the SKB is set according to the socket priority (the sk_priority field of the socket). The socket priority in turn can be set by calling the setsockopt() system call with the SO_PRIORITY socket option. Using the net_prio cgroup kernel module, you can define a rule which will set the priority for the SKB; see in the description of the sk_buff netprio_map field, later in this section, and also in Documentation/cgroup/netprio.txt. For forwarded packets, the priority is set according to TOS (Type Of Service) field in the IP header. There is a table named ip_tos2prio which consists of 16 elements. The mapping from TOS to priority is done by the rt_tos2priority() method, according to the TOS field of the IP header; see the ip_forward() method in net/ipv4/ip_forward.c and the ip_tos2prio definition in include/net/route.h.

- `__u8 local_df:1`

  Allow local fragmentation flag. If the value of the `pmtudisc` field of the socket which sends the packet is IP_PMTUDISC_DONT or IP_PMTUDISC_WANT, `local_df` is set to 1; if the value of the `pmtudisc` field of the socket is IP_PMTUDISC_DO or IP_PMTUDISC_PROBE, `local_df` is set to 0. See the implementation of the `__ip_make_skb()` method in net/ipv4/ip_output.c. Only when the packet `local_df` is 0 do you set the IP header don't fragment flag, IP_DF; see the `ip_queue_xmit()` method in net/ipv4/ip_output.c:

  ```
  . . .
  if (ip_dont_fragment(sk, &rt->dst) && !skb->local_df)
          iph->frag_off = htons(IP_DF);
      else
        iph->frag_off = 0;
  . . .
  ```

  The `frag_off` field in the IP header is a 16-bit field, which represents the offset and the flags of the fragment. The 13 leftmost (MSB) bits are the offset (the offset unit is 8-bytes) and the 3 rightmost (LSB) bits are the flags. The flags can be IP_MF (there are more fragments), IP_DF (do not fragment), IP_CE (for congestion), or IP_OFFSET (offset part).

  The reason behind this is that there are cases when you do not want to allow IP fragmentation. For example, in Path MTU Discovery (PMTUD), you set the DF (don't fragment) flag of the IP header. Thus, you don't fragment the outgoing packets. Any network device along the path whose MTU is smaller than the packet will drop it and send back an ICMP packet ("Fragmentation Needed"). Getting these ICMP "Fragmentation Needed" packets is required in order to determine the Path MTU. See more in Chapter 3. From userspace, setting IP_PMTUDISC_DO is done, for example, thus (the following code snippet is taken from the source code of the `tracepath` utility from the `iputils` package; the `tracepath` utility finds the path MTU):

  ```
  . . .
  int on = IP_PMTUDISC_DO;
  setsockopt(fd, SOL_IP, IP_MTU_DISCOVER, &on, sizeof(on));
  . . .
  ```

- `__u8 cloned:1`

  When the packet is cloned with the `__skb_clone()` method, this field is set to 1 in both the cloned packet and the primary packet. Cloning SKB means creating a private copy of the `sk_buff struct`; the data block is shared between the clone and the primary SKB.

- `__u8 ip_summed:2`

  Indicator of IP (Layer 3) checksum; can be one of these values:

  - CHECKSUM_NONE: When the device driver does not support hardware checksumming, it sets the `ip_summed` field to be CHECKSUM_NONE. This is an indication that checksumming should be done in software.

  - CHECKSUM_UNNECESSARY: No need for any checksumming.

- CHECKSUM_COMPLETE: Calculation of the checksum was completed by the hardware, for incoming packets.

- CHECKSUM_PARTIAL: A partial checksum was computed for outgoing packets; the hardware should complete the checksum calculation. CHECKSUM_COMPLETE and CHECKSUM_PARTIAL replace the CHECKSUM_HW flag, which is now deprecated.

- `__u8 nohdr:1`

  Payload reference only, must not modify header. There are cases when the owner of the SKB no longer needs to access the header at all. In such cases, you can call the `skb_header_release()` method, which sets the nohdr field of the SKB; this indicates that the header of this SKB should not be modified.

- `__u8 nfctinfo:3`

  Connection Tracking info. Connection Tracking allows the kernel to keep track of all logical network connections or sessions. NAT relies on Connection Tracking information for its translations. The value of the nfctinfo field corresponds to the `ip_conntrack_info` enum values. So, for example, when a new connection is starting to be tracked, the value of nfctinfo is IP_CT_NEW. When the connection is established, the value of nfctinfo is IP_CT_ESTABLISHED. The value of nfctinfo can change to IP_CT_RELATED when the packet is related to an existing connection—for example, when the traffic is part of some FTP session or SIP session, and so on. For a full list of `ip_conntrack_info` enum values see `include/uapi/linux/netfilter/nf_conntrack_common.h`. The nfctinfo field of the SKB is set in the `resolve_normal_ct()` method, `net/netfilter/nf_conntrack_core.c`. This method performs a Connection Tracking lookup, and if there is a miss, it creates a new Connection Tracking entry. Connection Tracking is discussed in depth in Chapter 9, which deals with the netfilter subsystem.

- `__u8 pkt_type:3`

  For Ethernet, the packet type depends on the destination MAC address in the ethernet header, and is determined by the `eth_type_trans()` method:

  - PACKET_BROADCAST for broadcast

  - PACKET_MULTICAST for multicast

  - PACKET_HOST if the destination MAC address is the MAC address of the device which was passed as a parameter

  - PACKET_OTHERHOST if these conditions are not met

  See the definition of the packet types in `include/uapi/linux/if_packet.h`.

- `__u8 ipvs_property:1`

  This flag indicates whether the SKB is owned by ipvs (IP Virtual Server), which is a kernel-based transport layer load-balancing solution. This field is set to 1 in the transmit methods of ipvs (`net/netfilter/ipvs/ip_vs_xmit.c`).

- `__u8 peeked:1`

  This packet has been already seen, so stats have been done for it—so don't do them again.

- __u8 nf_trace:1

    The netfilter packet trace flag. This flag is set by the packet flow tracing the netfilter module, xt_TRACE module, which is used to mark packets for tracing (net/netfilter/xt_TRACE.c).

    Helper method:

    - nf_reset_trace(struct sk_buff *skb): Sets the nf_trace of the specified skb to 0.

- __be16 protocol

    The protocol field is initialized in the Rx path by the eth_type_trans() method to be ETH_P_IP when working with Ethernet and IP.

- void (*destructor)(struct sk_buff *skb)

    A callback that is invoked when freeing the SKB by calling the kfree_skb() method.

- struct nf_conntrack *nfct

    The associated Connection Tracking object, if it exists. The nfct field, like the nfctinfo field, is set in the resolve_normal_ct() method. The Connection Tracking layer is discussed in depth in Chapter 9, which deals with the netfilter subsystem.

- int skb_iif

    The ifindex of the network device on which the packet arrived.

- __u32 rxhash

    The rxhash of the SKB is calculated in the receive path, according to the source and destination address of the IP header and the ports from the transport header. A value of zero indicates that the hash is not valid. The rxhash is used to ensure that packets with the same flow will be handled by the same CPU when working with Symmetrical Multiprocessing (SMP). This decreases the number of cache misses and improves network performance. The rxhash is part of the Receive Packet Steering (RPS) feature, which was contributed by Google developers (Tom Herbert and others). The RPS feature gives performance improvement in SMP environments. See more in Documentation/networking/scaling.txt.

- __be16 vlan_proto

    The VLAN protocol used—usually it is the 802.1q protocol. Recently support for the 802.1ad protocol (also known as Stacked VLAN) was added.

    The following is an example of creating 802.1q and 802.1ad VLAN devices in userspace using the ip command of the iproute2 package:

    ```
    ip link add link eth0 eth0.1000 type vlan proto 802.1ad id 1000
    ip link add link eth0.1000 eth0.1000.1000 type vlan proto 802.1q id 100
    ```

    Note: this feature is supported in kernel 3.10 and higher.

- __u16 vlan_tci

    The VLAN tag control information (2 bytes), composed of ID and priority.

Helper method:

- `vlan_tx_tag_present(__skb)`: This macro checks whether the VLAN_TAG_PRESENT flag is set in the `vlan_tci` field of the specified `__skb`.

- `__u16 queue_mapping`

Queue mapping for multiqueue devices.

Helper methods:

- `skb_set_queue_mapping (struct sk_buff *skh, u16 queue_mapping)`: Sets the specified `queue_mapping` for the specified skb.

- `skb_get_queue_mapping(const struct sk_buff *skb)`: Returns the `queue_mapping` of the specified skb.

- `__u8 pfmemalloc`

Allocate the SKB from PFMEMALLOC reserves.

Helper method:

- `skb_pfmemalloc()`: Returns `true` if the SKB was allocated from PFMEMALLOC reserves.

- `__u8 ooo_okay:1`

The `ooo_okay` flag is set to avoid ooo (out of order) packets.

- `__u8 l4_rxhash:1`

A flag that is set when a canonical 4-tuple hash over transport ports is used.

See the `__skb_get_rxhash()` method in `net/core/flow_dissector.c`.

- `__u8 no_fcs:1`

A flag that is set when you request the NIC to treat the last 4 bytes as Ethernet Frame Check Sequence (FCS).

- `__u8 encapsulation:1`

The encapsulation field denotes that the SKB is used for encapsulation. It is used, for example, in the VXLAN driver. VXLAN is a standard protocol to transfer Layer 2 Ethernet packets over a UDP kernel socket. It can be used as a solution when there are firewalls that block tunnels and allow, for example, only TCP or UDP traffic. The VXLAN driver uses UDP encapsulation and sets the SKB encapsulation to 1 in the `vxlan_init_net()` method. Also the `ip_gre` module and the `ipip` tunnel module use encapsulation and set the SKB encapsulation to 1.

- `__u32 secmark`

Security mark field. The `secmark` field is set by an `iptables` SECMARK target, which labels packets with any valid security context. For example:

```
iptables -t mangle -A INPUT -p tcp --dport 80 -j SECMARK --selctx
system_u:object_r:httpd_packet_t:s0
iptables -t mangle -A OUTPUT -p tcp --sport 80 -j SECMARK --selctx
system_u:object_r:httpd_packet_t:s0
```

In the preceding rule, you are statically labeling packets arriving at and leaving from port 80 as `httpd_packet_t`. See: `netfilter/xt_SECMARK.c`.

Helper methods:

- `void skb_copy_secmark(struct sk_buff *to, const struct sk_buff *from)`: Sets the value of the `secmark` field of the first specified SKB (`to`) to be equal to the value of the `secmark` field of the second specified SKB (`from`).

- `void skb_init_secmark(struct sk_buff *skb)`: Initializes the `secmark` of the specified `skb` to be 0.

The next three fields: `mark`, `dropcount`, and `reserved_tailroom` appear in a union.

- `__u32 mark`

  This field enables identifying the SKB by marking it.

  You can set the `mark` field of the SKB, for example, with the `iptables` MARK target in an iptables PREROUTING rule with the mangle table.

- `iptables -A PREROUTING -t mangle -i eth1 -j  MARK  --set-mark   0x1234`

  This rule will assign the value of 0x1234 to every SKB `mark` field for incoming traffic on eth1 before performing a routing lookup. You can also run an `iptables` rule which will check the `mark` field of every SKB to match a specified value and act upon it. Netfilter targets and `iptables` are discussed in Chapter 9, which deals with the netfilter subsystem.

- `__u32 dropcount`

  The dropcount counter represents the number of dropped packets (`sk_drops`) of the `sk_receive_queue` of the assigned sock object (`sk`). See the `sock_queue_rcv_skb()` method in `net/core/sock.c`.

- `_u32 reserved_tailroom`: Used in the `sk_stream_alloc_skb()` method.

- `sk_buff_data_t transport_header`

  The transport layer (L4) header.

  Helper methods:

  - `skb_transport_header(const struct sk_buff *skb)`: Returns the transport header of the specified `skb`.

  - `skb_transport_header_was_set(const struct sk_buff *skb)`: Returns 1 if the `transport_header` of the specified `skb` is set.

- `sk_buff_data_t network_header`

  The network layer (L3) header.

  Helper method:

  - `skb_network_header(const struct sk_buff *skb)`: Returns the network header of the specified `skb`.

- `sk_buff_data_t mac_header`

  The link layer (L2) header.

Helper methods:

- skb_mac_header(const struct sk_buff *skb): Returns the MAC header of the specified skb.

- skb_mac_header_was_set(const struct sk_buff *skb): Returns 1 if the mac_header of the specified skb was set.

- sk_buff_data_t tail

  The tail of the data.

- sk_buff_data_t end

  The end of the buffer. The tail cannot exceed end.

- unsigned char head

  The head of the buffer.

- unsigned char data

  The data head. The data block is allocated separately from the sk_buff allocation.

  See, in _alloc_skb(), net/core/skbuff.c:

  data = kmalloc_reserve(size, gfp_mask, node, &pfmemalloc);

  Helper methods:

  - skb_headroom(const struct sk_buff *skb): This method returns the headroom, which is the number of bytes of free space at the head of the specified skb (skb->data - skb->head). See Figure A-1.

  - skb_tailroom(const struct sk_buff *skb): This method returns the tailroom, which is the number of bytes of free space at the tail of the specified skb (skb->end - skb->tail). See Figure A-1.

Figure A-1 shows the headroom and the tailroom of an SKB.

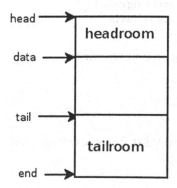

Figure A-1. *Headroom and tailroom of an SKB*

The following are some methods for handling buffers:

- `skb_put(struct sk_buff *skb, unsigned int len)`: Adds data to a buffer: this method adds len bytes to the buffer of the specified skb and increments the length of the specified skb by the specified len.

- `skb_push(struct sk_buff *skb, unsigned int len)`: Adds data to the start of a buffer; this method decrements the data pointer of the specified skb by the specified len and increments the length of the specified skb by the specified len.

- `skb_pull(struct sk_buff *skb, unsigned int len)`: Removes data from the start of a buffer; this method increments the data pointer of the specified skb by the specified len and decrements the length of the specified skb by the specified len.

- `skb_reserve(struct sk_buff *skb, int len)`: Increases the headroom of an empty skb by reducing the tail.

After describing some methods for handling buffers, I continue with listing the members of the sk_buff structure:

- `unsigned int truesize`

  The total memory allocated for the SKB (including the SKB structure itself and the size of the allocated data block).

- `atomic_t users`

  A reference counter, initialized to 1; incremented by the skb_get() method and decremented by the kfree_skb() method or by the consume_skb() method; the kfree_skb() method decrements the usage counter; if it reached 0, the method will free the SKB—otherwise, the method will return without freeing it.

  Helper methods:

  - `skb_get(struct sk_buff *skb)`: Increments the users reference counter by 1.

  - `skb_shared(const struct sk_buff *skb)`: Returns true if the number of users is not 1.

  - `skb_share_check(struct sk_buff *skb, gfp_t pri)`: If the buffer is not shared, the original buffer is returned. If the buffer is shared, the buffer is cloned, and the old copy drops a reference. A new clone with a single reference is returned. When being called from interrupt context or with spinlocks held, the pri parameter (priority) must be GFP_ATOMIC. If memory allocation fails, NULL is returned.

  - `consume_skb(struct sk_buff *skb)`: Decrements the users reference counter and frees the SKB if the users reference counter is zero.

struct skb_shared_info

The skb_shared_info struct is located at the end of the data block (skb_end_pointer(SKB)). It consists of only a few fields. Let's take a look at it:

```
struct skb_shared_info {
    unsigned char       nr_frags;
    __u8                tx_flags;
    unsigned short      gso_size;
    unsigned short      gso_segs;
    unsigned short      gso_type;
```

```
struct sk_buff           *frag_list;
struct skb_shared_hwtstamps hwtstamps;
__be32                   ip6_frag_id;
atomic_t                 dataref;
void *                   destructor_arg;
skb_frag_t               frags[MAX_SKB_FRAGS];
};
```

The following is a description of some of the important members of the skb_shared_info structure:

- nr_frags: Represents the number of elements in the frags array.

- tx_flags can be:

  - SKBTX_HW_TSTAMP: Generate a hardware time stamp.

  - SKBTX_SW_TSTAMP: Generate a software time stamp.

  - SKBTX_IN_PROGRESS: Device driver is going to provide a hardware timestamp.

  - SKBTX_DEV_ZEROCOPY: Device driver supports Tx zero-copy buffers.

  - SKBTX_WIFI_STATUS: Generate WiFi status information.

  - SKBTX_SHARED_FRAG: Indication that at least one fragment might be overwritten.

- When working with fragmentation, there are cases when you work with a list of sk_buffs (frag_list), and there are cases when you work with the frags array. It depends mostly on whether the Scatter/Gather mode is set.

  Helper methods:

  - skb_is_gso(const struct sk_buff *skb): Returns true if the gso_size of the skb_shared_info associated with the specified skb is not 0.

  - skb_is_gso_v6(const struct sk_buff *skb): Returns true if the gso_type of the skb_shared_info associated with the skb is SKB_GSO_TCPV6.

  - skb_shinfo(skb): A macro that returns the skb_shinfo associated with the specified skb.

  - skb_has_frag_list(const struct sk_buff *skb): Returns true if the frag_list of the skb_shared_info of the specified skb is not NULL.

  - dataref: A reference counter of the skb_shared_info struct. It is set to 1 in the method, which allocates the skb and initializes skb_shared_info (The __alloc_skb() method).

The net_device structure

The net_device struct represents the network device. It can be a physical device, like an Ethernet device, or it can be a software device, like a bridge device or a VLAN device. As with the sk_buff structure, I will list its important members. The net_device struct is defined in include/linux/netdevice.h:

- char name[IFNAMSIZ]

  The name of the network device. This is the name that you see with ifconfig or ip commands (for example eth0, eth1, and so on). The maximum length of the interface name is 16 characters. In newer distributions with biosdevname support, the naming scheme corresponds to the physical location of the network device. So PCI network devices are named p<slot>p<port>, according to the chassis labels, and embedded ports (on motherboard interfaces) are named em<port>—for example, em1, em2, and so on. There is a special suffix for SR-IOV devices and Network Partitioning (NPAR)–enabled devices. Biosdevname is developed by Dell: http://linux.dell.com/biosdevname. See also this white paper: http://linux.dell.com/files/whitepapers/consistent_ network_device_naming_in_linux.pdf.

Helper method:

- dev_valid_name(const char *name): Checks the validity of the specified network device name. A network device name must obey certain restrictions in order to enable creating corresponding sysfs entries. For example, it cannot be " . " or " .. "; its length should not exceed 16 characters. Changing the interface name can be done like this, for example: ip link set <oldDeviceName> p2p1 <newDeviceName>. So, for example, ip link set p2p1 name a12345678901234567 will fail with this message: Error: argument "a12345678901234567" is wrong: "name" too long. The reason is that you tried to set a device name that is longer than 16 characters. And running ip link set p2p1 name. will fail with RTNETLINK answers: Invalid argument, since you tried to set the device name to be "", which is an invalid value. See dev_valid_name() in net/core/dev.c.

- struct hlist_node name_hlist

  This is a hash table of network devices, indexed by the network device name. A lookup in this hash table is performed by dev_get_by_name(). Insertion into this hash table is performed by the list_netdevice() method, and removal from this hash table is done with the unlist_netdevice() method.

- char *ifalias

  SNMP alias interface name. Its length can be up to 256 (IFALIASZ).

  You can create an alias to a network device using this command line:

  ip link set <devName> alias myalias

  The ifalias name is exported via sysfs by /sys/class/net/<devName>/ifalias.

  Helper method:

  - dev_set_alias(struct net_device *dev, const char *alias, size_t len): Sets the specified alias to the specified network device. The specified len parameter is the number of bytes of specified alias to be copied; if the specified len is greater than 256 (IFALIASZ), the method will fail with -EINVAL.

- unsigned int irq

  The Interrupt Request (IRQ) number of the device. The network driver should call request_irq() to register itself with this IRQ number. Typically this is done in the probe() callback of the network device driver. The prototype of the request_irq() method is: int request_irq(unsigned int irq, irq_handler_t handler, unsigned long flags, const char *name, void *dev). The first argument is the IRQ number. The sepcified handler is the Interrupt Service Routine (ISR). The network driver should call the free_irq() method when it no longer uses this irq. In many cases, this irq is shared (the request_irq() method is called with the IRQF_SHARED flag). You can view the number of interrupts that occurred on each core by running cat /proc/interrupts. You can set the SMP affinity of the irq by echo irqMask > /proc/irq/<irqNumber>/smp_affinity.

In an SMP machine, setting the SMP affinity of interrupts means setting which cores are allowed to handle the interrupt. Some PCI network interfaces use Message Signaled Interrupts (MSIs). PCI MSI interrupts are never shared, so the IRQF_SHARED flag is not set when calling the request_irq() method in these network drivers. See more info in Documentation/PCI/MSI-HOWTO.txt.

- unsigned long state

  A flag that can be one of these values:

  - __LINK_STATE_START: This flag is set when the device is brought up, by the dev_open() method, and is cleared when the device is brought down.

  - __LINK_STATE_PRESENT: This flag is set in device registration, by the register_netdevice() method, and is cleared in the netif_device_detach() method.

  - __LINK_STATE_NOCARRIER: This flag shows whether the device detected loss of carrier. It is set by the netif_carrier_off() method and cleared by the netif_carrier_on() method. It is exported by sysfs via /sys/class/net/<devName>/carrier.

  - __LINK_STATE_LINKWATCH_PENDING: This flag is set by the linkwatch_fire_event() method and cleared by the linkwatch_do_dev() method.

  - __LINK_STATE_DORMANT: The dormant state indicates that the interface is not able to pass packets (that is, it is not "up"); however, this is a "pending" state, waiting for some external event. See section 3.1.12, "New states for IfOperStatus" in RFC 2863, "The Interfaces Group MIB."

  The state flag can be set with the generic set_bit() method.

  Helper methods:

  - netif_running(const struct net_device *dev): Returns true if the __LINK_STATE_START flag of the state field of the specified device is set.

  - netif_device_present(struct net_device *dev): Returns true if the __LINK_STATE_PRESENT flag of the state field of the specified device is set.

  - netif_carrier_ok (const struct net_device *dev): Returns true if the __LINK_STATE_NOCARRIER flag of the state field of the specified device is not set.

  These three methods are defined in include/linux/netdevice.h.

- netdev_features_t features

  The set of currently active device features. These features should be changed only by the network core or in error paths of the ndo_set_features() callback. Network driver developers are responsible for setting the initial set of the device features. Sometimes they can use a wrong combination of features. The network core fixes this by removing an offending feature in the netdev_fix_features() method, which is invoked when the network interface is registered (in the register_netdevice() method); a proper message is also written to the kernel log.

I will mention some net_device features here and discuss them. For the full list of net_device features, look in include/linux/netdev_features.h.

- NETIF_F_IP_CSUM means that the network device can checksum L4 IPv4 TCP/UDP packets.

- NETIF_F_IPV6_CSUM means that the network device can checksum L4 IPv6 TCP/UDP packets.

- NETIF_F_HW_CSUM means that the device can checksum in hardware all L4 packets. You cannot activate NETIF_F_HW_CSUM together with NETIF_F_IP_CSUM, or together with NETIF_F_IPV6_CSUM, because that will cause duplicate checksumming.

If the driver features set includes both NETIF_F_HW_CSUM and NETIF_F_IP_CSUM features, then you will get a kernel message saying "mixed HW and IP checksum settings." In such a case, the netdev_fix_features() method removes the NETIF_F_IP_CSUM feature. If the driver features set includes both NETIF_F_HW_CSUM and NETIF_F_IPV6_CSUM features, you get again the same message as in the previous case. This time, the NETIF_F_IPV6_CSUM feature is the one which is being removed by the netdev_fix_features() method. In order for a device to support TSO (TCP Segmentation Offload), it needs also to support Scatter/Gather and TCP checksum; this means that both NETIF_F_SG and NETIF_F_IP_CSUM features must be set. If the driver features set does not include the NETIF_F_SG feature, then you will get a kernel message saying "Dropping TSO features since no SG feature," and the NETIF_F_ALL_TSO feature will be removed. If the driver features set does not include the NETIF_F_IP_CSUM feature and does not include NETIF_F_HW_CSUM, then you will get a kernel message saying "Dropping TSO features since no CSUM feature," and the NETIF_F_TSO will be removed.

■ **Note** In recent kernels, if CONFIG_DYNAMIC_DEBUG kernel config item is set, you might need to explicitly enable printing of some messages, via <debugfs>/dynamic_debug/control interface. See Documentation/dynamic-debug-howto.txt.

- NETIF_F_LLTX is the LockLess TX flag and is considered deprecated. When it is set, you don't use the generic Tx lock (This is why it is called LockLess TX). See the following macro (HARD_TX_LOCK) from net/core/dev.c:

```
#define HARD_TX_LOCK(dev, txq, cpu) { \ if ((dev->features & NETIF_F_LLTX) == 0) { \
    __netif_tx_lock(txq, cpu); \
  } \
  }
```

NETIF_F_LLTX is used in tunnel drivers like VXLAN, VETH, and in IP over IP (IPIP) tunneling driver. For example, in the IPIP tunnel module, you set the NETIF_F_LLTX flag in the ipip_tunnel_setup() method (net/ipv4/ipip.c).

The NETIF_F_LLTX flag is also used in a few drivers that have implemented their own Tx lock, like the cxgb network driver.

In `drivers/net/ethernet/chelsio/cxgb/cxgb2.c`, you have:

```
static int __devinit init_one(struct pci_dev *pdev,
const struct pci_device_id *ent)
{
    . . .
    netdev->features |= NETIF_F_SG | NETIF_F_IP_CSUM |
                        NETIF_F_RXCSUM | NETIF_F_LLTX;
    . . .
}
```

- NETIF_F_GRO is used to indicate that the device supports GRO (Generic Receive Offload). With GRO, incoming packets are merged at reception time. The GRO feature improves network performance. GRO replaced LRO (Large Receive Offload), which was limited to TCP/IPv4. This flag is checked in the beginning of the `dev_gro_receive()` method; devices that do not have this flag set will not perform the GRO handling part in this method. A driver that wants to use GRO should call the `napi_gro_receive()` method in the Rx path of the driver. You can enable/disable GRO with ethtool, by `ethtool -K <deviceName> gro on`/ `ethtool -K <deviceName> gro off`, respectively. You can check whether GRO is set by running `ethtool -k <deviceName>` and looking at the gro field.

- NETIF_F_GSO is set to indicate that the device supports Generic Segmentation Offload (GSO). GSO is a generalization of a previous solution called TSO (TCP segmentation offload), which dealt only with TCP in IPv4. GSO can handle also IPv6, UDP, and other protocols. GSO is a performance optimization, based on traversing the networking stack once instead of many times, for big packets. So the idea is to avoid segmentation in Layer 4 and defer segmentation as much as possible. The sysadmin can enable/disable GSO with `ethtool`, by `ethtool -K <driverName> gso on`/`ethtool -K <driverName> gso off`, respectively. You can check whether GSO is set by running `ethtool -k <deviceName>` and looking at the gso field. To work with GSO, you should work in Scatter/Gather mode. The NETIF_F_SG flag must be set.

- NETIF_F_NETNS_LOCAL is set for network namespace local devices. These are network devices that are not allowed to move between network namespaces. The loopback, VXLAN, and PPP network devices are examples of namespace local devices. All these devices have the NETIF_F_NETNS_LOCAL flag set. A sysadmin can check whether an interface has the NETIF_F_NETNS_LOCAL flag set or not by `ethtool -k <deviceName>`. This feature is fixed and cannot be changed by `ethtool`. Trying to move a network device of this type to a different namespace results in an error (-EINVAL). For details, look in the `dev_change_net_namespace()` method (`net/core/dev.c`). When deleting a network namespace, devices that do not have the NETIF_F_NETNS_LOCAL flag set are moved to the default initial network namespace (`init_net`). Network namespace local devices that have the NETIF_F_NETNS_LOCAL flag set are not moved to the default initial network namespace (`init_net`), but are deleted.

- NETIF_F_HW_VLAN_CTAG_RX is for use by devices which support VLAN Rx hardware acceleration. It was formerly called NETIF_F_HW_VLAN_RX and was renamed in kernel 3.10, when support for 802.1ad was added. "CTAG" was added to indicate that this device differ from "STAG" device (Service provider tagging). A device driver that sets the NETIF_F_HW_VLAN_RX feature must also define the `ndo_vlan_rx_add_vid()` and `ndo_vlan_rx_kill_vid()` callbacks. Failure to do so will avoid device registration and result in a "Buggy VLAN acceleration in driver" kernel error message.

- NETIF_F_HW_VLAN_CTAG_TX is for use by devices that support VLAN Tx hardware acceleration. It was formerly called NETIF_F_HW_VLAN_TX and was renamed in kernel 3.10 when support for 802.1ad was added.

- NETIF_F_VLAN_CHALLENGED is set for devices that can't handle VLAN packets. Setting this feature avoids registration of a VLAN device. Let's take a look at the VLAN registration method:

```
static int register_vlan_device(struct net_device *real_dev, u16 vlan_id) {
    int err;
    . . .
    err = vlan_check_real_dev(real_dev, vlan_id);
```

The first thing the vlan_check_real_dev() method does is to check the network device features and return an error if the NETIF_F_VLAN_CHALLENGED feature is set:

```
int vlan_check_real_dev(struct net_device *real_dev, u16 vlan_id)
{
        const char *name = real_dev->name;

        if (real_dev->features & NETIF_F_VLAN_CHALLENGED) {
                pr_info("VLANs not supported on %s\n", name);
                return -EOPNOTSUPP;
        }
        . . .
}
```

For example, some types of Intel e100 network device drivers set the NETIF_F_VLAN_CHALLENGED feature (see e100_probe() in drivers/net/ethernet/intel/e100.c).

You can check whether the NETIF_F_VLAN_CHALLENGED is set by running ethtool -k <deviceName> and looking at the vlan-challenged field. This is a fixed value that you cannot change with the ethtool command.

- NETIF_F_SG is set when the network interface supports Scatter/Gather IO. You can enable and disable Scatter/Gather with ethtool, by ethtool -K <deviceName> sg on/ ethtool -K <deviceName> sg off, respectively. You can check whether Scatter/Gather is set by running ethtool -k <deviceName> and looking at the sg field.

- NETIF_F_HIGHDMA is set if the device can perform access by DMA to high memory. The practical implication of setting this feature is that the ndo_start_xmit() callback of the net_device_ops object can manage SKBs, which have frags elements in high memory. You can check whether the NETIF_F_HIGHDMA is set by running ethtool -k <deviceName> and looking at the highdma field. This is a fixed value that you cannot change with the ethtool command.

- netdev_features_t hw_features

    The set of features that are changeable features. This means that their state may possibly be changed (enabled or disabled) for a particular device by a user's request. This set should be initialized in the ndo_init() callback and not changed later.

- `netdev_features_t wanted_features`

  The set of features that were requested by the user. A user may request to change various offloading features—for example, by running ethtool -K eth1 rx on. This generates a feature change event notification (NETDEV_FEAT_CHANGE) to be sent by the netdev_features_change() method.

- `netdev_features_t vlan_features`

  The set of features whose state is inherited by child VLAN devices. For example, let's look at the rtl_init_one() method, which is the probe callback of the r8169 network device driver (see Chapter 14):

```
int rtl_init_one(struct pci_dev *pdev, const struct pci_device_id *ent)

{
    . . .
    dev->vlan_features=NETIF_F_SG|NETIF_F_IP_CSUM|NETIF_F_TSO|    NETIF_F_HIGHDMA;
    . . .
}
```

  (drivers/net/ethernet/realtek/r8169.c)

  This initialization means that all child VLAN devices will have these features. For example, let's say that your eth0 device is an r8169 device, and you add a VLAN device thus: vconfig add eth0 100. Then, in the initialization in the VLAN module, there is this code related to vlan_features:

```
static int vlan_dev_init(struct net_device *dev)
{
    . . .
    dev->features |= real_dev->vlan_features | NETIF_F_LLTX;
    . . .
}
```

  (net/8021q/vlan_dev.c)

  This means that it sets the features of the VLAN child device to be the vlan_features of the real device (which is eth0 in this case), which were set according to what you saw earlier in the rtl_init_one() method.

- `netdev_features_t hw_enc_features`

  The mask of features inherited by encapsulating devices. This field indicates what encapsulation offloads the hardware is capable of doing, and drivers will need to set them appropriately. For more info about the network device features, see Documentation/networking/netdev-features.txt.

- `ifindex`

  The ifindex (Interface index) is a unique device identifier. This index is incremented by 1 each time you create a new network device, by the dev_new_index() method. The first network device you create, which is almost always the loopback device, has ifindex of 1. Cyclic integer overflow is handled by the method that handles assignment of the ifindex number. The ifindex is exported by sysfs via /sys/class/net/<devName>/ifindex.

- `struct net_device_stats stats`

  The statistics `struct`, which was left as a legacy, includes fields like the number of `rx_packets` or the number of `tx_packets`. New device drivers use the `rtnl_link_stats64` struct (defined in `include/uapi/linux/if_link.h`) instead of the `net_device_stats` struct. Most of the network drivers implement the `ndo_get_stats64()` callback of `net_device_ops` (or the `ndo_get_stats()` callback of `net_device_ops`, when working with the older API).

  The statistics are exported via `/sys/class/net/<deviceName>/statistics`.

  Some drivers implement the `get_ethtool_stats()` callback. These drivers show statistics by `ethtool -S <deviceName>`

  See, for example, the `rtl8169_get_ethtool_stats()` method in `drivers/net/ethernet/realtek/r8169.c`.

- `atomic_long_t rx_dropped`

  A counter of the number of packets that were dropped in the RX path by the core network stack. This counter should not be used by drivers. Do not confuse the `rx_dropped` field of the `sk_buff` with the `dropped` field of the `softnet_data struct`. The `softnet_data` struct represents a per-CPU object. They are not equivalent because the `rx_dropped` of the `sk_buff` might be incremented in several methods, whereas the `dropped` counter of `softnet_data` is incremented only by the `enqueue_to_backlog()` method (`net/core/dev.c`). The dropped counter of `softnet_data` is exported by `/proc/net/softnet_stat`. In `/proc/net/softnet_stat` you have one line per CPU. The first column is the total packets counter, and the second one is the dropped packets counter.

For example:

```
cat /proc/net/softnet_stat
00000076 00000001 00000000 00000000 00000000 00000000 00000000 00000000 00000000 00000000
00000005 00000000 00000000 00000000 00000000 00000000 00000000 00000000 00000000 00000000
```

You see here one line per CPU (you have two CPUs); for the first CPU, you see 118 total packets (hex 0x76), where one packet is dropped. For the second CPU, you see 5 total packets and 0 dropped.

- `struct net_device_ops *netdev_ops`

  The `netdev_ops` structure includes pointers for several callback methods that you want to define if you want to override the default behavior. Here are some callbacks of `netdev_ops`:

  - The `ndo_init()` callback is called when network device is registered.

  - The `ndo_uninit()` callback is called when the network device is unregistered or when the registration fails.

  - The `ndo_open()` callback handles change of device state, when a network device state is being changed from down state to up state.

  - The `ndo_stop()` callback is called when a network device state is being changed to be down.

  - The `ndo_validate_addr()` callback is called to check whether the MAC is valid. Many network drivers set the generic `eth_validate_addr()` method to be the `ndo_validate_addr()` callback. The generic `eth_validate_addr()` method returns true if the MAC address is not a multicast address and is not all zeroes.

- The `ndo_set_mac_address()` callback sets the MAC address. Many network drivers set the generic `eth_mac_addr()` method to be the `ndo_set_mac_address()` callback of `struct net_device_ops` for setting their MAC address. For example, the VETH driver (`drivers/net/veth.c`) or the VXLAN driver (`drivers/nets/vxlan.c`).

- The `ndo_start_xmit()` callback handles packet transmission. It cannot be NULL.

- The `ndo_select_queue()` callback is used to select a Tx queue, when working with multiqueues. If the `ndo_select_queue()` callback is not set, then the `__netdev_pick_tx()` is called. See the implementaion of the `netdev_pick_tx()` method in `net/core/flow_dissector.c`.

- The `ndo_change_mtu()` callback handles modifying the MTU. It should check that the specified MTU is not less than 68, which is the minimum MTU. In many cases, network drivers set the `ndo_change_mtu()` callback to be the generic `eth_change_mtu()` method. The `eth_change_mtu()` method should be overridden if jumbo frames are supported.

- The `ndo_do_ioctl()` callback is called when getting an IOCTL request which is not handled by the generic interface code.

- The `ndo_tx_timeout()` callback is called when the transmitter was idle for a quite a while (for watchdog usage).

- The `ndo_add_slave()` callback is called to set a specified network device as a slave to a specified netowrk device. It is used, for example, in the team network driver and in the bonding network driver.

- The `ndo_del_slave()` callback is called to remove a previously enslaved network device.

- The `ndo_set_features()` callback is called to update the configuration of a network device with new features.

- The `ndo_vlan_rx_add_vid()` callback is called when registering a VLAN id if the network device supports VLAN filtering (the NETIF_F_HW_VLAN_FILTER flag is set in the device features).

- The `ndo_vlan_rx_kill_vid()` callback is called when unregistering a VLAN id if the network device supports VLAN filtering (the NETIF_F_HW_VLAN_FILTER flag is set in the device features).

■ **Note**   From kernel 3.10, the NETIF_F_HW_VLAN_FILTER flag was renamed to NETIF_F_HW_VLAN_CTAG_FILTER.

- There are also several callbacks for handling SR-IOV devices, for example, `ndo_set_vf_mac()` and `ndo_set_vf_vlan()`.

  Before kernel 2.6.29, there was a callback named `set_multicast_list()` for addition of multicast addresses, which was replaced by the `dev_set_rx_mode()` method. The `dev_set_rx_mode()` callback is called primarily whenever the unicast or multicast address lists or the network interface flags are updated.

- `struct ethtool_ops *ethtool_ops`

  The `ethtool_ops` structure includes pointers for several callbacks for handling offloads, getting and setting various device settings, reading registers, getting statistics, reading RX flow hash indirection table, WakeOnLAN parameters, and many more. If the network driver does not initialize the `ethtool_ops` object, the networking core provides a default empty ethtool_ops object named default_ethtool_ops. The management of ethtool_ops is done in net/core/ethtool.c.

Helper method:

- SET_ETHTOOL_OPS (netdev,ops): A macro which sets the specified ethtool_ops for the specified net_device.

You can view the offload parameters of a network interface device by running ethtool –k <deviceName>. You can set some offload parameters of a network interface device by running ethtool –K <deviceName> offloadParameter off/on. See man 8 ethtool.

- const struct header_ops *header_ops

  The header_ops struct include callbacks for creating the Layer 2 header, parsing it, rebuilding it, and more. For Ethernet it is eth_header_ops, defined in net/ethernet/eth.c.

- unsigned int flags

  The interface flags of the network device that you can see from userspace. Here are some flags (for a full list see include/uapi/linux/if.h):

  - IFF_UP flag is set when the interface state is changed from down to up.

  - IFF_PROMISC is set when the interface is in promiscuous mode (receives all packets). When running sniffers like wireshark or tcpdump, the network interface is in promiscuous mode.

  - IFF_LOOPBACK is set for the loopback device.

  - IFF_NOARP is set for devices which do not use the ARP protocol. IFF_NOARP is set, for example, in tunnel devices (see for example, in the ipip_tunnel_setup() method, net/ipv4/ipip.c).

  - IFF_POINTOPOINT is set for PPP devices. See for example, the ppp_setup() method, drivers/net/ppp/ppp_generic.c.

  - IFF_MASTER is set for master devices. See, for example, for bonding devices, the bond_setup() method in drivers/net/bonding/bond_main.c.

  - IFF_LIVE_ADDR_CHANGE flag indicates that the device supports hardware address modification when it's running. See the eth_mac_addr() method in net/ethernet/eth.c.

  - IFF_UNICAST_FLT flag is set when the network driver handles unicast address filtering.

  - IFF_BONDING is set for a bonding master device or bonding slave device. The bonding driver provides a method for aggregating multiple network interfaces into a single logical interface.

  - IFF_TEAM_PORT is set for a device used as a team port. The teaming driver is a load-balancing network software driver intended to replace the bonding driver.

  - IFF_MACVLAN_PORT is set for a device used as a macvlan port.

  - IFF_EBRIDGE is set for an Ethernet bridging device.

  The flags field is exported by sysfs via /sys/class/net/<devName>/flags.

Some of these flags can be set by userspace tools. For example, ifconfig <deviceName> -arp will set the IFF_NOARP network interface flag, and ifconfig <deviceName> arp will clear the IFF_NOARP flag. Note that you can do the same with the iproute2 ip command: ip link set dev <deviceName> arp on and ip link set dev <deviceName> arp off.

- unsigned int priv_flags

  The interface flags, which are invisible from userspace. For example, IFF_EBRIDGE for a bridge interface or IFF_BONDING for a bonding interface, or IFF_SUPP_NOFCS for an interface support sending custom FCS.

  Helper methods:

  - netif_supports_nofcs(): Returns true if the IFF_SUPP_NOFCS is set in the priv_flags of the specified device.

  - is_vlan_dev(struct net_device *dev): Returns 1 if the IFF_802_1Q_VLAN flag is set in the priv_flags of the specified network device.

- unsigned short gflags

  Global flags (kept as legacy).

- unsigned short padded

  How much padding is added by the alloc_netdev() method.

- unsigned char operstate

  RFC 2863 operstate.

- unsigned char link_mode

  Mapping policy to operstate.

- unsigned int mtu

  The network interface MTU (Maximum Transmission Unit) value. The maximum size of frame the device can handle. RFC 791 sets 68 as a minimum MTU. Each protocol has MTU of its own. The default MTU for Ethernet is 1,500 bytes. It is set in the ether_setup() method, net/ethernet/eth.c. Ethernet packets with sizes higher than 1,500 bytes, up to 9,000 bytes, are called Jumbo frames. The network interface MTU is exported by sysfs via /sys/class/net/<devName>/mtu.

  Helper method:

  - dev_set_mtu(struct net_device *dev, int new_mtu): Changes the MTU of the specified device to a new value, specified by the mtu parameter.

  The sysadmin can change the MTU of a network interface to 1,400, for example, in one of the following ways:

```
ifconfig <netDevice> mtu 1400
ip link set <netDevice> mtu 1400
echo 1400 > /sys/class/net/<netDevice>/mtu
```

  Many drivers implement the ndo_change_mtu() callback to change the MTU to perform driver-specific needed actions (like resetting the network card).

- **unsigned short type**

  The network interface hardware type. For example, for Ethernet it is ARPHRD_ETHER and is set in `ether_setup()` in `net/ethernet/eth.c`. For PPP interface, it is ARPHRD_PPP, and is set in the `ppp_setup()` method in `drivers/net/ppp/ppp_generic.c`. The type is exported by sysfs via `/sys/class/net/<devName>/type`.

- **unsigned short hard_header_len**

  The hardware header length. Ethernet headers, for example, consist of MAC source address, MAC destination address, and a type. The MAC source and destination addresses are 6 bytes each, and the type is 2 bytes. So the Ethernet header length is 14 bytes. The Ethernet header length is set to 14 (ETH_HLEN) in the `ether_setup()` method, `net/ethernet/eth.c`. The `ether_setup()` method is responsible for initializing some Ethernet device defaults, like the hard header len, Tx queue len, MTU, type, and more.

- **unsigned char perm_addr[MAX_ADDR_LEN]**

  The permanent hardware address (MAC address) of the device.

- **unsigned char addr_assign_type**

  Hardware address assignment type, can be one of the following:

  - NET_ADDR_PERM

  - NET_ADDR_RANDOM

  - NET_ADDR_STOLEN

  - NET_ADDR_SET

    By default, the MAC address is permanent (NET_ADDR_PERM). If the MAC address was generated with a helper method named `eth_hw_addr_random()`, the type of the MAC address is NET_ADD_RANDOM. The type of the MAC address is stored in the `addr_assign_type` member of the `net_device`. Also when changing the MAC address of the device, with `eth_mac_addr()`, you reset the `addr_assign_type` with ~NET_ADDR_RANDOM (if it was marked as NET_ADDR_RANDOM before). When a network device is registered (by the `register_netdevice()` method), if the `addr_assign_type` equals NET_ADDR_PERM, dev->perm_addr is set to be dev->dev_addr. When you set a MAC address, you set the `addr_assign_type` to be NET_ADDR_SET. This indicates that the MAC address of a device has been set by the `dev_set_mac_address()` method. The `addr_assign_type` is exported by sysfs via `/sys/class/net/<devName>/addr_assign_type`.

- **unsigned char addr_len**

  The hardware address length in octets. For Ethernet addresses, it is 6 (ETH_ALEN) bytes and is set in the `ether_setup()` method. The `addr_len` is exported by sysfs via `/sys/class/net/<deviceName>/addr_len`.

- **unsigned char neigh_priv_len**

  Used in the `neigh_alloc()` method, `net/core/neighbour.c`; `neigh_priv_len` is initialized only in the ATM code (`atm/clip.c`).

- `struct netdev_hw_addr_list uc`

  Unicast MAC addresses list, initialized by the `dev_uc_init()` method. There are three types of packets in Ethernet: unicast, multicast, and broadcast. Unicast is destined for one machine, multicast is destined for a group of machines, and broadcast is destined for all the machines in the LAN.

  Helper methods:

  - `netdev_uc_empty(dev)`: Returns 1 if the unicast list of the specified device is empty (its count field is 0).

  - `dev_uc_flush(struct net_device *dev)`: Flushes the unicast addresses of the specified network device and zeroes `count`.

- `struct netdev_hw_addr_list mc`

  Multicast MAC addresses list, initialized by the `dev_mc_init()` method.

  Helper methods:

  - `netdev_mc_empty(dev)`: Returns 1 if the multicast list of the specified device is empty (its count field is 0).

  - `dev_mc_flush(struct net_device *dev)`: Flushes the multicast addresses of the specified network device and zeroes the count field.

- `unsigned int promiscuity`

  A counter of the times a network interface card is told to work in promiscuous mode. With promiscuous mode, packets with MAC destination address which is different than the interface MAC address are not rejected. The `promiscuity` counter is used, for example, to enable more than one sniffing client; so when opening some sniffing clients (like `wireshark`), this counter is incremented by 1 for each client you open, and closing that client will decrement the promiscuity counter. When the last instance of the sniffing client is closed, `promiscuity` will be set to 0, and the device will exit from working in promiscuous mode. It is used also in the bridging subsystem, as the bridge interface needs to work in promiscuous mode. So when adding a bridge interface, the network interface card is set to work in promiscuous mode. See the call to the `dev_set_promiscuity()` method in `br_add_if()`, `net/bridge/br_if.c`.

  Helper method:

  - `dev_set_promiscuity(struct net_device *dev, int inc)`: Increments/decrements the `promiscuity` counter of the specified network device according to the specified increment. The `dev_set_promiscuity()` method can get a positive increment or a negative increment parameter. As long as the promiscuity counter remains above zero, the interface remains in promiscuous mode. Once it reaches zero, the device reverts back to normal filtering operation. Because promiscuity is an integer, the `dev_set_promiscuity()` method takes into account cyclic overflow of integer, which means it handles the case when the promiscuity counter is incremented when it reaches the maximum positive value an unsigned integer can reach.

- `unsigned int allmulti`

  The `allmulti` counter of the network device enables or disables the allmulticast mode. When selected, all multicast packets on the network will be received by the interface. You can set a network device to work in allmulticast mode by `ifconfig eth0 allmulti`. You disable the `allmulti` flag by `ifconfig eth0 -allmulti`.

Enabling/disabling the allmulticast mode can also be performed with the `ip` command:

```
ip link set p2p1 allmulticast on
ip link set p2p1 allmulticast off
```

You can also see the allmulticast state by inspecting the flags that are shown by the `ip` command:

```
ip addr show
flags=4610<BROADCAST,ALLMULTI,MULTICAST>  mtu 1500
```

Helper method:

- `dev_set_allmulti(struct net_device *dev, int inc)`: Increments/decrements the `allmulti` counter of the specified network device according to the specified increment (which can be a positive or a negative integer). The `dev_set_allmulti()` method also sets the IFF_ALLMULTI flag of the network device when setting the allmulticast mode and removes this flag when disabling the allmulticast mode.

The next three fields are protocol-specific pointers:

- `struct in_device __rcu *ip_ptr`

  This pointer is assigned to a pointer to `struct in_device`, which represents IPv4 specific data, in `inetdev_init()`, `net/ipv4/devinet.c`.

- `struct inet6_dev __rcu *ip6_ptr`

  This pointer is assigned to a pointer to `struct inet6_dev`, which represents IPv6 specific data, in `ipv6_add_dev()`, `net/ipv6/addrconf.c`.

- `struct wireless_dev *ieee80211_ptr`

  This is a pointer for the wireless device, assigned in the `ieee80211_if_add()` method, `net/mac80211/iface.c`.

- `unsigned long last_rx`

  Time of last Rx. It should not be set by network device drivers, unless really needed. Used, for example, in the bonding driver code.

- `struct list_head dev_list`

  The global list of network devices. Insertion to the list is done with the `list_netdevice()` method, when the network device is registered. Removal from the list is done with the `unlist_netdevice()` method, when the network device is unregistered.

- `struct list_head napi_list`

  NAPI stands for New API, a technique by which the network driver works in polling mode, and not in interrupt-driven mode, when it is under high traffic. Using NAPI under high traffic has been proven to improve performance. When working with NAPI, instead of getting an interrupt for each received packet, the network stack buffers the packets and from time to time triggers the poll method the driver registered with the `netif_napi_add()` method. When working with polling mode, the driver starts to work in interrupt-driven mode. When there is an interrupt for the first received packet, you reach the interrupt service routine (ISR), which is the method that was registered with `request_irq()`. Then the driver disables interrupts and notifies NAPI to take control, usually by calling the __napi_schedule() method from the ISR. See, for example, the cpsw_interrupt() method in drivers/net/ethernet/ti/cpsw.

When the traffic is low, the network driver switches to work in interrupt-driven mode. Nowadays, most network drivers work with NAPI. The napi_list object is the list of napi_ struct objects; The netif_napi_add() method adds napi_struct objects to this list, and the netif_napi_del() method deletes napi_struct objects from this list. When calling the netif_napi_add() method, the driver should specify its polling method and a weight parameter. The weight is a limit on the number of packets the driver will pass to the stack in each polling cycle. It is recommended to use a weight of 64. If a driver attempts to call netif_napi_add() with weight higher than 64 (NAPI_POLL_WEIGHT), there is a kernel error message. NAPI_POLL_WEIGHT is defined in include/linux/netdevice.h.

The network driver should call napi_enable() to enable NAPI scheduling. Usually this is done in the ndo_open() callback of the net_device_ops object. The network driver should call napi_disable() to disable NAPI scheduling. Usually this is done in the ndo_stop() callback of net_device_ops. NAPI is implemented using softirqs. This softirq handler is the net_rx_action() method and is registered by calling open_softirq(NET_RX_SOFTIRQ, net_rx_action) by the net_dev_init() method in net/core/dev.c. The net_rx_action() method invokes the poll method of the network driver which was registered with NAPI. The maximum number of packets (taken from all interfaces which are registered to polling) in one polling cycle (NAPI poll) is by default 300. It is the netdev_budget variable, defined in net/core/dev.c, and can be modified via a procfs entry, /proc/sys/net/core/netdev_budget. In the past, you could change the weight per device by writing values to a procfs entry, but currently, the /sys/class/net/<device>/weight sysfs entry is removed. See Documentation/sysctl/net.txt. I should also mention that the napi_complete() method removes a device from the polling list. When a network driver wants to return to work in interrupt-driven mode, it should call the napi_complete() method to remove itself from the polling list.

- struct list_head unreg_list

  The list of unregistered network devices. Devices are added to this list when they are unregistered.

- unsigned char *dev_addr

  The MAC address of the network interface. Sometimes you want to assign a random MAC address. You do that by calling the eth_hw_addr_random() method, which also sets the addr_assign_type to be NET_ADDR_RANDOM.

  The dev_addr field is exported by sysfs via /sys/class/net/<devName>/address.

  You can change dev_addr with userspace tools like ifconfig or ip of iproute2.

  Helper methods: Many times you invoke the following helper methods on Ethernet addresses in general and on dev_addr field of a network device in particular:

  - is_zero_ether_addr(const u8 *addr): Returns true if the address is all zeroes.

  - is_multicast_ether_addr(const u8 *addr): Returns true if the address is a multicast address. By definition the broadcast address is also a multicast address.

  - is_valid_ether_addr (const u8 *addr): Returns true if the specified MAC address is not 00:00:00:00:00:00, is not a multicast address, and is not a broadcast address (FF:FF:FF:FF:FF:FF).

- struct netdev_hw_addr_list dev_addrs

  The list of device hardware addresses.

- unsigned char broadcast[MAX_ADDR_LEN]

  The hardware broadcast address. For Ethernet devices, the broadcast address is initialized to 0XFFFFFFFF in the ether_setup() method, net/ethernet/eth.c. The broadcast address is exported by sysfs via /sys/class/net/<devName>/broadcast.

- struct kset *queues_kset

  A kset is a group of kobjects of a specific type, belonging to a specific subsystem.

  The kobject structure is the basic type of the device model. A Tx queue is represented by struct netdev_queue, and the Rx queue is represented by struct netdev_rx_queue. Each of them holds a kobject pointer. The queues_kset object is a group of all kobjects of the Tx queues and Rx queues. Each Rx queue has the sysfs entry /sys/class/net/<deviceName>/queues/<rx-queueNumber>, and each Tx queue has the sysfs entry /sys/class/net/<deviceName>/queues/<tx-queueNumber>. These entries are added with the rx_queue_add_kobject() method and the netdev_queue_add_kobject() method respectively, in net/core/net-sysfs.c. For more information about the kobject and the device model, see Documentation/kobject.txt.

- struct netdev_rx_queue *_rx

  An array of Rx queues (netdev_rx_queue objects), initialized by the netif_alloc_rx_queues() method. The Rx queue to be used is determined in the get_rps_cpu() method. See more info about RPS in the description of the rxhash field in the previous sk_buff section.

- unsigned int num_rx_queues

  The number of Rx queues allocated in the register_netdev() method.

- unsigned int real_num_rx_queues
  Number of Rx queues currently active in the device.

  Helper method:

  - netif_set_real_num_rx_queues (struct net_device *dev, unsigned int rxq): Sets the actual number of Rx queues used for the specified device according to the specified number of Rx queues. The relevant sysfs entries (/sys/class/net/<devName>/queues/*) are updated (only in the case that the state of the device is NETREG_REGISTERED or NETREG_UNREGISTERING). Note that alloc_netdev_mq() initializes num_rx_queues, real_num_rx_queues, num_tx_queues and real_num_tx_queues to the same value. One can set the number of Tx queues and Rx queues by using ip link when adding a device. For example, if you want to create a VLAN device with 6 Tx queues and 7 Rx queues, you can run this command:

    ```
    ip link add link p2p1 name p2p1.1 numtxqueues 6 numrxqueues 7 type vlan id 8
    ```

  - rx_handler_func_t __rcu *rx_handler

Helper methods:

- netdev_rx_handler_register(struct net_device *dev, rx_handler_func_t *rx_
  handler void *rx_handler_data)

The rx_handler callback is set by calling the netdev_rx_handler_register() method. It
is used, for example, in bonding, team, openvswitch, macvlan, and bridge devices.

- netdev_rx_handler_unregister(struct net_device *dev): Unregisters a receive
  handler for the specified network device.

- void __rcu *rx_handler_data

The rx_handler_data field is also set by the netdev_rx_handler_register() method
when a non-NULL value is passed to the netdev_rx_handler_register() method.

- struct netdev_queue __rcu *ingress_queue

Helper method:

- struct netdev_queue *dev_ingress_queue(struct net_device *dev): Returns the
  ingress_queue of the specified net_device (include/linux/rtnetlink.h).

- struct netdev_queue *_tx

An array of Tx queues (netdev_queue objects), initialized by the netif_alloc_netdev_
queues() method.

Helper method:

- netdev_get_tx_queue(const struct net_device *dev,unsigned int index): Returns
  the Tx queue (netdev_queue object), an element of the _tx array of the specified network
  device at the specified index.

- unsigned int num_tx_queues

Number of Tx queues, allocated by the alloc_netdev_mq() method.

- unsigned int real_num_tx_queues

Number of Tx queues currently active in the device.

Helper method:

- netif_set_real_num_tx_queues(struct net_device *dev, unsigned int txq): Sets
  the actual number of Tx queues used.

- struct Qdisc *qdisc

Each device maintains a queue of packets to be transmitted named qdisc. The Qdisc
(Queuing Disciplines) layer implements the Linux kernel traffic management. The default
qdisc is pfifo_fast. You can set a different qdisc using tc, the traffic control tool of the
iproute2 package. You can view the qdisc of your network device by the using the ip
command:

ip addr show <deviceName>

For example, running

```
ip addr show eth1
```

can give:

```
2: eth1: <BROADCAST,MULTICAST,UP,LOWER_UP> mtu 1500 qdisc pfifo_fast state UP qlen 1000
link/ether 00:e0:4c:53:44:58 brd ff:ff:ff:ff:ff:ff
inet 192.168.2.200/24 brd 192.168.2.255 scope global eth1
inet6 fe80::2e0:4cff:fe53:4458/64 scope link
valid_lft forever preferred_lft forever
```

In this example, you can see that a qdisc of pfifo_fast is used, which is the default.

- unsigned long tx_queue_len

  The maximum number of allowed packets per queue. Each hardware layer has its own tx_queue_len default. For Ethernet devices, tx_queue_len is set to 1,000 by default (see the ether_setup() method). For FDDI, tx_queue_len is set to 100 by default (see the fddi_setup() method in net/802/fddi.c).

  The tx_queue_len field is set to 0 for virtual devices, such as the VLAN device, because the actual transmission of packets is done by the real device on which these virtual devices are based. You can set the Tx queue length of a device by using the command ifconfig (this option is called txqueuelen) or by using the command ip link show (it is called qlen), in this way, for example:

  ```
  ifconfig  p2p1 txqueuelen 900
  ip link set txqueuelen 950 dev p2p1
  ```

  The Tx queue length is exported via the following sysfs entry: /sys/class/net/<deviceName>/tx_queue_len.

- unsigned long trans_start

  The time (in jiffies) of the last transmission.

- int watchdog_timeo

  The watchdog is a timer that will invoke a callback when the network interface was idle and did not perform transmission in some specified timeout interval. Usually the driver defines a watchdog callback which will reset the network interface in such a case. The ndo_tx_timeout() callback of net_device_ops serves as the watchdog callback. The watchdog_timeo field represents the timeout that is used by the watchdog. See the dev_watchdog() method, net/sched/sch_generic.c.

- int __percpu *pcpu_refcnt

  Per CPU network device reference counter.

  Helper methods:

  - dev_put(struct net_device *dev): Decrements the reference count.

  - dev_hold(struct net_device *dev): Increments the reference count.

- struct hlist_node index_hlist

  This is a hash table of network devices, indexed by the network device index (the ifindex field). A lookup in this table is performed by the dev_get_by_index() method. Insertion into this table is performed by the list_netdevice() method, and removal from this list is done with the unlist_netdevice() method.

- enum {...} reg_state

  An enum that represents the various registration states of the network device.

  Possible values:

  - NETREG_UNINITIALIZED: When the device memory is allocated, in the alloc_netdev_mqs() method.

  - NETREG_REGISTERED: When the net_device is registered, in the register_netdevice() method.

  - NETREG_UNREGISTERING: When unregistering a device, in the rollback_registered_many() method.

  - NETREG_UNREGISTERED: The network device is unregistered but it is not freed yet.

  - NETREG_RELEASED: The network device is in the last stage of freeing the allocated memory of the network device, in the free_netdev() method.

- NETREG_DUMMY: Used in the dummy device, in the init_dummy_netdev() method. See drivers/net/dummy.c.

- bool dismantle

  A Boolean flag that shows that the device is in dismantle phase, which means that it is going to be freed.

- enum {...} rtnl_link_state

  This is an enum that can have two values that represent the two phases of creating a new link:

  - RTNL_LINK_INITIALIZE: The ongoing state, when creating the link is still not finished.

  - RTNL_LINK_INITIALIZING: The final state, when work is finished.

  See the rtnl_newlink() method in net/core/rtnetlink.c.

- void (*destructor)(struct net_device *dev)

  This destructor callback is called when unregistering a network device, in the netdev_run_todo() method. It enables network devices to perform additional tasks that need to be done for unregistering. For example, the loopback device destructor callback, loopback_dev_free(), calls free_percpu() for freeing its statistics object and free_netdev(). Likewise the team device destructor callback, team_destructor(), also calls free_percpu() for freeing its statistics object and free_netdev(). And there are many other network device drivers that define a destructor callback.

- `struct net *nd_net`

  The network namespace this network device is inside. Network namespaces support was added in the 2.6.29 kernel. These features provide process virtualization, which is considered lightweight in comparison to other virtualization solutions like KVM and Xen. There is currently support for six namespaces in the Linux kernel. In order to support network namespaces, a structure called `net` was added. This structure represents a network namespace. The process descriptor (`task_struct`) handles the network namespace and other namespaces via a new member which was added for namespaces support, named `nsproxy`. This `nsproxy` includes a network namespace object called `net_ns`, and also four other namespace objects of the following namespaces: pid namespace, mount namespace, uts namespace, and ipc namespace; the sixth namespace, the user namespace, is kept in struct `cred` (the credentials object) which is a member of the process descriptor, `task_struct`).

  Network namespaces provide a partitioning and isolation mechanism which enables one process or a group of processes to have a private view of a full network stack of their own. By default, after boot all network interfaces belong to the default network namespace, `init_net`. You can create a network namespace with userspace tools using the `ip` command from `iproute2` package or with the `unshare` command of `util-linux`—or by writing your own userspace application and invoking the `unshare()` or the `clone()` system calls with the CLONE_NEWNET flag. Moreover, you can also change the network namespace of a process by invoking the `setns()` system call. This `setns()` system call and the `unshare()` system call were added specially to support namespaces. The `setns()` system call can attach to the calling process an existing namespace of any type (network namespace, pid namespace, mount namespace, and so on). You need CAP_SYS_ADMIN privilege to call `set_ns()` for all namespaces, except the user namespace. See `man 2 setns`.

  A network device belongs to exactly one network namespace at a given moment. And a network socket belongs to exactly one network namespace at a given moment. Namespaces do not have names, but they do have a unique inode which identifies them. This unique inode is generated when the namespace is created and can be read by reading a `procfs` entry (the command `ls -al /proc/<pid>/ns/` shows all the unique inode numbers symbolic links of a process—you can also read these symbolic links with the `readlink` command).

  For example, using the `ip` command, creating a new namespace called `ns1` is done thus:

  ```
  ip netns add myns1
  ```

  Each newly created network namespace includes only the loopback device and includes no sockets. Each device (like a bridge device or a VLAN device) that is created from a process that runs in that namespace (like a shell) belongs to that namespace.

Removing a namespace is done using the following command:

```
ip netns del myns1
```

■ **Note**   After deleting a namespace, all its physical network devices are moved to the default network namespace. Local devices (namespace local devices that have the NETIF_F_NETNS_LOCAL flag set, like PPP device or VXLAN device) are not moved to the default network namespace but are deleted.

Showing the list of all network namespaces on the system is done with this command:

```
ip netns list
```

Assigning the p2p1 interface to the myns1 network namespace is done by the command:

```
ip link set p2p1 netns myns1
```

Opening a shell in myns1 is done thus:

```
ip netns exec myns1 bash
```

With the unshare utility, creating a new namespace and starting a bash shell inside is done thus:

```
unshare --net bash
```

Two network namespaces can communicate by using a special virtual Ethernet driver, veth. (drivers/net/veth.c).

Helper methods:

- dev_change_net_namespace(struct net_device *dev, struct net *net, const char *pat): Moves the network device to a different network namespace, specified by the net parameter. Local devices (devices in which the NETIF_F_NETNS_LOCAL feature is set) are not allowed to change their namespace. This method returns -EINVAL for this type of device. The pat parameter, when it is not NULL, is the name pattern to try if the current device name is already taken in the destination network namespace. The method also sends a KOBJ_REMOVE uevent for removing the old namespace entries from sysfs, and a KOBJ_ADD uevent to add the sysfs entries to the new namespace. This is done by invoking the kobject_uevent() method specifying the corresponding uevent.

- dev_net(const struct net_device *dev): Returns the network namespace of the specified network device.

- dev_net_set(struct net_device *dev, struct net *net): Decrements the reference count of the nd_net (namespace object) of the specified device and assigns the specified network namespace to it.

The following four fields are members in a union:

- struct pcpu_lstats __percpu *lstats

  The loopback network device statistics.

- struct pcpu_tstats __percpu *tstats

  The tunnel statistics.

- struct pcpu_dstats __percpu *dstats

  The dummy network device statistics.

- struct pcpu_vstats __percpu *vstats

  The VETH (Virtual Ethernet) statistics.

- struct device dev

The device object associated with the network device. Every device in the Linux kernel is associated with a device object, which is an instance of the device structure. For more information about the device structure, I suggest you read the "Devices" section in Chapter 14 of *Linux Device Drivers*, 3rd Edition (O'Reilly, 2005) and Documentation/driver-model/overview.txt.

Helper methods:

- to_net_dev(d): Returns the net_device object that contains the specified device as its device object.

- SET_NETDEV_DEV (net, pdev): Sets the parent of the dev member of the specified network device to be that specified device (the second argument, pdev).

  With virtual devices, you do not call the SET_NETDEV_DEV() macro. As a result, entries for these virtual devices are created under /sys/devices/virtual/net.

  The SET_NETDEV_DEV() macro should be called before calling the register_netdev() method.

- SET_NETDEV_DEVTYPE(net, devtype): Sets the type of the dev member of the specified network device to be the specified type. The type is a device_type object.

  SET_NETDEV_DEVTYPE() is used, for example, in the br_dev_setup() method, innet/bridge/br_device.c:

```
static struct device_type br_type = {
.name = "bridge",
};

void br_dev_setup(struct net_device *dev)
{
    . . .
    SET_NETDEV_DEVTYPE(dev, &br_type);
    . . .

}
```

With the udevadm tool (udev management tool), you can find the device type, for example, for a bridge device named mybr:

```
udevadm info -q all -p /sys/devices/virtual/net/mybr

P: /devices/virtual/net/mybr

E: DEVPATH=/devices/virtual/net/mybr

E: DEVTYPE=bridge

E: ID_MM_CANDIDATE=1

E: IFINDEX=7

E: INTERFACE=mybr

E: SUBSYSTEM=net
```

- `const struct attribute_group *sysfs_groups[4]`

  Used by networking sysfs.

- `struct rtnl_link_ops *rtnl_link_ops`

  The rtnetlink link operations object. It consists of various callbacks for handling network devices, for example:

  - `newlink()` for configuring and registering a new device.
  - `changelink()` for changing parameters of an existing device.
  - `dellink()` for removing a device.
  - `get_num_tx_queues()` for getting the number of Tx queues.
  - `get_num_rx_queues()` for getting the number of Rx queues.

  Registration and unregistration of `rtnl_link_ops` object is done with the `rtnl_link_register()` method and the `rtnl_link_unregister()` method, respectively.

- `unsigned int gso_max_size`

  Helper method:

  - `netif_set_gso_max_size(struct net_device *dev, unsigned int size)`: Sets the specified `gso_max_size` for the specified network device.

- `u8 num_tc`

  The number of traffic classes in the net device.

Helper method:

- `netdev_set_num_tc(struct net_device *dev, u8 num_tc)`: Sets the `num_tc` of the specified network device (the maximum value of `num_tc` can be TC_MAX_QUEUE, which is 16).

- `int netdev_get_num_tc(struct net_device *dev)`: Returns the `num_tc` value of the specified network device.

- `struct netdev_tc_txq tc_to_txq[TC_MAX_QUEUE]`

- `u8 prio_tc_map[TC_BITMASK + 1];`

- `struct netprio_map __rcu *priomap`

The network priority `cgroup` module provides an interface to set the priority of network traffic. The cgroups layer is a Linux kernel layer that enables process resource management and process isolation. It enables assigning one task or several tasks to a system resource, like a networking resource, memory resource, CPU resource, and so on. The cgroups layer implements a Virtual File System (VFS) and is managed by filesystem operations like mounting/unmounting, creating files and directories, writing to cgroup VFS control files, and so forth. The cgroup project was started in 2005 by developers from Google (Paul Manage, Rohit Seth, and others). Some projects are based on cgroups usage, like `systemd` and `lxc` (Linux containers). Google has its own implementation of containers, based on cgroups. There is no relation between the cgroup implementation and the namespaces implementation. In the past, there was a namespace controller in cgroups but it was removed. No new system calls were added for cgroups implementations, and the cgroup code additions are not critical in terms of performance. There are two networking cgroups modules: `net_prio` and `net_cls`. These two `cgroup` modules are relatively short and simple.

Setting the priority of network traffic with the `netprio` cgroup module is done by writing an entry to a cgroup control file, `/sys/fs/cgroup/net_prio/<group>/net_prio.ifpriomap`. The entry is in the form "deviceName priority." It is true that an application can set the priority of its traffic via the `setsockopt()` system call with SO_PRIORITY, but this is not always possible. Sometimes you cannot change the code of certain applications. Moreover, you want to let the system administrator decide on priority according to site-specific setup. The `netprio` kernel module is a solution when using the `setsockopt()` system call with SO_PRIORITY is not feasible. The `netprio` module also exports another `/sys/fs/cgroup/netprio` entry, `net_prio.prioidx`. The `net_prio.prioidx` entry is a read-only file and contains a unique integer value that the kernel uses as an internal representation of this cgroup.

`netprio` is implemented in `net/core/netprio_cgroup.c`.

`net_cls` is implemented in `net/sched/cls_cgroup.c`.

The network classifier cgroup provides an interface to tag network packets with a class identifier (`classid`). Creating a `net_cls` cgroups instance creates a `net_cls.classid` control file. This `net_cls.classid` value is initialized to 0. You can set up rules for this classid with `tc`, the traffic control command of `iproute2`.

For more information, see `Documentation/cgroups/net_cls.txt`.

- struct phy_device *phydev

  The associated PHY device. The phy_device is the Layer 1 (the physical layer) device. It is defined in include/linux/phy.h. For many devices, PHY flow control parameters like autonegotiation, speed, or duplex can be configured via the PHY device with ethtool commands. See man 8 ethtool for more info.

- int group

  The group that the network device belongs to. It is initialized with INIT_NETDEV_GROUP (0) by default. The group is exported by sysfs via /sys/class/net/<devName>/netdev_group. The network device group filters are used for example in netfilter, in net/netfilter/xt_devgroup.c.

  Helper method:

  - void dev_set_group(struct net_device *dev, int new_group): Changes the group of the specified device to be the specified group.

- struct pm_qos_request pm_qos_req

  Power Management Quality Of Service request object, defined in include/linux/pm_qos.h.

  For more details about PM QoS, see Documentation/power/pm_qos_interface.txt.

Next I will describe the netdev_priv() method and the alloc_netdev() macro, which are used a lot in network drivers.

The netdev_priv(struct net_device *netdev) method returns a pointer to the end of the net_device. This area is used by drivers, which define a private network interface structure in order to store private data. For example, in drivers/net/ethernet/intel/e1000e/netdev.c:

```
static int e1000_open(struct net_device *netdev)
{
    struct e1000_adapter *adapter = netdev_priv(netdev);
    . . .
}
```

The netdev_priv() method is used also for software devices, like the VLAN device. So you have:

```
static inline struct vlan_dev_priv *vlan_dev_priv(const struct net_device *dev)
{
    return netdev_priv(dev);
}
```

(net/8021q/vlan.h)

- The `alloc_netdev(sizeof_priv, name, setup)` macro is for allocation and initialization of a network device. It is in fact a wrapper around `alloc_netdev_mqs()`, with one Tx queue and one Rx queue. `sizeof_priv` is the size of private data to allocate space for. The `setup` method is a callback to initialize the network device. For Ethernet devices, it is usually `ether_setup()`.

  For Ethernet devices, you can use the `alloc_etherdev()` or `alloc_etherdev_mq()` macros, which eventually invoke `alloc_etherdev_mqs()`; `alloc_etherdev_mqs()` is also a wrapper around `alloc_netdev_mqs()`, with the `ether_setup()` as the setup callback method.

- Software devices usually define a setup method of their own. So, in PPP you have the `ppp_setup()` method in `drivers/net/ppp/ppp_generic.c`, and for VLAN you have `vlan_setup(struct net_device *dev)` in `net/8021q/vlan.h`.

RDMA (Remote DMA)

The following sections describe the RDMA API for the following data structures:

- RDMA device
- Protection Domain (PD)
- eXtended Reliable Connected (XRC)
- Shared Receive Queue (SRQ)
- Address Handle (AH)
- Multicast Groups
- Completion Queue (CQ)
- Queue Pair (QP)
- Memory Window (MW)
- Memory Region (MR)

RDMA Device

The following methods are related to the RDMA device.

The ib_register_client() Method

The `ib_register_client()` method registers a kernel client that wants to use the RDMA stack. The specified callbacks will be called for every RDMA device that currently exists in the system and for every new device that will be detected or removed by the system (using hot-plug). It will return 0 on success or the errno value with the reason for the failure.

```
int ib_register_client(struct ib_client *client);
```

- `client`: A structure that describes the attributes of the registration.

The ib_client Struct:

The device registration attributes are represented by struct ib_client:

```
struct ib_client {
        char    *name;
        void (*add)    (struct ib_device *);
        void (*remove)(struct ib_device *);

        struct list_head list;
};
```

- name: The name of the kernel module to be registered.
- add: A callback to be called for each RDMA device that exists in the system and for every new RDMA device that will be detected by the kernel.
- remove: A callback to be called for each RDMA device being removed by the kernel.

The ib_unregister_client() Method

The ib_unregister_client() method unregisters a kernel module that wants to stop using the RDMA stack.

```
void ib_unregister_client(struct ib_client *client);
```

- device: A structure that describes the attributes of the unregistration.
- client: Should be the same object that was used when ib_register_client() was called.

The ib_get_client_data() Method

The ib_get_client_data() method returns the client context which was associated with the RDMA device using the ib_set_client_data() method.

```
void *ib_get_client_data(struct ib_device *device, struct ib_client *client);
```

- device: The RDMA device to get the client context from.
- client: The object that describes the attributes of the registration/unregistration.

The ib_set_client_data() Method

The ib_set_client_data() method sets a client context to be associated with the RDMA device.

```
void  ib_set_client_data(struct ib_device *device, struct ib_client *client,
            void *data);
```

- device: The RDMA device to set the client context with.
- client: The object that describes the attributes of the registration/unregistration.
- data: The client context to associate.

The INIT_IB_EVENT_HANDLER macro

The INIT_IB_EVENT_HANDLER macro initializes an event handler for the asynchronous events that may occur to the RDMA device. This macro should be used before calling the ib_register_event_handler() method:

```
#define INIT_IB_EVENT_HANDLER(_ptr, _device, _handler)          \
    do {                                              \
        (_ptr)->device  = _device;              \
        (_ptr)->handler = _handler;             \
        INIT_LIST_HEAD(&(_ptr)->list);          \
    } while (0)
```

- _ptr: A pointer to the event handler that will be provided to the ib_register_event_handler() method.

- _device: The RDMA device context; upon its events the callback will be called.

- _handler: The callback that will be called with every asynchronous event.

The ib_register_event_handler() Method

The ib_register_event_handler() method registers an RDMA event to be called with every handler asynchronous event. It will return 0 on success or the errno value with the reason for the failure.

```
int ib_register_event_handler  (struct ib_event_handler *event_handler);
```

- event_handler: The event handler that was initialized with the macro INIT_IB_EVENT_HANDLER. This callback may occur in interrupt context.

The ib_event_handler struct:

The RDMA event handler is represented by struct ib_event_handler:

```
struct ib_event_handler {
    struct ib_device *device;
    void            (*handler)(struct ib_event_handler *, struct ib_event *);
    struct list_head  list;
};
```

The ib_event Struct

The event callback is being called with the new event that happens to the RDMA device. This event is represented by struct ib_event.

```
struct ib_event {
    struct ib_device    *device;
    union {
        struct ib_cq    *cq;
        struct ib_qp    *qp;
```

```
        struct ib_srq    *srq;
        u8         port_num;
    } element;
    enum ib_event_type    event;
};
```

- device: The RDMA device to which the asynchronous event occurred.

- element.cq: If this is a CQ event, the CQ on which the asynchronous event occurred.

- element.qp: If this is a QP event, the QP on which the asynchronous event occurred.

- element.srq: If this is an SRQ event, the SRQ on which the asynchronous event occurred.

- element.port_num: If this is a port event, the port number on which the asynchronous event occurred.

- event: The type of the asynchronous event that was occurred. It can be:

    - IB_EVENT_CQ_ERR: CQ event. An error occurred to the CQ and no more Work Completions will be generated to it.

    - IB_EVENT_QP_FATAL: QP event. An error occurred to the QP that prevents it from reporting an error through a Work Completion.

    - IB_EVENT_QP_REQ_ERR: QP event. An incoming RDMA request caused a transport error violation in the targeted QP.

    - IB_EVENT_QP_ACCESS_ERR: QP event. An incoming RDMA request caused a requested error violation in the targeted QP.

    - IB_EVENT_COMM_EST: QP event. A communication established event occurred. An incoming message was received by a QP when it was in the RTR state.

    - IB_EVENT_SQ_DRAINED: QP event. Send Queue drain event. The QP's Send Queue was drained.

    - IB_EVENT_PATH_MIG: QP event. Path migration was completed successfully and the primary was changed.

    - IB_EVENT_PATH_MIG_ERR: QP event. There was an error when trying to perform path migration.

    - IB_EVENT_DEVICE_FATAL: Device event. There was an error with the RDMA device.

    - IB_EVENT_PORT_ACTIVE: Port event. The port state has become active.

    - IB_EVENT_PORT_ERR: Port event. The port state was active and it is no longer active.

    - IB_EVENT_LID_CHANGE: Port event. The LID of the port was changed.

    - IB_EVENT_PKEY_CHANGE: Port event. A P_Key entry was changed in the port's P_Key table.

    - IB_EVENT_SM_CHANGE: Port event. The Subnet Manager that manages this port was change.

    - IB_EVENT_SRQ_ERR: SRQ event. An error occurred to the SRQ.

    - IB_EVENT_SRQ_LIMIT_REACHED: SRQ event/SRQ limit event. The number of Receive Requests in the SRQ dropped below the requested watermark.

- IB_EVENT_QP_LAST_WQE_REACHED: QP event. Last Receive Request reached from the SRQ, and it won't consume any more Receive Requests from it.

- IB_EVENT_CLIENT_REREGISTER: Port event. The client should reregister to all services from the Subnet Administrator.

- IB_EVENT_GID_CHANGE: Port event. A GID entry was changed in the port's GID table.

The ib_unregister_event_handler() Method

The ib_unregister_event_handler() method unregisters an RDMA event handler. It will return 0 on success or the errno value with the reason for the failure.

```
int ib_unregister_event_handler(struct ib_event_handler *event_handler);
```

- event_handler: The event handler to be unregistered. It should be the same object that was registered with ib_register_event_handler().

The ib_query_device() Method

The ib_query_device() method queries the RDMA device for its attributes. It will return 0 on success or the errno value with the reason for the failure.

```
int ib_query_device(struct ib_device *device,
        struct ib_device_attr *device_attr);
```

- device: The RDMA device to be queried.

- device_attr: Pointer to a structure of an RDMA device attributes that will be filled.

The ib_device_attr struct:

The RDMA device attributes are represented by struct ib_device_attr:

```
struct ib_device_attr {
    u64             fw_ver;
    __be64          sys_image_guid;
    u64             max_mr_size;
    u64             page_size_cap;
    u32             vendor_id;
    u32             vendor_part_id;
    u32             hw_ver;
    int             max_qp;
    int             max_qp_wr;
    int             device_cap_flags;
    int             max_sge;
    int             max_sge_rd;
    int             max_cq;
    int             max_cqe;
    int             max_mr;
    int             max_pd;
```

```
int              max_qp_rd_atom;
int              max_ee_rd_atom;
int              max_res_rd_atom;
int              max_qp_init_rd_atom;
int              max_ee_init_rd_atom;
enum ib_atomic_cap    atomic_cap;
enum ib_atomic_cap    masked_atomic_cap;
int              max_ee;
int              max_rdd;
int              max_mw;
int              max_raw_ipv6_qp;
int              max_raw_ethy_qp;
int              max_mcast_grp;
int              max_mcast_qp_attach;
int              max_total_mcast_qp_attach;
int              max_ah;
int              max_fmr;
int              max_map_per_fmr;
int              max_srq;
int              max_srq_wr;
int              max_srq_sge;
unsigned int     max_fast_reg_page_list_len;
u16              max_pkeys;
u8               local_ca_ack_delay;
};
```

- fw_ver: A number which represents the FW version of the RDMA device. It can be evaluated as ZZZZYYXX: Zs are the major number, Ys are the minor number, and Xs are the build number.

- sys_image_guid: The system image GUID: Has a unique value for each system.

- max_mr_size: The maximum supported MR size.

- page_size_cap: Bitwise OR for all of supported memory page shifts.

- vendor_id: The IEEE vendor ID.

- vendor_part_id: Device's part ID, as supplied by the vendor.

- hw_ver: Device's HW version, as supplied by the vendor.

- max_qp: Maximum supported number of QPs.

- max_qp_wr: Maximum supported number of Work Requests in each non-RD QP.

- device_cap_flags: Supported capabilities of the RDMA device. It is a bitwise OR of the masks:

  - IB_DEVICE_RESIZE_MAX_WR: The RDMA device supports resize of the number of Work Requests in a QP.

  - IB_DEVICE_BAD_PKEY_CNTR: The RDMA device supports the ability to count the number of bad P_Keys.

  - IB_DEVICE_BAD_QKEY_CNTR: The RDMA device supports the ability to count the number of bad Q_Keys.

- IB_DEVICE_RAW_MULTI: The RDMA device supports raw packet multicast.

- IB_DEVICE_AUTO_PATH_MIG: The RDMA device supports Automatic Path Migration.

- IB_DEVICE_CHANGE_PHY_PORT: The RDMA device supports changing the QP's primary Port number.

- IB_DEVICE_UD_AV_PORT_ENFORCE: The RDMA device supports enforcements of the port number of UD QP and Address Handle.

- IB_DEVICE_CURR_QP_STATE_MOD: The RDMA device supports the current QP modifier when calling ib_modify_qp().

- IB_DEVICE_SHUTDOWN_PORT: The RDMA device supports port shutdown.

- IB_DEVICE_INIT_TYPE: The RDMA device supports setting InitType and InitTypeReply.

- IB_DEVICE_PORT_ACTIVE_EVENT: The RDMA device supports the generation of the port active asynchronous event.

- IB_DEVICE_SYS_IMAGE_GUID: The RDMA device supports system image GUID.

- IB_DEVICE_RC_RNR_NAK_GEN: The RDMA device supports RNR-NAK generation for RC QPs.

- IB_DEVICE_SRQ_RESIZE: The RDMA device supports resize of a SRQ.

- IB_DEVICE_N_NOTIFY_CQ: The RDMA device supports notification when N Work Completions exists in the CQ.

- IB_DEVICE_LOCAL_DMA_LKEY: The RDMA device supports Zero Stag (in iWARP) and reserved LKey (in InfiniBand).

- IB_DEVICE_RESERVED: Reserved bit.

- IB_DEVICE_MEM_WINDOW: The RDMA device supports Memory Windows.

- IB_DEVICE_UD_IP_CSUM: The RDMA device supports insertion of UDP and TCP checksum on outgoing UD IPoIB messages and can verify the validity of those checksum for incoming messages.

- IB_DEVICE_UD_TSO: The RDMA device supports TCP Segmentation Offload.

- IB_DEVICE_XRC: The RDMA device supports the eXtended Reliable Connected transport.

- IB_DEVICE_MEM_MGT_EXTENSIONS: The RDMA device supports memory management extensions support.

- IB_DEVICE_BLOCK_MULTICAST_LOOPBACK: The RDMA device supports blocking multicast loopback.

- IB_DEVICE_MEM_WINDOW_TYPE_2A: The RDMA device supports Memory Windows type 2A: association with a QP number.

- IB_DEVICE_MEM_WINDOW_TYPE_2B: The RDMA device supports Memory Windows type 2B: association with a QP number and a PD.

- `max_sge`: Maximum supported number of scatter/gather elements per Work Request in a non-RD QP.

- `max_sge_rd`: Maximum supported number of scatter/gather elements per Work Request in an RD QP.

- `max_cq`: Maximum supported number of CQs.

- `max_cqe`: Maximum supported number of entries in each CQ.

- `max_mr`: Maximum supported number of MRs.

- `max_pd`: Maximum supported number of PDs.

- `max_qp_rd_atom`: Maximum number of RDMA Read and Atomic operations that can be sent to a QP as the target of the operation.

- `max_ee_rd_atom`: Maximum number of RDMA Read and Atomic operations that can be sent to an EE context as the target of the operation.

- `max_res_rd_atom`: Maximum number of for incoming RDMA Read and Atomic operations that can be sent to this RDMA device as the target of the operation.

- `max_qp_init_rd_atom`: Maximum number of RDMA Read and Atomic operations that can be sent from a QP as the initiator of the operation.

- `max_ee_init_rd_atom`: Maximum number of RDMA Read and Atomic operations that can be sent from an EE context as the initiator of the operation.

- `atomic_cap`: Ability of the device to support atomic operations. Can be:

  - IB_ATOMIC_NONE: The RDMA device doesn't guarantee any atomicity at all.

  - IB_ATOMIC_HCA: The RDMA device guarantees atomicity between QPs in the same device.

  - IB_ATOMIC_GLOB: The RDMA device guarantees atomicity between this device and any other component.

- `masked_atomic_cap`: The ability of the device to support masked atomic operations. Possible values as described in `atomic_cap` earlier.

- `max_ee`: Maximum supported number of EE contexts.

- `max_rdd`: Maximum supported number of RDDs.

- `max_mw`: Maximum supported number of MWs.

- `max_raw_ipv6_qp`: Maximum supported number of Raw IPv6 Datagram QPs.

- `max_raw_ethy_qp`: Maximum supported number of Raw Ethertype Datagram QPs.

- `max_mcast_grp`: Maximum supported number of multicast groups.

- `max_mcast_qp_attach`: Maximum supported number of QPs that can be attached to each multicast group.

- `max_total_mcast_qp_attach`: Maximum number of total QPs that can be attached to any multicast group.

- `max_ah`: Maximum supported number of AHs.

- `max_fmr`: Maximum supported number of FMRs.

- `max_map_per_fmr`: Maximum supported number of map operations which are allowed per FMR.

- `max_srq`: Maximum supported number of SRQs.

- `max_srq_wr`: Maximum supported number of Work Requests in each SRQ.

- `max_srq_sge`: Maximum supported number of scatter/gather elements per Work Request in an SRQ.

- `max_fast_reg_page_list_len`: Maximum number of page list that can be used when registering an FMR using a Work Request.

- `max_pkeys`: Maximum supported number of P_Keys.

- `local_ca_ack_delay`: Local CA ack delay. This value specifies the maximum expected time interval between the local device receiving a message and transmitting the associated ACK or NAK.

The ib_query_port() Method

The `ib_query_port()` method queries the RDMA device port's attributes. It will return 0 on success or the errno value with the reason for the failure.

```
int ib_query_port(struct ib_device *device,
        u8 port_num, struct ib_port_attr *port_attr);
```

- device: The RDMA device to be queried.

- port_num: The port number to be queried.

- port_attr: A pointer to a structure of an RDMA port attributes which will be filled.

The ib_port_attr Struct

The RDMA port attributes are represented by struct `ib_port_attr`:

```
struct ib_port_attr {
    enum ib_port_state    state;
    enum ib_mtu    max_mtu;
    enum ib_mtu    active_mtu;
    int            gid_tbl_len;
    u32            port_cap_flags;
    u32            max_msg_sz;
    u32            bad_pkey_cntr;
    u32            qkey_viol_cntr;
    u16            pkey_tbl_len;
    u16            lid;
    u16            sm_lid;
    u8             lmc;
    u8             max_vl_num;
    u8             sm_sl;
    u8             subnet_timeout;
```

```
u8              init_type_reply;
u8              active_width;
u8              active_speed;
u8              phys_state;
};
```

- state: The logical port state. Can be:

  - IB_PORT_NOP: Reserved value.

  - IB_PORT_DOWN: Logical link is down.

  - IB_PORT_INIT: Logical link is initialized. The physical link is up but the Subnet Manager hasn't started to configure the port.

  - IB_PORT_ARMED: Logical link is armed. The physical link is up but the Subnet Manager started, and did not yet complete, configuring the port.

  - IB_PORT_ACTIVE: Logical link is active.

  - IB_PORT_ACTIVE_DEFER: Logical link is active but the physical link is down. The link tries to recover from this state.

- max_mtu: The maximum MTU supported by this port. Can be:

  - IB_MTU_256: 256 bytes.

  - IB_MTU_512: 512 bytes.

  - IB_MTU_1024: 1,024 bytes.

  - IB_MTU_2048: 2,048 bytes.

  - IB_MTU_4096: 4,096 bytes.

- active_mtu: The actual MTU that this port is configured with. Can be as max_mtu, mentioned earlier.

- gid_tbl_len: The number of entries in the port's GID table.

- port_cap_flags: The port supported capabilities. It is a bitwise OR of the masks:

  - IB_PORT_SM: An indication that the SM that manages the subnet is sending packets from this port.

  - IB_PORT_NOTICE_SUP: An indication that this port supports notices.

  - IB_PORT_TRAP_SUP: An indication that this port supports traps.

  - IB_PORT_OPT_IPD_SUP: An indication that this port supports Inter Packet Delay optional values.

  - IB_PORT_AUTO_MIGR_SUP: An indication that this port supports Automatic Path Migration.

  - IB_PORT_SL_MAP_SUP: An indication that this port supports SL 2 VL mapping table.

  - IB_PORT_MKEY_NVRAM: An indication that this port supports saving the M_Key attributes in Non Volatile RAM.

- IB_PORT_PKEY_NVRAM: An indication that this port supports saving the P_Key table in Non Volatile RAM.

- IB_PORT_LED_INFO_SUP: An indication that this port supports turning on and off the LED using management packets.

- IB_PORT_SM_DISABLED: An indication that there is an SM which isn't active in this port.

- IB_PORT_SYS_IMAGE_GUID_SUP: An indication that the port supports system image GUID.

- IB_PORT_PKEY_SW_EXT_PORT_TRAP_SUP: An indication that the SMA on the switch management port will monitor P_Key mismatches on each switch external port.

- IB_PORT_EXTENDED_SPEEDS_SUP: An indication that the port supports extended speeds (FDR and EDR).

- IB_PORT_CM_SUP: An indication that this port supports CM.

- IB_PORT_SNMP_TUNNEL_SUP: An indication that an SNMP tunneling agent is listening on this port.

- IB_PORT_REINIT_SUP: An indication that this port supports reinitialization of the node.

- IB_PORT_DEVICE_MGMT_SUP: An indication that this port supports device management.

- IB_PORT_VENDOR_CLASS_SUP: An indication that a vendor-specific agent is listening on this port.

- IB_PORT_DR_NOTICE_SUP: An indication that this port supports Direct Route notices.

- IB_PORT_CAP_MASK_NOTICE_SUP: An indication that this port supports sending a notice if the port's port_cap_flags is changed.

- IB_PORT_BOOT_MGMT_SUP: An indication that a boot manager agent is listening on this port.

- IB_PORT_LINK_LATENCY_SUP: An indication that this port supports link round trip latency measurement.

- IB_PORT_CLIENT_REG_SUP: An indication that this port is capable of generating the IB_EVENT_CLIENT_REREGISTER asynchronous event.

- max_msg_sz: The maximum supported message size by this port.

- bad_pkey_cntr: A counter for the number of bad P_Key from messages that this port received.

- qkey_viol_cntr: A counter for the number of Q_Key violations from messages that this port received.

- pkey_tbl_len: The number of entries in the port's P_Key table.

- lid: The port's Local Identifier (LID), as assigned by the SM.

- sm_lid: The LID of the SM.

- lmc: LID mask of this port.

- `max_vl_num`: Maximum number of Virtual Lanes supported by this port. Can be:

  - 1: 1 VL is supported: VL0

  - 2: 2 VLs are supported: VL0–VL1

  - 3: 4 VLs are supported: VL0–VL3

  - 4: 8 VLs are supported: VL0–VL7

  - 5: 15 VLs are supported: VL0–VL14

- `sm_sl`: The SL to be used when sending messages to the SM.

- `subnet_timeout`: The maximum expected subnet propagation delay. This duration of time calculation is 4.094*2^subnet_timeout.

- `init_type_reply`: The value that the SM configures before moving the port state to IB_PORT_ARMED or IB_PORT_ACTIVE to specify the type of the initialization performed.

- `active_width`: The port's active width. Can be:

  - IB_WIDTH_1X: Multiple of 1.

  - IB_WIDTH_4X: Multiple of 4.

  - IB_WIDTH_8X: Multiple of 8.

  - IB_WIDTH_12X: Multiple of 12.

- `active_speed`: The port's active speed. Can be:

  - IB_SPEED_SDR: Single Data Rate (SDR): 2.5 Gb/sec, 8/10 bit encoding.

  - IB_SPEED_DDR: Double Data Rate (DDR): 5 Gb/sec, 8/10 bit encoding.

  - IB_SPEED_QDR: Quad Data Rate (DDR): 10 Gb/sec, 8/10 bit encoding.

  - IB_SPEED_FDR10: Fourteen10 Data Rate (FDR10): 10.3125 Gb/sec, 64/66 bit encoding.

  - IB_SPEED_FDR: Fourteen Data Rate (FDR): 14.0625 Gb/sec, 64/66 bit encoding.

  - IB_SPEED_EDR: Enhanced Data Rate (EDR): 25.78125 Gb/sec.

- `phys_state`: The physical port state. There isn't any enumeration for this value.

The rdma_port_get_link_layer() Method

The `rdma_port_get_link_layer()` method returns the link layer of the RDMA device port. It will return the following values:

- IB_LINK_LAYER_UNSPECIFIED: Unspecified value, usually legacy value that indicates that this is an InfiniBand link layer.

- IB_LINK_LAYER_INFINIBAND: Link layer is InfiniBand.

- IB_LINK_LAYER_ETHERNET: Link layer is Ethernet. This indicates that the port supports RDMA Over Converged Ethernet (RoCE).

  ```
  enum rdma_link_layer rdma_port_get_link_layer(struct ib_device *device, u8 port_num);
  ```

- device: The RDMA device to be queried.
- port_num: The port number to be queried.

The ib_query_gid() Method

The ib_query_gid() method queries the RDMA device port's GID table. It will return 0 on success or the errno value with the reason for the failure.

```
int ib_query_gid(struct ib_device *device, u8 port_num, int index, union ib_gid *gid);
```

- device: The RDMA device to be queried.
- port_num: The port number to be queried.
- index: The index in the GID table to be queried.
- gid: A pointer to the GID union to be filled.

The ib_query_pkey() Method

The ib_query_pkey() method queries the RDMA device port's P_Key table. It will return 0 on success or the errno value with the reason for the failure.

```
int ib_query_pkey(struct ib_device *device,
        u8 port_num, u16 index, u16 *pkey);
```

- device: The RDMA device to be queried.
- port_num: The port number to be queried.
- index: The index in the P_Key table to be queried.
- pkey: A pointer to the P_Key to be filled.

The ib_modify_device() Method

The ib_modify_device() method modifies the RDMA device attributes. It will return 0 on success or the errno value with the reason for the failure.

```
int ib_modify_device(struct ib_device *device,
        int device_modify_mask,
        struct ib_device_modify *device_modify);
```

- device: The RDMA device to be modified.
- device_modify_mask: The device attributes to be changed. It is a bitwise OR of the masks:
  - IB_DEVICE_MODIFY_SYS_IMAGE_GUID: Modifies the system image GUID.
  - IB_DEVICE_MODIFY_NODE_DESC: Modifies the node description.
- device_modify: The RDMA attributes to be modified, as described immediately.

The ib_device_modify Struct

The RDMA device attributes are represented by struct ib_device_modify:

```
struct ib_device_modify {
    u64     sys_image_guid;
    char    node_desc[64];
};
```

- sys_image_guid: A 64-bit value of the system image GUID.
- node_desc: A NULL terminated string that describes the node description.

The ib_modify_port() Method

The ib_modify_port() method modifies the RDMA device port's attributes. It will return 0 on success or the errno value with the reason for the failure.

```
int ib_modify_port(struct ib_device *device,
            u8 port_num, int port_modify_mask,
            struct ib_port_modify *port_modify);
```

- device: The RDMA device to be modified.
- port_num: The port number to be modified.
- port_modify_mask: The port's attributes to be changed. It is a bitwise OR of the masks:
    - IB_PORT_SHUTDOWN: Moves the port state to IB_PORT_DOWN.
    - IB_PORT_INIT_TYPE: Sets the port InitType value.
    - IB_PORT_RESET_QKEY_CNTR: Resets the port's Q_Key violation counter.
- port_modify: The port attributes to be modified, as described in the next section.

The ib_port_modify struct:

The RDMA device attributes are represented by struct ib_port_modify:

```
struct ib_port_modify {
    u32     set_port_cap_mask;
    u32     clr_port_cap_mask;
    u8      init_type;
};
```

- set_port_cap_mask: The port capabilities bits to be set.
- clr_port_cap_mask: The port capabilities bits to be cleared.
- init_type: The InitType value to be set.

The ib_find_gid() Method

The `ib_find_gid()` method finds the port number and the index where a specific GID value exists in the GID table. It will return 0 on success or the errno value with the reason for the failure.

```
int ib_find_gid(struct ib_device *device, union ib_gid *gid,
        u8 *port_num, u16 *index);
```

- device: The RDMA device to be queried.

- gid: A pointer of the GID to search for.

- port_num: Will be filled with the port number that this GID exists in.

- index: Will be filled with the index in the GID table that this GID exists in.

The ib_find_pkey() Method

The `ib_find_pkey()` method finds the index where a specific P_Key value exists in the P_Key table in a specific port number. It will return 0 on success or the errno value with the reason for the failure.

```
int ib_find_pkey(struct ib_device *device,
        u8 port_num, u16 pkey, u16 *index);
```

- device: The RDMA device to be queried.

- port_num: The port number to search the P_Key in.

- pkey: The P_Key value to search for.

- index: The index in the P_Key table that this P_Key exists in.

The rdma_node_get_transport() Method

The `rdma_node_get_transport()` method returns the RDMA transport type of a specific node type. The available transport types can be:

- RDMA_TRANSPORT_IB: Transport is InfiniBand.

- RDMA_TRANSPORT_IWARP: Transport is iWARP.

The rdma_node_get_transport() Method

```
enum rdma_transport_type
rdma_node_get_transport(enum rdma_node_type node_type) __attribute_const__;
```

- node_type: The node type. Can be:RDMA_NODE_IB_CA: Node type is an InfiniBand Channel Adapter.

- RDMA_NODE_IB_SWITCH: Node type is an InfiniBand Switch.

- RDMA_NODE_IB_ROUTER: Node type is an InfiniBand Router.

- RDMA_NODE_RNIC: Node type is an RDMA NIC.

The ib_mtu_to_int() Method

The `ib_mtu_to_int()` method returns the number of bytes, as an integer, for MTU enumerations. It will return a positive value on success or –1 on a failure.

```
static inline int ib_mtu_enum_to_int(enum ib_mtu mtu);
```

- mtu: Can be an MTU enumeration, as described earlier.

The ib_width_enum_to_int() Method

The `ib_width_enum_to_int()` method returns the number of width multiple, as an integer, for an IB port enumerations. It will return a positive value on success or –1 on a failure.

```
static inline int ib_width_enum_to_int(enum ib_port_width width);
```

- width: Can be a port width enumeration, as described earlier.

The ib_rate_to_mult() Method

The `ib_rate_to_mult()` method returns the number of multiple of the base rate of 2.5 Gbit/sec, as an integer, for an IB rate enumerations. It will return a positive value on success or –1 on a failure.

```
int ib_rate_to_mult(enum ib_rate rate) __attribute_const__;
```

- rate: The rate enumeration to be converted. Can be:
    - IB_RATE_PORT_CURRENT: Current port's rate.
    - IB_RATE_2_5_GBPS: Rate of 2.5 Gbit/sec.
    - IB_RATE_5_GBPS: Rate of 5 Gbit/sec.
    - IB_RATE_10_GBPS: Rate of 10 Gbit/sec.
    - IB_RATE_20_GBPS: Rate of 20 Gbit/sec.
    - IB_RATE_30_GBPS: Rate of 30 Gbit/sec.
    - IB_RATE_40_GBPS: Rate of 40 Gbit/sec.
    - IB_RATE_60_GBPS: Rate of 60 Gbit/sec.
    - IB_RATE_80_GBPS: Rate of 80 Gbit/sec.
    - IB_RATE_120_GBPS: Rate of 120 Gbit/sec.
    - IB_RATE_14_GBPS: Rate of 14 Gbit/sec.
    - IB_RATE_56_GBPS: Rate of 56 Gbit/sec.
    - IB_RATE_112_GBPS: Rate of 112 Gbit/sec.
    - IB_RATE_168_GBPS: Rate of 168 Gbit/sec.
    - IB_RATE_25_GBPS: Rate of 25 Gbit/sec.

- IB_RATE_100_GBPS: Rate of 100 Gbit/sec.
- IB_RATE_200_GBPS: Rate of 200 Gbit/sec.
- IB_RATE_300_GBPS: Rate of 300 Gbit/sec.

The ib_rate_to_mbps() Method

The `ib_rate_to_mbps()` method returns the number of Mbit/sec, as an integer, for an IB rate enumerations. It will return a positive value on success or –1 on a failure.

```
int ib_rate_to_mbps(enum ib_rate rate) __attribute_const__;
```

- rate: The rate enumeration to be converted, as described earlier.

The ib_rate_to_mbps() Method

The `ib_rate_to_mbps()` method returns the IB rate enumerations for a multiple of the base rate of 2.5 Gbit/sec. It will return a positive value on success or –1 on a failure.

```
enum ib_rate mult_to_ib_rate(int mult) __attribute_const__;
```

- mult: The rate multiple to be converted, as described earlier.

Protection Domain (PD)

PD is an RDMA resource that associates QPs and SRQs with MRs and AHs with QPs. One can look at PD as a color, for example: red MR can work with a red QP, and red AH can work with a red QP. Working with green AH with a red QP will result in an error.

The ib_alloc_pd() Method

The `ib_alloc_pd()` method allocates a PD. It will return a pointer to the newly allocated PD on success or an ERR_PTR() which specifies the reason for the failure.

```
struct ib_pd *ib_alloc_pd(struct ib_device *device);
```

- device: The RDMA device that the PD will be associated with.

The ib_dealloc_pd() Method

The `ib_dealloc_pd()` method deallocates a PD. It will return 0 on success or the errno value with the reason for the failure.

```
int ib_dealloc_pd(struct ib_pd *pd);
```

- pd: The PD to be deallocated.

eXtended Reliable Connected (XRC)

XRC is an IB transport extension that provides better scalability, in the sender side, for Reliable Connected QPs than the original Reliable Transport can provide. Using XRC will decrease the number of QPs between two specific cores: when using RC QPs, for each core, in each machine, there is a QP. When using XRC, there will be one XRC QP in each host. When sending a message, the sender needs to specify the remote SRQ number that will receive the message.

The ib_alloc_xrcd() Method

The ib_alloc_xrcd() method allocates an XRC domain. It will return a pointer to the newly created XRC domain on success or an ERR_PTR() which specifies the reason for the failure.

```
struct ib_xrcd *ib_alloc_xrcd(struct ib_device *device);
```

- device: The RDMA device that this XRC domain will be allocated on.

The ib_dealloc_xrcd_cq() Method

The ib_dealloc_xrcd_cq() method deallocates an XRC domain. It will return 0 on success or the errno value with the reason for the failure:

```
int ib_dealloc_xrcd(struct ib_xrcd *xrcd);
```

- xrcd: The XRC domain to be deallocated.

Shared Receive Queue (SRQ)

SRQ is a resource that helps RDMA to be more scalable. Instead of managing the Receive Requests in the Receive Queues of many QPs, it is possible to manage them in a single Receive Queue, which all of them share. This will eliminate starvation in RC QPs or packet drops in unreliable transport types and will help to reduce the total posted Receive Requests, thus reducing the consumed memory. Furthermore, unlike a QP, an SRQ can have a watermark to allow a notification if the number of RRs in the SRQ dropped below a specify value.

The ib_srq_attr Struct

The SRQ attributes are represented by struct ib_srq_attr:

```
struct ib_srq_attr {
    u32     max_wr;
    u32     max_sge;
    u32     srq_limit;
};
```

- max_wr: The maximum number of outstanding RRs that this SRQ can hold.
- max_sge: The maximum number of scatter/gather elements that each RR in the SRQ can hold.
- srq_limit: The watermark limit that creates an asynchronous event if the number of RRs in the SRQ dropped below this value.

The ib_create_srq() Method

The ib_create_srq() method creates an SRQ. It will return a pointer to the newly created SRQ on success or an ERR_
PTR() which specifies the reason for the failure:

```
struct ib_srq *ib_create_srq(struct ib_pd *pd, struct ib_srq_init_attr *srq_init_attr);
```

- pd: The PD that this SRQ is being associated with.

- srq_init_attr: The attributes that this SRQ will be created with.

The ib_srq_init_attr Struct

The created SRQ attributes are represented by struct ib_srq_init_attr:

```
struct ib_srq_init_attr {
    void                (*event_handler)(struct ib_event *, void *);
    void                *srq_context;
    struct ib_srq_attr    attr;
    enum ib_srq_type    srq_type;

    union {
        struct {
            struct ib_xrcd *xrcd;
            struct ib_cq    *cq;
        } xrc;
    } ext;
};
```

- event_handler: A pointer to a callback that will be called in case of an affiliated asynchronous
event to the SRQ.

- srq_context: User-defined context that can be associated with the SRQ.

- attr: The SRQ attributes, as described earlier.

- srq_type: The type of the SRQ. Can be:

  - IB_SRQT_BASIC: For regular SRQ.

  - IB_SRQT_XRC: For XRC SRQ.

- ext: If srq_type is IB_SRQT_XRC, specifies the XRC domain or the CQ that this SRQ is
associated with.

The ib_modify_srq() Method

The ib_modify_srq() method modifies the attributes of the SRQ. It will return 0 on success or the errno value with
the reason for the failure.

```
int ib_modify_srq(struct ib_srq *srq, struct ib_srq_attr *srq_attr, enum ib_srq_attr_mask srq_attr_mask);
```

- `srq`: The SRQ to be modified.

- `srq_attr`: The SRQ attributes, as described earlier.

- `srq_attr_mask`: The SRQ attributes to be changed. It is a bitwise OR of the masks:

  - IB_SRQ_MAX_WR: Modify the number of RRs in the SRQ (that is, resize the SRQ). This can be done only if the device supports SRQ resize—that is, the IB_DEVICE_SRQ_RESIZE is set in the device flags.

  - IB_SRQ_LIMIT: Set the value of the SRQ watermark limit.

The ib_query_srq() Method

The `ib_query_srq()` method queries for the current SRQ attributes. It will return 0 on success or the errno value with the reason for the failure.

```
int ib_query_srq(struct ib_srq *srq, struct ib_srq_attr *srq_attr);
```

- `srq`: The SRQ to be queried.

- `srq_attr`: The SRQ attributes, as described earlier.

The ib_destory_srq() Method

The `ib_destory_srq()` method destroys an SRQ. It will return 0 on success or the errno value with the reason for the failure.

```
int ib_destroy_srq(struct ib_srq *srq);
```

- `srq`: The SRQ to be destroyed.

The ib_post_srq_recv() Method

The `ib_post_srq_recv()` method takes a linked list of Receive Requests and adds them to the SRQ for future processing. Every Receive Request is considered outstanding until a Work Completion is generated after its processing. It will return 0 on success or the errno value with the reason for the failure.

```
static inline int ib_post_srq_recv(struct ib_srq *srq, struct ib_recv_wr *recv_wr,
struct ib_recv_wr **bad_recv_wr);
```

- `srq`: The SRQ that the Receive Requests will be posted to.

- `recv_wr`: A linked list of Receive Request to be posted.

- `bad_recv_wr`: If there was an error with the handling of the Receive Requests, this pointer will be filled with the address of the Receive Request that caused this error.

The ib_recv_wr Struct

The Receive Request is represented by struct ib_recv_wr:

```
struct ib_recv_wr {
    struct ib_recv_wr       *next;
    u64             wr_id;
    struct ib_sge       *sg_list;
    int             num_sge;
};
```

- next: A pointer to the next Receive Request in the list or NULL, if this is the last Receive Request.

- wr_id: A 64-bit value that is associated with this Receive Request and will be available in the corresponding Work Completion.

- sg_list: The array of the scatter/gather elements, as described in the next section.

- num_sge: The number of entries in sg_list. The value zero means that the message size that can be saved has zero bytes.

The ib_sge Struct

The scatter/gather element is represented by struct ib_sge:

```
struct ib_sge {
    u64   addr;
    u32   length;
    u32   lkey;
};
```

- addr: The address of the buffer to access.

- length: The length of the address to access.

- lkey: The Local Key of the Memory Region that this buffer was registered with.

Address Handle (AH)

AH is an RDMA resource that describes the path from the local port to the remote port of the destination. It is being used for a UD QP.

The ib_ah_attr Struct

The AH attributes are represented by struct ib_ah_attr:

```
struct ib_ah_attr {
    struct ib_global_route      grh;
    u16                 dlid;
    u8                  sl;
    u8                  src_path_bits;
    u8                  static_rate;
    u8                  ah_flags;
    u8                  port_num;
};
```

- grh: The Global Routing Header attributes that are used for sending messages to another subnet or to a multicast group in the local or remote subnet.

- dlid: The destination LID.

- sl: The Service Level that this message will use.

- src_path_bits: The used source path bits. Relevant if LMC is used in this port.

- static_rate: The level of delay that should be done between sending the messages. It is used when sending a message to a remote node that supports a slower message rate than the local node.

- ah_flags: The AH flags. It is a bitwise OR of the masks:

  - IB_AH_GRH: GRH is used in this AH.

- port_num: The local port number that messages will be sent from.

The ib_create_ah() Method

The ib_create_ah() method creates an AH. It will return a pointer to the newly created AH on success or an ERR_PTR() which specifies the reason for the failure.

```
struct ib_ah *ib_create_ah(struct ib_pd *pd, struct ib_ah_attr *ah_attr);
```

- pd: The PD that this AH is being associated with.

- ah_attr: The attributes that this AH will be created with.

The ib_init_ah_from_wc() Method

The ib_init_ah_from_wc() method initializes an AH attribute structure from a Work Completion and a GRH structure. This is being done in order to return a message back for an incoming message of an UD QP. It will return 0 on success or the errno value with the reason for the failure.

```
int ib_init_ah_from_wc(struct ib_device *device, u8 port_num, struct ib_wc *wc,
        struct ib_grh *grh, struct ib_ah_attr *ah_attr);
```

- device: The RDMA device that the Work Completion came from and the AH to be created on.

- port_num: The port number that the Work Completion came from and the AH will be associated with.

- wc: The Work Completion of the incoming message.

- grh: The GRH buffer of the incoming message.

- ah_attr: The attributes of this AH to be filled.

The ib_create_ah_from_wc() Method

The `ib_create_ah_from_wc()` method creates an AH from a Work Completion and a GRH structure. This is done in order to return a message back for an incoming message of a UD QP. It will return a pointer to the newly created AH on success or an ERR_PTR() which specifies the reason for the failure.

```
struct ib_ah *ib_create_ah_from_wc(struct ib_pd *pd, struct ib_wc *wc, struct ib_grh *grh, u8 port_num);
```

- pd: The PD that this AH is being associated with.

- wc: The Work Completion of the incoming message.

- grh: The GRH buffer of the incoming message.

- port_num: The port number that the Work Completion came from and the AH will be associated with.

The ib_modify_ah() Method

The `ib_modify_ah()` method modifies the attributes of the AH. It will return 0 on success or the errno value with the reason for the failure.

```
int ib_modify_ah(struct ib_ah *ah, struct ib_ah_attr *ah_attr);
```

- ah: The AH to be modified.

- ah_attr: The AH attributes, as described earlier.

The ib_query_ah() Method

The `ib_query_ah()` method queries for the current AH attributes. It will return 0 on success or the errno value with the reason for the failure.

```
int ib_query_ah(struct ib_ah *ah, struct ib_ah_attr *ah_attr);
```

- ah: The AH to be queried

- ah_attr: The AH attributes, as described earlier.

The ib_destory_ah() Method

The `ib_destory_ah()` method destroys an AH. It will return 0 on success or the errno value with the reason for the failure.

```
int ib_destroy_ah(struct ib_ah *ah);
```

- ah: The AH to be destroyed.

Multicast Groups

Multicast groups are means to send a message from one UD QP to many UD QPs. Every UD QP that wants to get this message needs to be attached to a multicast group.

The ib_attach_mcast() Method

The ib_attach_mcast() method attaches a UD QP to a multicast group within an RDMA device. It will return 0 on success or the errno value with the reason for the failure.

```
int ib_attach_mcast(struct ib_qp *qp, union ib_gid *gid, u16 lid);
```

- qp: A handler of a UD QP to be attached to the multicast group.

- gid: The GID of the multicast group that the QP will be added to.

- lid: The LID of the multicast group that the QP will be added to.

The ib_detach_mcast() method

The ib_detach_mcast() method detaches a UD QP from a multicast group within an RDMA device. It will return 0 on success or the errno value with the reason for the failure.

```
int ib_detach_mcast(struct ib_qp *qp, union ib_gid *gid, u16 lid);
```

- qp: A handler of a UD QP to be detached from the multicast group.

- gid: The GID of the multicast group that the QP will be removed from.

- lid: The LID of the multicast group that the QP will be removed from.

Completion Queue (CQ)

A Work Completion specifies that a corresponding Work Request was completed and provides some information. about it: its status, the used opcode, its size, and so on. A CQ is an object that consists of Work Completions.

The ib_create_cq() Method

The ib_create_cq() method creates a CQ. It will return a pointer to the newly created CQ on success or an ERR_PTR() which specifies the reason for the failure.

```
struct ib_cq *ib_create_cq(struct ib_device *device, ib_comp_handler comp_handler,
void (*event_handler)(struct ib_event *, void *), void *cq_context, int cqe, int comp_vector);
```

- device: The RDMA device that this CQ is being associated with.

- comp_handler: A pointer to a callback that will be called when a completion event occur to the CQ.

- event_handler: A pointer to a callback that will be called in case of an affiliated asynchronous event to the CQ.

- cq_context: A user-defined context that can be associated with the CQ.

- cqe: The requested number of Work Completions that this CQ can hold.

- comp_vector: The index of the RDMA device's completion vector to work on. If the IRQ affinity masks of these interrupts are spread across the cores, this value can be used to spread the completion workload over all of the cores.

The ib_resize_cq() Method

The ib_resize_cq() method changes the size of the CQ to hold at least the new size, either by increasing the CQ size or decreasing it. Even if the user asks to resize a CQ, its size may not be resized.

```
int ib_resize_cq(struct ib_cq *cq, int cqe);
```

- cq: The CQ to be resized. This value cannot be lower than the number of Work Completions that exists in the CQ.

- cqe: The requested number of Work Completions that this CQ can hold.

The ib_modify_cq() Method

The ib_modify_cq() method changes the moderation parameter for a CQ. A Completion event will be generated if at least a specific number of Work Completion will enter the CQ or a timeout will expire. Using it may help to reduce the number of interrupts that happen to the RDMA device. It will return 0 on success or the -errno value with the reason for the failure.

```
int ib_modify_cq(structib_cq *cq, u16 cq_count, u16 cq_period);
```

- cq: The CQ to be modified.

- cq_count: The number of Work Completions that will be added to the CQ, since the last Completion event, that will trigger a CQ event.

- cq_period: The number of microseconds that will pass, since the last Completion event, that will trigger a CQ event.

The ib_peek_cq() Method

The ib_peek_cq() method returns the number of available Work Completions in the CQ. If the number of Work Completions in the CQ is equal to or greater than wc_cnt, it will return wc_cnt. Otherwise it will return the actual number of the Work Completions in the CQ. If an error occurred, it will return the errno value with the reason for the failure.

```
int ib_peek_cq(structib_cq *cq, intwc_cnt);
```

- cq: The CQ to peek.

- cq_count: The number of Work Completions that will added to the CQ, since the last Completion event, that will trigger a CQ event.

The ib_req_notify_cq() Method

The ib_req_notify_cq() method requests that a Completion event notification be created. Its return value can be:

- 0: This means that the notification was requested successfully. If IB_CQ_REPORT_MISSED_EVENTS was used, then a return value of 0 means that there aren't any missed events.

- Positive value is returned only when IB_CQ_REPORT_MISSED_EVENTS is used and there are missed events. The user should call the ib_poll_cq() method in order to read the Work Completions that exist in the CQ.

- Negative value is returned when an error occurred. The -errno value is returned, specifying the reason for the failure.

```
static inline int ib_req_notify_cq(struct ib_cq *cq,
                    enum ib_cq_notify_flags flags);
```

- cq: The CQ that this Completion event will be generated for.
- flags: Information about the Work Completion that will cause the Completion event notification to be created. Can be one of:
  - IB_CQ_NEXT_COMP: The next Work Completion that will be added to the CQ, after calling this method, will trigger the CQ event.
  - IB_CQ_SOLICITED: The next Solicited Work Completion that will be added to the CQ, after calling this method, will trigger the CQ event.

Both of those values can be bitwise ORed with IB_CQ_REPORT_MISSED_EVENTS in order to request a hint about missed events (that is, when calling this method and there are already Work Completions in this CQ).

The ib_req_ncomp_notif() Method

The ib_req_ncomp_notif() method requests that a Completion event notification be created when the number of Work Completions in the CQ equals wc_cnt. It will return 0 on success, or the errno value with the reason for the failure.

```
static inline int ib_req_ncomp_notif(struct ib_cq *cq, int wc_cnt);
```

- cq: The CQ that this Completion event will be generated for.
- wc_cnt: The number of Work Completions that the CQ will hold before a Completion event notification is generated.

The ib_poll_cq() Method

The ib_poll_cq() method polls Work Completions from a CQ. It reads the Work Completion from the CQ and removes them. The Work Completions are read in the order they were added to the CQ. It will return 0 or a positive number to indicate the number of Work Completions that were read or the -errno value with the reason for the failure.

```
static inline int ib_poll_cq(struct ib_cq *cq, int num_entries,
            struct ib_wc *wc);
```

- cq: The CQ to be polled.

- num_entries: The maximum number of Work Completions to be polled.

- wc: An array that the number of polled Work Completions will be stored in.

The ib_wc Struct

Every Work Completion is represented by struct ib_wc:

```
struct ib_wc {
    u64                 wr_id;
    enum ib_wc_status   status;
    enum ib_wc_opcode   opcode;
    u32                 vendor_err;
    u32                 byte_len;
    struct ib_qp            *qp;
    union {
        __be32          imm_data;
        u32             invalidate_rkey;
    } ex;
    u32                 src_qp;
    int                 wc_flags;
    u16                 pkey_index;
    u16                 slid;
    u8                  sl;
    u8                  dlid_path_bits;
    u8                  port_num;
};
```

- wr_id: A 64-bit value that was associated with the corresponding Work Request.

- status: Status of the ended Work Request. Can be:

  - IB_WC_SUCCESS: Operation completed successfully.

  - IB_WC_LOC_LEN_ERR: Local length error. Either sent message is too big to be handled or incoming message is bigger than the available Receive Request.

  - IB_WC_LOC_QP_OP_ERR: Local QP operation error. An internal QP consistency error was detected while processing a Work Request.

  - IB_WC_LOC_EEC_OP_ERR: Local EE context operation error. Deprecated, since RD QPs aren't supported.

  - IB_WC_LOC_PROT_ERR: Local protection error. The protection of the Work Request buffers is invalid to the requested operation.

  - IB_WC_WR_FLUSH_ERR: Work Request flushed error. The Work Request was completed when the QP was in the Error state.

  - IB_WC_MW_BIND_ERR: Memory Windows bind error. The operation of the Memory Windows binding failed.

  - IB_WC_BAD_RESP_ERR: Bad response error. Unexpected transport layer opcode returned by the responder.

- IB_WC_LOC_ACCESS_ERR: Local access error. A protection error occurred on local buffers during the processing of an RDMA Write With Immediate message.

- IB_WC_REM_INV_REQ_ERR: Remove invalid request error. The incoming message is invalid.

- IB_WC_REM_ACCESS_ERR: Remote access error. A protection error occurred to incoming RDMA operation.

- IB_WC_REM_OP_ERR: Remote operation error. The incoming operation couldn't be completed successfully.

- IB_WC_RETRY_EXC_ERR: Transport retry counter exceeded. The remote QP didn't send any Ack or Nack, and the timeout was expired after the message retransmission.

- IB_WC_RNR_RETRY_EXC_ERR: RNR retry exceeded. The RNR NACK return count was exceeded.

- IB_WC_LOC_RDD_VIOL_ERR: Local RDD violation error. Deprecated, since RD QPs aren't supported.

- IB_WC_REM_INV_RD_REQ_ERR: Remove invalid RD request. Deprecated, since RD QPs aren't supported.

- IB_WC_REM_ABORT_ERR: Remote aborted error. The responder aborted the operation.

- IB_WC_INV_EECN_ERR: Invalid EE Context number. Deprecated, since RD QPs aren't supported.

- IB_WC_INV_EEC_STATE_ERR: Invalid EE context state error. Deprecated, since RD QPs aren't supported.

- IB_WC_FATAL_ERR: Fatal error.

- IB_WC_RESP_TIMEOUT_ERR: Response timeout error.

- IB_WC_GENERAL_ERR: General error. Other error which isn't covered by one of the earlier errors.

- opcode: The operation of the corresponding Work Request that was ended with this Work Completion. Can be:

  - IB_WC_SEND: Send operation was completed in the sender side.

  - IB_WC_RDMA_WRITE: RDMA Write operation was completed in the sender side.

  - IB_WC_RDMA_READ: RDMA Read operation was completed in the sender side.

  - IB_WC_COMP_SWAP: Compare and Swap operation was completed in the sender side.

  - IB_WC_FETCH_ADD: Fetch and Add operation was completed in the sender side.

  - IB_WC_BIND_MW: Memory bind operation was completed in the sender side.

  - IB_WC_LSO: Send operation with Large Send Offload (LSO) was completed in the sender side.

  - IB_WC_LOCAL_INV: Local invalidate operation was completed in the sender side.

  - IB_WC_FAST_REG_MR: Fast registration operation was completed in the sender side.

  - IB_WC_MASKED_COMP_SWAP: Masked Compare and Swap operation was completed in the sender side.

- IB_WC_MASKED_FETCH_ADD: Masked Fetch and Add operation was completed in the sender side.

- IB_WC_RECV: Receive Request of an incoming send operation was completed in the receiver side.

- IB_WC_RECV_RDMA_WITH_IMM: Receive Request of an incoming RDMA Write with immediate operation was completed in the receiver side.

- vendor_err: A vendor-specific value that provides extra information about the reason for the error.

- byte_len: If this is a Work Completion that was created from the end of a Receive Request, the byte_len value indicates the number of bytes that were received.

- qp: Handle of the QP that got the Work Completion. It is useful when QPs are associated with an SRQ—this way you can know the handle associated with the QP, that its incoming message consumed the Receive Request from the SRQ.

- ex.imm_data: Out Of Band data (32 bits), in network order, that was sent with the message. It is available if IB_WC_WITH_IMM is set in wc_flags.

- ex.invalidate_rkey: The rkey that was invalidated. It is available if IB_WC_WITH_INVALIDATE is set in wc_flags.

- src_qp: Source QP number. The QP number that sent this message. Only relevant for UD QPs.

- wc_flags: Flags that provide information about the Work Completion. It is a bitwise OR of the masks:

  - IB_WC_GRH: Indicator that the message was received has a GRH and the first 40 bytes of the Receive Request buffers contains it. Only relevant for UD QPs.

  - IB_WC_WITH_IMM: Indicator that the received message has immediate data.

  - IB_WC_WITH_INVALIDATE: Indicator that a Send with Invalidate message was received.

  - IB_WC_IP_CSUM_OK: Indicator that the received message passed the IP checksum test done by the RDMA device. This is available only if the RDMA device supports IP checksum offload. It is available if IB_DEVICE_UD_IP_CSUM is set in the device flags.

- pkey_index: The P_Key index, relevant only for GSI QPs.

- slid: The source LID of the message. Only relevant for UD QPs.

- sl: The Service Level of the message. Only relevant for UD QPs.

- dlid_path_bits: The destination LID path bits. Only relevant for UD QPs.

- port_num: The port number from which the message came in. Only relevant for Direct Route SMPs on switches.

The ib_destory_cq() Method

The ib_destory_cq() method destroys a CQ. It will return 0 on success or the errno value with the reason for the failure.

```
int ib_destroy_cq(struct ib_cq *cq);
```

- cq: The CQ to be destroyed.

Queue Pair (QP)

QP is a resource that combines two Work Queues together: the Send Queue and the Receive Queue. Each queue acts as a FIFO. WRs that are being posted to each Work Queue will be processed by the order of their arrival. However, there isn't any guarantee about the order between the Queues. This resource is the resource that sends and receives packets.

The ib_qp_cap Struct

The QP's Work Queues sizes are represented by struct ib_qp_cap:

```
struct ib_qp_cap {
    u32    max_send_wr;
    u32    max_recv_wr;
    u32    max_send_sge;
    u32    max_recv_sge;
    u32    max_inline_data;
};
```

- max_send_wr: The maximum number of outstanding Work Requests that this QP can hold in the Send Queue.

- max_recv_wr: The maximum number of outstanding Work Requests that this QP can hold in the Receive Queue. This value is ignored if the QP is associated with an SRQ.

- max_send_sge: The maximum number of scatter/gather elements that each Work Request in the Send Queue will be able to hold.

- max_recv_sge: The maximum number of scatter/gather elements that each Work Request in the Receive Queue will be able to hold.

- max_inline_data: The maximum message size that can be sent inline.

The ib_create_qp() Method

The ib_create_qp() method creates a QP. It will return a pointer to the newly created QP on success or an ERR_PTR() which specifies the reason for the failure.

```
struct ib_qp *ib_create_qp(struct ib_pd *pd,
        struct ib_qp_init_attr *qp_init_attr);
```

- pd: The PD that this QP is being associated with.

- qp_init_attr: The attributes that this QP will be created with.

The ib_qp_init_attr Struct

The created QP attributes are represented by struct ib_qp_init_attr:

```
struct ib_qp_init_attr {
    void                    (*event_handler)(struct ib_event *, void *);
    void                *qp_context;
    struct ib_cq            *send_cq;
    struct ib_cq            *recv_cq;
    struct ib_srq            *srq;
    struct ib_xrcd            *xrcd;      /* XRC TGT QPs only */
    struct ib_qp_cap        cap;
    enum ib_sig_type        sq_sig_type;
    enum ib_qp_type        qp_type;
    enum ib_qp_create_flags    create_flags;
    u8                port_num; /* special QP types only */
};
```

- event_handler: A pointer to a callback that will be called in case of an affiliated asynchronous event to the QP.

- qp_context: User-defined context that can be associated with the QP.

- send_cq: A CQ that is being associated with the Send Queue of this QP.

- recv_cq: A CQ that is being associated with the Receive Queue of this QP.

- srq: A SRQ that is being associated with the Receive Queue of this QP or NULL if the QP isn't associated with an SRQ.

- xrcd: An XRC domain that this QP will be associated with. Relevant only if qp_type is IB_QPT_XRC_TGT.

- cap: A structure that describes the size of the Send and Receive Queues. This structure is described earlier.

- sq_sig_type: The signaling type of the Send Queue. It can be:

  - IB_SIGNAL_ALL_WR: Every posted Send Request to the Send Queue will end with a Work Completion.

  - IB_SIGNAL_REQ_WR: Only posted Send Requests to the Send Queue with an explicit request, i.e. set the IB_SEND_SIGNALED flag—will end with a Work Completion. This is called *selective signaling*.

- qp_type: The QP transport type. Can be:

  - IB_QPT_SMI: A Subnet Management Interface QP.

  - IB_QPT_GSI: A General Service Interface QP.

  - IB_QPT_RC: A Reliable Connected QP.

  - IB_QPT_UC: An Unreliable Connected QP.

  - IB_QPT_UD: An Unreliable Datagram QP.

  - IB_QPT_RAW_IPV6: An IPv6 raw datagram QP.

- IB_QPT_RAW_ETHERTYPE: An EtherType raw datagram QP.

- IB_QPT_RAW_PACKET: A raw packet QP.

- IB_QPT_XRC_INI: An XRC-initiator QP.

- IB_QPT_XRC_TGT: An XRC-target QP.

- create_flags: QP attributes flags. It is a bitwise OR of the masks:

  - IB_QP_CREATE_IPOIB_UD_LSO: The QP will be used to send IPoIB LSO messages.

  - IB_QP_CREATE_BLOCK_MULTICAST_LOOPBACK: Block loopback multicast packets.

- port_num: The RDMA device port number that this QP is associated with. Only relevant when qp_type is IB_QPT_SMI or IB_QPT_GS.

The ib_modify_qp() Method

The ib_modify_qp() method modifies the attributes of the QP. It will return 0 on success or the errno value with the reason for the failure.

```
int ib_modify_qp(struct ib_qp *qp,
    struct ib_qp_attr *qp_attr,
    int qp_attr_mask);
```

- qp: The QP to be modified.

- qp_attr: The QP attributes, as described earlier.

- qp_attr_mask: The QP attributes to be changed. Each mask specifies the attributes that will be modified in this QP transition, such as specifying which attributes in qp_attr will be used. It is a bitwise OR of the masks:

  - IB_QP_STATE: Modifies the QP state, specified in the qp_state field.

  - IB_QP_CUR_STATE: Modifies the assumed current QP state, specified in the cur_qp_state field.

  - IB_QP_EN_SQD_ASYNC_NOTIFY: Modifies the status of the request for notification when the QP state is SQD.drained, specified in the en_sqd_async_notify field.

  - IB_QP_ACCESS_FLAGS: Modifies the allowed incoming Remote operations, specified in the qp_access_flags field.

  - IB_QP_PKEY_INDEX: Modifies the index in the P_Key table that this QP is associated with in the primary path, specified in the pkey_index field.

  - IB_QP_PORT: Modifies the RDMA device's port number that QP's primary path is associated with, specified in the port_num field.

  - IB_QP_QKEY: Modifies the Q-Key of the QP, specified in the qkey field.

  - IB_QP_AV: Modifies the Address Vector attributes of the QP, specified in the ah_attr field.

  - IB_QP_PATH_MTU: Modifies the MTU of the path, specified in the path_mtu field.

  - IB_QP_TIMEOUT: Modifies the timeout to wait before retransmission, specified in the field timeout.

- IB_QP_RETRY_CNT: Modifies the number of retries of the QP for lack of Ack/Nack, specified in the retry_cnt field.

- IB_QP_RNR_RETRY: Modifies the number of RNR retry of the QP, specified in the rq_psn field.

- IB_QP_RQ_PSN: Modifies the start PSN of the received packets, specified in the rnr_retry field.

- IB_QP_MAX_QP_RD_ATOMIC: Modifies the number of RDMA Read and Atomic operations that this QP can process in parallel as an initiator, specified in the max_rd_atomic field.

- IB_QP_ALT_PATH: Modifies the alternate path of the QP, specified in the alt_ah_attr, alt_pkey_index, alt_port_num, and alt_timeout fields.

- IB_QP_MIN_RNR_TIMER: Modifies the minimum RNR timer that the QP will report to the remote side in the RNR Nak, specified in the min_rnr_timer field.

- IB_QP_SQ_PSN: Modifies the start PSN of the sent packets, specified in the sq_psn field.

- IB_QP_MAX_DEST_RD_ATOMIC: Modifies the number of RDMA Read and Atomic operations that this QP can process in parallel as an initiator, specified in the max_dest_rd_atomic field.

- IB_QP_PATH_MIG_STATE: Modifies the state of the path migration state machine, specified in the path_mig_state field.

- IB_QP_CAP: Modifies the size of the Work Queues in the QP (both Send and Receive Queues), specified in the cap field.

- IB_QP_DEST_QPN: Modifies the destination QP number, specified in the dest_qp_num field.

The ib_qp_attr Struct

The QP attributes are represented by struct ib_qp_attr:

```
struct ib_qp_attr {
    enum ib_qp_state    qp_state;
    enum ib_qp_state    cur_qp_state;
    enum ib_mtu         path_mtu;
    enum ib_mig_state   path_mig_state;
    u32                 qkey;
    u32                 rq_psn;
    u32                 sq_psn;
    u32                 dest_qp_num;
    int                 qp_access_flags;
    struct ib_qp_cap    cap;
    struct ib_ah_attr   ah_attr;
    struct ib_ah_attr   alt_ah_attr;
    u16                 pkey_index;
    u16                 alt_pkey_index;
    u8                  en_sqd_async_notify;
    u8                  sq_draining;
    u8                  max_rd_atomic;
```

```
u8              max_dest_rd_atomic;
u8              min_rnr_timer;
u8              port_num;
u8              timeout;
u8              retry_cnt;
u8              rnr_retry;
u8              alt_port_num;
u8              alt_timeout;
};
```

- qp_state: The state to move the QP to. Can be:
    - IB_QPS_RESET: Reset state.
    - IB_QPS_INIT: Initialized state.
    - IB_QPS_RTR: Ready To Receive state.
    - IB_QPS_RTS: Ready To Send state.
    - IB_QPS_SQD: Send Queue Drained state.
    - IB_QPS_SQE: Send Queue Error state.
    - IB_QPS_ERR: Error state.
- cur_qp_state: The assumed current state of the QP. Can be like qp_state.
- path_mtu: The size of the MTU in the path. Can be:
    - IB_MTU_256: 256 bytes.
    - IB_MTU_512: 512 bytes.
    - IB_MTU_1024: 1,024 bytes.
    - IB_MTU_2048: 2,048 bytes.
    - IB_MTU_4096: 4,096 bytes.
- path_mig_state: The path migration state machine, used in APM (Automatic Path Migration). Can be:
    - IB_MIG_MIGRATED: Migrated. The state machine of path migration is Migrated (initial state of migration was done).
    - IB_MIG_REARM: Rearm. The state machine of path migration is Rearm (attempt to try to coordinate the remote RC QP to move both local and remote QPs to Armed state).
    - IB_MIG_ARMED: Armed. The state machine of path migration is Armed (both local and remote QPs are ready to perform a path migration).
- qkey: The Q_Key of the QP.
- rq_psn: The expected PSN of the first packet in the Receive Queue. The value is 24 bits.
- sq_psn: The used PSN of the first packet in the Send Queue. The value is 24 bits.
- dest_qp_num: The QP number in the remote (destination) side. The value is 24 bits.

- qp_access_flags: The allowed incoming RDMA and Atomic operations. It is a bitwise OR of the masks:

  - IB_ACCESS_REMOTE_WRITE: Incoming RDMA Write operations are allowed.

  - IB_ACCESS_REMOTE_READ: Incoming RDMA Read operations are allowed.

  - IB_ACCESS_REMOTE_ATOMIC: Incoming Atomic operations are allowed.

- cap: The QP size. The number of Work Requests in the Receive and Send Queues. This can be done only if the device supports QP resize—that is, the IB_DEVICE_RESIZE_MAX_WR is set in the device flags. This structure is described earlier.

- ah_attr: Address vector of the primary path of the QP. This structure is described earlier.

- alt_ah_attr: Address vector of the alternate path of the QP. This structure is described earlier.

- pkey_index: The P_Key index of the primary path that this QP is associated with.

- alt_pkey_index: The P_Key index of the alternate path that this QP is associated with.

- en_sqd_async_notify: If value isn't zero, request that the asynchronous event callback will be called when the QP will moved to SQE.drained state.

- sq_draining: Relevant only for ib_query_qp(). If value isn't zero, the QP is in state SQD. drainning (and not SQD.drained).

- max_rd_atomic: The number of RDMA Read and Atomic operations that this QP can process in parallel as an initiator.

- max_dest_rd_atomic: The number of RDMA Read and Atomic operations that this QP can process in parallel as a destination.

- min_rnr_timer: The timeout to wait before resend the message again if the remote side responds with an RNR Nack.

- port_num: The RDMA device's Port number that this QP is associated with in the Primary path.

- timeout: The timeout to wait before resending the message again if the remote side didn't respond with any Ack or Nack in the primary path. The timeout is a 5-bit value, 0 is infinite time, and any other value means that the timeout will be 4.096 * 2 ^ timeout usec.

- retry_cnt: The number of times to (re)send the message if the remote side didn't respond with any Ack or Nack.

- rnr_retry: The number of times to (re)send the message if the remote side answered with an RNR Nack. 3 bits value, 7 means infinite retry. The value can be:

  - IB_RNR_TIMER_655_36: Delay of 655.36 milliseconds.

  - IB_RNR_TIMER_000_01: Delay of 0.01 milliseconds.

  - IB_RNR_TIMER_000_02: Delay of 0.02 milliseconds.

  - IB_RNR_TIMER_000_03: Delay of 0.03 milliseconds.

  - IB_RNR_TIMER_000_04: Delay of 0.04 milliseconds.

  - IB_RNR_TIMER_000_06: Delay of 0.06 milliseconds.

  - IB_RNR_TIMER_000_08: Delay of 0.08 milliseconds.

  - IB_RNR_TIMER_000_12: Delay of 0.12 milliseconds.

- IB_RNR_TIMER_000_16: Delay of 0.16 milliseconds.

- IB_RNR_TIMER_000_24: Delay of 0.24 milliseconds.

- IB_RNR_TIMER_000_32: Delay of 0.32 milliseconds.

- IB_RNR_TIMER_000_48: Delay of 0.48 milliseconds.

- IB_RNR_TIMER_000_64: Delay of 0.64 milliseconds.

- IB_RNR_TIMER_000_96: Delay of 0.96 milliseconds.

- IB_RNR_TIMER_001_28: Delay of 1.28 milliseconds.

- IB_RNR_TIMER_001_92: Delay of 1.92 milliseconds.

- IB_RNR_TIMER_002_56: Delay of 2.56 milliseconds.

- IB_RNR_TIMER_003_84: Delay of 3.84 milliseconds.

- IB_RNR_TIMER_005_12: Delay of 5.12 milliseconds.

- IB_RNR_TIMER_007_68: Delay of 7.68 milliseconds.

- IB_RNR_TIMER_010_24: Delay of 10.24 milliseconds.

- IB_RNR_TIMER_015_36: Delay of 15.36 milliseconds.

- IB_RNR_TIMER_020_48: Delay of 20.48 milliseconds.

- IB_RNR_TIMER_030_72: Delay of 30.72 milliseconds.

- IB_RNR_TIMER_040_96: Delay of 40.96 milliseconds.

- IB_RNR_TIMER_061_44: Delay of 61.44 milliseconds.

- IB_RNR_TIMER_081_92: Delay of 81.92 milliseconds.

- IB_RNR_TIMER_122_88: Delay of 122.88 milliseconds.

- IB_RNR_TIMER_163_84: Delay of 163.84 milliseconds.

- IB_RNR_TIMER_245_76: Delay of 245.76 milliseconds.

- IB_RNR_TIMER_327_68: Delay of 327.86 milliseconds.

- IB_RNR_TIMER_491_52: Delay of 391.52 milliseconds.

- alt_port_num: The RDMA device's Port number that this QP is associated with in the alternate path.

- alt_timeout: The timeout to wait before resend the message again if the remote side didn't respond with any Ack or Nack in the alternate path. 5-bit value, 0 is infinite time, and any other value means that the timeout will be 4.096 * 2 ^ timeout usec.

The ib_query_qp() Method

The ib_query_qp() method queries for the current QP attributes. Some of the attributes in qp_attr may change in subsequent calls to ib_query_qp() the state fields. It will return 0 on success or the errno value with the reason for the failure.

```
int ib_query_qp(struct ib_qp *qp, struct ib_qp_attr *qp_attr, int qp_attr_mask,
struct ib_qp_init_attr *qp_init_attr);
```

- qp: The QP to be queried.

- qp_attr: The QP attributes, as described earlier.

- qp_attr_mask: The mask of the mandatory attributes to query. Low-level drivers can use it as a hint for the fields to be queried, but they may also ignore it as well and fill the whole structure.

- qp_init_attr: The QP init attributes, as described earlier.

The ib_destory_qp() method destroys a QP. It will return 0 on success or the errno value with the reason for the failure.

```
int ib_destroy_qp(struct ib_qp *qp);
```

- qp: The QP to be destroyed.

The ib_open_qp() Method

The ib_open_qp() method obtains a reference to an existing sharable QP among multiple processes. The process that created the QP may exit, allowing transfer of the ownership of the QP to another process. It will return a pointer to the sharable QP on success or an ERR_PTR() which specifies the reason for the failure.

```
struct ib_qp *ib_open_qp(struct ib_xrcd *xrcd, struct ib_qp_open_attr *qp_open_attr);
```

- xrcd: The XRC domain that the QP will be associated with.

- qp_open_attr: The attributes of the existing QP to be opened.

The ib_qp_open_attr Struct

The shared QP attributes are represented by struct ib_qp_open_attr:

```
struct ib_qp_open_attr {
    void                    (*event_handler)(struct ib_event *, void *);
    void                    *qp_context;
    u32             qp_num;
    enum ib_qp_type     qp_type;
};
```

- event_handler: A pointer to a callback that will be called in case of an affiliated asynchronous event to the QP.

- qp_context: User-defined context that can be associated with the QP.

- qp_num: The QP number that this QP will open.

- qp_type: QP transport type. Only IB_QPT_XRC_TGT is supported.

The ib_close_qp() Method

The ib_close_qp() method releases an external reference to a QP. The underlying shared QP won't be destroyed until all internal references that were acquired by the ib_open_qp() method are released. It will return 0 on success or the errno value with the reason for the failure.

```
int ib_close_qp(struct ib_qp *qp);
```

- qp: The QP to be closed.

The ib_post_recv() Method

The ib_post_recv() method takes a linked list of Receive Requests and adds them to the Receive Queue for future processing. Every Receive Request is considered outstanding until a Work Completion is generated after its processing. It will return 0 on success or the errno value with the reason for the failure.

```
static inline int ib_post_recv(struct ib_qp *qp, struct ib_recv_wr *recv_wr, struct ib_recv_wr
**bad_recv_wr);
```

- qp: The QP that the Receive Requests will be posted to.

- recv_wr: A linked list of Receive Request to be posted.

- bad_recv_wr: If there was an error with the handling of the Receive Requests, this pointer will be filled with the address of the Receive Request that caused this error.

The ib_post_send() Method

The ib_post_send() method takes a linked list of Send Requests as an argument and adds them to the Send Queue for future processing. Every Send Request is considered outstanding until a Work Completion is generated after its processing. It will return 0 on success or the errno value with the reason for the failure.

```
static inline int ib_post_send(struct ib_qp *qp, struct ib_send_wr *send_wr, struct ib_send_wr
**bad_send_wr);
```

- qp: The QP that the Send Requests will be posted to.

- send_wr: A linked list of Send Requests to be posted.

- bad_send_wr: If there was an error with the handling of the Send Requests, this pointer will be filled with the address of the Send Request that caused this error.

The ib_send_wr Struct

The Send Request is represented by struct ib_send_wr:

```
struct ib_send_wr {
    struct ib_send_wr      *next;
    u64            wr_id;
    struct ib_sge      *sg_list;
    int            num_sge;
    enum ib_wr_opcode   opcode;
    int            send_flags;
    union {
        __be32        imm_data;
        u32        invalidate_rkey;
    } ex;
    union {
```

```
        struct {
            u64     remote_addr;
            u32     rkey;
        } rdma;
        struct {
            u64     remote_addr;
            u64     compare_add;
            u64     swap;
            u64     compare_add_mask;
            u64     swap_mask;
            u32     rkey;
        } atomic;
        struct {
            struct ib_ah    *ah;
            void            *header;
            int             hlen;
            int             mss;
            u32             remote_qpn;
            u32             remote_qkey;
            u16             pkey_index; /* valid for GSI only */
            u8          port_num;   /* valid for DR SMPs on switch only */
        } ud;
        struct {
            u64                 iova_start;
            struct ib_fast_reg_page_list    *page_list;
            unsigned int            page_shift;
            unsigned int            page_list_len;
            u32             length;
            int             access_flags;
            u32             rkey;
        } fast_reg;
        struct {
            struct ib_mw                *mw;
            /* The new rkey for the memory window. */
            u32                     rkey;
            struct ib_mw_bind_info          bind_info;
        } bind_mw;
    } wr;
    u32         xrc_remote_srq_num;     /* XRC TGT QPs only */
};
```

- **next**: A pointer to the next Send Request in the list or NULL, if this is the last Send Request.

- **wr_id**: 64-bit value that is associated with this Send Request and will be available in the corresponding Work Completion.

- **sg_list**: The array of the scatter/gather elements. As described earlier.

- **num_sge**: The number of entries in sg_list. The value zero means that the message size is zero bytes.

- opcode: The operation to perform. This affects the way that data is being transferred, the direction of it, and whether a Receive Request will be consumed in the remote side and which fields in the Send Request (send_wr) will be used. Can be:

  - IB_WR_RDMA_WRITE: RDMA Write operation.

  - IB_WR_RDMA_WRITE_WITH_IMM: RDMA Write with immediate operation.

  - IB_WR_SEND: Send operation.

  - IB_WR_SEND_WITH_IMM: Send with immediate operation.

  - IB_WR_RDMA_READ: RDMA Read operation.

  - IB_WR_ATOMIC_CMP_AND_SWP: Compare and Swap operation.

  - IB_WR_ATOMIC_FETCH_AND_ADD: Fetch and Add operation.

- IB_WR_LSO: Send an IPoIB message with LSO (let the RDMA device fragment the big SKBs to multiple MSS-sized packets).LSO is an optimization feature which allows to use large packets by reducing CPU overhead.

  - IB_WR_SEND_WITH_INV: Send with invalidate operation.

  - IB_WR_RDMA_READ_WITH_INV: RDMA Read with invalidate operation.

  - IB_WR_LOCAL_INV: Local invalidate operation.

  - IB_WR_FAST_REG_MR: Fast MR registration operation.

  - IB_WR_MASKED_ATOMIC_CMP_AND_SWP: Masked Compare and Swap operation.

  - IB_WR_MASKED_ATOMIC_FETCH_AND_ADD: Masked Fetch and Add operation.

  - IB_WR_BIND_MW: Memory bind operation.

- send_flags: Extra attributes for the Send Request. It is a bitwise OR of the masks:

  - IB_SEND_FENCE: Before performing this operation, wait until the processing of prior Send Requests has ended.

  - IB_SEND_SIGNALED: If the QP was created with selective signaling, when the processing of this Send Request is ended, a Work Completion will be generated.

  - IB_SEND_SOLICITED: Mark that a Solicited event will be created in the remote side.

  - IB_SEND_INLINE: Post this Send Request as inline—that is, let the low-level driver read the memory buffers in if sg_list instead of the RDMA device; this may increase the latency.

  - IB_SEND_IP_CSUM: Send an IPoIB message and calculate the IP checksum in HW (checksum offload).

- ex.imm_data: The immediate data to send. This value is relevant if opcode is IB_WR_SEND_WITH_IMM or IB_WR_RDMA_WRITE_WITH_IMM.

- ex.invalidate_rkey: The rkey to be invalidated. This value is relevant if opcode is IB_WR_SEND_WITH_INV.

The following union is relevant if opcode is IB_WR_RDMA_WRITE, IB_WR_RDMA_WRITE_WITH_IMM, or IB_WR_RDMA_READ:

- `wr.rdma.remote_addr`: The remote address that this Send Request is going to access.

- `wr.rdma.rkey`: The Remote Key (rkey) of the MR that this Send Request is going to access.

The following union is relevant if opcode is IB_WR_ATOMIC_CMP_AND_SWP, IB_WR_ATOMIC_FETCH_AND_ADD, IB_WR_MASKED_ATOMIC_CMP_AND_SWP, or IB_WR_MASKED_ATOMIC_FETCH_AND_ADD:

- `wr.atomic.remote_addr`: The remote address that this Send Request is going to access.

- `wr.atomic.compare_add`: If opcode is IB_WR_ATOMIC_FETCH_AND_ADD*, this is the value to add to the content of `remote_addr`. Otherwise, this is the value to compare the content of `remote_addr` with.

- `wr.atomic.swap`: The value to place in `remote_addr` if the value in it is equal to `compare_add`. This value is relevant if opcode is IB_WR_ATOMIC_CMP_AND_SWP or IB_WR_MASKED_ATOMIC_CMP_AND_SWP.

- `wr.atomic.compare_add_mask`: If opcode is IB_WR_MASKED_ATOMIC_FETCH_AND_ADD, this is the mask of the values to change when adding the value of `compare_add` to the content of `remote_addr`. Otherwise, this is the mask to use on the content of `remote_addr` when comparing it with swap.

- `wr.atomic.swap_mask`: This is the mask of the value in the content of `remote_addr` to change. Relevant only if opcode is IB_WR_MASKED_ATOMIC_CMP_AND_SWP.

- `wr.atomic.rkey`: The rkey of the MR that this Send Request is going to access.

The following union is relevant if the QP type that this Send Request is being posted to is UD:

- `wr.ud.ah`: The address handle that describes the path to the target node(s).

- `wr.ud.header`: A pointer that contains the header. Relevant if opcode is IB_WR_LSO.

- `wr.ud.hlen`: The length of `wr.ud.header`. Relevant if opcode is IB_WR_LSO.

- `wr.ud.mss`: The Maximum Segment Size that the message will be fragmented to. Relevant if opcode is IB_WR_LSO.

- `wr.ud.remote_qpn`: The remote QP number to send the message to. The enumeration IB_MULTICAST_QPN should be used if sending this message to a multicast group.

- `wr.ud.remote_qkey`: The remote Q_Key value to use. If the MSB of this value is set, then the value of the Q_Key will be taken from the QP attributes.

- `wr.ud.pkey_index`: The P_Key index that the message will be sent with. Relevant if QP type is IB_QPT_GSI.

- `wr.ud.port_num`: The port number that the message will be sent from. Relevant for Direct Route SMP on a switch.

The following union is relevant if opcode is IB_WR_FAST_REG_MR:

- `wr.fast_reg.iova_start`: I/O Virtual Address of the newly created FMR.

- `wr.fast_reg.page_list`: List of pages to allocate to map in the FMR.

- `wr.fast_reg.page_shift`: Log 2 of size of "pages" to be mapped.

- `wr.fast_reg.page_list_len`: The number of pages in `page_list`.

- wr.fast_reg.length: The size, in bytes, of the FMR.

- wr.fast_reg.access_flags: The allowed operations on this FMR.

- wr.fast_reg.rkey: The value of the remote key to be assigned to the FMR.

The following union is relevant if opcode is IB_WR_BIND_MW:

- wr.bind_mw.mw: The MW to be bounded.

- wr.bind_mw.rkey: The value of the remote key to be assigned to the MW.

- wr.bind_mw.bind_info: The bind attributes, as explained in the next section.

The following member is relevant if the QP type that this Send Request is being posted to is XRCTGT:

- xrc_remote_srq_num: The remote SRQ that will receive the messages.

The ib_mw_bind_info Struct

The MW binding attributes for both MW type 1 and type 2 are represented by struct ib_mw_bind_info.

```
struct ib_mw_bind_info {
    struct ib_mr      *mr;
    u64        addr;
    u64        length;
    int        mw_access_flags;
};
```

- mr: A Memory Region that this Memory Window will be bounded to.

- addr: The address where the Memory Window will start from.

- length: The length, in bytes, of the Memory Window.

- mw_access_flags: The allowed incoming RDMA and Atomic operations. It is a bitwise OR of the masks:

  - IB_ACCESS_REMOTE_WRITE: Incoming RDMA Write operations are allowed.

  - IB_ACCESS_REMOTE_READ: Incoming RDMA Read operations are allowed.

  - IB_ACCESS_REMOTE_ATOMIC: Incoming Atomic operations are allowed.

Memory Windows (MW)

Memory Windows are used as a lightweight operation to change the allowed permission of incoming remote operations and invalidate them.

The ib_alloc_mw() Method

The ib_alloc_mw() method allocates a Memory Window. It will return a pointer to the newly allocated MW on success or an ERR_PTR() which specifies the reason for the failure.

```
struct ib_mw *ib_alloc_mw(struct ib_pd *pd, enum ib_mw_type type);
```

- pd: The PD that this MW is being associated with.

- type: The type of the Memory Window. Can be:

  - IB_MW_TYPE_1: MW that can be bounded using a verb and supports only association of a PD.

  - IB_MW_TYPE_2: MW that can be bounded using Work Request and supports association of a QP number only or a QP number and a PD.

The ib_bind_mw() Method

The ib_bind_mw() method binds a Memory Window to a specified Memory Region with a specific address, size, and remote permissions. If there isn't any immediate error, the rkey of the MW will be updated to the new value, but the bind operation may still fail asynchronously (and end with completion with error). It will return 0 on success or the errno value with the reason for the failure.

```
static inline int ib_bind_mw(struct ib_qp *qp, struct ib_mw *mw, struct ib_mw_bind *mw_bind);
```

- qp: The QP that the bind WR will be posted to.

- mw: The MW to bind.

- mw_bind: The bind attributes, as explained next.

The ib_mw_bind Struct

The MW binding attributes for type 1 MW are represented by struct ib_mw_bind.

```
struct ib_mw_bind {
    u64                    wr_id;
    int                    send_flags;
    struct ib_mw_bind_info bind_info;
};
```

- wr_id: A 64-bit value that is associated with this bind Send Request The value of Work Request id (wr_id) will be available in the corresponding Work Completion.

- send_flags: Extra attribute for the bind Send Request, as explained earlier. Only IB_SEND_FENCE and IB_SEND_SIGNALED are supported here.

- bind_info: More attributes for the bind operation. As explained earlier.

The ib_dealloc_mw() Method

The ib_dealloc_mw() method deallocates an MW. It will return 0 on success or the errno value with the reason for the failure.

```
int ib_dealloc_mw(struct ib_mw *mw);
```

- mw: The MW to be deallocated.

Memory Region (MR)

Every memory buffer that is being accessed by the RDMA device needs to be registered. During the registration process, the memory will be pinned (prevented from being swapped out), and the memory translation information (from virtual addresses ➤ physical addresses) will be saved in the RDMA device. After the registration, every Memory Region has two keys: one for local access and one for remote access. Those keys will be used when specifying those memory buffers in Work Requests.

The ib_get_dma_mr() Method

The ib_get_dma_mr() method returns a Memory Region for system memory that is usable for DMA. Creating this MR isn't enough, and the ib_dma_*() methods below are needed in order to create or destroy addresses that the lkey and rkey of this MR will be used with. It will return a pointer to the newly allocated MR on success or an ERR_PTR() which specifies the reason for the failure.

```
struct ib_mr *ib_get_dma_mr(struct ib_pd *pd, int mr_access_flags);
```

- pd: The PD that this MR is being associated with.

- mr_access_flags: The allowed operations on this MR. Local Write is always supported in this MR. It is a bitwise OR of the masks:

  - IB_ACCESS_LOCAL_WRITE: Local write to this Memory Region is allowed.

  - IB_ACCESS_REMOTE_WRITE: Incoming RDMA Write operations to this Memory Region are allowed.

  - IB_ACCESS_REMOTE_READ: Incoming RDMA Read operations to this Memory Region are allowed.

  - IB_ACCESS_REMOTE_ATOMIC: Incoming Atomic operations to this Memory Region are allowed.

  - IB_ACCESS_MW_BIND: MW bind to this Memory Region is allowed.

  - IB_ZERO_BASED: Indication that the Virtual address is zero based.

The ib_dma_mapping_error() Method

The ib_dma_mapping_error() method checks if the DMA address that was returned from ib_dma_*() failed. It will return a non-zero value if there was any failure and zero if the operation finished successfully.

```
static inline int ib_dma_mapping_error(struct ib_device *dev, u64 dma_addr);
```

- dev: The RDMA device for which the DMA address was created by using an ib_dma_*() method.

- dma_addr: The DMA address to verify.

The ib_dma_map_single() Method

The ib_dma_map_single() method maps a kernel virtual address to a DMA address. It will return a DMA address that needed to be checked with the ib_dma_mapping_error() method for errors:

```
static inline u64 ib_dma_map_single(struct ib_device *dev, void *cpu_addr, size_t size, enum dma_
data_direction direction);
```

- dev: The RDMA device on which the DMA address will be created.

- cpu_addr: The kernel virtual address to map for DMA.

- size: The size, in bytes, of the region to map.

- direction: The direction of the DMA. Can be:

  - DMA_TO_DEVICE: DMA from the main memory to the device.

  - DMA_FROM_DEVICE: DMA from the device to main memory.

  - DMA_BIDIRECTIONAL: DMA from the main memory to the device or from the device to main memory.

The ib_dma_unmap_single() Method

The ib_dma_unmap_single() method unmaps a DMA mapping that was assigned using ib_dma_map_single():

```
static inline void ib_dma_unmap_single(struct ib_device *dev, u64 addr, size_t size, enum dma_data_
direction direction);
```

- dev: The RDMA device on which the DMA address was created.

- addr: The DMA address to unmap.

- size: The size, in bytes, of the region to unmap. This value must be the same value that was used in the ib_dma_map_single() method.

- direction: The direction of the DMA. This value must be the same value that was used in the ib_dma_map_single() method.

The ib_dma_map_single_attrs() Method

The ib_dma_map_single_attrs() method maps a kernel virtual address to a DMA address according to a DMA attributes. It will return a DMA address that is needed to be checked with the ib_dma_mapping_error() method for errors.

```
static inline u64 ib_dma_map_single_attrs(struct ib_device *dev, void *cpu_addr, size_t size, enum
dma_data_direction direction, struct dma_attrs *attrs);
```

- dev: The RDMA device on which the DMA address will be created.

- cpu_addr: The kernel virtual address to map for DMA.

- size: The size, in bytes, of the region to map.

- direction: The direction of the DMA. As described earlier.

- attrs: The DMA attributes for the mapping. If this value is NULL, this method behaves like the ib_dma_map_single() method.

The ib_dma_unmap_single_attrs() Method

The ib_dma_unmap_single_attrs() method unmaps a DMA mapping that was assigned using the ib_dma_map_single_attrs() method:

```
static inline void ib_dma_unmap_single_attrs(struct ib_device *dev, u64 addr, size_t size,
enum dma_data_direction direction, struct dma_attrs *attrs);
```

- dev: The RDMA device on which the DMA address was created.

- addr: The DMA address to unmap.

- size: The size, in bytes, of the region to unmap. This value must be the same value that was used in the ib_dma_map_single_attrs() method.

- direction: The direction of the DMA. This value must be the same value that was used in the ib_dma_map_single_attrs() method.

- attrs: The DMA attributes of the mapping. This value must be the same value that was used in the ib_dma_map_single_attrs() method. If this value is NULL, this method behaves like the ib_dma_unmap_single() method.

The ib_dma_map_page() Method

The ib_dma_map_page() method maps a physical page to a DMA address. It will return a DMA address that needs to be checked with the ib_dma_mapping_error() method for errors:

```
static inline u64 ib_dma_map_page(struct ib_device *dev, struct page *page, unsigned long offset,
size_t size, enum dma_data_direction direction);
```

- dev: The RDMA device on which the DMA address will be created.

- page: The physical page address to map for DMA.

- offset: The offset within the page that the registration will start from.

- size: The size, in bytes, of the region.

- direction: The direction of the DMA. As described earlier.

The ib_dma_unmap_page() Method

The ib_dma_unmap_page() method unmaps a DMA mapping that was assigned using the ib_dma_map_page() method:

```
static inline void ib_dma_unmap_page(struct ib_device *dev, u64 addr, size_t size, enum dma_data_
direction direction);
```

- dev: The RDMA device on which the DMA address was created.

- addr: The DMA address to unmap.

- size: The size, in bytes, of the region to unmap. This value must be the same value that was used in the ib_dma_map_page() method.

- direction: The direction of the DMA. This value must be the same value that was used in the ib_dma_map_page() method.

The ib_dma_map_sg() Method

The ib_dma_map_sg() method maps a scatter/gather list to a DMA address. It will return a non-zero value on success and 0 on a failure.

```
static inline int ib_dma_map_sg(struct ib_device *dev, struct scatterlist *sg, int nents, enum dma_
data_direction direction);
```

- dev: The RDMA device on which the DMA address will be created.

- sg: An array of the scatter/gather entries to map.

- nents: The number of scatter/gather entries in sg.

- direction: The direction of the DMA. As described earlier.

The ib_dma_unmap_sg() Method

The ib_dma_unmap_sg() method unmaps a DMA mapping that was assigned using the ib_dma_map_sg() method:

```
static inline void ib_dma_unmap_sg(struct ib_device *dev, struct scatterlist *sg, int nents, enum
dma_data_direction direction);
```

- dev: The RDMA device on which the DMA address was created.

- sg: An array of the scatter/gather entries to unmap. This value must be the same value that was used in the ib_dma_map_sg() method.

- nents: The number of scatter/gather entries in sg. This value must be the same value that was used in the ib_dma_map_sg() method.

- direction: The direction of the DMA. This value must be the same value that was used in the ib_dma_map_sg() method.

The ib_dma_map_sg_attr() Method

The ib_dma_map_sg_attr() method maps a scatter/gather list to a DMA address according to a DMA attributes. It will return a non-zero value on success and 0 on a failure.

```
static inline int ib_dma_map_sg_attrs(struct ib_device *dev, struct scatterlist *sg, int nents, enum
dma_data_direction direction, struct dma_attrs *attrs);
```

- dev: The RDMA device on which the DMA address will be created.

- sg: An array of the scatter/gather entries to map.

- nents: The number of scatter/gather entries in sg.

- direction: The direction of the DMA. As described earlier.

- attrs: The DMA attributes for the mapping. If this value is NULL, this method behaves like the ib_dma_map_sg() method.

The ib_dma_unmap_sg() Method

The ib_dma_unmap_sg() method unmaps a DMA mapping that was done using the ib_dma_map_sg() method:

```
static inline void ib_dma_unmap_sg_attrs(struct ib_device *dev, struct scatterlist *sg, int nents,
enum dma_data_direction direction, struct dma_attrs *attrs);
```

- dev: The RDMA device on which the DMA address was created.
- sg: An array of the scatter/gather entries to unmap. This value must be the same value that was used in the ib_dma_map_sg_attrs() method.
- nents: The number of scatter/gather entries in sg. This value must be the same value that was used in the ib_dma_map_sg_attrs() method.
- direction: The direction of the DMA. This value must be the same value that was used in the ib_dma_map_sg_attrs() method.
- attrs: The DMA attributes of the mapping. This value must be the same value that was used in the ib_dma_map_sg_attrs() method. If this value is NULL, this method behaves like the ib_dma_unmap_sg() method.

The ib_sg_dma_address() Method

The ib_sg_dma_address() method returns the DMA address from a scatter/gather entry.

```
static inline u64 ib_sg_dma_address(struct ib_device *dev, struct scatterlist *sg);
```

- dev: The RDMA device on which the DMA address was created.
- sg: A scatter/gather entry.

The ib_sg_dma_len() Method

The ib_sg_dma_len() method returns the DMA length from a scatter/gather entry.

```
static inline unsigned int ib_sg_dma_len(struct ib_device *dev, struct scatterlist *sg);
```

- dev: The RDMA device on which the DMA address was created.
- sg: A scatter/gather entry.

The ib_dma_sync_single_for_cpu() Method

The ib_dma_sync_single_for_cpu() method transfers a DMA region ownership to the CPU. This method must be called before the CPU accesses a DMA-mapped buffer in order to read or modify its content, and prevents the device from accessing it:

```
static inline void ib_dma_sync_single_for_cpu(struct ib_device *dev, u64 addr, size_t size,
enum dma_data_direction dir);
```

- dev: The RDMA device on which the DMA address was created.
- addr: The DMA address to sync.

- size: The size, in bytes, of the region.

- direction: The direction of the DMA. As described earlier.

The ib_dma_sync_single_for_device() Method

The ib_dma_sync_single_for_device() method transfers a DMA region ownership to the device. This method must be called before the device can access a DMA-mapped buffer again after the ib_dma_sync_single_for_cpu() method was called.

```
static inline void ib_dma_sync_single_for_device(struct ib_device *dev, u64 addr, size_t size, enum
dma_data_direction dir);
```

- dev: The RDMA device on which the DMA address was created.

- addr: The DMA address to sync.

- size: The size, in bytes, of the region.

- direction: The direction of the DMA. As described earlier.

The ib_dma_alloc_coherent() Method

The ib_dma_alloc_coherent() method allocates a memory block that can be accessible by the CPU and maps it for DMA. It will return the virtual address that the CPU can access on success or NULL in case of a failure:

```
static inline void *ib_dma_alloc_coherent(struct ib_device *dev, size_t size, u64 *dma_handle, gfp_t flag);
```

- dev: The RDMA device on which the DMA address will be created.

- size: The size, in bytes, of the memory to allocate and map.

- direction: The direction of the DMA. As described earlier.

- dma_handle: A pointer that will be filled with the DMA address of the region, if the allocation succeeds.

- flag: Memory allocation flags. Can be:

  - GFP_KERNEL: To allow blocking (not in interrupt, not holding SMP locks).

  - GFP_ATOMIC: Prevent blocking.

The ib_dma_free_coherent() method

The ib_dma_free_coherent() method frees a memory block that was allocated using the ib_dma_alloc_coherent() method:

```
static inline void ib_dma_free_coherent(struct ib_device *dev, size_t size, void *cpu_addr,
u64 dma_handle);
```

- dev: The RDMA device on which the DMA address was created.

- size: The size, in bytes, of the memory region. This value must be the same value that was used in the ib_dma_alloc_coherent() method.

- cpu_addr: The CPU memory address to free. This value must be the value that was returned by the ib_dma_alloc_coherent() method.

- dma_handle: The DMA address to free. This value must be the value that was returned by the ib_dma_alloc_coherent() method.

The ib_reg_phys_mr() Method

The ib_reg_phys_mr() method takes a set of physical pages, register them and prepare a virtual address that can be accessed by an RDMA device. It will return a pointer to the newly allocated MR on success or an ERR_PTR(), which specifies the reason for the failure.

```
struct ib_mr *ib_reg_phys_mr(struct ib_pd *pd, struct ib_phys_buf *phys_buf_array, int num_phys_buf,
int mr_access_flags, u64 *iova_start);
```

- pd: The PD that this MR is being associated with.

- phys_buf_array: An array of physical buffers to use in the Memory Region.

- num_phys_buf: The number of physical buffers in phys_buf_array.

- mr_access_flags: The allowed operations on this MR. As specified earlier.

- iova_start: A pointer to the requested I/O Virtual Address to be associated with the Region, which is allowed to begin anywhere within the first physical buffer. The RDMA device will set this value with the actual I/O virtual address of the Region. This value may be different from the requested one.

The ib_phys_buf Struct

The physical buffer is represented by struct ib_phys_buf.

```
struct ib_phys_buf {
    u64      addr;
    u64      size;
};
```

- addr: The physical address of the buffer.

- size: The size of the buffer.

The ib_rereg_phys_mr() Method

The ib_rereg_phys_mr() method modifies the attributes of an existing Memory Region. This method can be thought of as a call to the ib_dereg_mr() method, which was followed by a call to the ib_reg_phys_mr() method. Where possible, resources are reused instead of being deallocated and reallocated. It will return 0 on success or the errno value with the reason for the failure:

```
int ib_rereg_phys_mr(struct ib_mr *mr, int mr_rereg_mask, struct ib_pd *pd, struct ib_phys_buf
*phys_buf_array, int num_phys_buf, int mr_access_flags, u64 *iova_start);
```

- mr: The Memory Region to be reregistered.

- mr_rereg_mask: The Memory Region attributes to be changed. It is a bitwise OR of the masks:

    - IB_MR_REREG_TRANS: Modify the memory pages of this Memory Region.

    - IB_MR_REREG_PD: Modify the PD of this Memory Region.

    - IB_MR_REREG_ACCESS: Modify the allowed operations of this Memory Region.

- pd: The new Protection Domain that this Memory Region will be associated with.

- phys_buf_array: The new physical pages to be used.

- num_phys_buf: The number of physical pages to be used.

- mr_access_flags: The new allowed operations of this Memory Region.

- iova_start: The new I/O Virtual Address of this Memory Region.

The ib_query_mr() Method

The ib_query_mr() method retrieves the attributes of a specific MR. It will return 0 on success or the errno value with the reason for the failure.

```
int ib_query_mr(struct ib_mr *mr, struct ib_mr_attr *mr_attr);
```

- mr: The MR to be queried.

- mr_attr: The MR attributes as describe in the next section.

The MR attributes are represented by struct ib_mr_attr.

The ib_mr_attr Struct

```
struct ib_mr_attr {
    struct ib_pd    *pd;
    u64             device_virt_addr;
    u64             size;
    int             mr_access_flags;
    u32             lkey;
    u32             rkey;
};
```

- pd: The PD that the MR is associated with.

- device_virt_addr: The address of the virtual block that this MR covers.

- size: The size, in bytes, of the Memory Region.

- mr_access_flags: The access permissions of this Memory Region.

- lkey: The local key of this Memory Region.

- rkey: The remote key of this Memory Region.

The ib_dereg_mr() Method

The `ib_dereg_mr()` method deregisters an MR. This method may fail if a Memory Window is bounded to it. It will return 0 on success or the errno value with the reason for the failure:

```
int ib_dereg_mr(struct ib_mr *mr);
```

- mr: The MR to be deregistered.

■ ■ ■

Network Administration

This appendix reviews some of the most popular tools for network administration and debugging. These tools can help a lot in finding solutions to common problems and in developing, debugging, benchmarking, analyzing, troubleshooting, and researching network projects. Most of these tools have very good documentation resources, either with man pages or with wiki pages, and a lot of other information resources about them are on the Internet. Many of them have active mailing lists (for users and developers) and a bug reporting system. Some of the most commonly used tools are described here by specifying their purpose and relevant links, accompanied by several examples. The tools mentioned in this appendix appear in alphabetical order.

arp

This command is for ARP table management. Example of usage:

You can display the ARP table by running arp from the command-line. arp -n will display the ARP table without name resolution.

You can add static entries to the ARP table by:

```
arp -s 192.168.2.10 00:e0:4c:11:22:33
```

The arp utility belongs to the net-tools package. Website: http://net-tools.sourceforge.net.

arping

A utility to send ARP requests. The -D flag is for Duplicate Address Detection (DAD). The arping utility belongs to the iputils package. Website: http://www.skbuff.net/iputils/.

arptables

A userspace tool for configuring rules for a Linux-based ARP rules firewall. Website: http://ebtables.sourceforge.net/.

arpwatch

A userspace tool for monitoring ARP traffic. Website: http://ee.lbl.gov/.

ApacheBench (ab)

A command-line utility for measuring the performance of HTTP web servers. The ApacheBench tool is part of the Apache open source project. In many distributions (for example, Ubuntu) it is part of the `apache2-utils` package. Example of usage:

```
ab -n 100  http://www.google.com/
```

The `-n` option is the number of requests to perform for the benchmarking session.

brctl

A command-line utility for administration of Ethernet bridges, enabling the setup of a bridge configuration. The `brctl` utility belongs to the `bridge-utils` package. Examples for usage:

- `brctl addbr mybr`: Add a bridge named `mybr`.
- `brctl delbr mybr`: Delete the bridge named `mybr`.
- `brctl addif mybr eth1`: Add the `eth1` interface to the bridge.
- `brctl delif mybr eth1`: Delete the `eth1` interface from the bridge.
- `brctl show`: Show information about the bridge and its attached ports.

The maintainer of the `bridge-utils` package is Stephen Hemminger. Fetching the `git` repository can be done by:

```
git clone git://git.kernel.org/pub/scm/linux/kernel/git/shemminger/bridge-utils.git
```

Website: `http://www.linuxfoundation.org/collaborate/workgroups/networking/bridge`.

conntrack-tools

A set of userspace tools for management of netfilter connection tracking. It consists of a userspace daemon, conntrackd, and a command-line tool, conntrack. Website: `http://conntrack-tools.netfilter.org/`.

crtools

A utility for checkpoint/restore of a process. Website: `http://criu.org/Installation`.

ebtables

A userspace tool for configuring rules for a Linux-based bridging firewall. Website: `http://ebtables.sourceforge.net/`.

ether-wake

A utility to send Wake-On-LAN Magic Packets. The `ether-wake` utility belongs to the `net-tools` package.

ethtool

The ethtool utility provides a way to query or control network driver and hardware settings, get statistics, get diagnostic information, and more. With ethtool you can control parameters of Ethernet devices, such as speed, duplex, auto-negotiation and flow control. Many features of ethtool require support in the network driver code.

Examples:

- Output of ethtool eth0:

```
Settings for eth0:
        Supported ports: [ TP MII ]
        Supported link modes:   10baseT/Half 10baseT/Full
                                100baseT/Half 100baseT/Full
                                1000baseT/Half 1000baseT/Full
        Supported pause frame use: No
        Supports auto-negotiation: Yes
        Advertised link modes:  10baseT/Half 10baseT/Full
                                100baseT/Half 100baseT/Full
                                1000baseT/Half 1000baseT/Full
        Advertised pause frame use: Symmetric Receive-only
        Advertised auto-negotiation: Yes
        Speed: 10Mb/s
        Duplex: Half
        Port: MII
        PHYAD: 0
        Transceiver: internal
        Auto-negotiation: on
        Supports Wake-on: pumbg
        Wake-on: g
        Current message level: 0x00000033 (51)
                               drv probe ifdown ifup
        Link detected: no
```

- Getting offload parameters is done by: ethtool –k eth1.

- Setting offload parameters is done by: ethtool –K eth1 offLoadParamater.

- Querying the network device for associated driver information is done by: ethtool -i eth1.

- Showing statistics is done by: ethtool -S eth1 (note that not all the network device drivers implement this feature).

- Show permanent hardware (MAC) address: ethtool -P eth0.

The development of ethtool is done by sending patches to the netdev mailing list. The maintainer of ethtool as of this writing is Ben Hutchings. The ethtool project is developed over a git repository. It can be downloaded by: git clone git://git.kernel.org/pub/scm/network/ethtool/ethtool.git.

Website: www.kernel.org/pub/software/network/ethtool/.

git

A distributed version control system started by Linus Torvalds. Linux kernel development, as well as many Linux related projects, are managed by git. One can also use the git send-email command in order to send patches by mail. Website: http://git-scm.com/.

hciconfig

A command-line tool for configuring Bluetooth devices. With hciconfig, you can display information such as the Bluetooth interface type (BR/EDR or AMP), its Bluetooth address, its flags, and more. The hciconfig tool belongs to the bluez package. Example:

```
hciconfig
hci0:   Type: BR/EDR  Bus: USB
        BD Address: 00:02:72:AA:FB:94  ACL MTU: 1021:7   SCO MTU: 64:1
        UP RUNNING PSCAN
        RX bytes:964 acl:0 sco:0 events:41 errors:0
        TX bytes:903 acl:0 sco:0 commands:41 errors:0
```

Website: http://www.bluez.org/.

hcidump

A command-line utility for dumping raw HCI data coming from and going to a Bluetooth device. The hcidump utility belongs to the bluez-hcidump package. Website: http://www.bluez.org/.

hcitool

A command-line utility for configuring Bluetooth connections and for sending some special commands to Bluetooth devices. For example, you can scan for nearby Bluetooth devices by: hcitool scan. The hcitool utility belongs to the bluez-hcidump package.

ifconifg

The ifconfig command allows you to configure various network interface parameters, including the IP address of the device, the MTU, the MAC address, the Tx queue length (txqueuelen), flags, and more. The ifconfig tool belongs to the net-tools package, which is older than the iproute2 package (discussed later in this appendix). Here are three examples of usage:

- ifconfig eth0 mtu 1300: Change the MTU to 1300.

- ifconfig eth0 txqueuelen 1100: Change the Tx Queue length to 1100.

- ifconfig eth0 -arp: Disable the ARP protocol on eth0.

Website: http://net-tools.sourceforge.net.

ifenslave

A utility for attaching and detaching slave network devices to a bonding device. *Bonding* is putting multiple physical Ethernet devices into a single logical one, what is often termed as Link aggregation/Trunking/Link bundling. The source file is in Documentation/networking/ifenslave.c. You can attach eth0, for example, to a bonding device bond0 by:

```
ifenslave bond0 eth0
```

The ifenslave utility belongs to the iputils package, maintained by Yoshifuji Hideaki. Website: www.skbuff.net/iputils/.

iperf

The iperf project is an open source project that provides a benchmarking tool to measure TCP and UDP bandwidth performance. It allows you to tune various parameters. The iperf tool reports bandwidth, delay jitter, and datagram loss. It was originally developed by the Distributed Applications Support Team (DAST) at the National Laboratory for Applied Network Research (NLANR) in C++. It works in a client-server model. A new implementation from scratch, iperf3, which is not backwards compatible with the original iperf, is available from https://code.google.com/p/iperf/. The iperf3 is said to have a simpler code base. The iperf3 tool can report also the average CPU utilization of the client and the server.

Using iperf

Following is a simple example of using iperf for measuring TCP performance. On one device (which has an IP address of 192.168.2.104), run the next command, which starts the server side (by default, it is a TCP socket on port 5001):

```
iperf -s
```

On a second device, run the iperf TCP client to connect to the iperf server:

```
iperf -c 192.168.2.104
```

On the client side you will see the following:

```
------------------------------------------------------------
Client connecting to 192.168.2.104, TCP port 5001
TCP window size: 22.9 KByte (default)
------------------------------------------------------------
[  3] local 192.168.2.200 port 35146 connected with 192.168.2.104 port 5001
```

The default time interval is 10 seconds. After 10 seconds, the client will be disconnected, and you will see a message like this on the terminal:

```
[ ID] Interval       Transfer     Bandwidth
[  3]  0.0-10.3 sec  7.62 MBytes  6.20 Mbits/sec
```

You can tune many parameters of iperf, like these:

- -u: For using a UDP socket.
- -t: For using a different time interval in seconds instead of the default of 10 seconds.
- -T: Sets a TTL for multicast (the default is 1).
- -B: Bind to a host, an interface, or a multicast address.

See man iperf. Website: http://iperf.sourceforge.net/.

iproute2

The iproute2 package provides many tools for interaction between the userspace and the kernel networking subsystem. The most well-known is the ip command. It is based on netlink sockets (discussed in Chapter 2). With the ip command, you can perform various operations in a wide range of networking areas, and it has numerous options; see man 8 ip. Here are several examples of using the ip command for various tasks:

- Configuration of a network device with ip addr:

  - ip addr add 192.168.0.10/24 dev eth0: Sets an IP address on eth0.

  - ip addr show: Displays the addresses of all network interfaces (both IPv4 and IPv6).

  See man ip address.

- Configuration of a network device with ip link:

  - ip link add mybr type bridge: Creates a bridge named mybr.

  - ip link add name myteam type team: Creates a teaming device named myteam. (The teaming device driver aggregates multiple physical Ethernet devices into one logical one and is in fact the new bonding device. The teaming driver is discussed in Chapter 14.)

  - ip link set eth1 mtu 1450: Sets the MTU of eth1 to be 1450.

  See man ip link.

- Management of ARP tables (IPv4) and NDISC (IPv6) tables:

  - ip neigh show: Shows both the IPv4 neighbouring table (ARP table) and the IPv6 neighbouring table.

  - ip -6 neigh show: Shows only the IPv6 neighbouring table.

  - ip neigh flush dev eth0: Removes all entries from the neighboring tables associated with eth0.

  - ip neigh add 192.168.2.20 dev eth2 lladdr 00:11:22:33:44:55 nud permanent: Adds a permanent neighbour entry (parallel to adding static entries in an ARP table).

  - ip neigh change 192.168.2.20 dev eth2 lladdr 55:44:33:22:11:00 nud permanent: Updates a neighbour entry.

  See man ip neighbour.

- Management of the parameters for the neighbour tables:

  - ip ntable show: Displays the neighbour tables parameters.

  - ip ntable change name arp_cache locktime 1200 dev eth0: Changes the locktime parameter for the IPv4 neighbouring table associated with eth0.

  See man ip ntable.

- Network namespaces management:

  - ip netns add myNamespace: Adds a network namespace named myNamespace.

  - ip netns del myNamespace: Deletes the network namespace named myNamespace.

  - ip netns list: Shows all network namespaces on the host.

  - ip netns monitor: Displays a line of screen for each network namespace that is added or removed by the ip netns command.

See man `ip netns`.

- Configuration of multicast addresses:

  - `ip maddr show`: Shows all multicast addresses on the host (both IPv4 and IPv6).

  - `ip maddr add 00:10:02:03:04:05 dev eth1`: Adds a multicast address on `eth1`.

  See man `ip maddress`.

- Monitor netlink messages. For example:

  - `ip monitor route` displays on the screen messages about various network events like adding or deleting a route.

  See man `ip monitor`.

- Management of routing tables:

  - `ip route show`: Shows the routing table.

  - `ip route flush dev eth1`: Removes routing entries associated with `eth1` from the routing table.

  - `ip route add default via 192.168.2.1`: Adds 192.168.2.1 as a default gateway.

  - `ip route get 192.168.2.10`: Gets the route to 192.168.2.10 and displays it.

  See man `ip route`.

- Management of rules in the RPDB (Routing Policy DataBase). For example:

  - `ip rule add tos 0x02 table 200`: Adds a rule that sets the routing subsystem to perform a lookup in routing table 252 for packets whose TOS value is 0x02 (TOS is a field in the IPv4 header).

  - `ip rule del tos 0x02 table 200`: Deletes a specified rule from the RPDB.

  - `ip rule show`: Displays the rules in the RPDB.

  See man `ip rule`.

- Management of TUN/TAP devices:

  - `ip tuntap add tun1 mode tun`: Creates a TUN device named `tun1`.

  - `ip tuntap del tun1 mode tun`: Deletes a TUN device named `tun1`.

  - `ip tuntap add tap1 mode tap`: Creates a TAP device named `tap1`.

  - `ip tuntap del tap1 mode tap`: Deletes a TAP device named `tap1`.

- Management of IPsec policies:

  - `ip xfrm policy show`: Shows IPsec policies.

  - `ip xfrm state show`: Shows IPsec states.

  See man `ip xfrm`.

The `ss` tool is used to dump socket statistics. For example, running

```
ss -t -a
```

will show all TCP sockets:

```
State     Recv-Q Send-Q        Local Address:Port         Peer Address:Port
LISTEN    0      32                      *:ftp                     *:*
LISTEN    0      128                     *:ssh                     *:*
LISTEN    0      128             127.0.0.1:ipp                     *:*
ESTAB     0      0           192.168.2.200:ssh           192.168.2.104:52089
ESTAB     0      52          192.168.2.200:ssh           192.168.2.104:51352
ESTAB     0      0           192.168.2.200:ssh           192.168.2.104:51523
ESTAB     0      0           192.168.2.200:59532         107.21.231.190:http
LISTEN    0      128                   :::ssh                   :::*
LISTEN    0      128                   ::1:ipp                   :::*
CLOSE-WAIT 1     0                     ::1:48723                 ::1:ipp
```

There are other tools of iproute2:

- bridge: Shows/manipulates bridge addresses and devices. For example:

  - bridge fdb show: Displays forwarding entries.

  See man bridge.

- genl: Gets information (like id, header size, max attributes, and more) about registered generic netlink families. For example, running genl ctrl list can have this as a result:

```
Name: nlctrl
        ID: 0x10  Version: 0x2  header size: 0  max attribs: 7
        commands supported:
                #1:  ID-0x3
                Capabilities (0xe):
                  can doit; can dumpit; has policy

        multicast groups:
                #1:  ID-0x10  name: notify
```

- lnstat: Displays Linux network statistics.

- rtmon: Monitors Rtnetlink sockets.

- tc: Shows/manipulates traffic control settings. For example:

  - tc qdisc show: Running this command shows which queueing discipline (qdisc) entries are installed, for example:

```
qdisc pfifo_fast 0: dev eth1 root refcnt 2 bands 3 priomap  1 2 . . .
```

- This shows that the pfifo_fast qdisc is associated with the eth1 network device. The pfifo_fast qdisc, which is a classless queueing discipline, is the default qdisc in Linux.

  - tc -s qdisc show dev eth1: Shows statistics of the qdisc associated to eth1.

  See man tc.

  See: Linux Advanced Routing & Traffic Control HOWTO: www.lartc.org/howto/.

The development of iproute2 is done by sending patches to the netdev mailing list. The maintainer of ethtool as of this writing is Stephen Hemminger. The iproute2 is developed over a git repository, which can be downloaded by: git clone git://git.kernel.org/pub/scm/linux/kernel/git/shemminger/iproute2.git.

iptables and iptables6

The `iptables` and `iptables6` are administration tools for packet filtering and NAT management for IPv4 and IPv6, respectively. With `iptables`/`iptables6`, you can define lists of rules. Each such rule tells what should be done with the packet (for example, discard it or accept it). Each rule specifies some matching condition for a packet, for example, that it will be a UDP packet. Following are some examples for using the `iptables` command:

- `iptables -A INPUT -p tcp --dport=80 -j LOG --log-level 1`: The meaning of this rule is that incoming TCP packets with destination port 80 will be dumped to the syslog.

- `iptables –L`: Lists all rules in the filter table. (There is no table mentioned in the command, so it accesses the Filter table, which is the default table.)

- `iptables –t nat –L`: Lists all rules in the NAT table.

- `iptables –F`: Flushes the selected table.

- `iptables -t nat -A POSTROUTING -o eth0 -j MASQUERADE`: Sets a MASQUERADE rule.

Website: www.netfilter.org/.

ipvsadm

A tool for Linux Virtual Server administration. Website: www.linuxvirtualserver.org/software/ipvs.html.

iw

Shows/manipulates wireless devices and their configuration. The `iw` package is based on generic netlink sockets (see Chapter 2). For example, you can perform these operations:

- `iw dev wlan0 scan`: Scans for nearby wireless devices.

- `iw wlan0 station dump`: Displays statistics about a station.

- `iw list`: Gets information about a wireless device (such as band information and 802.11n information).

- `iw dev wlan0 get power_save` – get power save mode.

- `iw dev wlan0 set type ibss`: Changes the wireless interface mode to be ibss (Ad-Hoc).

- `iw dev wlan0 set type mesh`: Changes the wireless interface mode to be mesh mode.

- `iw dev wlan0 set type monitor`: Changes the wireless interface mode to be monitor mode.

- `iw dev wlan0 set type managed`: Changes the wireless interface mode to be managed mode.

See man iw.
Gitweb: http://git.kernel.org/cgit/linux/kernel/git/jberg/iw.git.
Website: http://wireless.kernel.org/en/users/Documentation/iw.

iwconfig

The old tool for administering wireless devices. The `iwconfig` belongs to the `wireless-tools` package and is based on IOCTLs. Website: www.hpl.hp.com/personal/Jean_Tourrilhes/Linux/Tools.html.

libreswan Project

An IPsec software solution which forked from openswan version 2.6.38. Website: `http://libreswan.org/`.

l2ping

A command-line utility for sending L2CAP echo requests and receiving answers over a Bluetooth device. The `l2ping` utility belongs to the `bluez` package. Website: `www.bluez.org/`.

lowpan-tools

A set of utilities to manage the Linux LoWPAN stack. Website: `http://sourceforge.net/projects/linux-zigbee/files/linux-zigbee-sources/0.3/`.

lshw

A utility that displays information about the hardware configuration of the machine. Website: `http://ezix.org/project/wiki/HardwareLiSter`.

lscpu

A utility for displaying information about the CPUs on the system. It is based on information from `/proc/cpuinfo` and `sysfs`. The `lscpu` belongs to the `util-linux` package.

lspci

A utility for displaying information about PCI buses in the system and devices connected to them. Sometimes you need to get some information about a PCI network device with the `lspci` command. The `lspci` utility belongs to the `pciutils` package. Website: `http://mj.ucw.cz/sw/pciutils/`.

mrouted

A multicast routing daemon, implementing the IPv4 Distance Vector Multicast Routing Protocol (DVMRP), which is specified in RFC 1075 from 1988. Website: `http://troglobit.com/mrouted.html`.

nc

A command-line utility that reads and writes data across networks. The `nc` belongs to the `nmap-ncat` package. Website: `http://nmap.org/`.

ngrep

A command-line tool, based on the well-known grep command, that allows you to specify extended expressions to match against data payloads of packets. It recognizes TCP, UDP, and ICMP across Ethernet, PPP, SLIP, FDDI, and null interfaces. Website: `http://ngrep.sourceforge.net/`.

netperf

Netperf is a networking benchmarking tool. Website: `www.netperf.org/netperf/`.

netsniff-ng

`netsniff-ng` is an open source project networking toolkit that, among other things, can help in analyzing network traffic, performing stress tests, generating packets at a very high speed, and more. It uses the PF_PACKET zero-copy RINGs (TX and RX). Among the tools it provides are the following:

- `netsniff-ng` is a fast zero-copy analyzer, pcap capturing and replaying tool. The `netsniff-ng` tool is Linux-specific and does not support other operating systems, unlike many of the tools mentioned in this appendix. Example: Running `netsniff-ng --in eth1 --out dump.pcap -s -b 0` creates a pcap file that can be read by `wireshark` or by `tcpdump`. The –s flag is for silence, and the –b 0 is for binding to CPU 0. See `man netsniff-ng`.

- `trafgen` is a zero-copy high performance network packet traffic generator utility.

- `ifpps` is a small utility that periodically provides top-like networking and system statistics from the kernel. `ifpps` gathers its data directly from `procfs` files.

- `bpfc` is a small Berkeley Packet Filter assembler and compiler.

Fetching the git repository: `git clone git://github.com/borkmann/netsniff-ng.git`. Website: `http://netsniff-ng.org/`.

netstat

The `netstat` tool enables you to print multicast memberships, routing tables, network connections, interface statistics, state of sockets, and more. The `netstat` tool belongs to the `net-tools` package. Useful flags:

- `netstat -s`: Displays summary statistics for each protocol.

- `netstat -g`: Displays multicast group membership information for IPv4 and IPv6.

- `netstat -r`: Shows the kernel IP routing table.

- `netstat -nl`: Shows the listening sockets (the -n flag is for showing numerical addresses instead of trying to determine symbolic host, port, or user names).

- `netstat -aw`: Shows all raw sockets.

- `netstat -ax`: Shows all Unix sockets.

- `netstat -at`: Shows all TCP sockets.

- `netstat -au`: Shows all UDP sockets.

Website: `http://net-tools.sourceforge.net`.

nmap (Network Mapper)

Nmap is an open source security project that provides a network exploration and probing tool and a security/port scanner. It has features like port scanning (detecting the open ports on target hosts), OS detection, detecting MAC addresses, and more. For example,

```
nmap www.google.com
```

can give output such as:

```
Starting Nmap 6.00 (http://nmap.org ) at 2013-09-26 16:37 IDT
Nmap scan report for www.google.com (212.179.154.227)
Host is up (0.013s latency).
Other addresses for www.google.com (not scanned): 212.179.154.221 212.179.154.251 212.179.154.232
212.179.154.237 212.179.154.216 212.179.154.231 212.179.154.241 212.179.154.247 212.179.154.222
212.179.154.226 212.179.154.236 212.179.154.246 212.179.154.212 212.179.154.217 212.179.154.242
Not shown: 998 filtered ports
PORT     STATE SERVICE
80/tcp  open  http
443/tcp open  https
Nmap done: 1 IP address (1 host up) scanned in 5.24 seconds
```

The nping utility of nmap can be used to generate raw packets for ARP poisoning, networking stress tests, and Denial of Service attacks, as well as to test connectivity like the ordinary ping utility. You can use the nping utility for setting IP options in generated traffic. See http://nmap.org/book/nping-man-ip-options.html. Website: http://nmap.org/.

openswan

An open source project implementing an IPsec-based VPN solution. It is based on the FreeS/WAN project. Website: www.openswan.org/projects/openswan.

OpenVPN

An open source project implementing VPN based on SSL/TLS. Website: www.openvpn.net/.

packeth

An Ethernet-based packet generator tool for Ethernet. The tool has both GUI and CLI. Website: http://packeth.sourceforge.net/packeth/Home.html.

ping

The well-known utility for testing connectivity by sending ICMP ECHO request messages. Here are four useful options that are also mentioned in this book:

- -Q tos: Enables setting Quality Of Service bits in an ICMP packet. Mentioned in this appendix in the explanation about tshark filters.

- -R: Sets the Record Route IP option (discussed in Chapter 4).

- -T: Sets the timestamp IP option (discussed in Chapter 4).

- -f: Flood ping.

- See man ping for more command-line options.

The ping utility belongs to the iputils package. Website: .www.skbuff.net/iputils/.

pimd

An open source lightweight stand-alone Protocol Independent Multicast - Sparse Mode (PIM-SM) v2 multicast daemon. Maintained by Joachim Nilsson. See http://troglobit.com/pimd.html. git repository: https://github.com/troglobit/pimd/.

poptop

PPTP Server for Linux. Website: http://poptop.sourceforge.net/dox/.

ppp

An open source PPP daemon. git repository: git://ozlabs.org/~paulus/ppp.git. Website: http://ppp.samba.org/download.html.

pktgen

The pktgen kernel module (net/core/pktgen.c) can generate packets at very high speed. Monitoring and controlling is done via writing to /proc/net/pktgen entries. For "HOWTO for the linux packet generator" see Documentation/networking/pktgen.txt.

radvd

This is a Router Advertisement Daemon for IPv6. It is an open source project maintained by Reuben Hawkins. It can be used for IPv6 stateless autoconfiguration and for renumbering. Website: www.litech.org/radvd/. git repository: https://github.com/reubenhwk/radvd.

route

A command-line tool for routing tables management. It belongs to the net-tools package, which is based on IOCTLs and which is older than the iproute2 package. Examples:

- route -n: Shows the routing table without name resolving.

- route add default gateway 192.168.1.1: Adds 192.168.1.1 as a default gateway.

- route -C: Displays the routing cache (keep in mind that the IPv4 routing cache was removed in kernel 3.6; see the "IPv4 Routing Cache" section in chapter 5).

See man route.

RP-PPPoE

An open source PPP over Ethernet (PPPoE) client for Linux and Solaris systems. Website: www.roaringpenguin.com/products/pppoe.

sar

A command-line tool to collect and report statistics about system activity. It is part of the sysstat package. As an example, running the following command will display four times the CPU statistics with interval of 1 second and the average at the end:

```
sar 1 4
Linux 3.6.10-4.fc18.x86_64 (a)   10/22/2013        _x86_64_         (2 CPU)

07:47:10 PM     CPU     %user     %nice   %system   %iowait    %steal      %idle
07:47:11 PM     all      0.00      0.00      0.00      0.00      0.00     100.00
07:47:12 PM     all      0.00      0.00      0.00      0.00      0.00     100.00
07:47:13 PM     all      0.00      0.00      0.00      0.00      0.00     100.00
07:47:14 PM     all      0.00      0.00      0.50      0.00      0.00      99.50
Average:        all      0.00      0.00      0.13      0.00      0.00      99.87
```

Website: http://sebastien.godard.pagesperso-orange.fr/.

smcroute

A command-line tool for multicast routing manipulation. Website: www.cschill.de/smcroute/.

snort

An open source project that provides a network intrusion detection system (IDS) and a network intrusion prevention system (IPS). Website: www.snort.org/.

suricata

An open source project that provides an IDS/IPS and a network security monitoring engine. Website: http://suricata-ids.org/.

strongSwan

An open source project that implements IPsec solutions for Linux, Android, and other operating systems. Both IKEv1 and IKEv2 are implemented. The maintainer is Professor Andreas Steffen. Website: www.strongswan.org/.

sysctl

The sysctl utility displays kernel parameters (including network parameters) at runtime. It can also set kernel parameters. For example, sysctl -a shows all kernel parameters. The sysctl utility belongs to the procps-ng package.

taskset

A command-line utility for setting or retrieving a process's CPU affinity. The taskset utility is from the util-linux package.

tcpdump

Tcpdump is an open source command-line protocol analyzer, available from www.tcpdump.org. It is based on a C/C++ network traffic capture library called libpcap. Like wireshark, it can write its results to a file and read them from a file and it supports filtering. Unlike wireshark, it does not have a front end GUI. However, its output files can be read by wireshark. Example of sniffing with tcpdump:

```
tcpdump -i eth1
```

Website: www.tcpdump.org.

top

The top utility provides a real-time view of the system (parameters like memory usage, CPU usage, and more) and a system summary. This utility is part of the procps-ng package. Website: https://gitorious.org/procps.

tracepath

The tracepath command traces a path to a destination address, discovering the MTU along this path. For IPv6 destination addresses, you can use tracepath6. The tracepath utility belongs to the iputils package. Website: www.skbuff.net/iputils/.

traceroute

Print the path that packets traverse to some destination. The traceroute utility uses the IP protocol's Time To Live (TTL) field to cause hosts on the packet path to return an ICMP TIME EXCEEDED response. The traceroute utility is discussed in Chapter 3, which deals with the ICMP protocol. Website: http://traceroute.sourceforge.net.

tshark

The tshark utility provides a command-line packet analyzer. It is part of the wireshark package. It has many command-line options. For example, you can write the output to a file with the –w option. You can set various filters to the packet filtering with tshark, some of which can be complex filters (as you will soon see). Example of setting a filter for capturing only ICMPv4 packets:

```
tshark -R icmp
Capturing on eth1
17.609101 192.168.2.200 -> 81.218.16.241 ICMP 98 Echo (ping) request  id=0x0dc6, seq=1/256, ttl=64
17.617101 81.218.16.241 -> 192.168.2.200 ICMP 98 Echo (ping) reply    id=0x0dc6, seq=1/256, ttl=58
```

You can also set a filter on a value of a field in the IPv4 header. For example, the following command sets a filter on the DS field in the IPv4 header:

```
tshark -R "ip.dsfield==0x2"
```

If from a second terminal you send traffic with DS field as 0x2 in the IPv4 header (such traffic can be sent, for example, with ping –Q 0x2 destinationAdderss), it will be displayed onscreen by tshark.

Example for filtering by source MAC address:

```
tshark ether src host 00:e0:4c:11:22:33
```

Example for filtering for UDP packets whose ports are in the port range 6000–8000:

```
tshark -R udp portrange 6000-8000
```

Example for setting a filter for capturing traffic where the source IP address is 192.168.2.200 and the port is 80 (it does not have to be TCP traffic only because here there is no filter set on some specified protocol):

```
tshark -i eth1 -f "src host 192.168.2.200 and port 80"
```

tunctl

tunctl is an older tool for creating TUN/TAP devices. It is available from http://tunctl.sourceforge.net. Note that you can also create or remove a TUN/TAP device with the ip command (see the iproute2 section earlier in this appendix) and with the openvpn command-line tool of the openvpn package:

```
openvpn --mktun --dev tun1
openvpn --rmtun --dev tun1
```

udevadm

You can get the network device type by running udevadm on its sysfs entry. For example, if the device has this entry under sysfs:

```
/sys/devices/virtual/net/eth1.100
```

then you can find that its DEVTYPE is VLAN:

```
udevadm info -q all -p  /sys/devices/virtual/net/eth1.100/

P: /devices/virtual/net/eth1.100
E: COMMENT=net device ()
E: DEVPATH=/devices/virtual/net/eth1.100
E: DEVTYPE=vlan
E: IFINDEX=4
E: INTERFACE=eth1.100
E: MATCHADDR=00:e0:4c:53:44:58
E: MATCHDEVID=0x0
```

```
E:  MATCHIFTYPE=1
E:  SUBSYSTEM=net
E:  UDEV_LOG=3
E:  USEC_INITIALIZED=28392625695
```

udevadm belongs to the udev package. Website: www.kernel.org/pub/linux/utils/kernel/hotplug/udev.html.

unshare

The unshare utility enables you to create a namespace and run a program within that namespace that is unshared from its parent. The unsare utility belongs to the util-linux package. For various command-line options of the unshare utility, see man unshare, Example of usage:

```
unshare -u /bin/bash
```

This will create a UTS namespace.

```
unshare --net /bin/bash
```

This will create a new network namespace, in which a bash process will be started. Gitweb: http://git.kernel.org/cgit/utils/util-linux/util-linux.git. Website: http://userweb.kernel.org/~kzak/util-linux/.

vconfig

The vconfig utility enables you to configure VLAN (802.1q) interface. Examples of usage:

- vconfig add eth2 100: Adds a VLAN interface. This will create a VLAN interface, eth2.100.

- vconfig rem eth2.100: Remove the eth2.100 VLAN interface.

- Note that you can also add and delete VLAN interfaces with the ip command, for example, like this:

  - ip link add link eth0 name eth0.100 type vlan id 100

- vconfig set_egress_map eth2.100 0 4: Map SKB priority of 0 to VLAN priority 4, so that outgoing packets which their SKB priority is 0 will be tagged with 4 as VLAN priority. The default VLAN priority is 0.

- vconfig set_ingress_map eth2.100 1 5: Map VLAN priority 5 to SKB priority of 1, so that incoming packets with VLAN priority of 5 will be queued with SKB priority of 1. The default SKB priority is 0.

See man vconfig.

Note that if VLAN support is compiled as a kernel module, then you must load the VLAN kernel module before trying to add the VLAN interface, by modprobe 8021q. Website: www.candelatech.com/~greear/vlan.html.

wpa_supplicant

Open source software that provides a wireless supplicant for Linux and other OSs. It supports WPA and WPA2. Website: http://hostap.epitest.fi/wpa_supplicant/.

wireshark

The `wireshark` project provides a free and open source analyzer ("sniffer"). It has two flavors: a front-end GTK+ based GUI and a command-line, the `tshark` utility (mentioned earlier in this appendix). It is available on many operating systems and evolves dynamically: when new features are added to existing protocols and new protocols are added, new parsers ("dissectors") are modified or added. Wireshark has many features:

- Enables defining a wide range of filters (ports, destination or source address, protocol identifier, fields in headers, and more).

- Enables sorting the result according to various parameters (protocol type, time, and so on).

- Saves the sniffer output to a file/read a sniffer output from a file.

- Reads/writes many different capture file formats: `tcpdump` (`libpcap`), Pcap NG, and more.

- Capture Filters and Display Filters.

Activating the `wireshark` or `thsark` sniffer puts the network interface to be in promiscuous mode to enable it to handle packets that are not destined to the local host. A lot of information is available in the man pages: `man wireshark` and `man tshark`. You can find more than 75 sniff samples of different protocols in `http://wiki.wireshark.org/SampleCaptures`. Wireshark users mailing list: `www.wireshark.org/mailman/listinfo/wireshark-users`. Website: `www.wireshark.org`. Wiki: `http://wiki.wireshark.org/`.

XORP

An Open Source project, implementing various routing protocols, like BGP, IGMP, OLSR, OSPF, PIM, and RIP. The name XORP is derived from eXtensible Open Router Platform. Website: `www.xorp.org/`.

APPENDIX C

■ ■ ■

Glossary

The following list of glossary terms are covered in this book.

ACL—Asynchronous Connection-oriented Link. A Bluetooth protocol.

ADB — Android Debug Bridge.

AVDTP—Audio/Video Distribution Transport Protocol. A Bluetooth protocol.

AEAD—Authenticated Encryption with Associated Data.

AES-NI—AES instruction set.

AH—Authentication Header protocol. Used in IPsec, has a protocol number 51.

AID—Association ID. A unique number that a wireless client gets when it associates to an Access Point. It is assigned by the Access Point, and it is in the range 1–2007.

AMP—Alternate MAC/PHY.

AMPDU—Aggregated Mac Protocol Data Unit. A type of packet aggregation in IEEE 802.11n.

AMSDU—Aggregated Mac Service Data Unit. A type of packet aggregation in IEEE 802.11n.

AOSP—Android Open Source Project.

AP—Access Point. In wireless networks, a wireless device to which wireless clients associate and which enables them to connect to a wired network.

API—Application Programming Interface. A set of methods and data structures that define the interface to a software layer, such as an interface for a library.

ABRO—Authoritative Border Router Option. Added for Neighbour Discovery Optimization for IPv6. See RFC 6775.

ABS—Android Builders Summit.

ARO—Address Registration Option. Added for Neighbour Discovery Optimization for IPv6. See RFC 6775.

ARP—Address Resolution Protocol. A protocol used to find the mapping between a network address (such as IPv4 address) into a link layer address (like a 48-bit Ethernet address).

ARPD—ARP daemon. A userspace daemon that implements the ARP functionality.

Ashmem—Android shared memory.

ASM—Any-Source Multicast. In the any-source model, you do not specify interest in receiving multicast traffic from a single particular source address or from a set of addresses.

BA—Block Acknowledgement mechanism used in IEEE 802.11n.

BGP—Border Gateway Protocol. A core routing protocol.

BLE—Bluetooth Low Energy.

BNEP—Bluetooth Network Encapsulation Protocol.

BTH—Base Transport Header. An InfiniBand header of 12 bytes. It specifies the source and destination QPs, the operation, packet sequence number, and partition.

CM—Communication Manager in the InfiniBand stack.

CIDR—Classless Inter-Domain Routing. A way to allocate Internet addresses used in inter-domain routing.

CQ—Completion Queue (InfiniBand).

CRIU — Checkpoint/Restore In Userspace. CRIU is a software tool, mainly implemented in userspace, with which you can freeze a running process and checkpoint it to a filesystem as a collection of files. You can then use these files to restore and run the application from the point where it was frozen. See `http://criu.org/Main_Page`.

CSMA/CD—Carrier Sense Multiple Access/Collision Detection. A Media Access Control method used in Ethernet networks.

CSMA/CA—Carrier Sense Multiple Access/Collision Avoidance. A Media Access Control method used in wireless networks.

CT—Connection Tracking. A netfilter layer that is the basis for NAT.

DAD—Duplicate Address Detection. The DAD is a mechanism that helps to detect the existence of double L3 addresses on different hosts on a LAN.

DAC—Duplicate Address Confirmation. An ICMPv6 type which was added in RFC 6775, with numeric value of 158.

DAR—Duplicate Address Request. An ICMPv6 type which was added in RFC 6775, with numeric value of 157.

DCCP—Datagram Congestion Control Protocol. An unreliable, congestion-controlled transport layer protocol. The use of DCCP would make sense, for instance, in applications that require low delays and where a small degree of data loss is permitted, like in telephony and streaming media applications.

DHCP—Dynamic Host Configuration Protocol. A protocol for configuring network device parameters like an IP address, a default route, and one or more DNS server addresses.

DMA—Direct Memory Access.

DNAT—Destination NAT. A NAT that changes the destination address.

DNS—Domain Name System. A system for translating domain names to IP addresses.

DSCP—Differentiated Services Code Point. A classifying mechanism.

DVMRP—Distance Vector Multicast Routing Protocol. A protocol for routing multicast datagrams. Suitable for use within an autonomous system. Defined in RFC 1075 from 1988.

ECN—Explicit Congestion Notification. See RFC 3168, "The Addition of Explicit Congestion Notification (ECN) to IP."

EDR—Enhanced Data Rate.

EGP—Exterior Gateway Protocol. A routing protocol which is now considered obsolete. It was first formalized in RFC 827 in 1982.

ERTM—Enhanced Retransmission Mode. A reliable protocol with error and flow control, used in Bluetooth.

ESP—Encapsulating Security Payload. Used in IPsec, has protocol number 50.

ETH—Extended Transport Header: An InfiniBand header with size from 4 to 28 bytes. This header represents an extra family of headers that may be present depending on the class of the service and the used operation.

ETSI—European Telecommunications Standards Institute.

FCS—Frame Check Sequence

FIB—Forwarding Information Base. The database that contains the routing tables information.

FMR—Fast Memory Region (InfiniBand).

FSF—Free Software Foundation.

FTP—File Transfer Protocol. A protocol for transferring files between two hosts, based on TCP.

GCC—GNU Compiler Collection.

GID—Global Identifier.

GMP—Group Management Protocol. A term that refers to both IGMP and MLD. See RFC 4604, section 1.

GRE—Generic Routing Encapsulation. A tunneling protocol.

GRH—Global Routing Header. An InfiniBand header of 40 bytes. It describes the source and destination port using GIDs, and its format is identical to the IPv6 header.

GRO—Generic Receive Offload. A technique with which incoming packets are merged at reception time into a bigger packet to improve performance.

GSO—Generic Segmentation Offload. A technique with which outgoing packets are segmented not in the transport layer but as close as possible to the network driver or in the network driver itself.

GUID—Global Unique Identifier.

HAL—Hardware Abstraction Layer.

HCA—Host Channel Adapter.

HCI—Host Controller Interface. Used, for example, in Bluetooth, PCI and more.

HDP—Health Device Profile. Used by Bluetooth.

HFP—Hands-Free Profile. Used by Bluetooth.

HoL Blocking—Head-of-line blocking is a performance-limiting phenomenon that occurs when a line of packets is held up by the first packet, for example, in multiple requests in HTTP pipelining.

HPC—High Performance Computing. Management of computer resources in a way that gives high performance for heavy tasks such as solving large-scale problems in science, engineering, or economics.

HS—High Speed.

HTTP—Hypertext Transfer Protocol. The basic protocol for accessing the World Wide Web.

HWMP— Hybrid Wireless Mesh Protocol. A routing protocol used in wireless Mesh networks that consists of two types of routing: *on-demand* routing and *proactive* routing.

iWARP—Internet Wide Area RDMA Protocol.

iSER—iSCSI extension for RDMA.

IANA—Internet Assigned Numbers Authority. Responsible for IP addressing, global coordination of the DNS Root, and other IP-related symbols and numbers. Operated by the Internet Corporation for Assigned Names and Numbers (ICANN).

IBTA—InfiniBand Trade Association.

ICMP—Internet Control Message Protocol. An IP protocol for control and informational messages. The well-known ping utility is based on ICMP. The ICMP protocol is known to be used in various types of security DoS attacks, like the Smurf attack.

ICE—Interactive Connectivity Establishment. Specified in RFC 5245. A protocol for NAT traversal.

ICRC—Invariant CRC. An InfiniBand header of 4 bytes. Covers all fields, which should not be changed as the packet travels in the subnet.

IDS—Intrusion Detection System.

IoT—Internet of Things. Networking of everyday objects.

IEEE—Institute of Electrical and Electronics Engineers.

IGMP—Internet Group Management Protocol. Multicast group memberships protocol.

IKE—Internet Key Exchange. A protocol for setting an IPsec Security Association.

IOMMU—I/O Memory Management Unit.

IP—Internet Protocol. The primary addressing and routing protocol for the Internet. IPv4 was first specified in RFC 791 from 1981, and IPv6 was first specified in RFC 1883 from 1995.

IPoIB—IP over InfiniBand.

IPS—Intrusion Prevention System.

ISAKMP—Internet Security Association & Key Management Protocol.

IOCTL—Input/Output Control. A system call that provides access from userspace to kernel.

IPC—Inter Process Communication. There are many different mechanisms for IPC, such as shared memory semaphores, message queues, and more.

IPCOMP—IP Payload Compression Protocol. A compressing protocol intended to reduce the size of data sent over a slow network connection. Using IPComp increases the overall communication performance between two network nodes.

IPsec—IP security. A set of protocols developed by the IETF for secure exchange of packets over the IP protocol. IPsec is mandatory in IPv6 according to the IPv6 spec and optional in IPv4, though many operating systems implemented it also in IPv4. IPsec uses two encryption modes: Transport and Tunnel.

IPVS—IP Virtual Server. A Linux kernel load balancing infrastructure, supports IPv4 and IPv6. See `http://www.linuxvirtualserver.org/software/ipvs.html`.

ISR—Interrupt Service Routine. An interrupt handler that is invoked when an interrupt is received.

ISM—Industrial, scientific, and medical radio band.

jumbo frames—Packets with size up to 9K. Some network interfaces allow using an MTU of up to 9K. Using jumbo frames can improve the network performance in some cases, such as in bulk data transfers.

KVM—Kernel-based Virtual Machine. A Linux virtualization project.

LACP—Link Aggregation Control Protocol.

LAN—Local Area Network. A network that connects a limited area, such as an office building.

LID—Local Identifier. A 16-bit value assigned to every subnet port by the Subnet Manager (InfiniBand).

L2CAP—Logical Link Control and Adaptation Protocol. Used in Bluetooth.

L2TP—Layer 2 Tunneling Protocol used by VPNs. L2TPv3 is specified in RFC 3931 (RFC 5641 has some updates).

LKML—Linux Kernel Mailing List.

LLCP—Logical Link Control Protocol. Used by NFC.

LLN—Low-power and Lossy Network.

LoWPAN—Low-power Wireless Personal Area Network.

LMP—Link Management Protocol. Controls the radio link between two Bluetooth devices.

LPM—Longest Prefix Match. An algorithm used by the routing subsystem.

LRH—Local Routing Header. An InfiniBand header of 8 bytes. It identifies the local source and destination ports of the packet. It also specifies the requested QoS attributes (SL and VL) of the message.

LRO—Large Receive Offload.

LR-WPAN—Low-Rate Wireless Personal Area Network. Used in IEEE 802.15.4.

LSB—Least significant bit.

LSRR—Loose Source Record Route.

LTE—Long Term Evolution.

MAC—Media Access Control. A sublayer of the Data Link Layer (L2) of the OSI model.

MAD—Management Datagram (InfiniBand).

MFC—Multicast Forwarding Cache. A data structure in the kernel that consists of multicast forwarding entries.

MIB—Management Information Base.

MLD—Multicast Listener Discovery protocol. Enables each IPv6 router to discover the presence of multicast listeners. The MLD protocol is specified in RFC 3810, from 2004.

MLME—MAC Layer Management Entity. A component in the IEEE 802.11 management layer responsible for operations such as scanning, authentication, association, and reassociation.

MR—Memory Region (InfiniBand).

MSF—Multicast Source Filtering. This is the feature to set filters so that multicast traffic from sources other than the expected ones will be dropped.

MSI—Message Signaled Interrupts.

MSS—Maximum Segment Size. A parameter of the TCP protocol.

MTU—Maximum transmission unit. The size of the largest packet that a network protocol can transmit.

MW—Memory Window (InfiniBand).

NAP—Network Access Point.

NAPI—New API. A technique by which network drivers are not interrupt-driven, but use polling. NAPI is discussed in Chapter 1.

NAT—Network Address Translation. A layer responsible for modifying IP headers. In Linux, support for IPv6 NAT was merged in kernel 3.7.

NAT-T—NAT traversal.

NCI—NFC Controller Interface.

ND / NDISC—Neighbour Discovery Protocol. Used in IPv6. Among its tasks: discovering network nodes on the same link, autoconfiguration of addresses, finding the Link Layer addresses of other nodes, and maintaining reachability information about other nodes.

NFC—Near Field Communication.

NDEF—NFC Data Exchange Format.

NIC—Network Interface Card, also known as Network Interface Controller or Network Adapter. The hardware network device.

NUMA—Non-Uniform Memory Access.

NPP—NDEF Push Protocol.

NPAR—NIC Partitioning. A technology that enables you to split up network card (NIC) traffic in partitions.

NUD—Network Unreachability Detection. A mechanism responsible for determining whether a neighbour can be reached.

OBEX—Object Exchange. A protocol for exchange of binary objects between devices, used in Bluetooth.

OEM—Original Equipment Manufacturer.

OFA—OpenFabrics Alliance.

OCF—Open Cryptography Framework.

OHA—Open Handset Alliance.

OOTB—Out of the Blue packet (a term of the SCTP protocol). A packet is an OOTB packet if it is correctly formed (that is, no checksum error), but the receiver is not able to identify the SCTP association to which the packet belongs (see section 8.4 in RFC 4960).

OPP—Object Push Profile. Used by Bluetooth.

OSI Model—Open Systems Interconnection.

OSPF—Open Shortest Path First. Interior gateway routing protocol developed for IP networks.

PADI—PPPoE Active Discovery Initiation.

PADO—PPPoE Active Discovery Offer.

PADR—PPPoE Active Discovery Request.

PADS—PPPoE Active Discovery Session.

PADT—PPPoE Active Discovery Terminate.

PAN—Personal Area Networking. A profile used in Bluetooth.

PCI—Peripheral Component Interconnect. A bus for attaching devices. Many network interface cards are PCI devices.

PD—Protection Domain.

PHDC—Personal Health Device Communication. Used by NFC.

PID—Process Identifier.

PIM—Protocol Independent Multicast Protocol. A multicast routing protocol.

PIM-SM—Protocol Independent Multicast—Sparse Mode.

PLME—Physical Layer Management Entity in IEEE 802.11.

PM—Power Management.

PPP—Point To Point data link protocol. A protocol for direct communication between two hosts.

PPPoE—PPP over Ethernet. The PPPoE protocol is specified in RFC 2516 from 1999.

PERR—Path Error. A message that informs about some failure in a wireless Mesh network routing.

PREP—Path Reply. A unicast packet sent as a reply to a PREQ message in a wireless Mesh network.

PREQ—Path Request. A broadcast packet sent when looking for some address in a wireless Mesh network.

PSK—Preshared Key.

Qdisc—Queuing Disciplines.

QP—Queue Pair (InfinBand).

RA—Router Alert. One of the IPv4 options. It notifies transit routers to more closely examine the contents of an IP packet. It is used by many protocols, such as IGMP, MLD, and more.

RANN—Root Announcement. A broadcast packet sent periodically by a Root Mesh point in a wireless Mesh network.

RARP—Reverse Address Resolution Protocol. A protocol used to find the mapping between a link layer address (like a 48-bit Ethernet address) to a network address (like an IPv4 address).

RC—A QP transport type in InfiniBand.

RDMA—Remote Direct Memory Access. A direct memory access from one host to another.

RDS—Reliable Datagram Socket. A reliable connectionless protocol developed by Oracle.

RFC—Request For Comments. A document that specifies Internet specifications, communications protocols, procedures, and events. The standardization process of RFCs is documented at `http://tools.ietf.org/html/rfc2026`, "The Internet Standards Process."

RFID—Radio Frequency ID.

RFCOMM—Radio Frequency Communications protocol. Used in Bluetooth.

RFS—Receive Flow Steering.

RIP—Routing Information Protocol: A distance-vector routing protocol.

RoCE—RDMA over Converged Ethernet.

RP—Rendezvous Point.

RPL—IPv6 Routing Protocol for Low-Power and Lossy Networks. The RPL protocol is specified in RFC 6550.

RPDB—Routing Policy DataBase.

RPF—Reverse Path Filter. A technique intended to prevent source address spoofing.

RPC—Remote Procedure Call.

RPS—Receive Packet Steering.

RS—Router Solicitations.

RSA—A cryptography algorithm. RSA stands for Ron Rivest, Adi Shamir, and Leonard Adleman, the people who developed it.

RTP—Real-time Transport Protocol. A protocol for transmitting audio and video over IP networks.

RTR—Ready To Receive. A state in InfiniBand QP State Machine.

RTS—Ready To Send. A state in InfiniBand QP State Machine.

SA—Security Association. A logical relationship between two hosts that consists of various parameters, such as cryptographic key, cryptographic algorithm, SPI, and more.

SACK—Selective Acknowledgments. See RFC 2018, "TCP Selective Acknowledgment Options," from 1996.

SAD—Security Association Database.

SAR—Segmentation and Reassembly.

SBC—Session Border Controllers.

SCO—Synchronous Connection Oriented link. A Bluetooth protocol.

SDP—Service Discovery Protocol. Used in Bluetooth.

SCTP—Stream Control Transmission Protocol. A transport protocol that has features of both UDP and TCP.

SE—Security Element (NFC).

SIG—Special Interest Group.

SIP—Session Initiation Protocol. A signaling protocol for VoIP, intended for creating and modifying VoIP sessions.

SLAAC—Stateless Address autoconfiguration. Specified in RFC 4862.

SKB —Socket Buffer. A kernel data structure representing a network packet (implemented by the `sk_buff` structure, `include/linux/skbuff.h`).

SL—Service Level. The QoS in InfiniBand is implemented using the SL to VL mapping and the resources for each VL.

SLAAC—Stateless Address Autoconfiguration.

SM—Subnet Manager.

SMA—Subnet Management Agent.

SME—System Management Entity in IEEE 802.11.

SMP—Symmetrical Multiprocessing. An architecture where two or more identical processors are connected to a single shared main memory.

SNAT—Source NAT. A NAT that changes the source address.

SNEP—Simple NDEF Exchange Protocol (SNEP) for exchanging NDEF-formatted data.

SNMP—Simple Network Management Protocol.

SPI—Security Parameter Index. Used by IPsec.

SPD—Security Policy Database.

SQD—Send Queue Drained. A state in InfiniBand QP State Machine.

SQE—Send Queue Error. A state in InfiniBand QP State Machine.

SRP—SCSI RDMA protocol.

SR-IOV—Single Root I/O Virtualization. A specification that allows a PCIe device to appear to be multiple separate physical PCIe devices.

SRQ—Shared Receive Queue (InfiniBand).

SSM—Source Specific Multicast.

STUN —Session Traversal Utilities for NAT.

SSP—Secure Simple Pairing. A security feature required by Bluetooth v2.1.

TCP—Transmission Control Protocol. The TCP protocol is the most commonly used transport protocol on the Internet today. Many protocols run on top of TCP, including FTP, HTTP, and more. TCP is specified in RFC 793 from 1981, and during the years since then there have been many protocol updates, variations, and additions to the base TCP protocol.

TIPC—Transparent Inter-process Communication protocol.
See http://tipc.sourceforge.net/.

TOS—Type Of Service.

TSO—TCP Segmentation Offload.

TTL—Time To Live. A counter in the IPv4 header (its counterpart in IPv6 is called Hop Limit) that is decremented in each forwarding device. When this counter reaches 0, an ICMP of Time Exceeded is sent back, and the packet is discarded. Both the `ttl` member of the IPv4 header and the `hop_limit` member of the IPv6 header are 8-bit fields.

TURN—Traversal Using Relays around NAT.

UC—Unreliable Connected. A QP transport type in InfiniBand.

UD—Unreliable Datagram. A QP transport type in InfiniBand.

UDP—User Datagram Protocol. UDP is an unreliable protocol, as there is no guarantee that packets will be delivered for upper layer protocols. There is no handshaking phase in UDP, in contrast to TCP. The UDP header is simple and consists of only 4 fields: source port, destination port, checksum, and length.

USAGI—UniverSAl playGround for Ipv6. A project that developed IPv6 and IPsec (for both IPv4 and IPv6) stacks for the Linux kernel.

UTS—Unix Time-sharing System.

VCRC—Variant CRC. An InfiniBand header of 2 bytes. Covers all the fields of the packet.

VETH—Virtual Ethernet. A network driver which enables communication between two network devices in different network namespaces.

VoIP—Voice Over IP.

VFS—Virtual File System.

VL—Virtual Lanes. A mechanism for creating multiple virtual links over a single physical link.

VLAN—Virtual Local Area Network.

VPN—Virtual Private Network.

VXLAN—Virtual Extensible Local Area Network. VXLAN is a standard protocol to transfer Layer 2 Ethernet packets over UDP. VXLAN is needed because there are cases where firewalls block tunnels and allow, for example, only TCP/UDP traffic.

WDS—Wireless Distribution System.

WLAN—Wireless LAN.

WOL—Wake On LAN.

WSN—Wireless Sensor Networks.

XRC—eXtended Reliable Connected. A QP transport type in InfiniBand.

XFRM—IPsec Transformer. A Linux kernel framework for handling IPsec transformations. The two most fundamental data structures of the XFRM framework are the XFRM policy and the XFRM state.

Index

■ **O**

Get the eBook for only $10!

> Now you can take the weightless companion with you anywhere, anytime. Your purchase of this book entitles you to 3 electronic versions for only $10.

This Apress title will prove so indispensible that you'll want to carry it with you everywhere, which is why we are offering the eBook in 3 formats for only $10 if you have already purchased the print book.

Convenient and fully searchable, the PDF version enables you to easily find and copy code—or perform examples by quickly toggling between instructions and applications. The MOBI format is ideal for your Kindle, while the ePUB can be utilized on a variety of mobile devices.

Go to www.apress.com/promo/tendollars to purchase your companion eBook.